9th Edition

Food for Fifty .

Grace Shugart

*Professor Emeritus of Hotel, Restaurant and Institution Management, and Dietetics
Kansas State University*

Mary Molt

*Assistant Director, Housing and Dining Services
Instructor of Hotel, Restaurant and Institution
    Management, and Dietetics
Kansas State University*

*Macmillan Publishing Company
New York*

*Maxwell Macmillan Canada
Toronto*

*Maxwell Macmillan International
New York   Oxford   Singapore   Sydney*

Cover art: Barbara Maslen
Editor: Kevin M. Davis
Developmental Editor: Carol S. Sykes
Production Editors: Sharon Rudd/Colleen Brosnan
Art Coordinator: Peter A. Robison
Cover Designer: Cathleen Norz
Production Buyer: Patricia A. Tonneman

This book was set in New Baskerville by Compset, Inc. and was printed and bound by Arcata Graphics/Halliday. The cover was printed by Lehigh Press, Inc.

Macmillan Publishing Company
866 Third Avenue
New York, New York 10022

Macmillan Publishing Company is part of the
Maxwell Communication Group of Companies.

Maxwell Macmillan Canada, Inc.
1200 Eglinton Avenue East, Suite 200
Don Mills, Ontario M3C 3N1

Library of Congress Cataloging-in-Publication Data
Shugart, Grace Severance
    Food for fifty / Grace Shugart, Mary Molt.   9th ed.
      p.   cm.
    Includes index.
    ISBN 0-02-410341-1
    1. Quantity cookery. 2. Menus. I. Molt, Mary. II. Title.
TX820.S45   1993
641.5′7—dc20   92-27391
                                                    CIP

Printing: 1 2 3 4 5 6 7 8 9 Year: 3 4 5 6 7

Preface .

Food for Fifty is designed as a text for use by students in quantity food production and as a reference for persons in foodservice management. Since the book's origin in 1937, revisions have been made to keep abreast of the changing foodservice industry. In the ninth edition, numerous recipes have been added. Special attention has been given to those recipes that reflect current food preferences and modern eating styles. In addition, each recipe has been evaluated for clarity of directions, and changes have been made where necessary. Nutritive values for protein, carbohydrate, fat, cholesterol, calories, sodium, iron, and calcium are included for each major recipe in this new edition.

Organization of the Book

Food for Fifty is divided into three major divisions. Part One, "Food Production Information," is intended as a guide to planning and preparing food in quantity. The section begins with a comprehensive table of amounts of food needed to serve 50, followed by tables of weights and measures, including metric conversion, and tables to assist in changing weights of recipe ingredients to volume measurement. Directions for increasing recipe yields are helpful when adapting recipes given in this book to different yields and for increasing home-size recipes for quantity production. Preparation guides include tables for cooking temperatures, food substitutions and equivalents, and pan and mixer bowl capacities.

Part Two, "Recipes," includes a wide variety of tested recipes given in yields of 50 portions and with many suggestions for variations of the basic recipes. Recipes are organized according to menu categories. Each recipe chapter begins with a discussion of general principles and production techniques for preparing the recipes in that section. New to this edition are nutritive values given for each major recipe.

Part Three, "Planning the Menu and Special Events," offers guidelines and procedures for planning meals, with special considerations for different types of foodservices.

Planning and serving special foodservice events, such as receptions, buffets, and banquets, are discussed, and guidelines for planning are provided.

At the back of the book are a list of menu planning suggestions (Appendix A), information for using herbs and spices in cooking (Appendix B), and a glossary of menu and cooking terms.

Distinctive Features of the Book

Food for Fifty has been recognized for many years as a dependable resource for foodservice students and managers. Part One is considered by many to be an indispensable reference for production information. Students find the various tables helpful when completing menu planning, purchasing, and food production assignments.

Dietitians, foodservice managers, and faculty members have for many years depended on the standardized recipes in *Food for Fifty*. Recipes are written in an easy-to-read format, with standardized procedures that allow quality products to be prepared consistently. Suggested variations for many of the recipes increase the value of this section. In revising the book, we have made an effort to lower fat and salt in recipes, where feasible, and to add recipes that include new foods on the market and are appropriate for today's dietary standards. We believe the users of this book will find the nutrition information helpful.

Menu planning information is given in concise terms in Part Three. The discussion of planning procedures and the menu suggestion list in Appendix A are helpful to students and to foodservice managers whose responsibilities include menu planning. Many foodservices are called upon today to provide food for special events, such as holiday meals, buffets, and coffees, receptions, and teas. Part Three offers suggestions for menus, organization, and service of these functions.

Using the Book

Food for Fifty is written for many users. Students in quantity food production and foodservice management use the text as a resource for learning the standards, skills, and techniques inherent in quality food production. Instructors find beneficial the basic menu planning and food production features that equip them with the tools necessary for designing teaching modules and supervising laboratories. The reliability of the recipes, tables, and charts in the book allows instructors to make assignments with confidence of a quality outcome. Additionally, the text provides a resource for instructing students on how to plan and serve special foodservice functions. Foodservice administrators, managers, and supervisors are also users of the text. *Food for Fifty* is a comprehensive resource for quantity recipes and technical food production information. The book serves as a foundation for the food production system.

The uses for *Food for Fifty* as both an instructional text and food production resource are unlimited. We believe the following examples of how the text can be used address many of the book's strengths.

- Amounts of food to purchase may be easily determined. Accurate calculations are achieved by using the purchasing and yield information in Part One and the standardized recipes in Part Two.

- While the recipes yield approximately 50 servings, they can be adjusted easily for other yields by using the recipe extension procedures in Part One.

- Menu planning is simplified by the lists of food item names, by menu categories, in both Appendix A and the Index. *Food for Fifty* also provides a comprehensive file of standardized recipes that can support the menu plan. General information on writing menus for various kinds of foodservices is included in the text.

- Variations are included for most recipes. Users are given suggestions for producing food products consistent with contemporary eating trends.

- Quality standards for food products may be established by using standardized recipes that produce a consistent quality product. Specific standards are available for some product categories.

- Food costs are easily established for recipes. Each recipe includes specific portion size information and instructions for ensuring accurate yields.

- Efficient labor procedures were considered for all recipes. Students and foodservice operators may use the recipes as a model for making products using the minimum amount of labor.

- Standardized recipes assure that accurate nutrition values can be assigned to serving portions. Users of the book can review the recipe's nutrient values and make adjustments if required for a specific population.

- *Food for Fifty* can be used for planning teas, receptions, and special functions. Part Three brings together general information and guidelines useful for organizing events. Parts One and Two support the planning function with food production information.

- Using *Food for Fifty* as a resource to direct accurate food production techniques is intended in the design of the recipes. Each recipe can be used for communicating the techniques necessary for producing a quality product. In addition, the material prefacing each recipe category provides general text information that supports the standardized techniques specified in the recipes.

Acknowledgments

Appreciation is extended to the many colleagues and friends who have, through the course of association with the authors, made this revision of *Food for Fifty* possible. Special acknowledgment is given to John Pence, Associate Director of Housing and Dining Services at Kansas State University, and his management staff for their support, advice, and creative ideas. Thanks are also due to the following reviewers for their helpful comments: Birgit Black, Texas Tech University; Carl P. Borchgrevink, Michigan State University; Peter D'Souza, University of Wisconsin-Stout; and Sandy Kapoor, California State Polytechnic University, Pomona.

Grace Shugart

Mary Molt

Contents .

Tables ▪

Figures ∎

Part One

Food Production Information .

1

Food Production Information

Information in this section is presented as a guide for ordering food, for adjusting recipes, and for the planning, preparation, and serving of food. Quantities to prepare are based on 50 average-size portions, as are most of the recipes, but adjustments may need to be made to fit individual situations. Rarely is 50 the exact number to be served, and the portion size will vary according to the type of foodservice and the needs of the individuals in the group. Tables are included that will assist with these recipe adjustments.

Most ingredients in the recipes are given in weights, but if volume measurements (teaspoons, tablespoons, cups, quarts, or gallons) are to be used, tables in this section will assist in converting from weights to measures. Metric measures were not used in the recipes, but charts for converting to metric are included.

Also given is basic information on cooking temperatures, food equivalents and substitutions, and equipment capacity. A guide for use of herbs and spices and a glossary of cooking and menu terms are found at the end of the book.

HOW TO USE TABLES AND GUIDES

Table 1.1—Amounts of Food to Serve 50   This table (pp. 11–25) suggests amounts of food to purchase and prepare for 50 persons, based on the portion size listed in the table. If larger or smaller servings are needed or if the number of portions required is other than 50, an adjustment in the amount to prepare or purchase must be made. Because preparation losses must be considered in determining the amount to purchase for 50 portions, the ready-to-serve raw yield or the yield of cooked product is given for some products, along with the amount as purchased (AP) to buy. The yields, which are given in decimal parts of a pound, can be converted to ounces by using Table 1.21 (p. 58).

Table 1.2—Yield in the Preparation of Fresh Fruits and Vegetables   When ordering fresh fruits and vegetables, the loss in preparation must be considered when determining the amount to buy. The approximate yield after preparation of one pound of fruit or vegetable, listed in this table (p. 26), is given in decimal parts of a pound but can be converted to ounces by referring to Table 1.21.

Table 1.3—Food Weights and Approximate Equivalents in Measure   Information in this table (pp. 27–38) is useful when converting recipe ingredients from weight to measure or vice versa and is helpful in adjusting or enlarging recipes.

Table 1.4—Basic Equivalents in Measures and Weights   Table 1.4 (p. 39) is useful when converting measures (gallons, quarts, or cups) to smaller units such as cups, tablespoons, or teaspoons. Metric equivalents are given for commonly used weights and measures.

Table 1.5—Weight and Approximate Measure Equivalents for Commonly Used Foods   In Table 1.5 (pp. 40–43), the equivalent measures (teaspoons, tablespoons, and cups) are given for selected ingredients, such as flour, salt, and sugar, that appear repeatedly in recipes. This information is the same as that given in Table 1.3 except that the equivalents are given for weights from 1 to 16 ounces.

Table 1.6—Metric Equivalents for Weight, Measure, and Temperature   Table 1.6 (p. 44) provides information that will be helpful in converting weights, measures, and temperatures as given in recipes to metric equivalents.

Table 1.7—Convection Oven Baking Times and Temperatures   Information in this table (p. 44) is useful when using convection ovens. Times and temperatures in recipes included in *Food for Fifty* have been tested using conventional ovens.

Table 1.8—Deep-Fat Frying Temperatures   Table 1.8 (p. 46) provides guidelines for the deep-fat frying of different types of menu items.

Table 1.9—Coatings for Deep Fat–Fried Foods   Proportions of ingredients are given (p. 47) for typical coatings for deep fat–fried foods.

Table 1.10—Dipper Equivalents   Approximate measure and weight for different-size dippers (scoops) are given (p. 47). Suggested uses for different food products are also included.

Table 1.11—Ladle Equivalents   Table 1.11 (p. 48) gives measures and approximate weights for different-size ladles and the size to use for different menu items.

Table 1.12—Cold Food Storage Temperatures   Recommended refrigerator and freezer temperatures are given (pp. 48–49) for safe storage of foods.

Table 1.13—Food Serving Temperatures   Serving temperatures in this table (p. 49) are those recommended for optimum food quality and safety.

Table 1.14—Mixer Bowl and Steam-Jacketed Kettle Sizes   This table (p. 50) is helpful in determining the size of mixer bowl and steam-jacketed kettle needed for selected food items in portions ranging from 50 to 500. If the equipment on hand is not large enough for the amount required, the recipe may need to be made in two or three batches.

Table 1.15—Pan Capacities for Baked Products   This table (p. 51) gives the maximum capacity of different-sized pans for baking breads, cakes, or pies and is useful when enlarging or adjusting recipes.

Table 1.16—Counter Pan Capacities   Capacities, suggested uses, and number of portions for different sizes of counter pans are given in this table (p. 52).

Table 1.17—Common Can Sizes   Can sizes, with approximate weight or measure and number of portions, are included in this table (pp. 52–53) as a purchasing guide.

Table 1.18—Ingredient Substitutions   This table (pp. 53–55) is useful when it is necessary to substitute one ingredient for another in a recipe.

Table 1.19—Ingredient Proportions   This table (p. 56) gives the relative proportion of ingredients in preparing certain types of foods. It is useful when evaluating recipes for the proper amount of leavening agents, seasonings, and thickening agents.

Table 1.20—Guide for Rounding Off Weights and Measures   When enlarging home-sized recipes, the resulting quantities may be difficult to measure. Table 1.20 (p. 57) aids in rounding fractions and complex measurements into amounts that are as simple as possible to weigh or measure while maintaining the accuracy needed for quality control.

Table 1.21—Ounces and Decimal Equivalents of a Pound   This table (p. 58) is useful when increasing or decreasing recipes. The multiplication or division of pounds and ounces is simplified if the ounces are converted first to decimal parts of a pound.

Tables 1.22–1.24—Direct-Reading Tables for Adjusting Recipes   These tables include amounts of ingredients needed for varying portions, from 25 to 500. Table 1.22 (pp. 61–63) is used when ingredient amounts are given in *weights* and portion yields are divisible by 25. In Table 1.23 (pp. 64–71) ingredients are stated in *volume* measurement (teaspoons, tablespoons, cups, quarts, and gallons) and portions are divisible by 25. Table 1.24 (pp. 74–77) is especially useful when enlarging home-sized recipes. Ingredients are in *volume* measurement for yields from 8 to 96 portions.

RECIPE ADJUSTMENT

Recipes often need to be adjusted to meet the requirements of an individual foodservice. For example, the number of portions may need to be increased from 50 to the exact number to be served, or an adjustment in portion size might better reflect the policy of the institution and the requirements of the clientele. Enlarging home-size recipes may require converting household measurements to weights and adjusting certain ingredient proportions as the recipes are expanded. These procedures, as well as directions for converting to metric weights and measures, are explained in the pages that follow.

Converting from U.S. Measurement to Metric

Two approaches are possible for converting recipes from U.S. to metric measures: soft conversion and hard conversion. *Soft* conversion translates weights and measures into their exact metric equivalents. An ounce would become 28.3 grams; a quart would be 0.95 liter. This method produces numbers that may be awkward to work with, and equipment may not be available to measure ingredients to the degree of accuracy required.

Hard conversion changes weights and measures to round metric sizes. For example, a 1-ounce portion would convert to either 25 or 30 grams, but not to 28.3 grams; 1 quart would be changed to 1 liter. This method may be satisfactory for recipes that are not sensitive to formula adjustments, such as soups and beverages, but may not be suitable for cakes, breads, and other products in which accurate ingredient ratios are critical. Testing recipes to evaluate acceptability is recommended when using the hard conversion method. (Table 1.6 shows metric conversions.)

Converting from Weight to Measure

Quantities of most dry ingredients in recipes in this book are given by weight in ounces and pounds. If accurate scales are not available, however, or if scales do not have graduations for weighing small amounts, the weights of ingredients may need to be converted to measures. A number of tables will be helpful:

- Table 1.3—Food Weights and Approximate Equivalents in Measure (p. 27)
- Table 1.4—Basic Equivalents in Measures and Weights (p. 39)
- Table 1.5—Weight (1–16 oz) and Measure Equivalents for Commonly Used Foods (p. 40)
- Table 1.20—A Guide for Rounding Off Weights and Measures (p. 57)
- Table 1.21—Ounces and Decimal Equivalents of a Pound (p. 58)

The following example illustrates the procedure for converting ingredients in Baking Powder Biscuits (p. 118) from weight to measure.

- Change 5 pounds flour to measure by multiplying by 4 cups. Turn to Table 1.3 (p. 27).
- The resulting 20 cups would be equivalent to 5 quarts. See Table 1.4 (p. 39). For ingredients other than flour, a gallon measure should be used.
- By referring to Table 1.5 (p. 40) the 5 ounces of baking powder and 1 pound 4 ounces of shortening may be converted quickly by finding the amount in the appropriate column or adding the columns together. The same information is in-

cluded in the longer table (Table 1.3, p. 27), but for conversion of small amounts of commonly used foods, Table 1.5 is useful.

Increasing and Decreasing Recipe Yields

Changing recipe yields in this book may be required to meet the needs of individual situations. Recipes may need to be adjusted to produce batch sizes compatible with preparation equipment, such as mixers, ovens, and steam-jacketed kettles, or consistent with pan sizes available. See Tables 1.14–1.16 for recommended equipment sizes and pan capacities. Recipes may also need adjustment as portion sizes are increased or decreased or as purchase units for ingredients change.

Three methods commonly used to adjust recipe yields are the *factor method*, the *percentage method*, and *direct-reading measurement tables.*

Factor Method

In the factor method, a conversion factor is determined and multiplied by each ingredient in the recipe. This process is explained in the following steps:

Step 1   Divide the desired yield by the known yield of the recipe being adjusted to obtain the conversion *factor.* For example, to increase a 50-portion recipe to 125 portions, divide 125 by 50 for a factor of 2.5

Step 2   Wherever possible, convert ingredients to weight. If amounts of some ingredients are too small to be weighed, leave them in measure.

Step 3   Multiply the amount of each ingredient in the original recipe by the factor. To work with decimal parts of a pound instead of ounces for this multiplication, Table 1.21 will be helpful.

Step 4   Multiply the original total weight of ingredients by the factor. Multiply the pounds and ounces separately.

Step 5   Add together the new weights of all ingredients for the adjusted recipe. If the answers in Steps 4 and 5 are not the same, an error exists and the calculations should be checked. (A slight difference may exist because of rounding the figures.)

Step 6   Change weights of any ingredients that can be more easily measured than weighed to measure.

Step 7   Check all amounts and use Table 1.20 for rounding off unnecessary fractions to simplify weights or measures as far as accuracy permits.

The following example illustrates the procedure for adjusting Baking Powder Biscuits from 100 biscuits to 500, using the factor method of adjustment:

Step 1   Derive the factor:

$$\frac{500 \text{ (new)}}{100 \text{ (original)}} = 5 \text{ (factor)}$$

Ingredients	Original recipe	Step 2: Convert to weight	Step 3: Multiply by factor	Steps 6 and 7: Change to measure and simplify
Flour, all-purpose	5 lb	5 lb	25 lb	25 lb
Baking powder	5 oz	5 oz	25 oz	1 lb 9 oz
Salt	2 Tbsp	1⅓ oz	6½ oz	6½ oz
Shortening, hydrogenated	1 lb 4 oz	1 lb 4 oz	6 lb 4 oz	6 lb 4 oz
Milk	1¾ qt	<u>3 lb 8 oz</u>	<u>17 lb 8 oz</u>	2 gal + ¾ qt
Steps 4 and 5:				
Total weight		10 lb 2 oz	50 lb 11 oz	

Percentage Method

The percentage method of recipe adjustment often is desirable, especially for large-volume production where batch sizes may vary greatly. Once the ingredient percentage has been established, it remains constant for all future adjustments. Recipe increases and decreases are made by multiplying the percentage of each ingredient by the total weight desired. Checking ingredients for proper recipe balance is possible, because the percentage of each ingredient is available. Some computer recipe systems use the percentage method of recipe adjustment. This process is explained in the following steps:

Step 1   Convert all ingredients from measure or pounds and ounces to pounds and tenths of a pound (see Tables 1.3 and 1.21). Make desired equivalent ingredient substitutions such as frozen whole eggs for fresh eggs, nonfat dry milk and water for liquid milk. Use edible portion (EP) weights when a difference exists between EP and as purchased (AP) weights (see Table 1.1). Individual meat items and other meats in entree recipes that do not require the meat to be cooked prior to combining with other ingredients are calculated on AP weight. Examples are pork chops, meat loaf, and Salisbury steak.

Step 2   Total the weight of ingredients in the recipe, using EP weight where applicable.

Step 3   Calculate the percentage of each ingredient in relation to the total weight, using the following formula:

$$\frac{\text{individual ingredient weight}}{\text{total weight}} = \text{percentage of each ingredient}$$

The sum of the percentages must equal 100.

Step 4   Check the ratio of ingredients. Standards have been established for ingredient proportions of many items. The ingredients should be in proper balance before going further.

Step 5   Establish the weight needed to give the desired number of servings. The weight will be determined by portion size multiplied by the desired number of servings to be prepared. This weight may need to be adjusted because of pan sizes or equipment capacity (see Tables 1.14–1.16).

Step 6   Handling loss must be added to the weight needed, and it may vary from 1 to 10 percent, depending on the product. Similar items produce predictable losses, and with some experimentation these losses can be assigned accurately. The formula for incorporating handling loss is as follows:

$$\text{total weight needed} = \frac{\text{desired yield}}{100 \text{ percent} - \text{assigned handling loss percent}}$$

For example, cake has a handling loss of approximately 2 percent, and 72 lb of batter is needed to make nine 18 × 26 × 2-inch pans. To determine the total amount of batter to be made, divide 72 lb by 98 percent (100 percent − 2 percent handling loss). Using this formula, a recipe calculated for 73.47 lb of batter is needed.

Step 7   Multiply each ingredient percentage by the total weight to give the exact amount of each ingredient needed. The total weight of ingredients should equal the weight needed as calculated in Step 6. Once the percentages of a recipe have been established, any number of servings can be calculated, and the ratio of ingredients to the total will remain the same.

Step 8   Unless scales are calibrated to read in pounds and tenths of a pound, convert to pounds and ounces (Table 1.21) or to measure (Table 1.3). Use Table 1.20 for rounding off unnecessary fractions. If volume measurements are required, Table 1.3 is helpful.

The following example illustrates the procedure for adjusting Baking Powder Biscuits (p. 118) from 100 biscuits to 500, using the percentage method of adjustment:

Ingredients	Original recipe	Step 1: Convert to decimal weights	Step 3: Calculate percentage	Step 7: Calculate weights	Step 8: Convert to pounds and ounces
Flour, all-purpose	5 lb	5.0 lb	49.276	25.52 lb	25 lb 8 oz
Baking powder	5 oz	0.313 lb	3.085	1.60 lb	1 lb 10 oz
Salt	2 Tbsp	0.0839 lb	0.827	0.43 lb	6¾ oz
Shortening, hydrogenated	1 lb 4 oz	1.25 lb	12.319	6.38 lb	6 lb 6 oz
Milk	1¾ qt	3.5 lb	34.493	17.86 lb	2¼ gal
Step 2:					
Total weight		10.1469 lb	100.00	51.79 lb	

Step 4   Check ratio of ingredients to see if they are within acceptable guidelines.

Step 5   Establish needed weight:

$$\frac{10.1469 \text{ (total weight of 100 biscuits)}}{100} = 0.1015 \text{ lb (weight per biscuit)}$$

500 (desired yield) $\times$ 0.1015 lb = 50.75 lb of dough needed before handling loss

Step 6   Calculate handling loss. Estimated handling loss 2 percent:

$$\frac{50.75 \text{ lb (desired yield)}}{98 \text{ percent}} = 51.79 \text{ lb total dough needed}$$
$$(100 \text{ percent} - 2 \text{ percent})$$

Enlarging Home-Size Recipes

Before enlarging a small recipe, be sure the recipe is appropriate for large-quantity production and that the same quality can be achieved in the larger amount. Appropriate equipment and pans also must be available. Quantity production procedures used in the particular foodservice may need to replace small-scale techniques.

Enlarging a small-quantity recipe in steps is more likely to be successful than increasing size too quickly. Following are suggestions for expanding home-size recipes:

Step 1   Prepare the product in the amount of the original recipe, following the quantities and procedures exactly and noting any procedures that are unclear or any problems that occur during preparation.

Step 2   Evaluate the product and decide if it is acceptable for the foodservice. If adjustments are necessary, revise the recipe and make the product again. Prepare the small-size amount until the product is satisfactory.

Step 3   Double the recipe or expand to an appropriate amount for the pan size that will be used, and prepare the product, making notations on the recipe of any changes you make. For example, additional cooking time may be needed for the larger amount. Use Table 1.24 for increasing recipe size. Evaluate the product and record the yield, portion size, and acceptability.

Step 4   Double the recipe again, or if the product is to be baked, calculate the quantities needed to prepare one baking pan of the size that will be used in the foodservice. Use Table 1.24 for increasing recipe size. If ingredients are to be weighed, home-size measures should be converted to pounds and ounces or to pounds and tenths of a pound before proceeding further. Prepare and evaluate the product as before.

Step 5   If the product is satisfactory, continue to enlarge by increments of 25 portions or by pans until approximately 100 portions are prepared. Recipes with larger yields should be evaluated for acceptability and adjustment made each time the yield is increased significantly.

TABLE 1.1 **Amounts of food to serve 50**[a]

Food	Serving portion	Amount for 50 portions	Miscellaneous information
BEVERAGES			
Cider	4 oz (½ cup)	2 gal	64 4-oz portions
Cocoa	6 oz (¾ cup)	2½ gal	50 6-oz portions
Unsweetened powder		8 oz	
Instant mix		2½ lb	
Coffee	6 oz (¾ cup)	2½ gal	
Regular or urn grind		1–1½ lb	
Freeze-dried		2–3 oz	
Instant		3 oz	
Lemonade	8 oz (1 cup)	3 gal	48 8-oz portions
Frozen concentrate		3 32-oz cans	dilute 1:4 parts water
Orange juice, see Juices			
Punch	4 oz (½ cup)	2–2½ gal	1 gal yields 32 4-oz portions
			2½ gal yields 50 4-oz portions plus 30 re-fills
Tea			
Hot	6 oz (¾ cup)	2½ gal	
Bulk		2 oz	Amount may vary with quality of tea
Iced	8 oz (1 cup)	3 gal	48 8-oz portions
1-oz bag		6 bags	6 1-oz bags make 3 gal
Instant		1–1½ oz	
Wine	See Tables 17–1 and 17–2		
BREAD AND CRACKERS			
Biscuits, baking powder	1 biscuit	4½ doz	
Dough ready for baking		5 lb	
Mix		2½ lb	
Bread			
1½-lb loaf	1 slice	2½ loaves	24 slices per loaf
2-lb pullman	1 slice	1½ loaves	36 slices per loaf
Breads, quick 5 × 9 × 2¾-inch loaves	1 slice	4 loaves	16 slices per loaf
Coffee cake, 12 × 18 × 2-inch	3 × 2¼-inch	2 pans	Cut 4 × 8
Batter, ready to bake		5–6 lb per pan	
Crackers			
Graham	2 crackers	1¾–2 lb	60–65 per lb
Saltines	4 crackers	1½ lb	150–160 per lb
Soda	2 crackers	1½–2 lb	65 per lb

[a]Abbreviations used: AP, as purchased; EP, edible portion.

TABLE 1.1   Continued

Food	Serving portion	Amount for 50 portions	Miscellaneous information
Muffins	1 muffin	4½ doz	
Batter, ready to bake		5 lb	
Mix		3½ lb	
Pancakes	3½ oz	7 qt batter	2 4-inch cakes
Mix		6 lb	
Rolls			
Breakfast, 3-oz	1 roll	4½ doz	
Dinner, 1½-oz	1 roll	4½ doz	
Frozen dough		10 lb	
Mix		5 lb	
Toast			
French	2 slices	7 lb bread	
Buttered or cinnamon	2 slices	7 lb bread	
Waffles	3 oz	6 qt batter	1 waffle
CEREALS			
Cooked cereal	⅔ cup	2 lb	2 gal cooked
Hominy grits	⅔ cup	2 lb	2 gal cooked
Cold cereal, flakes, crisp	1 oz (½–¾ cup)	3 lb	
Rice	½ cup	3–4 lb	6–8 qt cooked
See also Pasta			
DAIRY PRODUCTS			
Butter or margarine			
For sandwiches		1 lb	To butter 100 slices
For table	1–2 pats	1–1½ lb	
For vegetables	½–1 tsp	4–8 oz	
Cheese, cheddar, Monterey Jack, Swiss, provolone	1–1½ oz	3–5 lb	For sandwich or with cold cuts
Sandwich slices	1 oz	3¼ lb	
Cottage	2 oz (No. 20 dipper)	6½ lb	For salad or side dish
Cream	½ oz	2 lb	For salad or garnish
Dessert (cream, blue, Camembert)	1 oz	3 lb	
Cream			
Coffee		1–1½ qt	
Whipping	2 Tbsp	1½ pt	1½ qt whipped
Ice cream or sherbet, bulk	No. 12 dipper	2½ gal	Dish or sundae
	No. 16 dipper	1½ gal	With cake or cookie
	No. 20 dipper	1¼ gal	For à la mode
Milk			
Fluid	8 oz (1 cup)	3 gal	

TABLE 1.1 **Continued**

Food	Serving portion	Amount for 50 portions	Miscellaneous information
Nonfat dry	8 oz (1 cup)	3 lb	3.5 oz (1⅓ cups) dry milk per qt of water. Volume may vary with brand.
Nondairy creamer	1 tsp	3 oz	
Sherbet			See Ice cream
Sour cream	1 oz (2 Tbsp)	3 lb	For baked potato
	1 tsp	8 oz	For garnish
Whipped topping mix			
Dry	2 Tbsp	5 oz	
Frozen	2 Tbsp	18 oz (1½ qt)	
Liquid	2 Tbsp	1½ pt	1½ qt whipped
Yogurt	8 oz (1 cup)	25 lb	
DESSERTS			
Cakes			
Angel food	1 oz	3–4 10-inch cakes	12–14 cuts per cake
Pound or loaf, 5 × 9-inch	3 oz	4 loaves	
Sheet, 12 × 18 × 2-inch	3 × 2¼-inch	2 pans	Cut 4 × 8
Batter, ready to bake		4–5 lb each	
Sheet, 18 × 26 × 2-inch	3 × 2½-inch	1 pan	Cut 6 × 10
Batter, ready to bake		8–10 lb	
Cake mixes			
Angel food		4 lb	
Chocolate, white, yellow		5 lb	
Pies, 8-inch	⅙ pie	8 pies	Cut 6 pieces per pie
Filling			
Chiffon	3 cups per pie	6 qt	
Cream or custard	3 cups per pie	6 qt	
Fruit	3 cups (1 lb 8 oz per pie)	6 qt (10–12 lb)	
Meringue	4 oz per pie	2 lb	
Pastry			
1 crust	5 oz per pie	2 lb 8 oz	
2 crust	9 oz per pie	4 lb 8 oz	
Pies, 9-inch	⅛ pie	7 pies	Cut 8 pieces per pie
Filling			
Chiffon	3¾ cups per pie	6–7 qt	
Cream or custard	3¾ cups per pie	6–7 qt	
Fruit	3¾–4 cups (1 lb 14 oz)	6–7 qt (10–12 lb)	
Meringue	5–6 oz per pie	2–2¼ lb	

TABLE 1.1 Continued

Food	Serving portion	Amount for 50 portions	Miscellaneous information
Pies, continued			
Pastry			
1 crust	9 oz per pie	4 lb	
2 crust	16 oz per pie	7 lb	
Puddings	½ cup (4 oz)	6¼ qt	No. 10 dipper
Toppings, sauce	2–3 Tbsp	2–3 qt	
EGGS			
Eggs			
In shell	1 egg	4½ doz	
Fresh or frozen, whole	1 egg	5 lb (2½ qt)	
FISH AND SHELLFISH			
Fish			
Fillets and steaks, 4 per lb	3 oz	14–16 lb	1 lb AP = 0.70 lb cooked fish
Whole, dressed	3 oz	40 lb	1 lb AP = 0.27 lb cooked fish
Oysters, shucked	3–4 oz	1½–2 gal	1 lb AP = 0.38 lb cooked oysters
Scallops, frozen, to fry	3 oz	10–12 lb	
Shrimp			
Raw, in shell	2 oz	12½ lb	1 lb AP = 0.54 lb cooked shrimp
	3 oz	18–20 lb	
Raw, peeled and cleaned	3 oz	16 lb	1 lb peeled = 0.62 lb cooked shrimp
Cooked, peeled and cleaned	3 oz	10 lb	1 lb AP = 1.00 lb cooked shrimp
FRUITS			
Canned			
For pies, see Desserts			
For salad or dessert	3–4 oz (½ cup)	2–2½ No. 10 cans	For fruits such as peach or pear halves and sliced pineapple, depends on count per can
Fresh			
Apples	1 apple	½ box	Size 113
8 8-inch pies	⅙ pie	14–16 lb AP	1 lb AP = 0.91 lb ready to cook or serve raw with peels; 0.78 lb pared, cooked
7 9-inch pies	⅛ pie	16 lb AP	
Salad or dessert	3–3½ oz	15 lb AP	
Apricots	2	9 lb AP	Medium size 12 per lb

TABLE 1.1 **Continued**

Food	Serving portion	Amount for 50 portions	Miscellaneous information
Avocado	½	25 avocados	Medium size 2 per lb
Salad	3 slices	12 avocados	1 lb AP = 0.67 lb ready to serve raw
Bananas	1	16 lb AP	Small, 5–6 inch 1 lb AP = 0.65 lb ready to serve raw
Salad	3 oz	10 lb AP	Medium, 7–8 inch, 3 per lb
Blueberries	4 oz	12–14 lb AP	1 lb AP = 0.96 lb ready to serve raw
Cherries, sweet	3 oz	10 lb AP	1 lb AP = 0.98 lb ready to serve with pits; 0.84 lb pitted
Cranberries, for sauce	¼ cup	4 lb AP	1 lb AP = 0.95 lb ready to cook
Fruit cup (mixed fruits)	3 oz (⅓ cup)	9 lb (6 qt)	
Grapefruit	½	25 fruit	64 to 80 size
Salad	5 sections	21 fruit	12 sections per fruit 1 lb AP = 0.52 lb ready to serve raw
Grapes, seedless	4 oz	12–15 lb AP	1 lb AP = 0.97 lb ready to serve raw
With seeds			1 lb AP = 0.89 lb raw seeded
Kiwi	1 slice, for garnish	6–8 fruit	7–8 slices per fruit
Lemons			
For tea or fish	⅙ lemon	8–10 lemons	Medium, size 165
For lemonade	8-oz glass	3 doz	Medium, size 165
Limes			
Garnish	1 wedge	12 limes	4 wedges per lime
Limeade	8-oz glass	4½ doz	
Mangoes, cubed or sliced	½ cup	12½ lb AP	1 lb AP = 0.69 lb ready to serve raw
Melon			
Cantaloupe	½ melon	25 melons	
Fruit cup		5 melons	1 lb AP = 0.52 lb ready to serve raw
Salad slices		6 melons	
Casaba, honeydew, or persian	⅛ melon	7 melons	1 lb AP = 0.46 lb ready to serve raw
Watermelon	12–16 oz	38–50 lb AP	1 lb AP = 0.57 lb fruit without rind
Nectarines	1 nectarine (5 oz)	15–16 lb AP	1 lb AP = 0.91 lb ready to serve raw

TABLE 1.1 Continued

Food	Serving portion	Amount for 50 portions	Miscellaneous information
Oranges	1 orange	½ box	Size 113
Juice	4 oz (½ cup)	6¼ qt	16–18 doz size 113
Sections	5 sections	18 oranges	Size 150; 1 lb AP = 0.40 lb ready to serve, without membrane
Peaches	1 peach (4–5 oz)	12–15 lb AP	
Diced or sliced	½ cup	20 lb AP	1 lb AP = 0.76 lb ready to cook or serve raw
Pears	1 pear (5–6 oz)	17–19 lb AP	1 lb AP = 0.92 lb ready to cook or serve raw, unpared; 0.78 lb pared
Salad	3 slices	15–17 lb AP	8–10 slices per pear
Pineapple, cubed	½ cup	24 lb AP (6 pineapples)	1 lb AP = 0.54 lb ready to serve raw
Plums, Italian or purple	2 plums	12½ lb AP	Medium size, 8 per lb 1 lb AP = 0.94 lb ready to cook or serve raw
Rhubarb, 8 8-inch pies	⅙ pie	10–12 lb AP	1 lb AP = 0.86 lb ready to cook
7 9-inch pies	⅛ pie	12 lb AP	
Sauce	½ cup	14 lb AP	
Strawberries	4 oz	14 lb AP	1 lb AP = 0.88 lb ready to serve raw
Garnish	1 berry	1 qt AP	1 qt AP = about 1.32 lb ready to serve raw
Shortcake	¾ cup	8–9 qt AP	
Sundaes	½–¾ cup	6–8 qt AP	
Strawberries, frozen			
For pies, see Desserts			
For salad or dessert	4 oz (½ cup)	13–15 lb	
For topping	1½ oz	5 lb	
JUICES			
Fruit or vegetable	4 oz (½ cup)	6¼ qt	
	6 oz (¾ cup)	9½ qt	
Canned	4 oz	4 46-oz cans	
	6 oz	7 46-oz cans	
Frozen	4 oz	4–5 12-oz cans	Dilute 1:3 parts water
		2 32-oz cans	Dilute 1:3 parts water
	6 oz	7 12-oz cans	Dilute 1:3 parts water
		3 32-oz cans	Dilute 1:3 parts water

TABLE 1.1   Continued

Food	Serving portion	Amount for 50 portions	Miscellaneous information
MEAT			
Beef			
Brisket, corned, boneless	3 oz EP	25–30 lb AP	1 lb AP = 0.42 lb cooked lean meat
Brisket, fresh, boneless	3 oz EP	25–30 lb AP	1 lb AP = 0.46 lb cooked lean meat
Cubed, 1-inch, for stew	3 oz EP	12–15 lb AP	1 lb AP = 0.56 lb cooked lean meat
Ground, no more than 30% fat	3 oz EP	13–15 lb AP	1 lb AP = 0.70 lb cooked meat
Lean	3 oz EP	11–13 lb AP	1 lb AP = 0.8 lb cooked meat
Extra lean	3 oz EP	11–12 lb AP	1 lb AP = 0.85 lb cooked meat
Liver	3½ oz EP	16 lb AP	1 lb AP = 0.70 cooked liver
Roast			
Chuck, pot roast, boneless	3 oz EP	18 lb AP	1 lb AP = 0.70 lb lean cooked meat
With bone	3 oz EP	20–22 lb AP	1 lb AP = 0.45 lb cooked lean meat
Rib, standing	6 oz EP	45–50 lb AP	Bone in, oven prepared
Ribeye	3 oz EP	12–15 lb AP	1 lb AP = 0.75 lb lean cooked meat
Round, bottom boneless	3 oz EP	18 lb AP	1 lb AP = 0.78 lb cooked lean meat
Inside, boneless	3 oz EP	18 lb AP	1 lb AP = 0.73 lb cooked meat
Rump, boneless	3 oz EP	16–18 lb AP	1 lb AP = 0.62 lb cooked lean meat
Sirloin, boneless, trimmed	3 oz EP	16–18 lb AP	1 lb AP = 0.61 lb cooked lean meat
Short ribs, trimmed	3 oz EP	38–40 lb AP	1 lb AP = 0.25 lb cooked meat
Steaks			
Cubed, 4 per lb	3 oz EP	17 lb AP	
Flank, 4 per lb	3 oz EP	17 lb AP	1 lb AP = 0.67 lb cooked lean meat
Loin strip	8 oz AP	25 lb AP	Short cut, bone in
Round, boneless, 3 per lb	3½ oz EP	18–20 lb AP	1 lb AP = 0.59 lb cooked lean meat
Sirloin, boneless	3½ oz EP	14–16 lb AP	1 lb AP = 0.75 lb cooked lean meat

TABLE 1.1 Continued

Food	Serving portion	Amount for 50 portions	Miscellaneous information
Steaks, continued			
Tenderloin, trimmed	4 oz EP	14 lb AP	1 lb AP = 0.90 lb cooked lean meat
T-bone	8 oz AP 12 oz AP	25 lb AP 36–38 AP	
Lamb			
Chops, rib, 4 per lb	2 each	25 lb AP	1 lb AP = 0.46 lb cooked lean meat
Roast, leg, boneless	3 oz EP	15 lb AP	1 lb AP = 0.61 lb cooked lean meat
With bone	3 oz EP	22 lb AP	1 lb AP = 0.45 lb cooked lean meat
Pork, Fresh			
Chops, loin, with bone, 3 per lb	1 chop	17 lb AP	1 lb AP = 0.41 lb cooked lean meat
Cutlets, 3 or 4 per lb	3–3½ oz EP	12–15 lb AP	1 lb AP = 0.75 lb cooked meat
Roast, loin, boneless	3 oz EP	18–20 lb AP	1 lb AP = 0.54 lb cooked lean meat
With bone	3 oz EP	22–24 lb AP	1 lb AP = 0.41 lb cooked lean meat
Fresh ham, whole boneless	3 oz EP	18–20 lb AP	1 lb AP = 0.53 lb cooked lean meat
With bone	3 oz EP	20–22 lb AP	1 lb AP = 0.46 lb cooked lean meat
Shoulder, Boston butt, boneless	3 oz EP	18–20 lb AP	1 lb AP = 0.54 lb cooked lean meat
With bone	3 oz EP	19–21 lb AP	1 lb AP = 0.50 lb cooked lean meat
Shoulder, picnic, boneless	3 oz EP	20–22 lb AP	1 lb AP = 0.46 lb cooked lean meat
With bone	3 oz EP	25 lb AP	1 lb AP = 0.38 lb cooked lean meat
Sausage, bulk	2-oz pattie	12½–15 lb AP	1 lb AP = 0.47 lb cooked lean meat
Links, 12–16 per lb	2 links	7–8 lb AP	1 lb AP = 0.47 lb cooked lean meat
Spareribs	8–12 oz AP	25–40 lb AP	1 lb AP = 0.39 lb cooked meat
Pork, Cured			
Bacon, sliced			
Hotel pack	2 slices	4–5 lb	24 slices per lb
Sliced	2 slices	5–6 lb	17–20 slices per lb

TABLE 1.1   **Continued**

Food	Serving portion	Amount for 50 portions	Miscellaneous information
Canadian	2 slices (2 oz)	10 lb	16 slices per lb
Ham, boneless	3 oz EP	15 lb AP	1 lb AP = 0.63 lb cooked lean meat
With bone	3 oz EP	18–20 lb AP	1 lb AP = 0.53 lb cooked lean meat
Fully cooked, ready to eat	3 oz EP	15 lb AP	
Pullman, canned	3 oz EP	12–15 lb AP	1 lb AP = 0.64 lb cooked lean meat
Shoulder, Boston butt, boneless	3 oz EP	16 lb AP	1 lb AP = 0.60 lb cooked lean meat
Shoulder, picnic, boneless	3 oz EP	18 lb AP	1 lb AP = 0.53 lb cooked lean meat
Variety and Luncheon Meats			
Braunschweiger	2 oz	7 lb	
Frankfurters			
8 per lb	2 franks	12½ lb	
10 per lb	2 franks	10 lb	
Knockwurst	3 oz	10 lb	
Sliced luncheon meat	1 oz	3¼ lb	16 slices per lb
Veal			
Cubed, 1-inch for stew	2 oz EP	12–15 lb AP	1 lb AP = 0.65 lb cooked lean meat
Cutlets, 3 or 4 per lb	3–3½ oz EP	12½–15 lb AP	1 lb AP = 0.80 lb cooked lean meat
Ground	3–4 oz EP	15–18 lb AP	1 lb AP = 0.73 lb cooked lean meat
Roast, leg, boneless	3 oz EP	15–18 lb AP	1 lb AP = 0.61 lb cooked lean meat
Shoulder, boneless	3 oz EP	18 lb AP	1 lb AP = 0.59 lb cooked lean meat
PASTA			
Macaroni, noodles, and spaghetti	4 oz	4½–5 lb dry	12 lb cooked
In casseroles	2 oz	2–3 lb dry	6–7 lb cooked
POULTRY			
Chicken			
Fryer parts			
½ breast (without back)	5 oz AP	15–16 lb AP	1 lb AP = 0.66 lb cooked chicken
1 drumstick and thigh	6 oz AP	19–20 lb AP	
1 drumstick	3 oz AP	10 lb AP	1 lb AP = 0.49 lb cooked chicken
1 thigh	3 oz AP	10–11 lb AP	1 lb AP = 0.50 lb cooked chicken

TABLE 1.1   Continued

Food	Serving portion	Amount for 50 portions	Miscellaneous information
Chicken, continued			
2 wings	5 oz AP	15 lb AP	1 lb AP = 0.34 lb cooked chicken
Whole	¼ fryer	13 fryers	2½–3 lb each
	½ fryer	25 fryers	1¾–2 lb each
Whole, for stewing	3 oz cooked chicken without bone	26–28 lb AP	1 lb AP = 0.36 lb cooked chicken, not using neck and giblets; 0.41 lb using neck meat and giblets.
Cooked, diced	2 oz	6 lb 4 oz	
Turkey, dressed, whole for roasting	3 oz EP (slices)	40–50 lb AP	1 lb AP = 0.53 lb cooked turkey with skin, without neck and giblets; without skin 0.47 lb
Boneless roll, raw	3–4 oz EP	16–18 lb AP	1 lb AP = 0.66 lb cooked turkey meat
Boneless roll, cooked	3–4 oz EP	12–15 lb AP	1 lb AP = 0.92 lb cooked turkey meat
Breasts, whole, raw	3 oz EP	19 lb AP	1 lb AP = 0.64 lb turkey meat with skin; 0.57 lb without skin
Leg quarters	3 oz EP	19 lb AP	1 lb AP = 0.53 lb cooked turkey; without skin 0.48 lb
Ground	3 oz EP	11–12 lb	1 lb AP = 0.85 lb cooked meat
Tenderloin (steaks)	4 oz	14–15 lb	1 lb AP = 0.90 lb cooked meat
Wings	3–4 oz EP	30 lb	1 lb AP = 0.32 lb cooked meat (without skin)
Turkey ham, cooked	1½ oz	5 lb	
Turkey, cooked, cubed	1½–2 oz	5–6 lb EP (18–20 lb AP)	3¾–4½ qt
Canned, see Chicken			
RELISHES			
Catsup	1 oz	½ No. 10 can	1 No. 10 can = about 12 cups
	1 oz	5 14-oz bottles	
Mustard, prepared	½ tsp	½ cup	
Olives, green, whole	3	2 qt	88–90 per qt
Ripe, whole or pitted	3	1½ qt	120–150 per qt

TABLE 1.1 Continued

Food	Serving portion	Amount for 50 portions	Miscellaneous information
Pickles, dill, whole	1 pickle	2½ qt	
Dill or sweet, sliced	1 oz	2¼ qt	
Pickle relish	1 oz	2 qt	1 gal = about 58 oz drained
SALADS AND SALAD DRESSINGS			
Salads			
Bulky vegetable	1 cup	3 gal	
Fish or meat	½ cup	6–7 qt	
Fruit	⅓ cup	4¼ qt	
Gelatin	½ cup	1 12 × 20 × 2-inch pan	24-oz pkg flavored gelatin, 1 gal liquid
Potato	½ cup	6–7 qt	
Dressings			
Mixed in salad			
French, thin	1 Tbsp	3–4 cups	
Mayonnaise	1–2 Tbsp	1 qt	
Self-service			
Thousand Island, Roquefort, or Ranch	1–2 Tbsp	1½–2 qt	
French	1 Tbsp	1–1½ qt	
SAUCES			
Gravy	3–4 Tbsp	3–4 qt	
Meat accompaniment	2 Tbsp	2 qt	
Pudding	2–3 Tbsp	2–3 qt	
Vegetable	2–3 Tbsp	2–3 qt	
Salsa	2–3 Tbsp	2–3 qt	Condiment for Mexican entrees
SOUPS			
Soup			
First course	½–1 cup (4–8 oz)	2–3¼ gal	
Main course	1 cup (8 oz)	3¼ gal	
Soup			
Concentrated	1 cup (8 oz)	5 46-oz cans	
Soup base, paste		10 oz	For 2½ gal soup
SUGARS, JELLIES, SWEET, NUTS			
Candies, small	2 each	1 lb	
Honey	2 Tbsp	5 lb (2 qt)	
Jam or jelly	1 Tbsp	2–3 lb	
Marshmallows	3	1–1½ lb	
Nuts, mixed	1½ Tbsp	1–1½ lb	
Sugar, cubes	1–2 cubes	1½ lb	
Granulated	1½ tsp	12 oz	

TABLE 1.1   Continued

Food	Serving portion	Amount for 50 portions	Miscellaneous information
Syrup	¼ cup	3 qt	
Toppings for dessert	2 Tbsp	1½–2 qt	
VEGETABLES			
Canned	2½ oz	2 No. 10 cans	Most vegetables yield 60–70 oz drained weight
Dried			
Dehydrated potatoes			
Diced or sliced	3–4 oz	2–2½ lb AP	
Instant for mashing	4 oz	2–2¼ lb AP	
Dried beans	4 oz	5–6 lb AP	
Split peas or lentils	4 oz	4 lb AP	
Fresh			
Alfalfa sprouts	2 Tbsp	1 lb	
Asparagus	3 oz	18–20 lb AP	1 lb AP = 0.53 lb ready to cook; 0.50 lb cooked
Beans, green or wax	3 oz	10–12 lb AP	1 lb AP = 0.88 lb ready to cook
Bean sprouts	2 Tbsp	12 oz	
Beets, topped	3 oz	12–14 lb AP	1 lb AP = 0.77 lb peeled; 0.73 lb cooked slices
Broccoli	3 oz	16–20 lb AP	1 lb AP = 0.81 lb ready to cook
Brussels sprouts	3 oz	12–14 lb AP	1 lb AP = 0.76 lb ready to cook
Cabbage			
Green	1 wedge or 3 oz shredded	12–14 lb AP	1 lb AP = 0.89 lb ready to cook or serve raw
Red, chopped or shredded	2 oz	10 lb AP	1 lb AP = 0.64 lb ready to cook or serve raw
Carrots, without tops	3 oz	14–16 lb AP	1 lb AP = 0.70 lb ready to cook or serve raw; 0.60 lb cooked
Strips for relish	3 strips, 4 × ½ inch	4–5 lb	
Cauliflower	3 oz	16–18 lb AP	1 lb AP = 0.62 lb ready to cook or serve raw; 0.61 lb cooked

TABLE 1.1 Continued

Food	Serving portion	Amount for 50 portions	Miscellaneous information
Salad pieces	¼ cup	8 lb AP	1 medium head = about 6 cups (50–75 florets)
Celery, sliced	3 oz	12 lb AP	1 lb AP = 0.83 lb ready to cook or serve raw; 0.74 lb cooked
Sticks for relishes	4 sticks, 4 × ½ inch	4–5 lb AP	
Celery cabbage	2 oz	9 lb AP	1 lb AP = 0.93 lb ready to serve raw
Corn, on cob	1 ear	5 doz (25 lb with husks)	1 lb AP = 0.33 lb edible portion cooked
Cucumbers	1½ oz	5–6 lb AP	1 lb AP = 0.84 lb pared ready to serve raw
Eggplant	3 oz	12–15 lb AP	1 lb AP = 0.81 lb ready to cook
Endive, escarole	½ cup	8–10 lb AP	1 lb AP = 0.78 lb ready to serve
Lettuce			
Iceberg, wedges	⅙ head	8–10 heads	24 heads per crate
Broken, for salad	1 cup (2½ oz)	9½ lb AP	1 lb AP = 0.76 lb ready to serve
Garnish	1 leaf	4–5 lb AP	
Leaf, for garnish	1 leaf	3–4 lb AP	1 lb AP = 0.66 lb ready to serve
Bibb	2½ oz	9 lb	
Romaine, for salad	2½ oz	9 lb AP	1 lb AP = 0.64 lb ready to serve
Mushrooms, sliced	3 oz	12 lb AP	1 lb AP = 0.98 ready to serve raw or cook; 0.22 lb cooked
For sauce	1 oz	3–4 lb AP	
Onions			
Green, chopped for salad	¼ cup (with tops)	3½–4 lb AP	1 lb AP = 0.83 lb ready to serve raw with tops; 0.37 lb without tops
Mature	2 oz	7–8 lb AP	1 lb AP = 0.88 lb ready to serve raw or cook; 0.78 lb cooked
Whole, to bake	1 medium	12–15 lb AP	
Parsley, for garnish or seasoning		2 lb AP	1 lb AP = 0.92 lb ready to serve raw

TABLE 1.1   Continued

Food	Serving portion	Amount for 50 portions	Miscellaneous information
Parsnips	3 oz	12–15 lb AP	1 lb AP = 0.83 lb ready to cook
Peppers, green, red, and yellow strips	3 strips	4–5 lb AP	1 lb AP = 0.80 lb ready to cook or serve raw; 0.73 lb cooked
Chopped for salads	½ oz	1–2 lb AP	
Potatoes, sweet, or yams to bake	1 potato (4½–5 oz)	18–20 lb AP	1 lb AP = 0.61 lb baked, without skins
Candied	4 oz	20–25 lb AP	1 lb AP = 0.80 lb peeled, ready to cook
Mashed	4 oz	18 lb AP	
Potatoes, white, baked	1 potato	17–25 lb AP	1 lb AP = 0.74 lb baked potato without skins
Mashed	4 oz (½ cup)	15 lb AP	1 lb AP = 0.81 lb ready to cook pared
Steamed	4 oz (1 potato)	16–17 lb AP	
French fried	4–5 oz	16–20 lb AP	1 lb AP = 0.81 ready to cook
Radishes, without tops, for relishes	2 oz	6 lb AP	1 lb AP = 0.94 lb ready to serve raw
Salad greens	3 oz	10 lb	
Spinach	3 oz	12 lb AP	1 lb AP = 0.88 lb ready to cook or serve raw
For salad	1 oz	4–5 lb AP	
Squash, summer, yellow	3 oz	10 lb AP	1 lb AP = 0.95 ready to cook; 0.83 lb cooked
Zucchini	3 oz	10 lb AP	1 lb AP = 0.94 ready to cook; 0.86 lb cooked
Squash, winter, acorn	½ squash	20–25 lb AP	1 lb AP = 0.87 lb ready to cook in skin
Butternut	3 oz	12 lb AP	1 lb AP = 0.84 lb ready to cook pared
Hubbard, baked	2½-inch square	20–25 lb	
Mashed	3 oz	15 lb AP	1 lb AP = 0.64 lb ready to cook pared
Tomatoes	1 small	20 lb AP	
Sliced, salad	3 slices	15 lb AP	1 lb AP = 0.90 lb ready to cook or serve raw

TABLE 1.1 Continued

Food	Serving portion	Amount for 50 portions	Miscellaneous information
Diced	½ cup	10 lb AP	
Cherry, salad	1 oz	4 lb AP	1 lb AP = 0.97 lb stemmed
Turnips	3 oz	12–15 lb AP	1 lb AP = 0.79 lb ready to cook or serve raw; 0.78 lb cooked
Watercress	1½ oz	4–5 lb AP	1 lb AP = 0.92 lb ready to serve raw
Yams, see Potatoes, sweet			
Frozen			
Asparagus spears	3 oz	10 lb	
Beans, cut green or lima	3 oz	10 lb	
Broccoli	3 oz	10 lb	
Brussels sprouts	3 oz	10 lb	
Cauliflower	3 oz	10 lb	
Corn, whole kernel	3 oz	10 lb	
Peas	3 oz	10 lb	
Potatoes			
French fried	4 oz	12–13 lb	
Hashed brown	4 oz	12–13 lb	
Spinach	3 oz	10 lb	
MISCELLANEOUS			
Ice			
For water glasses	3–4 oz	10–12 lb	
For punch bowl		10 lb	
Potato chips	1 oz	3 lb	

TABLE 1.2   Approximate yield in the preparation of fresh fruits and vegetables (in lb)

Weight of ready to cook or ready to serve raw from 1 lb as purchased

Apples	0.78	Lettuce, head	0.76
Asparagus	0.53	Lettuce, leaf	0.66
Avocado	0.67	Lettuce, romaine	0.64
Bananas	0.65	Mangoes	0.69
Beans, green or wax	0.88	Mushrooms	0.98
Beans, lima	0.44	Nectarines	0.91
Beets	0.77	Okra	0.87
Blueberries	0.96	Onions, mature	0.88
Broccoli	0.81	Orange sections	0.40
Brussels sprouts	0.76	Papaya	0.62
Cabbage, green	0.87	Parsnips	0.83
Cabbage, red	0.64	Peaches	0.76
Cantaloupe, served without rind	0.52	Pears, served pared	0.78
Carrots	0.70	Peas, green	0.38
Cauliflower	0.62	Peppers, green	0.80
Celery	0.83	Pineapple	0.54
Chard, Swiss	0.92	Plums	0.94
Cherries, pitted	0.87	Potatoes, sweet	0.80
Chicory	0.89	Potatoes, white	0.81
Collards, leaves	0.57	Radishes, without tops	0.94
Collards, leaves and stems	0.74	Rhubarb, without leaves	0.86
Cranberries	0.95	Rutabagas	0.85
Cucumbers, pared	0.84	Spinach, partly trimmed	0.88
Eggplant	0.81	Squash, acorn or patty pan	0.87
Endive, escarole	0.78	Squash, butternut	0.84
Ginger, fresh	0.77	Squash, Hubbard	0.64
Grapefruit sections	0.52	Squash, summer	0.95
Grapes, seedless	0.97	Squash, zucchini	0.94
Honeydew melon, served without rind	0.46	Strawberries	0.88
		Tomatoes	0.99
Kale	0.67	Turnips, without tops	0.79
Kiwi	0.85	Watermelon	0.57

Adapted from *Food Buying Guide for School Food Service*, U.S. Department of Agriculture PA 1257, Washington, D.C., 1980.

Note

- *How to Use This Table*   To determine the amount of fruits or vegetables to yield the amount stated in a recipe as EP or as ready to cook in Table 15.1, Timetable for Boiling or Steaming Fresh Vegetables:

- Divide the weight of ready to cook or EP desired by the figure given in this table. For example, the recipe for Mashed Potatoes calls for 12 lb EP potatoes. To change the 12 lb EP to AP, divide 12 lb by 0.81, the ready to cook weight from 1 lb AP.

    12 lb EP divided by 0.81 lb = 14.8 or 15 lb to purchase

- For conversion to pounds and ounces, refer to Table 1.21.

TABLE 1.3   Food weights and approximate equivalents in measure

Food	Weight	Approximate measure
Alfalfa sprouts	1 lb	6 cups
Allspice, ground	1 oz	4½ Tbsp
Almonds, blanched, slivered, chopped	1 lb	3½ cups
Apples, canned, pie pack	1 lb	2 cups
Apples, fresh, AP[a]	1 lb	3–4 medium (113)
Apples, fresh, pared and sliced	1 lb	1 qt
Apples, pared and diced, 1½-inch cubes	1 lb	3½ cups
Applesauce	1 lb	2 cups
Apricots, canned halves, without juice	1 lb	2 cups or 12–20 halves
Apricots, canned, pie pack	1 lb	2 cups
Apricots, dried, AP	1 lb	3 cups
Apricots, dried, cooked, without juice	1 lb	4½–5 cups
Apricots, fresh	1 lb	5–8 apricots
Asparagus, canned, cuts	1 lb	2½ cups
Asparagus, canned tips, drained	1 lb	16–20 stalks
Asparagus, fresh	1 lb	16–20 stalks
Avocado	1 lb	2 medium
Bacon bits	1 lb	3⅓ cups
Bacon, cooked	1 lb	85–95 slices
Bacon, uncooked	1 lb	14–25 slices
Bacon, uncooked, diced	1 lb	2¼ cups
Baking powder	1 oz	2⅓ Tbsp
Baking powder	1 lb	2⅓ cups
Baking soda	1 oz	2⅓ Tbsp
Baking soda	1 lb	2⅓ cups
Bananas, AP	1 lb	3 medium
Bananas, diced	1 lb	2½–3 cups
Bananas, mashed	1 lb	2 cups
Barbecue sauce	1 lb	2 cups
Barley, pearl	1 lb	2 cups
Basil, sweet, dried	1 oz	1⅓ cups
Basil leaves, fresh (loosely packed)	1 oz	¾ cup
Bay leaves	1 oz	2 cups
Beans, baked	1 lb	2 cups

[a]AP denotes "as purchased," which refers to the status of the product before it is peeled, hulled, cored, or otherwise prepared for cooking.

TABLE 1.3   **Continued**

Food	Weight	Approximate measure
Beans, garbanzo, canned	1 lb	2½ cups
Beans, Great Northern, dried, AP	1 lb	2½ cups
Beans, green, cut, cooked	1 lb	3 cups
Beans, green, cut, frozen	1 lb	3 cups
Beans, kidney, dried, AP	1 lb	2½ cups
Beans, kidney, dried, 1 lb AP, after cooking	2 lb 6 oz	6–7 cups
Beans, lima, dried, AP	1 lb	2½ cups
Beans, lima, dried, 1 lb AP, after cooking	2 lb 9 oz	6 cups
Beans, lima, fresh, canned, or frozen	1 lb	3 cups
Beans, navy or black turtle, dried, AP	1 lb	2¼ cups
Beans, navy, dried, 1 lb AP, after cooking	2 lb 3 oz	5½–6 cups
Beans, pinto, dried, AP	1 lb	2½ cups
Bean sprouts, canned, drained	1 lb	1 qt
Bean sprouts, fresh	1 lb	2 qt
Beef, cooked, diced	1 lb	3 cups
Beef, dried, solid pack	1 lb	3¾ cups
Beef, ground, raw	1 lb	2 cups
Beef base (paste)	1 lb	2½ cups
Beets, cooked, diced or sliced	1 lb	2½–3 cups
Beets, fresh, medium	1 lb	3–4 beets
Blackberries, fresh, frozen, IQF[b]	1 lb	3½ cups
Blackberries or boysenberries, pie pack	1 lb	2½ cups
Blackeyed peas, dried	1 lb	2¾ cups
Blueberries, canned	1 lb	2 cups
Blueberries, fresh, frozen, IQF	1 lb	3 cups
Bran, all bran	1 lb	2 qt
Bran flakes	1 lb	3 qt
Bread, dry, broken	1 lb	8–9 cups
Bread, fresh	1 lb	8 oz dry crumbs
Bread, loaf	1 lb	16–18 slices, ½ inch each
Bread, sandwich	2 lb	36–40 slices, thin

[b]IQF denotes "individually quick frozen."

TABLE 1.3 Continued

Food	Weight	Approximate measure
Bread, soft, broken	1 lb	2½ qt
Bread crumbs, dry, ground	1 lb	4 cups (1 qt)
Bread crumbs, soft	1 lb	2 qt
Broccoli, florets	1 lb	4 cups
Broccoli, head	1 lb	1 medium
Brussels sprouts, AP	1 lb	1 qt
Butter	1 lb	2 cups
Buttermilk, dry	1 oz	¼ cup
Buttermilk, dry	1 lb	4 cups
Butterscotch chips	1 lb	2⅔ cups
Cabbage, raw, shredded	1 lb	1 qt lightly packed
Cabbage, AP, shredded, cooked	1 lb	1½ cups
Cake crumbs, soft	1 lb	6 cups
Cake mix	1 lb	4 cups
Cantaloupe	3 lb	1 melon, 6-inch diameter
Caraway seeds	1 oz	4 Tbsp
Carrots, diced, cooked	1 lb	3 cups
Carrots, diced, raw	1 lb	3–3¼ cups
Carrots, fresh	1 lb	4–5 medium
Carrots, ground, raw, EP[c]	1 lb	3 cups
Carrots, shredded	1 lb	4 cups
Carrots, sliced, frozen	1 lb	3½ cups
Catsup	1 lb	2 cups
Cauliflower, florets	1 lb	4 cups
Cauliflower, head	1 lb	1 medium
Cayenne pepper	1 oz	5 Tbsp
Celery, chopped	1 lb	3 cups
Celery, diced, EP	1 lb (1–2 bunches)	1 qt
Celery cabbage, shredded	1 lb	6 cups
Celery flakes, dried	1 oz	1⅓ cups
Celery salt	1 oz	2 Tbsp
Celery seed	1 oz	4 Tbsp
Cheese, cheddar or Swiss, shredded	1 lb	4 cups
Cheese, cottage	1 lb	2 cups
Cheese, cream	1 lb	2 cups
Cheese, loaf, slices	1 lb	16–20 slices
Cheese, mozzarella, shredded	1 lb	3½ cups

[c]EP denotes "edible portion," or the status of the product after it has been prepared for cooking or for serving raw.

TABLE 1.3 **Continued**

Food	Weight	Approximate measure
Cheese, Parmesan or Romano, grated	1 lb	3½ cups
Cherries, glacé, candied	1 lb	96 cherries or 2½ cups
Cherries, maraschino, drained	1 lb	50–60 cherries
Cherries, red, frozen	1 lb	2 cups
Cherries, red, pie pack, drained	1 lb	2½ cups
Cherries, Royal Anne, drained	1 lb	2½ cups
Chicken, cooked, cubed	1 lb	3 cups
Chicken, ready to cook	4–4½ lb	1 qt cooked, diced
Chicken base (paste)	1 lb	1¾ cups
Chili powder	1 oz	4 Tbsp
Chili sauce	1 lb	1⅓ cups
Chilis, green, diced	1 lb	2 cups
Chives, freeze-dried	1 oz	2⅞ cups
Chives, frozen	1 oz	⅓ cup
Chocolate, baking	1 lb	16 squares
Chocolate, grated	1 lb	3½ cups
Chocolate, melted	1 lb	2 cups (scant)
Chocolate chips	1 lb	3 cups
Chocolate wafers	1 lb	4 cups crumbs
Cilantro, fresh	1 oz	¾ cup
Cinnamon, ground	1 oz	4 Tbsp
Cinnamon, ground	1 lb	4 cups
Cinnamon sticks	1 oz	10 pieces
Citron, dried, chopped	1 lb	2½ cups
Cloves, ground	1 oz	4 Tbsp
Cloves, whole	1 oz	5 Tbsp
Cocoa	1 lb	4½ cups
Coconut, flaked or shredded	1 lb	4¾ cups
Coffee, ground coarse	1 lb	5–5½ cups
Coffee, instant	1 oz	½ cup
Corn, cream style, canned	1 lb	2 cups
Corn, whole kernel, canned, drained	1 lb	3 cups
Corn, whole kernel, frozen	1 lb	3 cups
Cornflake crumbs	1 lb	4½ cups
Cornflakes	1 lb	4 qt
Cornmeal, coarse	1 lb	3 cups
Cornmeal, 1 lb AP, dry, after cooking	6 lb	3 qt

TABLE 1.3   Continued

Food	Weight	Approximate measure
Cornstarch	1 oz	3 Tbsp
Cornstarch	1 lb	3 cups
Corn syrup	1 lb	1½ cups
Couscous	1 lb	2¼ cups
Crab in shell	1 lb	½ cup cooked meat
Crabmeat, flaked	1 lb	3½ cups
Cracked wheat	1 lb	3½ cups
Cracker crumbs, medium fine	1 lb	5–6 cups
Crackers, 2⅝ × 2⅝-inch	1 lb	65 crackers
Crackers, graham	1 lb	60–65 crackers
Crackers, graham, crumbs	1 lb	4 cups
Crackers, saltines, 2 × 2-inch	1 lb	150–160 crackers
Cranberries, cooked	1 lb	1¾ cups
Cranberries, raw	1 lb	4 cups
Cranberry relish	1 lb	1¾ cups
Cranberry sauce, jellied	1 lb	2 cups
Cream of tartar	1 oz	3 Tbsp
Cream of Wheat or farina, quick, AP	1 lb	2⅔ cups
Cream of Wheat or farina, 1 lb AP, after cooking	8 lb	1 gal
Cream, sour	1 lb	2 cups
Cream, whipping	1 pt	1 qt whipped
Croutons	1 lb	2¼ qt
Cucumbers	1 lb	2–3 large
Cucumbers, diced, EP	1 lb	3 cups
Cucumbers, sliced	1 lb	50–60 slices
Cumin, ground	1 oz	4 Tbsp
Currants, dried	1 lb	3 cups
Curry powder	1 oz	4½ Tbsp
Dates, pitted	1 lb	2½ cups
Dill seed	1 oz	4½ Tbsp
Dill weed	1 oz	¾ cup
Eggplant	1 lb	8 slices, 4 × ½-inch
Eggplant	1 lb	1 qt diced
Eggs, dried, whites	1 lb	5 cups
Eggs, dried, whole	1 lb	5⅓ cups
Eggs, dried, yolks	1 lb	5⅔ cups
Eggs, hard-cooked, chopped	1 lb	2⅔ cups
Eggs, hard-cooked, chopped	1 doz	3½ cups
Eggs, shelled, fresh or frozen, whole	1 lb (approximately 1¾ oz per egg)	2 cups (8–10 eggs)

TABLE 1.3 **Continued**

Food	Weight	Approximate measure
Eggs, shelled, fresh or frozen, whites	1 lb (approximately 1–1¼ oz per white)	2 cups (16–18 eggs)
Eggs, shelled, fresh or frozen, yolks	1 lb (approximately ½–¾ oz per yolk)	2 cups (22–26 eggs)
Eggs, whole, in shell[d]	1 lb	8–10 large eggs
Fennel seed	1 oz	4 Tbsp
Figs, dry, cut fine	1 lb	2½ cups
Flour, all-purpose or bread	1 lb	4 cups
Flour, cake or pastry, unsifted	1 lb	3¾ cups
Flour, rye	1 lb	4 cups
Flour, whole-wheat	1 lb	3¾–4 cups
Garlic, fresh	1 oz	6 large cloves
Garlic, fresh, minced	1 oz	3 Tbsp
Garlic powder	1 oz	3 Tbsp
Garlic salt	1 oz	2 Tbsp
Gelatin, granulated, flavored	1 lb	2¼ cups
Gelatin, granulated, unflavored	1 oz	3 Tbsp
Gelatin, granulated, unflavored	1 lb	3 cups
Ginger, candied, chopped	1 oz	2 Tbsp
Ginger, fresh, sliced	1 lb	3 cups
Ginger, ground	1 oz	4 Tbsp
Ginger, ground	1 lb	4 cups
Graham cracker crumbs	1 lb	4 cups
Grapefruit, medium	1 lb	1 grapefruit, 10–12 sections, ⅔ cup juice
Grapefruit sections	1 lb	2 cups
Grapes, cut, seeded, EP	1 lb	2¾ cups
Grapes, seedless, fresh	1 lb	2½ cups
Grapes, on stem	1 lb	1 qt
Grits, hominy	1 lb	3 cups
Grits, hominy, 1 lb AP, after cooking	6½ lb	3¼ qt
Ham, cooked, diced	1 lb	3 cups
Ham, cooked, ground	1 lb	2½ cups
Hominy, canned	1 lb	3 cups
Hominy grits, see Grits		
Honey	1 lb	1⅓ cups

[d]One case (30 doz) eggs weighs approximately 41–43 lb and yields approximately 35 lb liquid whole eggs

TABLE 1.3 **Continued**

Food	Weight	Approximate measure
Horseradish, prepared	1 oz	2 Tbsp
Ice cream	4½–6 lb	1 gal
Jam, jelly	1 lb	1⅓–1½ cups
Lemon juice	1 lb	2 cups (8–10 lemons)
Lemon peel, dried	1 oz	4 Tbsp
Lemon peel, fresh	1 oz	4 Tbsp
Lemon peel, fresh	1 lemon	2 Tbsp
Lemons, size 165	1 lb	4–5 lemons; yield, ¾ cup juice
Lettuce, average head	2 lb	1 head
Lettuce, chopped or shredded	1 lb	6–8 cups
Lettuce, leaf	1 lb	25–30 salad garnishes
Limes, fresh	1 lb	yield, ⅞ cup juice
Macaroni, 1-inch pieces, dry	1 lb	4 cups
Macaroni, 1 lb AP, after cooking	3 lb	2–2¼ qt
Macaroni, cooked	1 lb	3 cups
Mace	1 oz	4½ Tbsp
Margarine	1 lb	2 cups
Margarine, whipped	1 lb	2⅔ cups
Marjoram	1 oz	6 Tbsp
Marshmallows (1¼-inch)	1 lb	80–90
Marshmallows, miniature (10 miniature = 1 regular)	1 lb	8 cups
	1 oz	52
Mayonnaise	1 lb	2 cups (scant)
Meat, cooked, chopped	1 lb	2 cups
Milk, evaporated	1 lb	1¾ cups
Milk, fluid, whole	1 lb	2 cups
Milk, nonfat, dry	1 lb	6 cups
Milk, nonfat, dry	1 oz	6 Tbsp
Milk, sweetened, condensed	1 lb	1½ cups
Mincemeat	1 lb	2 cups
Molasses	1 lb	1⅓ cups
Monosodium glutamate	1 oz	2 Tbsp
Mushrooms, canned	1 lb	2 cups
Mushrooms, fresh, sliced	1 lb	6 cups raw (1¾ cups cooked)
Mustard, ground, dry	1 oz	5 Tbsp
Mustard, ground, dry	1 lb	5 cups
Mustard, prepared	1 oz	2 Tbsp

TABLE 1.3   Continued

Food	Weight	Approximate measure
Mustard seed	1 oz	2½ Tbsp
Noodles, cooked	1 lb	2¾ cups
Noodles, 1 lb AP, after cooking	3 lb	2 qt
Nutmeats	1 lb	4 cups
Nutmeg, ground	1 oz	3½ Tbsp
Oats, rolled, quick, AP	1 lb	5⅓ cups
Oats, rolled, 1 lb AP, after cooking	2½ lb	4 qt
Oil, vegetable	1 lb	2–2⅛ cups
Olives, AP	1 lb	⅔ cup chopped
Olives, green, small size, drained	1 lb	160 olives
Olives, green, stuffed	1 lb	2½ cups
Olives, ripe, sliced	1 lb	3⅓ cups
Olives, ripe, small size, drained	1 lb	160 olives
Onions, dehydrated	1 lb	8 lb raw (equivalent)
Onions, dehydrated, chopped	1 oz	5 Tbsp
Onions, dehydrated, chopped	1 lb	5–6 cups
Onions, fresh, chopped	1 lb	2½–3 cups
Onions, green, sliced	1 lb	2½–3 cups
Onions, mature, AP	1 lb	4–5 medium
Onion powder	1 oz	3 Tbsp
Onion salt	1 oz	2½ Tbsp
Onion soup mix	1 oz	2⅔ Tbsp
Onion soup mix	1 lb	2⅔ cups
Orange juice, frozen	6 oz	3 cups reconstituted
Orange juice, frozen	32 oz	4 qt reconstituted
Orange peel, dried	1 oz	4 Tbsp
Orange peel, fresh	1 medium orange	3 Tbsp grated peel
Oranges, medium (113)	1 lb	3–4 oranges, unpeeled; 5 oranges, peeled; 10–11 sections each; yield, 1 cup juice
Oranges	1 lb	2 cups bite-size pieces
Oregano, ground	1 oz	5 Tbsp
Oregano, leaf	1 oz	¾ cup

TABLE 1.3 **Continued**

Food	Weight	Approximate measure
Oysters, shucked	1 lb	2 cups
Paprika, ground	1 oz	4 Tbsp
Parsley, coarsely chopped	1 oz	¾ cup
Parsley flakes, dry	1 oz	1⅓ cups
Parsnips, AP	1 lb	4 medium
Pasta	1 lb	see p. 407
Peaches, canned, sliced, drained	1 lb	2 cups
Peaches, fresh, AP	1 lb	4 medium
Peaches, sliced, frozen	1 lb	2 cups
Peanut butter	1 lb	2 cups
Peanuts, chopped, no skins	1 lb	3 cups
Peanuts, shelled	1 lb	3¼ cups
Pears, canned, drained, diced	1 lb	2½ cups
Pears, canned, large halves, drained	1 lb 14 oz	1 qt (9 halves)
Pears, fresh AP	1 lb	3–4 medium
Peas, cooked, drained	1 lb	2¼ cups
Peas, dried, 1 lb after cooking	2½ lb	5½ cups
Peas, split, dried, AP	1 lb	2⅓ cups
Pecans, chopped	1 lb	4 cups
Pecans, shelled, pieces	1 lb	4 cups
Pepper, cayenne	1 oz	5 Tbsp
Pepper, ground, black or white	1 oz	4 Tbsp
Pepper, ground, black or white	1 lb	4 cups
Peppercorns	1 oz	6 Tbsp
Peppers, green	1 lb	2–3 medium
Peppers, green, chopped	1 lb	3 cups
Peppers, green, dried flakes	1 oz	¾ cup
Pickle relish	1 lb	2 cups
Pickles, chopped	1 lb	3 cups
Pickles, halves, 3-inch	1 lb	3 cups or 36 halves
Pimiento, chopped	1 lb	2 cups
Pineapple, canned, crushed	1 lb	2 cups
Pineapple, canned, slices, drained	1 lb	8–12 slices
Pineapple, canned, tidbits	1 lb	2 cups
Pineapple, fresh	2–4 lb	1 pineapple, 2–4 cups, cubed
Pineapple, frozen, chunks	1 lb	2 cups
Poppy seed	1 oz	3 Tbsp

TABLE 1.3   Continued

Food	Weight	Approximate measure
Potato chips	1 lb	4–5 qt
Potato chips, crushed	1 lb	2 qt
Potatoes, dehydrated, diced	1 lb	5⅛ cups
Potatoes, dehydrated, flakes	1 lb	5 cups
Potatoes, dehydrated, granules	1 lb	2¼ cups
Potatoes, dehydrated, slices	1 lb	9⅔ cups
Potatoes, fresh, white, AP	1 lb	3 medium
Potatoes, fresh, white, cooked	1 lb	2½ cups
Potatoes, raw, white, cubed	1 lb	2¾ cups
Potatoes, sweet	1 lb	3 medium
Potatoes, sweet, cooked	1 lb	2 cups
Poultry seasoning, ground	1 oz	6 Tbsp
Prunes, dried, size 30/40, AP	1 lb	2½ cups
Prunes, dried, 1 lb AP, after cooking	2 lb	3–4 cups
Prunes, pitted, cooked	1 lb	3¼ cups
Pudding mix, dry, instant	1 lb	2½ cups
Pudding mix, dry, regular	1 lb	2⅔ cups
Pumpkin, cooked	1 lb	2 cups
Radishes, AP	1 lb	45–50
Raisins, AP	1 lb	3 cups
Raisins, 1 lb AP, after cooking	1 lb 12 oz	1 qt
Raisins, chopped	1 lb	2⅔ cups
Raspberries, fresh AP, or frozen IQF	1 lb	3 cups
Raspberries, with syrup	1 lb	2 cups
Red-hots	1 lb	2¼ cups
Rhubarb, raw, 1-inch pieces	1 lb	4 cups
Rhubarb, 1 lb EP, after cooking		2½ cups
Rice, brown, AP	1 lb	2½ cups
Rice, converted, AP	1 lb	2½ cups
Rice, cooked	1 lb	2¼ cups
Rice, 1 lb AP, after cooking	3½ lb	2 qt
Rice, precooked, AP	1 lb	4½ cups
Rice, regular, AP	1 lb	2⅓ cups
Rice, wild	1 lb	2⅔ cups
Rice, wild, 1 lb AP, after cooking	1 lb	5 cups
Rice cereal, crisp	1 lb	4 qt
Rosemary leaves	1 oz	9 Tbsp

TABLE 1.3 Continued

Food	Weight	Approximate measure
Rutabagas, raw, cubed, EP	1 lb	3⅓ cups
Sage, finely ground	1 oz	8 Tbsp (½ cup)
Sage, rubbed	1 oz	⅔ cup
Salad dressing, cooked	1 lb	2 cups
Salmon, canned	1 lb	2 cups
Salt	1 oz	1½ Tbsp
Salt	1 lb	1½ cups
Sauerkraut	1 lb	3 cups packed
Sausage, bulk, AP	1 lb	2 cups
Sausages, link, small	1 lb	16–17
Sesame seed	1 oz	3 Tbsp
Sherbet	6 lb	1 gal
Shortening, hydrogenated fat	1 lb	2¼ cups
Shrimp, cleaned, cooked, peeled	1 lb	3¼ cups
Soda, baking	1 oz	2⅓ Tbsp
Spaghetti, cooked	1 lb	2⅔ cups
Spaghetti, 1 lb AP, after cooking	3 lb	2 qt
Spinach, canned or frozen	1 lb	2 cups
Spinach, raw	1 lb	5 qt lightly packed
Spinach, raw, chopped	1 lb	3¼ qt
Spinach, 1 lb AP, after cooking	13 oz	2¾ cups
Squash, Hubbard, cooked	1 lb	2 cups
Squash, summer	1 lb	4 cups
Starch, waxy maize	1 oz	3 Tbsp
Strawberries, fresh or frozen, IQF	1 lb	3 cups
Strawberries, sliced, frozen, with syrup	1 lb	2 cups
Suet, ground	1 lb	3¾ cups
Sugar, brown, lightly packed	1 lb	3 cups
Sugar, brown, solid pack	1 lb	2 cups
Sugar, cubes	1 lb	96 cubes
Sugar, granulated	1 lb	2¼ cups
Sugar, granulated	1 oz	2¼ Tbsp
Sugar, powdered, unsifted	1 lb	3¼ cups
Sugar, powdered, XXXX sifted	1 lb	3¾ cups
Syrup, corn or maple	1 lb	1½ cups
Tapioca, quick cooking	1 lb	3 cups
Tapioca, 1 lb AP, after cooking		7½ cups

TABLE 1.3 Continued

Food	Weight	Approximate measure
Tarragon, leaf	1 oz	1 cup
Tea, bulk	1 lb	6 cups
Tea, instant	1 oz	½ cup
Thyme, ground	1 oz	6 Tbsp
Thyme, leaves	1 oz	½ cup
Tomatoes, canned	1 lb	2 cups
Tomatoes, fresh	1 lb	3–4 medium, 16 slices
Tomatoes, fresh, diced	1 lb	2¼ cups
Tomato paste	1 lb	2 cups
Tortillas, corn, 8-inch	1 lb	16
Tortillas, flour, 8-inch	1 lb	12
Tortillas, flour, 10-inch	1 lb	9
Tuna, canned	1 lb	2 cups
Turkey, AP, dressed weight	14 lb	11–12 cups diced, cooked meat
Turmeric, ground	1 oz	4 Tbsp
Turnips, AP	1 lb	2–3
Vanilla and other extracts	1 oz	2 Tbsp
Vinegar	1 lb	2 cups
Walnuts, English, shelled	1 lb	4 cups
Water	1 lb	2 cups
Watercress, EP	1 oz	½ cup
Watermelon	1 lb	1-inch slice, 6-inch diameter
Wheat germ	1 lb	5⅓ cups
Whipped topping, liquid	1 lb	2 cups
Yeast, compressed	1 oz	1 pkg
Yeast, dry	¼ oz	1 envelope
Yeast, dry, regular or instant	1 oz	3 Tbsp + 1 tsp
Yeast, dry, regular or instant	1 lb	3⅓ cups
Yogurt	1 lb	2 cups
Zucchini, fresh, shredded	1 lb	3¼ cups

TABLE 1.4   Basic equivalents in measures and weights

Equivalents	*Abbreviations used in this book*[a]	
1 Tbsp = 3 tsp in liquids ½ fl oz	bu	bushel
⅛ cup = 2 Tbsp, in liquids 1 fl oz	fl oz	fluid ounce
¼ cup = 4 Tbsp, in liquids 2 fl oz	gal	gallon
⅓ cup = 5 Tbsp + 1 tsp	g	gram
½ cup = 8 Tbsp, in liquids 4 fl oz	kg	kilogram
⅔ cup = 10 Tbsp + 2 tsp	L	liter
¾ cup = 12 Tbsp, in liquids 6 fl oz	lb	pound
1 cup = 16 Tbsp, in liquids 8 fl oz	mL	milliliter
1 pt = 2 cups, in liquids 16 fl oz	oz	ounce
1 qt = 2 pt = 4 cups	pk	peck
1 gal = 4 qt	pt	pint
1 lb = 16 oz	qt	quart
1 pk = 8 qt, approximately 12½ lb	Tbsp	tablespoon
1 bu = 4 pk, approximately 50 lb	tsp	teaspoon

METRIC

1 g = 0.035 oz
1 kg = 2.2 lb
1 oz = 28 g
1 lb = 454 g
1 mL = ⅕ tsp
1 L = 1.06 qt
1 cup = 240 mL
1 qt = 0.95 L
1 gal = 3.8 L

[a]Periods are usually not used in abbreviations for quantity recipes.

TABLE 1.5   Weight (1–16 oz) and approximate measure equivalents for commonly used foods

Food item	1 oz	2 oz	3 oz	4 oz
Baking powder	2⅓ Tbsp	¼ cup + 1 tsp	⅓ cup + 2 Tbsp	½ cup + 1 Tbsp
Baking soda	2⅓ Tbsp	¼ cup + 1 tsp	⅓ cup + 2 Tbsp	½ cup + 1 Tbsp
Bread crumbs, dry	¼ cup	½ cup	¾ cup	1 cup
Butter or margarine	2 Tbsp	¼ cup	⅓ cup + 2 tsp	½ cup
Celery, chopped	¼ cup	½ cup	¾ cup	1 cup
Cornstarch	3½ Tbsp	⅓ cup + 2 Tbsp	⅔ cup	¾ cup + 2 Tbsp
Eggs, whole, whites or yolks, fresh or frozen	2 Tbsp	¼ cup	⅓ cup + 2 tsp	½ cup
Flour, all-purpose, unsifted	¼ cup	½ cup	¾ cup	1 cup
Flour, cake, unsifted	¼ cup	½ cup	½ cup + 3 Tbsp	¾ cup + 3 Tbsp
Milk, nonfat dry	⅓ cup	¾ cup	1 cup + 2 Tbsp	1½ cups
Nutmeats	¼ cup	½ cup	¾ cup	1 cup
Onion, chopped	2 Tbsp	¼ cup	⅓ cup + 2 tsp	½ cup
Salt	1½ Tbsp	3 Tbsp	¼ cup + 1½ tsp	⅓ cup + 2 tsp
Shortening, hydrogenated fat	2 Tbsp + 1 tsp	¼ cup + 2 tsp	⅓ cup + 2 Tbsp	½ cup + 1 Tbsp
Sugar, brown, light pack	3 Tbsp	⅓ cup + 2 tsp	½ cup + 1 Tbsp	¾ cup
Sugar, granulated	2¼ Tbsp	¼ cup	¼ cup + 3 Tbsp	½ cup + 1 Tbsp
Sugar, powdered	3 Tbsp	⅓ cup + 2 tsp	½ cup + 1 tsp	¾ cup
Yeast, dry	3 Tbsp + 1 tsp	⅓ cup + 1 Tbsp	½ cup + 2 Tbsp	¾ cup + 1 Tbsp

5 oz	6 oz	7 oz	8 oz
¾ cup	¾ cup + 2 Tbsp	1 cup + 1 tsp	1 cup + 3 Tbsp
¾ cup	¾ cup + 2 Tbsp	1 cup + 1 tsp	1 cup + 3 Tbsp
1¼ cups	1½ cups	1¾ cups	2 cups
½ cup + 2 Tbsp	¾ cup	¾ cup + 2 Tbsp	1 cup
1¼ cups	1½ cups	1¾ cups	2 cups
1 cup + 2 Tbsp	1¼ cup + 1 Tbsp	1½ cup + 1 Tbsp	1¾ cups
½ cup + 2 Tbsp	¾ cup	¾ cup + 2 Tbsp	1 cup
1¼ cups	1½ cups	1¾ cups	2 cups
1 cup + 3 Tbsp	1¼ cups + 3 Tbsp	1½ cups + 2 Tbsp	1¾ cups + 2 Tbsp
1¾ cups + 2 Tbsp	2¼ cups	2½ cups + 2 Tbsp	3 cups
1¼ cups	1½ cups	1¾ cups	2 cups
½ cup + 2 Tbsp	¾ cup	¾ cup + 2 Tbsp	1 cup
⅓ cup + 2 Tbsp	½ cup + 1 Tbsp	⅔ cup	¾ cup
⅔ cup + 1 Tbsp	¾ cup + 2 Tbsp	1 cup	1 cup + 2 Tbsp
¾ cup + 3 Tbsp	1 cup + 2 Tbsp	1¼ cups + 1 Tbsp	1½ cups
½ cup + 3 Tbsp	¾ cup + 2 Tbsp	1 cup	1 cup + 2 Tbsp
¾ cup + 3 Tbsp	1 cup + 2 Tbsp	1¼ cups + 1 Tbsp	1½ cups
1 cup + 2 tsp	1¼ cups	1½ cups	1⅔ cups

Continued

TABLE 1.5 Continued

Food item	9 oz	10 oz	11 oz	12 oz
Baking powder	1¼ cups + 1 Tbsp	1½ cups	1½ cups + 2 Tbsp	1¾ cups
Baking soda	1¼ cups + 1 Tbsp	1½ cups	1½ cups + 2 Tbsp	1¾ cups
Bread crumbs, dry	2¼ cups	2½ cups	2¾ cups	3 cups
Butter or margarine	1 cup + 2 Tbsp	1¼ cups	1⅓ cups + 1 Tbsp	1½ cups
Celery, chopped	2¼ cups	2½ cups	2¾ cups	3 cups
Cornstarch	2 cups	2 cups + 3 Tbsp	2⅓ cups + 2 Tbsp	2½ cups + 2 Tbsp
Eggs, whole, whites or yolks, fresh or frozen	1 cup + 2 Tbsp	1¼ cups	1⅓ cups + 1 Tbsp	1½ cups
Flour, all-purpose, unsifted	2¼ cups	2½ cups	2¾ cups	3 cups
Flour, cake, un-sifted	2 cups + 2 Tbsp	2¼ cups + 2 Tbsp	2½ cups + 1 Tbsp	2¾ cups
Milk, nonfat dry	3¼ cups + 2 Tbsp	3¾ cups	4 cups + 2 Tbsp	4½ cups
Nutmeats	2¼ cups	2½ cups	2¾ cups	3 cups
Onion, chopped	1 cup + 2 Tbsp	1¼ cups	1⅓ cups + 1 Tbsp	1½ cups
Salt	¾ cup + 2 Tbsp	¾ cup + 3 Tbsp	1 cup + 1 Tbsp	1 cup + 2 Tbsp
Shortening, hydro-genated fat	1¼ cups	1⅓ cups + 1 Tbsp	1½ cups + 1 Tbsp	1⅔ cups
Sugar, brown, light pack	1⅔ cups	1¾ cups + 2 Tbsp	2 cups + 1 Tbsp	2¼ cups
Sugar, granulated	1¼ cups	1¼ cups + 3 Tbsp	1½ cups + 1 Tbsp	1½ cups + 3 Tbsp
Sugar, powdered	1⅔ cups	1¾ cups + 2 Tbsp	2 cups + 1 Tbsp	2¼ cups
Yeast, dry	1¾ cups + 2 Tbsp	2 cups + 1 Tbsp	2¼ cups + 1 Tbsp	2½ cups

13 oz	14 oz	15 oz	16 oz
1¾ cups + 2 Tbsp	2 cups + 1 Tbsp	2 cups + 3 Tbsp	2⅓ cups
1¾ cups + 2 Tbsp	2 cups + 1 Tbsp	2 cups + 3 Tbsp	2⅓ cups
3¼ cups	3½ cups	3¾ cups	4 cups
1½ cups + 2 Tbsp	1¾ cups	1¾ cups + 2 Tbsp	2 cups
3¼ cups	3½ cups	3¾ cups	4 cups
2¾ cups + 2 Tbsp	3 cups + 1 Tbsp	3¼ cups + 1½ tsp	3½ cups
1½ cups + 2 Tbsp	1¾ cups	1¾ cups + 2 Tbsp	2 cups
3¼ cups	3½ cups	3¾ cups	4 cups
3 cups + 1 Tbsp	3¼ cups + 1 Tbsp	3½ cups	3¾ cups
4¾ cups + 2 Tbsp	5¼ cups	5½ cups + 2 Tbsp	6 cups
3¼ cups	3½ cups	3¾ cups	4 cups
1½ cups + 2 Tbsp	1¾ cups	1¾ cups + 2 Tbsp	2 cups
1¼ cups	1¼ cups + 1 Tbsp	1⅓ cups + 1 Tbsp	1½ cups
1¾ cups + 1 Tbsp	2 cups	2 cups + 2 Tbsp	2¼ cups
2⅓ cups + 2 Tbsp	2½ cups + 2 Tbsp	2¾ cups + 1 Tbsp	3 cups
1¾ cups + 1 Tbsp	2 cups	2 cups + 2 Tbsp	2¼ cups
2⅓ cups + 2 Tbsp	2½ cups + 2 Tbsp	2¾ cups + 1 Tbsp	3 cups
2⅔ cups + 1 Tbsp	2¾ cups + 3 Tbsp	3 cups + 2 Tbsp	3⅓ cups

TABLE 1.6 **Metric equivalents for weight, measure, and temperature**

Weight		Measure		Temperature	
U.S.	Metric[a]	U.S.	Metric[b]	°F	°C[c]
1 oz	28 g	1 tsp	5 mL	32	0
1½ oz	43 g	1 Tbsp	15 mL	100	38
2 oz	57 g	¼ cup (4 Tbsp)	60 mL	150	65
2½ oz	70 g	⅓ cup (5⅓ Tbsp)	80 mL	200	95
3 oz	85 g	½ cup (8 Tbsp)	120 mL	250	121
3⅓ oz	100 g	⅔ cup (10⅔ Tbsp)	160 mL	275	135
4 oz (¼ lb)	114 g	¾ cup (12 Tbsp)	180 mL	300	150
5 oz	142 g	1 cup (16 Tbsp)	240 mL	325	165
6 oz	170 g	2 cups (1 pint)	480 mL	350	175
7 oz	198 g	4 cups (1 qt)	0.95 L	365	190
8 oz (½ lb)	227 g	2 qt (½ gal)	1.89 L	400	205
9 oz	255 g	4 qt (1 gal)	3.79 L	425	220
10 oz	284 g			450	230
11 oz	312 g			475	245
12 oz (¾ lb)	340 g			500	260
13 oz	369 g				
14 oz	397 g				
15 oz	425 g				
1 lb (16 oz)	454 g				
2 lb	908 g				
2 lb 4 oz	1.02 kg				

[a]Basic formula used to calculate metric weights: 1 oz = 28.35 g. Resulting figures were rounded to nearest gram and to two decimal places for kilograms. Abbreviations used: oz = ounce; lb = pound; g = gram; kg = kilogram. To change grams to kilograms, move decimal three places to left: e.g., 28 g = 0.028 kg.
[b]Basic formulas used to calculate metric volume: 1 Tbsp = 14.8 mL, rounded to 15 mL; 1 cup = 237 mL, rounded to 240 mL; 1 qt = 0.95 L (4 × 237 ÷ 1000). Abbreviations used: tsp = teaspoon; Tbsp = tablespoon; pt = pint; qt = quart; gal = gallon; mL = milliliter; L = liter.
[c]To convert from °F to °C, the following formula is used: (°F − 32) × ⁵⁄₉ = °C.

TABLE 1.7 **Convection oven baking times and temperatures**

Product	Oven temperature		Approximate baking time
	°F	°C	
MEATS			
Steamship round (50 lb, medium)	250–275	120–135	8–9 hr
Rolled beef roast (12–15 lb)	275	135	2½ hr
Standing rib, choice (20 lb, trimmed, rare)	250–300	120–150	2¾ hr
Lasagna	250–275	130	90 min
Hot dogs, 10 per lb (18 × 26-inch pan)	325	165	10–15 min
Baked stuffed pork chops	375	190	20–30 min
Bacon (on racks in 18 × 26-inch pans)	400	205	5–7 min

TABLE 1.7   **Continued**

Product	Oven temperature		Approximate baking time
	°F	°C	
POULTRY			
Chicken breast and thigh	350	175	40 min
Chicken (2½ lb quartered)	350	175	30 min
Turkey, rolled (18 lb rolls)	310	155	3¾ hr
Turkey, whole (16–20 lb)	275–300	135–150	4–5 hr
FISH AND SHELLFISH			
Halibut steaks, codfish (frozen 5 oz)	350	175	20 min
Lobster tails (frozen)	425	220	9 min
POTATOES			
Baked potatoes (120 count)	400	205	50 min
Oven roasted potatoes (sliced or diced)	325	165	10 min
BAKED GOODS			
Frozen pies (22 oz)	400	205	30–35 min
Frozen pies (46 oz)	350	175	45–50 min
Fresh apple pie (20 oz)	350–375	175–190	25–30 min
Pumpkin pies	300	150	30–35 min
Fruit cobbler	300	150	30 min
Apple turnovers	350	175	15 min
Corn bread	335	170	20–25 min
Bread (24 1-lb loaves)	350	175	30 min
French bread	375	190	18–20 min
Yeast rolls	350	175	25 min
Croissant	325	165	15–18 min
Danish	335	170	12 min
Sheet cakes (5 lb batter per pan)	325	165	20–25 min
Chocolate cake	335	170	20 min
Fruit cakes	275	135	70 min
Brownies	325	165	20 min
Cookies	325–350	165–175	10–15 min
Cream puffs	350	175	20–25 min

Notes

- Actual times and temperatures may vary from those shown. They are affected by weight of load, temperature of the product, recipe, and type of pan.

- For menu items not listed, use recommended time and temperature for conventional oven but reduce the temperature setting by 25°–50°F and reduce the total bake/roast time by approximately 10–15 percent.

TABLE 1.8   Deep-fat frying temperatures

Type of product	Preparation[a]	Temperature[b] °F	Temperature[b] °C	Frying time[c] (minutes)
BREADS				
Doughnuts	See p. 142	375	190	3–5
French toàst	See p. 144	360	180	3–4
Fritters	See p. 144	375	190	2–5
Sandwiches	Batter	350–375	175–190	3–4
FISH				
Fillets or pieces	Egg and crumb or batter	360–375	180–190	4–6
Oysters	Egg and crumb	375	190	2–4
Scallops	Egg and crumb	360–375	180–190	3–4
Shrimp	Batter or egg and crumb	360–375	180–190	3–5
FRUIT				
Bananas	Batter	375	190	1–3
POULTRY				
Chicken, pieces	Light coating or egg and crumb			
Fryers(1½–2 lb)		350	175	10–12
Fryers (2–2½ lb)		350	175	12–15
Chicken, half	Light coating or egg and crumb			
Fryers (1½–2 lb)		350	175	12–15
Turkey or chicken cutlets	Egg and crumb	325–350	165–175	5–8
VEGETABLES				
Cauliflower, precooked	See p. 668	370	185	3–5
Eggplant	See p. 668	370	185	5–7
Mushrooms	See p. 668	370	185	4–6
Onion rings	Batter	350	175	3–4
Potatoes, ½ inch strips	See p. 672			
Complete fry		365	182	6–8
Blanching		360	180	3–5
Browning		375	190	2–3
Frozen, fat-blanched		375	190	2–3
Zucchini	See p. 668	370	185	4–6

[a]See Table 1.9 for light coating, egg and crumb, and batter.
[b]If food is frozen, use lower temperatures listed and allow additional cooking time. At high altitudes, the lower boiling point of water in foods requires lowering of temperatures for deep-fat frying.
[c]The exact frying time will vary with the equipment used, size and temperature of the food pieces, and the amount of food placed in fryer at one time. If fryer is overloaded, foods may become grease-soaked.

Note   ■   Use fat with a high smoking temperature. Filter fat regularly, at least daily or more often if fryer is in constant use. The breakdown of fat may be caused by using the fat for too long a period, cooking food at too high a temperature, failing to filter the fat regularly, or inadvertently getting salt into the fryer when salting food.

TABLE 1.9   Coatings for deep-fat fried foods

Ingredient	Light coating[d]	Egg and crumb[e]	Batter[f]
Eggs[a]		3	6
Milk[b]	1 cup	1 cup	2 cups
Flour, all-purpose or whole wheat	1 lb	8 oz (optional)	12 oz
Salt[c]	2 tsp	1 tsp	2 tsp
Bread crumbs, fine		12 oz	
Baking powder			
Shortening, melted, or vegetable oil			2 tsp
Seasonings		As desired	3 Tbsp

[a]Cholesterol can be lowered by substituting egg whites for all or part of the eggs.
[b]Water may be substituted for milk, except in batter.
[c]Seasoned salt (p. 599) may be substituted.
[d]Dip prepared food in milk. Dredge with seasoned flour.
[e]Dip prepared food in flour (may omit), then in mixture of beaten egg and milk. Drain. Roll in crumbs to cover (see Figure 10.2).
[f]Combine flour, salt, and baking powder. Add milk, beaten eggs, and shortening. Dip prepared foods in batter.

TABLE 1.10   Dipper equivalents

Dipper number[a]	Approximate measure	Approximate weight	Suggested use
6	10 Tbsp (⅔ cup)	6 oz	Entree salads
8	8 Tbsp (½ cup)	4–5 oz	Entrees
10	6 Tbsp (⅜ cup)	3–4 oz	Desserts, meat patties
12	5 Tbsp (⅓ cup)	2½–3 oz	Croquettes, vegetables, muffins, desserts, salads
16	4 Tbsp (¼ cup)	2–2¼ oz	Muffins, desserts, croquettes
20	3⅕ Tbsp	1¾–2 oz	Muffins, cupcakes, sauces, sandwich fillings
24	2⅔ Tbsp	1½–1¾ oz	Cream puffs
30	2⅕ Tbsp	1–1½ oz	Large drop cookies
40	1½ Tbsp	¾ oz	Drop cookies
60	1 Tbsp	½ oz	Small drop cookies, garnishes
100	Scant 2 tsp		Tea cookies

[a]Portions per quart.

Note   ■   These measurements are based on food leveled off in the dipper. If food is left rounded in the dipper, the measure and weight are closer to those of the next-larger dipper.

TABLE 1.11   **Ladle equivalents**

Approximate weight	Approximate measure	Approximate portions per quart	Suggested use
1 oz	⅛ cup	32	Sauces, salad dressings
2 oz	¼ cup	16	Gravies, some sauces
4 oz	½ cup	8	Stews, creamed dishes
6 oz	¾ cup	5	Stews, creamed dishes, soup
8 oz	1 cup	4	Soup

Note   ■   These measurements are based on food leveled off in the ladle. If food is left rounded in the ladle, the measure and weight are closer to those of the next-larger ladle.

TABLE 1.12   **Cold food storage temperatures**

Food	Refrigerator		Freezer	
	°F	Days	°F	Months
DAIRY/EGGS				
Ice cream			−10	3
Milk	32	7		
Eggs in shell	40	21		
Raw yolks/whites	40	2–4		
Liquid pasteurized (opened)	40	3		
FRESH MEATS				
Beef roast/steaks	32	3–5	0 to −20	6–12
Pork roast	32	3–5	0 to −20	3–6
Pork chops	32	3–5	0 to −20	3–4
Hamburger/ground pork	32	1–2	0 to −20	3–4
Beef cubes	32	1–2	0 to −20	3–4
COOKED MEATS				
Browned meats	35	3–4	0 to −20	2–3
Bacon	35	7	0 to −20	1
Frankfurters				
Unopened package	32	14	0 to −20	1–2
Opened package	32	7	0 to −20	1–2
Luncheon meats	32	3–5	0 to −20	1–2

TABLE 1.12 **Continued**

Food	Refrigerator °F	Days	Freezer °F	Months
FRESH POULTRY AND FISH				
Chicken/turkey				
Whole	32	1–2	0 to −20	12
Pieces	32	1–2	0 to −20	9
Fish	32	1	0 to −20	3
COOKED POULTRY				
With broth or gravy	35	1–2	0 to −20	6
Pieces, no gravy	35	3–4	0 to −20	4
Cooked dishes	35	3–4	0 to −20	4–6
Fried chicken	35	3–4	0 to −20	4

TABLE 1.13 **Food serving temperatures**

Food	Serving temperature °F
DAIRY	
Ice Cream	10
Milk	34–38
FRESH MEATS (ROASTS)	150–165[a]
COOKED MEATS (SERVED HOT OR COLD)	Below 40 or above 150
FRESH OR COOKED POULTRY AND FISH	Below 40 or above 165
DESSERTS	
Refrigerator desserts	36
Pastries and cakes	60–70[b]
SALADS	34–38
SOUPS, CASSEROLES, VEGETABLES	160–180
HOT BEVERAGES	185–195

[a]Temperature will depend on the doneness of meat. Rare roast beef may be served at a temperature lower than 150°F but does pose some food-safety risk.
[b]Some pastries may be served warm, 100°–125°F, but food products that are potential food safety risks should not be held at temperatures between 40° and 140°F for more than 30 minutes. Examples are custard or pumpkin pie.

TABLE 1.14   Recommended mixer bowl and steam-jacketed kettle sizes for selected products

	50 portions	*100 portions*	*200 portions*	*500 portions*
Breads, yeast	7 lb/12 qt MB[a]	14 lb/12 qt MB	28 lb/20 qt MB	70 lb/60 qt MB
Quick	10 lb/12 qt MB	20 lb/20 qt MB	40 lb/60 qt MB	100 lb/80 qt MB
Cakes, angel food	6 lb/12 qt MB	12 lb/30 qt MB	24 lb/60 qt MB	60 lb/2 batch sizes, 60 qt MB
Other	8 lb/12 qt MB	16 lb/20 qt MB	32 lb/30 qt MB	80 lb/80 qt MB
Cookies	5 lb/5 qt MB	10 lb/12 qt MB	20 lb/30 qt MB	50 lb/60 qt MB
Pastry	7 lb/12 qt MB	14 lb/20 qt MB	28 lb/30 qt MB	70 lb/80 qt MB
Pie fillings				
Fruit	12 lb/10 qt SJK 10 qt SP	24 lb/20 qt SJK 20 qt SP	48 lb/20 gal SJK	70 lb/20 gal SJK
Frozen/chiffon	12 lb/20 qt MB	24 lb/60 qt MB	48 lb/80 qt MB	120 lb/2 batch sizes, 80 qt MB
Puddings/pie fillings	12 lb/10 qt SJK 10 qt SP	24 lb/20 qt SJK 10 qt SP	48 lb/20 gal SJK	120 lb/20 gal SJK
Scrambled eggs	10 lb/12 qt MB	20 lb/20 qt MB	40 lb/60 qt MB	100 lb/2 batch sizes, 60 qt MB
Cheese soufflé	14 lb/30 qt MB	28 lb/60 qt MB	56 lb/2 batch sizes, 60 qt MB	140 lb/3 batch sizes, 80 qt MB
Meat loaf	12 lb/20 qt MB	24 lb/30 qt MB	48 lb/60 qt MB	120 lb/2 batch sizes, 80 qt MB
Spaghetti sauce	19 lb/20 qt SJK 15 qt SP	38 lb/20 gal SJK 20 qt SP	76 lb/20 gal SJK	190 lb/40 gal SJK
Pasta (and cooking water)	45 lb/20 gal SJK 25 qt SP	90 lb/20 gal SJK	180 lb/40 gal SJK	450 lb/80 gal SJK
Salad dressing	8 lb/12 qt MB	16 lb/20 qt MB	32 lb/60 qt MB	80 lb/80 qt MB
Soups/stews	25 lb/20 qt SJK 15 qt SP	50 lb/20 gal SJK 25 qt SP	100 lb/20 gal SJK	250 lb/40 gal SJK
Mashed potatoes	15 lb/20 qt MB	30 lb/30 qt MB	60 lb/80 qt MB	150 lb/3 batch sizes, 80 qt MB
Whipped cream or topping	1½ qt/5 qt MB	3 qt/12 qt MB	6 qt/30 qt MB	15 qt/60 qt MB

[a]Abbreviations used: MB = mixer bowl; SJK = steam-jacketed kettle; SP = stock pot.

TABLE 1.15   Pan capacities for baked products

Pan size	Maximum capacity	Portion	Suggested use
18 × 26 × 2-inch (cake pan)	8–10 lb	Cut 6 × 10 (3 × 2½ inches)	Cakes
18 × 26 × 1-inch (sheet pan)	4–6 lb	Cut 6 × 10 (3 × 2½ inches) Panned 8 × 12 Dropped 3 × 5	Sheet cakes, bar cookies Dinner rolls Cookies
13 × 18 × 1-inch (half sheet pan)	2–3 lb	Cut 5 × 6 (2½ × 3 inches)	Sheet cakes, bar cookies
12 × 18 × 2-inch	4–5 lb	Cut 5 × 6 (2½ × 3 inches)	Cakes
10-inch tube	2–2½ lb	Cut $\frac{1}{14}$	Chiffon cakes
9-inch round (cake)	1½ lb	Cut $\frac{1}{16}$	Layer cakes, corn bread
8-inch round (cake)	1¼ lb	Cut $\frac{1}{12}$–$\frac{1}{14}$	Layer cakes
9-inch round (pie)	1½ lb	Cut $\frac{1}{8}$	Pies
8-inch round (pie)	1 lb	Cut $\frac{1}{6}$	Pies
5 × 6 × 4 inches (loaf)	3–5 lb	Cut $\frac{1}{24}$–$\frac{1}{32}$ Cut $\frac{1}{24}$	Quick breads, yeast breads Cakes
5 × 8 × 4 inches (loaf)	1½–2½ lb	Cut $\frac{1}{12}$–$\frac{1}{16}$ Cut $\frac{1}{12}$	Quick breads, yeast breads Cakes
5 × 9 × 2¾ inches (loaf)	1½–2 lb	Cut $\frac{1}{16}$	Quick breads, yeast breads, cakes

Notes

- The product volume/weight ratio will dictate the weight per pan.
- See recipes for specific instructions.
- A formula for determining scaling weight of cakes is given on p. 185.

TABLE 1.16   Counter pan capacities

Pan size	Depth (in inches)	Maximum capacity lb	Maximum capacity qt	Cut	Number of portions 1 oz	Number of portions 2 oz	Number of portions 4 oz	Number of portions 8 oz	Suggested use
Full size 20 × 12 inches	2	12–15	8	48 (3 × 2½-inch)			67	33	Baked entrees Baked desserts
	4	24–30	14	24 (3 × 3⅓-inch) 32 (3 × 2½-inch)			113	56	Baked entrees Baked entrees
Half size 10 × 12 inches	2½	6–7	4	12 (3 × 3-inch) 16 (3 × 2½-inch)			34 34	17 17	Baked entrees Baked entrees
	4	12–15	6½				53	27	Baked entrees
	6		10				80	40	Vegetables
One-third size 6⅞ × 12¾ inches	2				85	42			Salad bar items
	4				134	67			Condiments
	6				197	98			Sauces
One-fourth size 6⅜ × 10 ⅜ inches	2				60	30			Salad bar items
	4				96	48			Condiments
	6				146	73			Sauces

TABLE 1.17   Common can sizes

Can size (industry term)	Approximate net weight or fluid measure	Approximate cups per can	Approximate number of 4 oz portions	Principal products
No. 10	6 lb–7 lb 5 oz	9–12	25	Institutional size for fruits, vegetables
No. 5 Squat	4 lb–4¼ lb	8	16–20	Institutional size for canned fish, sweet potatoes
No. 3 Cyl	46 fl oz or 5 fl oz	5¼	10–12	Fruit and vegetable juices, condensed soups

TABLE 1.17   Continued

Can size (industry term)	Approximate net weight or fluid measure	Approximate cups per can	Approximate number of 4 oz portions	Principal products
No. 2½	26–30 oz	3½	5–7	Fruits, some vegetables
No. 2	18 fl oz or 20 oz	2½	5	Juices, fruits, ready-to-serve soups
No. 303	1 lb	2	4	Fruits, vegetables, ready-to-serve soups
No. 300	14–16 oz	1¾	3–4	Some fruits and meat products
No. 1 (Picnic)	10½–12 oz	1¼	2–3	Condensed soups
8 oz	8 oz	1	2	Ready-to-serve soups, fruits, vegetables

Notes   ■   When substituting one can for another size, one No. 10 can is approximately equivalent to:

7 No. 303 (1 lb) cans

5 No. 2 (1 lb 4 oz) cans

4 No. 2½ (1 lb 13 oz) cans

2 No. 3 (46 to 50 oz) cans

TABLE 1.18   Ingredient substitutions (approximate)

Recipe item	Amount	Substitute ingredient
Baking powder	1 tsp	¼ tsp baking soda + ½ tsp cream of tartar ¼ tsp baking soda + ½ cup buttermilk or sour milk (to replace ½ cup of the liquid)
Butter or margarine	1 lb	14 oz hydrogenated shortening + 1 tsp salt 14 oz (1⅜ cups) oil + 1 tsp salt
Buttermilk	1 cup	1 Tbsp lemon juice or vinegar + enough whole milk to make 1 cup (let stand 5 minutes before using) or 1 cup unflavored yogurt
Celery, fresh	8 oz	4 oz celery flakes, dry

TABLE 1.18 Continued

Recipe item	Amount	Substitute ingredient
Chocolate, unsweetened	1 oz (1 square)	3 Tbsp cocoa + 1 Tbsp (½ oz) fat
Cocoa	3 Tbsp	1 oz chocolate; reduce fat in recipe by 1 Tbsp
Cornstarch (thickening)	1 Tbsp 1 oz 1 Tbsp 1 oz	2 Tbsp flour, all-purpose 2 oz flour, all-purpose 2 tsp waxy maize starch ¾ oz waxy maize starch

Cream
  Half and half
  Whipping
	
	1 cup
	1 cup
		
		¾ cup milk + 2–3 Tbsp fat
		¾ cup milk + ⅓ cup fat

Flour, all-purpose	1 cup (4 oz)	1½ cups bread flour 1 cup + 2 Tbsp cake flour 1 cup rye or whole wheat flour 1 cup less 2 Tbsp cornmeal 1 cup rolled oats 1½ cups bread crumbs
Flour, all-purpose (thickening)	1 oz	1⅓ oz quick-cooking tapioca ½ cup cornmeal ⅔ oz cornstarch ½ oz waxy maize starch, arrowroot ¾ oz bread crumbs
Flour, cake	1 cup (4 oz)	1 cup less 2 Tbsp all-purpose flour
Garlic	1 medium clove	⅛ tsp garlic powder ½ tsp garlic, minced, dry ½ tsp garlic salt
Green peppers, fresh, chopped	8 oz EP	1 oz green pepper flakes, dry
Herbs, fresh	1 Tbsp	1 tsp whole dried ¼ tsp ground
Honey	1 cup	1¼ cup granulated sugar + ¼ cup liquid
Milk, fluid, whole	1 cup 1 qt	1 oz (⅓ cup) nonfat dry milk + water to make 1 cup + 1 Tbsp fat (optional) ½ cup evaporated milk + ½ cup water 4 oz nonfat dry milk + water to make 1 qt + 1¼ oz fat (optional)

TABLE 1.18 Continued

Recipe item	Amount	Substitute ingredient
Milk, sour[a]	1 cup	1 Tbsp vinegar or lemon juice + sweet milk to make 1 cup
Onions, fresh, chopped	8 oz EP	1 oz dehydrated onions, chopped or minced[b]
Mushrooms, fresh	1 lb (6 cups)	3 cups processed mushrooms
Parsley, fresh, chopped	8 oz EP	3 oz parsley flakes, dry
Sour cream	1 cup	1 cup yogurt
Stock, chicken or beef	1 gal	3 oz concentrated soup base + 1 gal water (commercial products may vary in strength; follow manufacturer's directions)
Sugar, granulated	1 cup (8 oz)	1⅓ cups brown sugar 1½ cups powdered sugar 1¼–1½ cups corn syrup less ¼–½ cup liquid in recipe 1 cup honey less ¼–⅓ cup liquid in recipe 1⅓ cups molasses less ⅓ cup liquid in recipe
Tapioca, quick-cooking	1 Tbsp	1 Tbsp all-purpose flour (for thickening)
Yeast, active dry	¼ oz (1 pkg) 1 oz	1 cake compressed 2 oz compressed
Yeast, instant		See manufacturer's directions for conversion from active dry or compressed

[a]To substitute buttermilk or sour milk for sweet milk, add ½ tsp baking soda and decrease baking powder by 2 tsp per cup of milk.

[b]Rehydrate onions unless they are to be used in a recipe in which there is a large volume of liquid. To rehydrate, cover onions with water, using the ratio of 1 oz dehydrated onions (½ cup) to ¾ cup water. Let stand 20–30 minutes.

TABLE 1.19 Ingredient proportions

Function	Ingredient	Relative proportion
Leavening agents	Baking powder	1½–2 Tbsp to 1 lb flour
	Baking soda	2 tsp to 1 qt sour milk or molasses
	Yeast	½–1 envelope dry (⅛–¼ oz) to 1 lb flour (varies with ingredients and time allowed)
Seasonings	Salt	1–2 tsp to 1 lb flour
		1¼ tsp to 1 lb meat
		2 tsp to 1 qt water (for cereal)
		2½ tsp to 1 pt liquid (for rolls)
Thickening agents	Eggs	4–6 whole eggs to 1 qt milk
		8–12 egg yolks to 1 qt milk
		8–12 egg whites to 1 qt milk
	Flour	½ oz to 1 qt liquid—very thin sauce (cream soups, starchy vegetables)
		1 oz to 1 qt liquid—thin sauce (cream soups, nonstarchy vegetables)
		2 oz to 1 qt liquid—medium sauce (creamed foods, gravy)
		3–4 oz to 1 qt liquid—thick sauce (soufflés)
		4–5 oz to 1 qt liquid—very thick sauce (croquettes)
		1 lb to 1 qt liquid—pour batter (popovers)
		2 lb to 1 qt liquid—drop batter (cake muffins)
		3 lb to 1 qt liquid—soft dough (biscuits, rolls)
		4 lb to 1 qt liquid—stiff dough (pastry, cookies, noodles)
	Gelatin, granulated, unflavored	2 Tbsp to 1 qt liquid—plain gelatins (gelatin and fruit juices)
		2 Tbsp to 1 qt liquid—whips (gelatin and fruit juices whipped)
		3 Tbsp to 1 qt liquid—fruit gelatins (gelatin, fruit juices, and chopped fruit)
		3 Tbsp to 1 qt liquid—vegetable gelatins (gelatin, liquid, and chopped vegetables)
		3 Tbsp to 1 qt liquid—sponges (gelatin, fruit juice, and beaten egg whites)
		4 Tbsp to 1 qt liquid—Bavarian cream (gelatin, fruit juice, fruit pulp, and whipped cream)

Note   ■   See Table 1.18 for ingredient substitutions.

TABLE 1.20   Guide for rounding off weights and measures

If the total amount of an ingredient is	*Round it to*
WEIGHTS	
Less than 2 oz	Measure unless weight is ¼-, ½-, or ¾-oz amounts
2–10 oz	Closest ¼ oz or convert to measure
More than 10 oz but less than 2 lb 8 oz	Closest ½ oz
2 lb 8 oz–5 lb	Closest full ounce
More than 5 lb	Closest ¼ lb
MEASURES	
Less than 1 Tbsp	Closest ⅛ tsp
More than 1 Tbsp but less than 3 Tbsp	Closest ¼ tsp
3 Tbsp–½ cup	Closest ½ tsp or convert to weight
More than ½ cup but less than ¾ cup	Closest full tsp or convert to weight
More than ¾ cup but less than 2 cups	Closest full Tbsp or convert to weight
2 cups–2 qt	Nearest ¼ cup
More than 2 qt but less than 4 qt	Nearest ½ cup
1–2 gal	Nearest full cup or ¼ qt
More than 2 gal but less than 10 gal[a]	Nearest full quart
More than 10 gal but less than 20 gal[a]	Closest ½ gal
More than 20 gal[a]	Closest full gallon

[a]For baked goods or products in which accurate ratios are critical, always round to the nearest full cup or ¼ qt.

Note   ■   This table is intended to aid in rounding fractions and complex measurements into amounts that are as simple as possible to weigh or measure while maintaining the accuracy needed for quality control.

TABLE 1.21   Ounces and decimal equivalents of a pound

Ounces	Decimal part of a pound	Ounces	Decimal part of a pound
¼	0.016	8¼	0.516
½	0.031	8½	0.531
¾	0.047	8¾	0.547
1	0.063	9	0.563
1¼	0.078	9¼	0.578
1½	0.094	9½	0.594
1¾	0.109	9¾	0.609
2	0.125	10	0.625
2¼	0.141	10¼	0.641
2½	0.156	10½	0.656
2¾	0.172	10¾	0.672
3	0.188	11	0.688
3¼	0.203	11¼	0.703
3½	0.219	11½	0.719
3¾	0.234	11¾	0.734
4	0.250	12	0.750
4¼	0.266	12¼	0.766
4½	0.281	12½	0.781
4¾	0.297	12¾	0.797
5	0.313	13	0.813
5¼	0.328	13¼	0.828
5½	0.344	13½	0.844
5¾	0.359	13¾	0.859
6	0.375	14	0.875
6¼	0.391	14¼	0.891
6½	0.406	14½	0.906
6¾	0.422	14¾	0.922
7	0.438	15	0.938
7¼	0.453	15¼	0.953
7½	0.469	15½	0.969
7¾	0.484	15¾	0.984
8	0.500	16	1.000

Note   ■ This table is useful when increasing or decreasing recipes. The multiplication or division of pounds and ounces is simplified if the ounces are converted to decimal parts of a pound. For example, when multiplying 1 lb 9 oz by 3, first change the 9 oz to 0.563 lb, using the table. Thus, the 1 lb 9 oz becomes 1.563 lb, which multiplied by 3 is 4.683 lb or 4 lb 11 oz.

Direct-Reading Measurement Tables

Recipe adjustment may be made by using tables that have been developed for different numbers of portions. Using these charts requires minimal calculation. Table 1.22 can be used when the desired yields are divisible by 25 and the ingredients are given in *weights*. Table 1.23 is used when recipe ingredients are given in *volume measurements* and the yields can be divided by 25. Table 1.24 has yields that can be divided by 8 and is useful in enlarging home-size recipes. Following are instructions for using direct-reading measurement tables.

Directions for Using Tables 1.22 and 1.23

The choice of Tables 1.22 or 1.23 depends on whether the recipe ingredients are given in weights (ounces and pounds) or in volume measurements (teaspoons, tablespoons, cups, quarts, or gallons). Table 1.22 is used for converting weighed ingredients using recipe yields that are divisible by 25. Table 1.23 is used for converting volume measures of ingredients using recipe yields that are divisible by 25. To adjust recipes, follow these steps:

1. Locate the column that corresponds to the original yield of the recipe to be adjusted. For example, assume the original recipe yields 100 portions. Locate the "100" column across the top of the chart on Table 1.22.

2. Go down this column to the amount of the ingredient required (or to the closest number to that figure) in the recipe to be adjusted. If the recipe for 100 portions requires 21 lb of ground beef, for example, go down the column headed 100 to the figure "21."

3. Then go across the page, in line with that amount, to the column that is headed to correspond with the yield desired. For example, if only 75 portions are desired, begin with the 21 lb figure in the "100" column and slide across to the column headed "75" and read that figure. It indicates that 15 lb 12 oz of ground beef would be required to make 75 portions with this recipe.

4. Record this figure as the amount of the ingredient required for the new yield of the recipe. Repeat steps 1, 2, and 3 for each ingredient in the original recipe to obtain the adjusted ingredient weight needed for the new yield. Follow the same procedure using Table 1.23 in adjusting ingredient amounts indicated in volume measures. Yields can be either increased or decreased in this manner.

5. If two columns need to be combined to obtain the desired yield, follow steps 1 through 4 and add together the amounts given in the two columns to obtain the amount required for the adjusted yield. For example, to find the amount of ground beef for 225 portions of our hypothetical recipe, locate the figures in columns headed "200" and "25" and add them together. In this example it would be 42 lb + 5 lb 4 oz, so the required total for ground beef would be 47 lb 4 oz.

6. The figures given in these tables are given in exact weights including fractional ounces. After making yield adjustments for every ingredient, refer to Table 1.20 for rounding off fractional amounts that are not of sufficient proportion to change product quality.

Abbreviations used in the charts include the following:

- oz = ounce
- lb = pound
- tsp = teaspoon
- Tbsp = tablespoon
- qt = quart
- gal = gallon
- (r) = slightly rounded
- (s) = scant

Equivalents helpful in using the charts include:

- 3 tsp = 1 Tbsp
- 4 Tbsp = ¼ cup
- 5 Tbsp + 1 tsp = ⅓ cup
- 8 Tbsp = ½ cup
- 10 Tbsp + 2 tsp = ⅔ cup
- 12 Tbsp = ¾ cup
- 16 Tbsp = 1 cup
- 4 cups = 1 qt
- 4 qt = 1 gal

TABLE 1.22 Direct-reading table for adjusting weight ingredients of recipes divisible by 25[a]

25	50	75	100	200	300	400	500
*[b]	*	*	¼ oz	½ oz	¾ oz	1 oz	1¼ oz
*	*	*	½ oz	1 oz	1½ oz	2 oz	2½ oz
*	*	*	¾ oz	1½ oz	2¼ oz	3 oz	3¾ oz
¼ oz	½ oz	¾ oz	1 oz	2 oz	3 oz	4 oz	5 oz
*	*	*	1¼ oz	2½ oz	3¾ oz	5 oz	6¼ oz
*	¾ oz	*	1½ oz	3 oz	4½ oz	6 oz	7½ oz
*	*	*	1¾ oz	3½ oz	5¼ oz	7 oz	8¾ oz
½ oz	1 oz	1½ oz	2 oz	4 oz	6 oz	8 oz	10 oz
*	*	1¾ oz	2¼ oz	4½ oz	6¾ oz	9 oz	11¼ oz
*	1¼ oz	2 oz	2½ oz	5 oz	7½ oz	10 oz	12½ oz
*	*	2 oz	2¾ oz	5½ oz	8¼ oz	11 oz	13¾ oz
¾ oz	1½ oz	2¼ oz	3 oz	6 oz	9 oz	12 oz	15 oz
*	*	2½ oz	3¼ oz	6½ oz	9¾ oz	13 oz	1 lb ¼ oz
*	1¾ oz	2¾ oz	3½ oz	7 oz	10½ oz	14 oz	1 lb 1½ oz
1 oz	2 oz	2¾ oz	3¾ oz	7½ oz	11¼ oz	15 oz	1 lb 2¾ oz
1 oz	2 oz	3 oz	4 oz	8 oz	12 oz	1 lb	1 lb 4 oz
1 oz	2¼ oz	3¼ oz	4¼ oz	8½ oz	12¾ oz	1 lb 1 oz	1 lb 5¼ oz
*	2½ oz	3½ oz	4½ oz	9 oz	13½ oz	1 lb 2 oz	1 lb 6½ oz
*	2½ oz	3½ oz	4¾ oz	9½ oz	14¼ oz	1 lb 3 oz	1 lb 7¾ oz
1¼ oz	2½ oz	3¾ oz	5 oz	10 oz	15 oz	1 lb 4 oz	1 lb 9 oz
*	2¾ oz	4¼ oz	5½ oz	11 oz	1 lb ½ oz	1 lb 6 oz	1 lb 11½ oz
1½ oz	3 oz	4½ oz	6 oz	12 oz	1 lb 2 oz	1 lb 8 oz	1 lb 14 oz
*	3¼ oz	4¾ oz	6½ oz	13 oz	1 lb 3½ oz	1 lb 10 oz	2 lb ½ oz
1¾ oz	3½ oz	5¼ oz	7 oz	14 oz	1 lb 5 oz	1 lb 12 oz	2 lb 3 oz
2 oz	3¾ oz	5¾ oz	7½ oz	15 oz	1 lb 6½ oz	1 lb 14 oz	2 lb 5½ oz
2 oz	4 oz	6 oz	8 oz	1 lb	1 lb 8 oz	2 lb	2 lb 8 oz
2¼ oz	4¼ oz	6½ oz	8½ oz	1 lb 1 oz	1 lb 9½ oz	2 lb 2 oz	2 lb 10½ oz
2¼ oz	4½ oz	6¾ oz	9 oz	1 lb 2 oz	1 lb 11 oz	2 lb 4 oz	2 lb 13 oz
2½ oz	4¾ oz	7¼ oz	9½ oz	1 lb 3 oz	1 lb 12½ oz	2 lb 6 oz	2 lb 15½ oz
2½ oz	5 oz	7½ oz	10 oz	1 lb 4 oz	1 lb 14 oz	2 lb 8 oz	3 lb 2 oz
2¾ oz	5½ oz	8¼ oz	11 oz	1 lb 6 oz	2 lb 1 oz	2 lb 12 oz	3 lb 7 oz
3 oz	6 oz	9 oz	12 oz	1 lb 8 oz	2 lb 4 oz	3 lb	3 lb 12 oz
3¼ oz	6½ oz	9¾ oz	13 oz	1 lb 10 oz	2 lb 7 oz	3 lb 4 oz	4 lb 1 oz
3½ oz	7 oz	10½ oz	14 oz	1 lb 12 oz	2 lb 10 oz	3 lb 8 oz	4 lb 6 oz
3¾ oz	7½ oz	11¼ oz	15 oz	1 lb 14 oz	2 lb 13 oz	3 lb 12 oz	4 lb 11 oz
4 oz	8 oz	12 oz	1 lb	2 lb	3 lb	4 lb	5 lb
4½ oz	9 oz	13½ oz	1 lb 2 oz	2 lb 4 oz	3 lb 6 oz	4 lb 8 oz	5 lb 10 oz

[a]To be used with Table 1.23, which is similarly constructed for volume measures.
[b]An asterisk (*) means these amounts cannot be weighed accurately without introducing errors.

TABLE 1.22   Continued

25	50	75	100	200	300	400	500
5 oz	10 oz	15 oz	1 lb 4 oz	2 lb 8 oz	3 lb 12 oz	5 lb	6 lb 4 oz
5½ oz	11 oz	1 lb ½ oz	1 lb 6 oz	2 lb 12 oz	4 lb 2 oz	5 lb 8 oz	6 lb 14 oz
6 oz	12 oz	1 lb 2 oz	1 lb 8 oz	3 lb	4 lb 8 oz	6 lb	7 lb 8 oz
6½ oz	13 oz	1 lb 3½ oz	1 lb 10 oz	3 lb 4 oz	4 lb 14 oz	6 lb 8 oz	8 lb 2 oz
7 oz	14 oz	1 lb 5 oz	1 lb 12 oz	3 lb 8 oz	5 lb 4 oz	7 lb	8 lb 12 oz
7½ oz	15 oz	1 lb 6½ oz	1 lb 14 oz	3 lb 12 oz	5 lb 10 oz	7 lb 8 oz	9 lb 6 oz
8 oz	1 lb	1 lb 8 oz	2 lb	4 lb	6 lb	8 lb	10 lb
8½ oz	1 lb 1 oz	1 lb 9½ oz	2 lb 2 oz	4 lb 4 oz	6 lb 6 oz	8 lb 8 oz	10 lb 10 oz
9 oz	1 lb 2 oz	1 lb 11 oz	2 lb 4 oz	4 lb 8 oz	6 lb 12 oz	9 lb	11 lb 4 oz
9½ oz	1 lb 3 oz	1 lb 12½ oz	2 lb 6 oz	4 lb 12 oz	7 lb 2 oz	9 lb 8 oz	11 lb 14 oz
10 oz	1 lb 4 oz	1 lb 14 oz	2 lb 8 oz	5 lb	7 lb 8 oz	10 lb	12 lb 8 oz
11 oz	1 lb 6 oz	2 lb 1 oz	2 lb 12 oz	5 lb 8 oz	8 lb 4 oz	11 lb	13 lb 12 oz
12 oz	1 lb 8 oz	2 lb 4 oz	3 lb	6 lb	9 lb	12 lb	15 lb
13 oz	1 lb 10 oz	2 lb 7 oz	3 lb 4 oz	6 lb 8 oz	9 lb 12 oz	13 lb	16 lb 4 oz
14 oz	1 lb 12 oz	2 lb 10 oz	3 lb 8 oz	7 lb	10 lb 8 oz	14 lb	17 lb 8 oz
15 oz	1 lb 14 oz	2 lb 13 oz	3 lb 12 oz	7 lb 8 oz	11 lb 4 oz	15 lb	18 lb 12 oz
1 lb	2 lb	3 lb	4 lb	8 lb	12 lb	16 lb	20 lb
1 lb 1 oz	2 lb 2 oz	3 lb 3 oz	4 lb 4 oz	8 lb 8 oz	12 lb 12 oz	17 lb	21 lb 4 oz
1 lb 2 oz	2 lb 4 oz	3 lb 6 oz	4 lb 8 oz	9 lb	13 lb 8 oz	18 lb	22 lb 8 oz
1 lb 3 oz	2 lb 6 oz	3 lb 9 oz	4 lb 12 oz	9 lb 8 oz	14 lb 4 oz	19 lb	23 lb 12 oz
1 lb 4 oz	2 lb 8 oz	3 lb 12 oz	5 lb	10 lb	15 lb	20 lb	25 lb
1 lb 5 oz	2 lb 10 oz	3 lb 15 oz	5 lb 4 oz	10 lb 8 oz	15 lb 12 oz	21 lb	26 lb 4 oz
1 lb 6 oz	2 lb 12 oz	4 lb 2 oz	5 lb 8 oz	11 lb	16 lb 8 oz	22 lb	27 lb 8 oz
1 lb 7 oz	2 lb 14 oz	4 lb 5 oz	5 lb 12 oz	11 lb 8 oz	17 lb 4 oz	23 lb	28 lb 12 oz
1 lb 8 oz	3 lb	4 lb 8 oz	6 lb	12 lb	18 lb	24 lb	30 lb
1 lb 10 oz	3 lb 4 oz	4 lb 14 oz	6 lb 8 oz	13 lb	19 lb 8 oz	26 lb	32 lb 8 oz
1 lb 12 oz	3 lb 8 oz	5 lb 4 oz	7 lb	14 lb	21 lb	28 lb	35 lb
1 lb 14 oz	3 lb 12 oz	5 lb 10 oz	7 lb 8 oz	15 lb	22 lb 8 oz	30 lb	37 lb 8 oz
2 lb	4 lb	6 lb	8 lb	16 lb	24 lb	32 lb	40 lb
2 lb 2 oz	4 lb 4 oz	6 lb 6 oz	8 lb 8 oz	17 lb	25 lb 8 oz	34 lb	42 lb 8 oz
2 lb 4 oz	4 lb 8 oz	6 lb 12 oz	9 lb	18 lb	27 lb	36 lb	45 lb
2 lb 6 oz	4 lb 12 oz	7 lb 2 oz	9 lb 8 oz	19 lb	28 lb 8 oz	38 lb	47 lb 8 oz
2 lb 8 oz	5 lb	7 lb 8 oz	10 lb	20 lb	30 lb	40 lb	50 lb
2 lb 12 oz	5 lb 8 oz	8 lb 4 oz	11 lb	22 lb	33 lb	44 lb	55 lb
3 lb	6 lb	9 lb	12 lb	24 lb	36 lb	48 lb	60 lb
3 lb 4 oz	6 lb 8 oz	9 lb 12 oz	13 lb	26 lb	39 lb	52 lb	65 lb
3 lb 8 oz	7 lb	10 lb 8 oz	14 lb	28 lb	42 lb	56 lb	70 lb
3 lb 12 oz	7 lb 8 oz	11 lb 4 oz	15 lb	30 lb	45 lb	60 lb	75 lb

TABLE 1.22 Continued

25	50	75	100	200	300	400	500
4 lb	8 lb	12 lb	16 lb	32 lb	48 lb	64 lb	80 lb
4 lb 4 oz	8 lb 8 oz	12 lb 12 oz	17 lb	34 lb	51 lb	68 lb	85 lb
4 lb 8 oz	9 lb	13 lb 8 oz	18 lb	36 lb	54 lb	72 lb	90 lb
4 lb 12 oz	9 lb 8 oz	14 lb 2 oz	19 lb	38 lb	57 lb	76 lb	95 lb
5 lb	10 lb	15 lb	20 lb	40 lb	60 lb	80 lb	100 lb
5 lb 4 oz	10 lb 8 oz	15 lb 12 oz	21 lb	42 lb	63 lb	84 lb	105 lb
5 lb 8 oz	11 lb	16 lb 8 oz	22 lb	44 lb	66 lb	88 lb	110 lb
5 lb 12 oz	11 lb 8 oz	17 lb 4 oz	23 lb	46 lb	69 lb	92 lb	115 lb
6 lb	12 lb	18 lb	24 lb	48 lb	72 lb	96 lb	120 lb
6 lb 4 oz	12 lb 8 oz	18 lb 12 oz	25 lb	50 lb	75 lb	100 lb	125 lb
7 lb 8 oz	15 lb	22 lb 8 oz	30 lb	60 lb	90 lb	120 lb	150 lb
8 lb 12 oz	17 lb 8 oz	26 lb 4 oz	35 lb	70 lb	105 lb	140 lb	175 lb
10 lb	20 lb	30 lb	40 lb	80 lb	120 lb	160 lb	200 lb
11 lb 4 oz	22 lb 8 oz	33 lb 12 oz	45 lb	90 lb	135 lb	180 lb	225 lb
12 lb 8 oz	25 lb	37 lb 8 oz	50 lb	100 lb	150 lb	200 lb	250 lb

Used with permission from *Quantity Food Preparation: Standardizing Recipes and Controlling Ingredients.* Copyright 1983 by the American Dietetic Association, Chicago.

TABLE 1.23   Direct-reading table for adjusting recipes with ingredient amounts given in volume measurement and divisible by 25[a]

25	50	75	100
¼ tsp	½ tsp	¾ tsp	1 tsp
¼ tsp (r)	½ tsp (r)	1 tsp (s)	1¼ tsp
¼ tsp + ⅛ tsp	¾ tsp	1 tsp + ⅛ tsp	1½ tsp
½ tsp (s)	¾ tsp (r)	1¼ tsp (r)	1¾ tsp
½ tsp	1 tsp	1½ tsp	2 tsp
½ tsp (r)	1 tsp + ⅛ tsp	1¾ tsp (s)	2¼ tsp
½ tsp + ⅛ tsp	1¼ tsp	2 tsp (s)	2½ tsp
¾ tsp (s)	1¼ tsp + ⅛ tsp	2 tsp (r)	2¾ tsp
¾ tsp	1½ tsp	2¼ tsp	1 Tbsp
1 tsp + ⅛ tsp	2¼ tsp	1 Tbsp + ¼ tsp + ⅛ tsp	1½ Tbsp
1½ tsp	1 Tbsp	1½ Tbsp	2 Tbsp
1¾ tsp + ⅛ tsp	1 Tbsp + ¾ tsp	1 Tbsp + 2½ tsp + ⅛ tsp	2½ Tbsp
2¼ tsp	1½ Tbsp	2 Tbsp + ¾ tsp	3 Tbsp
2¼ tsp + ⅛ tsp	1 Tbsp + 2¼ tsp	2 Tbsp + 1½ tsp + ⅛ tsp	3½ Tbsp
1 Tbsp	2 Tbsp	3 Tbsp	¼ cup
1 Tbsp + 1 tsp	2 Tbsp + 2 tsp	¼ cup	⅓ cup
2 Tbsp	¼ cup	¼ cup + 2 Tbsp	½ cup
2 Tbsp + 2 tsp	⅓ cup	½ cup	⅔ cup
3 Tbsp	6 Tbsp	½ cup + 1 Tbsp	¾ cup
¼ cup	½ cup	¾ cup	1 cup
¼ cup + 1 Tbsp	½ cup + 2 Tbsp	¾ cup + 3 Tbsp	1¾ cups
⅓ cup	⅔ cup	1 cup	1⅓ cups
⅓ cup + 2 tsp	¾ cup	1 cup + 2 Tbsp	1½ cups

[a]To be used with Table 1.22, which is similarly constructed for weight measures.

200	300	400	500
2 tsp	1 Tbsp	1 Tbsp + 1 tsp	1 Tbsp + 2 tsp
2½ tsp	1 Tbsp + ¾ tsp	1 Tbsp + 2 tsp	2 Tbsp + ¼ tsp
1 Tbsp	1½ Tbsp	2 Tbsp	2½ Tbsp
1 Tbsp + ½ tsp	1 Tbsp + 2¼ tsp	2 Tbsp + 1 tsp	2 Tbsp + 2¾ tsp
1 Tbsp + 1 tsp	2 Tbsp	2 Tbsp + 2 tsp	3 Tbsp + 1 tsp
1½ Tbsp	2 Tbsp + ¾ tsp	3 Tbsp	3 Tbsp + 2¼ tsp
1 Tbsp + 2 tsp	2½ Tbsp	3 Tbsp + 1 tsp	4 Tbsp + ½ tsp
1 Tbsp + 2½ tsp	2 Tbsp + 2¼ tsp	3 Tbsp + 2 tsp	4 Tbsp + 1¾ tsp
2 Tbsp	3 Tbsp	¼ cup	5 Tbsp
3 Tbsp	¼ cup + 1½ tsp	⅓ cup + 2 tsp	¼ cup + 3½ Tbsp
¼ cup	¼ cup + 2 Tbsp	½ cup	½ cup + 2 Tbsp
¼ cup + 1 Tbsp	¼ cup + 3½ Tbsp	½ cup + 2 Tbsp	¾ cup + ½ Tbsp
⅓ cup + 2 tsp	½ cup + 1 Tbsp	¾ cup	¾ cup + 3 Tbsp
¼ cup + 3 Tbsp	½ cup + 2½ Tbsp	¾ cup + 2 Tbsp	1 cup + 1½ Tbsp
½ cup	¾ cup	1 cup	1¼ cups
⅔ cup	1 cup	1⅓ cups	1⅔ cups
1 cup	1½ cups	2 cups	2½ cups
1⅓ cups	2 cups	2⅔ cups	3⅓ cups
1½ cups	2¼ cups	3 cups	3¾ cups
2 cups	3 cups	1 qt	1¼ qt
2½ cups	3¾ cups	1¼ qt	1½ qt + ¼ cup
2⅔ cups	1 qt	1¼ qt + ⅓ cup	1½ qt + ⅔ cup
3 cups	1 qt + ½ cup	1½ qt	1¾ qt + ½ cup

Continued

TABLE 1.23 Continued

25	50	75	100
6 Tbsp + 2 tsp	¾ cup + 4 tsp	1¼ cups	1⅔ cups
¼ cup + 3 Tbsp	¾ cup + 2 Tbsp	1¼ cups + 1 Tbsp	1¾ cups
½ cup	1 cup	1½ cups	2 cups
½ cup + 1 Tbsp	1 cup + 2 Tbsp	1½ cups + 3 Tbsp	2¼ cups
½ cup + 4 tsp	1 cup + 2 Tbsp + 2 tsp	1¾ cups	2⅓ cups
½ cup + 2 Tbsp	1¼ cups	1¾ cups + 2 Tbsp	2½ cups
⅔ cup	1⅓ cups	2 cups	2⅔ cups
½ cup + 3 Tbsp	1¼ cups + 2 Tbsp	2 cups + 1 Tbsp	2¾ cups
¾ cup	1½ cups	2¼ cups	3 cups
¾ cup + 1 Tbsp	1½ cups + 2 Tbsp	2¼ cups + 3 Tbsp	3¼ cups
¾ cup + 4 tsp	1⅔ cups	2½ cups	3⅓ cups
¾ cup + 2 Tbsp	1¾ cups	2½ cups + 2 Tbsp	3½ cups
¾ cup + 2 Tbsp + 2½ tsp	1¾ cups + 4 tsp	2¾ cups + ½ tsp	3⅔ cups
¾ cup + 3 Tbsp	1¾ cups + 2 Tbsp	2¾ cups + 1 Tbsp	3¾ cups
1 cup	2 cups	3 cups	1 qt
1¼ cups	2½ cups	3¾ cups	1¼ qt
1½ cups	3 cups	1 qt + ½ cup	1½ qt
1¾ cups	3½ cups	1¼ qt + ¼ cup	1¾ qt
2 cups	1 qt	1½ qt	2 qt

200	300	400	500
3⅓ cups	1¼ qt	1½ qt + ⅔ cup	2 qt + ⅓ cup
3½ cups	1¼ qt + ¼ cup	1¾ qt	2 qt + ¾ cup
1 qt	1½ qt	2 qt	2½ qt
1 qt + ½ cup	1½ qt + ¾ cup	2¼ qt	2¾ qt + ¼ cup
1 qt + ⅔ cup	1¾ qt	2¼ qt + ⅓ cup	2¾ + ⅔ cup
1¼ qt	1¾ qt + ½ cup	2½ qt	3 qt + 1½ cups
1¼ qt + ⅓ cup	2 qt	2½ qt + ⅔ cup	3 qt + 1⅓ cups
1¼ qt + ½ cup	2 qt + ¼ cup	2¾ qt	3¼ qt + ¾ cup
1½ qt	2¼ qt	3 qt	3¾ qt
1½ qt + ½ cup	2¼ qt + ¾ cup	3¼ qt	1 gal + ¼ cup
1½ qt + ⅔ cup	2½ qt	3¼ qt + ⅓ cup	1 gal + ⅔ cup
1¾ qt	2½ qt + ½ cup	3½ qt	1 gal + 1½ cups
1¾ qt + ⅓ cup	2¾ qt	3½ qt + ⅔ cup	1 gal + 1⅔ cups
1¾ qt + ½ cup	3 qt + ¼ cup	1 gal	1 gal + 3¾ cups
2 qt	3 qt	1 gal	1¼ gal
2½ qt	3¾ qt	1¼ gal	1½ gal + 1 cup
3 qt	1 gal + 2 cups	1½ gal	1¾ gal + 2 cups
3½ qt	1¼ gal + 1 cup	1¾ gal	2 gal + 3 cups
1 gal	1½ gal	2 gal	2½ gal

Continued

TABLE 1.23 **Continued**

25	50	75	100
2¼ cups	1 qt + ½ cup	1½ qt + ¾ cup	2¼ qt
2½ cups	1¼ qt	1¾ qt + ½ cup	2½ qt
2¾ cups	1¼ qt + ½ cup	2 qt + ¼ cup	2¾ qt
3 cups	1½ qt	2¼ qt	3 qt
3¼ cups	1½ qt + ½ cup	2¼ qt + ¾ cup	3¼ qt
3½ cups	1¾ qt	2½ qt + ½ cup	3½ qt
3¾ cups	1¾ qt + ½ cup	2¾ qt + ¼ cup	3¾ qt
1 qt	2 qt	3 qt	1 gal
1¼ qt	2½ qt	3¾ qt	1¼ gal
1½ qt	3 qt	1 gal + 2 cups	1½ gal
1¾ qt	3½ qt	1¼ gal + 1 cup	1¾ gal
2 qt	1 gal	1½ gal	2 gal
2¼ qt	1 gal + 2 cups	1½ gal + 3 cups	2¼ gal
2½ qt	1¼ gal	1¾ gal + 2 cups	2½ gal
2¾ qt	1¼ gal + 2 cups	2 gal + 1 cup	2¾ gal
3 qt	1½ gal	2¼ gal	3 gal
3 qt + 1 cup	1½ gal + 2 cups	2¼ gal + 3 cups	3¼ gal
3½ qt	1¾ gal	2½ gal + 2 cups	3½ gal
3½ qt + 1 cup	1¾ gal + 2 cups	2¾ gal + 1 cup	3¾ gal

200	300	400	500
1 gal + 2 cups	1½ gal + 3 cups	2¼ gal	2¾ gal + 1 cup
1¼ gal	1¾ gal + 2 cups	2½ gal	3 gal + 2 cups
1¼ gal + 2 cups	2 gal + 1 cup	2¾ gal	3¼ gal + 3 cups
1½ gal	2¼ gal	3 gal	3¾ gal
1½ gal + 2 cups	2¼ gal + 3 cups	3¼ gal	4 gal + 1 cup
1¾ gal	2½ gal + 2 cups	3½ gal	4¼ gal + 2 cups
1¾ gal + 2 cups	2¾ gal + 1 cup	3¾ gal	4½ gal + 3 cups
2 gal	3 gal	4 gal	5 gal
2½ gal	3¾ gal	5 gal	6¼ gal
3 gal	4½ gal	6 gal	7½ gal
3½ gal	5¼ gal	7 gal	8¾ gal
4 gal	6 gal	8 gal	10 gal
4½ gal	6¾ gal	9 gal	11¼ gal
5 gal	7½ gal	10 gal	12½ gal
5½ gal	8¼ gal	11 gal	13¾ gal
6 gal	9 gal	12 gal	15 gal
6½ gal	9¾ gal	13 gal	16¼ gal
7 gal	10½ gal	14 gal	17½ gal
7½ gal	11¼ gal	15 gal	18¾ gal

Continued

TABLE 1.23   Continued

25	50	75	100
1 gal	2 gal	3 gal	4 gal
1 gal + 1 cup	2 gal + 2 cups	3 gal + 3 cups	4¼ gal
1 gal + 2 cups	2¼ gal	3¼ gal + 2 cups	4½ gal
1 gal + 3 cups	2¼ gal + 2 cups	3½ gal + 1 cup	4¾ gal
1¼ gal	2½ gal	3¾ gal	5 gal
1¼ gal + 1 cup	2½ gal + 2 cups	3¾ gal + 3 cups	5¼ gal
1¼ gal + 2 cups	2¾ gal	4 gal + 2 cups	5½ gal
1¼ gal + 3 cups	2¾ gal + 2 cups	4¼ gal + 1 cup	5¾ gal
1½ gal	3 gal	4½ gal	6 gal
1½ gal + 1 cup	3 gal + 2 cups	4½ gal + 3 cups	6¼ gal
1½ gal + 2 cups	3¼ gal	4¾ gal + 2 cups	6½ gal
1½ gal + 3 cups	3¼ gal + 2 cups	5 gal + 1 cup	6¾ gal
1¾ gal	3½ gal	5¼ gal	7 gal

200	300	400	500
8 gal	12 gal	16 gal	20 gal
8½ gal	12¾ gal	17 gal	21¼ gal
9 gal	13½ gal	18 gal	22½ gal
9½ gal	14¼ gal	19 gal	23¾ gal
10 gal	15 gal	20 gal	25 gal
10½ gal	15¾ gal	21 gal	26¼ gal
11 gal	16½ gal	22 gal	27½ gal
11½ gal	17¼ gal	23 gal	28¾ gal
12 gal	18 gal	24 gal	30 gal
12½ gal	18¾ gal	25 gal	31¼ gal
13 gal	19½ gal	26 gal	32½ gal
13½ gal	20¼ gal	27 gal	33¾ gal
14 gal	21 gal	28 gal	35 gal

Used with permission from *Quantity Food Preparation Receipes and Controlling Ingredients.* Copyright 1983 by The American Dietetic Association, Chicago.

Directions for Using Table 1.24

Many quantity recipes can be expanded from home-size recipes. Table 1.24 is useful when enlarging small-quantity recipes. Instructions for using this table follow:

1. Locate column that corresponds to the yield of the recipe to be increased. For example, if the recipe yields 8 portions, use the figures in the first column under the heading 8.

2. Locate the ingredient amount for each ingredient to be adjusted. Example: the original recipe of 8 portions calls for 1 Tbsp sugar. Find 1 Tbsp in the column marked 8.

3. Locate the amount on the same line under the heading for the desired yield. Example: To increase the original recipe for 8 servings to 24, locate under the 24 column heading the number on the same line with the 1 Tbsp in the 8 column. In the case of 1 Tbsp sugar for 8 portions the enlarged amount is 3 Tbsp.

4. Repeat this procedure for each ingredient in the recipe. Refer to Table 1.20 for rounding off awkward fractions and complicated measurements.

Abbreviations in this table include:

- tsp = teaspoon
- Tbsp = tablespoon
- qt = quart
- gal = gallon
- (b) = too small for accurate measure; use caution
- (r) = slightly rounded
- (s) = scant

Measuring spoon sizes are:

- 1 Tbsp
- 1 tsp
- ½ tsp
- ¼ tsp
- for ¾ tsp combine ½ tsp + ¼ tsp
- for ⅛ tsp use half of the ¼ tsp

Equivalents include:

- 3 tsp = 1 Tbsp
- 4 Tbsp = ¼ cup
- 5 Tbsp + 1 tsp = ⅓ cup
- 8 Tbsp = ½ cup
- 10 Tbsp + 2 tsp = ⅔ cup
- 12 Tbsp = ¾ cup
- 16 Tbsp = 1 cup
- 4 cups = 1 qt
- 4 qt = 1 gal

TABLE 1.24 Direct-reading table for increasing home-size recipes with ingredient amounts given in volume measurement and divisible by 8

8	16	24	32
(b)	(b)	⅛ tsp	⅛ tsp (r)
(b)	⅛ tsp (r)	¼ tsp	¼ tsp (r)
¼ tsp (s)	¼ tsp (r)	½ tsp	¾ tsp (s)
¼ tsp	½ tsp	¾ tsp	1 tsp
¼ tsp (r)	¾ tsp (s)	1 tsp	1¼ tsp (r)
½ tsp (s)	¾ tsp (r)	1¼ tsp	1¾ tsp (s)
½ tsp	1 tsp	1½ tsp	2 tsp
½ tsp (r)	1¼ tsp (s)	1¾ tsp	2¼ tsp (r)
¾ tsp (s)	1¼ tsp (r)	2 tsp	2¾ tsp (r)
¾ tsp	1½ tsp	2¼ tsp	1 Tbsp
¾ tsp (r)	1¾ tsp (s)	2½ tsp	1 Tbsp + ¼ tsp (r)
1 tsp (s)	1¾ tsp (r)	2¾ tsp	1 Tbsp + ¾ tsp (s)
1 tsp	2 tsp	1 Tbsp	1 Tbsp + 1 tsp
1½ tsp	1 Tbsp	1½ Tbsp	2 Tbsp
2 tsp	1 Tbsp + 1 tsp	2 Tbsp	2 Tbsp + 2 tsp
2½ tsp	1 Tbsp + 2 tsp	2½ Tbsp	3 Tbsp + 1 tsp
1 Tbsp	2 Tbsp	3 Tbsp	¼ cup
1 Tbsp + ½ tsp	2 Tbsp + 1 tsp	3½ Tbsp	¼ cup + 2 tsp
1 Tbsp + 1 tsp	2 Tbsp + 2 tsp	¼ cup	⅓ cup
1 Tbsp + 2¼ tsp	3 Tbsp + 2¾ tsp	⅓ cup	¼ cup + 3 Tbsp
2 Tbsp + 2 tsp	⅓ cup	½ cup	⅔ cup
3 Tbsp + 1¾ tsp	⅓ cup + 5 tsp	⅔ cup	¾ cup + 2 Tbsp
¼ cup	½ cup	¾ cup	1 cup
⅓ cup	⅔ cup	1 cup	1⅓ cups
⅓ cup + 4 tsp	¾ cup + 4 tsp	1¼ cups	1⅔ cups
⅓ cup + 5¼ tsp	⅔ cup + 3½ Tbsp	1⅓ cups	1¾ cups + 1¼ tsp
½ cup	1 cup	1½ cups	2 cups
½ cup + 2¼ tsp	1 cup + 5¼ tsp	1⅔ cups	2 cups + 3½ Tbsp
½ cup + 4 tsp	1 cup + 3 Tbsp	1¾ cups	2⅓ cups
⅔ cup	1⅓ cups	2 cups	2⅔ cups

48	64	96
¼ tsp	¼ tsp (r)	½ tsp
½ tsp	¾ tsp (s)	1 tsp
1 tsp	1¼ tsp (r)	2 tsp
1½ tsp	2 tsp	1 Tbsp
2 tsp	2¾ tsp (s)	1 Tbsp + 1 tsp
2½ tsp	1 Tbsp + ¼ tsp	1 Tbsp + 2 tsp
1 Tbsp	1 Tbsp + 1 tsp	2 Tbsp
1 Tbsp + ½ tsp	1 Tbsp + 1¾ tsp	2 Tbsp + 1 tsp
1 Tbsp + 1 tsp	1 Tbsp + 2¼ tsp	2 Tbsp + 2 tsp
1 Tbsp + 1½ tsp	2 Tbsp	3 Tbsp
1 Tbsp + 2 tsp	2 Tbsp + ¾ tsp	3 Tbsp + 1 tsp
1 Tbsp + 2½ tsp	2 Tbsp + 1¼ tsp	3 Tbsp + 2 tsp
2 Tbsp	2 Tbsp + 2 tsp	¼ cup
3 Tbsp	¼ cup	⅓ cup + 2 tsp
¼ cup	⅓ cup	½ cup
¼ cup + 1 Tbsp	⅓ cup + 4 tsp	½ cup + 2 Tbsp
⅓ cup + 2 tsp	½ cup	¾ cup
¼ cup + 3 Tbsp	½ cup + 4 tsp	¾ cup + 2 Tbsp
½ cup	⅔ cup	1 cup
⅔ cup	¾ cup + 2 Tbsp	1⅓ cups
1 cup	1⅓ cups	2 cups
1⅓ cups	1¾ cups	2⅔ cups
1½ cups	2 cups	3 cups
2 cups	2⅔ cups	1 qt
2½ cups	3⅓ cups	1¼ qt
2⅔ cups	3½ cups + 2½ tsp	1¼ qt + ⅓ cup
3 cups	1 qt	1½ qt
3⅓ cups	4¼ cups + 3 Tbsp	1½ qt + ⅔ cup
3½ cups	1 qt + ⅔ cup	1¾ qt
1 qt	1¼ qt + ⅓ cup	2 qt

Continued

TABLE 1.24 Continued

8	16	24	32
¾ cup	1½ cups	2¼ cups	3 cups
¾ cup + 1¼ tsp	1½ cups + 2¾ tsp	2⅓ cups	3 cups + 2 Tbsp
¾ cup + 4 tsp	1⅔ cups	2½ cups	3⅓ cups
⅔ cup + 3½ Tbsp	1¾ cups + 1¼ tsp	2⅔ cups	3½ cups + 1 Tbsp
⅔ cup + ¼ cup	1¾ cups + 4 tsp	2¾ cups	3⅔ cups
1 cup	2 cups	3 cups	1 qt
1 cup + 4 tsp	2 cups + 2½ Tbsp	3¼ cups	1 qt + ⅓ cup
1 cup + 5¼ tsp	2 cups + 3½ Tbsp	3⅓ cups	4¼ cups + 3 Tbsp
1 cup + 2 Tbsp + 2 tsp	2¼ cups + 4 tsp	3½ cups	1 qt + ⅔ cup
1 cup + 3½ Tbsp	2¼ cups + 3 Tbsp	3⅔ cups	4¾ cups + 2 Tbsp
1¼ cups	2½ cups	3¾ cups	1¼ qt
1⅓ cups	2⅔ cups	1 qt	1¼ qt + ⅓ cup
1⅔ cups	3⅓ cups	1¼ qt	1½ qt + ⅔ cup
2 cups	1 qt	1½ qt	2 qt
2⅓ cups	1 qt + ⅔ cup	1¾ qt	2¼ qt + ⅓ cup
2⅔ cups	1¼ qt + ⅓ cup	2 qt	2½ qt + ⅔ cup
3 cups	1½ qt	2¼ qt	3 qt
3⅓ cups	1½ qt + ⅔ cup	2½ qt	3¼ qt + ⅓ cup
3⅔ cups	1¾ qt + ⅓ cup	2¾ qt	3½ qt + ⅔ cup
1 qt	2 qt	3 qt	1 gal
1 qt + ⅓ cup	2 qt + ⅔ cup	3¼ qt	1 gal + 1⅓ cups
1 qt + ⅔ cup	2¼ qt + ⅓ cup	3½ qt	1 gal + 2⅔ cups
1¼ qt	2½ qt	3¾ qt	1¼ gal
1¼ qt + ⅓ cup	2½ qt + ⅔ cup	1 gal	1¼ gal + 1⅓ cups
1½ qt + ⅔ cup	3¼ qt + ⅓ cup	1¼ gal	1½ gal + 2⅔ cups
2 qt	1 gal	1½ gal	2 gal

48	64	96
1 qt + ½ cup	1½ qt	2¼ qt
1 qt + ⅔ cup	1½ qt + ¼ cup	2¼ qt + ⅓ cup
1¼ qt	1½ qt + ⅔ cup	2½ qt
1¼ qt + ⅓ cup	1¾ qt + 2 Tbsp	2½ qt + ⅔ cup
1¼ qt + ½ cup	1¾ qt + ⅓ cup	2¾ qt
1½ qt	2 qt	3 qt
1½ qt + ½ cup	2 qt + ⅔ cup	3¼ qt
1½ qt + ⅔ cup	2 qt + ¾ cup + 2 Tbsp	3¼ qt + ⅓ cup
1¾ qt	2¼ qt + ⅓ cup	3½ qt
1¾ qt + ⅓ cup	2¼ qt + ¾ cup	3 qt + 2⅔ cups
1¾ qt + ½ cup	2½ qt	3 qt + 3 cups
2 qt	2¾ qt + ⅓ cup	1 gal
2½ qt	3¼ qt + ⅓ cup	1¼ gal
3 qt	1 gal	1½ gal
3½ qt	1 gal + 2⅔ cups	1¾ gal
1 gal	1¼ gal + 1⅓ cups	2 gal
1 gal + 2 cups	1½ gal	2¼ gal
1¼ gal	1½ gal + 2⅔ cups	2½ gal
1¼ gal + 2 cups	1¾ gal + 1⅓ cups	2¾ gal
1½ gal	2 gal	3 gal
1½ gal + 2 cups	2 gal + 2⅔ cups	3¼ gal
1¾ gal	2¼ gal + 1⅓ cups	3½ gal
1¾ gal + 2 cups	2½ gal	3¾ gal
2 gal	2½ gal + 2⅔ cups	4 gal
2½ gal	3¼ gal + 1⅓ cups	5 gal
3 gal	4 gal	6 gal

Part Two

Recipes ∎

RECIPE INFORMATION

Yield

The recipes in this book produce servings for 50 people unless otherwise stated. Factors that may affect yield include portioning, ingredient weighing error, mistakes in calculating increased or decreased quantities, abnormal handling loss, and variation in the edible portion (EP) and as purchased (AP) factors for food products such as fresh produce and meats.

A standard counter pan 12 × 20 inches has been indicated for many recipes. For baked desserts and some bread products, either a 12 × 18-inch or 18 × 26-inch pan is specified, as they are standard bakeware sizes. Weight of product per pan may need to be changed if pans other than those specified in the recipe are used. Care should be taken to scale products so that portion weight will be accurate and recipe yield remains correct. Tables 1.15 and 1.16 give capacities of baking and counter pans.

The number of servings per pan will depend on the portion size desired. Many standard-sized baking or counter pans will yield from 24 to 32 servings per pan, and where these size pans are indicated, the recipes generally are calculated for 48 or 64 servings. Yield adjustments may be made by cutting the servings into sizes that will yield the desired number of portions. Portion size is included in each recipe, and the yield is given in number of portions, volume produced, and/or number of pans. Some foodservices may wish to adjust the yield based on the clientele to be served.

Ingredients

In most cases, the type of ingredient used in testing the recipes has been specified; for example, granulated, brown, or powdered sugar, and all-purpose or cake flour. High-ratio and/or hydrogenated shortenings were used in cake and pastry recipes; margarine or butter in cookies, some quick breads, and most sauce recipes. Solid fats such as margarine, butter, and hydrogenated fats were used interchangeably in recipes that specify "shortening." Corn, soybean, or cottonseed oil was used in recipes that specify salad or vegetable oil. Sodium aluminum sulfate–type baking powder (double acting) and active dry yeast were used for leavening.

Fresh eggs, large size, weighing approximately 2 ounces unshelled (1¾ oz shelled) were used in the preparation of the recipes. Eggs are specified by both number and weight. In many foodservices, frozen eggs are used, in which case the eggs are weighed or measured. If the eggs are to be measured, the number and weight may easily be converted to volume by referring to Table 1.3.

Nonfat dry milk is indicated in some recipes, but in those specifying fluid milk, dry milk may be substituted. Table 1.18 gives a formula for conversion. In most cases, it is not necessary to rehydrate the dry milk, since it is mixed with other dry ingredients, and water is added in place of the fluid milk. The amount of fat in the recipe may need to be increased slightly.

Nutrition Information

Recipes in this book include nutritional values for calories; grams of carbohydrate, fat, and protein; and milligrams of cholesterol, sodium, iron, and calcium. Values are for the recipe portion listed at the top of each recipe. Total percentage of calories contributed by protein, carbohydrate, and fat for each portion also is listed. The nutritive values are approximate and are intended to be used as a general guideline. Values may vary if ingredients used are different from those used in the nutritional value data base. Differences also may occur if ingredient amounts are adjusted or procedures are changed.

Weights and Measures

Quantities of dry ingredients weighing more than 1 ounce are given by weight in ounces (oz) and pounds (lb). Weights are for foods as purchased (AP) unless otherwise stated. Liquid ingredients are indicated by measure, teaspoons (tsp), tablespoons (Tbsp), cups (cups), quarts (qt), and gallons (gal).

Accurate weighing and measuring of ingredients are essential for a satisfactory product. Weighing is more accurate than measuring and is recommended whenever possible, but reliable scales are essential. A table model scale with a 15- to 20-pound capacity and 1/4- to 1/2-ounce graduations (or an electronic digital readout scale with a 15- to 20-pound capacity) is suitable for weighing ingredients for 50 portions.

Standard measuring equipment should be used to ensure accuracy, and measurements should be level. Use the largest appropriate measure to reduce the possibility of error and to save time. For example, use a one-gallon measure once instead of a one-quart measure four times. Flour is the exception: Use measure no larger than one quart for flour.

Cooking Time and Temperature

The cooking time given in each recipe is based on the size of pan and the amount of food in the pan. If a smaller or larger pan is used, an adjustment in cooking time may be necessary. The number of pans placed in the oven at one time also may affect the length of baking time; the larger the number of pans or the colder a product, the longer the cooking time. In convection ovens, the temperature as specified for a conventional oven should be reduced by 25°–50°F and the total bake/roast time by 10–15 percent.

Abbreviations Used in Recipes

AP	as purchased	oz	ounce
EP	edible portion	psi	pounds per square inch
°F	degrees Fahrenheit	pt	pint
1 oz	fluid ounce	qt	quart
gal	gallon	tsp	teaspoon
lb	pound	Tbsp	tablespoon

2

Appetizers and Party Foods

Appetizer in this book describes foods offered before a meal, as well as foods served informally for parties, receptions, and other functions where people serve themselves from a variety of offerings. In either case the appetizers should be attractive in appearance, pleasing in flavor, and tastefully displayed.

Appetizers may be selected from one or more of the following categories:

Hors d'oeuvres are attractive hot and cold finger foods that may include crisp fresh fruits and vegetables, pickles, olives, cheese, fish, sausages, deviled eggs, or a combination of these.

Crudités are raw vegetables, attractively displayed and garnished, and usually served with a dip. Presentation is important. Broad, flat dishes, baskets, silver trays and shallow, decorative pans may be used for the container. Vegetables are arranged with consideration for shape, color, balance, and overall decorative appeal. A low-calorie appetizer may be prepared by arranging crudités attractively around a hollowed-out vegetable filled with a yogurt dip (p. 89). Although vegetables used for crudités are served raw, the appearance of certain vegetables such as asparagus and carrots is brightened if they are blanched first (p. 495).

Dips, hot or cold, are accompaniments to fruits, vegetables, crackers, or chips. They should complement the foods being served with them.

Canapés are made by spreading a well-seasoned mixture of eggs, cheese, fish, or meat on a canapé base. Bases include toasted or untoasted bread slices cut into various shapes, crackers, chips, tiny biscuits, or puff pastry shells. Fruit and nut breads make good bases for many canapé mixtures.

Cocktails are made of pieces of fruit, fruit or vegetable juices, and carbonated or alcoholic beverages. Nonalcoholic beverages may be referred to as mocktails. Cocktails may be made also of seafood such as oysters, shrimp, crab, or lobster and served with a seasoned sauce.

Soup appetizers are light and generally served as a first course at the dining table. Hot or cold broth or cream soups may be served and should complement the remainder of the meal.

Table 2.1 is a general guide for quantities of appetizers needed to serve 50 people. Table 2.2 suggests foods appropriate for serving entree party trays to 50 people. The type of group being served, time of day, type of event and duration, and number of different items offered may necessitate increasing or decreasing the amount of food recommended.

TABLE 2.1   Suggestions for appetizers

Food item	Guide to serving quantities for 50
BEVERAGES	
Punch	2–2½ gal, recipes pp. 100–110
Wine	See Tables 17.1 and 17.2, p. 711
CANAPÉ SPREADS AND FILLINGS	
Chicken salad spread	Recipe p. 562, prepare ¼ recipe
Ham salad spread	Recipe p. 561, prepare ¼ recipe
Tuna salad spread	Recipe p. 526, prepare ¼ recipe
Miniature puffs	Recipe p. 291, prepare ½ recipe
COCKTAILS	
Broiled grapefruit	25 fruit
Fruit cup	10 lb
Melon balls or cubes	10 lb
Punch	2 gal, recipes pp. 100–110
Shrimp cocktail	Recipe for sauce p. 593
DIPS	
Artichoke, hot	Recipe p. 87
Artichoke and crab, hot	Recipe p. 87
Basic, and variations	Recipe p. 88–89
Garden dressing (dip)	Recipe p. 543
Layered Mexican	Recipe p. 90
Nacho	Recipe p. 323
Salsa	Recipe p. 589
Summer fruit	Recipe p. 89
Vegetable	Recipe p. 552
Yogurt	Recipes p. 552
HORS D'OEUVRES	
Apple and cheese wedges	1½ lb cheese, 8 apples, cut in wedges
Carrot curls	3–4 lb
Celery sticks	3–4 lb
Cheese ball, party, with crackers	Recipe p. 91; 125–150 crackers
Cheese balls, hot	Recipe p. 319, prepare ½ recipe, use No. 40 dipper
Cheese cubes	5 lb

TABLE 2.1   Continued

Food item	Guide to serving quantities for 50
Hors d'Oeuvres (continued)	
Cheese olive balls	Recipe p. 92
Cherry tomatoes	2 lb
Chips	5 lb
Cocktail sausages	3–5 lb
Crudité party trays	12–15 lb assorted vegetables
Deviled eggs	Recipe p. 318, prepare ½ recipe
Fruit chunks	8 lb
Marinated mushrooms	Recipe p. 504
Meatballs in barbecue sauce	Recipe p. 370, prepare ⅓ recipe, use No. 70 dipper
Mixed nuts	1–1½ lb
Party mix	3 lb
Sausage balls	100, recipe p. 92
Vegetable relishes	See p. 487 for ideas
Whole shrimp, with cocktail sauce	3–5 lb shrimp, recipe for sauce p. 598, prepare ½ recipe
Soups	
Bouillon	Recipe p. 616, prepare ½ recipe for 4 oz portion
French onion	Recipe p. 629, prepare ½ recipe for 4 oz portion
Gazpacho	Recipe p. 638
Vichyssoise	Recipe p. 639, prepare ½ recipe for 4 oz portion

Notes

- The quantity of appetizers needed for 50 portions will depend on the group being served, the type of function, and the number of different items offered. If food items are served in combination with other foods, adjust the amounts to yield the approximate total weight or total number recommended. Example: Carrot curls, in combination with celery sticks, require a total weight of 3–4 lb.

- Preparing appetizers for an attractive buffet requires careful planning. Choosing foods that need last-minute preparation, along with those that can be produced in advance, is suggested. Following are useful guidelines for production planning:

    Canapés, spreads, and fillings: Highly perishable fillings should be made shortly before serving.
    Cocktails: Prepare fruit one day in advance. Cook and chill shrimp one day in advance. Make and chill beverages one to three days in advance.
    Dips: Prepare and chill one to three days in advance. Store in glass or other inert-material container.
    Hors d'oeuvres: Prepare vegetable relishes one day in advance; store in cold water. To freshen, cover with ice for 30 minutes before serving. Marinate vegetables one day in advance. Prepare cheese balls one to five days in advance; cover tightly. Cut cheese cubes no more than one day in advance; cover tightly.
    Soups: Prepare cold soups one to two days in advance, hot soups soon before serving.

TABLE 2.2   Entree party trays

Meat and cheese trays (approximate amount to serve 50)			
Meat (shaved or thinly sliced)	Cheese (thinly sliced)	Bread (thinly sliced bread or buns)	Spreads/other
Choose 10 lb:	Choose 3 lb:	Choose 125 small slices or 75 buns:	Use suggested amount:

Cold cuts
Corned beef
Roast beef
Ham
Pastrami
Turkey
	American
	Cheddar
	Edam
	Gouda
	Monterey
	  Jack
	Muenster
	Provolone
	Swiss
	See p. 306
	  for addi-
	  tional
	  cheeses
		Small buns
		Sliced bread
		  Pumpernickel
		  Rye
		  White
		  Whole wheat
			Margarine or butter,
			  softened, 1 lb
			Mayonnaise or salad
			  dressing, 1½ cups
			Prepared mustard,
			  1 cup
			Horseradish, 1 cup
			Leaf lettuce, 3 lb
			Alfalfa sprouts, 1 lb
			Tomatoes, sliced,
			  7 lb
			Onions, sliced, 2 lb

Vegetable trays and dips (approximate amount to serve 50; see Notes)		
Vegetables	Relishes	Dips
Choose 5 lb:	Choose 3 lb:	Choose 1–1½ qt:

Asparagus spears
Broccoli florets
Baby carrots
Carrot sticks or slices
Cauliflower florets
Celery sticks
Cherry tomatoes
Cucumber spears or circles
Green beans
Green onions
Jicama
Kohlrabi
Mushrooms
Pea pods
Radish roses
Red, green, or yellow bell
  peppers
Zucchini spears
	Black or green olives
	Dill spears
	Pickled beets
	Pickled eggs
	Pickled vegetables
	Sweet pickles
	Garnishes
	  Chives
	  Flowers
	  Herbs
	  Scallions
		Hot artichoke
		Blue cheese
		Creamy herb
		Creamy onion
		Dill
		Garden (prepare ½ recipe)
		Italian
		Picante
		Seafood
		Summer fruit
		Yogurt

Notes

- Meat and cheese may be rolled, folded, or stacked and garnished with leaf lettuce, parsley, and colorful vegetables. Vegetables look appealing when cut in creative shapes and garnished with crisp greens.
- Arranging food neatly so the tray will remain attractive is important. Including larger quantities of more-popular items will make food trays appear well supplied throughout the serving period. Color and flavor combinations also should be considerations for determining placement of food items.
- Crudité trays may require two or three times the amount of vegetables for an attractive display to be arranged and garnished.
- Blanching asparagus, broccoli, cauliflower, and green beans heightens their flavor and appearance (p. 495).

APPETIZER RECIPES

HOT ARTICHOKE DIP

Yield: 50 portions   *Portion:* 1½ oz
Oven: 350°F   *Bake:* 20–25 minutes

Ingredient	Amount	Procedure
Artichoke hearts, canned	2 lb 10 oz	Drain and chop artichoke hearts.
Garlic clove, mashed	3 cloves	Stir remaining ingredients into artichoke hearts.
Mayonnaise	2 cups	
Worcestershire sauce	1½ tsp	
Parmesan cheese, grated	3 cups	
Pepper, white	¼ tsp	

Pour into 2 one-quart ovenproof bowls or pans.
Bake at 350°F for 20–25 minutes.
Serve warm with chips or crackers.

Approximate nutritive values per portion

Calories (kcal)	Protein (grams)	Carbohydrate (grams)	Fat (grams)	Cholesterol (mg)	Sodium (mg)	Iron (mg)	Calcium (mg)
91	1.6 (7%)	5 (22%)	7.4 (72%)	3	148	0.3	11

Variation

- **Hot Crab and Artichoke Dip.**   Add 1 lb chopped crabmeat before baking.

BASIC DIP ◼

Yield: 50 portions

Ingredient	Amount	Procedure
Cream cheese	8 oz	Mix cream cheese until softened, using flat beater.
Sour cream	1 lb 8 oz	Add sour cream. Mix until smooth. Add ingredients for variations from following chart. Mix until evenly distributed. Chill.

Note	◼ Dip may be thinned by adding a small quantity of buttermilk or milk.

BASIC DIP VARIATIONS ◼

Variation	Ingredients added to basic dip	Serve with
Avocado (guacamole) (see Notes)	(Delete cream cheese; reduce sour cream to 8 oz) 1 lb 8 oz avocado pulp 1 Tbsp lemon juice 3 oz onion, finely chopped 2 Tbsp fresh cilantro, finely chopped ¼ tsp garlic powder 8 oz fresh tomatoes, diced	Tortilla chips Nacho chips
Blue Cheese	8 oz blue cheese, crumbled 1½ tsp lemon juice 2 Tbsp onion, finely chopped ½ cup buttermilk or milk	Crackers Fresh vegetables Chips
Creamy Herb	¼ cup fresh onion, finely chopped ¼ cup snipped fresh parsley ¼ cup chives, chopped 1 Tbsp Worcestershire sauce ¼ tsp garlic powder	Fresh vegetables
Creamy Onion	2 oz dry onion soup mix ½ oz snipped fresh parsley or chives	Chips
Dill	1½ Tbsp chopped onion 1 Tbsp dill weed 1½ tsp Beau Monde seasoning	Fresh vegetables
Italian	1½ oz dry Italian salad dressing mix ½ oz snipped fresh parsley	Fresh vegetables

Picante	(Delete sour cream; increase cream cheese to 2 lb) 8 oz salsa (see Notes) ¼ cup fresh cilantro, chopped 1 oz stuffed olives, chopped	Tortilla chips Nacho chips Fresh vegetables Spread for canapés
Seafood	8 oz cooked shrimp, clam, or crab, finely chopped 1 oz dry onion soup mix 2 oz chili sauce 1½ Tbsp horseradish	Crackers Toasted party bread
Summer Fruit	(Delete cream cheese) 8 oz brown sugar or honey 1½ tsp vanilla	Fresh fruit
Yogurt, Vegetable Yogurt, Fruit	see p. 552 see p. 552	Fresh vegetables Fresh fruit

Notes

- Chunky avocado dip may be made by deleting sour cream and using 2 lb cubed fresh avocados.
- More salsa may be added to Picante for a thinner dip.

LAYERED MEXICAN DIP

Yield: 50 portions or 3 14-inch platters   *Portion:* 4 oz

Ingredient	Amount	Procedure
Bean dip	4 lb (6 10½-oz cans)	
Avocado pulp	3 lb	Blend. Save for later step.
Lemon juice	6 Tbsp	
Salt	1 tsp	
Pepper, black	1½ tsp	
Sour cream	1 lb 8 oz	Blend. Save for later step.
Mayonnaise	1½ cups	
Taco seasoning	3¾ oz	
Tomatoes, fresh, diced	3 lb	
Green onions, sliced	9 oz	
Ripe olives, sliced	1 lb 4 oz	
Cheddar cheese, shredded	12 oz	

1. Spread 1 lb 5 oz bean dip on each of 3 14-inch round platters.

2. Spread 1 lb avocado mixture over bean dip layer.

3. Spread 12 oz sour cream mixture over avocado layer.

4. Sprinkle rest of ingredients over each platter in the following order: tomatoes, green onions, olives, and cheese.

5. Serve with tortilla or nacho chips. Platter of dip will keep well in the refrigerator for up to two days.

Approximate nutritive values per portion

Calories (kcal)	Protein (grams)	Carbohydrate (grams)	Fat (grams)	Cholesterol (mg)	Sodium (mg)	Iron (mg)	Calcium (mg)
212	5.3 (10%)	8.4 (15%)	18 (75%)	14	786	1.2	101

Notes

- Refried Beans (½ recipe, p. 654) may be substituted for purchased bean dip.

- Salsa may be substituted for diced tomatoes, taco seasoning, and mayonnaise. Use 7½ cups salsa (2½ cups on each tray).

PARTY CHEESE BALL

Yield: 50 portions   *Portion:* 1½ oz

Ingredient	Amount	Procedure
Cream cheese, softened	1 lb	Mix all ingredients until smooth, using flat beater. Shape into two balls, 2 lb 4 oz each. Chill.
Blue cheese, crumbled	1 lb 8 oz	
Sharp cheddar cheese, shredded	2 lb	
Onion, finely minced	3 oz	
Worcestershire sauce	1 tsp	

Approximate nutritive values per portion

Calories (kcal)	Protein (grams)	Carbohydrate (grams)	Fat (grams)	Cholesterol (mg)	Sodium (mg)	Iron (mg)	Calcium (mg)
154	8.1 (21%)	1 (2%)	13.1 (76%)	39	331	0.3	211

Notes
- Ball may be rolled in chopped pecans, snipped fresh parsley, or paprika.
- Cheese mixture may be shaped into a long roll. After chilling, slice and serve on crackers or other canapé base.

SAUSAGE BALLS

Yield: 50 portions   *Portion:* 2 balls
Oven: 350°F   *Bake:* 20–25 minutes, both steps

Ingredient	Amount	Procedure
Pork sausage, bulk	2 lb	Form sausage into 100 1-inch balls, using a No. 70 dipper. Place on baking sheet. Bake at 350°F for 15 minutes. Drain on paper towels.
Cheddar cheese, grated	1 lb	Combine cheese, margarine, flour, and seasonings in mixer bowl, using flat beater.
Margarine, softened	8 oz	
Flour, all-purpose	12 oz	
Salt	½ tsp	
Paprika	2 tsp	
		Wrap 2 Tbsp (No. 70 dipper) of dough around each sausage ball. Place on ungreased baking sheet. Bake at 350°F for 8–10 minutes. Serve hot.

Approximate nutritive values per portion

Calories (kcal)	Protein (grams)	Carbohydrate (grams)	Fat (grams)	Cholesterol (mg)	Sodium (mg)	Iron (mg)	Calcium (mg)
145	5.7 (16%)	5.5 (15%)	11 (69%)	21	296	0.6	73

Note   ■ Balls may be frozen after wrapping with dough. Bake while still frozen at 400°F for 12–15 minutes.

Variation   ■ **Cheese Olive Puffs.**   Wrap dough around large stuffed green olives. Bake same as for Sausage Balls.

3

Beverages

COFFEE

The type of coffee-making equipment used in a foodservice determines the method of preparation and the grind of coffee. The urn is used when large quantities of coffee are required, as on a rapidly moving cafeteria line or for a large catered function. Where the service is spread over a longer period, coffee may be prepared in small batches in a drip coffee maker.

The equipment selected should make a clear, rich brew, hold the coffee at a consistent temperature, and provide the quantity needed at an appropriate speed with minimal labor. Regardless of the method used, certain precautions should be observed:

1. Select a blend of coffee that is appropriate to the clientele and the type of event. Flavored coffees are available and are often served after dessert and for special events. Choose a grind that is suitable for the coffee brewing equipment.

2. Use fresh coffee. Coffee loses its strength and flavor rapidly after it is ground and exposed to air. Large amounts should not be accumulated. Coffee should be protected from exposure to heat, moisture, and air. Coffee not needed for immediate use should be stored in the freezer.

3. Use a proportion of fresh, cold water to coffee that makes a brew of the strength preferred by the clientele. A proportion of 2½ gallons of water per pound of coffee makes a commonly accepted brew. Use 3 gallons of water per pound of coffee when a milder flavor is preferred. See p. 95 for coffee recipes.

4. Measure coffee accurately. The number of servings per pound of coffee varies with the quality of the coffee bean, equipment used, and cup size. A pound of high-quality coffee should yield about 50 6-ounce portions when properly brewed.

5. Have the water cold, freshly drawn, accurately measured, and brought to a temperature of 195°–200°F. Water that is too hot will extract bitter solids. Water that is too cold will not extract enough flavor and the coffee will be too cold for serving.

6. Hold coffee at a temperature of 185°–190°F for not more than one hour, and do not allow it to boil.

7. Serve coffee very hot. The consumer often judges a foodservice by the quality of its coffee, and temperature is important to its acceptance.

8. Plan production so that coffee is always fresh.

9. Clean the urn or other equipment immediately after each use, following instructions that come with the equipment.

TEA

Three main types of tea are available, produced by variations in processing. *Black* tea derives its color from a special processing treatment that allows the leaves to oxidize. This turns the leaves black and produces a rich brew. English Breakfast and Orange Pekoe are familiar black teas. *Oolong* tea is semioxidized. Its leaves are brown and green, and it brews light in color. *Green* tea is made from leaves that are dried without fermenting. The brew is pale green in color. Flavored and other specialty teas are also available. Tea is packaged in bulk as loose tea and in tea bags of various sizes.

Tea is brewed by the process of infusion, in which boiling water is poured over tea leaves or bags. The mixture is allowed to stand until the desired concentration is reached. The tea bags are then removed, or the tea leaves are strained out.

A stainless steel or earthenware container is preferable for brewing tea. Use freshly drawn cold water, heated just to the boiling point. For iced tea, make the brew stronger than for hot tea to compensate for the melting of the ice added at the time of service. Keep the tea at room temperature, because cloudiness develops in refrigerated tea.

PUNCH

Punch may be made easily from frozen or canned juices in various combinations. Lemonade (p. 102) or Basic Fruit Punch (p. 100) make good bases for many other fruit drinks when combined with fresh, frozen, canned, or powdered juices of the desired flavor.

The amount of sugar needed varies with the sugar concentration of the juices and individual preference. A recipe for Simple Syrup for sweetening punch is given on p. 101. If time does not allow making the syrup, the sugar may be added directly to the punch and stirred until the sugar is dissolved.

For punch that is to be served iced, the ingredients should be refrigerated. The chilled ingredients may be combined several hours in advance of service. If ginger ale or other carbonated beverage is to be used, however, it should be chilled and added just before serving.

Punch may be served from a bowl and kept cold by adding ice cubes, or it may be poured over an ice mold (p. 101). It may also be served as a nonalcoholic cocktail in appropriate glassware and garnished. See p. 110 for a few suggestions for nonalcoholic cocktails that use recipes in this book.

The amount of punch or iced beverage to prepare depends on the size of the punch cup or glass, the number of guests to be served, and whether second servings will be offered. Service from a punch bowl requires slightly more punch than if it is to be poured from a pitcher for individual service. It is always desirable to have extra chilled, unopened cans of the main punch ingredients to facilitate serving a larger crowd than anticipated.

Most recipes in this book were developed for 2–2½ gallons of punch. Each gallon will yield 32 one-half cup portions. Punch cups vary in size from three to six ounces, so it is important that the size be considered in determining the correct amount of punch to prepare.

BEVERAGE RECIPES

COFFEE

Yield: 50 portions or 2½ gal   *Portion:* 6 oz (¾ cup)

Ingredient	Amount	Procedure
Coffee	1 lb	Use proper blend and grind for the coffee maker used.
Water, cold	2½ gal	Use method recommended by the manufacturer of the coffee maker.

Note   ■   The amount of water will vary with the brand of coffee and the strength preferred.

Variations   ■   **Iced Coffee.**   Increase coffee to 2 lb. Pour over ice in glasses. Coffee may be cooled to room temperature but should not be refrigerated. Flavorings may be added for variety; i.e. vanilla, almond.

■   **Instant Coffee.**   Use 3 oz instant coffee or 2 oz freeze-dried to 2½ gal boiling water. Dissolve the coffee in a small amount of boiling water and add to the remaining hot water. Keep hot just below the boiling point, 185°–190°F.

■   **Steeped Coffee.**   Tie regular grind coffee loosely in a cloth bag. Immerse bag in cold water, which has been measured into a stainless steel kettle or stock pot. Heat to boiling point. Boil 3 minutes or until of desired strength. Remove coffee bag. Cover container and hold over low heat to keep at serving temperature.

HOT TEA

Yield: 50 portions or 2½ gal   *Portion:* 6 oz (¾ cup)

Ingredient	Amount	Procedure
Tea bags, 1-oz	2	Place tea bags in a stainless steel, enamel, or earthenware container.
Water, cold	2½ gal	Bring water to a boil, pour over tea. Steep for 3 minutes. Remove bags.

Notes

- If bulk tea is used, tie loosely in a bag.
- The amount of tea to be used will vary with the quality.
- Instant tea (¾–1 oz) may be used in place of the tea bags. The exact amount will vary according to the strength desired.

SPICED TEA

Yield: 48 portions or 1½ gal   *Portion:* 4 oz (½ cup)

Ingredient	Amount	Procedure
Water, boiling	1½ gal	Mix all ingredients except tea.
Sugar, granulated	1 lb 8 oz	Simmer 20 minutes.
Lemon juice	¼ cup	Strain.
Lemon peel, grated	1 lemon	
Orange juice	1 cup	
Orange peel, grated	1 orange	
Cloves, whole	4 tsp	
Cinnamon sticks	8	
Tea bag, 1-oz	1	Add tea bag to hot liquid. Steep for 5 minutes. Remove tea bag. Serve hot.

Approximate nutritive values per portion							
Calories (kcal)	Protein (grams)	Carbohydrate (grams)	Fat (grams)	Cholesterol (mg)	Sodium (mg)	Iron (mg)	Calcium (mg)
57	0.1 (0%)	15.6 (99%)	0 (0%)	0	7	0.1	6

Variation

- **Russian Tea.** Use only 1¼ gal water. Add 1 qt grape juice when adding other juice.

ICED TEA

Yield: 48 portions or 3 gal   *Portion:* 8 oz (1 cup)

Ingredient	Amount	Procedure
Tea bags, 1-oz	6	Place tea bags in enamel, stainless steel, or earthenware container.
Water, boiling	1 gal	Pour boiling water over tea bags. Steep 4–6 minutes. Remove bags.
Water, cold	2 gal	Pour hot tea into cold water.
Ice, chipped or cubed	10–15 lb	Fill 12-oz glasses with ice. Pour tea over ice just before serving.

Notes

- Always pour the hot tea concentrate into the cold water. Do not refrigerate or ice the tea prior to service. Cloudiness develops in tea that has been refrigerated.
- Instant tea (1 to 1½ oz) may be used in place of the tea bags.
- Six to seven lemons, cut in eighths, may be served with the tea.
- Iced tea may be garnished with lemon or orange slices or mint leaves.

COCOA

Yield: 50 portions or 2½ gal   *Portion:* 6 oz (¾ cup)

Ingredient	Amount	Procedure
Sugar, granulated Cocoa Salt	1 lb 8 oz 8 oz ½ tsp	Mix sugar, cocoa, and salt.
Water	1 qt	Add water and mix until smooth. Boil approximately 3 minutes or to form a thin syrup.
Milk	2½ gal	Heat milk. Stir in syrup.
Vanilla	1 tsp	Just before serving, add vanilla and stir until well mixed.

Approximate nutritive values per portion

Calories (kcal)	Protein (grams)	Carbohydrate (grams)	Fat (grams)	Cholesterol (mg)	Sodium (mg)	Iron (mg)	Calcium (mg)
180	7.3 (15%)	25.3 (52%)	7 (32%)	26	121	1.7	240

Notes
- A marshmallow or 1 tsp whipped cream may be added to each cup if desired.
- Cocoa syrup may be made in amounts larger than this recipe and stored in the refrigerator for three or four days. To serve, add 1 qt cocoa syrup to each 2 gal hot milk.

Variations
- **Hot Chocolate.**   Substitute 10 oz unsweetened baking chocolate for cocoa. Add to water and stir until melted.
- **Instant Hot Cocoa.**   Dissolve 2½ lb instant cocoa powder in 2 gal boiling water.
- **Mexican Chocolate.**   Follow hot chocolate recipe. Substitute 1 gal of hot coffee for 1 gal of milk. Add 1 oz (¼ cup) ground cinnamon.

FRENCH CHOCOLATE

Yield: 64 portions or 3 gal   *Portion:* 6 oz (¾ cup)

Ingredient	Amount	Procedure
Unsweetened chocolate Water, cold	1 lb 2 oz 3 cups	Combine chocolate and water. Cook over direct heat, stirring constantly, for 5 minutes or until chocolate is melted. Remove from heat. Beat with a wire whip until smooth.
Sugar, granulated Salt	2 lb 8 oz ½ tsp	Add sugar and salt to chocolate mixture. Return to heat. Cook over hot water 20–30 minutes or until thick. Chill.
Whipping cream	3½ cups	Whip cream. Fold into cold chocolate mixture.
Milk	2½ gal	Heat milk to scalding. To serve, place 1 Tbsp (rounded) chocolate mixture in each serving cup. Add hot milk to fill cup. Stir until well blended. Serve immediately.

Approximate nutritive values per portion

Calories (kcal)	Protein (grams)	Carbohydrate (grams)	Fat (grams)	Cholesterol (mg)	Sodium (mg)	Iron (mg)	Calcium (mg)
245	6.1 (9%)	27.7 (42%)	14.1 (48%)	38	97	0.6	197

Notes

- The milk must be kept very hot during the serving period.
- The chocolate mixture may be stored for 24 hours in the refrigerator.
- To make in quantity, prepare chocolate syrup and add hot milk. Whip cream to soft peaks and fold into hot chocolate. Keep hot.

BASIC FRUIT PUNCH

Yield: 80 portions or 2½ gal   *Portion:* 4 oz (½ cup)

Ingredient	Amount	Procedure
Sugar, granulated	2 lb 8 oz	Mix sugar and water.
Water	1 qt	Bring to boil. Cool.
Orange juice, frozen, undiluted	3 cups (2 12-oz cans)	Combine juices and water. Add sugar syrup and stir until mixed. Chill.
Lemon juice, frozen, undiluted	3 cups (2 12-oz cans)	
Water, cold	1½ gal	

Approximate nutritive values per portion							
Calories (kcal)	Protein (grams)	Carbohydrate (grams)	Fat (grams)	Cholesterol (mg)	Sodium (mg)	Iron (mg)	Calcium (mg)
75	0.4 (2%)	19.8 (97%)	0.1 (1%)	0	2	0	6

Notes
- If time does not allow making and cooling syrup, the sugar may be added to the cold punch and stirred until dissolved. Increase cold water to 1¾ gal.
- Ginger ale may be substituted for part or all of the water. Chill and add just before serving.

Variations
- **Golden Punch.**   Reduce orange and lemon juice to one 12-oz can each. Add two 46-oz cans pineapple juice.
- **Ginger Ale Fruit Punch.**   Use 1½ qt lemon juice, 1½ qt orange juice, 1 qt pineapple juice, and 1 gal water. Increase sugar to 3 lb. Add 2 qt ginger ale just before serving. Lime, orange, lemon, or raspberry sherbet may be added to punch just before serving.
- **Sparkling Grape Punch.**   Reduce orange and lemon juice to one 12-oz can each. Add two 12-oz cans frozen grape juice. Just before serving, add two 20-oz bottles of ginger ale.

ICE MOLD

Yield: 1 mold

Ingredient	Amount	Procedure
Ice mold Punch, juice, lemon- ade	1	Select mold that will fit in punch bowl. Fill mold with liquid, half to two-thirds full. Freeze.
Garnishes	See Notes	Add garnishes and enough liquid to partially cover garnishes. Freeze.
		After thin layer of liquid and fruit are frozen, fill mold with liquid and freeze until firm.
		To unmold ice ring, dip the mold in warm water until the ice slips out easily. Place the ring in very cold punch, garnished side up. Replace mold as necessary.

Notes
- Some attractive garnishes include: strawberries; cherries; pineapple; grapes; orange, lemon or lime slices; mint; ivy; and fresh flowers.
- If water is the liquid, use distilled or boiled tap water. Allow boiled water to set and de-aerate about 15 minutes.
- For a very decorative ice mold, use two or three layers of garnish. Freeze the garnish in place before adding the layers of liquid.

SIMPLE SYRUP

Yield: 2 qt

Ingredient	Amount	Procedure
Sugar, granulated Water	2 lb 1 qt	Mix sugar and water. Boil for 3 minutes. Chill before using in punch.

Notes
- For a thicker syrup, increase sugar to 2 lb 8 oz and add 1 Tbsp corn syrup.
- May be stored in the refrigerator for use in beverages or where recipe specifies Simple Syrup.

LEMONADE

Yield: 48 portions or 3 gal   *Portion:* 8 oz (1 cup)

Ingredient	Amount	Procedure
Lemon juice	1¼ qt (approximately 30 lemons)	Mix lemon juice and sugar.
Sugar, granulated	2 lb 8 oz	
Water, cold	2¼ gal	Add water. Stir until sugar is dissolved. Chill.

Approximate nutritive values per portion

Calories (kcal)	Protein (grams)	Carbohydrate (grams)	Fat (grams)	Cholesterol (mg)	Sodium (mg)	Iron (mg)	Calcium (mg)
94	0.1 (0%)	25.3 (99%)	0.1 (1%)	0	11	0.1	6

Notes

- Three 6-oz cans undiluted frozen lemon juice may be substituted for fresh lemon juice. Increase water to 2½ gal.
- Three 32-oz cans frozen lemonade concentrate, diluted 1:4 parts water, will yield 60 1-cup portions.
- Lemonade makes a good base for fruit punch.

BANANA PUNCH

Yield: 64 portions or 2 gal   *Portion:* 4 oz (½ cup)

Ingredient	Amount	Procedure
Sugar, granulated	2 lb	Mix sugar and water.
Water, hot	1½ qt	Boil for 3 minutes. Cool.
Orange juice, frozen, undiluted	1½ cups (1 12-oz can)	Combine juices, fruits, and water. Add cooled sugar syrup. Chill.
Lemon juice, frozen, undiluted	¾ cup (1 6-oz can)	
Water, cold	1 qt	
Pineapple, crushed	3 qt (1 No. 10 can)	
Bananas, ripe, mashed	6 medium	
Ginger ale, chilled	1 qt	Add ginger ale just before serving.

Approximate nutritive values per portion

Calories (kcal)	Protein (grams)	Carbohydrate (grams)	Fat (grams)	Cholesterol (mg)	Sodium (mg)	Iron (mg)	Calcium (mg)
104	.4 (2%)	27.1 (97%)	0.1 (1%)	0	3	0.2	11

Notes
- Mixture may be frozen before ginger ale is added and held for use later.
- Two 46-oz cans of unsweetened pineapple juice and one 12-oz can lemonade may be substituted for the crushed pineapple and lemon juice.

Variation
- **Banana Slush Punch.** Mix and freeze juices, syrup, and mashed bananas. To serve, fill glass about half full of partially frozen slush and add chilled ginger ale.

CRANBERRY PUNCH ∎

Yield: 80 portions or 2½ gal   *Portion:* 4 oz (½ cup)

Ingredient	Amount	Procedure
Cranberry juice	3 qt	Mix juices and water. Chill.
Pineapple juice	3 qt (2 46-oz cans)	
Lemonade, frozen, undiluted	1 qt (1 32-oz can)	
Water, cold	1 qt	
Ginger ale, chilled	3 28-oz bottles	Add ginger ale just before serving.

Approximate nutritive values per portion							
Calories (kcal)	Protein (grams)	Carbohydrate (grams)	Fat (grams)	Cholesterol (mg)	Sodium (mg)	Iron (mg)	Calcium (mg)
75	0.1 (1%)	19.2 (99%)	0 (0%)	0	5	0.2	9

SANGRIA ∎

Yield: 80 portions or 3¾ gal   *Portion:* 6 oz

Ingredient	Amount	Procedure
Grape juice, frozen, undiluted	3 12-oz cans	Combine juices and water. Stir well. Refrigerate until time of service.
Orange juice, frozen, undiluted	3 12-oz cans	
Lemonade, frozen, undiluted	3 12-oz cans	
Water	5 qt	
Club soda	7 qt	Just before service, combine juice mixture, club soda, and sliced fruit.
Oranges, thinly sliced	10	
Lemons, thinly sliced	9	
Limes, thinly sliced	6	

Serve punch and sliced fruit in a stemmed goblet.

Approximate nutritive values per portion							
Calories (kcal)	Protein (grams)	Carbohydrate (grams)	Fat (grams)	Cholesterol (mg)	Sodium (mg)	Iron (mg)	Calcium (mg)
79	0.7 (3%)	20.8 (95%)	0.1 (1%)	0	21	0.3	27

Note   ∎   May be garnished with skewered fruit.

SPARKLING APRICOT-PINEAPPLE PUNCH

Yield: 80 portions or 2½ gal   *Portion:* 4 oz (½ cup) ■

Ingredient	Amount	Procedure
Apricot nectar	3 qt (2 46-oz cans)	Combine juices and water. Chill.
Pineapple juice, un-sweetened	3 qt (2 46-oz cans)	
Lemon or lime juice, frozen, undiluted	1½ cups	
Water, cold	2 qt	
Ginger ale, chilled	2 qt	Add ginger ale just before serving.

Approximate nutritive values per portion

Calories (kcal)	Protein (grams)	Carbohydrate (grams)	Fat (grams)	Cholesterol (mg)	Sodium (mg)	Iron (mg)	Calcium (mg)
54	0.3 (2%)	13.9 (96%)	0.1 (2%)	0	4	0.3	11

MOCK PIÑA COLADA

Yield: 96 portions or 3 gal   *Portion:* 4 oz (½ cup) ■

Ingredient	Amount	Procedure
Vanilla ice cream mix, liquid, un-frozen	2 gal	Combine, using wire whip. Place in punch bowl.
Milk	3 qt	
Coconut extract	½ cup	
Rum extract	5 Tbsp	
Pineapple juice	1 qt	
Maraschino cherries, with stems	50	Serve in punch cup or stemmed glass. Garnish with maraschino cherry.

Approximate nutritive values per portion

Calories (kcal)	Protein (grams)	Carbohydrate (grams)	Fat (grams)	Cholesterol (mg)	Sodium (mg)	Iron (mg)	Calcium (mg)
202	4.3 (8%)	21.2 (41%)	11.5 (50%)	75	86	0.2	148

Note   ■   Softened vanilla ice cream may be substituted for ice cream mix.

BLUSHING PINEAPPLE PUNCH

Yield: 50 portions or 1¾ gal   *Portion:* 4 oz (½ cup)

Ingredient	Amount	Procedure
Sugar, granulated	6 oz	Cook sugar, water, and cinnamon candies over low heat, stirring until candies are dissolved.
Water	1½ cups	
Cinnamon candies (red-hots)	6 oz	
Pineapple juice	1 gal	Combine pineapple juice and cinnamon candy syrup.
Ginger ale	2 qt	Add ginger ale and ice just before serving.
Ice	8 oz	

Approximate nutritive values per portion

Calories (kcal)	Protein (grams)	Carbohydrate (grams)	Fat (grams)	Cholesterol (mg)	Sodium (mg)	Iron (mg)	Calcium (mg)
84	0.3 (1%)	21.2 (99%)	0 (0%)	0	4	0.3	15

Variation   ■ **Red-Hot Tea.** Use following ingredients in place of those in recipe: 12 oz cinnamon candies dissolved in 5½ qt hot water. Add 16 oz concentrated orange juice and lemon juice to taste. Serve hot.

WASSAIL

Yield: 80 portions or 2½ gal   *Portion:* 4 oz (½ cup)

Ingredient	Amount	Procedure
Sugar, granulated	2 lb 8 oz	Mix sugar, water, and spices.
Water	2½ qt	Boil 10 minutes.
Cloves, whole	1½ tsp	Cover and let stand one hour in a warm place.
Cinnamon sticks	10	Strain.
Allspice berries	10	
Crystallized ginger, chopped	2 oz	
Orange juice, strained	2 qt	When ready to serve, add juices and cider. Heat quickly to boiling point.
Lemon juice, strained	1¼ qt	
Apple cider	5 qt	

| Crabapples or small oranges | 6–10 | To serve, pour hot mixture over fruit, studded with cloves, in a punch bowl. |
| Cloves, whole | | If using a glass bowl, temper by filling with warm water to prevent cracking when hot punch is poured in. |

Approximate nutritive values per portion

Calories (kcal)	Protein (grams)	Carbohydrate (grams)	Fat (grams)	Cholesterol (mg)	Sodium (mg)	Iron (mg)	Calcium (mg)
103	0.4 (1%)	26.7 (97%)	0.1 (1%)	0	3	0.3	14

FRESH CRANBERRY WARMER

Yield: 50 portions or 3 gal   *Portion:* 8 oz

Ingredient	Amount	Procedure
Cranberries, fresh	2 lb 4 oz (3 12-oz pkg)	Cook cranberries until soft.
Water	2 qt	Strain, forcing pulp through the sieve. Reserve strained liquid for next step.
Water	2 qt	Combine. Cook until red hots dissolve.
Sugar, granulated	1 lb	Remove cloves and add liquid strained from cooked cranberries.
Red hots (cinammon candies)	1 lb	
Cloves, whole	24	
Orange juice, frozen, undiluted	12 oz	Add undiluted concentrate and water.
Lemonade frozen, undiluted	12 oz	Strain and heat before serving.
Water	1½ gal	
Red food coloring	few drops	

Approximate nutritive values per portion

Calories (kcal)	Protein (grams)	Carbohydrate (grams)	Fat (grams)	Cholesterol (mg)	Sodium (mg)	Iron (mg)	Calcium (mg)
102	0.2 (1%)	26.8 (99%)	0.1 (0%)	0	6	0.1	8

TOMATO JUICE COCKTAIL

Yield: 72 portions or 2¼ gal   *Portion:* 4 oz (½ cup)

Ingredient	Amount	Procedure
Tomato juice	8½ qt (6 46-oz cans)	Mix all ingredients. Chill.
Lemon juice	¾ cup	
Worcestershire sauce	3 Tbsp	
Hot pepper sauce	½ tsp	
Celery salt	3 Tbsp	

Approximate nutritive values per portion

Calories (kcal)	Protein (grams)	Carbohydrate (grams)	Fat (grams)	Cholesterol (mg)	Sodium (mg)	Iron (mg)	Calcium (mg)
21	0.9 (15%)	5.1 (83%)	1 (3%)	0	645	0.7	12

HOT SPICED TOMATO JUICE

Yield: 64 portions or 2 gal   *Portion:* 4 oz (½ cup)

Ingredient	Amount	Procedure
Tomato juice	4¼ qt (3 46-oz cans)	Add onions, celery, and seasonings to tomato juice. Simmer for about 15 minutes. Strain.
Onions, chopped	8 oz	
Celery stalks, cut in 1-inch pieces	6	
Bay leaves	3	
Cloves, whole	12	
Salt	1 tsp	
Dry mustard	1 Tbsp	
Consommé	1 gal	Add consommé to tomato mixture and reheat. Serve hot.

Approximate nutritive values per portion

Calories (kcal)	Protein (grams)	Carbohydrate (grams)	Fat (grams)	Cholesterol (mg)	Sodium (mg)	Iron (mg)	Calcium (mg)
21	1.9 (33%)	3.7 (63%)	0.1 (4%)	0	430	0.5	11

Note   ■   Two 50-oz cans condensed beef or chicken consommé, diluted with 2 qt water, may be used.

SPICED CIDER

Yield: 80 portions or 2½ gal   *Portion:* 4 oz (½ cup)

Ingredient	Amount	Procedure
Cinnamon sticks	10	Tie cinnamon, cloves, and allspice loosely in a clean
Cloves, whole	2½ Tbsp	white cloth to make a spice bag.
Allspice berries	2½ Tbsp	
Apple cider	2½ gal	Add spice bag, sugar, and mace to cider.
Sugar, brown (see Note)	12 oz	Bring slowly to the boiling point. Simmer for about 15 minutes.
Mace	½ tsp	Remove spices. Serve hot or chilled.

Approximate nutritive values per portion

Calories (kcal)	Protein (grams)	Carbohydrate (grams)	Fat (grams)	Cholesterol (mg)	Sodium (mg)	Iron (mg)	Calcium (mg)
74	0.1 (0%)	18.7 (98%)	0.1 (2%)	0	5	0.6	13

Note
- If a very sweet cider is used, omit or reduce brown sugar.

Variations
- **Cider Punch.** Omit spices. Substitute 1 qt reconstituted frozen orange juice and 1 qt pineapple juice for an equal amount of cider. Garnish with thin slices of orange.

- **Hot Mulled Orange Cider.** Combine 2 gal apple cider, 1½ qt reconstituted frozen orange juice, and 1 cup reconstituted frozen lemon juice. Add 2 sticks cinnamon, 1½ tsp ground cinnamon, 1½ tsp whole cloves, and 10 oz sliced fresh orange peels, which have been tied in a clean white cloth. Bring to a boil. Reduce heat and simmer for 15 minutes. Remove spice bag. Serve hot.

- **Spiced Cranberry Juice.** Substitute cranberry juice for apple cider. Reduce brown sugar to 4 oz.

NONALCOHOLIC COCKTAILS

Cocktail	Beverage to use	Garnish	Glassware
Apple Cooler	Spiced Cider (p. 109)	Apple on a skewer	Goblet
Citrus Spritzer	Ginger Ale Fruit Punch (p. 100)	Orange and lemon on skewer with maraschino cherry	Stemmed glass
Chocolate Mint Warmer	French Chocolate (p. 99)	Crème de menthe syrup Mint leaf	Cup or mug
Hot Apple Toddy	Spiced Cider (p. 109)	Cinnamon stick	Mug
Piña Colada	Mock Piña Colada (p. 105)	Pineapple and maraschino cherry on skewer	Stemmed glass
Tomato Juice Cocktail	Tomato Juice Cocktail (p. 108)	Celery stalk	Tumbler

Note   ■   Recipe yields may need to be adjusted, depending on the size of glassware used.

4

Breads

QUICK BREADS

Basic ingredients in all quick breads are flour, liquid, a leavening agent, and flavorings. Fat and eggs are usually included also. The type and quantity of each of these ingredients and their interaction affect the characteristics of the finished product. They may be classified, according to the proportion of flour to liquid, as:

- *pour batter:* pancakes, waffles, popovers, crepes
- *drop batter:* muffins, pan breads, drop biscuits
- *soft dough:* rolled and cut biscuits

Quick breads are leavened by baking powder, baking soda, or steam, which act quickly, requiring them to be baked at once. If a double-acting baking powder is used, quick breads may be mixed, panned, refrigerated, and then baked as needed during the serving period, although they will have slightly decreased volume. A variety of sweet and savory quick breads may be made from basic biscuit and muffin recipes by adding fruits, nuts, and other flavorings.

Quick-bread mixes may be prepared by sifting together the dry ingredients, which generally include nonfat dry milk, and then cutting in the shortening. Such a mix may be made on days when the work load is light and stored for periods up to six weeks without refrigeration, or longer if refrigerated. Many foodservices use some type of commercial mix. The decision to purchase a mix or to prepare from scratch depends on the amount of time and skilled labor available, food inventories, and the cost and quality of the mix.

Pans for quick breads should be greased on the bottoms only. A coating mixture may be prepared and brushed on (p. 195), or the pans may be coated with a vegetable spray. Muffin pans with paper baking cups are often used.

Methods of Mixing

Ingredients for most quick breads are combined by the muffin or biscuit method, although the cake method is used for some loaf breads. Most quick bread ingredients should be mixed only to blend, with as little handling as possible.

Muffin Method

The muffin method is used for muffins, pancakes, waffles, and popovers.

1. Mix the dry ingredients in a mixer bowl. If dry milk is used, add it to the other dry ingredients.
2. Combine beaten eggs, milk, and melted or liquid fat and add to the dry ingredients all at once.
3. Mix at low speed only enough to dampen the dry ingredients.

The mixture should be slightly lumpy and appear undermixed when put into the pan. Excess mixing causes gluten to develop and carbon dioxide to be lost, resulting in the formation of long "tunnels" in the baked product. Effects of overmixing are less evident in rich muffins and loaf breads that contain a high proportion of fat and sugar, or when the batter is made with cake or pastry flour. The batter should be dipped into pans carefully to avoid additional mixing.

Biscuit Method

The biscuit method is used mainly for baking powder biscuits.

1. Combine dry ingredients in a mixer bowl.
2. Cut fat into the flour with flat beater or pastry knife.
3. Add liquid and mix to form a soft dough.
4. Knead dough on low speed for 15–30 seconds (or on a lightly floured board for 15–20 strokes) to develop the gluten. Kneading contributes to making a good volume biscuit with a crumb that peels off in flakes. Overkneading or working in extra flour when kneading by hand may result in a biscuit that is compact and less tender. The volume can be affected also by the temperature of the liquid used and the amount of standing time before baking.

Conventional Method

The conventional method, described on p. 181, may be used for coffee cakes, loaf breads, and rich muffins.

Quality Standards for Quick Breads

Quality standard: Golden brown color, slightly rounded with pebbly top, well-proportioned shape; tender crust, even grain, with no tunnels; moist crumb, breaks easily without crumbling; light and tender; good flavor.

Deviation	Possible Cause
Pale color	Overmixing, oven temperature too low
Rough surface	Undermixing, too much flour
Peaked shape	Wrong size pans, overmixing, incorrect liquid measurement, oven temperature too high
Undersized	Incorrect proportion of ingredients, inaccurate measurements, improper mixing, too hot water (leavening gone), oven temperature too low, too large a proportion of acidic ingredients (blueberries, oranges, etc.) or dough held too long before baking when using acidic ingredients, too much flour used when rolling biscuits
Texture coarse, tunneled	Incorrect proportion of ingredients, inaccurate measurements, overmixing
Dry	Too much flour or too little liquid, oven temperature too low, overbaking
Tough, elastic	Overmixing, too little liquid
Unpleasant flavor	Not enough salt, too much baking powder or soda, poor-quality fat or flavorings

YEAST BREADS

Ingredients

An understanding of the functions of the main ingredients in yeast-raised doughs is essential to the production of good bread and rolls.

Flour

Flour used for baked products must contain enough protein to make an elastic framework of gluten that will stretch and hold the air bubbles of carbon dioxide gas formed as the dough ferments. *Bread flour* is made from hard wheat and contains more protein than other flour. It is used for making breads and pasta when strength and elasticity are required. *All-purpose flour* is milled from a blend of hard and soft wheats and contains enough protein to provide the gluten essential to make good rolls and yeast breads. An all-purpose flour, unless otherwise noted, was used in testing the recipes in this book. *Whole wheat, rye,* and *specialty flours* add variety to breads. These flours should be combined with a high-protein flour because they do not have enough protein to effect proper gluten formation.

Yeast

Yeast is added to dough for its leavening effect, as well as to enhance the flavor and texture of the finished product. In the fermentation process, sugar in the dough is fermented, and carbon dioxide, ethanol, and other by-products such as lactic acid and acetic acid are released. Fermentation is controlled very carefully by monitoring time, temperature and humidity throughout the mixing and rising process. When the yeast cells reach about 140°F, as they do soon after baking begins, the cells are destroyed and fermentation ceases. The continued rising is a result of heat expanding the gases trapped within the gluten structure.

There are three types of yeast used for yeast bread doughs: compressed, active dry, and instant active dry. *Compressed yeast* is generally purchased in one pound cakes. It is highly perishable and may be held for two to three weeks under refrigeration (30°–40°F). The longer the storage time, the more yeast activity lost. Compressed yeast is softened in lukewarm water (95°F) before adding to the other ingredients.

Active dry yeast is manufactured from a different strain of bakers' yeast than compressed and is dehydrated at low temperatures. The yeast does not require refrigeration and remains active in cool dry storage. Some yeast activity is lost during storage and is proportional to the time being stored. In order to obtain maximum activity it is essential that active dry yeast be rehydrated with water that ranges in temperature between 105°–115°F. When substituting active dry yeast for compressed yeast, use 60–70 percent of the compressed yeast weight plus enough water to make up the difference.

The difference between active dry yeast and *instant active dry yeast* is a result of the yeast's genetics and method of processing. The yeast produced from this recent development is slightly less sensitive to temperature extremes at the time of mixing and does not require a separate step for rehydrating prior to use. Three methods are recommended for adding instant active dry yeast to dough. Method one: Mix all ingredients except yeast for one minute, add yeast and continue to mix as usual. Method two: Add yeast to the other dry ingredients and mix thoroughly to combine before the water is added and mixing is continued as usual. Method three: Rehydrate the yeast with five times its weight of water at 95°F for 10 minutes, proceed as usual. Instant active yeast is always vacuum packed. Stored unopened it loses only a very small amount of activity.

Liquid

The amount of liquid necessary to produce an optimum dough varies with the flour and generally is related to the flour's protein content. Flours with high protein values absorb more water than low-protein flour.

The liquid used for yeast breads generally is milk or water, although potato water and fruit juice may be used. Milk improves the browning and nutritive value of the bread and tends to delay staling. If fresh milk is used, it is scalded to stop enzyme action that may produce undesirable characteristics, then cooled to the appropriate temperature. Nonfat dry milk may be mixed with the dry ingredients or reconstituted and used in liquid form. The nutritive value of bread may be increased by the addition of extra quantities of dry milk.

The temperature of the liquid used has an effect on the end-point dough temperature after mixing. When using high-speed mixers or making large quantities, it is necessary to calculate the water temperature based on factors such as friction heat generated by the equipment, flour temperature, and room temperature. For quantities used in this book, however, the following guidelines for water temperature are recommended: luke-warm (95°F) for compressed yeast, warm (105°–110°F) for active dry yeast, and very warm (120°F) for instant active dry yeast that is mixed with flour and other ingredients.

Other Ingredients

Although used in small quantities, other ingredients influence the quality of the finished product. Salt is added for flavor and also helps to control the rate of fermentation. Sugar, a ready source of food for the yeast, accelerates the action of the yeast. Although the addition of a small amount of sugar makes the dough rise faster, too much sugar inhibits yeast activity. Granulated sugar generally is used for bread making, but honey, corn syrup, brown sugar, and molasses are also used, especially in dark whole-grain bread, sweet rolls, or coffee cake. Fat is added to improve flavor, tenderness, browning, and keeping quality. Fat in large amounts, or if added directly to the yeast, will slow its action. Eggs affect flavor, richness, tenderness, and color.

Bread Bases

Commercially available bread bases may include ingredients for dough conditioning, fla-voring, and coloring, as well as flour, salt, eggs, and seeds or nuts. These bases generally require mixing with flour, yeast, and liquid. Mixing and proofing time and techniques may differ from standard procedures, so the manufacturer's instructions should be fol-lowed.

Mixing the Dough

Mixing and kneading of dough has three important functions: to uniformly distribute the ingredients into a homogeneous mass, develop the gluten structure that will entrap the carbon dioxide gas, and develop the dough into a continuous gluten network that will have maximum gas-holding capacity. A repeated stretching-and-folding motion, per-formed always in the same direction, is the most effective way to produce quality bread with high volume; a soft, silky, and uniform grain and texture; and good keeping quality. Dividing, rounding, sheeting, and shaping all have a beneficial effect on bread quality because they too contribute to the mixing functions.

The mixing speed and length of time will vary with the size of mixer and amount of dough. Overmixing and allowing the dough temperature to get too high will produce a product with a dense texture and low volume. Generally dough is mixed only until it leaves the sides and bottom of the bowl. When mixed adequately, a small piece of dough may be stretched, without tearing, to resemble a membrane (sometimes referred to as the membrane test).

Moisture content of the flour may vary, making it necessary to adjust slightly the amount of flour called for in the recipe. Reserving some of the flour specified and adding it as needed toward the end of the mixing process is suggested. Enough flour should be added to produce a soft—but not sticky—dough. Dough for rolls is usually softer than for loaf bread.

Fermentation of Dough

The flavor and texture of the bread depend on the fermentation process. Fermentation begins when the dough is mixed and continues until the yeast is killed by the heat of the oven (approximately 140°F). After mixing is completed, the dough should be set in a warm place (80°–85°F), with a relative humidity near 75 percent. The length of the fermentation period depends on the type of product, amount of yeast, strength of the flour, amount of sugar and temperature of the dough and proofing area. Usually 1 to 1½ hours are required for the dough to double in bulk for the first time.

After the dough has doubled, air must be forced out and the dough returned to its original bulk. This may be done with a mixer using a dough arm or by hand for small amounts of dough. This process continues to decrease the size of the air bubbles and help form a good grain and texture in the finished product. Dough at this stage may be retarded by chilling and held in a refrigerator for use at a later time. It is important to cover the dough tightly so that moisture is not lost and a dry, tough skin does not develop on the surface.

Shaping and Baking

After the dough has fermented until double and the air bubbles are forced out, it is time to be formed into the desired shape. A rest period of 10–15 minutes allows the gluten structure to relax and makes shaping easier (see p. 146 for recipes and directions for shaping). When panning rolls or bread, the distance apart will affect the shape, size, and amount of crust in the final product. Individual preference should be considered.

Panned bread or rolls should rise (proof) at 90°–100°F and 80–85 percent humidity until double in bulk. A general test for assessing how long to proof is to press the dough lightly with a finger. When proofed for the correct length of time, a slight indentation remains. When not proofed long enough, the dough will spring back, leaving no indentation. Overproofed dough will collapse when pressed with a finger. Too short a proofing period will produce a dense, undersized product with a tough crust; too long a proofing period will cause an open, crumbly, texture with low volume and unpleasant flavor.

Crust texture may be determined partly by the treatment applied prior to baking and during the early stages in the oven. For a crisp crust, spray loaves or rolls with cold water before baking and again after about 10 minutes in the oven. An egg-white glaze (one slightly beaten egg white with one teaspoon of water) also may be used to produce a crisp crust. For a shiny, golden crust, brush loaves or rolls with egg or egg-yolk glaze (one slightly beaten egg or egg yolk with one tablespoon of water or milk) prior to baking. For a soft or tender crust, brush with melted butter or margarine immediately after baking; and to give baked sweet rolls a shiny, glossy appearance brush with simple syrup, then glaze as usual.

Most bread is baked at 375°–400°F. Rich and sweet doughs may overbrown quickly and may need to be baked at a slightly lower temperature, 350°F. Generally, small rolls, spaced apart, are baked at a higher temperature than larger loaves so that they become browned in the short time it takes to bake them. For best volume and texture, preheat the oven before baking yeast breads. The final expansion of the dough, called "oven spring," occurs in the first 10–15 minutes of baking in a hot oven. The bread is usually done when tapping the crust produces a hollow sound and the sides, bottom, and top are golden brown. Remove bread from the pans immediately and place on a wire rack to prevent steaming and softening of the crust. Cool the loaves uncovered.

Freezing Yeast Doughs and Breads

Yeast doughs can be frozen up to six weeks before or after shaping. Sugar and yeast are usually increased slightly. It is important that the dough be frozen quickly and covered tightly. Some quality loss can be expected when freezing dough using techniques available in most bakeries. Commercial processors are able to achieve better results.

To freeze baked bread and rolls, allow to cool to room temperature, then wrap and freeze. Frozen baked products should be allowed to return to room temperature before being warmed or used.

Quality Standards for Yeast Breads

Quality standard: Symmetrical, uniform shape, rounded top, good volume; smooth, tender crust; golden brown color; fine, even grain, free from large air bubbles, thin cell walls; moist, silky, elastic crumb; nutlike flavor.

Deviation	*Possible Cause*
Excessive volume	Too much yeast, too little salt, oven temperature too low, protein content of flour too high, overproofing
Poor volume	Protein content of flour too low, not enough yeast, over- or underdeveloped gluten, over- or underproofing, too much salt
Pale color	Not enough sugar, overfermented dough, oven temperature too low, crust formed before baking
Dark color	Excessive sugar or milk, oven temperature too high, baking time too long
Cracked	Overmixing, improper shaping, formation of dried crust before baking, cooling too fast
Coarse texture	Not enough flour, slack dough, underkneading, proofing period too long or at too high a temperature, oven temperature too low, temperature of dough out of mixer too high
Heavy texture	Yeast partially killed, underkneading, poor distribution of ingredients, too-cool proofing temperature, too-short proofing period, excessive dough in pan
Crumbly, dry	Too-stiff dough, oven temperature too low, underkneading
Poor flavor	Flat: too little salt
	Yeasty: too-long proofing period, proofing temperature too warm
	Sour: too-long proofing period, poor quality ingredients

QUICK BREAD RECIPES

BAKING POWDER BISCUITS ■

Yield: 100 2½-inch biscuits or 130 2-inch biscuits
Oven: 425°F   *Bake:* 15 minutes

Ingredient	Amount	Procedure
Flour, all-purpose Baking powder Salt	5 lb 5 oz 2 Tbsp	Combine flour, baking powder, and salt in mixer bowl. Mix on low speed until blended, approximately 10 seconds, using flat beater.
Shortening, hydrogenated	1 lb 4 oz	Add shortening to flour mixture. Mix on low speed for one minute. Stop and scrape sides and bottom of bowl. Mix one minute longer. The mixture will be crumbly.
Milk	1¾ qt	Add milk. Mix on low speed to form a soft dough, about 30 seconds. Do not overmix. Dough should be as soft as can be handled.

1. Place one half of dough on lightly floured board or table. Knead lightly 15–20 times.
2. Roll to ¾-inch thickness. Biscuits will approximately double in height during baking. Cut with a 2½-inch (or 2-inch) cutter; or cut into 2-inch squares with a knife. When using round hand cutters, cut straight down and do not twist to produce the best shape. Space the cuts close together to minimize scraps. Use of a roller cutter or cutting the dough into squares eliminates or reduces scraps. The scraps can be rerolled, but the biscuits may not be as tender.
3. Place on ungreased baking sheets ½ inch apart for crusty biscuits, just touching for softer biscuits. Repeat, using remaining dough.
4. Bake at 425°F for 15 minutes, or until golden brown.
5. Biscuits may be held 2–3 hours in the refrigerator until time to bake.

Approximate nutritive values per 2½-inch biscuit							
Calories (kcal)	Protein (grams)	Carbohydrate (grams)	Fat (grams)	Cholesterol (mg)	Sodium (mg)	Iron (mg)	Calcium (mg)
145	2.9 (8%)	18.5 (51%)	6.5 (40%)	2	278	1	114

Note   ■ 7 oz nonfat dry milk and 1¾ qt water may be substituted for fluid milk. Combine dry milk with other dry ingredients. Increase shortening to 1 lb 6 oz.

Variations   ■ **Buttermilk Biscuits.** Substitute cultured buttermilk (or 7 oz dry buttermilk and 1¾ qt water) for milk. Add 1 Tbsp baking soda to dry ingredients.

■ **Butterscotch Biscuits.** Divide dough into 8 parts. Roll each part into a rectangle ¼ inch thick. Spread with melted margarine or butter and brown sugar. Roll the dough as for jelly roll. Cut off slices ¾ inch thick. Bake at 375°F for 15 minutes.

- **Cheese Biscuits.**   Reduce shortening to 1 lb and add 1 lb grated cheddar cheese.
- **Cinnamon Raisin Biscuits.**   Substitute 2 lb 8 oz margarine for shortening. Combine 8 oz sugar and 2½ Tbsp cinnamon with dry ingredients. Add 1 lb 12 oz raisins to mixture after margarine has been mixed in. When baked, ice with Powdered Sugar Glaze (p. 228).
- **Drop Biscuits.**   Increase milk to 2 qt. Drop by spoon or No. 30 dipper onto greased baking sheets.
- **Orange Biscuits.**   Proceed as for Butterscotch Biscuits. Spread with orange marmalade.
- **Raisin Biscuits.**   Reduce shortening to 14 oz and use ½ cup less milk; add 4 whole eggs, beaten, 3 Tbsp grated orange rind, 8 oz sugar, and 8 oz chopped raisins.
- **Scotch Scones.**   Add 10 oz sugar and 7 oz currants to dry ingredients. Add 5 eggs, beaten, mixed with the milk. Cut dough in squares and then cut diagonally to form triangles. Brush lightly with milk before baking.
- **Shortcake.**   Increase shortening to 1 lb 12 oz. Add 8 oz sugar.
- **Whole-Wheat Biscuits.**   Substitute 2 lb whole-wheat flour for 2 lb all-purpose flour.

BASIC MUFFINS (MUFFIN METHOD)

Yield: 50 muffins   *Portion:* 2¼ oz
Oven: 400°F   *Bake:* 20–25 minutes

Ingredient	Amount	Procedure
Flour, all-purpose	2 lb 8 oz	Combine dry ingredients in mixer bowl.
Baking powder	2 oz	Blend on low speed for 10 seconds, using flat beater.
Salt	1 Tbsp	
Sugar, granulated	6 oz	
Eggs, beaten	4 (7 oz)	Combine eggs, milk, and melted shortening.
Milk	1½ qt	Add to dry ingredients. Mix on low speed only long enough to blend, about 15 seconds.
Oil or melted short- ening	8 oz (1 cup)	Batter will still be lumpy.
		Portion batter with No. 16 dipper into greased muffin pans, about ⅔ full. Batter should be dipped all at once with as little handling as possible. The dipped muffin batter may be refrigerated for up to 24 hours and baked as needed. See Notes.
		Bake at 400°F for 20–25 minutes, or until golden brown.
		Remove muffins from pans as soon as baked.

Approximate nutritive values per portion

Calories (kcal)	Protein (grams)	Carbohydrate (grams)	Fat (grams)	Cholesterol (mg)	Sodium (mg)	Iron (mg)	Calcium (mg)
161	3.8 (10%)	22.4 (56%)	6.1 (34%)	21	261	1	113

Notes
- 6 oz nonfat dry milk and 1½ qt water may be substituted for fluid milk. Combine dry milk with other dry ingredients. Increase fat to 9 oz.
- No. 24 dipper yields 6½ dozen muffins.
- For best results, bake muffins immediately. If refrigerated, let come to room temperature before baking or they will have peaks formed or exploding tops.
- If adding acidic fruits, bake immediately. Acidic fruits will affect the leavening action.

Variations
- **Apple Muffins.** Add 1 lb chopped, peeled apples. Fold into batter.
- **Apricot Muffins.** Add 1 lb cooked apricots, drained and chopped. Fold into batter.
- **Blueberry Muffins.** Carefully fold 1 lb well-drained blueberries into the batter. Increase sugar to 10 oz. Bake immediately.
- **Cherry Muffins.** Add 1 lb well-drained, cooked cherries. Fold into batter.

- **Cornmeal Muffins.**   Substitute 1 lb white cornmeal for 1 lb flour.
- **Cranberry Muffins.**   Sprinkle 4 oz granulated sugar over 1 lb chopped raw cranberries. Fold into batter. Bake immediately.
- **Currant Muffins.**   Add 8 oz chopped currants. Fold into batter.
- **Date Muffins.**   Add 1 lb chopped dates. Fold into batter.
- **Jelly Muffins.**   Drop ¼–½ tsp jelly on top of each muffin just before placing in the oven.
- **Nut Muffins.**   Add 10 oz chopped nuts. Fold into batter.
- **Raisin Nut Muffins.**   Add 6 oz chopped nuts and 6 oz chopped raisins. Fold into batter.
- **Spiced Muffins.**   Add 1½ tsp cinnamon, 1 tsp ginger, and ½ tsp allspice to dry ingredients.
- **Whole-Wheat Muffins.**   Substitute 12 oz whole-wheat flour for 12 oz white flour. Add ¼ cup molasses with liquid ingredients.

BASIC MUFFINS (CAKE METHOD)

Yield: 50 3-oz muffins or 70 2¼-oz muffins
Oven: 350°F　*Bake:* 18–20 minutes

Ingredient	Amount	Procedure
Sugar, granulated Shortening	1 lb 3 oz 14 oz	Cream sugar and shortening until fluffy, about 10 minutes, using flat beater.
Eggs	5 (9 oz)	Add eggs slowly to creamed mixture. Mix until blended. Scrape sides of bowl.
Flour, all-purpose Baking powder Salt	3 lb 3 oz 3 oz 1 Tbsp	Combine dry ingredients.
Milk Vanilla	1½ qt 1 Tbsp	Add milk and vanilla alternately with dry ingredients to creamed mixture. Do not overmix.
		Grease bottoms of muffin pans or line with paper baking cups. Portion batter into pans with No. 12 dipper for 3-oz muffins or No. 16 dipper for 2¼-oz muffins. Bake at 350°F for 18–20 minutes.

Approximate nutritive values per 3-oz muffin							
Calories (kcal)	Protein (grams)	Carbohydrate (grams)	Fat (grams)	Cholesterol (mg)	Sodium (mg)	Iron (mg)	Calcium (mg)
244	4.6 (7%)	34.8 (57%)	9.7 (36%)	26	319	1.4	150

Note
- 6 oz nonfat dry milk and 1½ qt water may be substituted for fluid milk. Combine dry milk with flour.

Variations
- **Chocolate Chip Muffins.**　Add 1 lb chocolate chips to batter.
- **Coconut Muffins.**　Add 1 lb flaked coconut to batter.
- **Honey Streusel Topping for Muffins.**　Combine 8 oz brown sugar, 8 oz margarine or butter, 2 Tbsp honey, and ¼ tsp salt. Stir in 1 lb all-purpose flour. Sprinkle on top of muffins before baking.
- For other variations, see Basic Muffins (Muffin method), p. 120.

BANANA WHOLE-WHEAT MUFFINS

Yield: 50 muffins   *Portion:* 2¼ oz
Oven: 350°F   *Bake:* 35–40 minutes

Ingredient	Amount	Procedure
Sugar, granulated	1 lb 9 oz	Cream sugar and shortening on medium speed until
Shortening	13 oz	fluffy, using flat beater.
Eggs	7 (12 oz)	Add eggs and vanilla to creamed mixture and mix
Vanilla	1 Tbsp	thoroughly.
		Scrape sides of bowl.
Bananas, mashed	2 lb 11 oz	Add bananas. Mix on medium speed for 10 minutes.
Flour, whole-wheat	10 oz	Combine dry ingredients.
Flour, all-purpose	1 lb 8 oz	Add to banana mixture.
Baking soda	3½ tsp	Mix on low speed only until blended. Scrape sides of
Salt	1½ tsp	bowl as needed.
		Portion batter into greased muffin pans with No. 16 dipper.
		Bake at 350°F for 35–40 minutes.

Approximate nutritive values per portion

Calories (kcal)	Protein (grams)	Carbohydrate (grams)	Fat (grams)	Cholesterol (mg)	Sodium (mg)	Iron (mg)	Calcium (mg)
222	3.01 (5%)	34.8 (61%)	8.4 (33%)	29	131	1	8

Variation   ■   **Banana Muffins.**   Delete whole-wheat flour. Increase all-purpose flour to 2 lb 2 oz.

OATMEAL MUFFINS

Yield: 50 muffins   *Portion:* 2¼ oz
Oven: 400°F   *Bake:* 15–20 minutes

Ingredient	Amount	Procedure
Rolled oats	14 oz	Combine rolled oats and buttermilk in mixer bowl. Let
Buttermilk	1¼ qt	stand one hour.
Eggs, beaten	5 (9 oz)	Combine eggs, sugar, and shortening.
Sugar, brown	1 lb 4 oz	Add to rolled-oat mixture. Mix 30 seconds.
Oil or melted short-	1 lb	Scrape sides of bowl.
ening		
Flour, all-purpose	1 lb 4 oz	Combine dry ingredients.
Baking powder	5 tsp	Add to rolled-oat mixture. Mix on low speed only until
Salt	2½ tsp	dry ingredients are moistened, about 15 seconds.
Baking soda	2½ tsp	
		Portion batter with No. 16 dipper into greased muffin pans (⅔ full).
		Bake at 400°F for 15–20 minutes.
		Remove from pans as soon as baked.

Approximate nutritive values per portion

Calories (kcal)	Protein (grams)	Carbohydrate (grams)	Fat (grams)	Cholesterol (mg)	Sodium (mg)	Iron (mg)	Calcium (mg)
212	3.9 (7%)	26.2 (49%)	10.4 (44%)	23	213	1	65

Notes

- 4 oz dry buttermilk and 1¼ qt water may be substituted for liquid buttermilk.
- Flavor may be varied by the addition of 1 tsp cinnamon to the dry ingredients.
- No. 24 dipper yields 7 dozen muffins.

Variation

- **Oatmeal Fruit Muffins.**   Add 1 lb raisins, chopped dates, or other fruit. Fold into batter.

POPPY SEED–YOGURT MUFFINS

Yield: 50 muffins   *Portion:* 2¼ oz
Oven: 400°F   *Bake:* 18–22 minutes

Ingredient	Amount	Procedure
Flour, all-purpose	2 lb 8 oz	Blend. Set aside for later step.
Poppy seeds	¼ cup	
Salt	2 tsp	
Baking soda	3½ tsp	
Sugar, granulated	1 lb 12 oz	Cream sugar and margarine on medium speed until light and fluffy, using flat beater.
Margarine	12 oz	
Eggs	1 lb (9)	Combine and add gradually to creamed mixture. Mix until smooth.
Vanilla	4 tsp	
Lemon juice	1½ tsp	
Yogurt, plain	2 lb 3 oz	Add yogurt alternately with dry ingredients from first step, blending after each addition. Portion into prepared muffin pans, using No. 16 dipper. Bake at 400°F for 18–22 minutes. Cool briefly before removing from pans.

Approximate nutritive values per portion

Calories (kcal)	Protein (grams)	Carbohydrate (grams)	Fat (grams)	Cholesterol (mg)	Sodium (mg)	Iron (mg)	Calcium (mg)
222	4.7 (8%)	35 (63%)	7.2 (29%)	40	233	1	57

Variation   ■ **Glazed Poppy Seed–Yogurt Muffins.**   Combine ¾ cup lemon juice and 2 Tbsp granulated sugar. Brush on baked muffins.

FRENCH BREAKFAST PUFFS

Yield: 50 puffs   *Portion:* 2¼ oz
Oven: 350°F   *Bake:* 20–25 minutes

Ingredient	Amount	Procedure
Margarine	1 lb 2 oz	Cream margarine and sugar on medium speed until light and fluffy, using flat beater.
Sugar, granulated	1 lb 10 oz	
Eggs	6 (10 oz)	Add eggs to creamed mixture. Blend on low speed, then beat on medium speed for 3–5 minutes.
Flour, all-purpose	2 lb 8 oz	Combine dry ingredients.
Baking powder	2½ Tbsp	
Salt	1 Tbsp	
Nutmeg, ground	1½ tsp	
Nonfat dry milk	3 oz	
Water	3⅓ cups	Add dry ingredients and water alternately, on low speed, to creamed mixture.
		Portion batter into greased muffin pans with No. 16 dipper. Bake at 350°F for 20–25 minutes.
Sugar, granulated	1 lb 10 oz	Mix sugar and cinnamon.
Cinnamon, ground	2 Tbsp	
Margarine, melted	1 lb 4 oz	When muffins are baked, remove from pans. Roll in melted margarine, then in sugar-cinammon mixture.

Approximate nutritive values per portion							
Calories (kcal)	Protein (grams)	Carbohydrate (grams)	Fat (grams)	Cholesterol (mg)	Sodium (mg)	Iron (mg)	Calcium (mg)
364	3.8 (4%)	48.3 (52%)	18.2 (44%)	24	392	1	66

Notes
- 3½ cups fluid milk may be used in place of the nonfat dry milk and water.
- For small, tea-sized muffins, dip batter with No. 40 dipper into small (1½-inch) muffin pans.

Variations
- **Apple Nut Muffins.** Add 1 lb chopped apples and 8 oz chopped nuts.
- **Plain Cake Muffins.** Delete nutmeg. Do not roll in sugar and cinnamon.

BISHOP'S BREAD

Yield: 64 portions or 2 pans 12 × 18 × 2-inch   *Portion:* 3 × 2¼-inch
Oven: 365°F   *Bake:* 35–45 minutes

Ingredient	Amount	Procedure
Shortening Sugar, brown	1 lb 3 lb 2 oz	Cream shortening and sugar on medium speed for 5 minutes, using flat beater.
Flour, all-purpose Salt Cinnamon, ground	2 lb 14 oz 2 tsp 1 Tbsp	Combine flour, salt, and cinnamon. Add to creamed mixture and mix until well blended. Remove 1 lb 12 oz of the mixture to sprinkle on top later.
Flour, all-purpose Baking powder Baking soda	1 lb 2 oz 5 tsp 1½ tsp	Combine flour, baking powder, and soda.
Eggs, beaten Buttermilk	5 (9 oz) 1½ qt	Combine eggs and buttermilk. Add alternately with dry ingredients to creamed mixture. Scrape sides of bowl. Mix on low speed about 30 seconds. (Batter will not be smooth.)
		Scale batter into 2 greased 12 × 18 × 2-inch baking pans, 5 lb per pan. Sprinkle 14 oz of the reserved topping over batter in each pan. Bake at 365°F for 35–45 minutes. Cut 4 × 8.

Approximate nutritive values per portion

Calories (kcal)	Protein (grams)	Carbohydrate (grams)	Fat (grams)	Cholesterol (mg)	Sodium (mg)	Iron (mg)	Calcium (mg)
264	4.2 (6%)	44.3 (67%)	7.9 (27%)	18	1.45	2	68

Notes

- May be baked in one 18 × 26 × 2-inch pan. Cut 6 × 10 for 60 portions 3 × 2½-inch.

- 4 oz dry buttermilk and 1 qt water may be substituted for fluid buttermilk.

BLUEBERRY COFFEE CAKE ◼

Yield: 64 portions or 2 pans 12 × 18 × 2-inch   *Portion:* 3 × 2¼-inch
Oven: 350°F   *Bake:* 45 minutes

Ingredient	Amount	Procedure
Sugar, brown Sugar, granulated Flour, all-purpose Cinnamon, ground Margarine, soft	12 oz 4 oz 4 oz 2 tsp 4 oz	Combine sugars, flour, cinnamon, and margarine. Mix on low speed to a coarse crumb consistency, about 5 minutes, using flat beater. Set aside for final step.
Shortening Sugar, granulated	14 oz 2 lb 10 oz	Cream shortening and sugar on medium speed for about 10 minutes.
Eggs	7 (12 oz)	Add eggs to creamed mixture and continue mixing, 3–5 minutes.
Flour, all-purpose Baking powder Salt	3 lb 6 oz 2 oz 1 Tbsp	Combine flour, baking powder, and salt.
Milk	3½ cups	Add dry ingredients and milk alternately to creamed mixture. Mix on low speed for 3 minutes. Scrape sides of bowl. Mix on medium speed 10 seconds.
Blueberries, frozen or canned (well-drained and rinsed)	2 lb	Carefully fold blueberries into batter. (Berries may be sprinkled on top of batter.)
		Scale into 2 greased 12 × 18 × 2-inch baking pans, 4 lb 12 oz per pan. Crumble topping mixture evenly over top of batter, 10 oz per pan. Bake at 350°F for 45 minutes. Cut 4 × 8.

Approximate nutritive values per portion							
Calories (kcal)	Protein (grams)	Carbohydrate (grams)	Fat (grams)	Cholesterol (mg)	Sodium (mg)	Iron (mg)	Calcium (mg)
219	3.9 (7%)	31.1 (57%)	8.9 (36%)	24	2.21	2	85

Notes   ◼   May be baked in one 18 × 26 × 2-inch pan. Cut 6 × 10 for 60 portions 3 × 2½-inch.

- 3 oz nonfat dry milk and 3½ cups water may be substituted for fluid milk. Add dry milk to other dry ingredients. Increase shortening to 15 oz.
- After cake is baked, thin Powdered Sugar Glaze (p. 228) may be drizzled in a fine stream over the top to form an irregular design.
- Recipe can be used for blueberry muffins. Sprinkle blueberries on top.

DUTCH APPLE COFFEE CAKE

Yield: 64 portions or 2 pans 12 × 20 × 2-inch   *Portion:* 3 × 2½-inch
Oven: 365°F   *Bake:* 50–60 minutes

Ingredient	Amount	Procedure
Sugar, granulated Shortening Eggs	2 lb 8 oz 12 oz 8 (14 oz)	Cream sugar, shortening, and eggs on medium speed for 10 minutes, using flat beater.
Flour, all-purpose Baking powder Salt	2 lb 8 oz 2 oz 2 tsp	Combine dry ingredients and mix until well blended.
Milk	1 qt	Add milk and dry ingredients alternately to creamed mixture. Mix on low speed for 3 minutes. Scrape sides of bowl. Mix on medium speed for 10 seconds.
Apples, frozen or canned Margarine, melted Sugar, granulated Cinnamon, ground	2 lb 8 oz 2 oz 1 lb 2 oz 2 Tbsp	Drain apples and chop. Combine with margarine, sugar, and cinnamon.
		Scale batter into 2 greased 12 × 20 × 2-inch baking pans, 4 lb 6 oz per pan. Spread 1 lb 14 oz apple mixture over batter in each pan. Bake at 365°F for 50–60 minutes. Cut 4 × 8.

Approximate nutritive values per portion							
Calories (kcal)	Protein (grams)	Carbohydrate (grams)	Fat (grams)	Cholesterol (mg)	Sodium (mg)	Iron (mg)	Calcium (mg)
243	3.2 (5%)	42.6 (68%)	7.4 (27%)	28	180	1	84

Notes

- Cake batter may be mixed and panned the day before using. Refrigerate overnight, then add topping and bake.
- 4 oz nonfat dry milk and 1 qt water may be substituted for fluid milk.

COFFEE CAKE

Yield: 64 portions or 2 pans 12 × 18 × 2-inch   *Portion:* 3 × 2¼-inch
Oven: 350°F   *Bake:* 25 minutes

Ingredient	Amount	Procedure
Margarine	10 oz	Place margarine, sugar, flour, cinnamon, and salt in mixer bowl.
Sugar, granulated	1 lb 4 oz	
Flour, all-purpose	3 oz	Mix on low speed until crumbly, using flat beater. Set aside, to be used later as topping.
Cinnamon, ground	1 oz	
Salt	1½ tsp	
Flour, all-purpose	3 lb 6 oz	Combine dry ingredients in mixer bowl.
Baking powder	2 oz	
Sugar, granulated	2 lb	
Salt	1⅔ Tbsp	
Eggs, beaten	6 (10 oz)	Combine eggs and milk.
Milk	1¼ qt	Add to dry ingredients.
		Mix on low speed until dry ingredients are just moistened.
Shortening, melted and cooled	1 lb 10 oz	Add shortening and mix on low speed for one minute.
		Scale dough into 2 greased 12 × 18 × 2-inch baking pans, 4 lb 2 oz per pan.
		Sprinkle with reserved topping mixture, 1 lb per pan.
		Bake at 350°F for 25 minutes or until done.
		Cut 4 × 8.

Approximate nutritive values per portion

Calories (kcal)	Protein (grams)	Carbohydrate (grams)	Fat (grams)	Cholesterol (mg)	Sodium (mg)	Iron (mg)	Calcium (mg)
332	3.8 (5%)	43.9 (62%)	16.4 (44%)	21	363	1	93

Notes

- 5 oz nonfat dry milk and 1¼ qt water may be substituted for the fluid milk. Combine dry milk with other dry ingredients. Increase shortening to 1 lb 12 oz.

- May be baked in one 18 × 26 × 2-inch pan. Cut 6 × 10 for 60 portions 3 × 2½ inches.

- If used for breakfast, may be mixed and panned the day before. Refrigerate until morning, then bake. Allow 5–10 minutes extra time because batter will be cold.

WALNUT COFFEE CAKE

Yield: 4 cakes   *Portion:* 16 slices per cake
Oven: 350°F   *Bake:* 45–50 minutes

Ingredient	Amount	Procedure
Sugar, granulated	3 lb	Cream sugar and margarine on medium speed until light and fluffy, using flat beater.
Margarine	1 lb	
Eggs	16 (1 lb 12 oz)	Add eggs slowly to creamed mixture, beating well after each addition.
Vanilla	1 Tbsp	Add vanilla.
Flour, all-purpose	3 lb	Mix flour, baking powder, and salt together.
Baking powder	4 Tbsp	
Salt	2 tsp	
Milk	1 qt	Add milk alternately with dry ingredients to creamed mixture. Combine thoroughly after each addition.
Sugar, brown	2 lb	Combine brown sugar, margarine, flour, cinnamon, and walnuts for crumb mixture.
Margarine	4 oz	
Flour, all-purpose	2 oz	
Cinnamon, ground	1 Tbsp	
Walnuts, chopped	1 lb	
		Scale 1 lb 4 oz batter into each of 4 greased 10-inch tube pans.
		Sprinkle 6 oz crumb mixture over batter.
		Spread with 1 lb 4 oz batter.
		Top with 6 oz crumb mixture.
		Bake at 350°F for 45–50 minutes.
		Cool slightly. Remove from pans.
		Ice with Powdered Sugar Glaze (p. 228) if desired.
		Slice 16 servings per cake.

Approximate nutritive values per portion

Calories (kcal)	Protein (grams)	Carbohydrate (grams)	Fat (grams)	Cholesterol (mg)	Sodium (mg)	Iron (mg)	Calcium (mg)
349	6.1 (7%)	53.9 (60%)	13.1 (33%)	55	233	2	82

Note   ■   4 oz nonfat dry milk and 1 qt water may be substituted for the fluid milk.

CORN BREAD

Yield: 64 portions or 2 pans 12 × 18 × 2-inch   *Portion:* 3 × 2¼-inch
Oven: 350°F   *Bake:* 35 minutes

Ingredient	Amount	Procedure
Cornmeal, yellow	2 lb 3 oz	Combine dry ingredients in mixer bowl.
Flour, all-purpose	2 lb 5 oz	Blend on low speed, using flat beater.
Baking powder	3½ oz	
Salt	2½ Tbsp	
Sugar, granulated	10 oz	
Eggs, beaten	9 (1 lb)	Combine eggs, milk, and shortening.
Milk	1¾ qt	Add to dry ingredients. Mix on low speed only until
Shortening, melted and cooled	10 oz	dry ingredients are moistened.
		Scale batter into 2 greased 12 × 18 × 2-inch baking pans, 5 lb per pan. Bake at 350°F for 35 minutes. Cut 4 × 8.

Approximate nutritive values per portion

Calories (kcal)	Protein (grams)	Carbohydrate (grams)	Fat (grams)	Cholesterol (mg)	Sodium (mg)	Iron (mg)	Calcium (mg)
200	4.7 (9%)	30.6 (61%)	6.7 (30%)	34	433	1.4	138

Notes
- 7 oz nonfat dry milk and 1¾ qt water may be substituted for fluid milk. Mix dry milk with other dry ingredients. Increase shortening to 11 oz.
- May be baked in one 18 × 26 × 2-inch pan. Cut 6 × 10 for 60 portions 3 × 3½ inches.
- May be baked in corn stick or muffin pans. Reduce baking time to 15–20 minutes.
- White cornmeal may be used.

SPOON BREAD

Yield: 50 portions or 2 pans 12 × 20 × 2-inch   *Portion:* 4 oz
Oven: 350°F   *Bake:* 45–60 minutes

Ingredient	Amount	Procedure
Milk	5¾ qt	Scald milk by heating to point just below boiling.
Cornmeal, yellow	1 lb 12 oz	Add cornmeal and salt to milk, stirring briskly with a
Salt	1 oz (1½ Tbsp)	wire whip. Cook 10 minutes, or until thick.

Eggs, beaten	25 (2 lb 12 oz)	Add eggs slowly to cornmeal mixture, while stirring.
Margarine, melted Baking powder	6 oz 2 oz	Add margarine and baking powder to cornmeal mixture. Stir to blend.
		Pour batter into 2 greased 12 × 20 × 2-inch baking pans, 8 lb per pan. Place in pans of hot water. Bake at 350°F for 45–60 minutes or until set. Serve at once.

Approximate nutritive values per portion

Calories (kcal)	Protein (grams)	Carbohydrate (grams)	Fat (grams)	Cholesterol (mg)	Sodium (mg)	Iron (mg)	Calcium (mg)
190	8.1 (17%)	18 (38%)	9.6 (45%)	121	430	1	221

Note   ■ Serve with crisp bacon, Creamed Chicken (p. 462), or Creamed Ham (p. 394).

BOSTON BROWN BREAD

Yield: 64 portions or 8 round loaves, 3¼ × 4½ inches   *Portion:* ½-inch slice
Steam Pressure: 5 lb   *Steam:* 1¼–1½ hours

Ingredient	Amount	Procedure
Cornmeal, yellow Flour, whole wheat Flour, all-purpose Salt Baking soda	1 lb 12 oz 12 oz 1 oz (1½ Tbsp) 1½ Tbsp	Combine dry ingredients in mixer bowl. Blend on low speed for 10 seconds, using flat beater.
Buttermilk Molasses	1½ qt 2¼ cups	Blend buttermilk and molasses. Add all at once to dry ingredients. Mix on low speed only until ingredients are blended.
		Fill 8 greased 3¼ × 4½-inch cans ¾ full. Cover tightly with aluminum foil. Steam for 1¼–1½ hours. Cut 8 slices per loaf.

Approximate nutritive values per portion

Calories (kcal)	Protein (grams)	Carbohydrate (grams)	Fat (grams)	Cholesterol (mg)	Sodium (mg)	Iron (mg)	Calcium (mg)
99	2.4 (10%)	20.9 (85%)	0.6 (5%)	0.8	245	2.5	107

Notes   ■ 12 oz raisins may be added.

■ May be baked as loaves. Add 3 Tbsp melted fat. Scale into three 5 × 9-inch loaf pans, 2 lb 8 oz per pan. Bake at 375°F for one hour.

NUT BREAD

Yield: 80 portions or 5 loaves 5 × 9-inch   *Portion:* ½-inch slice
Oven: 350°F   *Bake:* 50 minutes

Ingredient	Amount	Procedure
Flour, all-purpose	3 lb	Combine dry ingredients and nuts in mixer bowl.
Baking powder	1 oz	Mix on low speed until blended, using flat beater.
Salt	1 Tbsp	
Sugar, granulated	1 lb 8 oz	
Pecans or walnuts, chopped	1 lb	
Eggs, beaten	6 (10 oz)	Combine eggs, milk, and shortening.
Milk	1½ qt	Add to dry ingredients.
Oil or melted short-ening	4 oz	Mix on low speed only until blended.
		Scale batter into 5 greased loaf pans (5 × 9 × 2¾-inch), approximately 1 lb 14 oz per pan. Bake at 350°F for about 50 minutes. Cut 16 slices per loaf.

Approximate nutritive values per portion							
Calories (kcal)	Protein (grams)	Carbohydrate (grams)	Fat (grams)	Cholesterol (mg)	Sodium (mg)	Iron (mg)	Calcium (mg)
158	4.2 (10%)	23.2 (57%)	5.7 (32%)	18	129	1	52

Note   ■   5 oz nonfat dry milk and 1½ qt water may be substituted for fluid milk. Combine dry milk with other dry ingredients. Increase shortening to 6 oz.

DATE NUT BREAD

Yield: 64 portions or 4 loaves 5 × 9-inch   *Portion:* ½-inch slice
Oven: 350°F   *Bake:* 50 minutes

Ingredient	Amount	Procedure
Dates, chopped	1 lb 8 oz	Add water and soda to dates. Let stand 20 minutes.
Baking soda	1½ Tbsp	
Water, boiling	3¼ cups	
Shortening	3 oz	Cream shortening and sugar on medium speed for 5 minutes, using flat beater.
Sugar, granulated	1 lb 12 oz	
Eggs	4 (7 oz)	Add eggs and vanilla to creamed mixture. Mix on medium speed for 2 minutes.
Vanilla	1½ Tbsp	

Flour, all-purpose	2 lb	Combine flour, salt, and nuts.
Salt	1½ tsp	Add alternately with dates to creamed mixture.
Pecans or walnuts, chopped	8 oz	

Scale batter into 4 greased loaf pans (5 × 9 × 2¾-inch), approximately 2 lb per pan.
Bake at 350°F for about 50 minutes.
Cut 16 slices per loaf.

Approximate nutritive values per portion

Calories (kcal)	Protein (grams)	Carbohydrate (grams)	Fat (grams)	Cholesterol (mg)	Sodium (mg)	Iron (mg)	Calcium (mg)
166	2.9 (7%)	31.6 (73%)	3.8 (20%)	13	113	0.9	9

BANANA NUT BREAD

Yield: 64 portions or 4 loaves 5 × 9-inch   *Portion:* ½-inch slice
Oven: 350°F   *Bake:* 50 minutes

Ingredient	*Amount*	*Procedure*
Margarine	10 oz	Cream margarine and sugar on medium speed for 5 minutes, using flat beater.
Sugar, granulated	1 lb 10 oz	
Eggs	5 (9 oz)	Add eggs to creamed mixture. Beat 2 minutes.
Bananas, mashed	1 lb 10 oz	Add bananas. Beat 1 minute.
Flour, all-purpose	2 lb	Combine dry ingredients and nuts.
Baking powder	4 Tbsp	
Salt	2 tsp	
Baking soda	½ tsp	
Pecans or walnuts, chopped	8 oz	
Milk	¾ cup	Add dry ingredients and milk to creamed mixture. Mix on low speed for 1 minute.

Scale batter into 4 greased loaf pans (5 × 9 × 2¾-inch), approximately 2 lb per pan.
Bake at 350°F for 50 minutes.
Cut 16 slices per loaf.

Approximate nutritive values per portion

Calories (kcal)	Protein (grams)	Carbohydrate (grams)	Fat (grams)	Cholesterol (mg)	Sodium (mg)	Iron (mg)	Calcium (mg)
169	2.5 (6%)	26 (60%)	6.7 (34%)	17	173	0.8	45

CRANBERRY NUT BREAD

Yield: 80 portions or 5 loaves 5 × 9-inch   *Portion:* ½-inch slice
Oven: 350°F   *Bake:* 50 minutes

Ingredient	Amount	Procedure
Cranberries, raw	1 lb 4 oz	Wash and sort cranberries.
Orange peel	7 oz	Coarsely grind cranberries and orange peel.
Flour, all-purpose	2 lb 8 oz	Combine dry ingredients in mixer bowl.
Sugar, granulated	2 lb 4 oz	Blend on low speed for 10 seconds or until mixed, using flat beater.
Baking powder	1 oz	
Salt	2 tsp	
Baking soda	2 tsp	
Eggs, beaten	5 (9 oz)	Combine and add to dry ingredients.
Orange juice	1½ cups	Mix on low speed only until dry ingredients are moistened.
Water	3¾ cups	
Vegetable oil	½ cup	
Pecans or walnuts, chopped	1 lb	Add nuts and cranberry mixture to batter. Mix on low speed until blended. Batter may be lumpy.
		Scale batter into 5 greased loaf pans (5 × 9 × 2¾-inch), approximately 2 lb per pan.
		Bake at 350°F for about 50 minutes.
		Cut 16 slices per loaf.

Approximate nutritive values per portion

Calories (kcal)	Protein (grams)	Carbohydrate (grams)	Fat (grams)	Cholesterol (mg)	Sodium (mg)	Iron (mg)	Calcium (mg)
160	2.4 (6%)	26.7 (64%)	5.7 (31%)	14	114	0.9	34

PUMPKIN BREAD

Yield: 80 portions or 5 loaves 5 × 9-inch   *Portion:* ½-inch slice
Oven: 350°F   *Bake:* 50 minutes

Ingredient	Amount	Procedure
Sugar, granulated	2 lb 12 oz	Combine sugar, oil, pumpkin, and eggs in mixer bowl.
Vegetable oil	2 cups	Cream on medium speed for 10 minutes, using flat
Pumpkin, canned	2 lb 6 oz	beater.
Eggs	9 (15 oz)	Scrape sides of bowl and beater.
Flour, all-purpose	2 lb 2 oz	Combine dry ingredients.
Baking soda	4 tsp	
Baking powder	2 tsp	
Salt	1 Tbsp	
Cinnamon, ground	1 Tbsp	
Nutmeg, ground	1 tsp	
Water	1¼ cups	Add dry ingredients and water alternately to creamed mixture.
		Mix 3 minutes on low speed. Scrape sides of bowl.
		Scale batter into 5 greased loaf pans (5 × 9 × 2¾-inch), approximately 1 lb 15 oz per pan.
		Bake at 350°F for 50 minutes or until done.
		Cool 30 minutes before removing from pans.
		Cut 16 slices per loaf.

Approximate nutritive values per portion

Calories (kcal)	Protein (grams)	Carbohydrate (grams)	Fat (grams)	Cholesterol (mg)	Sodium (mg)	Iron (mg)	Calcium (mg)
164	2.1 (5%)	26 (62%)	6.2 (33%)	23	136	0.8	14

Note   ■   8 oz raisins or chopped nuts may be added.

PANCAKES

Yield: 7 qt batter or 100 cakes (50 portions)   *Portion:* 2 4-inch cakes

Ingredient	Amount	Procedure
Flour, all-purpose	4 lb 8 oz	Place dry ingredients in mixer bowl.
Baking powder	4 oz	Mix on low speed until well blended, using flat beater.
Salt	2 Tbsp	
Sugar, granulated	12 oz	
Eggs	12 (1 lb 5 oz)	In another bowl, beat eggs until light.
Milk	3½ qt	Add milk and melted shortening to eggs.
Shortening, melted and cooled, or vegetable oil	12 oz	Add to dry ingredients.Mix on low speed for 30 seconds.
		If necessary, thin with milk.
		Use No. 16 dipper to place batter on griddle, which has been preheated to 350°F.
		Cook until surface of cake is full of bubbles and golden brown.
		Turn pancakes and finish cooking.

Approximate nutritive values per portion

Calories (kcal)	Protein (grams)	Carbohydrate (grams)	Fat (grams)	Cholesterol (mg)	Sodium (mg)	Iron (mg)	Calcium (mg)
296	8 (11%)	41.9 (57%)	10.7 (33%)	60	532	2	238

Note

■ 14 oz nonfat dry milk and 3½ qt water may be substituted for the fluid milk. Add dry milk to other dry ingredients. Increase shortening to 1 lb.

Variations

■ **Apple Pancakes.**   Add 1 lb chopped cooked apples and 1 tsp cinnamon or nutmeg.

■ **Blueberry Pancakes.**   Fold 1 lb individually quick frozen (IQF) blueberries or well-drained and rinsed canned blueberries carefully into batter after cakes are mixed. Handle carefully to avoid mashing berries. If a large batch is being prepared, add berries to a small portion of the batter at one time. Serve with Blueberry Syrup, p. 611.

■ **Buttermilk Pancakes.**   Substitute buttermilk for milk. Add 1 Tbsp baking soda to dry ingredients. 14 oz dry buttermilk and 3½ qt water may be substituted for fluid buttermilk. Add dry buttermilk and soda to other dry ingredients. Increase shortening to 1 lb.

■ **Pecan Pancakes.**   Add 1 lb chopped pecans.

WHOLE-WHEAT PANCAKES

Yield: 2½ gal batter or 100 cakes (50 portions)   *Portion:* 2 cakes
Griddle: 350°F

Ingredient	Amount	Procedure
Flour, whole wheat	3 lb	Combine dry ingredients in mixer bowl. Mix, using flat beater, until blended.
Flour, all-purpose	2 lb 12 oz	
Sugar, granulated	8 oz	
Salt	2 oz (3 Tbsp)	
Baking powder	4 oz	
Baking soda	5½ tsp	
Nonfat dry milk	1 lb 2 oz	
Vegetable oil	3 cups	Add to dry ingredients, mixing just until large lumps disappear.
Water	1 gal + 2 cups	
Eggs	2 lb (18 eggs)	Portion batter with No. 12 dipper onto greased preheated griddle.
		Bake until edges start to dry and bubbles appear on top surface.
		Flip and bake other side.

Approximate nutritive values per portion

Calories (kcal)	Protein (grams)	Carbohydrate (grams)	Fat (grams)	Cholesterol (mg)	Sodium (mg)	Iron (mg)	Calcium (mg)
382	12.2 (13%)	49.4 (51%)	15.7 (36%)	79	784	2.5	295

Note   ■ 1¼ gal fluid milk may be substituted for nonfat dry milk and water. Add milk along with vegetable oil and eggs.

PANCAKE MIX

Yield: 12 lb mix

Ingredient	Amount	Procedure
Flour, all-purpose	9 lb	Combine ingredients in mixer bowl.
Baking powder	8 oz	Blend well, using flat beater or whip.
Salt	¼ cup	Store in covered container.
Sugar, granulated	1 lb 8 oz	
Nonfat dry milk	1 lb 8 oz	

Variation   ■ **Buttermilk Pancake Mix.** Substitute 1 lb 8 oz dry buttermilk for nonfat dry milk and add 2 Tbsp baking soda.

PANCAKES FROM MIX

Ingredient	30 cakes	50 cakes	100 cakes	200 cakes
Pancake mix	2 lb	3 lb	6 lb	12 lb
Eggs, beaten	4 (7 oz)	6 (10 oz)	12 (1 lb 5 oz)	24 (2 lb 10 oz)
Water	1 qt	1½ qt	3 qt	1½ gal
Oil or melted shortening	4 oz	6 oz	12 oz	1 lb 8 oz

To use mix

1. Weigh appropriate amount of mix as given in the table.
2. Add beaten eggs, water, and cooled melted fat.
3. Stir only until mix is dampened.
4. Place on hot griddle with No. 16 dipper.
5. Cook until cake is full of bubbles. Turn and finish cooking.

WAFFLES

Yield: 6 qt batter or 50–60 waffles   *Portion:* 1 waffle

Ingredient	Amount	Procedure
Flour, all-purpose	3 lb	Combine dry ingredients in mixer bowl.
Baking powder	3 oz	Blend on low speed for 10 seconds, using flat beater.
Salt	2 Tbsp	
Sugar, granulated	4 oz	
Egg yolks	18 (11 oz)	Combine egg yolks, milk, and melted shortening.
Milk	2¼ qt	Add to dry ingredients.
Oil or melted shortening	1 lb (2 cups)	Mix on low speed just enough to moisten dry ingredients.
Egg whites	18 (1 lb 5 oz)	Beat egg whites until stiff but not dry. Fold into batter.
		Use No. 10 dipper to place batter on preheated waffle iron. Bake about 4 minutes.

Approximate nutritive values per portion							
Calories (kcal)	Protein (grams)	Carbohydrate (grams)	Fat (grams)	Cholesterol (mg)	Sodium (mg)	Iron (mg)	Calcium (mg)
223	6 (11%)	23.4 (42%)	11.6 (47%)	78	427	1.4	159

Note   ■ 9 oz nonfat dry milk and 2¼ qt water may be substituted for fluid milk. Mix dry milk with dry ingredients. Increase shortening to 1 lb 2 oz.

Variation   ■ **Pecan Waffles.** Add 6 oz chopped pecans.

CREPES

Yield: 50 portions or 5 qt batter   *Portion:* 2 crepes

Ingredient	Amount	Procedure
Flour, all-purpose Salt	2 lb 8 oz 1 oz (1½ Tbsp)	Combine flour and salt in mixer bowl.
Eggs	24 (2 lb 10 oz)	Beat eggs until fluffy.
Milk Margarine, melted	2¾ qt 6 oz	Add milk and margarine to eggs. Add to flour and mix until smooth. Batter will be thinner than pancake batter.
		Portion batter with No. 20 (1¾ oz) dipper onto lightly greased hot griddle. Brown lightly on both sides. Crepes will roll best if they are not overbrowned. Stack, layered with waxed paper, until ready to use.

Approximate nutritive values per portion

Calories (kcal)	Protein (grams)	Carbohydrate (grams)	Fat (grams)	Cholesterol (mg)	Sodium (mg)	Iron (mg)	Calcium (mg)
176	7.1 (16%)	20.1 (46%)	7.1 (37%)	109	281	1.4	81

Notes

- Crepes may be folded or rolled around desired filling. (See recipe for Chicken Crepes, p. 461.)

- If used for dessert crepes, add 3 Tbsp sugar to dry ingredients. Fill with fruit filling.

CAKE DOUGHNUTS

Yield: 8 dozen doughnuts   *Portion:* 1 doughnut
Deep-fat fryer: 375°F   *Fry:* 3–4 minutes

Ingredient	Amount	Procedure
Eggs	6 (10 oz)	Beat eggs until light.
Sugar, granulated Oil or melted short- ening	1 lb 4 oz 3 oz	Add sugar and melted shortening to eggs. Mix on medium speed about 10 minutes.
Flour, all-purpose Baking powder Salt Nutmeg, ground Ginger, ground Orange peel, grated	3 lb 4 oz 3 oz 2½ tsp 2 tsp ¼ tsp 1 Tbsp	Combine dry ingredients.
Milk	1 qt	Add dry ingredients and milk alternately to egg mixture. Mix to form a soft dough. Add more flour if dough is too soft to handle. Chill.
		Roll dough to ⅜-inch thickness on floured board or table. Cut with floured 2½-inch doughnut cutter. Fry in deep fat for 3–4 minutes.
Sugar, granulated	8 oz	Sprinkle with sugar when partially cool.

Approximate nutritive values per portion

Calories (kcal)	Protein (grams)	Carbohydrate (grams)	Fat (grams)	Cholesterol (mg)	Sodium (mg)	Iron (mg)	Calcium (mg)
127	2.3 (7%)	20.8 (65%)	4.1 (28%)	14	153	0.8	72

Note   ■ 4 oz nonfat dry milk and 1 qt water may be substituted for fluid milk. Mix dry milk with the dry ingredients. Increase shortening to 4 oz.

Variation ■ **Chocolate Doughnuts.** Substitute 2 oz cocoa for 2 oz flour.

DUMPLINGS

Yield: 50 portions   *Portion:* 2 dumplings
Steam pressure: 5 lb   *Steam:* 12–15 minutes

Ingredient	Amount	Procedure
Flour, all-purpose Baking powder Salt	2 lb 8 oz 3 oz (6 Tbsp) 2 Tbsp	Combine dry ingredients in mixer bowl. Mix on low speed until blended, using flat beater.
Eggs, beaten Milk	6 (10 oz) 5½ cups	Combine eggs and milk. Add to dry ingredients. Mix on low speed only until blended.
		Portion batter with No. 24 dipper, onto trays. Do not cover trays. Steam for 12–15 minutes.

Approximate nutritive values per portion

Calories (kcal)	Protein (grams)	Carbohydrate (grams)	Fat (grams)	Cholesterol (mg)	Sodium (mg)	Iron (mg)	Calcium (mg)
109	3.9 (15%)	18.9 (71%)	1.7 (14%)	28	381	1.1	106

Notes
- 5 oz nonfat dry milk and 5½ cups water may be substituted for the fluid milk. Add dry milk to other dry ingredients.
- Serve with meat stew or stewed chicken. Mixture may be dropped onto hot meat mixture in counter pans and steamed.

Variation
- **Spaetzles (Egg Dumplings).** Use 1 lb 4 oz flour, 1 tsp baking powder, 1½ tsp salt, 6 eggs, and 3 cups milk. Mix as above. Drop small bits of dough or press through a colander into 3 gal simmering soup. Cook approximately 5 minutes. Soup must be very hot to cook dumplings.

FRENCH TOAST ■

Yield: 50 slices   *Portion:* 1 slice

Ingredient	Amount	Procedure
Eggs	24 (2 lb 10 oz)	Beat eggs.
Milk Salt Sugar, granulated	1½ qt 1 Tbsp 4 oz	Add milk, salt, and sugar to eggs. Mix well.
Bread slices, day old	50	Dip bread into egg mixture. Do not let bread soak. Fry on a well-greased griddle or in deep fat at 360°F until golden brown. Serve sprinkled with powdered sugar.

Approximate nutritive values per portion							
Calories (kcal)	Protein (grams)	Carbohydrate (grams)	Fat (grams)	Cholesterol (mg)	Sodium (mg)	Iron (mg)	Calcium (mg)
144	6.4 (17%)	15.2 (41%)	6.7 (41%)	105	331	1.2	66

Variations
- **Batter-Fried French Toast.** Use 1-inch thick bread slices. Cut into triangles or leave whole. Dip in mixture made from 18 eggs (2 lb), 1¼ qt milk, ⅓ cup vegetable oil, 2 lb 8 oz all-purpose flour, 1 oz (1½ Tbsp) salt, and 1 oz (2⅓ Tbsp) baking powder. Fry in deep fat at 350–375°F until golden brown. Dredge in powdered sugar. Serve with warm maple syrup.
- **Cinnamon French Toast.** Add 1 tsp cinnamon to egg mixture.

FRITTERS ■

Yield: 50 portions   *Portion:* 2 fritters
Deep-fat fryer: 375°F   *Fry:* 4–6 minutes

Ingredient	Amount	Procedure
Flour, all-purpose Baking powder Salt Sugar, granulated	4 lb 4 oz 1 Tbsp 2 oz	Combine dry ingredients in mixer bowl. Mix on low speed for 10 seconds or until mixed, using flat beater.
Eggs, beaten Milk Oil or melted short-ening	12 (1 lb 5 oz) 2 qt 6 oz (¾ cup)	Combine eggs, milk, and melted shortening. Add to dry ingredients. Mix only enough to moisten dry ingredients.
		Portion batter with No. 30 dipper into hot deep fat. Fry at 375°F for 4–6 minutes. Serve with syrup.

Approximate nutritive values per portion							
Calories (kcal)	Protein (grams)	Carbohydrate (grams)	Fat (grams)	Cholesterol (mg)	Sodium (mg)	Iron (mg)	Calcium (mg)
251	6.5 (10%)	31.4 (50%)	10.8 (39%)	56	390	1.8	202

Note   ■ 8 oz nonfat dry milk and 2 qt water may be substituted for fluid milk. Add dry milk to other dry ingredients.

Variations   ■ **Apple Fritters.**   Add 3 lb tart raw apple, peeled and finely chopped, and 1 tsp cinnamon (optional).

■ **Banana Fritters.**   Add 3 lb bananas, mashed.

■ **Corn Fritters.**   Add 2 qt whole kernel corn, drained.

■ **Fruit Fritters.**   Add 1 qt drained fruit: peach, pineapple, or other fruit.

■ **Green Chili Fritters.**   Add 2 lb 8 oz chopped green chilies, drained. Serve with nacho sauce (Nachos, p. 323). Make ¼ recipe.

CHEESE STRAWS

Yield: 6 dozen 4 × 1-inch straws
Oven: 350°F   *Bake:* 10–15 minutes

Ingredient	Amount	Procedure
Butter or margarine	6 oz	Cream butter on medium speed until soft.
Cheddar cheese, sharp, shredded	8 oz	Blend in cheese.
Flour, all-purpose	8 oz	Combine dry ingredients and add to cheese mixture on low speed.
Baking powder	2 tsp	
Salt	1 tsp	
Pepper, cayenne	¼ tsp	
Eggs, beaten	3	Add eggs and water, combined.
Water	2 Tbsp	Mix on low speed to form a stiff dough. Chill.
		Roll ¼ inch thick and cut into strips 4 inches long and 1 inch wide. Place on ungreased baking sheet. Bake at 350°F for 10–15 minutes.

Approximate nutritive values per portion							
Calories (kcal)	Protein (grams)	Carbohydrate (grams)	Fat (grams)	Cholesterol (mg)	Sodium (mg)	Iron (mg)	Calcium (mg)
44	1.4 (13%)	2.5 (23%)	3.2 (65%)	12	82	0.2	30

Variation   ■ **Caraway Cheese Straws.**   Add 2 tsp caraway seeds to flour before mixing.

YEAST BREAD RECIPES

WHITE BREAD ■

Yield: 16 1½-lb loaves
Oven: 400°F   *Bake:* 30–40 minutes

Ingredient	Amount	Procedure
Yeast, active dry	5 oz	Soften yeast in warm water.
Water, warm (110°F)	3 cups	Let stand 10 minutes.
Sugar, granulated	10 oz	Combine sugar, salt, dry milk, water, and shortening.
Salt	5 oz	Add softened yeast.
Nonfat dry milk	14 oz	Mix on medium speed until blended, using dough arm.
Water, lukewarm	1 gal	
Shortening, melted	12 oz	
Flour, all-purpose	15 lb	Add flour. Mix on low speed about 10 minutes or until dough is smooth and elastic and small blisters appear on the surface.

1. Let dough rise in a warm place (80°F) approximately 2 hours, or until double in bulk.

2. Punch down dough by pulling the dough up on all sides, folding over the center and pressing down, then turning over in the bowl. Shape into 16 loaves, 1 lb 8 oz each (Figure 4.1). Place in greased 5 × 9 × 2¾ loaf pans.

3. Let rise approximately 1½ hours, or until double in bulk.

4. Bake at 400°F for 30–40 minutes or until loaves are golden brown and sound hollow when tapped (Figure 4.2).

5. Brush tops of loaves with melted margarine or butter.

Approximate nutritive values per loaf

Calories (kcal)	Protein (grams)	Carbohydrate (grams)	Fat (grams)	Cholesterol (mg)	Sodium (mg)	Iron (mg)	Calcium (mg)
1917	56.4 (12%)	359 (76%)	25.6 (12%)	4	3587	21.2	399

Notes
- 1¼ gal fresh milk may be substituted for the water and dry milk. Scald milk, combine with sugar, salt, and shortening. Cool to lukewarm before adding to other ingredients.

- The dough temperature should be about 80°F when mixed.

- Mixing may be simplified by combining dry yeast with sugar, salt, dry milk, and 2 lb of the flour. Mix thoroughly. In mixer bowl, combine very warm water (120°F) and shortening. Blend on low speed. Add yeast-flour mixture while mixing on low speed. Add remaining flour gradually, mixing until a smooth, elastic dough is formed.

- Shortening may be increased to 1 lb and sugar to 12 oz if a richer dough is desired.
- A variety of shapes may be made from the dough (Figures 4.3 and 4.4).

Variations

- **Buffet Submarine Buns.** Scale dough into 1-lb portions. Shape into 18-inch long loaves. (See Figure 4.1 for shaping instructions.) Use for Submarine Sandwiches (p. 564).
- **Butter Slices.** Divide dough into thirds. Roll ⅓ inch thick. Cut with 3-inch biscuit cutter or shape into long rolls and cut into slices. Dip in melted margarine or butter. Stand pieces on edge in 5 × 9 × 2¾-inch loaf pans (8 pieces per pan). Let rise and bake.
- **Cinnamon Bread.** After dough has been divided and scaled into loaves, roll each into a rectangular sheet. Brush with melted margarine or shortening; sprinkle generously with cinnamon and sugar. Roll as for Jelly Roll. Seal edge of dough and place in greased loaf pans sealed edge down. Sprinkle top with cinnamon and sugar.
- **Raisin Bread.** Add 3 lb raisins to dough after mixing.
- **Sandwich Ring Bread.** Scale fermented dough into 11-oz balls and shape each ball into a 16-inch rope. Braid 3 ropes together and pinch ends to seal. Shape braided ropes into a 15-inch circle with a 5-inch center hole (work ends together to form a smooth ring). Proof ring in a warm place until double in bulk (30–40 minutes). Bake at 375°F until done (about 20 minutes).
- **Whole-Wheat Bread.** Substitute whole-wheat flour for half of the all-purpose flour.

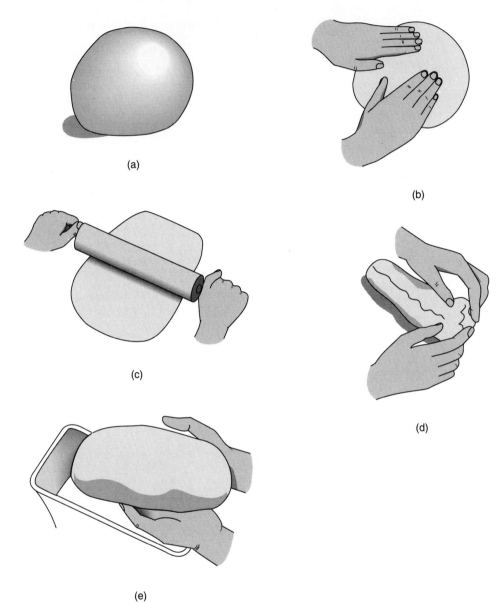

(a)

(b)

(c)

(d)

(e)

FIGURE 4.1   Shaping bread loaves: (a) Divide into 1 lb 8 oz balls. (b) Press dough by hand to force out air bubbles. (c) Roll dough to flatten. (d) Seal by pinching ends together. (e) Place in pans.

FIGURE 4.2   Well-shaped baked bread loaf, showing fine grain and evenly browned top and sides. Photo provided by Kansas Wheat Commission.

FIGURE 4.3   Basic bread or roll dough is shaped easily into a variety of products. Photo supplied by Fleischmann's Yeast, Inc.

FIGURE 4.4   Varying bread shapes and toppings. Photo supplied by
Fleischmann's Yeast, Inc.

WHOLE-WHEAT BREAD ▪

Yield: 5 1½-lb loaves
Oven: 365°F   *Bake:* 30–35 minutes

Ingredient	Amount	Procedure
Yeast, active dry	1¼ oz	Combine yeast, water, and sugar.
Water, warm (110°F)	1¾ cup	Let stand 10 minutes.
Sugar, granulated	1 Tbsp	
Water, hot	1 qt	Combine water, milk, sugar, salt, and shortening in mixer bowl, using dough arm.
Nonfat dry milk	5 oz	
Sugar, granulated	5 oz	Mix until shortening is softened.
Salt	1½ oz	
Shortening	6 oz	
Flour, all-purpose	3 lb	Add enough flour to mixture in mixer bowl to make a thin, smooth batter. Add yeast mixture. Mix 15 minutes on medium speed.
Flour, whole-wheat	1 lb	Add remaining all-purpose flour and whole-wheat flour in small amounts to make a soft dough that pulls itself from side of bowl. Mix on low speed about 10 minutes or until dough is smooth and elastic and small blisters appear on the surface.

1. Let dough rise (proof) in warm place for about two hours or until double in bulk.
2. Punch down dough. Scale into 5 portions 1 lb 8 oz each.
3. Shape into loaves. Place in greased 5 × 9 × 2¾-inch loaf pans. Let rise until double in size.
4. Bake at 365°F for 30–35 minutes.
5. Remove bread from oven. Brush with melted margarine.

Approximate nutritive values per loaf

Calories (kcal)	Protein (grams)	Carbohydrate (grams)	Fat (grams)	Cholesterol (mg)	Sodium (mg)	Iron (mg)	Calcium (mg)
1859	50.5 (11%)	326 (71%)	37.8 (18%)	5	3468	18	431

Note   ▪ Recipe may be used for Whole-Wheat Rolls. See p. 160 for procedure. Recipe makes approximately 100 1½-oz rolls. Bake at 375°F for 20–25 minutes.

Variation

- **Cornmeal Bread.**   Delete whole-wheat flour. Add 1 lb cornmeal.

- **Egg Bread.**   Delete whole-wheat flour. Increase all-purpose flour to 3 lb 12 oz. Add 5 eggs (8 oz), beaten.

- **Jalapeño Cheese Bread.**   Delete whole-wheat flour. Increase all-purpose flour to 4 lb. Increase yeast to 1½ oz. Reduce nonfat dry milk to 1 oz. Add 3 oz seeded jalapeño peppers, finely chopped; 8 oz green chilies, chopped; 10 oz shredded cheddar cheese; and 8 oz shredded processed cheese.

- **White Loaves.**   Delete whole-wheat flour. Increase all-purpose flour to 4 lb.

FRENCH BREAD

Yield: 5 loaves 1 lb 12 oz
Oven: 425°F   *Bake:* 25–30 minutes

Ingredient	Amount	Procedure
Yeast, active dry	1½ oz	Combine yeast, water, and sugar.
Water, warm (110°F)	2 cups	Stir to dissolve yeast. Let stand 10 minutes.
Sugar, granulated	2 oz	
Water, warm	3 cups	Add to yeast mixture. Mix until blended, using dough
Shortening	3 oz	arm.
Salt	1¾ oz	
Flour, all-purpose	5 lb	Add flour all at once. Mix on low speed to blend. Mix on medium speed for 7–10 minutes, or until sides of bowl are clean and dough makes a rhythmic slapping sound against side of bowl.

1. Let dough rise (proof) in a warm place for about 2 hours, or until double in bulk.
2. Punch down dough by pulling the dough up on all sides, folding over the center and pressing down, then turning over in the bowl.
3. Divide into 5 portions, 1 lb 12 oz each. On lightly floured surface, roll or pat dough to a 12 × 6-inch rectangle.
4. Starting with longer side, roll up tightly, pressing dough into roll with each turn. Pinch edges and ends to seal.
5. Place on greased baking sheet sprinkled with cornmeal.
6. Proof until double in bulk.
7. With sharp knife, make 2 or 3 diagonal slashes across top of loaf.
8. Spray or brush with cold water.
9. Bake at 425°F for 25–30 minutes until golden brown. Spray or brush loaf with cold water several times during baking for a crisp crust.

Approximate nutritive values per loaf

Calories (kcal)	Protein (grams)	Carbohydrate (grams)	Fat (grams)	Cholesterol (mg)	Sodium (mg)	Iron (mg)	Calcium (mg)
1868	50.5 (11%)	361 (79%)	21.4 (10%)	0	3862	22.4	99

Notes
- For a shiny, golden crust, brush loaves before baking with an egg glaze made from one slightly beaten egg and 1 Tbsp of water or milk.
- After baking, leave uncovered at room temperature to keep the crust crisp.

DILLY BREAD

Yield: 5 1½-lb loaves
Oven: 375°F   *Bake:* 30–35 minutes

Ingredient	Amount	Procedure
Yeast, active dry	1¼ oz	Combine yeast, water, and sugar.
Water, warm (110°F)	½ cup	Stir to dissolve yeast.
Sugar, granulated	3 oz	Let stand for later step.
Cottage cheese, cream style	1 lb 12 oz	Combine cottage cheese and water in mixer bowl.
Water, warm	1¼ cups	
Vegetable oil	¼ cup	Add oil, onion, dill weed, and eggs to cottage cheese mixture. Mix to blend, using dough arm.
Dehydrated chopped onion	½ oz	
Dill weed	1 Tbsp	Add yeast mixture.
Eggs, whole	3 (6 oz)	
Flour, all-purpose	4 lb 2 oz	Combine dry ingredients. Add enough to cottage cheese mixture to make a smooth batter. Scrape sides of bowl occasionally.
Salt	1 Tbsp	
Baking soda	½ tsp	Add remaining flour gradually until dough pulls itself from sides of bowl. Dough will be sticky.
		Proof until double in bulk.
		Scale dough into 5 portions, 1 lb 8 oz each. Shape into loaves.
		Place in greased 5 × 9 × 2¾-inch loaf pans.
		Proof until double in size.
		Bake at 375°F for 30–35 minutes.
		Brush with melted margarine.

Approximate nutritive values per loaf

Calories (kcal)	Protein (grams)	Carbohydrate (grams)	Fat (grams)	Cholesterol (mg)	Sodium (mg)	Iron (mg)	Calcium (mg)
1768	66.1 (15%)	313 (72%)	25.1 (13%)	169	2058	19.5	197

ENGLISH MUFFIN BREAD ■

Yield: 5 1½-lb loaves
Oven: 375°F   *Bake:* 40–50 minutes

Ingredient	Amount	Procedure
Water, hot Vegetable oil	2 cups 1½ cups	Combine water and oil in mixer bowl.
Flour, all-purpose Sugar, granulated Salt Eggs, beaten	2 lb 6 oz 2 oz 6 (10 oz)	Add flour, sugar, salt, and eggs to water-oil mixture.
Yeast, active dry Water, warm (110°F)	1¼ oz 1½ cups	Dissolve yeast in warm water. Add to flour mixture. Mix on medium speed for 2 minutes, using dough arm.
Flour, all-purpose	2 lb	Add enough remaining flour to make a stiff batter. Cover and let rise until light and double in bulk. Punch down dough.
Cornmeal	2 oz	Grease 5 loaf pans (5 × 9 × 2¾-inch). Sprinkle with cornmeal. Scale 1 lb 8 oz dough per pan. Shape and place in pans. Sprinkle with cornmeal. Cover. Let rise until double in bulk. Bake at 375°F for 40–50 minutes or until loaf sounds hollow when tapped lightly.

Approximate nutritive values per loaf

Calories (kcal)	Protein (grams)	Carbohydrate (grams)	Fat (grams)	Cholesterol (mg)	Sodium (mg)	Iron (mg)	Calcium (mg)
2173	48.5 (9%)	323 (60%)	75 (31%)	242	4483	19.1	117

OATMEAL BREAD

Yield: 5 1½-lb loaves
Oven: 375°F   *Bake:* 30–35 minutes

Ingredient	Amount	Procedure
Yeast, active dry Water, warm (110°F) Sugar, granulated	1¼ oz 1 cup 2 tsp	Combine yeast, water, and sugar. Let stand 10 minutes.
Water, hot Rolled oats Molasses Shortening Salt	3 cups 6 oz 1 cup 6 oz 2 Tbsp	Combine in mixer bowl, using dough arm.
Flour, all-purpose	3 lb 8 oz	Add enough flour to rolled oats mixture to make a smooth, thin batter.
Eggs	4 (7 oz)	Add eggs and yeast mixture to batter. Mix 15 minutes on medium speed. Add remaining flour in small amounts, on low speed, to make a soft dough. Let rest 10 minutes. Knead on low speed for 10 minutes or until smooth and elastic, or until a small piece of dough can be stretched to resemble a thin membrane. Let rise until double in bulk.
Rolled oats	4 oz	Grease 5 loaf pans (5 × 9 × 2¾-inch). Coat each pan with ¼ cup rolled oats. Punch down dough. Scale 1 lb 8 oz dough for each pan and shape into a loaf. Place in prepared pans.
Egg whites Water	2 (2 oz) 1 Tbsp	Combine egg whites and water. Brush on loaves and sprinkle with rolled oats. Let rise until double in bulk. Bake at 375°F for 30–35 minutes.

Approximate nutritive values per loaf

Calories (kcal)	Protein (grams)	Carbohydrate (grams)	Fat (grams)	Cholesterol (mg)	Sodium (mg)	Iron (mg)	Calcium (mg)
1926	51.1 (11%)	327 (68%)	44.7 (21%)	169	2651	21.7	225

Variation   ■   **Molasses Bran Bread.**   Delete rolled oats and eggs. Increase water to 1 qt. Add 10 oz whole wheat flour, 3 oz unprocessed bran, 1½ tsp ground ginger, and 4 oz non-fat dry milk.

POTATO BREAD

Yield: 5 1½-lb loaves
Oven: 375°F   *Bake:* 30–35 minutes

Ingredient	Amount	Procedure
Instant potatoes Water, boiling	5 oz 2 cups	Pour boiling water over potatoes. Set aside for later step.
Yeast, active dry Water, warm (110°F) Sugar, granulated	1 oz 1 cup 1 tsp	Combine yeast, water, and sugar. Let stand 10 minutes.
Water, hot Nonfat dry milk Shortening Sugar, granulated Salt	1½ cups 4 oz 8 oz 8 oz 2 Tbsp	Combine water, milk, shortening, sugar, and salt in mixer bowl, using dough arm to mix and soften shortening. Add potato mixture and mix until well blended.
Flour, all-purpose	3 lb 8 oz	Add enough flour to make a smooth batter. Add yeast mixture. Mix on medium speed for 15 minutes.
Eggs, beaten	5 (8 oz)	Add eggs and mix thoroughly. Add remaining flour in small amounts on low speed to make a soft dough. Proof until double in bulk.
		Punch down dough. Scale into 5 loaves, 1 lb 8 oz each. Place in greased baking pans (5 × 9 × 2¾-inch). Proof until double in size. Bake at 375°F for 30–35 minutes.

Approximate nutritive values per loaf

Calories (kcal)	Protein (grams)	Carbohydrate (grams)	Fat (grams)	Cholesterol (mg)	Sodium (mg)	Iron (mg)	Calcium (mg)
2010	51.1 (10%)	326 (65%)	54.3 (24%)	197	3347	16.8	440

Note
■ Dough may be shaped into rolls. Recipe makes approximately 100 1½-oz rolls. Bake at 375°F for 20–25 minutes.

Variation
■ **Portuguese Sweet Bread.**   Delete nonfat dry milk. Substitute 6 oz margarine for shortening. Increase sugar to 10 oz and eggs to 6 (10 oz).

SWEDISH RYE BREAD

Yield: 5 1½-lb loaves
Oven: 375°F   *Bake:* 40–50 minutes

Ingredient	Amount	Procedure
Yeast, active dry	2¼ oz	Combine yeast, water, and brown sugar. Let stand 10 minutes.
Water, warm (110°F)	2 cups	
Sugar, brown	1 oz	
Water, hot	3 cups	Combine in mixer bowl. Mix thoroughly until shortening is softened.
Salt	1 Tbsp	
Sugar, brown	6 oz	
Molasses	6 oz (½ cup)	
Shortening	3 oz	
Flour, all-purpose	3 lb 8 oz	Combine flours. Add enough to mixture in mixer bowl to make a thin, smooth batter.
Flour, rye	12 oz	Add yeast mixture. Mix on medium speed for 10 minutes, using dough arm.
		Reduce mixer speed. Add remaining flour in small amounts to make a soft dough that pulls itself from sides of bowl.
		Mix for about 10 minutes, until smooth and elastic, or until a small piece of dough can be stretched to resemble a thin membrane.
		Let rise until double in bulk.
		Punch down dough.
		Shape into 5 loaves, 1 lb 8 oz each.
		Place in 5 greased loaf pans (5 × 9 × 2¾-inch). Let rise until double in bulk.
		Bake at 375°F for 40–50 minutes or until bread sounds hollow when tapped lightly.

Approximate nutritive values per loaf

Calories (kcal)	Protein (grams)	Carbohydrate (grams)	Fat (grams)	Cholesterol (mg)	Sodium (mg)	Iron (mg)	Calcium (mg)
1791	47.8 (11%)	354 (78%)	21.9 (11%)	0	1311	23.9	189

Variations
- **Caraway Rye Bread.** Add 2 Tbsp caraway seeds to dough.
- **Limpa Rye Bread.** Decrease all-purpose flour to 2 lb and increase rye flour to 2 lb. Add 2 Tbsp fennel seed and 2 Tbsp grated orange peel.
- **Rye Rolls.** Shape into 1½-oz rolls. Yield: 7 dozen.

BASIC ROLL DOUGH

Yield: 8 dozen rolls   *Portion:* 1½ oz
Oven: 400°F   *Bake:* 15–25 minutes

Ingredient	Amount	Procedure
Water, warm (110°F)	1 cup	Combine sugar and water. Add yeast.
Sugar, granulated	1 tsp	Let stand 10 minutes.
Yeast, active dry	1½ oz	
Water, hot	1¼ qt	Place hot water, dry milk, sugar, salt, and shortening in mixer bowl.
Nonfat dry milk	5 oz	
Sugar, granulated	4 oz	Mix thoroughly, using dough arm, until shortening is softened.
Salt	2 oz	
Shortening	8 oz	
Eggs, beaten	4 (7 oz)	Add eggs and softened yeast.
Flour, all-purpose	4 lb 12 oz (variable)	Add flour to make a moderately soft dough. Mix on low speed for about 10 minutes until smooth and satiny or until a small piece of dough can be stretched to resemble a thin membrane.

1. Turn into lightly greased bowl, then turn over to grease top. Cover. Let rise in warm place (80°F) until double in bulk.

2. Punch down. Divide into thirds for ease in handling. Shape into 1½-oz rolls or into desired shapes. (See Variations.)

3. Let rise until double in bulk.

4. Bake at 400°F for 15–25 minutes or until golden brown.

Approximate nutritive values per portion							
Calories (kcal)	Protein (grams)	Carbohydrate (grams)	Fat (grams)	Cholesterol (mg)	Sodium (mg)	Iron (mg)	Calcium (mg)
117	3.3 (11%)	19.3 (67%)	2.8 (22%)	9	241	1.1	24

Notes

- 1¼ qt fluid milk may be used in place of nonfat dry milk and hot water. Scald milk, then add sugar, salt, and shortening, and cool to lukewarm.

- Mixing may be simplified by combining dry yeast with sugar, salt, dry milk, and 2 lb of the flour. Mix thoroughly. In mixer bowl combine 1½ qt very warm water (120°F), shortening, and beaten eggs. Blend on low speed. Add remaining flour gradually, mixing until a smooth, elastic dough is formed.

- 3–4 hours are required for mixing and rising. For a quicker rising dough, increase yeast to 2 oz.

Variations

- **Bowknots.** Roll 1½-oz portions of dough into strips 9 inches long. Tie loosely into a single knot (see Figure 4.5).

- **Braids.**   Roll dough ¼ inch thick and cut in strips 6 inches long and ½ inch wide. Braid 3 strips, fold under, and pinch to seal (see Figure 4.6).

- **Butterhorns.**   Proceed as for Crescents, but do not form crescent shape.

- **Caramel Crowns.**   Increase sugar in dough to 9 oz. Scale dough into balls 1½ oz each. Drop into mixture of 1 lb 4 oz sugar and 3 Tbsp cinnamon to coat balls. Arrange 18 balls in each of 5 greased tube pans, into which 2 oz pecans, halves or coarsely chopped, have been placed. The pan should be about ⅓ full. Let rise until double in bulk. Bake at 350°F for 30 minutes. Immediately loosen from pan with a spatula. Invert pans to remove. Cool. Serve irregular side up to resemble a crown. Garnish with maraschino cherries.

- **Cloverleaf Rolls.**   Pinch off 1-oz pieces of dough and roll into smooth balls. Fit into greased muffin pans, 3 balls per cup (see Figure 4.7).

- **Crescents.**   Weigh dough into 12-oz portions. Roll each into a circle ⅛ inch thick and 8 inches in diameter. Cut into 12 triangles and brush top with melted margarine or butter. Beginning at base, roll each triangle, keeping point in middle of roll and bringing ends toward each other to form a crescent shape. Place on greased baking sheets 1½ inches apart (see Figure 4.8).

- **Dinner or Pan Rolls.**   Shape dough into 1½-oz balls and place on well-greased baking sheets. Cover. Let rise until light. Brush with mixture made of egg yolk and milk—1 egg yolk to 1 Tbsp milk (see Figure 4.9).

- **Fan Tan or Butterflake Rolls.**   Weigh dough into 12-oz pieces. Roll out into very thin rectangular sheet. Brush with melted margarine or butter. Cut in strips about 1 inch wide. Pile 6 or 7 strips together. Cut 1½-inch pieces and place on end in greased muffin pans.

- **Gooey Buns.**   Grease sides of one 18 × 26 × 2-inch baking sheet. Combine in kettle or saucepan 8 oz margarine, 1 lb 8 oz brown sugar, and ¾ cup corn syrup. Cook until sugar is dissolved. Pour into prepared pan. Cool. If desired, sprinkle 1 lb pecans over mixture. Place 1½-oz portions of dough 8 × 12 on sugar mixture. Let rise. Bake at 375°F for 20–25 minutes. Remove from oven and turn upside down onto 18 × 26 × 1-inch baking sheet.

- **Half-and-Half Rolls.**   Proceed as for Twin Rolls. Use 1 round plain dough and 1 round whole wheat dough for each roll.

- **Hamburger Buns.**   Divide dough into 2 portions. Roll each piece of dough into a strip 1½ inches in diameter. Cut strips into pieces approximately 2½ oz each. Round the pieces into balls (Figure 4.10). Place balls in rows on greased baking sheets 1½–2 inches apart. Let stand 10–15 minutes, then flatten to desired thickness with finger, rolling pin, or another baking sheet.

- **Hot Cross Buns.**   Divide dough into thirds. Roll ½ inch thick. Cut rounds 3 inches in diameter. Brush tops with beaten egg. Score top of bun to make a cross before baking, or make a cross on top with frosting after baking. (See p. 171 for variation.)

- **Hot Dog Buns.**   Divide dough into 2 portions. Roll each piece of dough into a strip 1½ inches in diameter. Cut strips of dough into pieces approximately 2½ oz each. Round pieces of dough; roll into pieces approximately 4½ inches long. Place in rows on greased baking sheets ½ inch apart.

- **Parker House Rolls.**   Divide dough into thirds. Roll dough to ⅓ inch thickness. Cut rounds 2–2½ inches in diameter with a biscuit cutter. Let dough rest a few minutes after cutting. Brush with melted butter or margarine. Crease the rolls across the center with the dull edge of a table knife. Fold over and press down on the folded edge (see Figure 4.11).

- **Popcorn Rolls.**   Shape dough into 1½-oz balls. Place on greased baking sheets. Snip top of each ball twice with scissors.

- **Poppy Seed Rolls.**   (a) Proceed as for Twists. Substitute poppy seed for sugar and cinnamon. (b) Proceed as for Cinnamon Rolls (p. 176). Substitute poppy seed for sugar, cinnamon, and raisins.

- **Ribbon Rolls.**   Weigh dough into 12-oz pieces. Roll ¼ inch thick. Spread with melted margarine. Place on top of this a layer of whole-wheat dough rolled to the same thickness. Repeat, using the contrasting dough until 5 layers thick. Cut with a 1½-inch cutter. Place in greased muffin pans with cut surface down.

- **Rosettes.**   Follow directions for Bowknots. After tying, bring one end through center and the other over the side.

- **Sesame Rolls.**   Proceed as for Twin Rolls. Brush tops with melted margarine and sprinkle with sesame seeds.

- **Twin Rolls.**   Weigh dough into 12-oz pieces. Roll ⅝ inch thick. Cut rounds 1 inch in diameter. Brush with melted margarine. Place on end in well-greased muffin pans, allowing 2 rounds for each roll.

- **Twists.**   Weigh dough into 12-oz pieces. Roll ⅓ inch thick, spread with melted margarine, sugar, and cinnamon. Cut into strips ⅓ × 8 inches, bring both ends together, and twist dough.

- **Whole-Wheat Rolls.**   Substitute 2 lb 6 oz whole-wheat flour for 2 lb 6 oz of the all-purpose flour. Proceed as for Basic Roll Dough.

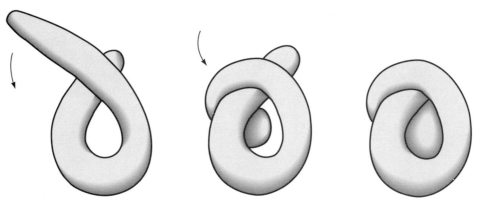

FIGURE 4.5 Shaping Bowknot Rolls.

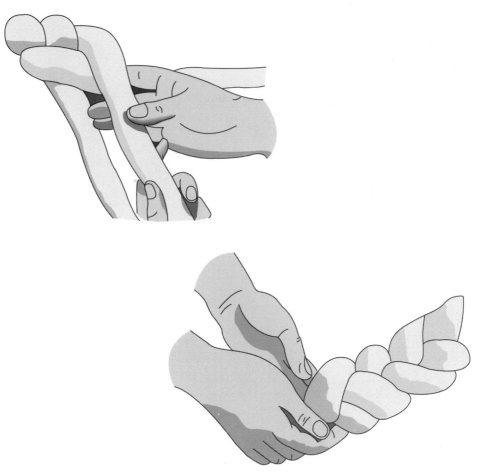

FIGURE 4.6 Braiding yeast dough.

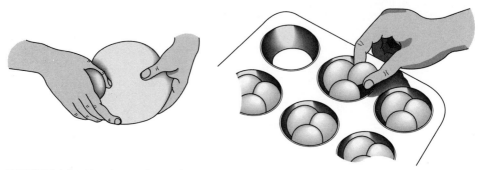

FIGURE 4.7   Shaping and panning Cloverleaf Rolls.

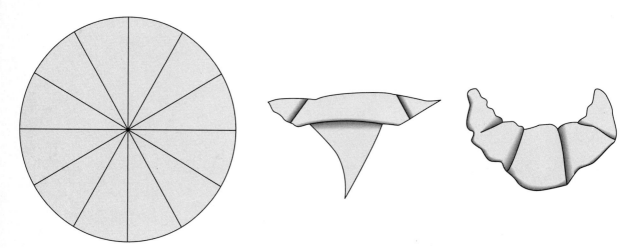

FIGURE 4.8   Shaping Crescent Rolls.

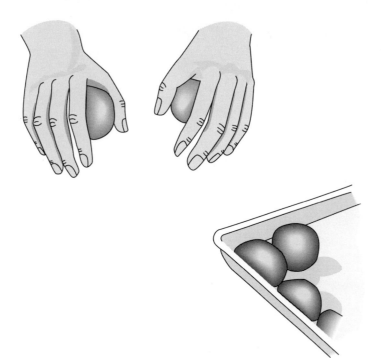

FIGURE 4.9   Shaping Dinner or Pan Rolls.

FIGURE 4.10 Bread or roll dough may be shaped into buns and topped with caraway seeds, coarse salt, or other topping. Used by permission of Red Star Yeast Products, Universal Foods Corporation.

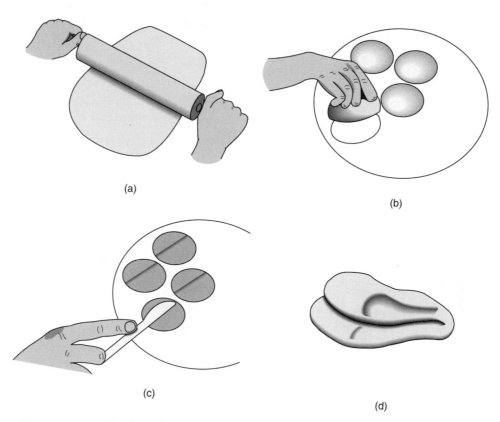

(a)

(b)

(c)

(d)

FIGURE 4.11   Shaping Parker House Rolls. (a) Divide dough into thirds. Roll to ⅓ inch thickness and brush with melted margarine. (b) Cut into circles with cutter. (c) Crease rolls with back of table knife. (d) Fold over and press down on folded edge.

BUTTER BUNS

Yield: 9–10 dozen buns   *Portion:* 1¾ oz
Oven: 400°F   *Bake:* 15–20 minutes

Ingredient	Amount	Procedure
Sugar, granulated	1 lb	Place sugar, salt, and margarine in mixer bowl.
Salt	1 oz	
Margarine or butter	1 lb 8 oz	
Milk	3 cups	Scald milk by heating to a point just below boiling. Add to ingredients in mixer bowl and mix. Cool to lukewarm.
Yeast, active dry	2 oz	Soften yeast in warm water.
Water, warm (110°F)	1 cup	
Eggs	12 (1 lb 5 oz)	Beat eggs and yolks.
Egg yolks	16 (10 oz)	Add eggs, lemon extract, and yeast to milk mixture. Mix until blended.
Lemon extract (optional)	4 tsp	
Flour, all-purpose	4 lb 8 oz	Add flour and mix thoroughly, using dough arm. Let dough rise until double in bulk. Portion with No. 30 dipper into greased muffin pans. Let rise 1 hour. Bake at 400°F for 15–20 minutes.

Approximate nutritive values per portion

Calories (kcal)	Protein (grams)	Carbohydrate (grams)	Fat (grams)	Cholesterol (mg)	Sodium (mg)	Iron (mg)	Calcium (mg)
145	3.4 (9%)	18.3 (50%)	6.5 (40%)	55	164	1	19

Note   ■ 3 oz nonfat dry milk and 3 cups water may be substituted for the fluid milk. Combine dry milk with the flour. Increase margarine to 1 lb 9 oz.

RAISED MUFFINS

Yield: 8 dozen muffins   *Portion:* 2 oz
Oven: 350°F   *Bake:* 20 minutes

Ingredient	Amount	Procedure
Sugar, granulated Salt Shortening	12 oz 2 oz 9 oz	Place sugar, salt, and shortening in mixer bowl.
Milk	1½ qt	Scald milk by heating to point just below boiling. Add to mixture in mixer bowl. Cool to lukewarm.
Yeast, active dry Water, warm (110°F)	1½ oz 1½ cups	Soften yeast in warm water.
Eggs, beaten	12 (1 lb 5 oz)	Add eggs and softened yeast to milk mixture.
Flour, all-purpose	2 lb	Add flour. Beat on medium speed for 10 minutes, using flat beater. Let rise in warm place for 1½ hours.
Flour, all-purpose	2 lb 12 oz (variable)	Add remaining flour. Beat until batter is smooth. Portion with No. 20 dipper into greased muffin pans. Let rise until double in bulk (about 1 hour). Bake at 350°F for 20 minutes.

Approximate nutritive values per portion

Calories (kcal)	Protein (grams)	Carbohydrate (grams)	Fat (grams)	Cholesterol (mg)	Sodium (mg)	Iron (mg)	Calcium (mg)
138	3.8 (11%)	21.7 (63%)	4 (26%)	28	245	1.2	26

Note   ■   6 oz nonfat dry milk and 1½ qt water may be substituted for the fluid milk. Combine dry milk with the first portion of flour.

BASIC SWEET ROLL DOUGH

Yield: 8 dozen rolls   *Portion:* 2 oz
Oven: 375°F   *Bake:* 20–25 minutes

Ingredient	Amount	Procedure
Yeast, active dry	2 oz	Soften yeast in warm water.
Water, warm (110°F)	1½ cups	
Water, hot	3 cups	Combine hot water, dry milk, sugar, shortening, and
Nonfat dry milk	3 oz	salt in mixer bowl.
Sugar, granulated	1 lb	Mix until shortening is softened, using dough arm.
Shortening	1 lb	Cool to lukewarm.
Salt	1¾ oz	
Eggs, beaten	9 (1 lb)	Add eggs and yeast to mixture in bowl. Blend.
Flour, all-purpose	5–6 lb (variable)	Add flour gradually on low speed. Mix on medium speed to a smooth dough, 5–6 minutes. Do not overmix. Dough should be moderately soft.

1. The dough temperature just after mixing should be 78°–82°F.
2. Place dough in lightly greased bowl. Grease top of dough, cover, and let rise in warm place until double in bulk, about 2 hours.
3. Punch down and let rise again, about 1 hour.
4. Punch down and divide into portions for rolls. Let rest 10 minutes.
5. Scale 2 oz per roll. Shape (see Variations) and let rise until rolls are almost double in bulk, about 45 minutes.
6. Bake at 375°F for 20–25 minutes.

Approximate nutritive values per portion

Calories (kcal)	Protein (grams)	Carbohydrate (grams)	Fat (grams)	Cholesterol (mg)	Sodium (mg)	Iron (mg)	Calcium (mg)
166	3.8 (9%)	25.3 (61%)	5.5. (30%)	20	212	1.4	19

Notes
- Mixing may be simplified by combining dry yeast with sugar, salt, dry milk, and 2 lb of the flour. Mix thoroughly. Combine eggs, very warm water (120°F), and melted shortening. Add yeast-flour mixture on low speed. Add remaining flour gradually, mixing until a smooth, elastic dough is formed.
- 3 cups fluid milk may be used in place of nonfat dry milk and hot water. Scald milk, then add sugar, salt, and shortening, and cool to lukewarm.
- For a quicker rising dough, increase yeast to 3 oz.

Variations
- **Cherry Nut Rolls.**   Add 1 tsp nutmeg, ½ tsp almond or lemon extract, 1 lb chopped glacé cherries, and 1 lb chopped pecans to dough. Shape into 1-oz balls. When baked, cover with glaze made of orange juice and powdered sugar.

- **Cinnamon Twists.**   Combine 1 lb granulated sugar and 1 Tbsp cinnamon. Melt 4 oz margarine. Dip 2-oz portions of dough into melted margarine, then roll in sugar-cinnamon mixture. Elongate and twist dough portions into 3-inch-long rolls. Place side by side in two 13 × 18-inch baking pans. Bake at 375°F for 20–25 minutes.

- **Coffee Cake.**   Scale 4 lb dough and roll out to size of 18 × 26 × 1-inch baking sheet. Cover top of dough with melted margarine or butter and topping (see p. 180). Fruit fillings may be used also.

- **Crullers.**   Roll dough ⅓ inch thick. Cut into strips ½ × 8 inches. Bring two ends together and twist dough. Let rise, then fry in deep fat. Ice with Powdered Sugar Glaze (p. 228) or dip in fine granulated sugar.

- **Danish Pastry.**   Roll a 5-lb piece of dough into a rectangular shape about ¼ inch thick. Start at one edge and cover completely ⅔ of the dough with small pieces of hard butter, margarine, or special Danish pastry shortening. The latter is stable at bakeshop temperature and is easier to use than butter or margarine. Use 2–5 oz per lb of dough.

  Fold the unbuttered ⅓ portion of dough over an equal portion of buttered dough. Fold the remaining ⅓ buttered dough over the top to make 3 layers of dough separated by a layer of fat. Roll out dough ¼ inch thick. This completes the first roll. Repeat folding and rolling two or more times. Do not allow the fat to become soft while working with the dough. Let dough rest 45 minutes. Make into desired shapes.

- **Hot Cross Buns.**   Add to dough 8 oz chopped glacé cherries, 8 oz raisins, 2 Tbsp cinnamon, ¼ tsp cloves, and ¼ tsp nutmeg. Shape into round buns, 1 oz per bun. When baked, make a cross on top with Powdered Sugar Glaze (Figure 4.12).

- **Kolaches.**   Add 2 Tbsp freshly grated lemon peel to dough. Shape dough into 1-oz balls. Place on lightly greased baking sheet. Let rise until light. Press down center to make cavity and fill with 1 tsp filling. Brush with melted margarine or butter and sprinkle with chopped nuts. Suggested fillings: chopped cooked prunes and dried apricots cooked with sugar and cinnamon; poppy seed mixed with sugar and milk; apricot or peach marmalade.

- **Long Johns.**   Roll out dough to a thickness of ½ inch. Cut dough into rectangular pieces ½ × 4 inches. Let rise until double in bulk. Fry in deep fat.

- **Swedish Braids.**   Add to dough 1 lb chopped candied fruit, 8 oz pecans, and ½ tsp cardamom seed. Weigh dough into 1¾ lb portions and braid. Place on greased 18 × 26 × 1-inch baking sheets, 4 per pan. When baked, brush with Powdered Sugar Glaze (p. 228) made with milk in place of water.

FIGURE 4.12 Yeast breads are made festive by various shapes and icings such as hot cross buns or frosted can-shaped loaves. Used by permission of Red Star Yeast Products, Universal Foods Corporation.

FRUIT COFFEE RINGS

Yield: 8 rings
Oven: 350°F   *Bake:* 30 minutes

Ingredient	Amount	Procedure
Basic Roll Dough (p. 160) or Basic Sweet Roll Dough (p. 170)	10 lb (1 recipe)	Let dough rise until double in bulk. Divide dough into 1½-lb portions. Roll out each portion into a rectangular strip 9 × 14 × ⅓ inches.
Filling (see below)	2 qt	Spread each strip with 1 cup filling. Roll as for Cinnamon Rolls. Arrange in ring mold or 10-inch tube pan. Cut slashes in dough with scissors about 1 inch apart (Figure 4.13). Let rise until double in bulk. Bake at 350°F for 25–30 minutes. Brush with Powdered Sugar Glaze (p. 228).

Suggested Fillings

■ Use 2 qt Apricot Filling (p. 229) or apricot preserves, Fig Filling (p. 229), Prune-Date Filling (p. 229), orange marmalade, or a mixture of 1 lb margarine or butter and 1 lb honey whipped together until light and fluffy. Dough may be shaped in a twist (see Figure 4.14).

FIGURE 4.13   Yeast dough may be filled and shaped into a coffee ring. Used by permission of Red Star Yeast Products, Universal Foods Corporation.

FIGURE 4.14 Nuts, raisins, or other fruits may be added to bread or sweet roll dough and shaped in a twist. Photo supplied by Fleischmann's Yeast, Inc.

CINNAMON ROLLS

Yield: 5 dozen rolls   *Portion:* 3 oz
Oven: 375°F   *Bake:* 20–25 minutes

Ingredient	Amount	Procedure
Basic Roll Dough (p. 160) or Basic Sweet Roll Dough (p. 170)	10 lb (1 recipe)	Let dough rise until double in bulk. Divide dough into 8 portions, 1 lb 4 oz each. Roll each portion into rectangular sheet 9 × 14 × ⅓ inches.
Margarine or butter, melted	12 oz	Spread each sheet with melted margarine.
Sugar, granulated Cinnamon, ground	2 lb 1 oz (4 Tbsp)	Combine sugar and cinnamon. Sprinkle 6 oz over each sheet. Roll as for Jelly Roll (see Figure 4.15). Cut into 1-inch slices. Place cut side down on greased baking sheets, in muffin pans, or round pans (see Figure 4.16). Let rise until double in bulk, about 45 minutes. Bake at 375°F for 20–25 minutes. After removing from oven, spread tops with Powdered Sugar Glaze (p. 228) made with milk in place of water, Peanut Butter Glaze (p. 227), or Chocolate Glaze (p. 227).

Approximate nutritive values per portion

Calories (kcal)	Protein (grams)	Carbohydrate (grams)	Fat (grams)	Cholesterol (mg)	Sodium (mg)	Iron (mg)	Calcium (mg)
351	5.8 (7%)	53.2 (60%)	13.3 (34%)	32	393	2.2	37

Note
- 8 oz brown sugar may be substituted for part of granulated sugar.

Variations
- **Butterfly Rolls.**   Cut rolled dough into 2-inch slices. Press each roll across center parallel to the cut side, with the back of a large knife handle. Press or flatten out the folds of each end. Place on greased baking sheets 1½ inches apart.

- **Butterscotch Rolls.**   Use brown sugar and omit cinnamon, if desired. Cream 8 oz margarine or butter, 1 lb 8 oz brown sugar, and 1 tsp salt. Gradually add 1 cup water, blending thoroughly. Spread 10 oz mixture over each of 4 greased 18 × 26 × 1-inch baking sheets or place 1 Tbsp mixture into each greased muffin pan cup. Place rolls cut side down in pans.

- **Caramel Pecan Rolls.**   Melt 12 oz margarine. Add 1 lb chopped pecans, 2 lb 6 oz brown sugar, and 12 oz light corn syrup. Stir to mix. Scale 1 lb 10 oz into each 12 × 18 × 2-inch pan. Place rolls cut side down onto caramel mixture.

- **Cinnamon Raisin Rolls.** Use brown sugar in place of granulated sugar and add 8 oz raisins to filling.

- **Double Cinnamon Buns.** Proceed as for Butterfly Rolls. Roll sheet of dough from both sides to form a double roll.

- **Glazed Marmalade Rolls.** Omit cinnamon. Dip cut slices in additional melted margarine or butter and granulated sugar. When baked, glaze with orange marmalade mixed with powdered sugar until of a consistency to spread. Apricot marmalade, strawberry jam, or other preserves may be used for the glaze.

- **Honey Rolls.** Substitute honey filling for sugar and cinnamon. Whip 1 lb margarine or butter and 1 lb honey until light and fluffy.

- **Jumbo Cinnamon Rolls.** Use 24 lb dough, 3 lb granulated sugar mixed with 5 Tbsp cinnamon, and 1 lb margarine or butter. Divide dough into four 6-lb portions. Roll each portion into approximately 26 × 26-inch square. Spread with 4 oz softened margarine and sprinkle with 1½ cups sugar-cinnamon mixture. Roll into a 26-inch-long roll. Cut into 12 slices 2 inches thick. Pan 2 × 4 in 12 × 18-inch baking pans. Proof until double in bulk. Bake at 350°F for 25 minutes or until done. Ice with Powdered Sugar Glaze (p. 228).

- **Orange Rolls.** Omit cinnamon. Spread with mixture of 1 lb 8 oz granulated sugar and 1 cup fresh grated orange peel. When baked, brush with a glaze made of powdered sugar and orange juice. If desired, use a filling made by creaming 1 lb margarine or butter, 2 Tbsp fresh grated orange peel, 2 lb granulated sugar, and ¾ cup undiluted frozen orange juice concentrate. Spread on dough.

- **Pecan Rolls.** Coarsely chop 1 lb 8 oz pecans. Sprinkle 8 oz over bottom of each of three 12 × 18 × 2-inch baking pans. Combine 2 lb margarine or butter, 2 Tbsp cinnamon, ⅓ cup corn syrup, ⅓ cup water, and 2 lb 8 oz brown sugar. Cook over medium heat until margarine melts. Pour over chopped nuts, 1 lb 12 oz per pan. Place rolls cut side down on mixture.

- **Sugared Snails.** Proceed as for Butterfly Rolls, rolling dough thinner before adding sugar filling. Cut rolled dough into slices ¾ inch thick. Dip cut surface of each roll in granulated sugar. Place on greased baking sheets ½ inch apart, with sugared side up. Allow to stand 10–15 minutes, then flatten before baking.

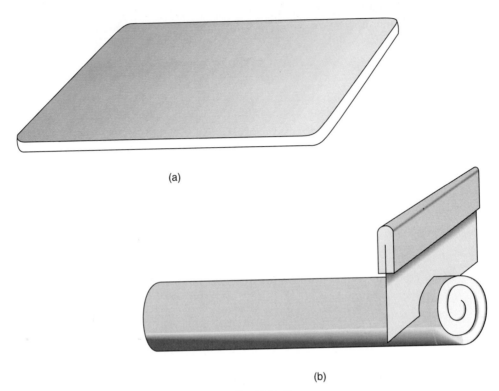

(a)

(b)

FIGURE 4.15 Preparing Cinnamon Rolls. (a) Roll dough into rectangular sheets, brush with melted margarine, and sprinkle with sugar-cinnamon mixture. (b) Roll up as for jelly roll. Cut into 1-inch slices.

FIGURE 4.16   Cinnamon Rolls baked in a round pan. Photo supplied by
Fleischmann's Yeast, Inc.

FILLINGS OR TOPPINGS FOR COFFEE CAKE AND SWEET ROLLS

1. **Almond Filling.** Mix 1 lb almond paste, 1 lb granulated sugar, 12 oz margarine or butter, and 4 oz flour. Add 2 eggs and beat until smooth.

2. **Butter Cinnamon Topping.** Cream 8 oz margarine or butter, 1 lb granulated sugar, 3 Tbsp cinnamon, and ½ tsp salt. Add 4 beaten eggs and 3 oz flour and blend.

3. **Butter Crunch Topping.** Blend 1 lb granulated sugar, 1 lb margarine or butter, ½ tsp salt, 3 oz honey, and 2 lb flour together to form a crumbly mixture.

4. **Crumb Topping.** Mix 8 oz margarine or butter, 12 oz granulated sugar, ½ tsp cinnamon, and 12 oz flour until crumbly. Add 4 oz chopped nuts if desired.

5

Desserts

CAKES AND ICINGS

Cakes may be classified according to two major types: butter or shortened cakes and foam or sponge cakes. Butter cakes contain butter, margarine, or other shortening and usually are leavened with baking powder or with baking soda and an acid. True sponge cakes are leavened chiefly by air incorporated in beaten eggs, although modified sponge cakes may have baking powder added.

A properly balanced formula, correct temperature of ingredients, accurate measurements, controlled mixing of ingredients, proper relationship of batter to pan, and correct oven temperature and baking time are essential to good cake making. Cake flour yields better volume and finer texture than all-purpose flour and was used in testing recipes in this section, unless otherwise specified. If all-purpose flour is used, see Table 1.18 for substitution guidelines.

Methods of Mixing Butter or Shortened Cakes

For all methods of mixing, weigh or measure ingredients accurately and have them at room temperature.

Conventional Method

1. Cream shortening and sugar on medium speed, using flat beater, for about 10 minutes or until light and fluffy.
2. Add eggs and beat 3–5 minutes on high speed. Stop mixer and scrape sides and bottom of bowl and beater. Removing the beater to make sure bottom of bowl is scraped is recommended.

3. Combine flour, leavening, and other dry ingredients. Add alternately with the liquid to the creamed mixture.

4. Mix on low speed until thoroughly blended. Scrape sides of bowl and beater occasionally for even mixing.

Dough-Batter Method

1. Cream flour, baking powder, and shortening on low speed for 2 minutes, using flat beater. Scrape sides of bowl and beater. Mix for 3 minutes.

2. Add sugar, salt, and half the milk. Mix 2 minutes. Scrape bowl and beater. Mix 3 minutes.

3. Combine egg, flavoring, and remaining milk. Add half to flour mixture. Mix 30 seconds. Scrape bowl and beater. Mix 1 minute.

4. Add remaining egg mixture. Mix 1 minute. Scrape bowl and beater. Mix 2½ minutes.

This method requires less time and fewer utensils than the conventional method and yields a good product. See p. 200 for White Cake made by the dough-batter method.

Dry Blending and Wetting Method

1. Blend dry ingredients in mixer bowl and mix on low speed for 1 minute, using flat beater.

2. Add 60 percent of the water to the dry ingredients. Mix slightly; flour is not completely hydrated.

3. Add fat and mix on low speed for 1 minute, then on medium speed for 4 minutes.

4. Add 10 percent of the water. Mix 1 minute on low speed, then 3 minutes on medium speed.

5. Add remainder of water (30 percent), eggs, and flavoring. Mix 3 minutes on low speed.

This method of mixing produces a cake with good volume and fine texture. Converting water from weight to liquid measurements may produce awkward numbers. A small adjustment of the three liquid additions may need to be made for easy measurement, but the total weight of water should be the same as the amount specified in the recipe. See p. 199 for White Cake made by the dry blending and wetting method of mixing.

Muffin Method

1. Mix dry ingredients, including dry milk if used, in a mixer bowl.

2. Combine liquids (beaten eggs, milk or water, and melted shortening or oil).

3. Add liquids all at once to dry ingredients. Mix at low speed only enough to combine ingredients.

This method is quick and most successful when the cake is used soon after baking.

Methods of Mixing Foam or Sponge Cakes

Angel Food Cakes

1. Sift the flour with part of the sugar. This step helps the flour mix more evenly with the foam.

2. Beat the egg whites, using the whip attachment, until they form soft peaks. Egg whites should be at room temperature and all utensils used for whipping must be dry and free from fat or grease. Salt and cream of tartar are added near the beginning of the beating process.

3. Gradually beat in the sugar that was not mixed with the flour. Continue to beat until the egg whites form stiff, glossy peaks. Do not overbeat.

4. Fold in the flour/sugar mixture carefully to minimize loss of air from the foam. Fold until it is absorbed, but no longer.

5. Place in ungreased tube, loaf, or sheet pans and bake immediately.

Sponge Cakes

All egg-foam cakes are similar in that they contain little or no shortening and depend for most or all of their leavening on the air trapped in beaten eggs. However, the whole-egg foams and egg-yolk foams are handled differently from those made with egg whites alone. In sponge cakes, the sugar and liquid are added to the eggs or egg yolks and beaten until light. Dry ingredients are folded in. Chiffon cakes contain baking powder, which is mixed with the flour, and a small amount of fat in the form of vegetable oil that is added to the egg yolks and liquid. The beaten egg whites are folded into the batter.

Cake Mixes

Prepared cake mixes offer the foodservice a wide variety of products that can be produced with fewer and less-skilled employees than cakes prepared "from scratch." However, care should be given to the selection of the mix, and the instructions for preparation should be followed carefully to ensure high-quality products. The formulas in commercial mixes are balanced, and deviations such as the substitution of milk for water or the addition of eggs may change the finished product.

Scaling Batter

Pan Preparation

Prepare pans before mixing cake batters, so that cakes can be baked without delay as soon as they are mixed.

1. For butter cakes, grease pans and line with parchment cake liners or grease and dust with flour. For best results, use a solid shortening. Oil will cause the cake to stick to the pan. A commercial vegetable spray may be used, or a coating mixture may be prepared and brushed on the pans (p. 195). Sides of the pan should be left ungreased unless cakes are to be removed from the pan for layers.

2.   For angel food cakes and other foam cakes, do not grease the pan. The batter must be able to cling to the sides to rise.

Scaling

Butter or other shortened cakes usually are baked as sheet cakes for ease of preparation and serving but may be baked in layers or as cupcakes. Layer cakes may be made by cutting 18 × 26-inch sheet cakes in half or layering two 13 × 18-inch sheet cakes. (See Figure 5.1 for layering and icing a sheet cake.)

The correct amount of cake batter per pan is important in producing a cake with consistently high quality and volume. Table 5.1 gives approximate weights of batter for selected pan sizes. The proper scaling weight for different batters, however, can be determined by actual baking tests and experimentation. Once it has been determined, scaling weights for all pan sizes using the same batter can be calculated mathematically. The formula follows.

FIGURE 5.1   Layering and icing a sheet cake. (a) Remove sheet cake from pan after loosening sides. Place top side down on inverted baking sheet. Spread icing evenly over cake. (b) Carefully turn second cake onto iced layer. (c) Remove cake liner if used. (d) Ice top and sides of cake.

Step 1   Experiment, using any pan, to determine the proper scaling weight.

Step 2   Determine the volume of the pan used, expressed as cubic inches.

square or rectangular pan volume = length × width × height
round pan volume = 3.14 × radius squared × height

Step 3   Determine the cubic inches per ounce of batter (factor) by dividing the cubic inches (as found in Step 2) by the ounces of batter determined to be correct by experimentation in Step 1.

$$\text{factor} = \frac{\text{cubic inches in pan}}{\text{correct scaling weight per pan}}$$

Step 4   Find the proper scaling weight of the particular batter calculated for any pan by dividing the known factor into the pan volume.

$$\frac{\text{volume of cake pan to be used}}{\text{factor}} = \text{proper scaling weight of batter}$$

The following example illustrates the procedure for calculating proper scaling weight for a cake. The proper scaling weight of a 6 × 1½-inch round chocolate cake was determined to be 8 ounces. What would be the scaling weight for the same batter in a 10 × 1½-inch round pan?

Step 1   Through experimentation, it was determined that 8 oz in a 6 × 1½-inch pan was correct.

Step 2   Volume = 3.14 × 3^2 × 1.5 = 42 cubic inches.

Step 3   42 cubic inches ÷ 8 ounces = 5.25 cubic inches per ounce = factor

Step 4   10-inch pan volume = 3.14 × 5 × 1.5 = 118 cubic inches. 118 cubic inches ÷ 5.25 (factor) = 22.5 ounces scaling weight

Baking

Cake structure is fragile, so proper baking conditions are essential for quality products. The following are guidelines for producing quality cakes.

1. Preheat the oven.

2. Make sure oven and shelves are level.

3. Make sure batter is level in the pan and pan is filled in corners.

4. Do not let pans touch each other in the oven. If pans touch, air circulation is inhibited and the cakes rise unevenly.

5. Bake at correct temperature. Too high a temperature can cause tunneling in the cakes, cakes with a cracked top crust, or excessively high peaks. Too low an oven temperature can cause a pale top crust, a top crust that is sticky, or low volume.

6. Do not open ovens or disturb cakes until they have finished rising and are partially browned. In a convection oven, sheet cakes should be turned halfway through the baking time to ensure uniform baking and symmetry.

TABLE 5.1 **Approximate scaling weights and yields for cakes**

Pan size	Approximate weight per pan	Yield	Type of cake
12 × 18 × 2 inches	4–5 lb	30 portions (5 × 6) 32 portions (4 × 8)	Butter, sheet
13 × 18 × 1 inches (half-size baking sheet)	2–2½ lb	48 portions (6 × 8)	Butter, layer
13 × 18 × 1 inches	1¼–1½ lb	12 portions	Sponge or foam, sheet
18 × 26 × 2 inches	8–10 lb	60 portions (6 × 10) 64 portions (8 × 8)	Butter, sheet
8-inch round	16–20 oz per layer	16 portions (2 layers)	Butter, layer
9-inch round	20–24 oz per layer	16 portions (2 layers)	Butter, layer
10-inch tube	28–40 oz	14–16 portions	Foam, sponge
Cupcakes	1¾ oz each		Butter

Note   ■   See p. 187 for scaling weights for icings and fillings.

7. Test for doneness. Cakes are fully baked when cake center springs back when touched lightly. A cake tester inserted near the center of the cake will come out clean. Shortened cakes will shrink away from sides of pan slightly.

Cooling and Removing from Pans

1. Cool butter layer cakes 10–15 minutes before removing from pans. Cool cakes completely before icing.

2. Sheet cakes may be left in the pans and iced when cool or removed from the pan and layered (Figure 5.1).

3. Invert pans of angel food cakes or sponge cakes and cool completely. Be sure the edges of the pan are supported so that the top of the cake does not rest on the table. When cool, loosen cake from sides of pan with spatula or knife and pull out carefully.

Icings and Fillings

The presentation of cakes may be varied by the use of different icings and fillings. The amount to use will depend on the kind of cake to be iced and the individual preference of the patrons. Table 5.2 may serve as a guide. Sheet cakes usually are iced in their baking pans. Layered sheet cakes should be removed from the pans before icing (Figure 5.1). If possible, cakes should be iced as soon as they have cooled to help prevent drying. If uniced cakes will not be used within a short time, they should be covered and kept in a closed cabinet or freezer. To freeze cakes, cover with plastic wrap or put in an airtight container. It is best to freeze cakes uniced. Figure 5.2 suggests cutting configurations for cakes.

TABLE 5.2   Approximate scaling weights for icings and fillings

Pan size	Approximate weight per pan
13 × 18 × 2-inch	1 lb 8 oz (3 cups)
18 × 26 × 2-inch	3 lb (1½ qt)
9-inch layer	1 lb (2 cups)
	⅔ cup in the middle
	1¼ cups top and sides
10-inch tube	12 oz (1½ cups)

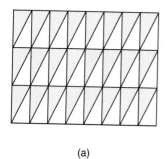

(a)

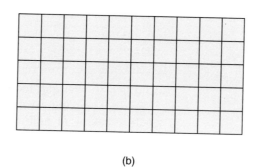

(b)

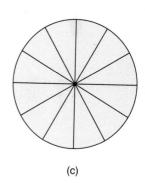

(c)

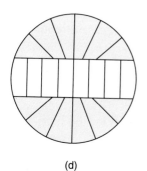

(d)

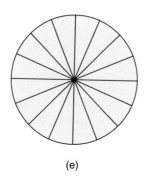

(e)

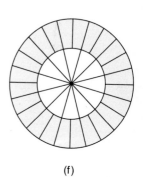

(f)

FIGURE 5.2 Suggested cutting configurations for cakes: (a) 18 × 26-inch baking sheet, 48 portions; (b) 18 × 26-inch baking sheet, 60 portions; (c) 8- to 12-inch round, 12 portions; (d) 10- to 12-inch round, 20 portions; (e) 8- to 12-inch round, 16 portions; (f) 10- to 12-inch round, 36 portions.

Quality Standards for Cakes

Quality standards for butter cakes: Smooth surface, slightly rounded top, high volume; fine-grained, small, evenly distributed cell walls, light but not crumbly; soft texture, velvety, moist, light, tender crumb; delicate, sweet, well-blended flavor. Cakes other than chocolate should be a golden-brown color.

Deviation	Possible Cause
Peaked or cracked	Too much flour, too little liquid, overmixing, oven temperature too high
Flat top	Oven temperature too low. (Some cakes used for layering are formulated for a flat top.)
Pale color	Too little sugar, too much liquid, wrong type pan, underbaked, oven temperature too low
Too dark color	Too much sugar, oven temperature too high, overbaking
Low volume	Too much shortening, too much liquid, insufficient leavening, undermixing, wrong size pan, too long standing time before baking or holding too long in a warm room, oven temperature too high
Large cells	Too little liquid, too much shortening, under- or overmixing, oven temperature too low
Compact texture	Overbeating
Crumbly texture	Too much shortening or sugar, too little liquid, insufficient mixing
Tunnels	Too much egg, too little sugar, overmixing, oven temperature too high, excessive bottom heat
Dry	Too little sugar, too much leavening, overbaking
Soggy	Too much shortening, undermixing, underbaking, improper cooling before covering
Tough	Too much shortening, protein content of flour too high, improper balance of ingredients, overmixed, overbaked, oven temperature too high
Unpleasant flavor	Flat, too little salt, rancid fat
Shrinkage	Oven temperature too low, overbaked

Quality standards for angel, sponge, or chiffon cakes: Thin, golden brown crust, rounded top, slightly split in the middle; fine texture, with thin cell walls, light in weight in proportion to size; moist, tender crumb; delicate flavor.

Deviation	Possible Cause
Thick, hard crust	Oven temperature too low, overbaked
Sticky crust	Too much sugar, insufficient baking
Large cracks	Too stiff a mixture, overbeaten eggs, oven temperature too high
Undersized, heavy	Grease on equipment or bowl, overbeating or underbeating egg whites, overmixing, improper balance of ingredients, oven temperature too high, cakes removed from pan too soon after baking, underbaked
Dry	Overbeaten egg whites, too much flour, too little sugar, overbaked, oven temperature too low
Tough	Oven temperature too high, overmixing, sugar content too high, too much flour or wrong type used
Coarse	Overbeaten egg whites, insufficient mixing, oven temperature too low

COOKIES

Cookies are made in a variety of shapes, sizes, and textures. They may be crisp, soft, or chewy, depending on the proportion of ingredients, the method of mixing, and baking time and temperature.

Proportion of Ingredients

Crisp cookies generally have a low proportion of liquid and a high sugar and fat content. Soft cookies have a high proportion of liquid and are lower in fat and sugar. Chewy cookies have high sugar and liquid content but are low in fat and have a high proportion of eggs. Some cookies are best when the dough spreads some during baking, while others must hold their shape. A high sugar or liquid content may increase cookie spread during baking.

Methods of Mixing

Most cookies are prepared by one of the following methods:

Creaming Method   Cream shortening, sugar, and flavorings at low speed until blended. The amount of creaming can affect the texture of the cookies. A short creaming time is used for a chewy cookie; for a cookie with cakelike texture, the shortening and sugar are creamed until light and fluffy. The amount of creaming may also affect the spread of the cookie while it is baking. After the creaming is completed, blend in the eggs and liquid, then the flour and leavening. Mix the dough only until ingredients are combined.

One-Stage Method   Place all ingredients in the mixer and mix at low speed until blended.

Sponge Method   Beat eggs (white, yolks, or whole) until light. Add the remaining ingredients and blend, being careful not to overmix or deflate the eggs.

Shaping

Drop cookies are made from a soft dough, which is portioned onto prepared baking sheets with a dipper. A No. 40 dipper, which was used for most of the recipes in this book, makes a medium-sized cookie, approximately 2½–3 inches in diameter and weighing about ¾ oz. Larger cookies may be made by using a No. 20 or No. 30 dipper, and Nos. 60 or 70 make tea cookies. If using the recipe for larger or smaller cookies, the yield may need to be adjusted by using the procedure on p. 7.

Bar cookies are made from a soft dough or batter that is spread evenly on prepared baking pans. Most recipes in this section suggest using two 13 × 18 × 1-inch pans (half baking sheet) or one 18 × 26 × 1-inch pan (baking sheet). The 13 × 18-inch pan will yield 30 2½ × 3-inch bars by cutting 5 × 6. An 18 × 26-inch pan may be cut 6 × 10 to yield 60 bars 3 × 2½ inches or 8 × 12 for 96 cookies.

Rolled cookies are made from a stiff dough that has been chilled thoroughly. The dough is rolled out to ⅛ inch thickness on a lightly floured board and cut with a cookie cutter.

Refrigerator cookies are made by shaping dough into rolls of uniform size (1–2 inches in diameter) and chilling, then cutting into slices. Use of a slicing machine ensures uniform thickness. The dough may be made into rolls, wrapped in waxed or parchment paper, refrigerated or frozen and baked as needed.

Molded or pressed cookies are made by shaping dough into small balls, which is then flattened by pressing with a mold or other flat utensil dipped in sugar. Cookies may be shaped also with a cookie press or, if using a soft dough, with a pastry bag.

Baking

Pans are prepared by lightly greasing or lining with baking pan liners. A heavily greased pan increases the spread of the cookie. Some high-fat cookies can be baked on ungreased pans. Most cookies are baked at a relatively high temperature. Too low a temperature increases spreading and may produce dry, pale cookies. Too high a temperature decreases spreading and may burn the edges or bottoms.

Cookies should be watched carefully to prevent overbaking or burning. To test for doneness, touch center of the cookie lightly with a finger. If almost no imprint remains and the cookie is browned it is done. Fudge-type bars will be done when the top has a dull crust, and cakelike bars when a pick inserted in the center comes out clean. Soft cookies should be removed from the oven when they are still soft to the touch.

In most cases, to prevent sticking, the cookies should be removed from pans while they are still warm. If baking pan liners are used, the cookies may be left on the pan to cool. Very soft cookies, however, should not be removed until they are cool and firm enough to handle. Cookies should be completely cooled before storing.

Storing

Proper storage is important to maintain the quality and freshness of cookies. Crisp cookies may become soft if they absorb moisture, so they should be stored loosely covered away from moisture. Soft cookies should be stored tightly covered because they will become dry if allowed to lose moisture. All cookies are best if served soon after baking.

Quality Standards for Cookies

Quality standards for drop cookies: Uniform shape and color; good flavor; crisp or chewy texture (true to type of cookie).

Deviation	Possible Cause
Misshapen	Improper dropping of dough, oven temperature too high or too low, improper mixing
Excessive spreading	Too much liquid, too much fat and sugar, liquid fat substituted for solid fat, overcreaming, dough too warm, incorrect oven temperature, not peaked when dropped, cookies panned too close together
Dry, crumbly texture	Incorrect proportion of ingredients, inaccurate measuring, poor mixing or baking techniques, incorrect oven temperature

Quality standards for bar cookies: Uniform, well-cut shape; rich, moist eating quality; thin, delicate crust; appealing flavor.

Deviation	Possible Cause
Crumbles when cut	Cut while too warm
Dry, crumbly texture	Overbaking, improper proportion of ingredients
Hard, crusty top	Overmixed, overbaked

Quality standards for rolled cookies: Retains shape of cutter; lightly browned surface; crisp or soft texture, depending on thickness.

Deviation	Possible Cause
Tough	Excessive rerolling
Dry	Rolling in too much flour or rerolling

Quality standards for pressed and molded cookies: Well-defined pattern and shape; tender, crisp texture; rich, buttery flavor; delicately browned color.

Deviation	Possible Cause
Misshapen	Improper use of cookie press or poor molding, dough too cold or too warm, dough placed on hot baking sheet, oven temperature too low
Crumbly, dry	Incorrect proportion of ingredients, insufficient shaping

Quality standards for refrigerator cookies: Uniform thin slices, lightly browned surface, crisp and crunchy texture, rich flavor.

Deviation	Possible Cause
Irregular shape	Improper molding of dough roll, dough not chilled before slicing, improper slicing technique
Too soft	Cut too thick

PIES

A good pie has a tender crust that cuts easily and a filling that will just hold its shape when cut. Pie crust is an uncomplicated mixture, consisting of four ingredients: flour, shortening, water, and salt. The quality of the crust depends on the mixing technique as well as the type and proportion of ingredients.

Ingredients

Tenderness depends largely on the kind of flour, the amount of fat and water used, and the amount of mixing. Choice of flour is important in pastry making. Gluten is developed from the protein present in wheat flours and gives structure and strength to baked goods. Pastry flour, which is made from soft wheat, has enough protein to produce the desired structure and flakiness, yet is low enough in protein to yield a tender product if handled properly. All-purpose flour, which is a blend of soft and hard wheats, contains enough protein to provide the gluten essential to make good pastry and is the type of flour used in recipes in this book.

Regular hydrogenated shortening is the fat used most often for pie crusts because it has the right plasticity to produce a flaky crust. It is firm and moldable enough to make a workable dough. The tenderness of pastry increases with the proportion of fat, but excess fat may cause the crust to be too tender to remove from the pan. Shortening should be cool when added to the flour. If it is warm, it blends too quickly with the flour.

Addition of a liquid, generally water, develops some gluten in the flour and gives structure and flakiness to the dough. Excess water gives a less tender product, but if not enough water is used, the crust will not hold together. The water should be cold (35–40°F) when added to the flour/fat mixture.

Salt, which is added mainly for flavor, is dissolved in the water before adding to the mix in order to ensure even distribution.

Mixing

Pastry is mixed by cutting the fat into the flour, then adding water and salt. The type of crust produced is partially determined by the method of combining the fat and flour. For a *flaky* crust, the fat and flour are mixed until small lumps are formed throughout the mixture. A *mealy* crust results when the fat and flour are thoroughly mixed until the mixture resembles cornmeal. Overmixing after the water has been added or using too much flour when rolling toughens pastry.

Pie dough should be kept cool during mixing and makeup. Chilling the dough for several hours, or until 50–60°F, allows the water to become distributed better throughout the dough and hardens the shortening so that it is less likely to soften during handling and shaping operations.

A pie crust mix, made by cutting the fat into the flour and salt mixture, may be stored in the refrigerator for four to six weeks and used as needed by adding water to make fresh pie crusts. If freezer storage is adequate, crusts may be made and frozen unbaked until needed.

Quality Standards for Pastry

Quality standards: Golden brown color, blistery surface, uniform, attractive edges, fits pan well; flaky or mealy texture, cuts easily, pleasant bland flavor.

Deviation	*Possible Cause*
Smooth surface	Overhandling, too much flour when rolling
Shrunken	Stretched crust when easing into pan, overmixing, protein content of flour too high, too much water
Tough	Too much water, overmixing, overhandling, protein content of flour too high
Not flaky	Temperature of dough too high, shortening too soft, overmixing
Too tender	Undermixing, not enough liquid, too much shortening
Soggy bottom crust	Baked too short a time, too much fat in crust, oven temperature too low or not enough bottom heat, using a filling that is too hot
Compact	Underbaking, too much liquid
Dry	Shortening cut in too finely, not enough liquid

OTHER DESSERTS

Although cakes, cookies, and pies remain popular, today's foodservices offer a wide variety of other desserts, such as fruit cobblers and crisps, cheesecake, frozen yogurt and ice cream, and fresh fruits in a variety of presentations. Recipes for many of these desserts are included in this section, as are the time-tested custards and other puddings, gelatin desserts, and refrigerator desserts used in many foodservices.

Basic custard consists of milk, sugar, eggs, and flavoring and may be of two types. Soft or stirred custard is cooked slowly over low heat, while stirring, until it is slightly thickened. It remains pourable when cooked. Baked custard, which is not stirred, is baked until it sets and becomes firm. Custards should be cooked to an internal temperature of 181–185°F. If heated beyond this point, the custard may curdle and become watery. Cooking baked custards in a water bath, in which the custard cups or baking pan are placed in a pan of hot water, helps prevent curdling.

Cream puddings contain starch thickeners as well as eggs, resulting in a thicker, more stable product. The thickener may be cornstarch, flour, tapioca, or a cereal product. These desserts require sweetening, usually sugar. Too much sugar interferes with the thickening of the eggs and the starch; therefore, a properly balanced formula is important. To make a cream pudding, the milk is added slowly to the combined dry ingredients, while stirring with a wire whip. The mixture is stirred occasionally and cooked until thickened in a steam-jacketed or other kettle over low heat to prevent scorching. The method of adding the eggs is also important to a smooth pudding. To avoid curdling when the eggs are added, a small amount of the hot mixture is first added to the beaten eggs, then this mixture is stirred into the rest of the pudding. Cream puddings should be smooth and creamy.

Gelatin desserts, usually in the form of a fruit gelatin or Bavarian Cream, are served as dessert choices in many institutions. A basic recipe for Fruit Gelatin Salad on p. 514 gives proportions for gelatin and fruit and instructions for preparing gelatin mixtures. Bavarian cream has whipped cream folded in.

Fruit offers a wide range of dessert possibilities and may be served fresh, poached, baked, as a sauce or combined with other ingredients to make a baked dessert such as strawberry shortcake, fruit cobbler, or fruit crisp. A fresh-fruit and cheese plate, with in-season fresh fruit and cheese attractively displayed, is a popular dessert. Suggestions for a fruit and cheese dessert are given on p. 301.

CAKE RECIPES

COATING FOR BAKING PANS

Yield: 2 lb 12 oz

Ingredient	Amount	Procedure
Shortening	1 lb	Mix shortening until creamy.
Flour, all-purpose	12 oz	Add flour gradually, whipping until smooth. Start on low mixer speed, then move to medium.
Vegetable oil	2 cups	Add oil very slowly and whip until light and frothy. Store at room temperature in tightly closed containers. Apply to pans with pastry brush. Use to grease cake pans or cookie sheets.

ANGEL FOOD CAKE

Yield: 42 portions or 3 10-inch cakes   *Portion:* 14 slices per cake
Oven: 350°F   *Bake:* 50–55 minutes

Ingredient	Amount	Procedure
Egg whites, fresh or frozen	2 lb 8 oz (5 cups)	Beat egg whites on high speed for 1 minute, using whip attachment. Be sure utensils are free from grease.
Salt Cream of tartar	1 tsp 2 Tbsp	Add salt and cream of tartar. Continue beating until egg whites are just stiff enough to hold their shape.
Sugar, granulated	1 lb 8 oz	Add sugar slowly while beating on medium speed.
Vanilla Almond extract (optional)	1 Tbsp 1 tsp	Add flavorings. Continue beating on high speed for 2 minutes, or until mixture will stand in stiff peaks.
Sugar, granulated Flour, cake	12 oz 12 oz	Mix sugar and flour. Sift three times. Gradually add to egg whites on low speed. Continue folding 2 minutes after last addition. Scale into 3 ungreased tube cake pans, 1 lb 12 oz per pan. Bake at 350°F for 50–55 minutes or at 400°F for 35 minutes. Invert cakes to cool.

Approximate nutritive values per portion							
Calories (kcal)	Protein (grams)	Carbohydrate (grams)	Fat (grams)	Cholesterol (mg)	Sodium (mg)	Iron (mg)	Calcium (mg)
136	3.5 (10%)	31 (89%)	0.07 (0%)	0	96	0.6	3

Note   ■ To add sugar-flour mixture by hand, remove bowl from machine and fold mixture into meringue, using wire whip or spatula, adding 1 cup at a time. Mix about 5 strokes after each addition.

Variations   ■ **Chocolate Angel Food Cake.** Substitute 1½ oz cocoa for 1½ oz flour.

■ **Frozen-Filled Angel Food Cake.** Cut each cake crosswise into 3 slices. Spread 1 pt softened strawberry ice cream on first layer and cover with cake slice. Spread second slice with 1 pt softened pistachio ice cream. Top with remaining slice. Frost top and sides with sweetened whipped cream (1 cup cream, 2 Tbsp powdered sugar, and ½ tsp vanilla per cake). Cover with toasted coconut. Freeze. Remove from freezer 1 hour before serving. Other ice cream or sherbet may be used.

■ **Orange-Filled Angel Food Cake.** Cut each cake crosswise into 3 slices. Spread Orange Filling (p. 231) between layers, and ice top and sides with Orange Icing (p. 224).

YELLOW ANGEL FOOD (EGG YOLK SPONGE CAKE)

Yield: 42 portions or 3 10-inch cakes   *Portion:* 14 slices per cake
Oven: 350°F   *Bake:* 30–45 minutes

Ingredient	Amount	Procedure
Egg yolks	1 lb 8 oz (3 cups)	Beat egg yolks on medium speed, using whip attachment.
Water, boiling	2 cups	Add water to egg yolks. Beat on high speed until light, about 5 minutes.
Sugar, granulated	1 lb	Sift sugar. Add to egg mixture gradually, beating on high speed while adding.
Flour, cake Sugar, granulated	12 oz 12 oz	Combine flour and sugar. Add on low speed to egg mixture.
Flour, cake Baking powder Salt	10 oz 4½ tsp 1 tsp	Mix flour, baking powder, and salt.
Lemon juice Fresh lemon peel, grated	3 Tbsp 1 Tbsp	On low speed, gradually add flour alternately with lemon juice and peel to egg mixture.
Vanilla Lemon extract	1 Tbsp 1½ tsp	Add flavoring and continue mixing on low speed for 2 minutes.
		Scale into 3 ungreased tube cake pans, 1 lb 14 oz per pan. Bake at 350°F for 30–45 minutes. Immediately upon removal from oven, invert cakes to cool.

Approximate nutritive values per portion

Calories (kcal)	Protein (grams)	Carbohydrate (grams)	Fat (grams)	Cholesterol (mg)	Sodium (mg)	Iron (mg)	Calcium (mg)
184	3.9 (8%)	31 (67%)	5.1 (25%)	208	90	1.7	45

ORANGE CHIFFON CAKE

Yield: 42 portions or 3 10-inch cakes   *Portion:* 14 slices per cake
Oven: 350°F   *Bake:* 45–50 minutes

Ingredient	Amount	Procedure
Flour, cake Baking powder Salt Sugar, granulated	1 lb 8 oz 1½ oz (3 Tbsp) 2 tsp 1 lb 3 oz	Combine dry ingredients in mixer bowl. Mix on low speed for about 10 seconds, or until blended, using flat beater.
Egg yolks, beaten Vegetable oil Water	1 lb (2 cups) 1½ cups 1½ cups	Combine egg yolks, salad oil, and water. Add to dry ingredients. Mix on medium speed until smooth.
Orange juice Orange peel, grated	1 cup 2 Tbsp	Add orange juice and peel gradually. Mix well after each addition, but avoid overmixing.
Egg whites Cream of tartar	1 lb 4 oz (2½ cups) 2 tsp	Whip egg whites until foamy. Add cream of tartar and continue beating until egg whites form soft peaks.
Sugar, granulated	1 lb 2 oz	Add sugar gradually and continue beating until very stiff. Fold gently into batter. Scale into 3 ungreased tube cake pans, 2 lb 12 oz per pan. Bake at 350°F for 45–50 minutes. Immediately on removal from oven, invert cakes to cool.
Orange Icing (p. 224)	1½ qt	When cake has cooled, remove from pan and ice.

Approximate nutritive values per portion

Calories (kcal)	Protein (grams)	Carbohydrate (grams)	Fat (grams)	Cholesterol (mg)	Sodium (mg)	Iron (mg)	Calcium (mg)
414	4.7 (4%)	66.2 (62%)	15.6 (33%)	139	268	1.6	61

Variations

- **Cocoa Chiffon Cake.** Omit orange juice and peel. Add 5 oz cocoa to dry ingredients. Increase water to 2⅓ cups. Add 1 Tbsp vanilla.

- **Walnut Chiffon Cake.** Omit orange juice and peel. Increase water to 2⅓ cups. Add 2 Tbsp vanilla and 12 oz finely chopped walnuts. Ice with Burnt Butter Icing (p. 221).

WHITE CAKE (DRY BLENDING METHOD)

Yield: 60 portions or 2 pans 12 × 18 × 2 inches   *Portion:* 2½ × 3 inches
Oven: 350°F   *Bake:* 25–30 minutes

Ingredient	Amount	Procedure
Flour, cake	1 lb 13 oz	Combine dry ingredients in mixer bowl. Mix on low speed for 1 minute.
Sugar, granulated	2 lb 5 oz	
Nonfat dry milk	3 oz	
Salt	4 tsp	
Baking powder	1¾ oz	
Water	1¾ cups	Add water. Mix slightly.
Shortening	1 lb	Add shortening. Mix 1 minute on low speed. Mix 4 minutes on medium speed.
Water	½ cup	Add water. Mix 1 minute on low speed. Scrape bowl. Mix 3 minutes on medium speed. Scrape bowl and beater.
Egg whites	1 lb	Add eggs, water, and vanilla. Mix 3 minutes on low speed.
Eggs, whole	3 oz	
Water	1 cup	
Vanilla	2 Tbsp	
		Scale batter into 2 greased 12 × 18 × 2-inch pans, 4 lb per pan. Bake at 350°F for 25–30 minutes. Cool and frost.

Approximate nutritive values per portion

Calories (kcal)	Protein (grams)	Carbohydrate (grams)	Fat (grams)	Cholesterol (mg)	Sodium (mg)	Iron (mg)	Calcium (mg)
132	2.6 (8%)	12.3 (38%)	7.8 (54%)	6	247	1	74

Note ■ May be baked in one 18 × 26 × 2-inch pan. Cut 6 × 10 for 60 portions.

Variations ■ See p. 200.

WHITE CAKE (DOUGH-BATTER METHOD)

Yield: 60 portions or 2 pans 12 × 18 × 2 inches   *Portion:* 2½ × 3 inches
Oven: 350°F   *Bake:* 35–40 minutes

Ingredient	Amount	Procedure
Flour, cake	2 lb 4 oz	Place flour, baking powder, and shortening in mixer bowl.
Baking powder	1½ oz	
Shortening, hydro-genated	1 lb 2 oz	Mix on low speed for 2 minutes, using flat beater. Scrape sides of bowl. Mix 3 minutes.
Sugar, granulated	2 lb 4 oz	Combine sugar, salt, and milk. Add to flour mixture.
Salt	1 Tbsp	Mix on low speed 2 minutes.
Milk	2 cups	Scrape sides of bowl. Mix 3 minutes.
Egg whites	12 (14 oz)	Combine egg whites, milk, and vanilla.
Milk	1⅓ cups	Add half to mixture in bowl. Mix on low speed for 30 seconds.
Vanilla	2 Tbsp	Scrape sides of bowl. Mix 1 minute.
		Add remaining egg-milk mixture. Mix on low speed for 1 minute.
		Scrape sides of bowl. Mix 2½ minutes.
		Scale batter into 2 greased 12 × 18 × 2-inch pans, 5 lb 7 oz per pan.
		Bake at 350°F for 35–40 minutes.
		Cool and ice.
		Cut 5 × 6.

Approximate nutritive values per portion

Calories (kcal)	Protein (grams)	Carbohydrate (grams)	Fat (grams)	Cholesterol (mg)	Sodium (mg)	Iron (mg)	Calcium (mg)
214	2.5 (5%)	31.3 (58%)	9.1 (38%)	2	196	1.3	64

Notes
- 3 oz nonfat dry milk and 3⅓ cups water may be substituted for fluid milk. Increase shortening to 1 lb 3 oz. Mix dry milk with flour.
- May be baked in one 18 × 26 × 2-inch pan. Cut 6 × 10 for 60 portions.
- For six 9-inch layer pans, scale 1 lb 6 oz per pan.

Variations
- **Chocolate Chip Cake.**   Add 12 oz chocolate chips to batter.
- **Coconut Lime Cake.**   Scale into six 9-inch layer cake pans. When baked, cool, then spread Lime Filling (p. 231) between layers. Ice with Ice Cream Icing (p. 222). Sprinkle with toasted flaked coconut.
- **Cupcakes.**   Portion batter with No. 20 dipper into muffin pans or paper baking cups. Yield: 7 dozen.

- **Lady Baltimore Cake.**   Bake cake in layers. Prepare one recipe Ice Cream Icing (p. 222). To 1½ qt icing, add 1 tsp orange juice, 4 oz macaroon crumbs, 5 oz chopped almonds, and 6 oz chopped raisins. Spread on bottom layers; place second layers on top and spread with filling. Ice tops and sides with remaining frosting.
- **Poppy Seed Cake.**   Add 6 oz poppy seeds that have been soaked in part of the milk. Ice with Chocolate Icing (p. 223).
- **Silver White Cake.**   Scale batter into six 9-inch layer cake pans. When baked, cool and then spread Lemon Filling (p. 231) between layers. Ice with Ice Cream Icing (p. 222).
- **Starburst Cake.**   Bake in two 12 × 18 × 2-inch pans. While cake is warm, perforate top with a meat fork every half inch. Prepare 2 qt flavored gelatin, and while still liquid slowly pour 1 qt over each cake. Cool and ice with Ice Cream Icing (p. 222) or other white icing.

YELLOW CAKE

Yield: 60 portions or 2 pans 12 × 18 × 2 inches   *Portion:* 2½ × 3 inches
Oven: 350°F   *Bake:* 35–40 minutes

Ingredient	Amount	Procedure
Flour, cake	2 lb 5 oz	Place flour, baking powder, and shortening in mixer bowl.
Baking powder	3¾ Tbsp	
Shortening, hydro-genated	1 lb	Mix on low speed for 2 minutes, using flat beater. Scrape sides of bowl. Mix 3 minutes.
Sugar, granulated	2 lb 13 oz	Combine sugar, salt, and milk. Add to flour mixture.
Salt	2 tsp	Mix on low speed 2 minutes.
Milk	2 cups	Scrape sides of bowl. Mix 3 minutes.
Eggs	8 (14 oz)	Combine eggs, milk, and vanilla.
Milk	2½ cups	Add half to flour mixture. Mix on low speed 30 seconds.
Vanilla	2 Tbsp	Scrape sides of bowl. Mix 1 minute. Add remaining egg mixture. Mix 1 minute. Scrape sides of bowl. Mix 2½ minutes.
		Scale batter into 2 greased 12 × 18 × 2-inch baking pans 4 lb 10 oz per pan. Bake at 350°F for 35–40 minutes. Cut 5 × 6.

Approximate nutritive values per portion

Calories (kcal)	Protein (grams)	Carbohydrate (grams)	Fat (grams)	Cholesterol (mg)	Sodium (mg)	Iron (mg)	Calcium (mg)
233	2.9 (5%)	36.1 (61%)	9 (34%)	31	143	1.4	62

Notes

- 4 oz nonfat dry milk and 4½ cups water may be substituted for fluid milk. Add dry milk to flour mixture. Divide water as stated in recipe.
- May be baked in one 18 × 26 × 2-inch pan. Cut 6 × 10 for 60 portions.
- For layer cakes, scale 1 lb 9 oz batter into each of six 9-inch layer cake pans.
- For cupcakes, portion with No. 30 dipper into muffin pan. Yield 8½ dozen.

Variations

- **Boston Cream Pie.** For two 12 × 18-inch pies, scale batter into 4 pans, 2 lb 5 oz each. When baked, spread Custard Filling (p. 230) on 2 cakes, 3 lb 3 oz each. Place other cakes on top. Cover with Chocolate Glaze (p. 227), 1 lb per cake. Cut 5 × 6.

    For two 18 × 26-inch pies, scale 4 lb 10 oz into each of 2 pans. Use 6 lb 6 oz Custard Filling and 2 lb Chocolate Glaze. Cut 6 × 10.

    For 9-inch layers, scale batter into 8 pans, 1 lb 2 oz per pan. Use ½ recipe Custard Filling. Spread 1½ cups on each of 4 layers. Use ½ recipe Chocolate Glaze, spreading ½ cup on each pie.

    Powdered sugar sifted over top of pies may be substituted for Chocolate Glaze.

- **Cottage Pudding.**   Cut cake into squares and serve with No. 20 dipper of fruit, lemon, nutmeg, or other sauce.

- **Dutch Apple Cake.**   After the cake batter is poured into baking pans, arrange 2 lb 8 oz peeled sliced apples in rows over each pan. Sprinkle over top of each pan 4 oz granulated sugar and 1 tsp cinnamon, mixed.

- **Lazy Daisy Cake.**   Mix 1 lb 2 oz melted margarine or butter, 2 lb brown sugar, 2 lb coconut, and 1½ cups half and half, or enough to moisten to consistency for spreading. Spread over baked cake, 3 lb per pan, and brown under the broiler or in the oven.

- **Marble Cake.**   Divide batter into 2 portions after mixing. To 1 portion add 3 Tbsp cocoa, 1 Tbsp cinnamon, and 1 tsp nutmeg. Place batters alternately in cake pans; swirl with knife.

- **Pineapple Upside-Down Cake.**   Mix 1 No. 10 can drained crushed pineapple (or tidbits), 8 oz melted margarine or butter, 12 oz brown sugar, and 8 oz chopped nuts. Pour 4 lb 3 oz in each 12 × 18-inch baking pan. Pour cake batter over mixture. Apricots or peaches may be substituted for pineapple.

- **Praline Cake.**   Substitute chopped pecans for coconut in Lazy Daisy Cake.

CARROT CAKE

Yield: 60 portions or 2 pans 12 × 18 × 2 inches   *Portion:* 2½ × 3 inches
Oven: 325°F   *Bake:* 40–45 minutes

Ingredient	Amount	Procedure
Sugar, granulated Vegetable oil Eggs	2 lb 6 oz 2½ cups 1 lb (9)	Combine sugar, oil, and eggs. Beat 2 minutes on medium speed, using flat beater.
Flour, all-purpose Salt Baking soda Cinnamon, ground	1 lb 12 oz 1 oz (1½ Tbsp) ⅔ oz (5 tsp) ⅔ oz (3 Tbsp)	Combine dry ingredients. Add to oil mixture and beat 1 minute.
Carrots, raw, grated Nuts, chopped	2 lb 8 oz 1 lb	Add carrots and nuts. Mix until blended.
		Scale batter into 2 greased 12 × 18 × 2-inch pans, 5 lb per pan. Bake at 325°F for 40–45 minutes. Ice with Cream Cheese Icing (p. 224). Cut 5 × 6.

Approximate nutritive values per portion

Calories (kcal)	Protein (grams)	Carbohydrate (grams)	Fat (grams)	Cholesterol (mg)	Sodium (mg)	Iron (mg)	Calcium (mg)
261	4 (6%)	31.9 (47%)	14 (47%)	32	246	1.2	36

Note   ■ May be baked in one 18 × 26 × 2-inch pan cut 6 × 10 for 60 portions.

APPLESAUCE CAKE

Yield: 60 portions or 2 pans 12 × 18 × 2 inches   *Portion:* 2½ × 3 inches
Oven: 350°F   *Bake:* 40–45 minutes

Ingredient	Amount	Procedure
Shortening, hydro-genated	1 lb	Cream shortening and sugar on medium speed for 10 minutes, using flat beater.
Sugar, granulated	1 lb 14 oz	
Eggs	8 (14 oz)	Add eggs to creamed mixture. Mix on medium speed for 5 minutes.
Flour, cake	1 lb 12 oz	Combine dry ingredients.
Baking powder	2½ Tbsp	
Salt	1¾ tsp	
Baking soda	½ tsp	
Cinnamon, ground	2½ tsp	
Cloves, ground	1 tsp	
Nutmeg, ground	1 tsp	
Water	2½ cups	Add dry ingredients alternately with water on low speed to creamed mixture, ending with dry ingredients.
Applesauce	2½ cups	Add remaining ingredients. Mix on low speed only to blend.
Raisins	1 lb 4 oz	
Nuts, chopped	10 oz	
		Scale batter into 2 greased 12 × 18 × 2-inch baking pans, 5 lb per pan. Bake at 350°F for 40–45 minutes. Cool and ice. See Notes for suggested icings. Cut 5 × 6.

Approximate nutritive values per portion

Calories (kcal)	Protein (grams)	Carbohydrate (grams)	Fat (grams)	Cholesterol (mg)	Sodium (mg)	Iron (mg)	Calcium (mg)
243	3.2 (5%)	35.4 (56%)	10.9 (39%)	28	116	1.5	48

Notes
- May be baked in one 18 × 26 × 2-inch pan. Cut 6 × 10 for 60 portions.
- This cake is too tender to bake in layers.
- Suggested icings: Ice Cream Icing (p. 222) or Cream Cheese Icing (p. 224).

BANANA CAKE

Yield: 48 portions or 3 2-layer cakes (9-inch)   *Portion:* 16 slices per cake
Oven: 350°F   *Bake:* 25–30 minutes

Ingredient	Amount	Procedure
Shortening, hydro-genated	1 lb	Cream shortening, sugar, and vanilla on medium speed for 10 minutes, using flat beater.
Sugar, granulated	2 lb	
Vanilla	1 Tbsp	
Eggs	8 (14 oz)	Add eggs to creamed mixture and mix on medium speed for 3 minutes, then add bananas and mix for an additional 2 minutes.
Bananas, mashed	2 lb (4 cups)	
Flour, cake	2 lb	Combine dry ingredients.
Salt	1¼ tsp	
Baking powder	3⅓ Tbsp	
Baking soda	2 tsp	
Buttermilk	1 cup	Add dry ingredients alternately with buttermilk on low speed. Mix on medium speed 2–3 minutes.
		Scale batter into 6 greased 9-inch layer cake pans, 1 lb 6 oz per pan. Bake at 350°F for 25–30 minutes. Cool. Remove from pans and ice. See Notes for suggesting icings.

Approximate nutritive values per portion

Calories (kcal)	Protein (grams)	Carbohydrate (grams)	Fat (grams)	Cholesterol (mg)	Sodium (mg)	Iron (mg)	Calcium (mg)
256	2.9 (5%)	38.7 (59%)	10.6 (36%)	35	167	1.6	52

Notes

- May be baked in two 12 × 18 × 2-inch pans, scaled 4 lb 3 oz per pan. Cut 5 × 6 for 30 portions per pan.
- For sheet cake, bake in one 18 × 26 × 2-inch pan. Cut 6 × 10 for 60 portions. Suggested icings: Creamy Icing (p. 224) or Cream Cheese Icing (p. 224).

BURNT SUGAR CAKE

Yield: 60 portions or 2 pans 12 × 18 × 2 inches   *Portion:* 2½ × 3 inches
Oven: 375°F   *Bake:* 35–40 minutes

Ingredient	Amount	Procedure
Sugar, granulated Shortening, hydro- genated	2 lb 11 oz 1 lb	Cream shortening and sugar on medium speed for 10 minutes, using flat beater.
Egg yolks	8 (5 oz)	Add egg yolks to creamed mixture and mix on medium speed for 5 minutes.
Milk Water Burnt sugar syrup (see Notes) Vanilla	2 cups 2 cups ⅔ cup 4 tsp	Combine liquids.
Flour, cake Baking powder Salt	2 lb 2 oz 2⅔ Tbsp 1¼ tsp	Combine dry ingredients. On low speed, add to creamed mixture alternately with liquids. Scrape sides of bowl. Mix 2 minutes.
Egg whites	8 (9 oz)	Beat egg whites until they form soft peaks. Fold into batter on low speed.
		Scale batter into 2 greased 12 × 18 × 2-inch baking pans, 4 lb 8 oz per pan. Bake at 375°F for 35–40 minutes. Cool and ice. See Notes for suggested icings. Cut 5 × 6.

Approximate nutritive values per portion

Calories (kcal)	Protein (grams)	Carbohydrate (grams)	Fat (grams)	Cholesterol (mg)	Sodium (mg)	Iron (mg)	Calcium (mg)
229	2.4 (4%)	36.5 (62%)	8.7 (33%)	31	98	1.3	41

Notes

- **Burnt Sugar Syrup.**   Place ⅓ cup granulated sugar in pan and melt slowly, stirring constantly. Cook until light brown (caramelized), being careful not to scorch. Add ⅓ cup boiling water. Cook slowly until a syrup is formed. For larger amounts, use 1 lb sugar and 2 cups boiling water.

- May be baked in one 18 × 26 × 2-inch pan cut 6 × 10; or in eight 9-inch layers, scaled 1 lb 2 oz per pan.

- Suggested icings: Burnt Butter Icing (p. 221), Creamy Icing (p. 224), Cream Cheese Icing (p. 224), or Ice Cream Icing (p. 222).

CHOCOLATE CAKE

Yield: 60 portions or 2 pans 12 × 18 × 2 inches   *Portion:* 2½ × 3 inches
Oven: 350°F   *Bake:* 25–30 minutes

Ingredient	Amount	Procedure
Flour, cake	1 lb 8 oz	Combine dry ingredients in mixer bowl.
Cocoa	5 oz	Mix on low speed for 1 minute, using flat beater.
Sugar, granulated	2 lb 5 oz	
Nonfat dry milk	2½ oz	
Salt	1 Tbsp	
Baking powder	1 oz	
Baking soda	3½ tsp	
Water	1½ cups	Add to dry ingredients.
Shortening	1 lb	Mix on low speed for 1 minute.
		Mix on medium speed for 3 minutes.
		Scrape sides of bowl and beater.
Water	1½ cups	Add and mix on low speed for 1 minute.
		Mix on medium speed for 2 minutes.
Eggs	10 (1 lb 2 oz)	Blend in eggs. Mix on low speed for 2 minutes.
Water	1 cup	
Vanilla	¼ cup	
		Scale batter into 2 greased 12 × 18 × 2-inch baking pans, 4 lb 2 oz per pan.
		Bake at 350°F for 25–30 minutes.
		Cool and ice. See Notes for suggested icings.
		Cut 5 × 6.

Approximate nutritive values per portion

Calories (kcal)	Protein (grams)	Carbohydrate (grams)	Fat (grams)	Cholesterol (mg)	Sodium (mg)	Iron (mg)	Calcium (mg)
198	2.9 (6%)	28.8 (56%)	8.7 (38%)	36	221	1.8	55

Notes
- Cake may be baked in one 18 × 26 × 2-inch pan. Cut 6 × 10 for 60 servings.
- Suggested icings: Chocolate Butter Cream Icing (p. 223), Mocha Icing (p. 226), or Ice Cream Icing (p. 222).

FUDGE CAKE

Yield: 48 portions or 3 2-layer cakes (9-inch)   *Portion:* 16 slices per cake
Oven: 350°F   *Bake:* 25–30 minutes

Ingredient	Amount	Procedure
Shortening, hydrogenated	12 oz	Cream shortening, sugar, and vanilla on medium speed for 10 minutes, using flat beater.
Sugar, granulated	2 lb	
Vanilla	1 Tbsp	
Eggs	6 (10 oz)	Add eggs and mix on medium speed for 5 minutes.
Cocoa	5 oz	Mix cocoa and hot water.
Water, hot	1½ cups	
Flour, cake	1 lb 12 oz	Combine flour, salt, and soda.
Salt	1 tsp	
Baking soda	1½ Tbsp	
Buttermilk	3 cups	Add dry ingredients alternately with buttermilk and cocoa to creamed mixture on low speed. Scrape sides of bowl and beater. Continue mixing until smooth and ingredients are mixed.
		Scale batter into 6 greased 9-inch layer cake pans, 1 lb 4 oz per pan. Bake at 350°F for 25–30 minutes. Cool. Remove from pans and ice. See Notes.

Approximate nutritive values per portion

Calories (kcal)	Protein (grams)	Carbohydrate (grams)	Fat (grams)	Cholesterol (mg)	Sodium (mg)	Iron (mg)	Calcium (mg)
215	3.2 (6%)	34.4 (61%)	8.2 (33%)	26	147	2.3	28

Notes
- For 12 × 18-inch layer cake, scale into two 12 × 18 × 2-inch or two 13 × 18 × 1-inch pans, 3 lb 13 oz per pan. When baked and cooled, ice one cake, then remove cake from pan and place on top (see Figure 5.1). Ice top and sides.
- Suggested icings: Chocolate Butter Cream Icing (p. 223), Ice Cream Icing (p. 222), or Mocha Icing (p. 226).

Variations
- **Chocolate Cupcakes.**   Portion with No. 20 dipper into muffin pans or paper liners. Yield: 5 dozen.
- **Chocolate Sheet Cake.**   Bake in one 18 × 26 × 2-inch baking pan. Cut 6 × 10 for 60 portions.

GERMAN SWEET CHOCOLATE CAKE ■

Yield: 60 portions or 2 pans 12 × 18 × 2 inches   *Portion:* 2½ × 3 inches
Oven: 350°F   *Bake:* 40–45 minutes

Ingredient	Amount	Procedure
German sweet choc- olate	10 oz	Melt chocolate in water. Cool. Add vanilla. Set aside.
Water, boiling	1¼ cups	
Vanilla	2½ tsp	
Shortening, hydro- genated	1 lb 4 oz	Cream shortening and sugar on medium speed for 10 minutes, using flat beater.
Sugar, granulated	2 lb 8 oz	
Egg yolks	10 (6 oz)	Add egg yolks one at a time. Beat well after each addition. Add chocolate mixture and blend.
Flour, cake	1 lb 9 oz	Combine flour, salt, and soda.
Salt	1¼ tsp	
Baking soda	2½ tsp	
Buttermilk	2½ cups	Add dry ingredients alternately with buttermilk to creamed mixture. Mix on low speed until smooth. Scrape sides of bowl.
Egg whites	10 (11 oz)	Beat egg whites until stiff peaks form. Fold into batter on low speed. Do not overmix. Scale batter into 2 greased 12 × 18 × 2-inch baking pans, 4 lb 7 oz per pan. Bake at 350°F for 40–45 minutes.
Coconut Pecan Icing (p. 221)	2 qt	When cool, ice with Coconut Pecan Icing. Cut 5 × 6.

Approximate nutritive values per portion

Calories (kcal)	Protein (grams)	Carbohydrate (grams)	Fat (grams)	Cholesterol (mg)	Sodium (mg)	Iron (mg)	Calcium (mg)
375	4 (4%)	43.5 (45%)	22.1 (51%)	63	146	1.4	48

Notes
- ■ May be baked in one 18 × 26 × 2-inch pan. Cut 6 × 10 for 60 portions.
- ■ For four 2-layer cakes, scale into eight 9-inch layer cake pans, 1 lb 1 oz per pan. Cut 16 slices per cake for 64 portions.

PEANUT BUTTER CAKE

Yield: 60 portions or 1 pan 18 × 26 × 2 inches   *Portion:* 2½ × 3 inches
Oven: 350°F   *Bake:* 30–35 minutes

Ingredient	Amount	Procedure
Margarine	9 oz	Cream margarine, peanut butter, and sugar for 15 minutes, using flat beater. Scrape bottom and sides of bowl after each 5 minutes.
Peanut butter, creamy	12 oz	
Sugar, granulated	2 lb 2 oz	
Eggs	8 oz (5)	Add to creamed mixture.
Vanilla	2 Tbsp	
Flour, all-purpose	1 lb 12 oz	Combine flour, baking powder, and salt.
Baking powder	½ oz (3½ tsp)	
Baking soda	1 oz (2⅓ Tbsp)	
Buttermilk	4⅔ cups	Add dry ingredients and buttermilk alternately to creamed mixture. Scrape bottom and sides of bowl after each addition.
		Scale 8 lb batter into one 18 × 26 × 2-inch baking pan. Bake at 350°F for 30–35 minutes or until cake springs back when lightly depressed in the center.
Peanut Butter Icing (p. 225)	2 qt	Ice with Peanut Butter Icing.

Approximate nutritive values per portion

Calories (kcal)	Protein (grams)	Carbohydrate (grams)	Fat (grams)	Cholesterol (mg)	Sodium (mg)	Iron (mg)	Calcium (mg)
331	4.5 (5%)	51.8 (61%)	12.8 (34%)	16	257	0.8	45

Notes
- ½ oz (1 Tbsp) caramel food color may be added for a darker color.
- May be baked in two 12 × 18 × 2-inch pans. Scale 4 lb batter per pan.

PINEAPPLE CASHEW CAKE ◼

Yield: 40 portions or 3 2-layer cakes (9-inch)   *Portion:* 16 slices per cake
Oven: 350°F   *Bake:* 25–30 minutes

Ingredient	Amount	Procedure
Margarine or butter	1 lb 2 oz	Cream margarine, sugar, and vanilla on medium speed for 10 minutes, using flat beater.
Sugar, granulated	1 lb 14 oz	
Vanilla	1 Tbsp	
Egg yolks	10 (6 oz)	Add egg yolks in 3 portions, while creaming. Mix 2 minutes.
Flour, cake	1 lb 14 oz	Combine flour, baking powder, and salt.
Baking powder	1½ oz	
Salt	1½ tsp	
Milk	2¼ cups	Add dry ingredients alternately with milk on low speed to creamed mixture.
Crushed pineapple, drained	1 lb	Add pineapple to batter. Mix on low speed only to blend.
Egg whites	10 (11 oz)	Beat egg whites on high speed until stiff but not dry. Fold into batter on low speed. Scale batter into 6 greased 9-inch layer cake pans, 1 lb 5 oz per pan. Bake at 350°F for 25–30 minutes.
Pineapple Butter Icing (p. 220)	2 qt	When cool, remove cake from pans. Cover with icing and sprinkle with toasted cashews.
Cashew nuts, toasted, coarsely chopped	8 oz	

Approximate nutritive values per portion

Calories (kcal)	Protein (grams)	Carbohydrate (grams)	Fat (grams)	Cholesterol (mg)	Sodium (mg)	Iron (mg)	Calcium (mg)
515	4.9 (4%)	72.9 (55%)	24 (41%)	56	450	2.1	105

Note   ◼ May be baked in one 18 × 26 × 2-inch pan, cut 6 × 10 for 60 portions; or in two 12 × 18 × 2-inch pans, scaled 4 lb per pan, and cut 5 × 6 for 30 portions per pan.

FRUITCAKE

Yield: 64 portions or 4 loaves 5 × 9 inches   *Portion:* ½-inch slice
Oven: 300°F   *Bake:* 2½ hours

Ingredient	Amount	Procedure
Shortening, hydro-genated	8 oz	Cream shortening and sugar on medium speed for 10 minutes, using flat beater.
Sugar, granulated	1 lb	
Eggs	4 (7 oz)	Add eggs to creamed mixture. Mix 5 minutes.
Jelly	8 oz	Add ingredients in order listed.
Cinnamon, ground	2 tsp	Mix on low speed only until fruit is coated with flour mixture.
Cloves, ground	2 tsp	
Raisins	2 lb	
Currants	1 lb	
Dates, chopped	1 lb	
Nuts	8 oz	
Flour, cake	1 lb 4 oz	
Baking soda	2 tsp	Dissolve soda in cold coffee.
Coffee, brewed, cold	1½ cups	Add to other ingredients and mix until blended.
		Scale batter into 4 loaf pans (5 × 9 × 2¾ inches) lined with 2 layers of heavy waxed paper, 2 lb 3 oz per pan.
		Bake at 300°F for 2½ hours.
		Cut 16 slices per cake.

Approximate nutritive values per portion

Calories (kcal)	Protein (grams)	Carbohydrate (grams)	Fat (grams)	Cholesterol (mg)	Sodium (mg)	Iron (mg)	Calcium (mg)
192	2.5 (5%)	34.8 (69%)	5.9 (26%)	13	33	1.3	26

Notes
- May be steamed for 4 hours.
- Store in a container with a tight cover. Most fruitcakes mellow in flavor if kept about 2 weeks before using.

GINGERBREAD

Yield: 60 portions or 2 pans 12 × 18 × 2 inches   *Portion:* 2½ × 3 inches
Oven: 350°F   *Bake:* 40 minutes

Ingredient	Amount	Procedure
Shortening, hydro-genated	14 oz	Cream shortening and sugar on medium speed for 10 minutes, using flat beater.
Sugar, granulated	14 oz	
Molasses	3½ cups	Add molasses and mix on low speed until blended.
Flour, cake	2 lb 4 oz	Combine dry ingredients.
Baking soda	2 Tbsp	
Salt	1½ tsp	
Cinnamon, ground	1 Tbsp	
Cloves, ground	1 Tbsp	
Ginger, ground	1 Tbsp	
Water, hot	3¾ cups	Add dry ingredients alternately with water to creamed mixture.
Eggs, beaten	7 (12 oz)	Add eggs and mix on low speed 2 minutes. Scale batter into 2 greased 12 × 18 × 2-inch baking pans, 4 lb 3 oz per pan. Bake at 350°F for 40 minutes. Sprinkle with powdered sugar and serve warm or serve with Lemon Sauce (p. 608). Cut 5 × 6.

Calories (kcal)	Protein (grams)	Carbohydrate (grams)	Fat (grams)	Cholesterol (mg)	Sodium (mg)	Iron (mg)	Calcium (mg)
201	2.1 (4%)	32.3 (63%)	7.4 (32%)	24	146	2.2	39

Approximate nutritive values per portion

Note ■ May be baked in one 18 × 26 × 2-inch pan. Cut 6 × 10 for 60 portions.

Variations ■ **Almond Meringue Gingerbread.** Cover baked Gingerbread with Meringue (p. 259). Sprinkle with slivered or chopped almonds and brown in 375°F oven.

■ **Ginger Muffins.** Measure into greased muffin pans with No. 20 dipper. Yield: 7 dozen.

■ **Praline Gingerbread.** Combine 1 lb melted margarine or butter, 2 lb brown sugar, 2 lb chopped pecans, and 1½–2 cups cream. Spread 2 lb 12 oz mixture over each pan. Brown under broiler, or return to oven and heat until topping is slightly browned.

POUND CAKE

Yield: 48 portions or 2 cakes (10-inch tube pans)   *Portion:* 24 slices per cake
Oven: 325°F   *Bake:* 1 hour 15 minutes

Ingredient	Amount	Procedure
Flour, cake Sugar, granulated Salt Baking powder	1 lb 10 oz 2 lb 1 Tbsp ½ tsp	Combine dry ingredients in mixer bowl. Blend on low speed for 1 minute, using flat beater.
Eggs	10 (1 lb 2 oz)	Add eggs to dry ingredients. Mix until ingredients are mixed evenly and lumps disappear. Batter will be stiff.
Shortening Milk	1 lb 2 oz ¼ cup	Add shortening and milk to mixture in bowl. Cream on medium speed until very light, about 10 minutes.
Milk Almond extract Vanilla	1½ cups 1½ tsp 1½ tsp	Add milk and extracts slowly. Mix on low speed for 2–3 minutes or just until blended.
		Scale batter into 2 greased 10-inch tube pans, 3 lb 6 oz per pan. Bake at 325°F for 1 hour 15 minutes to 1 hour 25 minutes, or until cake tests done. Drop bottom of cake pans onto counter from a distance of 2–3 inches as cakes are removed from oven to produce a compact texture. Cool. Remove from pans. Cut into 24 slices.

Approximate nutritive values per portion

Calories (kcal)	Protein (grams)	Carbohydrate (grams)	Fat (grams)	Cholesterol (mg)	Sodium (mg)	Iron (mg)	Calcium (mg)
243	2.9 (5%)	31.5 (51%)	12.1 (44%)	46	155	1.3	21

Note

- May be baked in four loaf pans (5 × 9 × 2¾ inches), 1 lb 10 oz batter per pan. Cut in 12 slices.

PUMPKIN CAKE

Yield: 48 portions or 3 cakes (10-inch tube pans)   *Portion:* 16 slices per cake
Oven: 350°F   *Bake:* 60–70 minutes

Ingredient	Amount	Procedure
Eggs	12 (1 lb 4 oz)	Beat eggs on medium speed until blended.
Sugar, granulated	2 lb 10 oz	Add sugar to eggs gradually, beating on high speed until thick and lemon colored.
Vegetable oil	1 qt	Add oil very slowly on low speed.
Flour, all-purpose	2 lb 10 oz	Combine dry ingredients in a separate bowl.
Baking powder	2 Tbsp	
Baking soda	2 Tbsp	
Salt	1 Tbsp	
Cinnamon, ground	3 Tbsp	
Pumpkin, canned	3 lb	On low speed, add pumpkin alternately with dry ingredients, beginning and ending with dry ingredients.
		Scale batter into 3 ungreased 10-inch tube pans, 3 lb 12 oz per pan. Bake at 350°F for 60–70 minutes. When cool, remove from pans and drizzle with Powdered Sugar Glaze (p. 228).

Approximate nutritive values per portion

Calories (kcal)	Protein (grams)	Carbohydrate (grams)	Fat (grams)	Cholesterol (mg)	Sodium (mg)	Iron (mg)	Calcium (mg)
373	4.4 (5%)	46.6 (49%)	19.7 (46%)	50	289	1.9	46

CHOCOLATE ROLL

Yield: 48 portions or 4 pans 12 × 18 × 2 inches   *Portion:* 1-inch slice
Oven: 325°F   *Bake:* 20 minutes

Ingredient	Amount	Procedure
Egg yolks	24 (14 oz)	Beat egg yolks on high speed, using flat beater.
Sugar, granulated	2 lb 4 oz	Add sugar and continue beating until mixture is lemon colored, thick, and fluffy.
Unsweetened chocolate, melted Vanilla	12 oz 2 Tbsp	Add chocolate and vanilla. Blend on low speed.
Flour, cake Baking powder Salt	9 oz 1 Tbsp 1½ tsp	Combine flour, baking powder, and salt. Add to creamed mixture on low speed.
Egg whites	24 (1 lb 11 oz)	Beat egg whites on high speed until they form rounded peaks. Fold into cake mixture on low speed. Scale batter, 1 lb 7 oz per pan, into 4 greased 12 × 18 × 2-inch pans lined with baking liners. Bake at 325°F for 20 minutes.
		When baked, remove from pans and quickly remove baking liner. Trim edges if hard. Roll (Figure 5.3) and let stand a few minutes. Unroll and spread with one of the fillings suggested (see Note). Roll up securely. Cover with a thin layer of Chocolate Icing (p. 222).

Approximate nutritive values per portion

Calories (kcal)	Protein (grams)	Carbohydrate (grams)	Fat (grams)	Cholesterol (mg)	Sodium (mg)	Iron (mg)	Calcium (mg)
174	4.3 (9%)	28.2 (60%)	6.3 (31%)	106	115	1.2	31

Note   ■ Suggested fillings: Custard Filling (p. 230) or whipped cream, plain or flavored with peppermint.

Variation   ■ **Ice Cream Roll.** Spread with a thick layer of softened vanilla ice cream. Roll up securely and wrap in waxed paper. Place in freezer for several hours before serving.

JELLY ROLL

Yield: 48 portions or 4 pans 12 × 18 × 2 inches   *Portion:* 1-inch slice
Oven: 375°F   *Bake:* 12 minutes

Ingredient	Amount	Procedure
Eggs	27 (3 lb)	Beat eggs on high speed for 1–2 minutes, using flat beater.
Sugar, granulated Vanilla	3 lb 1 Tbsp	Add sugar and vanilla to eggs. Beat 10–15 minutes.
Flour, cake Cream of tartar Baking powder Salt	1 lb 8 oz 2 Tbsp 2 Tbsp 2 tsp	Mix dry ingredients. Fold on low speed into egg-sugar mixture.
		Scale batter, 1 lb 14 oz per pan, into 4 greased 12 × 18 × 2-inch baking pans lined with baking liners. Bake at 375°F for 12 minutes.
		When baked, turn onto a cloth or heavy paper covered with powdered sugar (Figure 5.3). Quickly remove baking liners and trim edges if hard. Immediately roll cakes tightly.
Jelly or Custard Filling (p. 230)	1 qt	When cooled but not cold, unroll, spread with jelly or Custard Filling, 1 cup per roll. Roll firmly and wrap with waxed paper.
Sugar, powdered	1 lb	Sprinkle top of each roll with 4 oz powdered sugar. Slice each roll into 12 portions.

Approximate nutritive values per portion

Calories (kcal)	Protein (grams)	Carbohydrate (grams)	Fat (grams)	Cholesterol (mg)	Sodium (mg)	Iron (mg)	Calcium (mg)
305	4.7 (6%)	66.7 (85%)	2.9 (9%)	121	165	1.9	45

Note   ■ May be baked in two 18 × 26 × 1-inch pans, scaled 3 lb 12 oz per pan.

Variation   ■ **Apricot Roll.** Cover cakes with Apricot Filling (p. 229) and roll. Cover outside with sweetened whipped cream or whipped topping and toasted coconut.

FIGURE 5.3   Rolling and filling a jelly roll. (a) Turn baked cake onto a cloth sprinkled with powdered sugar. Remove waxed or parchment paper. (b) While still warm, roll tightly. (c) When cooled but not cold, unroll and spread with filling. (d) Roll firmly. (e) Sprinkle finished jelly roll with powdered sugar.

PUMPKIN CAKE ROLL

Yield: 50 portions or 2 rolls   *Portion:* cut 25 per roll
Oven: 375°F   *Bake:* 15 minutes

Ingredient	Amount	Procedure
Eggs	18 (2 lb)	Whip eggs on high speed until thick and lemon colored, using flat beater.
Sugar, granulated	2 lb 13 oz	Add sugar gradually while mixing on medium speed.
Pumpkin, canned Lemon juice	2 lb 3 oz 2 Tbsp	Add pumpkin and lemon juice to egg mixture, mixing until blended.
Flour, all-purpose Baking powder Salt Cinnamon, ground Ginger, ground Nutmeg, ground	1 lb 2 oz 1 oz 1 Tbsp 1 oz 4 tsp 1 Tbsp	Combine dry ingredients in a bowl. Fold into pumpkin mixture. Scale batter, 4 lb per pan, into 2 greased 28 × 26 × 1-inch baking pans lined with baking liners. Bake at 375°F for 15 minutes or until cake tests done.
Sugar, powdered	6 oz	Sift powdered sugar generously onto a large white cloth. Loosen edges of cake and turn onto cloth. Remove paper (Figure 5.3). Roll cake and cloth up jelly roll fashion. Cool.
Cream cheese, softened Margarine	2 lb 10 oz	Beat cream cheese and margarine until creamy, using flat beater.
Sugar, powdered Vanilla	1 lb 6 oz 1 Tbsp	Add sugar and vanilla to cream cheese mixture. Beat until smooth and creamy. Unroll cooled cake. Spread cream cheese filling over unrolled cakes, 2 lb per cake. Reroll cake.
Nuts, chopped	2 cups	Garnish with 1 cup nuts sprinkled over each roll. Chill. Cut each roll into 25 portions.

Approximate nutritive values per portion

Calories (kcal)	Protein (grams)	Carbohydrate (grams)	Fat (grams)	Cholesterol (mg)	Sodium (mg)	Iron (mg)	Calcium (mg)
267	6.1 (6%)	53.5 (56%)	15.7 (37%)	97	318	1.7	90

Note   ■   If needed, sift additional powdered sugar over top of rolled cake.

ICING RECIPES

BOILED ICING

Yield: 2 qt

Ingredient	Amount	Procedure
Sugar, granulated Water, hot	2 lb 1¼ cups	Combine sugar and water. Stir until sugar is dissolved. Boil without stirring to soft ball stage (238°F).
Egg whites	4 (4 oz)	Beat egg whites on high speed until stiff but not dry, using wire whip attachment. Gradually pour syrup over egg whites while beating. Continue beating until icing is of consistency to spread.
Vanilla	1 Tbsp	Add vanilla. Spread on cake at once.

Approximate nutritive values per cup

Calories (kcal)	Protein (grams)	Carbohydrate (grams)	Fat (grams)	Cholesterol (mg)	Sodium (mg)	Iron (mg)	Calcium (mg)
500	1.7 (1%)	130 (99%)	0 (0%)	0	29	0	1

Variations   ■   See variations of Ice Cream Icing, p. 222.

BURNT BUTTER ICING

Yield: 1¼ qt

Ingredient	Amount	Procedure
Butter or margarine	9 oz	Heat butter in sauce pan until golden brown.
Sugar, powdered, sifted	1 lb 8 oz	Add sugar to butter and blend.
Vanilla Water, hot	1 Tbsp ½ cup	Add vanilla and water. Beat until of spreading consistency. Add more water if necessary.

Approximate nutritive values per cup

Calories (kcal)	Protein (grams)	Carbohydrate (grams)	Fat (grams)	Cholesterol (mg)	Sodium (mg)	Iron (mg)	Calcium (mg)
899	0.4 (0%)	137 (59%)	41.5 (40%)	112	425	0.2	13

Note   ■   This amount will ice 8 dozen 1½-inch cookies. If used for cake, increase by one-fourth.

ICE CREAM ICING

Yield: 2½ qt

Ingredient	Amount	Procedure
Sugar, granulated Water, hot	1 lb 8 oz 1 cup	Combine sugar and water. Boil without stirring to soft ball stage (238°F).
Egg whites	9 (10 oz)	Beat egg whites until frothy, using wire whip attachment.
Sugar, powdered, sifted	3 oz	Add powdered sugar to egg whites and beat on high speed to consistency of meringue. Add hot syrup slowly and continue beating until mixture is thick and creamy.
Sugar, powdered, sifted Vanilla	8 oz 1 Tbsp	Add powdered sugar and vanilla. Beat until smooth. Add more sugar if necessary to make icing hold its shape when spread.

Approximate nutritive values per cup

Calories (kcal)	Protein (grams)	Carbohydrate (grams)	Fat (grams)	Cholesterol (mg)	Sodium (mg)	Iron (mg)	Calcium (mg)
394	3 (3%)	100 (97%)	0 (0%)	0	48	0	2

Note   ■ This icing may be kept several days in a covered container in the refrigerator.

Variations   ■ **Bittersweet Icing.**   Melt 8 oz unsweetened chocolate over hot water. Gradually stir in 1½ oz margarine or butter. When slightly cool, pour over white icing to form a design.

■ **Candied Fruit Icing.**   Add 8 oz chopped candied fruit.

■ **Chocolate Icing.**   Add 8 oz melted chocolate.

■ **Coconut Icing.**   Frost cake. Sprinkle with 4 oz dry shredded coconut.

■ **Maple Nut Icing.**   Delete vanilla. Flavor with 1½ tsp maple flavoring. Add 6 oz chopped nuts.

■ **Maraschino Cherry Icing.**   Delete vanilla. Add ½ tsp almond extract and 8 oz chopped maraschino cherries.

■ **Peppermint Icing.**   Add 8 oz finely crushed peppermint candy.

CHOCOLATE BUTTER CREAM ICING

Yield: 2 qt

Ingredient	Amount	Procedure
Margarine or butter	1 lb 8 oz	Cream margarine on medium speed until fluffy.
Evaporated milk	½ cup	Add milk and blend.
Sugar, powdered, sifted	1 lb 8 oz	Add sugar gradually. Mix on medium speed until smooth.
Unsweetened chocolate, melted	6 oz	Add chocolate and vanilla. Beat on high speed until light and fluffy.
Vanilla	1 tsp	

Approximate nutritive values per cup

Calories (kcal)	Protein (grams)	Carbohydrate (grams)	Fat (grams)	Cholesterol (mg)	Sodium (mg)	Iron (mg)	Calcium (mg)
1219	4.7 (1%)	108 (34%)	92.5 (65%)	5	938	1.9	96

Note ■ Milk may be substituted for evaporated milk.

COCONUT PECAN ICING

Yield: 2 qt

Ingredient	Amount	Procedure
Evaporated milk	2 cups	Combine milk, egg yolks, sugar, and margarine.
Egg yolks, beaten	6 (4 oz)	Cook in steam-jacketed kettle or over hot water until thickened.
Sugar, granulated	1 lb	
Margarine	8 oz	
Pecans, finely chopped	12 oz	Add pecans, coconut, and vanilla.
Coconut, flaked	12 oz	Cool, then beat well until thick enough to spread.
Vanilla	2 tsp	

Approximate nutritive values per cup

Calories (kcal)	Protein (grams)	Carbohydrate (grams)	Fat (grams)	Cholesterol (mg)	Sodium (mg)	Iron (mg)	Calcium (mg)
1173	13.3 (4%)	102 (33%)	84.8 (62%)	229	400	2.7	244

CREAM CHEESE ICING

Yield: 1¾ qt

Ingredient	Amount	Procedure
Cream cheese, softened	12 oz	Blend cream cheese, margarine, and milk on medium speed until smooth.
Margarine, softened	2 oz	
Milk	¼ cup	
Sugar, powdered, sifted	2 lb 12 oz	Add sugar gradually to cheese-margarine mixture. Add vanilla and beat until smooth and of spreading consistency.
Vanilla	1 Tbsp	

Approximate nutritive values per cup							
Calories (kcal)	Protein (grams)	Carbohydrate (grams)	Fat (grams)	Cholesterol (mg)	Sodium (mg)	Iron (mg)	Calcium (mg)
927	4.1 (2%)	181 (76%)	24 (23%)	55	228	0.8	53

Variation   ■ **Orange Cheese Icing.** Substitute 1 Tbsp orange juice and 1 Tbsp grated orange peel for vanilla.

CREAMY ICING

Yield: 1½ qt

Ingredient	Amount	Procedure
Margarine	12 oz	Cream margarine on medium speed for 1 minute or until soft.
Evaporated milk	½ cup	Add milk and vanilla. Mix until blended.
Vanilla	1 Tbsp	
Sugar, powdered, sifted	2 lb	Add sugar gradually. Whip on medium speed until mixture is smooth and creamy.

Approximate nutritive values per cup							
Calories (kcal)	Protein (grams)	Carbohydrate (grams)	Fat (grams)	Cholesterol (mg)	Sodium (mg)	Iron (mg)	Calcium (mg)
1025	1.9 (1%)	155 (59%)	47.3 (40%)	6	558	0.2	72

Note   ■ Milk or cream may be substituted for evaporated milk.

Variations   ■ **Cocoa Icing.** Increase liquid to 1¼ cups. Add 6 oz cocoa sifted with the sugar.

■ **Lemon Butter Icing.** Substitute ¼ cup lemon juice for an equal amount of milk, and 1½ Tbsp fresh grated lemon peel for the vanilla.

■ **Orange Butter Icing.** Substitute ½ cup orange juice for an equal amount of milk, and 1 Tbsp fresh grated orange peel for the vanilla.

ORANGE ICING

Yield: 1½ qt

Ingredient	Amount	Procedure
Margarine	8 oz	Cream margarine until fluffy.
Sugar, powdered, sifted	2 lb 8 oz	Add sugar gradually on medium speed. Mix until creamy.
Vanilla	2 Tbsp	Add remaining ingredients. Blend until smooth.
Salt	½ tsp	
Orange juice	¼ cup	
Lemon juice	¼ cup	
Orange peel, grated	1 tsp	

Approximate nutritive values per cup

Calories (kcal)	Protein (grams)	Carbohydrate (grams)	Fat (grams)	Cholesterol (mg)	Sodium (mg)	Iron (mg)	Calcium (mg)
1020	0.4 (0%)	193 (74%)	30.5 (26%)	0	538	0.3	15

PEANUT BUTTER ICING

Yield: 2 qt

Ingredient	Amount	Procedure
Sugar, powdered, sifted	3 lb	Cream powdered sugar and shortening for 5 minutes.
Margarine	10 oz	
Peanut butter, creamy	5 oz	Add to creamed mixture. Cream until fluffy. Spread on Peanut Butter Cake (p. 211).
Water, warm	¾ cup	
Vanilla	1 Tbsp	

Approximate nutritive values per cup

Calories (kcal)	Protein (grams)	Carbohydrate (grams)	Fat (grams)	Cholesterol (mg)	Sodium (mg)	Iron (mg)	Calcium (mg)
1078	4.4 (2%)	174 (63%)	44.3 (36%)	0	87	0.5	6

Note   ■   ½ oz (1 Tbsp) caramel food color may be added for a darker color.

PINEAPPLE ICING (FOR PINEAPPLE CASHEW CAKE)

Yield: 2 qt

Ingredient	Amount	Procedure
Margarine	1 lb	Blend in mixer bowl, using flat beater.
Sugar, powdered	1 lb 4 oz	
Salt	¼ tsp	
Pineapple juice	¾ cup	Add pineapple juice. Mix to blend.
Sugar, powdered	1 lb 6 oz	Add sugar in three additions. Beat on medium speed until light and of the desired consistency.

Approximate nutritive values per cup

Calories (kcal)	Protein (grams)	Carbohydrate (grams)	Fat (grams)	Cholesterol (mg)	Sodium (mg)	Iron (mg)	Calcium (mg)
1048	0.6 (0%)	167 (62%)	46 (38%)	0	603	0.3	21

Note ■ Crushed pineapple may be substituted for pineapple juice. Add additional juice in small quantities until icing is of spreading consistency.

MOCHA ICING

Yield: 2 qt

Ingredient	Amount	Procedure
Hot coffee, strong	1½ cups	Add coffee to margarine and cocoa. Mix on medium speed until blended.
Margarine, softened	3 oz	
Cocoa	4 oz	
Sugar, powdered, sifted	3 lb	Add sugar, salt, and vanilla. Mix until smooth. Add more sugar if necessary to make icing hold its shape when spread.
Salt	¼ tsp	
Vanilla	½ tsp	

Approximate nutritive values per cup

Calories (kcal)	Protein (grams)	Carbohydrate (grams)	Fat (grams)	Cholesterol (mg)	Sodium (mg)	Iron (mg)	Calcium (mg)
870	3.3 (1%)	204 (88%)	11.3 (11%)	0	204	5.8	30

Note ■ Instant coffee, 2 Tbsp dissolved in 1½ cups hot water, may be used in place of brewed coffee.

CHOCOLATE GLAZE

Yield: 1 qt

Ingredient	Amount	Procedure
Unsweetened chocolate	4 oz	Melt chocolate and margarine over low heat.
Margarine	3 oz	
Sugar, powdered, sifted	1 lb 5 oz	Add sugar, vanilla, and water gradually.
Vanilla	1 Tbsp	Beat until smooth. If needed, add boiling water, a few drops at a time, to make spreading consistency.
Water, boiling	½ cup	

Approximate nutritive values per cup

Calories (kcal)	Protein (grams)	Carbohydrate (grams)	Fat (grams)	Cholesterol (mg)	Sodium (mg)	Iron (mg)	Calcium (mg)
877	3.2 (1%)	159 (68%)	32.1 (31%)	0	204	2.2	30

PEANUT BUTTER GLAZE

Yield: 5½ cups

Ingredient	Amount	Procedure
Margarine, melted	3 oz	Cream margarine and peanut butter.
Peanut butter	8 oz	
Sugar, powdered, sifted	1 lb 10 oz	Add sugar and milk alternately to make spreading consistency.
Milk	1 cup	Spread over rolls.

Approximate nutritive values per cup

Calories (kcal)	Protein (grams)	Carbohydrate (grams)	Fat (grams)	Cholesterol (mg)	Sodium (mg)	Iron (mg)	Calcium (mg)
897	11.8 (5%)	145 (62%)	34.6 (33%)	6	366	0.9	72

POWDERED SUGAR GLAZE

Yield: 5 cups

Ingredient	Amount	Procedure
Sugar, powdered	2 lb	Mix until smooth, adding more water if necessary.
Corn syrup, white	½ cup	Cover tightly until needed. Stir before using.
Water, warm	¾ cup	
Vanilla	2 tsp	

Approximate nutritive values per cup

Calories (kcal)	Protein (grams)	Carbohydrate (grams)	Fat (grams)	Cholesterol (mg)	Sodium (mg)	Iron (mg)	Calcium (mg)
667	0 (0%)	172 (100%)	0 (0%)	0	22	1.2	13

Notes
- Use for icing baked rolls or products requiring a thin icing.
- Thin, if necessary, to spread.

FILLING RECIPES

CHOCOLATE CREAM FILLING

Yield: 3 qt

Ingredient	Amount	Procedure
Chocolate chips	2 lb 4 oz (3 12-oz pkg)	Combine chocolate chips, orange juice, and sugar. Melt over hot water. Cool.
Orange juice or water	1 cup	
Sugar, granulated	8 oz	
Cream, whipping	1½ qt	Whip cream until stiff. Fold into chocolate mixture.

Approximate nutritive values per cup

Calories (kcal)	Protein (grams)	Carbohydrate (grams)	Fat (grams)	Cholesterol (mg)	Sodium (mg)	Iron (mg)	Calcium (mg)
825	6.7 (3%)	80.5 (36%)	61 (61%)	133	43	2.3	109

Note
- Use as filling for Orange Cream Puffs (p. 291).

Variation
- **Chocolate Mousse.** Whip 10 egg whites to a soft peak and fold into chocolate-whipped cream mixture. Chill. May be frozen.

DATE FILLING

Yield: 1½ qt

Ingredient	Amount	Procedure
Dates, pitted, chopped	2 lb	Combine dates, water, and sugar. Cook until mixture is thick. Cool.
Water	2¼ cups	
Sugar, granulated	12 oz	

Approximate nutritive values per cup

Calories (kcal)	Protein (grams)	Carbohydrate (grams)	Fat (grams)	Cholesterol (mg)	Sodium (mg)	Iron (mg)	Calcium (mg)
487	2.3 (2%)	130 (97%)	0.5 (1%)	0	6	1.4	39

Notes
- Use as cake or cookie filling.
- To add flavor, 6 oz jelly or ¼ cup orange juice may be used in place of ¼ cup of the water.

APRICOT FILLING

Yield: 2 qt

Ingredient	Amount	Procedure
Apricots, dried	2 lb	Cook apricots and water together. When cooked, chop apricots.
Water	2 cups	
Sugar, granulated	1 lb	Add sugar, flour, salt, and lemon juice to apricots. Cook to a paste.
Flour, all-purpose	4 oz	
Salt	½ tsp	
Lemon juice	½ cup	
Margarine	1 lb	Blend margarine into hot mixture.

Approximate nutritive values per cup

Calories (kcal)	Protein (grams)	Carbohydrate (grams)	Fat (grams)	Cholesterol (mg)	Sodium (mg)	Iron (mg)	Calcium (mg)
839	5.5 (2%)	124 (56%)	41.2 (42%)	0	609	5.4	66

Variations
- **Fig Filling.** Substitute 2 lb dried figs, cooked and chopped, for the apricots. Increase lemon juice to 1 cup.
- **Prune-Date Filling.** Substitute 1 lb cooked, pitted, and chopped prunes and 1 lb chopped dates for the apricots.

CUSTARD FILLING

Yield: 4 qt

Ingredient	Amount	Procedure
Cornstarch Sugar, granulated Salt	6 oz 1 lb ½ tsp	Combine dry ingredients.
Milk, cold	2 cups	Add cold milk to dry ingredients and stir until smooth.
Milk, hot	2½ qt	Add cold mixture to hot milk, stirring constantly with wire whip. Cook over hot water until thick.
Eggs, beaten	10 (1 lb)	Add, while stirring, a small amount of hot mixture to the beaten eggs. Add to remainder of hot mixture, stirring constantly. Cook 7 minutes.
Vanilla	2 tsp	Remove from heat. Add vanilla. Cool.

Approximate nutritive values per cup

Calories (kcal)	Protein (grams)	Carbohydrate (grams)	Fat (grams)	Cholesterol (mg)	Sodium (mg)	Iron (mg)	Calcium (mg)
304	9.6 (12%)	47.1 (61%)	9 (26%)	146	194	0.5	233

Notes
- Use as a filling for cakes, Cream Puffs (p. 291), Chocolate Roll (p. 217), and Eclairs (p. 291).
- To fill three 9-inch layer cakes, use ⅓ recipe.

LEMON FILLING

Yield: 1¾ qt

Ingredient	Amount	Procedure
Sugar, granulated	1 lb	Heat sugar and water to boiling point.
Water	3 cups	
Cornstarch	2½ oz	Blend cornstarch and cold water.
Water, cold	¾ cup	Gradually add to boiling sugar and water while stirring with a wire whip.
		Cook until thickened and clear, stirring constantly.
Egg yolks, beaten	4 (3 oz)	Stir a small amount of hot mixture into egg yolks, then blend egg yolks into hot mixture with wire whip.
		Cook 5–8 minutes while stirring.
Salt	¾ tsp	Add remaining ingredients. Stir to blend.
Lemon juice	½ cup	Cool.
Fresh lemon peel, grated	2 tsp	
Margarine	1 oz (2 Tbsp)	

Approximate nutritive values per cup

Calories (kcal)	Protein (grams)	Carbohydrate (grams)	Fat (grams)	Cholesterol (mg)	Sodium (mg)	Iron (mg)	Calcium (mg)
358	2.2 (2%)	75.6 (81%)	7.1 (17%)	156	281	0.5	25

Variations

- **Lime Filling.** Substitute fresh lime for the lemon. Add a few drops of green food coloring.

- **Orange Filling.** Substitute orange juice for the water and fresh orange peel for the lemon peel. Reduce lemon juice to 3 Tbsp.

MARMALADE NUT FILLING

Yield: 1 qt

Ingredient	Amount	Procedure
Margarine	2 oz	Melt margarine.
Walnuts, pieces	1 lb	Add nuts. Cook and stir until nuts are toasted.
Sugar, brown	6 oz	Add sugar and cinnamon. Cook until heated through.
Cinnamon, ground	1 tsp	
Orange marmalade	1 lb	Add marmalade. Mix well.

Approximate nutritive values per cup							
Calories (kcal)	Protein (grams)	Carbohydrate (grams)	Fat (grams)	Cholesterol (mg)	Sodium (mg)	Iron (mg)	Calcium (mg)
1012	22.2 (8%)	110 (41%)	60.5 (51%)	0	134	5.6	110

Note ■ Use for filling in fruit ring or sweet rolls.

PRUNE FILLING

Yield: 1½ qt

Ingredient	Amount	Procedure
Prunes, pitted, cooked and chopped	2 cups	Add cream, margarine, and eggs to prunes. Heat over hot water.
Sour cream	1 cup	
Margarine	2 oz	
Eggs, beaten ·	4 (7 oz)	
Sugar, granulated	1 lb	Mix dry ingredients. Add to prune mixture.
Salt	½ tsp	Cook and stir over hot water until thick. Cool.
Flour, all-purpose	1 oz (¼ cup)	

Approximate nutritive values per cup							
Calories (kcal)	Protein (grams)	Carbohydrate (grams)	Fat (grams)	Cholesterol (mg)	Sodium (mg)	Iron (mg)	Calcium (mg)
555	6.5 (4%)	97.5 (67%)	18.4 (28%)	152	318	1.5	79

Note ■ 8 oz chopped nuts may be added.

Variation ■ **Apricot Filling.** Substitute dried apricots for prunes.

DROP COOKIE RECIPES

BUTTERSCOTCH DROP COOKIES

Yield: 8 dozen cookies   *Portion:* ¾ oz per cookie
Oven: 375°F   *Bake:* 10–15 minutes

Ingredient	Amount	Procedure
Margarine Sugar, brown	8 oz 1 lb	Cream margarine and brown sugar on medium speed for 5 minutes, using flat beater.
Eggs Vanilla	4 (7 oz) 2 tsp	Add eggs and vanilla to creamed mixture. Mix on medium speed until well blended.
Flour, all-purpose Baking powder Baking soda Salt	1 lb 4 oz 1 tsp 2 tsp 1 tsp	Combine dry ingredients.
Sour cream	1 lb	Add dry ingredients alternately with sour cream to dough. Mix on low speed until blended.
Walnuts, chopped	8 oz	Add nuts. Mix until blended. Chill dough until firm.
		Portion with No. 40 dipper 3 × 5 onto lightly greased or parchment-paper-lined 18 × 26-inch baking sheets. Bake at 375°F for 10–12 minutes. Cover with Burnt Butter Icing (p. 221) while cookies are still warm.

Approximate nutritive values per cookie

Calories (kcal)	Protein (grams)	Carbohydrate (grams)	Fat (grams)	Cholesterol (mg)	Sodium (mg)	Iron (mg)	Calcium (mg)
84	1.6 (8%)	9.6 (45%)	4.5 (47%)	11	71	0.5	16

Variations

- **Butterscotch Squares.** Spread batter in 12 × 18 × 2-inch baking pan. Bake at 325°F for 25 minutes.
- **Chocolate Drop Cookies.** Add 4 oz unsweetened chocolate, melted, to creamed mixture.

COCONUT MACAROONS

Yield: 9 dozen cookies   *Portion:* ½ oz per cookie
Oven: 325°F   *Bake:* 15 minutes

Ingredient	Amount	Procedure
Egg whites	8 (9 oz)	Beat egg whites and salt on high speed until frothy, using whip attachment.
Salt	⅛ tsp	
Sugar, granulated	12 oz	Combine sugars and add gradually to egg whites.
Sugar, powdered	12 oz	
Vanilla	2 tsp	Add vanilla. Continue beating on high speed until stiff.
Coconut, shredded	1 lb 6 oz	Carefully fold in coconut on low speed. Portion with No. 60 dipper 4 × 6 onto lightly greased or parchment-paper-lined 18 × 26-inch baking sheets. Bake at 325°F for 15 minutes.

Approximate nutritive values per cookie

Calories (kcal)	Protein (grams)	Carbohydrate (grams)	Fat (grams)	Cholesterol (mg)	Sodium (mg)	Iron (mg)	Calcium (mg)
53	0.5 (3%)	8.8 (66%)	1.8 (31%)	0	23	0.1	0

CHOCOLATE CHIP COOKIES

Yield: 10 dozen cookies   *Portion:* ¾ oz per cookie
Oven: 375°F   *Bake:* 8–10 minutes

Ingredient	Amount	Procedure
Margarine	12 oz	Cream margarine and sugars on medium speed for 5 minutes, using flat beater.
Sugar, granulated	8 oz	
Sugar, brown	8 oz	
Eggs	4 (7 oz)	Add eggs and vanilla to creamed mixture and beat until light and fluffy.
Vanilla	2 tsp	
Flour, all-purpose	1 lb 4 oz	Combine dry ingredients. Add on low speed to creamed mixture.
Salt	1 tsp	
Baking soda	2 tsp	
Nuts, coarsely chopped	1 lb	Add nuts and chocolate chips. Mix until blended.
Chocolate chips	1 lb 8 oz	

Portion with No. 40 dipper 3 × 5 onto lightly greased or parchment-paper-lined 18 × 26-inch baking sheets.
Bake at 375°F for 8–10 minutes.

Approximate nutritive values per cookie

Calories (kcal)	Protein (grams)	Carbohydrate (grams)	Fat (grams)	Cholesterol (mg)	Sodium (mg)	Iron (mg)	Calcium (mg)
103	1.7 (6%)	11.9 (44%)	6 (50%)	7	61	0.6	16

Note
- For jumbo cookies, use No. 20 dipper. Bake at 365°F for 12–15 minutes.

BUTTERSCOTCH PECAN COOKIES

Yield: 10 dozen cookies   *Portion:* ¾ oz per cookie
Oven: 375°F   *Bake:* 10–12 minutes

Ingredient	Amount	Procedure
Margarine Sugar, brown	1 lb 2 lb	Cream margarine and sugar on medium speed for 5 minutes, using flat beater.
Eggs Vanilla	4 (7 oz) 1 Tbsp	Add eggs and vanilla to creamed mixture. Mix on low speed until blended.
Flour, all-purpose Pecans, chopped	1 lb 8 oz 1 lb	Add flour and pecans. Mix on low speed until blended.

Portion with No. 40 dipper 3 × 5 onto lightly greased or parchment-paper-lined 18 × 26-inch baking sheets.
Bake at 375°F for 10–12 minutes.

Approximate nutritive values per cookie

Calories (kcal)	Protein (grams)	Carbohydrate (grams)	Fat (grams)	Cholesterol (mg)	Sodium (mg)	Iron (mg)	Calcium (mg)
104	1.1 (4%)	12.4 (47%)	5.8 (49%)	7	40	0.6	11

OATMEAL COOKIES

■

Yield: 8 dozen cookies   *Portion:* ¾ oz per cookie
Oven: 375°F   *Bake:* 8–11 minutes

Ingredient	*Amount*	*Procedure*
Margarine Sugar, brown Sugar, granulated	1 lb 4 oz 8 oz 8 oz	Cream margarine and sugars on medium speed for 5 minutes, using flat beater.
Eggs Vanilla	2 (4 oz) 2 tsp	Add eggs and vanilla to creamed mixture. Continue to cream until well mixed.
Flour, all-purpose Salt Baking soda	12 oz 1 tsp 2 tsp	Combine dry ingredients. Add to creamed mixture.
Rolled oats, un-cooked	1 lb	Add oats. Mix on low speed until blended.
Raisins, softened	12 oz	Add raisins. Mix only to blend. Portion with No. 40 dipper 3 × 5 onto lightly greased or parchment-paper-lined 18 × 26-inch baking sheets. Flatten slightly. Bake at 375°F for 8–9 minutes for a chewy cookie, 10–11 minutes for a crisp cookie.

Approximate nutritive values per cookie

Calories (kcal)	Protein (grams)	Carbohydrate (grams)	Fat (grams)	Cholesterol (mg)	Sodium (mg)	Iron (mg)	Calcium (mg)
87	0.7 (3%)	10.4 (47%)	4.9 (50%)	5	93	0.4	7

Notes
- For variety, add 8 oz chopped nuts, chocolate chips, or coconut.
- 2 tsp cinnamon may be added.

PEANUT BUTTER COOKIES

Yield: 9 dozen cookies   *Portion:* ¾ oz per cookie
Oven: 375°F   *Bake:* 8 minutes

Ingredient	Amount	Procedure
Margarine	1 lb	Cream margarine and sugars on medium speed for 5 minutes, using flat beater.
Sugar, granulated	1 lb	
Sugar, brown	10 oz	
Eggs	4 (7 oz)	Add eggs and vanilla.
Vanilla	2 tsp	Continue beating until blended.
Peanut butter	1 lb 2 oz	Add peanut butter to creamed mixture. Blend on low speed.
Flour, all-purpose	1 lb	Combine dry ingredients.
Baking soda	2 tsp	Add to creamed mixture. Mix on low speed until well blended.
Salt	1 tsp	
		Portion dough with No. 40 dipper 3 × 5 onto lightly greased or parchment-paper-lined 18 × 26-inch baking sheets. Flatten with tines of a fork. Bake at 375°F for 8 minutes.

Approximate nutritive values per cookie

Calories (kcal)	Protein (grams)	Carbohydrate (grams)	Fat (grams)	Cholesterol (mg)	Sodium (mg)	Iron (mg)	Calcium (mg)
102	1.9 (7%)	11 (42%)	6 (51%)	8	100	0.4	7

Variations
- **Chocolate Chip Peanut Butter Cookies.** Add 1 lb chocolate chips.
- **Chunky Peanut Butter Cookies.** Use chunky peanut butter or add 12 oz chopped peanuts.

JUMBO CHUNK CHOCOLATE COOKIES

Yield: 5 dozen cookies   *Portion:* 3½ oz
Oven: 350°F   *Bake:* 10–12 minutes

Ingredient	Amount	Procedure
Sugar, brown	1 lb 8 oz	Cream sugars and shortening on medium speed for 5 minutes, using flat beater.
Sugar, granulated	1 lb	
Shortening	2 lb	
Eggs, beaten	9 (1 lb)	Add eggs and vanilla to creamed mixture.
Vanilla	1½ Tbsp	
Flour, all-purpose	2 lb 8 oz	Combine dry ingredients and add to creamed mixture. Mix thoroughly.
Baking soda	4 tsp	
Salt	4 tsp	
Semisweet chocolate chunks	4 lb 12 oz	Add chocolate and nuts.
Nuts, chopped	1 lb	
		Portion with No. 20 dipper 3 × 5 onto lightly greased or parchment-paper-lined 18 × 26-inch baking sheets. Flatten slightly. Bake at 350°F for 10–12 minutes.

Approximate nutritive values per cookie

Calories (kcal)	Protein (grams)	Carbohydrate (grams)	Fat (grams)	Cholesterol (mg)	Sodium (mg)	Iron (mg)	Calcium (mg)
501	6.9 (5%)	56.1 (42%)	31.4 (53%)	32	212	2.9	51

Note   ■   These cookies are best when served the same day they are baked.

DROP MOLASSES COOKIES

Yield: 8 dozen cookies   *Portion:* ¾ oz per cookie
Oven: 350°F   *Bake:* 8–10 minutes

Ingredient	Amount	Procedure
Flour, all-purpose	2 lb	Stir together flour, soda, and spices.
Baking soda	2⅔ Tbsp	Set aside.
Cinnamon, ground	¼ cup	
Cloves, ground	1 tsp	
Nutmeg, ground	1 tsp	
Ginger, ground	2 tsp	
Salt	2 tsp	
Oil or melted short- ening	1 lb 8 oz	Combine shortening and sugar in mixer bowl. Beat on medium speed for 5 minutes, using flat beater.
Sugar, granulated	2 lb	
Eggs	4 (7 oz)	Add eggs, one at a time, beating well after each addition.
Molasses	1 cup	Add molasses gradually to egg mixture. Add dry ingredients gradually on low speed and mix well.
		Portion with No. 40 dipper 3 × 5 onto lightly greased or parchment-paper-lined 18 × 26-inch baking sheets. Bake at 350°F for 8–10 minutes.

Approximate nutritive values per cookie

Calories (kcal)	Protein (grams)	Carbohydrate (grams)	Fat (grams)	Cholesterol (mg)	Sodium (mg)	Iron (mg)	Calcium (mg)
145	1.3 (3%)	19.1 (52%)	7.4 (45%)	9	116	0.7	12

Note   ■   Cookies will be soft in center.

PEANUT COOKIES

Yield: 9 dozen cookies   *Portion:* ¾ oz per cookie
Oven: 350°F   *Bake:* 12–15 minutes

Ingredient	Amount	Procedure
Margarine	12 oz	Cream margarine and sugars on medium speed for 5 minutes, using flat beater.
Sugar, granulated	8 oz	
Sugar, brown	1 lb	
Eggs	4 (7 oz)	Add eggs and vanilla. Mix for 5 minutes.
Vanilla	2 tsp	
Flour, all-purpose	12 oz	Combine dry ingredients.
Baking soda	1 tsp	Add to creamed mixture.
Salt	1 tsp	
Rolled oats, quick, uncooked	10 oz	Add rolled oats and peanuts. Mix until blended.
Peanuts, salted	1 lb	

Portion dough with No. 40 dipper 3 × 5 onto lightly greased or parchment-paper-lined 18 × 26-inch baking sheets.
Bake at 350°F for 12–15 minutes.

Approximate nutritive values per cookie

Calories (kcal)	Protein (grams)	Carbohydrate (grams)	Fat (grams)	Cholesterol (mg)	Sodium (mg)	Iron (mg)	Calcium (mg)
95	2.1 (9%)	11.1 (45%)	5.1 (46%)	8	61	0.5	10

SNICKERDOODLES

Yield: 8 dozen cookies   *Portion:* ¾ oz per cookie
Oven: 375°F   *Bake:* 8–10 minutes

Ingredient	Amount	Procedure
Margarine	1 lb	Cream margarine and sugar on medium speed for 5 minutes, using flat beater.
Sugar, granulated	1 lb 8 oz	
Eggs	4 (7 oz)	Add eggs to creamed mixture. Mix thoroughly.
Flour, all-purpose	1 lb 6 oz	Mix dry ingredients. Add to creamed mixture.
Cream of tartar	4 tsp	Mix on low speed until well-blended.
Baking soda	2 tsp	
Salt	½ tsp	

Sugar, granulated	8 oz	Combine sugar and cinnamon.
Cinnamon	5 Tbsp	Portion dough with No. 40 dipper.
		Roll in sugar-cinnamon mixture.
		Place 3 × 5 onto lightly greased or parchment-paper-lined 18 × 26-inch baking sheets.
		Bake at 375°F for 8–10 minutes or until lightly browned but still soft. These cookies puff up at first, then flatten out with crinkled tops.

Approximate nutritive values per cookie

Calories (kcal)	Protein (grams)	Carbohydrate (grams)	Fat (grams)	Cholesterol (mg)	Sodium (mg)	Iron (mg)	Calcium (mg)
97	1 (4%)	14.8 (59%)	4.1 (37%)	9	76	0.5	8

DROP SUGAR COOKIES

Yield: 8 dozen cookies   *Portion:* ¾ oz per cookie
Oven: 375°F   *Bake:* 8–10 minutes

Ingredient	Amount	Procedure
Shortening	1 lb	Cream fats and sugar, starting on low speed, progressing to medium, then high speed for 5 minutes. Use flat beater.
Margarine or butter	1 lb 2 oz	
Sugar, granulated	2 lb	
Eggs	3 (5 oz)	Add eggs and vanilla to creamed mixture and mix thoroughly.
Vanilla	4 tsp	
Flour, all-purpose	1 lb 14 oz	Combine dry ingredients.
Cream of tartar	2 tsp	Add gradually to creamed mixture.
Baking soda	2½ tsp	Blend well.
Salt	½ tsp	
		Portion with No. 40 dipper 3 × 5 onto lightly greased or parchment-paper-lined 18 × 26-inch baking sheets.
		Bake at 375°F for 8–10 minutes.

Approximate nutritive values per cookie

Calories (kcal)	Protein (grams)	Carbohydrate (grams)	Fat (grams)	Cholesterol (mg)	Sodium (mg)	Iron (mg)	Calcium (mg)
150	1.1 (3%)	16.3 (43%)	9.2 (54%)	6	85	0.4	4

Notes
- Cookies will be soft in center.
- For jumbo cookies, use No. 20 dipper.

WHOLE WHEAT SUGAR COOKIES

Yield: 8 dozen cookies   *Portion:* ¾ oz per cookie
Oven: 375°F   *Bake:* 8–10 minutes

Ingredient	Amount	Procedure
Margarine	1 lb	Cream margarine and sugar for 5 minutes or until light
Sugar, granulated	2 lb	and fluffy, using flat beater.
Eggs	4 (7 oz)	Add eggs, vanilla, and milk. Mix well.
Vanilla	4 tsp	
Milk	½ cup	
Flour, whole wheat	2 lb	Combine dry ingredients.
Baking powder	4 tsp	Add gradually to creamed mixture.
Baking soda	2 tsp	Blend well.
Salt	2 tsp	
Nutmeg, ground	2 tsp	
Orange peel, grated	4 Tbsp	
Sugar, granulated	4 oz	Portion with No. 40 dipper 3 × 5 onto lightly greased
Cinnamon, ground	2 tsp	or parchment-paper-lined 18 × 26-inch baking sheets.
		Flatten slightly and sprinkle with sugar and cinnamon mixture.
		Bake at 375°F for 8–10 minutes.

Approximate nutritive values per cookie

Calories (kcal)	Protein (grams)	Carbohydrate (grams)	Fat (grams)	Cholesterol (mg)	Sodium (mg)	Iron (mg)	Calcium (mg)
113	1.3 (5%)	18.2 (63%)	4.2 (32%)	9	122	0.5	14

Note   ■   Cookies will be soft in center.

BAR COOKIE RECIPES

BROWNIES

Yield: 60 portions or 2 pans 12 × 18 × 1 inches   *Portion:* 2½ × 3 inches
Oven: 325°F   *Bake:* 20 minutes

Ingredient	Amount	Procedure
Eggs	15 (1 lb 10 oz)	Beat eggs on high speed for 5 minutes, using flat beater.
Sugar, granulated Shortening, melted Margarine, melted Vanilla	2 lb 4 oz 10 oz 8 oz 2 Tbsp	Add sugar, fats, and vanilla to eggs. Mix on medium speed for 5 minutes.
Flour, cake Cocoa Baking powder Salt	14 oz 10 oz 2 tsp ½ tsp	Combine dry ingredients. Add to creamed mixture. Mix on low speed about 5 minutes.
Nuts, chopped	12 oz	Add nuts to batter. Mix to blend.
		Scale batter into 2 lightly greased 12 × 18 × 1-inch baking pans, 3 lb 8 oz per pan. Bake at 325°F for 20 minutes. Do not overbake. Should be soft to touch when done. While warm, sprinkle with powdered sugar, or cool and cover with a thin layer of mocha or chocolate frosting if desired.

Approximate nutritive values per cookie

Calories (kcal)	Protein (grams)	Carbohydrate (grams)	Fat (grams)	Cholesterol (mg)	Sodium (mg)	Iron (mg)	Calcium (mg)
219	4.2 (7%)	26.4 (45%)	12.5 (48%)	52	82	2.5	37

Notes

- 12 oz unsweetened chocolate may be substituted for the cocoa. Melt and add to the fat-sugar-egg mixture.
- 13 oz all-purpose flour may be substituted for cake flour.
- 2 lb chopped dates may be added.
- May be baked in one 18 × 26 × 1-inch baking sheet.

COCONUT PECAN BARS

Yield: 96 portions or 2 pans 12 × 18 × 1 inches   *Portion:* 2 × 2¼ inches
Oven: 350°F   *Bake:* 15–20 minutes, first layer; 20–25 minutes, second layer

Ingredient	Amount	Procedure
Margarine	1 lb 8 oz	Blend margarine, brown sugar, and flour on low speed until mixture resembles coarse meal, using flat beater.
Sugar, brown	12 oz	
Flour, all-purpose	1 lb 4 oz	
		Press even layer of mixture into two 12 × 18 × 1-inch baking pans, 1 lb 12 oz per pan.
		Bake at 350°F until light brown, 15–20 minutes.
Eggs, beaten	8 (14 oz)	Combine remaining ingredients to form topping.
Flour, all-purpose	4 oz	
Baking powder	1 Tbsp	
Salt	2 tsp	
Sugar, brown	2 lb 8 oz	
Vanilla	1 Tbsp	
Coconut, shredded or flaked	8 oz	
Pecans, chopped	12 oz	
		Spread topping over baked crust, 3 lb per pan.
		Bake 20–25 minutes.
		Ice with Orange Icing (p. 224) if desired.
		Cut 6 × 8.

Approximate nutritive values per cookie

Calories (kcal)	Protein (grams)	Carbohydrate (grams)	Fat (grams)	Cholesterol (mg)	Sodium (mg)	Iron (mg)	Calcium (mg)
178	1.7 (4%)	22.2 (48%)	9.7 (48%)	18	136	1	26

Note   ■ May be baked in one 18 × 26 × 1-inch baking sheet.

Variation   ■ **Dreamland Bars.**   Reduce coconut to 4 oz. Increase pecans to 1 lb. Add 12 oz chopped maraschino cherries and 1 lb chopped dates. Combine 2 oz margarine or butter and 8 oz powdered sugar. Spread over top. Bake.

DATE BARS

Yield: 60 portions or 2 pans 12 × 18 × 1 inches   *Portion:* 2½ × 3 inches
Oven: 350°F   *Bake:* 25–30 minutes

Ingredient	Amount	Procedure
Egg yolks	12 (7 oz)	Beat egg yolks on high speed until lemon colored, using flat beater.
Sugar, granulated	2 lb	Add sugar to yolks gradually and continue beating after each addition.
Flour, all-purpose Baking powder Salt	1 lb 1½ Tbsp ½ tsp	Combine flour, baking powder, and salt.
Dates, chopped Nuts, chopped	3 lb 1 lb	Add dates and nuts to flour mixture. Combine with egg-sugar mixture.
Egg whites	12 (14 oz)	Beat egg whites on high speed until they form soft peaks, using wire whip attachment. Fold into batter.
		Spread batter evenly into 2 lightly greased 12 × 18 × 1-inch baking pans, 4 lb 3 oz per pan. Bake at 350°F for 25–30 minutes.
Sugar, powdered	6 oz	Sift powdered sugar over top of warm baked bars. Cut 5 × 6.

Approximate nutritive values per cookie

Calories (kcal)	Protein (grams)	Carbohydrate (grams)	Fat (grams)	Cholesterol (mg)	Sodium (mg)	Iron (mg)	Calcium (mg)
217	3.9 (7%)	42.1 (73%)	5.1 (20%)	42	54	1	47

Note   ■   May be baked in one 18 × 26 × 1-inch baking sheet. Cut 6 × 10.

BUTTERSCOTCH SQUARES

Yield: 60 portions or 2 pans 12 × 18 × 1 inches   *Portion:* 2½ × 3 inches
Oven: 325°F   *Bake:* 25 minutes

Ingredient	Amount	Procedure
Margarine	1 lb	Cream margarine and sugar on medium speed for 5 minutes, using flat beater.
Sugar, brown	2 lb 8 oz	
Eggs	10 (1 lb)	Add eggs, one at a time, and vanilla. Mix on low speed until blended.
Vanilla	1 Tbsp	
Flour, all-purpose	1 lb 8 oz	Combine dry ingredients. Add to creamed mixture. Mix on low speed until blended.
Baking powder	2 Tbsp	
Salt	1 tsp	
Nuts, chopped (optional)	12 oz	Add nuts to batter. Mix to blend.
		Spread batter evenly in 2 lightly greased 12 × 18 × 1-inch baking pans, 3 lb 6 oz per pan. Bake at 325°F for 25 minutes. Cut 5 × 6.

Approximate nutritive values per cookie							
Calories (kcal)	Protein (grams)	Carbohydrate (grams)	Fat (grams)	Cholesterol (mg)	Sodium (mg)	Iron (mg)	Calcium (mg)
212	3.3 (6%)	28.3 (53%)	9.9 (41%)	32	152	1.5	57

Note   ■ May be baked in one 18 × 26 × 1-inch baking sheet. Cut 6 × 10.

Variation ■ **Butterscotch Chocolate Chip Brownies.**   Add 1 lb chocolate chips.

OATMEAL DATE BARS

Yield: 96 portions or 2 pans 12 × 18 × 1 inches   *Portion:* 2 × 2¼ inches
Oven: 325°F   *Bake:* 45 minutes

Ingredient	Amount	Procedure
Margarine	1 lb 10 oz	Cream margarine and sugar on medium speed for 5 minutes, using flat beater.
Sugar, brown	2 lb 12 oz	
Flour, all-purpose	2 lb	Combine dry ingredients. Add to creamed mixture. Mix on low speed until crumbly.
Rolled oats, quick, uncooked	1 lb 8 oz	
Baking soda	2⅔ Tbsp	Spread 2 lb 10 oz prepared mixture into each of two 12 × 18 × 1-inch baking pans. Flatten to an even layer.

| Date Filling (p. 229) | 3 qt | Spread date filling over oatmeal mixture, 1½ qt per pan.
Cover with remainder of dough, 1 lb 4 oz per pan.
Bake at 325°F for 45 minutes.
Cut 6 × 8 into bars. |

Approximate nutritive values per cookie

Calories (kcal)	Protein (grams)	Carbohydrate (grams)	Fat (grams)	Cholesterol (mg)	Sodium (mg)	Iron (mg)	Calcium (mg)
244	2.6 (4%)	45.5 (72%)	6.8 (24%)	0	146	1.4	2.5

Notes
- May be baked in one 18 × 26 × 1-inch baking sheet. Cut 8 × 12.
- Crushed pineapple or cooked dried apricots may be used in place of dates in the filling.

MARSHMALLOW KRISPIE SQUARES

Yield: 60 portions or 2 pans 12 × 18 × 1 inches   *Portion:* 2½ × 3 inches

Ingredient	Amount	Procedure
Margarine Marshmallows Vanilla	1 lb 4 lb 1 Tbsp	Melt margarine. Add marshmallows and vanilla. Stir until completely melted. Cook over low heat 3 minutes longer, stirring constantly. Remove from heat.
Rice Krispies	2 lb 8 oz	Stir Rice Krispies into marshmallow mixture until well-coated. Using buttered spatula, press mixture evenly into 2 lightly greased 12 × 18 × 1-inch baking pans, 3 lb per pan. Cut while warm, 5 × 6.

Approximate nutritive values per cookie

Calories (kcal)	Protein (grams)	Carbohydrate (grams)	Fat (grams)	Cholesterol (mg)	Sodium (mg)	Iron (mg)	Calcium (mg)
225	2.4 (4%)	41.1 (71%)	6.2 (24%)	0	309	1.7	10

Note
- May be made in one 18 × 26 × 1-inch baking sheet. Cut 5 × 6.

Variations
- **Chocolate Marshmallow Squares.** Cover squares with a thin, rich chocolate icing.
- **Peanut Butter Squares.** Add 1 lb 2 oz peanut butter to marshmallow mixture. Proceed as above. Frost with Chocolate Glaze (p. 227).

PRESSED, MOLDED, AND ROLLED COOKIE RECIPES

BUTTER TEA COOKIES

Yield: 10 dozen cookies
Oven: 375°F   *Bake:* 10–12 minutes

Ingredient	Amount	Procedure
Butter Sugar, granulated	1 lb 9 oz	Cream butter and sugar on medium speed for 5 minutes, using flat beater.
Egg yolks Vanilla	6 (4 oz) 1 tsp	Add egg yolks and vanilla to creamed mixture. Mix on medium speed until blended.
Flour, all-purpose	1 lb 4 oz	Add flour and mix on low speed. Chill dough.
		Shape with cookie press onto ungreased baking sheets. Bake at 375°F for 10–12 minutes.

Approximate nutritive values per cookie							
Calories (kcal)	Protein (grams)	Carbohydrate (grams)	Fat (grams)	Cholesterol (mg)	Sodium (mg)	Iron (mg)	Calcium (mg)
66	0.7 (5%)	5.8 (41%)	3.4 (54%)	20	32	0.3	3

Variation   ■ **Thimble Cookies.**   Roll dough into 1-inch balls. Dip in egg white and roll in finely chopped pecans. Bake 3 minutes at 325°F, then make indentation in center of cookies and fill with jelly. Bake 10–12 minutes longer.

CHOCOLATE TEA COOKIES

Yield: 10 dozen cookies
Oven: 350°F   *Bake:* 6–10 minutes

Ingredient	Amount	Procedure
Margarine Sugar, granulated	1 lb 12 oz	Cream margarine and sugar on medium speed for 5 minutes, using flat beater.
Eggs Vanilla	2 (4 oz) 1 Tbsp	Add eggs and vanilla to creamed mixture. Blend on medium speed for 5 minutes.
Flour, all-purpose Baking powder Salt Cocoa	1 lb 2 oz 1 tsp ¼ tsp 1 oz (¼ cup)	Combine dry ingredients. Add to creamed mixture and mix on low speed until blended. Chill dough.

Shape dough with cookie press onto ungreased baking
sheets.

Bake at 350°F for 6–10 minutes.

Approximate nutritive values per cookie

Calories (kcal)	Protein (grams)	Carbohydrate (grams)	Fat (grams)	Cholesterol (mg)	Sodium (mg)	Iron (mg)	Calcium (mg)
55	0.6 (4%)	6.3 (44%)	3.2 (51%)	4	44	0.3	4

SANDIES

Yield: 8 dozen cookies
Oven: 325°F   *Bake:* 20 minutes

Ingredient	Amount	Procedure
Margarine or butter Sugar, granulated Vanilla	12 oz 3 oz 1 tsp	Cream margarine, sugar, and vanilla on medium speed for 5 minutes, using flat beater.
Flour, all-purpose Salt	1 lb 2 oz 1 tsp	Add flour and salt to creamed mixture. Mix on low speed until blended.
Water Pecans, finely chopped	1 Tbsp 8 oz	Add water and pecans and blend. Chill dough.
		Shape dough into small balls ¾ inch in diameter. If mixture crumbles so it will not stick together, add a small amount of melted margarine. Place on lightly greased or parchment-paper-lined baking sheets. Bake at 325°F until lightly browned, about 20 minutes.
Sugar, powdered, sifted	8 oz (approximate)	Roll in powdered sugar while still hot.

Approximate nutritive values per cookie

Calories (kcal)	Protein (grams)	Carbohydrate (grams)	Fat (grams)	Cholesterol (mg)	Sodium (mg)	Iron (mg)	Calcium (mg)
73	0.8 (4%)	7.8 (42%)	4.5 (54%)	0	56	0.3	3

Variation   ■   **Frosty Date Balls.**   Add 1 lb finely chopped pitted dates.

BUTTERSCOTCH REFRIGERATOR COOKIES

Yield: 8 dozen cookies
Oven: 375°F   *Bake:* 8–10 minutes

Ingredient	Amount	Procedure
Margarine	8 oz	Cream fats and sugars on medium speed for 5 minutes, using flat beater.
Shortening	8 oz	
Sugar, granulated	12 oz	
Sugar, brown	1 lb	
Eggs	4 (7 oz)	Add eggs and vanilla to creamed mixture. Mix on medium speed for 5 minutes.
Vanilla	2 tsp	
Flour, all-purpose	2 lb	Combine dry ingredients.
Cream of tartar	2 tsp	
Baking soda	2 tsp	
Dates, finely chopped	8 oz	Add dry ingredients, dates, and nuts to dough. Mix on low speed until well-blended.
Nuts, chopped	8 oz	
		Form dough into three 2-lb rolls, 2 inches in diameter. Wrap in waxed paper. Chill several hours.
		Slice cookies ⅛ inch thick. Place on ungreased baking sheets.
		Bake at 375°F for 8–10 minutes.

Approximate nutritive values per cookie

Calories (kcal)	Protein (grams)	Carbohydrate (grams)	Fat (grams)	Cholesterol (mg)	Sodium (mg)	Iron (mg)	Calcium (mg)
127	1.8 (5%)	17.6 (54%)	5.8 (40%)	9	44	0.7	14

CRISP GINGER COOKIES

Yield: 8 dozen cookies
Oven: 375°F   *Bake:* 8–10 minutes

Ingredient	Amount	Procedure
Molasses Sugar, granulated	1 cup 8 oz	Combine molasses and sugar. Boil 1 minute. Cool.
Shortening	8 oz	Place shortening and molasses in mixer bowl. Blend on medium speed, using flat beater.
Eggs	2 (4 oz)	Add eggs and mix thoroughly.
Flour, all-purpose Salt Baking soda Ginger, ground	1 lb 12 oz (or more) ½ tsp 1 tsp 2 tsp	Combine dry ingredients. Add to molasses-egg mixture. Mix on low speed until well-blended.
		Form dough into two rolls 2 inches in diameter. Wrap in waxed paper. Chill thoroughly. Cut into ⅛-inch slices. Place on lightly greased baking sheets. Bake at 375°F for 8–10 minutes.

Approximate nutritive values per cookie

Calories (kcal)	Protein (grams)	Carbohydrate (grams)	Fat (grams)	Cholesterol (mg)	Sodium (mg)	Iron (mg)	Calcium (mg)
70	1 (6%)	10.9 (62%)	2.6 (33%)	5	22	0.6	7

Note   ■   Dough may be rolled and cut with cookie cutter.

OATMEAL CRISPIES

Yield: 8 dozen cookies
Oven: 350°F   *Bake:* 12–15 minutes

Ingredient	Amount	Procedure
Flour, all-purpose	12 oz	Combine flour, salt, and soda in mixer bowl.
Salt	2 tsp	
Baking soda	2 tsp	
Shortening	1 lb	Add shortening, sugars, eggs, and vanilla to flour mixture.
Sugar, granulated	1 lb	Mix on low speed about 5 minutes, using flat beater.
Sugar, brown	1 lb	
Eggs	4 (7 oz)	
Vanilla	2 tsp	
Rolled oats, quick, uncooked	1 lb	Add rolled oats and nuts. Mix on low speed to blend.
Nuts, chopped	8 oz	Shape dough into three 2-lb rolls, 2 inches in diameter. Wrap in waxed paper and chill.
		Cut dough into slices ¼ inch thick. Place 2 inches apart on ungreased baking sheets. Bake at 350°F for 12–15 minutes.

Approximate nutritive values per cookie							
Calories (kcal)	Protein (grams)	Carbohydrate (grams)	Fat (grams)	Cholesterol (mg)	Sodium (mg)	Iron (mg)	Calcium (mg)
125	1.9 (6%)	15.7 (49%)	6.5 (45%)	9	66	0.6	15

Note   ■ For smaller cookies form into four 1½-inch rolls and slice ⅛ inch thick. Yield: approximately 25 dozen.

Variation   ■ **Oatmeal Coconut Crispies.**   Add 1 cup flaked coconut.

ROLLED SUGAR COOKIES

Yield: 10 dozen cookies   *Portion:* 2-inch cookie
Oven: 375°F   *Bake:* 7 minutes

Ingredient	Amount	Procedure
Margarine or butter Sugar, granulated	1 lb 1 lb	Cream margarine and sugar on medium speed for 5 minutes, using flat beater.
Eggs Vanilla	4 (7 oz) 1 Tbsp	Add eggs and vanilla to creamed mixture. Blend on medium speed for 2 minutes.
Flour, all-purpose Salt Baking powder	1 lb 8 oz 2 tsp 2 tsp	Combine dry ingredients. Add to creamed mixture. Mix on low speed until blended.
Flour, all-purpose Sugar, granulated	4 oz 2 oz	Mix flour and sugar. Roll dough ⅛ inch thick on a surface that has been lightly dusted with flour-sugar mixture. Cut into desired shapes. Place on ungreased baking sheets. Bake at 375°F for 7 minutes or until lightly browned.

Approximate nutritive values per cookie

Calories (kcal)	Protein (grams)	Carbohydrate (grams)	Fat (grams)	Cholesterol (mg)	Sodium (mg)	Iron (mg)	Calcium (mg)
70	0.9 (5%)	9.4 (53%)	3.3 (42%)	7	78	0.3	6

Variations

- **Christmas Wreath Cookies.** Cut rolled dough with doughnut cutter. Brush with beaten egg and sprinkle with chopped nuts. Decorate with candied cherry rings and pieces of citron arranged to represent holly.

- **Coconut Cookies.** Cut rolled dough with round cookie cutter. Brush with melted margarine or butter and sprinkle with shredded coconut, plain or tinted with food coloring.

- **Filled Cookies.** Cut dough with round cutter. Cover half with Fig or Date Filling (p. 229). Brush edges with milk and cover with remaining cookies. Press edges together with tines of a fork.

- **Pinwheel Cookies.** Divide dough into 2 portions. Add 2 oz melted unsweetened chocolate to one portion. Roll each portion into the same size sheet, ⅛ inch thick. Place chocolate dough over the white dough and press together. Roll as for jelly roll. Chill thoroughly. Cut into thin slices.

PIE RECIPES

PASTRY ◼

Yield: 50 lb dough

Ingredient	Amount	Procedure
Flour, all-purpose	25 lb	Mix flour and shortening on low speed, using flat beater.
Shortening, hydro-genated	18 lb	Mix until fat particles are the size of small peas for a flaky crust. For a mealy crust, mixture should resemble cornmeal.
Ice water	3¾ qt	Add water and salt to flour-fat mixture.
Salt	12 oz	Mix on low speed only until dough will hold together.

Approximate nutritive values per pound							
Calories (kcal)	Protein (grams)	Carbohydrate (grams)	Fat (grams)	Cholesterol (mg)	Sodium (mg)	Iron (mg)	Calcium (mg)
2269	23.4 (4%)	173 (30%)	166 (65%)	0	2643	10.5	51

Notes
- For seven 9-inch one-crust pies, use 4 lb; for seven 9-inch two-crust pies, use 7 lb. See pp. 254 and 256 for directions for preparation.
- For eight 8-inch one-crust pies, use 2 lb 8 oz; for eight 8-inch two-crust pies, use 4 lb 8 oz. See pp. 254 and 256 for directions for preparation.

PASTRY FOR ONE-CRUST PIES ◼

Yield: 56 portions or 4 lb dough or 7 9-inch pies   *Portion:* cut 8 per pie

Ingredient	Amount	Procedure
Flour, all-purpose	2 lb	Mix flour and shortening on low speed for 1 minute, using pastry knife or flat beater.
Shortening, hydro-genated	1 lb 6 oz	Scrape sides of bowl and continue mixing until shortening is evenly distributed, 1 to 2 minutes.
Ice water	1–1¼ cups	Dissolve salt in smaller amount of water (use reserved amount of water if needed).
Salt	1 oz (1½ Tbsp)	Add to flour mixture. Mix on low speed only until a dough is formed, about 40 seconds. Portion into 9-oz balls for 9-inch pies. See Note for 8-inch pies.

To Make a One-Crust Pie:

1. Roll dough into a circle 2 inches larger than pie pan.
2. Fit pastry loosely into pan so that there are no air spaces between the crust and pan (Figure 5.4).
3. Trim, allowing ½ inch extra to build up edge.
4. For custard-type pie, crimp edge, add filling, and bake according to the recipe.
5. For cream or chiffon pies, crimp edge (Figure 5.4) and prick crust with fork. Bake according to directions that follow.
6. Bake in a hot oven (425°F) for 10 minutes or until light brown. Cool. A second pan may be placed over the crust for the first part of baking, then removed and the crust allowed to brown. The second pan helps to keep the crust in shape.
7. Fill baked crust with desired filling.

Approximate nutritive values per portion

Calories (kcal)	Protein (grams)	Carbohydrate (grams)	Fat (grams)	Cholesterol (mg)	Sodium (mg)	Iron (mg)	Calcium (mg)
157	1.6 (4%)	12.4 (31%)	11.3 (64%)	0	172	0.7	4

Note

■ For eight 8-inch pies, use 1 lb 3 oz flour, 13 oz shortening, 1 cup water, and 2½ tsp salt. Scale 5 oz for each crust. To serve, cut pies in six portions.

FIGURE 5.4   Preparing pastry for a baked pie shell. Holes are made in shells to keep them flat during baking.

PASTRY FOR TWO-CRUST PIES

Yield: 56 portions or 7 lb dough or 7 9-inch pies   *Portion:* cut 8 per pie

Ingredient	Amount	Procedure
Flour, all-purpose Shortening, hydro- genated	3 lb 6 oz 2 lb 7 oz	Mix flour and shortening on low speed for one minute, using pastry knife or flat beater. Scrape sides of bowl and continue mixing until shortening is evenly distributed, 1–2 minutes.
Ice water Salt	1¾–2 cups 1¾ oz (2½ Tbsp)	Dissolve salt in smaller amount of water (use reserved amount of water if needed). Add to flour mixture. Mix on low speed only until a dough is formed, about 40 seconds. Portion into 9-oz balls for bottom crust and 7-oz for top crust. See Notes for 8-inch pies.

To Make a Two-Crust Pie:

1. Roll each ball of dough into a circle. Place pastry for bottom crust in pie pans, easing into pans without stretching the dough.

2. Trim off overhanging dough. If desired, leave ½ inch extra pastry around the edge and fold over to make a pocket of pastry to prevent fruit juices from running out.

3. Add desired filling.

4. Moisten edge of bottom crust with water (Figure 5.5).

5. Cover with top crust, in which slits or vents have been cut near the center to allow steam to escape.

6. Trim top pastry to extend ½ inch beyond edge of pan.

7. Fold edge of top pastry under edge of lower pastry, then seal by pressing the two crusts together and fluting with fingertips.

8. If desired, brush top crusts with milk and sprinkle with sugar.

9. Bake as directed in the recipe.

Approximate nutritive values per portion							
Calories (kcal)	Protein (grams)	Carbohydrate (grams)	Fat (grams)	Cholesterol (mg)	Sodium (mg)	Iron (mg)	Calcium (mg)
274	2.8 (4%)	20.8 (30%)	20 (66%)	0	286	1.3	6

Notes

- For eight 8-inch pies, use 2 lb flour, 1 lb 8 oz shortening, 1½–1¾ cups water, and 1 oz (1½ Tbsp) salt. Scale 5 oz for bottom crust and 4 oz for top crust. To serve, cut into six portions.

- Using scrap dough is often necessary. Using no more than 50 percent of scrap dough and restricting its use to bottom crusts is recommended. Care must be taken to handle the dough as little as possible.

Variation

- **Cheddar Cheese Pastry.**   Use 2 lb 8 oz flour, 1 lb 13 oz shortening, 1 lb 14 oz shredded cheddar cheese, ¾ cup water, and 1½ oz salt. Add cheese after flour and shortening have been mixed.

FIGURE 5.5   Preparing pastry for a two-crust pie. (a) Moistening edge of crust. (b) Placing top crust on filled pie. (c) Pressing top crust to seal tightly. (d) Fluting edge of pie.

GRAHAM CRACKER CRUST

Yield: 56 portions or 7 9-inch pies   *Portion:* cut 8 per pie
Oven: 375°F   *Bake:* 5 minutes

Ingredient	Amount	Procedure
Graham cracker crumbs	2 lb	Mix all ingredients.
Sugar, granulated	15 oz	Pat 9 oz crumb mixture evenly into each pie pan. For 8-inch crusts, see Notes.
Margarine, melted	15 oz	Bake at 375°F for about 5 minutes.

Approximate nutritive values per portion

Calories (kcal)	Protein (grams)	Carbohydrate (grams)	Fat (grams)	Cholesterol (mg)	Sodium (mg)	Iron (mg)	Calcium (mg)
147	1.2 (3%)	19.2 (52%)	7.3 (44%)	0	148	0.6	9

Notes
- For eight 8-inch shells, use 1 lb 5 oz crumbs, 10 oz sugar, and 10 oz melted margarine. Portion 5 oz per shell.
- Vanilla wafer crumbs or chocolate cookie crumbs may be substituted for graham cracker crumbs.
- Crusts may be refrigerated several hours instead of baking.

Variation
- **Chocolate Crumb Crust.**   Add 6 oz cocoa to graham cracker crumbs and sugar. Mix, then add melted margarine.

MERINGUE FOR PIES

Yield: 56 portions or meringue for 7 9-inch pies   *Portion:* cut 8 per pie
Oven: 375°F   *Bake:* 10–12 minutes

Ingredient	Amount	Procedure
Egg whites, at room temperature	16 (2 cups/1 lb)	Add salt and cream of tartar to egg whites. Whip past frothy stage, on high speed, approximately 1½ minutes, using wire whip attachment.
Salt	½ tsp	
Cream of tartar	½ tsp	
Sugar, granulated	1 lb	Add sugar gradually while beating. Beat until sugar has dissolved. The meringue should be stiff enough to hold peaks but not dry.
		Spread meringue on filled pies while filling is hot, 5–6 oz per pie. The meringue should touch all edges of the crust. Brown in oven at 375°F for 10–12 minutes or until golden brown.

Approximate nutritive values per portion

Calories (kcal)	Protein (grams)	Carbohydrate (grams)	Fat (grams)	Cholesterol (mg)	Sodium (mg)	Iron (mg)	Calcium (mg)
36	0.9 (9%)	8.6 (91%)	0 (0%)	0	34	0	1

Notes

- For 8-inch pies, use 4 oz per pie.
- For proper volume, egg whites must have no yolk mixed in them, and the beater and bowl must be free of any trace of fat. Even a small trace of fat will prevent the whites from foaming properly.
- Egg whites should be at room temperature before beating. The meringue will be higher and lighter.

MERINGUE SHELLS

Yield: 50 shells   *Portion:* 3 oz
Oven: 275°F   *Bake:* 1 hour

Ingredient	Amount	Procedure
Egg whites	28 (3 cups/1 lb 8 oz)	Add salt and cream of tartar to egg whites. Beat on high speed until frothy, using wire whip attachment.
Salt	1 tsp	
Cream of tartar	1 tsp	
Sugar, granulated	3 lb	Add sugar ½ cup at a time, beating on high speed between each addition until sugar is dissolved and mixture will hold its shape, 20–30 minutes.
		Place mixture on greased and floured baking sheets with No. 10 dipper and shape into nests with spoon; or place on pans with pastry tube. Bake at 275°F for about 1 hour. Watch carefully the last 15–20 minutes to avoid overcooking. Meringues should be white, not brown. If overcooked, they are too brittle. Serve ice cream or fruit in the center.

Approximate nutritive values per portion

Calories (kcal)	Protein (grams)	Carbohydrate (grams)	Fat (grams)	Cholesterol (mg)	Sodium (mg)	Iron (mg)	Calcium (mg)
109	1.4 (5%)	27.4 (95%)	0 (0%)	0	65	0	1

Variations

- **Angel Pie.** Place meringue in well-greased and floured pie pans, about 1¼ qt per pan. Use spoon to build up sides. After baking fill each shell with 3 cups Cream Pie filling (p. 268), Lemon Pie filling (p. 271), or Chocolate Pie filling (p. 269). Then top with a thin layer of whipped cream.

- **Meringue Sticks.** Force mixture through pastry tube to form sticks. Sprinkle with chopped nuts. Bake.

PIES MADE WITH CANNED FRUIT

Yield: 56 portions or 7 9-inch pies   *Portion:* cut 8 per pie
Oven: 400°F   *Bake:* 30 minutes

Ingredient	Amount	Procedure
Pastry for Two-Crust Pies (p. 256)	7 lb	Make pastry. Divide into 9-oz balls for bottom crust and 7-oz balls for top crusts. Roll and place bottom crusts in seven 9-inch pie pans. For 8-inch pies, see Notes.
Fruit, pie pack	2 No. 10 cans	Drain fruit. Measure liquid and add water to make 2 qt. Bring 1½ qt of the liquid to boiling point.
Cornstarch	8 oz	Mix remaining liquid with cornstarch and add gradually to hot liquid, while stirring with a wire whip. Cook until thick and clear.
Sugar, granulated Salt	3 lb 8 oz 2 tsp	While still hot, add sugar and salt. Mix thoroughly and bring to boiling point. Add drained fruit and mix carefully to avoid breaking or mashing fruit. Cool slightly.
		Scale 1 lb 12 oz–2 lb (3½–4 cups) filling into each unbaked pie shell. Moisten edge of bottom crust with water. Cover with top crust. Seal edge, trim, and flute edges (Figure 5.5). Bake at 400°F for 30 minutes or until crust is browned.

Notes
- For eight 8-inch pies, make 4 lb 8 oz dough for crusts and portion into 5 oz for bottom crust and 4 oz for top crust. For filling, use 1½ No. 10 cans fruit, 3 lb sugar (variable), 6 oz cornstarch, and 1½ tsp salt. Drain liquid from fruit and add water to make 1½ qt liquid. Scale 1 lb–1 lb 8 oz (approximately 3 cups) filling per pie.
- Suggested fillings: apple, apricot, blackberry, cherry, gooseberry, or peach.
- Other thickening agents may be used, such as waxy maize (6 oz total for 9-inch or 4½ oz total for 8-inch pies) or tapioca (9 oz total for 9-inch or 7½ oz total for 8-inch pies).

PIES MADE WITH FROZEN FRUIT

Yield: 56 portions or 7 9-inch pies   *Portion:* cut 8 per pie
Oven: 400°F   *Bake:* 30–40 minutes

Ingredient	Amount	Procedure
Pastry for Two-Crust Pies (p. 256)	7 lb	Make pastry. Divide into 9-oz balls for bottom crust, 7-oz balls for top crust. Roll and place bottom crusts in seven 9-inch pie pans. For 8-inch pies, see Notes.
Fruit, frozen	10 lb	Thaw fruit. Measure juice. If necessary, add water to bring total liquid to 1½–2 qt according to consistency desired.
Sugar, granulated Cornstarch or waxy maize (see Notes)	See Table 5.3 See Table 5.3	Combine sugar and starch. Add to hot liquid, stirring with wire whip.
Seasonings	See Table 5.3	Add seasonings to thickened liquid and pour over fruit. Mix carefully to avoid breaking or mashing fruit.
		Scale 1 lb 12 oz–2 lb (3½–4 cups) filling into each unbaked pie shell. Moisten edge of bottom crust with water. Cover with top crust in which slits have been made for steam to escape. Seal edge, trim and flute edges (see Figure 5.5). Bake at 400°F for 30–40 minutes or until fruit is done and crust is golden brown.

Notes
- Allow 2–3 oz cornstarch or 2–2½ oz waxy maize per qt of liquid. Use of waxy maize or other waxy starch products results in a translucent soft gel through which the fruit shows clearly. The color is brighter and the gel is less opaque and less rigid, making it ideal for thickening fruit fillings. It is important to use a waxy starch if the pies are to be frozen.
- For eight 8-inch pies, use 4 lb 8 oz pastry, portioned 5 oz for bottom crust and 4 oz for top crust. Portion 1 lb–1 lb 8 oz (approximately 3 cups) filling per pie.

TABLE 5.3   Guide for using frozen fruit in pies or cobblers (seven 9-inch pies)

| Fruit 10 lb | Sugar[a] | Thickening | | Seasonings |
		Cornstarch[a]	Waxy maize[a]	
Apples	1 lb 8 oz	3 oz	2½ oz	Salt, 1 tsp; nutmeg, 1 tsp; cinnamon, 1 Tbsp; butter, 2 oz
Apricots	2 lb	5½ oz	4 oz	Cinnamon, 2 tsp
Berries	2½–3½ lb	6½ oz	5 oz	Lemon juice, 2 Tbsp; salt, 1 tsp
Blueberries	3 lb	8 oz	6 oz	Salt, 1 tsp; butter, 2 oz; lemon juice, 1½ cups; cinnamon, 1 tsp
Blue plums	2–2½ lb	5½ oz	4 oz	Salt, 1 tsp; butter, 2 oz
Cherries	1 lb 12 oz	7 oz	5 oz	Salt, 1 tsp
Gooseberries	6 lb	14 oz	10 oz	Salt, ½ tsp
Peaches	1 lb 6 oz	5½ oz	4 oz	Butter, 1 oz; salt, 1 tsp; almond extract, ¼ tsp; cinnamon, 1 tsp; nutmeg, 1 tsp
Pineapple	2 lb	5½ oz	4 oz	Salt, 1 tsp
Rhubarb	5 lb	7 oz	5 oz	Salt, 1 tsp
Strawberries	2 lb	12 oz	8½ oz	Lemon juice, ¾ cup; red color, ¾ tsp

[a]The amount of sugar and cornstarch or waxy maize added to the fruit will vary according to the pack of the fruit and individual preferences of flavor and consistency. Frozen fruits packed without the addition of sugar are known as "dry pack." When sugar is added during the freezing process, the ratio is usually 3, 4, or 5 parts by weight of fruit to 1 part by weight of sugar. Use less thickening for cobblers. Some fruits are available individually quick frozen (IQF) without added sugar.

FRESH APPLE PIE

Yield: 56 portions or 7 9-inch pies   *Portion:* cut 8 per pie
Oven: 400°F   *Bake:* 45 minutes

Ingredient	Amount	Procedure
Pastry for Two-Crust Pies (p. 256)	7 lb	Make pastry. Divide into 9-oz balls for bottom crust, 7-oz for top crust. Roll and place bottom crusts in seven 9-inch pie pans. For 8-inch pies, see Notes.
Apples, tart, fresh	12 lb (EP) 15 lb (AP)	Peel, core, and slice apples.
Sugar, granulated Flour, all-purpose Cinnamon	3 lb 4 oz 1 Tbsp	Combine sugar, fruit, and cinnamon. Add to apples and mix carefully.
Margarine	8 oz	Portion 2 lb 4 oz filling into each unbaked crust. Add 1 oz margarine to each pie. Moisten edge of bottom crust. Cover with perforated top crust. Seal edge, trim excess dough, and flute edges (see Figure 5.5). Bake at 400°F for 45 minutes or until apples are tender.

Approximate nutritive values per portion

Calories (kcal)	Protein (grams)	Carbohydrate (grams)	Fat (grams)	Cholesterol (mg)	Sodium (mg)	Iron (mg)	Calcium (mg)
459	3.3 (3%)	61.7 (52%)	23.6 (45%)	0	325	1.6	16

Notes
- For eight 8-inch pies, use 4 lb 8 oz dough for crust and portion 5 oz for bottom crust and 4 oz for top crust. Portion filling, 2 lb per pie.
- Suggested apples are Jonathan, Granny Smith, and Winesap.

Variation
- **Apple Crumb Pie.**   Omit top crust. Sprinkle apples with **Streusel Topping:** Mix 1 lb flour, 1 lb 10 oz sugar, 2 oz nonfat dry milk, and 1 tsp salt. Cut in 10 oz margarine or butter and add 6 oz chopped pecans. Use 1 cup per pie. Bake until apples are tender and topping is brown.

SOUR CREAM APPLE NUT PIE

Yield: 56 portions or 7 9-inch pies   *Portion:* cut 8 per pie
Oven: 450°F, 350°F   *Bake:* 10 minutes, 55 minutes

Ingredient	Amount	Procedure
Pastry for One-Crust Pies (p. 254)	4 lb	Make pastry. Line seven 9-inch pie pans, 9 oz per pan. For 8-inch pies, see Note.
Sour cream	3 lb	Combine and mix until thoroughly blended.
Sugar, granulated	8 oz	
Flour, all-purpose	6 oz	
Eggs	4 (6 oz)	
Vanilla	2 Tbsp	
Salt	1 tsp	
Apples, sliced, frozen	8 lb 8 oz	Combine apples and sour cream mixture, being careful not to break apples.
		Scale 1 lb 12 oz filling into each unbaked crust. Bake at 450°F for 10 minutes. Reduce temperature to 350°F and continue baking until filling is slightly puffed and golden brown, about 40 minutes.

Topping

Ingredient	Amount	Procedure
Flour, all-purpose	5 oz	Combine flour, sugars, and cinnamon.
Sugar, brown	4 oz	
Sugar, granulated	5 oz	
Cinnamon	2 Tbsp	
Margarine	5 oz	Add margarine to dry ingredients. Mix until crumbly.
Walnuts, coarsely chopped	8 oz	Add nuts. Mix in. Scale 3½ oz topping over each pie and bake for 15 minutes.

Approximate nutritive values per portion							
Calories (kcal)	Protein (grams)	Carbohydrate (grams)	Fat (grams)	Cholesterol (mg)	Sodium (mg)	Iron (mg)	Calcium (mg)
345	4.6 (5%)	35.6 (40%)	21.3 (54%)	24	253	1.5	45

Note ■ For eight 8-inch pies, use 2 lb 8 oz dough portioned 5 oz per pie. For filling, scale apple mixture 1 lb 8 oz per pie and topping 3 oz per pie.

RAISIN PIE

Yield: 56 portions or 7 9-inch pies   *Portion:* cut 8 per pie
Oven: 400°F   *Bake:* 30 minutes

Ingredient	Amount	Procedure
Pastry for Two-Crust Pies (p. 256)	7 lb	Make pastry. Divide into 9-oz balls for bottom crust, 7-oz for top crust. Roll and place bottom crusts in seven 9-inch pie pans. For 8-inch pies, see Note.
Raisins Water, hot	4 lb 4½ qt	Simmer raisins in water until plump. Cool slightly.
Sugar, granulated Cornstarch Salt	2 lb 4 oz 6 oz 2 tsp	Combine sugar, cornstarch, and salt. Add to raisins and cook until thickened. Remove from heat.
Lemon juice Margarine	6 Tbsp 3 oz	Add lemon juice and margarine to raisin mixture. Cool slightly.
		Portion 2 lb 4 oz (3½–4 cups) filling into each unbaked crust. Moisten edge of bottom crust. Cover with perforated top crust. Seal edge, trim excess dough, and flute edges (see Figure 5.5). Bake at 400°F for 30 minutes or until crust is golden brown.

Approximate nutritive values per portion

Calories (kcal)	Protein (grams)	Carbohydrate (grams)	Fat (grams)	Cholesterol (mg)	Sodium (mg)	Iron (mg)	Calcium (mg)
462	3.9 (3%)	67.7 (57%)	21.4 (40%)	0	384	1.9	25

Note   ■   For eight 8-inch pies, use 4 lb 8 oz dough, portioned 5 oz for bottom crust and 4 oz for top crust. For filling, portion 1 lb 14 oz (3–3½ cups) filling per pie.

Variation   ■   **Dried Apricot Pie.**   Use 5 lb dried apricots. Cover with hot water; let stand 1 hour. Cook slowly without stirring until tender. Combine 4 lb granulated sugar and 2½ oz cornstarch. Mix with ½ cup cold water. Add to fruit a few minutes before it is done. Continue cooking until juice is clear. Proceed as for Raisin Pie.

RHUBARB PIE

Yield: 56 portions or 7 9-inch pies   *Portion:* cut 8 per pie
Oven: 400°F   *Bake:* 35 minutes

Ingredient	Amount	Procedure
Rhubarb, fresh or frozen	10 lb (EP)	If fresh rhubarb is used, wash and trim. Do not peel. Cut in 1-inch pieces.
Sugar, granulated Tapioca, quick-cooking Salt Orange peel, grated	5 lb 8 oz 6 oz 2 tsp 3 Tbsp	Combine and stir into rhubarb. Let stand 30 minutes.
Pastry for Two-Crust Pies (p. 256)	7 lb	Make pastry. Divide into 9-oz balls for bottom crust, 7-oz for top crust. Roll and place bottom crusts in seven 9-inch pie pans, 9 oz per pan. For 8-inch pies, see Notes.
Margarine, melted	5 oz	Portion 2 lb 4 oz filling into each unbaked crust. Distribute margarine over filling in each pie. Moisten edges with cold water. Cover with top crust or pastry strips. Press edges together. Bake at 400°F for 35 minutes or until crust is golden brown and fruit is tender.

Approximate nutritive values per portion

Calories (kcal)	Protein (grams)	Carbohydrate (grams)	Fat (grams)	Cholesterol (mg)	Sodium (mg)	Iron (mg)	Calcium (mg)
488	3.6 (3%)	72 (57%)	22.2 (40%)	0	390	1.5	78

Notes
- For eight 8-inch pies, use 4 lb 8 oz dough portioned 5 oz for bottom crust and 4 oz for top crust. Scale 1 lb 14 oz filling per pie.
- 8 oz cornstarch or 5 oz waxy maize starch may be substituted for the tapioca.

RHUBARB CUSTARD PIE

Yield: 56 portions or 7 9-inch pies   *Portion:* cut 8 per pie
Oven: 375°F   *Bake:* 45–50 minutes

Ingredient	Amount	Procedure
Pastry for One-Crust Pies (p. 254)	4 lb	Make pastry. Line seven 9-inch pie pans, 9 oz per pan. Flute edges. For 8-inch pies, see Notes.
Rhubarb, fresh or frozen	8 lb (EP)	If fresh rhubarb is used, wash and trim. Do not peel. Cut into ¼-inch pieces.
Eggs, beaten	12 (1 lb 5 oz)	Add eggs to rhubarb.
Sugar, granulated Flour, all-purpose Salt Lemon peel, grated	4 lb 8 oz 9 oz 1 tsp 1 tsp	Mix dry ingredients. Add to rhubarb mixture. Scale 2 lb (4½ cups) filling into each unbaked crust. Bake at 375°F for 45–50 minutes or until custard is set.

Approximate nutritive values per portion

Calories (kcal)	Protein (grams)	Carbohydrate (grams)	Fat (grams)	Cholesterol (mg)	Sodium (mg)	Iron (mg)	Calcium (mg)
340	4 (5%)	55.4 (63%)	12.5 (32%)	45	226	1.3	66

Notes
- For eight 8-inch pies, use 2 lb 8 oz dough, portioned 5 oz per pie. Use 1 lb 12 oz filling per pie.
- May be topped with Meringue (p. 259).
- Unbaked pie may be covered with a top crust or a latticed top made of ⅛-inch pastry strips.

CREAM PIE

Yield: 56 portions or 7 9-inch pies   *Portion:* cut 8 per pie
Oven: 425°F for pastry, 375°F for meringue   *Bake:* 10 minutes, 12 minutes

Ingredient	Amount	Procedure
Pastry for One-Crust Pies (p. 254)	4 lb	Make pastry. Line seven 9-inch pie pans, 9 oz per pan. For 8-inch pies, see Note. Flute edges and prick crust with fork (Figure 5.4). Bake at 425°F for 10 minutes or until light brown. Cool.
Milk	3¾ qt	Heat milk to boiling point in a steam-jacketed or other large kettle.

Sugar, granulated	2 lb 12 oz	Mix sugar, cornstarch, and salt.
Cornstarch	13 oz	Add cold milk and stir until smooth.
Salt	2½ tsp	Add to hot milk gradually, stirring briskly with a wire
Milk, cold	1¼ qt	whip.
		Cook until smooth and thick, approximately 10 minutes.
Egg yolks, beaten	20 (13 oz)	Add, while stirring, a small amount of hot mixture to the egg yolks.
		Add to remaining hot mixture, stirring constantly. Stir slowly and cook 5–10 minutes.
		Remove from heat.
Margarine	5 oz	Stir in margarine and vanilla.
Vanilla	2½ Tbsp	Pour 2 lb (4 cups) filling into each baked pie shell.
Egg whites	20 (1 lb 6 oz)	Prepare Meringue (p. 259).
Salt	½ tsp	Cover each filled pie with 5 oz meringue.
Sugar, granulated	1 lb 4 oz	Bake at 375°F for 10–12 minutes or until meringue is
Cream of tartar	½ tsp	golden brown.

Approximate nutritive values per portion

Calories (kcal)	Protein (grams)	Carbohydrate (grams)	Fat (grams)	Cholesterol (mg)	Sodium (mg)	Iron (mg)	Calcium (mg)
430	7.2 (7%)	58.4 (54%)	19.3 (40%)	102	396	1.1	126

Note

- For eight 8-inch pies, use 2 lb 8 oz dough, portioned 5 oz per pie. Use 1 lb 12 oz (3½ cups) filling per pie.

Variations

- **Banana Cream Pie.** Slice 1 large banana into each pie shell before adding cream filling.

- **Chocolate Cream Pie.** Add 6 oz cocoa or 8 oz unsweetened chocolate. Increase sugar to 3 lb. If using cocoa, mix with cornstarch and sugar. If using chocolate, melt and add to hot milk.

- **Coconut Cream Pie.** Add 10 oz toasted coconut to filling and sprinkle 2 oz coconut over meringue.

- **Date Cream Pie.** Add 3 lb chopped, pitted dates to cooked filling.

- **Fruit Glazed Pie.** Use frozen blueberries, strawberries, or cherries. Thaw 6 lb frozen fruit and drain. Measure 1 qt fruit syrup, adding water if needed to make that amount. Add slowly to a mixture of 6 oz sugar, 4 oz cornstarch, and ¾ cup lemon juice. Cook until thick and clear. Cool slightly. Add drained fruit. Spread over cream pies.

- **Nut Cream Pie.** Add ½ cup chopped pecans or other nuts.

- **Pineapple Cream Pie.** Add 3½ cups crushed pineapple, drained, to cooked filling.

BUTTERSCOTCH CREAM PIE ∎

Yield: 56 portions or 7 9-inch pies   *Portion:* cut 8 per pie
Oven: 425°F for pastry, 375°F for meringue   *Bake:* 10 minutes, 12 minutes

Ingredient	Amount	Procedure
Pastry for One-Crust Pies (p. 254)	4 lb	Make pastry. Line seven 9-inch pie pans, 9 oz per pan. For 8-inch pies, see Notes. Flute edges and prick crust with fork (Figure 5.4). Bake at 425°F for 10 minutes or until light brown.
Margarine Sugar, brown	1 lb 2 lb 8 oz	Melt margarine. Stir in sugar. Cook over low heat to 220°F, stirring occasionally.
Milk	3 qt	Add milk slowly to margarine-sugar mixture while stirring with wire whip. Stir until all sugar is dissolved. Heat mixture to boiling.
Cornstarch Flour, all-purpose Salt	6 oz 6 oz 1 Tbsp	Combine cornstarch, flour, and salt.
Milk, warm Eggs, whole Egg yolks	1 qt 5 (9 oz) 10 (6 oz)	Combine milk and eggs. Add to cornstarch and flour mixture and mix. Add to the hot mixture while stirring. Cook until thick. Remove from heat.
Margarine Vanilla	4 oz 2 Tbsp	Add margarine and vanilla. Cool partially. Fill baked pie shells, 1 lb 12 oz (3½ cups) per pie.
Egg whites Salt Sugar, granulated Cream of tartar	16 (1 lb 2 oz) ½ tsp 1 lb ½ tsp	Prepare Meringue (p. 259). Cover each filled pie with 5 oz meringue. Bake at 375°F for 10–12 minutes, or until meringue is golden brown.

Approximate nutritive values per portion

Calories (kcal)	Protein (grams)	Carbohydrate (grams)	Fat (grams)	Cholesterol (mg)	Sodium (mg)	Iron (mg)	Calcium (mg)
425	6.4 (6%)	48.8 (45%)	23.2 (49%)	68	463	1.8	115

Notes
- For eight 8-inch pies, use 2 lb 8 oz dough portioned 5 oz per pie. Use 1 lb 8 oz (3 cups) filling per pie.
- Recipe may be used for pudding. Omit flour and increase cornstarch to 8 oz.

LEMON PIE

Yield: 56 portions or 7 9-inch pies   *Portion:* cut 8 per pie
Oven: 425°F pastry, 375°F meringue   *Bake:* 10 minutes, 12 minutes

Ingredient	Amount	Procedure
Pastry for One-Crust Pies (p. 254)	4 lb	Make pastry. Line seven 9-inch pie pans, 9 oz per pan. For 8-inch pies, see Note. Flute edges and prick bottom and sides of crust with fork. Bake at 425°F for 10 minutes or until light brown.
Water Salt Lemon rinds, grated	2¼ qt 2 tsp 3	Heat water, salt, and lemon peel to boiling point.
Sugar, granulated Cornstarch Water, cold	3 lb 8 oz 12 oz 3 cups	Mix sugar and cornstarch. Add cold water and stir until mixed. Add slowly to boiling water, stirring constantly with wire whip. Cook until thickened and clear. Remove from heat.
Egg yolks, beaten	16 (1½ cups)	Add, while stirring, a small amount of hot mixture to egg yolks. Add to remaining hot mixture, stirring constantly. Return to heat and cook about 5 minutes. Remove from heat.
Margarine Lemon juice	3 oz 1½ cups	Add margarine and lemon juice. Blend. Scale into baked pie shells, 1 lb 10 oz (3½ cups) per pie.
Egg whites Salt Sugar, granulated Cream of tartar	16 (1 lb 2 oz) ½ tsp 1 lb ½ tsp	Prepare Meringue (p. 259). Cover each pie with 5 oz meringue. Bake at 375°F for 10–12 minutes, or until meringue is golden brown.

Approximate nutritive values per portion

Calories (kcal)	Protein (grams)	Carbohydrate (grams)	Fat (grams)	Cholesterol (mg)	Sodium (mg)	Iron (mg)	Calcium (mg)
351	3.5 (4%)	5.5 (61%)	1.4 (35%)	61	302	1	14

Note   ■   For eight 8-inch pies, use 2 lb 8 oz dough portioned 5 oz per pie. Use 3 cups filling per pie.

CUSTARD PIE

Yield: 56 portions or 7 9-inch pies   *Portion:* cut 8 per pie
Oven: 450°F, 350°F   *Bake:* 15 minutes, 20 minutes

Ingredient	Amount	Procedure
Pastry for One-Crust Pies (p. 254)	4 lb	Make pastry. Line seven 9-inch pie pans, 9 oz per pan. For 8-inch pies, see Note. Flute edges.
Eggs Sugar, granulated Salt Vanilla	30 (3 lb 4 oz) 1 lb 14 oz 1¼ tsp 2½ Tbsp	Beat eggs slightly. Add sugar, salt, and vanilla. Mix.
Milk, scalded	1¼ gal	Add hot milk, slowly at first, then more rapidly. Pour into unbaked pie shells, 1 qt per pie.
Nutmeg, ground	2 tsp	Sprinkle nutmeg over top of pies. Bake at 450°F for 15 minutes. Reduce heat to 350°F and bake for 20 minutes, or until a knife inserted halfway between the edge and center comes out clean.

Approximate nutritive values per portion

Calories (kcal)	Protein (grams)	Carbohydrate (grams)	Fat (grams)	Cholesterol (mg)	Sodium (mg)	Iron (mg)	Calcium (mg)
310	7.9 (10%)	32.2 (41%)	16.9 (49%)	124	296	1.2	121

Note   ■ For eight 8-inch pies, use 2 lb 8 oz dough portioned 5 oz per pie. For filling, use 24 (2 lb 8 oz) eggs, 1 lb 8 oz sugar, 1 tsp salt, 2 Tbsp vanilla, and 1 gal milk, portioned 3 cups per pie.

Variation   ■ **Coconut Custard Pie.**   Add 1 lb flaked coconut. Omit nutmeg.

PUMPKIN PIE

Yield: 56 portions or 7 9-inch pies   *Portion:* cut 8 per pie
Oven: 450°F, 350°F   *Bake:* 15 minutes, 30 minutes

Ingredient	Amount	Procedure
Pastry for One-Crust Pies (p. 254)	4 lb	Make pastry. Line seven 9-inch pie pans, 9 oz per pan. For 8-inch pies, see Notes. Flute edges.
Eggs, beaten Pumpkin	14 (1 lb 8 oz) 2½ qt (3 No. 2½ cans)	Combine eggs and pumpkin in mixer bowl.
Sugar, granulated Sugar, brown Ginger, ground Cinnamon, ground Salt	1 lb 12 oz 10 oz 1½ tsp 1½ Tbsp 1 Tbsp	Combine sugars and seasonings. Add to pumpkin mixture.
Milk, hot	2¾ qt	Add milk to pumpkin mixture. Mix. Pour into unbaked pie shells, 1 qt per pie. Bake at 450°F for 15 minutes. Reduce heat to 350°F and bake for 30 minutes, or until a knife inserted halfway between the edge and center comes out clean.

Approximate nutritive values per portion

Calories (kcal)	Protein (grams)	Carbohydrate (grams)	Fat (grams)	Cholesterol (mg)	Sodium (mg)	Iron (mg)	Calcium (mg)
293	5.3 (7%)	37.5 (50%)	14.2 (43%)	58	329	1.8	86

Notes
- For eight 8-inch pies, use 2 lb 8 oz pastry portioned 5 oz per pie. Use 3½ cups filling per pie.
- Undiluted evaporated milk may be substituted for fresh milk.
- One pound chopped pecans may be sprinkled over tops of pies after 15 minutes of baking. Continue baking.

Variation
- **Praline Pumpkin Pie.** Mix 12 oz finely chopped pecans, 14 oz brown sugar, and 8 oz margarine or butter. Pat 4 oz of mixture into each unbaked pie shell before pouring in filling.

PECAN PIE

Yield: 56 portions or 7 9-inch pies   *Portion:* cut 8 per pie
Oven: 350°F   *Bake:* 40 minutes

Ingredient	Amount	Procedure
Pastry for One-Crust Pies (p. 254)	4 lb	Make pastry. Line seven 9-inch pie pans, 9 oz per pan. For 8-inch pies, see Note. Flute edges.
Sugar, granulated Margarine Salt	5 lb 5 oz 1 Tbsp	Cream sugar, margarine, and salt on medium speed until fluffy, using flat beater.
Eggs, beaten	30 (3 lb 4 oz)	Add eggs to creamed mixture and mix well.
Corn syrup, white Vanilla	1¼ qt 3 Tbsp	Add corn syrup and vanilla. Blend thoroughly.
Pecan halves or pieces	2 lb	Place 4½ oz pecans in each unbaked pie shell. Pour 1 lb 8 oz (3 cups) egg-sugar mixture over pecans. Bake at 350°F for 40 minutes, or until filling is set.

Approximate nutritive values per portion

Calories (kcal)	Protein (grams)	Carbohydrate (grams)	Fat (grams)	Cholesterol (mg)	Sodium (mg)	Iron (mg)	Calcium (mg)
563	6.2 (4%)	77.9 (54%)	26.9 (42%)	112	365	2.6	37

Note   ■   For eight 8-inch pies, use 2 lb 8 oz pastry portioned 5 oz per pie. Use 2½ cups filling and 4 oz pecans per pie.

PECAN CREAM CHEESE PIE

Yield: 56 portions or 7 9-inch pies   *Portion:* 8 per pie
Oven: 375°F, 350°F   *Bake:* 10 minutes, 40–45 minutes

Ingredient	Amount	Procedure
Pastry for One-Crust Pies (p. 254)	4 lb	Make pastry. Line seven 9-inch pie pans, 5 oz per pan. For 8-inch pies, see Note. Flute edges and prick crust with fork (Figure 5.4). Bake at 375°F for 10 minutes or until set. Cool.
Cream cheese, softened	3 lb 12 oz	Combine cream cheese and sugar in mixer bowl. Beat on medium until smooth, using flat beater.
Sugar, granulated	1 lb	
Eggs	7 (12 oz)	Add eggs, salt, and vanilla to creamed mixture. Beat until smooth.
Salt	1 tsp	
Vanilla	2 Tbsp	Spread 12 oz filling into each pie shell.
Pecan pieces	2 lb 3 oz	Sprinkle 5 oz pecans over cream cheese layer.
Eggs	11 (1 lb 4 oz)	Combine eggs, sugar, corn syrup, and vanilla in mixer bowl. Mix until blended.
Sugar, brown	8 oz	
Corn syrup	2 lb 8 oz	Scale 10 oz (approximately 1 cup) over pecans.
Vanilla	1 Tbsp	Bake at 350°F for 40–45 minutes. Cool. Refrigerate overnight.

Approximate nutritive values per portion

Calories (kcal)	Protein (grams)	Carbohydrate (grams)	Fat (grams)	Cholesterol (mg)	Sodium (mg)	Iron (mg)	Calcium (mg)
512	7.4 (6%)	43.3 (33%)	35.6 (61%)	103	337	2.6	55

Note   ■   For eight 8-inch pies, use 2 lb 8 oz pastry portioned 5 oz per pie. For the filling, portion 11 oz cream cheese filling, 8 oz (1 cup) syrup mixture, and 4 oz pecans per pie.

CHOCOLATE CHIFFON PIE

Yield: 56 portions or 7 9-inch pies   *Portion:* cut 8 per pie
Oven: 425°F pastry   *Bake:* 10 minutes

Ingredient	Amount	Procedure
Pastry for One-Crust Pies (p. 254)	4 lb	Make pastry. Line seven 9-inch pie pans, 9 oz per pan. For 8-inch pies, see Notes. Flute edges and prick crust with a fork (Figure 5.4) Bake at 425°F for 10 minutes or until light brown.
Gelatin, unflavored Water, cold	1½ oz 1½ cups	Sprinkle gelatin over water. Let stand 10 minutes.
Unsweetened chocolate Water, boiling	8 oz 3 cups	Melt chocolate. Add hot water slowly. Stir until mixed. Add gelatin and stir until dissolved.
Egg yolks, beaten Sugar, granulated Salt	24 (1 lb) 1 lb 8 oz 1½ tsp	Combine egg yolks, sugar, and salt. Cook until mixture begins to thicken.
Vanilla	2 Tbsp	Add vanilla and chocolate to egg mixture. Chill until mixture begins to congeal.
Egg whites Sugar, granulated	24 (1 lb 12 oz) 1 lb 8 oz	Beat egg whites until frothy. Gradually add sugar and beat at high speed until meringue can be formed into soft peaks. Fold into chocolate mixture. Scale into baked pie shells, 1 lb (4 cups) per pie. Refrigerate.
Cream, whipping Sugar, granulated	1 qt ¼ cup	Just before serving, whip cream. Add sugar. Spread 1 cup whipped cream over each pie.

Approximate nutritive values per portion

Calories (kcal)	Protein (grams)	Carbohydrate (grams)	Fat (grams)	Cholesterol (mg)	Sodium (mg)	Iron (mg)	Calcium (mg)
362	6 (6%)	39.8 (43%)	21.2 (51%)	123	263	1.4	32

Notes
- Use of pasteurized frozen egg yolks and whites is recommended.
- For eight 8-inch pies, use 2 lb 8 oz pastry portioned 5 oz per pie. For filling, use 12 oz (3 cups) per pie.
- Graham Cracker Crust (p. 258) may be used in place of pastry.

Variations
- **Chocolate Peppermint Chiffon Pie.** Cover pie with whipped cream to which 1 lb crushed peppermint candy sticks has been added.
- **Chocolate Refrigerator Dessert.** Use ⅔ recipe Chocolate Chiffon Pie. Spread 12

oz vanilla wafer crumbs over bottom of 12 × 20 × 2-inch pan. Pour in chocolate chiffon mixture and cover with 1 lb 12 oz crumbs.

- **Frozen Chocolate Chiffon Pie.**   Fold in 3 cups cream, whipped. Pile into pastry or graham cracker crust. Spread over tops of pies 1½ cups cream, whipped and sweetened with 3 Tbsp sugar. Freeze. Serve frozen.

STRAWBERRY CHIFFON PIE

Yield: 56 portions or 7 9-inch pies   *Portion:* cut 8 per pie
Oven: 425°F pastry   *Bake:* 10 minutes

Ingredient	Amount	Procedure
Pastry for One-Crust Pies (p. 254)	4 lb	Make pastry. Line seven 9-inch pie pans, 9 oz per pan. For 8-inch pies, see Notes. Flute edges and prick crust with fork (Figure 5.4). Bake at 425°F for 10 minutes or until light brown.
Strawberries, sliced frozen	3 lb 12 oz	Drain strawberries. Reserve juice.
Strawberry gelatin Water, boiling	1 lb 4 oz 1¼ qt	Dissolve gelatin in boiling water.
Strawberry juice drained from berries Lemon juice	2 lb (1 qt) ⅔ cup	Add enough water to reserved juice to make 1 qt. Combine lemon and strawberry juices. Add to gelatin mixture. Chill until partially set. Stir occasionally.
Whipped topping	3 cups	Whip topping stiff but not dry. Whip gelatin mixture until soft peaks form. Fold in whipped topping.
Egg whites Salt Sugar, granulated	10 (12 oz) 1 tsp 12 oz	Add salt to egg whites. Beat until soft peaks form. Gradually add sugar. Beat until stiff peaks form. Fold in gelatin mixture. Fold strawberries into mixture. Portion 1 lb 4 oz filling into each baked pie shell. Chill until firm.

Approximate nutritive values per portion

Calories (kcal)	Protein (grams)	Carbohydrate (grams)	Fat (grams)	Cholesterol (mg)	Sodium (mg)	Iron (mg)	Calcium (mg)
294	6.7 (9%)	29.3 (42%)	15.3 (49%)	14	472	1	18

Note

- Use of pasteurized frozen egg whites is recommended.
- For eight 8-inch pies, use 2 lb 8 oz pastry portioned 5 oz per pie. For the filling, use 1 lb per pie.

LEMON CHIFFON PIE

Yield: 56 portions or 7 9-inch pies   *Portion:* cut 8 per pie
Oven: 425°F pastry   *Bake:* 10 minutes

Ingredient	Amount	Procedure
Pastry for One-Crust Pies (p. 254)	4 lb	Make pastry. Line seven 9-inch pie pans, 9 oz per pan. For 8-inch pies, see Note. Flute edges and prick crust with fork (Figure 5.4). Bake at 425°F for 10 minutes or until light brown.
Gelatin, unflavored Water, cold	1½ oz 1¾ cups	Sprinkle gelatin over water. Let stand 10 minutes.
Egg yolks, beaten Sugar, granulated Salt Lemon juice	21 (13 oz) 1 lb 8 oz 2 tsp 2½ cups	Add sugar, salt, and lemon juice to egg yolks. Cook in steam-jacketed kettle or over hot water until consistency of custard. Remove from heat. Add softened gelatin. Stir until dissolved.
Lemon peel, grated	2 Tbsp	Add lemon peel. Chill until mixture begins to congeal.
Egg whites Sugar, granulated	21 (1 lb 8 oz) 1 lb 2 oz	Beat egg whites until frothy. Gradually add sugar and beat until meringue will form soft peaks. Fold into lemon mixture. Scale into baked pie shells, 1 lb (4 cups) per pie. Refrigerate.
Cream, whipping Sugar, granulated	1 qt ½ cup	Just before serving, whip cream. Spread 1 cup cream over each pie.

Approximate nutritive values per portion

Calories (kcal)	Protein (grams)	Carbohydrate (grams)	Fat (grams)	Cholesterol (mg)	Sodium (mg)	Iron (mg)	Calcium (mg)
347	5.4 (6%)	38.9 (44%)	19.7 (50%)	109	296	1.1	29

Notes
- Use of pasteurized frozen egg yolks and whites is recommended.
- For eight 8-inch pies, use 2 lb 8 oz pastry portioned 5 oz per pie. For the filling, use 12 oz (3 cups) per pie.
- Graham Cracker Crust (p. 258) may be used in place of pastry.

Variations
- **Frozen Lemon Pie.**   Increase sugar in custard to 2 lb. Delete sugar from meringue. Beat egg whites and fold into 2 qt cream, whipped. Fold into chilled lemon mixture. Pour into Graham Cracker Crusts (p. 258). Freeze. Serve frozen.
- **Lemon Refrigerator Dessert.**   Crush 3 lb 8 oz vanilla wafers. Spread half of crumbs in bottom of 12 × 20 × 2-inch pan. Pour chiffon pie mixture over crumbs and cover with remaining crumbs.
- **Orange Chiffon Pie.**   Substitute 2 cups orange juice for 2 cups lemon juice. Substitute grated orange peel for lemon peel.

ICE CREAM PIE

Yield: 56 portions or 7 9-inch pies   *Portion:* cut 8 per pie
Oven: 500°F   *Bake:* 2–3 minutes

Ingredient	Amount	Procedure
Graham Cracker Crust (p. 258)	1 recipe	Prepare seven 9-inch crusts. For 8-inch pies, see Notes.
Vanilla ice cream	2 gal	Soften ice cream. Dip into prepared crusts, using 4½ cups per pie. Freeze several hours.
Egg whites Salt Sugar, granulated Vanilla	24 (2 lb 10 oz) ¾ tsp 1 lb 8 oz 1½ tsp	Add salt to egg whites. Beat until frothy, using whip attachment. Add sugar gradually, beating at high speed until sugar has dissolved. Add vanilla. Cover pies with meringue, 9 oz per pie. Brown quickly (2–3 minutes) in oven at 500°F. Return to freezer if not served immediately.
Chocolate Sauce (p. 606)	1½ qt	Serve with chocolate sauce or fresh strawberries.

Approximate nutritive values per portion

Calories (kcal)	Protein (grams)	Carbohydrate (grams)	Fat (grams)	Cholesterol (mg)	Sodium (mg)	Iron (mg)	Calcium (mg)
462	7.1 (6%)	63.9 (54%)	21.3 (40%)	36	323	1	133

Notes
- Use of pasteurized frozen egg whites is recommended.
- For eight 8-inch pies, portion 1 qt ice cream per pie. Cover with 8 oz meringue.
- Pastry crust, baked, may be used in place of graham cracker crust.
- Other flavors of ice cream may be used.

Variation
- **Raspberry Alaska Pie.**   Thicken three 40-oz packages frozen red raspberries with 2 oz cornstarch. Make thin layers of thickened berries and ice cream in graham cracker crusts, using about half of the berries. Proceed as for Ice Cream Pie. Spoon remaining berries over individual servings of pie.

FROZEN MOCHA ALMOND PIE ■

Yield: 56 portions or 7 9-inch pies   *Portion:* cut 8 per pie

Ingredient	Amount	Procedure
Graham Cracker Crust (p. 258)	1 recipe	Prepare seven 9-inch crusts. For 8-inch pies, see Note.
Gelatin, unflavored Water, cold	1½ oz 1 cup	Sprinkle gelatin over water. Let stand 10 minutes.
Egg yolks, beaten Sugar, granulated Salt Coffee, hot	18 (11 oz) 1 lb 8 oz 1 Tbsp 2 qt	Add sugar, salt, and coffee to egg yolks. Cook in steam-jacketed kettle or over hot water until mixture coats spoon. Remove from heat. Add softened gelatin. Stir until dissolved. Chill until mixture is consistency of unbeaten egg whites.
Egg whites Cream of tartar Sugar, granulated	18 (1 lb 5 oz) 1½ tsp 1 lb 8 oz	Add cream of tartar to egg whites. Beat until frothy. Add sugar gradually and beat on high speed until consistency of meringue. Fold into gelatin mixture.
Cream, whipping Sugar, granulated	1 qt ¼ cup	Whip cream. Add sugar to one-third of the whipped cream. Save for topping.
Almonds, toasted Vanilla	1 lb 2 Tbsp	Add almonds and vanilla to remaining whipped cream. Fold into gelatin mixture. Pour into prepared crusts. Spread remaining whipped cream over pies and freeze. Remove from freezer 15–20 minutes before serving.

Approximate nutritive values per portion

Calories (kcal)	Protein (grams)	Carbohydrate (grams)	Fat (grams)	Cholesterol (mg)	Sodium (mg)	Iron (mg)	Calcium (mg)
369	5.9 (6%)	47 (50%)	18.5 (44%)	90	291	1.1	52

Note   ■ Use of pasteurized frozen egg yolks and whites is recommended.

   ■ For eight 8-inch pies, use 2 lb 8 oz pastry, portioned 5 oz per pie. Portion filling 3 cups per pie.

OTHER DESSERT RECIPES

BUTTERSCOTCH PUDDING

Yield: 50 portions or 6 qt   *Portion:* ½ cup

Ingredient	Amount	Procedure
Margarine Sugar, brown	10 oz 3 lb 4 oz	Cook margarine and sugar in steam-jacketed kettle until sugar starts to dissolve.
Water, warm	1 qt	Add water slowly, while stirring. Turn off heat.
Milk	2½ qt	Add milk to warm mixture.
Cornstarch Flour, all-purpose Salt Milk	6 oz 2½ oz ½ tsp 3 cups	Combine dry ingredients in mixer bowl. Add milk to make a smooth paste. Slowly add to warm sugar-milk mixture, stirring constantly. Cook until mixture thickens. Turn off heat.
Eggs	8 (14 oz)	Beat eggs on medium speed for 3 minutes. Add some of the hot mixture to the beaten eggs while still beating. Gradually add egg mixture to hot mixture. Turn on heat. Cook to 185°F. (Eggs must be cooked thoroughly or mixture will thin upon standing.)
Vanilla	2 Tbsp	Stir in vanilla. Cover with plastic wrap or waxed paper while cooling to prevent formation of film. Serve with No. 10 dipper (rounded).

Approximate nutritive values per portion

Calories (kcal)	Protein (grams)	Carbohydrate (grams)	Fat (grams)	Cholesterol (mg)	Sodium (mg)	Iron (mg)	Calcium (mg)
221	3.3 (6%)	35.9 (64%)	7.5 (30%)	42	126	1.2	107

CHOCOLATE PUDDING

Yield: 50 portions or 6 qt   *Portion:* ½ cup

Ingredient	*Amount*	*Procedure*
Sugar, granulated	2 lb 6 oz	Combine dry ingredients.
Flour, all-purpose	6 oz	
Cornstarch	3 oz	
Salt	1 tsp	
Cocoa	8 oz	
Milk	1 gal	Pour milk into steam-jacketed kettle or stock pot. Gradually add dry ingredients while stirring briskly with a wire whip. Heat to boiling point, then cook until thickened, about 20 minutes. Stir occasionally. Remove from heat.
Margarine	8 oz	Add margarine and vanilla. Blend.
Vanilla	2 Tbsp	Cover with plastic wrap or waxed paper while cooling to prevent formation of film. Serve with No. 10 dipper (rounded).

Approximate nutritive values per portion

Calories (kcal)	Protein (grams)	Carbohydrate (grams)	Fat (grams)	Cholesterol (mg)	Sodium (mg)	Iron (mg)	Calcium (mg)
191	3.8 (8%)	32.1 (63%)	6.7 (30%)	11	127	1.8	102

Variations
- **Chocolate Banana Pudding.**   Slice 12 bananas into cooled pudding.
- **Chocolate Pudding with Chips.**   Stir 8 oz peanut butter, butterscotch, or chocolate chips into cooled pudding.

TAPIOCA CREAM PUDDING

Yield: 50 portions or 6 qt   *Portion:* ½ cup

Ingredient	Amount	Procedure
Milk	1 gal	Heat milk to boiling point in a steam-jacketed kettle or stock pot.
Tapioca, quick-cooking	9 oz	Add tapioca gradually while stirring with a wire whip. Cook until clear, stirring frequently.
Eggs yolks, beaten Sugar, granulated Salt	10 (6 oz) 1 lb 2 tsp	Mix egg yolks, sugar, and salt. Add slowly to hot mixture while stirring. Cook about 10 minutes. Remove from heat.
Egg whites Sugar, granulated	10 (12 oz) 4 oz	Beat egg whites until frothy. Add sugar and beat on high speed to form a meringue.
Vanilla	2 Tbsp	Fold egg whites and vanilla into tapioca mixture. Serve with No. 10 dipper (rounded).

Approximate nutritive values per portion

Calories (kcal)	Protein (grams)	Carbohydrate (grams)	Fat (grams)	Cholesterol (mg)	Sodium (mg)	Iron (mg)	Calcium (mg)
127	3.9 (12%)	20 (62%)	3.7 (26%)	54	137	0.2	99

Variation ■ **Fruit Tapioca Cream.** Add 1 qt chopped canned peaches or crushed pineapple, drained. Add ½ tsp almond extract for peach tapioca.

VANILLA CREAM PUDDING

Yield: 50 portions or 6 qt   *Portion:* ½ cup

Ingredient	Amount	Procedure
Milk Sugar, granulated	3 qt 1 lb	Heat milk and sugar in steam-jacketed kettle.
Sugar, granulated Cornstarch Salt Milk, cold	1 lb 4 oz 6 oz 1½ tsp 2¼ qt	Combine dry ingredients with cold milk in mixer bowl. Whip until smooth. Add to hot milk mixture slowly, stirring constantly with a wire whip. Cook mixture until it is thickened and there is no starch taste, approximately 10 minutes.
Egg yolks, beaten	20 (12 oz)	Add, while stirring, a small amount of hot mixture to the beaten eggs. Add to remainder of hot mixture in kettle, stirring constantly. Stir slowly and cook about 2 minutes. Remove from heat.
Margarine Vanilla	4 oz 2 Tbsp	Stir in margarine and vanilla. Cover with waxed paper while cooling to prevent formation of film. Serve with No. 10 dipper (rounded).

Approximate nutritive values per portion

Calories (kcal)	Protein (grams)	Carbohydrate (grams)	Fat (grams)	Cholesterol (mg)	Sodium (mg)	Iron (mg)	Calcium (mg)
195	4.5 (9%)	28.6 (58%)	7.4 (33%)	101	139	0.3	133

Variations

- **Banana Cream Pudding.**   Add 12 bananas, sliced, to cooled pudding.
- **Chocolate Cream Pudding.**   Add 6 oz sugar and 8 oz cocoa.
- **Coconut Cream Pudding.**   Add 8 oz shredded coconut just before serving.
- **Pineapple Cream Pudding.**   Add 1 qt crushed pineapple, well drained.

BAKED DATE PUDDING

Yield: 54 portions or 1 pan 12 × 20 × 2 inches   *Portion:* 3 oz
Oven: 350°F   *Bake:* 45 minutes

Ingredient	Amount	Procedure
Dates Water, hot	2 lb 4 oz 2½ cups	Pour hot water over dates in mixer bowl. Cover and let dates steam for 15 minutes. Mix on low speed and then on medium speed until dates are broken into small pieces.
Sugar, granulated Flour, all-purpose Baking powder Nonfat dry milk Salt Walnuts, coarsely chopped	1 lb 1 lb 1½ oz 2 oz 1½ tsp 12 oz	Combine dry ingredients in bowl and stir until blended. Add to date mixture. Mix on low speed only until blended. Scale into well-greased 12 × 20 × 2-inch baking pan.
Sugar, brown Margarine Water, boiling	1 lb 4 oz 2 oz 1½ qt	Mix sugar, margarine, and water. Heat to boiling point. Pour hot sauce over batter in pan. Do not stir. Bake at 350°F for 45 minutes. Cool.
		Cut 6 × 9 for 54 portions or 6 × 8 for 48 portions. Serve with whipped cream or whipped topping.

Approximate nutritive values per portion

Calories (kcal)	Protein (grams)	Carbohydrate (grams)	Fat (grams)	Cholesterol (mg)	Sodium (mg)	Iron (mg)	Calcium (mg)
204	3.1 (6%)	40.3 (75%)	4.6 (19%)	0	159	1.2	84

LEMON CAKE PUDDING

Yield: 60 portions or 2 pans 12 × 20 × 2 inches   *Portion:* 2½ × 3 inches
Oven: 350°F   *Bake:* 1 hour

Ingredient	Amount	Procedure
Egg yolks Lemon juice Margarine, softened	35 (1 lb 6 oz) 5 cups 3 oz	Beat egg yolks, lemon juice, and margarine together until lemon colored.
Sugar, granulated Flour, all-purpose Salt	6 lb 1 lb 3 oz 1 oz (1½ Tbsp)	Combine sugar, flour, and salt.
Milk	3 qt	Add dry ingredients and milk alternately to egg mixture on low speed, ending with dry ingredients.
Egg whites	27 (2 lb)	Beat egg whites on high speed, until stiff, using wire whip attachment. Blend into egg mixture on low speed.
		Pour pudding into two 12 × 20 × 2-inch counter pans, 9 lb 8 oz per pan. Set filled pans in two other counter pans that have been filled half full with boiling water. Bake at 350°F for 1 hour. Cut 5 × 6.

Approximate nutritive values per portion

Calories (kcal)	Protein (grams)	Carbohydrate (grams)	Fat (grams)	Cholesterol (mg)	Sodium (mg)	Iron (mg)	Calcium (mg)
292	6 (8%)	56.2 (74%)	6.1 (18%)	140	231	0.8	79

CHEESECAKE

Yield: 48 portions or 6 8-inch cakes   *Portion:* cut 8 per cake
Oven: 350°F   *Bake:* 45 minutes

Ingredient	Amount	Procedure
Graham cracker crumbs	1 lb 8 oz	Combine crumbs, sugar, and melted margarine. Place 1 cup crumb mixture into each of six 8-inch pie pans or six 6 × 6-inch square cake pans. Press crumbs to sides and bottom of pans.
Sugar, granulated	12 oz	
Margarine, melted	12 oz	
Cream cheese	4 lb 8 oz	Let cheese stand until it reaches room temperature. Cream until smooth, using flat beater.
Eggs	11 (1 lb 3 oz)	Add eggs slowly to cream cheese while beating.
Sugar, granulated	1 lb 2 oz	Add sugar and vanilla to cheese mixture. Beat on high speed for about 5 minutes. Place about 3 cups filling in each shell. Bake at 350°F for 30–35 minutes. Do not overbake.
Vanilla	2 Tbsp	
Sour cream	1¼ qt	Mix sour cream, sugar, and vanilla. Spread 1 cup topping on each cake.
Sugar, granulated	4 oz	
Vanilla	1½ tsp	
Graham cracker crumbs	4 oz	Sprinkle with a few graham cracker crumbs. Bake 10 minutes.

Approximate nutritive values per portion

Calories (kcal)	Protein (grams)	Carbohydrate (grams)	Fat (grams)	Cholesterol (mg)	Sodium (mg)	Iron (mg)	Calcium (mg)
411	6.7 (6%)	34.5 (33%)	28 (61%)	105	299	1.3	78

Variation ■ **Cheesecake with Fruit Glaze.** Cover baked cheesecake with the following glaze: Thaw and drain 6 lb frozen strawberries, raspberries, or cherries. Measure 1 qt fruit syrup, adding water if needed to make that amount. Add slowly to mixture of 4 oz cornstarch, 6 oz granulated sugar, and ¾ cup lemon juice. Cook until thick and clear. Cool slightly. Add drained fruit. Spread over cheesecakes. Canned fruit pie fillings may be used for the glaze.

BAKED CUSTARD

Yield: 50 custards   *Portion:* 4 oz
Oven: 325°F   *Bake:* 40–45 minutes

Ingredient	Amount	Procedure
Eggs	20 (2 lb 3 oz)	Beat eggs slightly, using wire whip attachment.
Sugar, granulated	1 lb 4 oz	Add sugar, salt, cold milk, and vanilla.
Salt	½ tsp	Mix on low speed only until blended.
Milk, cold	1 qt	
Vanilla	2 Tbsp	
Milk	1 gal	Scald milk by bringing to point just below boiling. Add to egg mixture and blend.
Nutmeg	2 tsp	Pour mixture into custard cups that have been arranged in baking pans. Sprinkle nutmeg over tops. Pour hot water around cups. Bake at 325°F for 40–45 minutes or until a knife inserted in custard comes out clean.

Approximate nutritive values per portion

Calories (kcal)	Protein (grams)	Carbohydrate (grams)	Fat (grams)	Cholesterol (mg)	Sodium (mg)	Iron (mg)	Calcium (mg)
134	5.7 (17%)	16.4 (48%)	5.3 (35%)	98	94	0.3	127

Note
- Custard may be baked in a 12 × 20 × 2-inch pan set in a pan of hot water. Cut 5 × 8 for 40 portions.

Variations
- **Bread Pudding.**   Pour liquid mixture over 1 lb dry bread cubes and let stand until bread is softened. Add 1 lb raisins if desired. Bake. Day-old sweet rolls may be substituted for bread.
- **Caramel Custard.**   Add 1 cup Burnt Sugar Syrup (p. 207) slowly to scalded milk and stir carefully until melted.
- **Rice Custard.**   Use ½ Baked Custard recipe, adding 1 lb rice (AP) cooked, 1 lb raisins, and 3 oz melted margarine or butter.

FLOATING ISLAND

Yield: 50 portions or 6 qt   *Portion:* ½ cup (4 oz)

Ingredient	Amount	Procedure
Milk	4½ qt	Heat milk to boiling point.
Sugar, granulated Cornstarch Salt	1 lb 4 oz ½ tsp	Combine sugar, cornstarch, and salt. Add gradually to hot milk, stirring briskly with wire whip. Cook over hot water or in steam-jacketed kettle until slightly thickened.
Egg yolks, beaten Vanilla	27 (1 lb 2 oz) 2 Tbsp	Gradually stir egg yolks and vanilla into hot mixture. Continue cooking until thickened, about 5 minutes.
Egg whites Sugar, granulated	27 (1 lb 14 oz) 12 oz	Beat egg whites on high speed past the frothy stage, approximately 1½ minutes, using wire whip attachment. Add sugar gradually, while beating. Beat until sugar has dissolved and mixture resembles meringue. Drop by spoonfuls onto hot water and bake at 375°F until set.
		Cool custard slightly and pour into sherbet dishes; or dip, using a No. 10 dipper. Lift meringues from water with a fork and place on top of portioned custards. Add dash of nutmeg. Chill before serving.

Approximate nutritive values per portion

Calories (kcal)	Protein (grams)	Carbohydrate (grams)	Fat (grams)	Cholesterol (mg)	Sodium (mg)	Iron (mg)	Calcium (mg)
169	6.4 (15%)	22.6 (53%)	6.1 (32%)	143	98	0.4	120

Variation   ■ **Creamy Custard Sauce with Fruit.** Ladle 3 oz custard over fresh fruit. Suggested combinations are: sliced bananas, blueberries and sliced peaches; or cubed pineapple, raspberries, and sliced peaches.

CHRISTMAS PUDDING

Yield: 48 portions   *Portion:* 3 oz
Steam pressure: 5–6 lb   *Steam:* 40–45 minutes

Ingredient	Amount	Procedure
Carrots, raw, peeled	1 lb 4 oz (EP)	Peel and grate carrots and potatoes.
Potatoes, raw, peeled	1 lb 11 oz (EP)	
Sugar, granulated	2 lb	Cream sugar and margarine on medium speed, using flat beater.
Margarine	1 lb	
Raisins	1 lb 4 oz	Add raisins, dates, and nuts to creamed mixture.
Dates, chopped	1 lb 4 oz	Add carrots and potatoes.
Nuts, chopped	12 oz	Mix on low speed until blended.
Flour, all-purpose	1 lb	Combine dry ingredients.
Baking soda	4 tsp	Add to fruit mixture. Mix on low speed until blended.
Cinnamon	1 Tbsp	
Cloves	1 Tbsp	
Nutmeg	1 Tbsp	
Salt	¼ tsp	
		Portion mixture with No. 16 dipper into greased muffin pans.
		Cover each filled pan with an inverted empty muffin pan.
		Steam for 40–45 minutes.
		Serve warm with Vanilla Sauce (p. 608), Hard Sauce (p. 609), or Nutmeg Sauce (p. 608)
		Garnish with holly leaf and whole cranberries for Christmas.

Approximate nutritive values per portion

Calories (kcal)	Protein (grams)	Carbohydrate (grams)	Fat (grams)	Cholesterol (mg)	Sodium (mg)	Iron (mg)	Calcium (mg)
303	3.5 (4%)	50.3 (63%)	11.6 (33%)	0	177	1.3	40

Variation   ■ **Flaming Pudding.** Dip sugar cube in lemon extract. Place on hot pudding and light just before serving.

CREAM PUFFS

Yield: 50 portions   *Portion:* 1 puff
Oven: 425°F, 325°F   *Bake:* 15 minutes, 30 minutes

Ingredient	Amount	Procedure
Margarine or butter Water, boiling	1 lb 1 qt	Melt margarine in boiling water.
Flour, all-purpose Salt	1 lb 3 oz 1 tsp	Add flour and salt all at once to boiling mixture. Beat vigorously. Remove from heat as soon as mixture leaves sides of pan. Transfer to mixer bowl. Cool slightly.
Eggs	16 (1 lb 12 oz)	Add eggs one at a time, beating on high speed after each addition.
		Drop batter with No. 24 dipper onto greased baking sheets. Bake at 425°F for 15 minutes. Reduce heat to 325°F and bake 30 minutes longer.
		When ready to use, make a cut in top of each puff with a sharp knife. Fill with Custard Filling (p. 230), using a No. 16 dipper. Top with Chocolate Sauce (p. 606) if desired.

Approximate nutritive values per portion

Calories (kcal)	Protein (grams)	Carbohydrate (grams)	Fat (grams)	Cholesterol (mg)	Sodium (mg)	Iron (mg)	Calcium (mg)
128	3.2 (10%)	8.5 (27%)	9 (63%)	68	149	0.7	13

Variations

- **Butterscotch Cream Puffs.** Fill cream puffs with Butterscotch Pudding (p. 281). Top with Butterscotch Sauce (p. 605) if desired.

- **Eclairs.** Shape cream puff mixture by piping with a pastry tube, ¾ inch wide and 4 inches long. Bake. Split lengthwise. Proceed as for Cream Puffs. When filled, ice with Chocolate Glaze (p. 227).

- **Ice Cream Puffs.** Fill puffs with vanilla ice cream and serve with Chocolate Sauce (p. 606).

- **Orange Cream Puffs with Chocolate Filling.** Add ½ cup grated orange peel and 10 oz chopped almonds to cream puff mixture. Bake. Fill with Chocolate Cream Filling (p. 228) or Chocolate Pudding (p. 282).

- **Puff Shells.** Make bite-size shells with pastry tube or No. 100 dipper. Bake. Fill with chicken, fish, or ham salad. Yield: approximately 200 puffs.

PINEAPPLE BAVARIAN CREAM

Yield: 60 portions or 2 pans 12 × 20 × 2 inches   *Portion:* 2½ × 3 inches

Ingredient	Amount	Procedure
Gelatin, unflavored Water, cold	3 oz 1 qt	Sprinkle gelatin over water. Let stand 10 minutes.
Crushed pineapple Sugar, granulated	1 No. 10 can 1 lb 12 oz	Heat pineapple and sugar to boiling point.
Lemon juice	¼ cup	Add gelatin to pineapple mixture. Stir until dissolved. Add lemon juice. Chill until mixture begins to congeal.
Whipping cream	1 qt	Whip cream and fold into pineapple mixture. Pour into 50 individual molds or two 12 × 20 × 2-inch pans. Cut 5 × 6.

Approximate nutritive values per portion

Calories (kcal)	Protein (grams)	Carbohydrate (grams)	Fat (grams)	Cholesterol (mg)	Sodium (mg)	Iron (mg)	Calcium (mg)
127	1.7 (5%)	20.4 (61%)	5 (34%)	18	8	0.3	18

Note   ■ May be used for pie filling.

Variations ■ **Apricot Bavarian Cream.** Substitute 3 lb dried apricots, cooked, or 6 lb canned apricots, sieved, for the crushed pineapple.

■ **Strawberry Bavarian Cream.** Substitute 6 lb fresh or frozen sliced strawberries for pineapple.

RUSSIAN CREAM

Yield: 50 portions or 5 qt   *Portion:* 4 oz

Ingredient	Amount	Procedure
Gelatin, unflavored Water, cold	1½ oz 1¼ qt	Sprinkle gelatin over cold water. Let stand 10 minutes.
Light cream (half-and-half) Sugar, granulated	1½ qt 2 lb	Combine half-and-half and sugar. Heat until warm in steam-jacketed kettle or over hot water. Stir in softened gelatin. Heat until gelatin and sugar are dissolved but do not boil. Cool.
Sour cream Vanilla	2 lb 8 oz 2½ Tbsp	When mixture begins to thicken, fold in sour cream and vanilla, which have been beaten until smooth. Chill.
Raspberries, frozen	5 lb	Dip pudding with No. 12 dipper. Serve with No. 30 dipper of partially defrosted raspberries.

Approximate nutritive values per portion

Calories (kcal)	Protein (grams)	Carbohydrate (grams)	Fat (grams)	Cholesterol (mg)	Sodium (mg)	Iron (mg)	Calcium (mg)
206	2.6 (5%)	32.4 (61%)	8.2 (34%)	21	26	0.4	64

APPLE CRISP ■

Yield: 64 portions or 2 pans 12 × 20 × 2 inches   *Portion:* 3 × 2½ inches
Oven: 350°F   *Bake:* 45–50 minutes

Ingredient	Amount	Procedure
Apples, sliced	15 lb (EP)	Mix sugar and lemon juice with apples.
Sugar, granulated	12 oz	Arrange in 2 greased 12 × 20 × 2-inch baking pans, 8
Lemon juice	⅓ cup	lb per pan.
Margarine, soft	1 lb 4 oz	Combine remaining ingredients and mix until crumbly.
Flour, all-purpose	12 oz	Spread evenly over apples, 2 lb 4 oz per pan.
Rolled oats, quick-cooking, uncooked	12 oz	Bake at 350°F for 45–50 minutes. Serve with whipped cream, ice cream, or cheese.
Sugar, brown	2 lb	Cut 4 × 8.

Approximate nutritive values per portion

Calories (kcal)	Protein (grams)	Carbohydrate (grams)	Fat (grams)	Cholesterol (mg)	Sodium (mg)	Iron (mg)	Calcium (mg)
239	1.7 (3%)	43 (69%)	7.9 (28%)	0	88	1.2	26

Notes

- Fresh, frozen, or canned apples may be used.
- 1 tsp cinnamon or nutmeg may be added to the topping.
- 8 oz finely chopped pecans may be added to the topping.

Variations

- **Cheese Apple Crisp.**   Add 8 oz grated cheese to topping mixture.
- **Cherry Crisp.**   Substitute frozen pie cherries for apples. Increase granulated sugar to 1 lb. Add ½ tsp almond extract.
- **Fresh Fruit Crisp.**   Combine 3 lb granulated sugar, 12 oz flour, 1 Tbsp nutmeg, and 1 Tbsp cinnamon. Add to 15 lb fresh fruit, peeled and sliced. Top with mixture of 2 lb 6 oz margarine, 2 lb 8 oz brown sugar, and 2 lb 6 oz flour. Cream margarine, add brown sugar and flour, and mix until of dough consistency. Spread over fruit. Bake. Serve warm with cream.
- **Peach Crisp.**   Substitute sliced peaches for apples.

BAKED APPLES

Yield: 50 portions *Portion:* 1 apple
Oven: 375°F *Bake:* 45 minutes

Ingredient	Amount	Procedure
Apples	50	Wash and core apples. Peel down about one-fourth of the way from the top. Place in baking pans, peeled-side up.
Sugar, granulated Water, hot Salt Cinnamon, ground	3 lb 3 cups 1 tsp 1 Tbsp	Mix sugar, water, salt, and cinnamon. Pour over apples. Bake at 375°F until tender, about 45 minutes, basting occasionally while cooking to glaze. Test for doneness with a pointed knife inserted in the apple.

Approximate nutritive values per portion

Calories (kcal)	Protein (grams)	Carbohydrate (grams)	Fat (grams)	Cholesterol (mg)	Sodium (mg)	Iron (mg)	Calcium (mg)
183	0.3 (1%)	48.4 (97%)	0.5 (2%)	0	44	0.3	12

Notes

- Use apples of uniform size, suitable for baking, such as Rome Beauty or Jonathan.
- Amount of sugar will vary with tartness of apples.
- ½ cup red cinnamon candies may be substituted for cinnamon.
- Apple centers may be filled with chopped dates, raisins, nuts, or mincemeat.
- 3 oz margarine or butter may be added to the syrup for flavor.

APPLE DUMPLINGS

Yield: 50 dumplings   *Portion:* 1 dumpling
Oven: 350°F   *Bake:* 25–30 minutes

Ingredient	Amount	Procedure
Pastry (p. 256)	7 lb	Make pastry. Scale into 10-oz balls. Chill for 10 minutes or more.
Flour, all-purpose Sugar, granulated Salt Cinnamon, ground	10 oz 6 lb 1 Tbsp 1 Tbsp	Make sauce. Combine flour, sugar, salt, and cinnamon.
Water, hot	1½ gal	Add dry ingredients to water while stirring with a wire whip. Cook until thickened.
Margarine	1 lb	Add margarine and stir until margarine is melted. Remove from heat.
Vanilla	2 Tbsp	Add vanilla.
Apples, medium size	50	Wash, core, and peel apples.
Margarine	1 lb 8 oz	Roll pastry to ⅛-inch thickness. Position apple on dough and cut a circle approximately 7 inches in diameter around it. Insert 1 Tbsp margarine into center of each apple. Push toward center of apple.
Sugar, granulated Cinnamon, ground Nutmeg, ground	1 lb 5 oz 1½ Tbsp 2 tsp	Combine sugar, cinnamon, and nutmeg. Use mixture to fill centers of apples. Enclose the apple in the cut dough, pinching to seal the edges. Turn the apple over so that the bottom is the top and make three slashes in the top of the apple. Place in lightly greased baking pans. Bake for 15 minutes at 350°F. Baste dumplings with one-half of the sauce and bake 10–15 minutes longer or until golden brown. Serve dumplings with additional warm sauce as desired.

Approximate nutritive values per portion

Calories (kcal)	Protein (grams)	Carbohydrate (grams)	Fat (grams)	Cholesterol (mg)	Sodium (mg)	Iron (mg)	Calcium (mg)
823	4.2 (2%)	116 (54%)	41.3 (44%)	0	668	2	32

Notes
- Apples may be wrapped with dough and frozen for later use. To serve, make sauce and bake as directed but allow 15–20 minutes longer baking time.
- Sliced apples, frozen or fresh, may be used in place of whole apples. Cut pastry into 6-inch squares. Place No. 10 dipper of fruit in the center and sprinkle with sugar-cinnamon mixture. Fold corners of pastry to the center and on top of fruit and seal edges to together. Bake as directed for Apple Dumplings.

APPLESAUCE

Yield: 50 portions   *Portion:* ½ cup (4 oz)

Ingredient	Amount	Procedure
Apples, tart	15 lb (AP)	Wash, peel and core apples. Cut into quarters.
Water	1 qt	Add water to apples. Cook slowly until soft.
Sugar, granulated	3 lb	Add sugar and stir until dissolved. Serve with No. 10 dipper (rounded).

Approximate nutritive values per portion

Calories (kcal)	Protein (grams)	Carbohydrate (grams)	Fat (grams)	Cholesterol (mg)	Sodium (mg)	Iron (mg)	Calcium (mg)
182	0.3 (1%)	48 (97%)	0.5 (2%)	0	2	0.2	10

Notes
- Thin slices of lemon, lemon juice, or 1 tsp cinnamon may be added.
- Peaches or pears may be substituted for apples.
- Apples may be cooked unpeeled.
- Amount of sugar will vary with tartness of apples.

Variation
- **Apple Compote.** Combine sugar and water and heat to boiling point. Add apples and cook until transparent.

FRUIT COBBLER

Yield: 64 portions or 2 pans 12 × 20 × 2 inches   *Portion:* 3 × 2½ inches
Oven: 425°F   *Bake:* 30 minutes

Ingredient	Amount	Procedure
Fruit, frozen	10 lb	Drain fruit. Reserve juice.
Juice drained from fruit, plus water to make total amount needed	2 qt	Heat juice and water to boiling point.
Sugar, granulated Cornstarch Seasonings	1–2 lb (see Table 5.3, p. 263) 6 oz See Table 5.3, p. 263	Mix sugar, cornstarch, salt, and seasonings, if any.
Water, cold	2 cups	Add cold water to dry ingredients and stir until smooth. Add to hot juice while stirring briskly with a wire whip. Cook until thickened.
		Add cooked, drained fruit to thickened juice. Mix carefully to prevent breaking or mashing fruit. Cool. Pour into two 12 × 20 × 2-inch baking pans, 9 lb 6 oz per pan.
Pastry (p. 254) or Biscuit Topping for Fruit Cobbler (p. 299)	3 lb	Roll pastry or topping to fit pans. Place on top of fruit. Seal edges to sides of pan. Perforate top. Bake at 425°F for 30 minutes or until top is browned. Cut 4 × 8.

Approximate nutritive values per portion

Calories (kcal)	Protein (grams)	Carbohydrate (grams)	Fat (grams)	Cholesterol (mg)	Sodium (mg)	Iron (mg)	Calcium (mg)
192	1.3 (3%)	30 (60%)	8.2 (37%)	2	144	0.7	8

Notes
- Use cherries, berries, peaches, apricots, apples, plums, or other fruits.
- The amount of sugar will vary with the tartness of the fruit.
- For canned fruit, see p. 261.

Variations   ■   **Fruit Slices.**   Use 2 lb 12 oz pastry. Line an 18 × 26 × 2-inch baking pan with 1 lb 8 oz of the pastry. Add fruit filling prepared as for cobbler. Moisten edges of dough and cover with crust made of remaining pastry. Trim and seal edges and perforate top. Bake at 400°F for 1–1¼ hours.

■   **Peach Cobbler with Hard Sauce.**   Use 10 lb frozen sliced peaches, thawed, and mixed with 1 lb sugar, 1 tsp nutmeg, 4 oz flour, and 6 oz margarine, melted. Top with pastry crust and bake. Serve warm with Hard Sauce (p. 609) or ice cream.

BISCUIT TOPPING FOR FRUIT COBBLER

Yield: topping for two 12 × 20-inch pans or 64 portions

Ingredient	Amount	Procedure
Flour, all-purpose	1 lb 6 oz	Blend dry ingredients in mixer bowl.
Baking powder	1 oz	
Salt	1 tsp	
Sugar, granulated	3 oz	
Nonfat dry milk	2 tsp	
Shortening	8 oz	Cut shortening into dry ingredients on low speed until it appears as coarse as cornmeal.
Eggs	2 (4 oz)	Beat eggs. Add water and blend.
Water	1¼ cups	Add to flour-shortening mixture.
		Blend on low speed until a soft dough is formed.
		Scale 1 lb 8 oz dough per pan. Roll to fit 12 × 20-inch pan.
		Roll onto rolling pin. Place over filling in pan, allowing dough to extend up edge of pan, about 1 inch all around (to allow for shrinkage).
		Cut several slits in dough.
Milk	¼ cup	Brush top of each pan with 2 Tbsp milk and 2 Tbsp sugar.
Sugar, granulated	2 oz	

Approximate nutritive values per portion

Calories (kcal)	Protein (grams)	Carbohydrate (grams)	Fat (grams)	Cholesterol (mg)	Sodium (mg)	Iron (mg)	Calcium (mg)
79	1.3 (6%)	9.9 (50%)	3.8 (44%)	8	81	0.5	32

OLD-FASHIONED STRAWBERRY SHORTCAKE

Yield: 50 individual shortcakes   *Portion:* 1 shortcake + ¾ cup (6 oz) strawberries
Oven: 375°F   *Bake:* 15 minutes

Ingredient	Amount	Procedure
Strawberries, fresh Sugar, granulated	9 qt 2 lb (variable)	Wash, drain, and stem strawberries. Slice and sweeten. Adjust sugar according to sweetness of berries.
Flour, all-purpose Baking powder Salt Sugar	4 lb 5 oz 1 Tbsp 1 lb 5 oz	Mix dry ingredients in mixer bowl.
Margarine or butter	2 lb	Cut margarine into dry ingredients, using pastry blender or flat beater. Mixture should have coarse, mealy consistency.
Milk	1½ qt	Stir milk quickly into flour mixture. Mix just enough to moisten.
		Portion dough with No. 20 dipper onto ungreased baking sheets. Place about 2 inches apart to allow for spreading. Bake at 375°F for 12–15 minutes or until golden brown.
Cream, half-and-half, or whipping cream	1½ qt (3 qt if whipped)	To serve, dip ¾ cup (6 oz) strawberries over shortcake. Serve with cream or top with whipped cream.

Approximate nutritive values per portion

Calories (kcal)	Protein (grams)	Carbohydrate (grams)	Fat (grams)	Cholesterol (mg)	Sodium (mg)	Iron (mg)	Calcium (mg)
466	6.4 (5%)	68.8 (58%)	19.7 (37%)	15	611	2.1	271

Note   ■   For frozen strawberries, use 12 lb. Portion ½ cup over shortcake.

FRUIT AND CHEESE DESSERT

Yield: 50 portions   *Portion:* 2⅓–3 oz

Ingredient	Amount	Procedure

Fruit—choose from:
  Apples, cut in
  wedges
  Bananas, cut in
  chunks
  Kiwi fruit, cut in
  wedges
  Pears, quartered
  Pineapple spears
  Strawberries
	5–6 lb	Select fruit in season that offers contrast in color and texture.
		Arrange attractively on a platter or tray.

Dessert cheese—
  choose from:
  Blue
  Brie
  Camembert
  Gruyère
  Port du Salut
	3–4 lb	Place cheese on the platter with the fruit or along side.
		Cut cheese into serving pieces or provide knife or cheese server so guests may serve themselves.
		Garnish. Seasonal garnishes are appropriate.

Dessert crackers or wafers	2–2½ lb	Serve with dessert crackers or wafers.

Approximate nutritive values per portion

Calories (kcal)	Protein (grams)	Carbohydrate (grams)	Fat (grams)	Cholesterol (mg)	Sodium (mg)	Iron (mg)	Calcium (mg)
242	10.9 (17%)	25.8 (41%)	11.5 (41%)	32	435	1	206

6

Eggs and Cheese

Eggs, cheese, and milk are basic ingredients in many quantity recipes, and their cookery requires carefully controlled temperatures and cooking times.

EGGS

Market Forms

Fresh Eggs

The quality of an egg is indicated by grade and is not related to size. Federal quality standards, determined by both interior and exterior quality, classify fresh shell eggs as AA, A, and B. Grades AA and A are best for poaching, frying, and cooking in the shell because the yolks are firm, round, and high, and the thick white stands high around the yolk.

Eggs are classified also according to size and are available as jumbo (30 oz per doz), extra large (27 oz per doz), large (24 oz per doz), medium (21 oz per doz), and small (18 oz per doz). Recipes in this book were tested using large eggs. Substituting smaller or larger eggs in recipes where exact proportions are important will require some calculation based on weights. Table 1.3 gives additional information on weights for whole eggs, whites, and yolks.

Eggs are susceptible to bacterial growth, so proper storage, handling, and cooking are important in maintaining quality. Fresh eggs deteriorate rapidly at room temperature and should be refrigerated at 40°F or below. If kept under proper refrigeration they will retain their quality for three weeks. Eggs should be kept in their case to prevent loss of moisture and should be stored away from foods with strong odors.

Processed Eggs

Although fresh shell eggs are used extensively for table service, processed eggs are convenient to use in many food products and eliminate the time-consuming task of breaking eggs. Whole eggs, whites, yolks, and various blends are available in liquid, frozen, and dried forms. All egg products must be processed in sanitary facilities under USDA supervision and bear the USDA inspection mark. They must be pasteurized and are routinely analyzed for salmonella contamination. Processed eggs may be contaminated easily and care must be taken to handle them properly.

Frozen Eggs   Eggs may be purchased frozen whole or in the form of whites or yolks, and they are available in containers of various sizes. High-quality eggs are used for frozen eggs, and they are suitable for omelets, scrambled eggs, and French toast, as well as for baking.

Frozen egg products should be transferred to refrigerators or freezers immediately upon delivery. Store frozen eggs at 0°F or below, and when defrosting, leave in the refrigerator. Never thaw at room temperature. If 30-lb cans are used, they require two to three days to defrost in the refrigerator. Use defrosted eggs promptly. Refrigerate any unused portion and use within one to three days.

Dried Eggs   Dried eggs are used less frequently than frozen and fresh eggs and are used primarily for baking. They should be stored in a cool, dry place where the temperature does not exceed 50°F, preferably in the refrigerator. After opening a package, any unused portion should be refrigerated in a container with a close-fitting lid.

Reconstitute only the amount that will be used immediately. Dried eggs may be blended with water; more often they are combined with other dry ingredients in the recipe and the amount of water needed to reconstitute is added. Reconstituted eggs should be used immediately or refrigerated promptly in an airtight container and used within an hour.

See Table 1.3 for substituting processed for shell eggs.

Egg Cookery

Important rules in egg cooking are to use low temperatures and short cooking times. Eggs should be cooked until the white is completely coagulated (set) and the yolk begins to thicken. It is not necessary to cook eggs until hard or rubbery to kill bacteria that may be present. Egg white coagulates between 140°F and 149°F. Whole eggs cooked until the white is set (completely coagulated and firm) and the yolk is beginning to thicken (no longer runny but not hard) are considered to have met necessary time and temperature requirements for safety.

Poached, soft- or hard-cooked, and scrambled eggs should be prepared as close to service as possible by batch cooking or cooking to order. If eggs must be held on a hot counter, they should be undercooked slightly to compensate for the additional heating that will occur. Directions for cooking eggs are given beginning on p. 308.

CHEESE AND MILK

Cheese Cookery

Cheese used in cooking should be appropriate in flavor and texture to the item being prepared and should blend well with other ingredients. Aged natural cheese or processed cheese blends more readily than green or unripened cheese. Processed cheese is a blend of fresh and aged natural cheeses that have been melted, pasteurized, and mixed with an emulsifier. It has no rind or waste, is easy to slice, and melts readily. During processing, however, it loses some of the characteristic flavor of natural cheese. For this reason, a natural cheese with a more pronounced flavor may be preferred for cheese sauce and as an addition to other cooked foods where a distinctive cheese flavor is desired.

Cheese to be combined with other ingredients usually is ground, shredded, or diced to expedite melting and blending. Cheese melts in a 300°–325°F oven, so baked dishes containing cheese should be cooked at a temperature no higher than 350°F. Excessive temperature and prolonged cooking cause cheese to toughen and become stringy and the fat to separate. When making cheese sauce, the cheese should be added after the white sauce is completely cooked and the mixture heated only enough to melt the cheese. When cheese is used as a topping, a thin layer of buttered bread crumbs will protect it from the heat and from becoming stringy.

Because it is available in many forms, cheddar cheese is commonly used in quantity food preparation and ranges in flavor from mild to very sharp. Cheese may be used for appetizers, sandwiches, and salads, or with crackers and fruit for dessert (see p. 301 for dessert suggestions). Table 6.1 lists some of the most common cheeses.

Milk Cookery

Milk should be heated or cooked at a low temperature. At high temperatures the protein in milk coagulates, leaving a film on the surface and a coating on the sides of the kettle. This coating tends to scorch when milk is heated over direct heat. To prevent formation of this coating, milk should be heated over water, in a steamer, or in a steam-jacketed kettle. Whipping the milk to form a foam or tightly covering the pan and heating the milk to below boiling temperature help to prevent formation of a surface film.

Curdling may be caused by holding the milk at high temperature or by adding foods containing acids and tannins. For example, the tannins in potatoes often cause curdling of the milk used in scalloped potatoes. Milk in combination with ham or certain vegetables, such as asparagus, green beans, carrots, peas, or tomatoes, may curdle. Curdling may be lessened by limiting the salt used, adding the milk in the form of a white sauce, keeping the temperature below boiling, and shortening the cooking time. Danger of curdling in tomato soup may be lessened by adding the tomato to the milk, by having both the milk and tomato hot when they are combined, or by thickening the milk or tomato juice before they are combined.

Dry milk is substituted often for fluid milk in quantity cooking because dry milk is comparatively lower in cost and easy to handle and store. It is available as whole milk, nonfat milk, and buttermilk. Nonfat dry milk is pure, fresh milk from which the fat and water have been removed. It has better keeping qualities than dry whole milk, although both should be kept dry and cool. Once reconstituted, dry milk should be refrigerated.

When dry milk is used in recipes that contain a large proportion of dry ingredients, such as bread, biscuits, and cakes, the only change in method would be to mix the unsifted dry milk with the other dry ingredients and use water in place of fluid milk. For best results, dry milk should be weighed, not measured. Package directions for reconstituting dry milk solids should be followed. A general guide is to use 3.5 ounces, by weight, of instant or regular spray process nonfat dry milk plus 3¾ cups water to make 1 quart liquid milk; or 1 pound plus 3¾ quarts water to make 1 gallon. The same proportion is used for dry buttermilk. For some foods, additional fat (1.2 oz per quart of liquid) should be added. Additional amounts of nonfat dry milk may be added to some foods to supplement their nutritional value, although excessive amounts that affect palatability should not be used.

TABLE 6.1   Guide to natural cheeses

Type	Fat grams per ounce (approx.)	Characteristics	Mode of serving
American	9	Mild flavor; semisoft to soft; smooth, plastic body	In sandwiches, on crackers
Bel Paese		Mild to moderately robust flavor; soft; smooth waxy body	On crackers, with fruit, in sandwiches; as such (dessert)
Blue (bleu)	8	Tangy, piquant flavor; semisoft, pasty sometimes crumbly texture; white interior marbled or streaked with blue veins of mold; resembles Roquefort	In dips, salad dressings, and cooked foods; as such (dessert)
Brick	8	Mild to moderately sharp flavor; semisoft to medium firm, elastic texture; creamy white-to-yellow interior; brownish exterior; slices well without crumbling	In salads and sandwiches; as such (dessert)
Brie	8	Mild to pungent flavor; soft, smooth texture; creamy yellow interior; edible thin brown and white crust	As such (dessert)
Camembert		Distinctive mild to tangy flavor; smooth texture, almost fluid when fully ripened; creamy yellow interior; edible thin white or gray-white crust	As such (dessert)
Cheddar	9	Mild to very sharp flavor; hard, smooth, firm body; can be crumbly; light cream to orange	As such; in sandwiches, cooked foods
Colby	9	Mild to mellow flavor, similar to cheddar; softer body and more open texture than cheddar; light cream to orange	As such; in sandwiches, cooked foods
Cottage	5 (creamed)	Mild, slightly acid flavor; soft, open texture with tender curds of varying size; white to creamy white	As such; in salads, dips, cooked foods
Cream	10	Delicate, slightly acid flavor; soft, smooth texture; white	As such; in salads, in sandwiches, in dips, on crackers

TABLE 6.1 **Continued**

Type	Fat grams per ounce (approx.)	Characteristics	Mode of serving
Edam	7	Mellow, nutlike, sometimes salty flavor; rather firm, rubbery texture; creamy yellow or medium yellow-orange interior; surface coated with red wax; usually shaped like a flattened ball	As such; on crackers, with fresh fruit
Feta		Salty; soft, flaky, similar to very dry, high-acid cottage cheese; white	As such; in cooked foods
Gouda	7	Mellow, nutlike flavor, similar to Edam; smooth texture, often containing small holes; creamy yellow or medium yellow-orange interior; usually has a red wax coating; usually shaped like a flattened ball	As such; on crackers, with fresh fruit, in cooked dishes
Gruyère		Nutlike, salty flavor, similar to Swiss but sharper; firm, smooth texture with small holes or eyes; light yellow	As such (dessert); fondue
Monterey Jack	9	Very mild flavor; semisoft (whole milk), hard (lowfat or skim milk); smooth texture with small openings throughout; creamy white	As such; in sandwiches; grating cheese if made from lowfat or skim milk
Mozzarella	5 (part skim)	Delicate, mild flavor; semisoft, plastic texture; creamy white	Generally used in cooking, on pizza, or as such
Muenster	9	Mild to mellow flavor; semisoft; smooth, waxy body, numerous small mechanical openings; yellow, tan, or white surface; creamy white interior	As such; in sandwiches
Neufchâtel	7	Soft, smooth, creamy	As such; in sandwiches, dips, salads
Parmesan	7	Sharp, distinctive flavor; very hard, granular texture; yellowish white	Grated cheese on salads, soups, and pasta dishes
Port du Salut		Mellow to robust flavor similar to Gouda; semisoft, smooth elastic texture; creamy white or yellow	As such (dessert); with fresh fruit; on crackers
Provolone	8	Bland, acid flavor to sharp and piquant, usually smoked; hard, stringy texture; cuts without crumbling; plastic	As such (dessert) after it has ripened for 6 to 9 months; grating cheese
Ricotta	10 (part skim)	Bland but semisweet; soft, moist, and grainy or dry	As such; in cooked foods; as seasoning when grated
Romano		Sharp, peppery, piquant flavor; semisoft pasty, sometimes crumbly texture; white interior streaked with blue-green veins of mold	In salad dressings, on crackers; as such (dessert)
Roquefort		See Blue	
Swiss, Emmentaler	8	Mild, sweet, nutlike flavor; hard, smooth with large gas holes or eyes; pale yellow	As such; in sandwiches, with salads; fondue

Based on information from the National Dairy Council, Rosemont, IL.

EGG AND CHEESE RECIPES

PROCEDURE FOR COOKING EGGS ■

Method	Equipment and procedure
HARD- OR SOFT-COOKED (IN SHELL)	*Kettle:*

HARD- OR SOFT-COOKED (IN SHELL)

Kettle:
1. Place eggs in wire baskets and lower into kettle of boiling water. Simmer (do not boil), timing as follows:

	Soft-cooked	*Hard-cooked*
	5–7 minutes	10–15 minutes

2. Immerse hard-cooked eggs in cold water or serve immediately. Serve soft-cooked eggs immediately after cooking.

Steamer:
1. Place eggs in perforated counter pans, 3 doz per 12 × 20 × 2-inch pan.
2. Place in steamer and time as follows:

Pressure	*Soft-cooked*	*Hard-cooked*
5 lb	5–7 minutes	8–10 minutes
15 lb	4–6 minutes	7–9 minutes
0 lb	6–8 minutes	9–10 minutes

3. Immerse in cold water or serve immediately.

HARD-COOKED (OUT OF SHELL)

Steamer:
1. Crack eggs into a 12 × 20 × 2-inch solid, greased counter pan. Eggs should be thick enough in pans so whites come up to level of yolks (4 doz per pan).
2. Place in steamer and time as follows:

Pressure	*Hard-cooked*
5 lb	6–8 minutes
15 lb	5–7 minutes
0 lb	6–8 minutes

3. Remove from steamer and drain off any accumulated condensate. Chop and cool.

POACHED

Fry pan or kettle:
1. Break eggs into individual dishes. Carefully slide eggs into simmering water in fry pan or other shallow pan. The addition of 1 Tbsp salt or 2 tsp vinegar to the water increases the speed of coagulation and helps maintain shape.
2. Keep water at simmering (not boiling) temperature. Cook 5 minutes.
3. Remove eggs with slotted spoon.

Steamer:

1. Break eggs into water in 12 × 10 × 2-inch counter pans.
2. Place eggs into steamer and time as follows:

Pressure	*Soft-poached*
5 lb	3–4 minutes
15 lb	2–3 minutes
0 lb	3–5 minutes

3. To serve, lift out of water into a warmed pan.

FRIED

Skillet or griddle:

1. Break eggs into individual dishes. Slide carefully into hot fat in skillet or on griddle.
2. Cook over low heat until of desired hardness, 5–7 minutes:

Sunnyside: 7 minutes at a cooking surface temperature of 250°F.
Over easy: 3 minutes at a cooking surface temperature of 250°F on one side, then turn the egg and fry for another 2 minutes on the other side.

SCRAMBLED

See recipe, p. 310.

Notes

- Hard-cooked eggs will peel easier if the raw eggs have been held in the refrigerator for 24 hours before cooking. A greenish color may appear on the yolks of hard-cooked eggs when the eggs have been overcooked or allowed to cool slowly in the cooking water. Cooking the eggs for the minimum length of time required to make them solid and cooling them in cold running water or ice water help to prevent this color formation.

- Cook scrambled eggs in small batches (no larger than 3 quarts) until no visible liquid egg remains. Do not combine raw egg mixture with cooked scrambled eggs.

- Do not combine eggs that have been held in a steam table pan with a fresh batch of eggs. Always use a fresh steam table pan.

- The practice of breaking large quantities of eggs together and holding for a period of time greatly increases the risk of bacterial contamination.

- Never leave eggs or egg-containing products at room temperature for more than one hour (including preparation and service).

- Hold cold egg dishes below 40°F.

- Hold hot dishes above 140°F. Do not hold hot foods on buffet line for longer than 30 minutes.

- When refrigerating a large quantity of a hot egg-rich dish or leftover, divide into several shallow containers so it will cool quickly.

SCRAMBLED EGGS

Yield: 50 portions   *Portion:* 3 oz

Ingredient	Amount	Procedure
Eggs	75 (8 lb 3 oz)	Break eggs into mixer bowl. If using frozen eggs, defrost. Beat slightly on medium speed, using wire whip attachment.
Milk Salt	1½ qt 2 Tbsp	Add milk and salt to eggs. Beat until blended.
Margarine	8 oz	Melt margarine in fry pan, griddle, or steam-jacketed kettle. Pour in egg mixture (see Notes). Cook over low heat, stirring occasionally, until of desired consistency. Eggs should be glossy. Serve with No. 10 dipper.

Approximate nutritive values per portion

Calories (kcal)	Protein (grams)	Carbohydrate (grams)	Fat (grams)	Cholesterol (mg)	Sodium (mg)	Iron (mg)	Calcium (mg)
162	10.3 (26%)	2.3 (6%)	12.1 (68%)	320	407	1.1	75

Notes

- The type of equipment used will determine batch size. Eggs should be cooked in small batches and held for a minimum amount of time before serving.

- **Steamer method.**   Melt 4 oz margarine in each of two steamer or counter pans. Pour egg mixture into pans. Steam for 6–8 minutes at 5 lb pressure until desired degree of hardness is reached.

- **Oven method.**   Melt 4 oz margarine in each of two counter or baking pans. Pour egg mixture into pans. Bake approximately 20 minutes at 350°F, stirring once after 10 minutes of baking.

- For lower cholesterol, egg whites may be substituted for half of the whole eggs.

Variations

- **Scrambled Eggs and Cheese.**   Add 1 lb grated cheddar cheese.
- **Scrambled Eggs and Chipped Beef.**   Add 1 lb chopped chipped beef. Reduce salt to 1 Tbsp or less.
- **Scrambled Eggs and Ham.**   Add 1 lb 4 oz chopped cooked ham. Reduce salt to 1 Tbsp or less.

CREAMED EGGS

Yield: 50 portions   *Portion:* 5 oz

Ingredient	Amount	Procedure
Eggs, hard-cooked (p. 308)	75	Peel eggs. Set aside for later step.
Margarine Flour, all-purpose Salt Pepper, white	1 lb 8 oz 1 oz (1½ Tbsp) ¼ tsp	Melt margarine. Add flour, salt, and pepper. Stir until smooth. Cook for 5 minutes.
Milk	1 gal	Add milk gradually, stirring constantly with wire whip. Cook until thickened.
		Slice or quarter hard-cooked eggs. When ready to serve, pour hot sauce over eggs. Mix carefully. Reheat to serving temperature.

Approximate nutritive values per portion

Calories (kcal)	Protein (grams)	Carbohydrate (grams)	Fat (grams)	Cholesterol (mg)	Sodium (mg)	Iron (mg)	Calcium (mg)
242	12.5 (21%)	8.1 (14%)	17.5 (66%)	330	410	1.3	135

Variations

- **Curried Eggs.**   Substitute chicken broth for 2 qt of the milk. Add 2 Tbsp curry powder. May be served with steamed rice or chow mein noodles.

- **Eggs à la King.**   Substitute Chicken Stock for 2 qt of the milk. Add 1 lb mushrooms that have been sautéed, 12 oz chopped green peppers, and 8 oz chopped pimiento.

- **Goldenrod Eggs.**   Mash or rice egg yolks. Add sliced whites to sauce. Serve on toast. Sprinkle mashed yolks over the top.

- **Scotch Woodcock.**   Add 1 lb sharp Cheddar cheese to sauce. Cut eggs in half lengthwise and place in pans. Pour sauce over eggs. Cover with buttered crumbs. Bake until heated through and crumbs are brown.

BAKED OMELET

Yield: 48 portions or 2 pans 12 × 20 × 2 inches   *Portion:* 3 oz
Oven: 325°F   *Bake:* 45 minutes

Ingredient	Amount	Procedure
Margarine	12 oz	Melt margarine. Add flour and seasonings. Stir until smooth.
Flour, all-purpose	8 oz	
Salt	2 Tbsp	Cook 5 minutes.
Pepper, white	½ tsp	
Milk	3 qt	Add milk gradually, stirring constantly with a wire whip. Cook until thick.
Egg yolks, beaten	24 (15 oz)	Add egg yolks and mix well with wire whip.
Egg whites	24 (1 lb 12 oz)	Beat egg whites until they form rounded peaks. Fold into egg yolk mixture.
		Pour mixture into 2 greased 12 × 20 × 2-inch baking pans, 5 lb per pan.
		Set pans in counter pans with 3 cups of hot water in each.
		Bake at 325°F for 45 minutes or until set.
		Cut 4 × 6.

Approximate nutritive values per portion

Calories (kcal)	Protein (grams)	Carbohydrate (grams)	Fat (grams)	Cholesterol (mg)	Sodium (mg)	Iron (mg)	Calcium (mg)
146	5.8 (16%)	6.9 (19%)	10.5 (65%)	122	394	0.6	91

Variations

- **Bacon Omelet.** Fry 1 lb 8 oz diced bacon; substitute bacon fat for margarine in white sauce. Add diced bacon to egg mixture.

- **Cheese Omelet.** Add 12 oz grated cheese before placing pans in ovens.

- **Cheese and Bacon Omelet.** Combine 8 lb eggs, 1 Tbsp (¾ oz) salt, and 1 Tbsp white pepper and mix on low speed just until blended. Portion with No. 12 dipper onto lightly greased preheated grill. Cook until set. Portion 1 oz shredded processed cheese and ½ oz cooked crumbled bacon over each omelet. Fold omelet with spatula. Place in 12 × 20 × 2-inch pans. Cover and keep hot. Prepare 3 lb cheese and 1 lb 8 oz bacon for 50 omelets.

- **Grilled Cheese Omelet.** Combine 11 lb eggs, 1½ Tbsp (1 oz) salt, and 1 Tbsp white pepper and mix on low speed just until blended. Portion with No. 8 dipper onto lightly greased preheated grill. As omelet begins to set, portion 1½ oz shredded processed cheese over each (4 lb 8 oz for 50 omelets). Fold omelet with spatula and place in 12 × 20 × 2-inch pans. Cover and keep hot.

- **Ham Omelet.**   Add 3 lb finely diced cooked ham. Reduce salt to 1 Tbsp or less.
- **Jelly Omelet.**   Spread 1 lb tart jelly over cooked omelet.
- **Mushroom and Cheese Omelet.**   Add 8 oz grated cheese and 6 oz sliced mushrooms.
- **Spanish Omelet.**   Add 8 oz chopped green chilies to egg mixture. Serve with Spanish Sauce (p. 592).

POTATO OMELET

Yield: 56 portions or 2 pans 12 × 20 × 2 inches   *Portion:* 6 oz
Oven: 325°F   *Bake:* 1 hour

Ingredient	Amount	Procedure
Bacon slices	50	Arrange bacon, slightly overlapping, in baking pans. Cook in oven at 400°F until crisp. Remove from pans. Place on paper towels to absorb fat.
Potatoes, cooked, diced	9 lb (EP)	Brown potatoes slightly in bacon fat. Remove to 2 greased 12 × 20 × 2-inch baking pans, 4 lb 8 oz per pan.
Eggs, beaten Salt Pepper, white Pepper, cayenne Milk, hot	36 (3 lb 15 oz) 2 oz 1 tsp few grains 3 qt	Combine eggs, milk, and seasonings. Pour over potatoes.
		Bake at 325°F for 1 hour. Serve as soon as removed from oven. Cut 4 × 7. Place a slice of crisp bacon on top of each serving.

Approximate nutritive values per portion

Calories (kcal)	Protein (grams)	Carbohydrate (grams)	Fat (grams)	Cholesterol (mg)	Sodium (mg)	Iron (mg)	Calcium (mg)
180	8.9 (20%)	18.6 (41%)	7.8 (39%)	148	552	0.8	85

Note   ■   4 oz chopped green pepper and 4 oz chopped onion may be added.

Variation   ■   **Potato-Ham Omelet.**   Omit bacon. Add 4 lb diced cooked ham to potatoes. Reduce salt to 1 Tbsp.

CHINESE OMELET

Yield: 48 portions or 2 pans 12 × 20 × 2 inches   *Portion:* 4 oz
Oven: 325°F   *Bake:* 45 minutes

Ingredient	Amount	Procedure
Rice, long-grain	2 lb (AP)	Cook rice according to directions on p. 430.
Water	2½ qt	
Salt	1 Tbsp	
Margarine or vegetable oil	1 Tbsp	
Margarine	4 oz	Melt margarine. Add flour and salt. Stir until smooth.
Four, all-purpose	2 oz	Cook 5 minutes.
Salt	1 tsp	
Milk	1 qt	Add milk gradually, stirring constantly with wire whip. Cook until thickened.
Cheddar cheese, sharp, shredded	1 lb	Add cheese to white sauce. Stir until cheese is melted.
Egg yolks	24 (15 oz)	Beat egg yolks until light and fluffy. Add seasonings.
Mustard, dry	1 tsp	Add to cheese sauce. Stir until smooth.
Salt	2 Tbsp	Add rice and mix to blend.
Paprika	1 tsp	
Egg whites	24 (1 lb 12 oz)	Beat egg whites until they form soft peaks. Fold into rice mixture.
		Pour into 2 greased 12 × 20 × 2-inch pans, 7 lb per pan. Bake at 325°F for 45 minutes or until set. Cut 4 × 6. Serve with Cheese Sauce (p. 582) or Tomato Sauce (p. 591).

Approximate nutritive values per portion							
Calories (kcal)	Protein (grams)	Carbohydrate (grams)	Fat (grams)	Cholesterol (mg)	Sodium (mg)	Iron (mg)	Calcium (mg)
185	7.7 (17%)	17.8 (39%)	8.9 (44%)	126	570	1.1	122

EGG AND SAUSAGE BAKE

Yield: 48 portions or 2 pans 12 × 20 × 2 inches   *Portion:* 6 oz
Oven: 325°F   *Bake:* 1 hour

Ingredient	Amount	Procedure
Bread, sliced	2 lb 8 oz	Cut bread in cubes. Cover bottoms of 2 greased 12 × 20 × 2-inch baking pans with bread cubes. Pans should be well covered.
Sausage, bulk	9 lb	Brown sausage. Drain well.
Cheddar cheese, shredded	2 lb 8 oz	Spread cheese and sausage over bread cubes.
Eggs, beaten Milk Mustard, dry	42 (4 lb 8 oz) 3 qt 1½ Tbsp	Combine eggs, milk, and mustard. Pour over mixture in pans, 2½ qt per pan. May be mixed, covered, and refrigerated overnight.
		Bake uncovered at 325°F for 1 hour or until set. If browning too fast, cover with foil. Cut 4 × 6.

Approximate nutritive values per portion

Calories (kcal)	Protein (grams)	Carbohydrate (grams)	Fat (grams)	Cholesterol (mg)	Sodium (mg)	Iron (mg)	Calcium (mg)
568	32.1 (23%)	15.1 (11%)	41.7 (66%)	285	1483	2.7	309

Note

- Chopped ham or bacon may be substituted for sausage.

Variations

- **Sausage-Potato Bake.**   Substitute frozen hashed brown potatoes, for bread cubes.
- **Egg-Potato Bake.**   Delete sausage. Substitute frozen hashed brown potatoes for bread cubes.

QUICHE

Yield: 48 portions or 12 8-inch quiches   *Portion:* ¼ quiche
Oven: 375°F   *Bake:* 25–30 minutes

Ingredient	Amount	Procedure
Flour, all-purpose	1 lb 13 oz	Make pastry according to directions on p. 254.
Salt	1 Tbsp	Line twelve 8-inch pie pans with pastry, 5 oz per pan.
Shortening	1 lb 4 oz	Partially bake shells at 375°F for about 10 minutes.
Water, cold	1¼ cups	
Eggs	30 (3 lb 4 oz)	Beat eggs. Add cream, milk, and seasonings.
Cream or half-and-half	2 qt	
Milk	2 qt	
Salt	1½ tsp	
Pepper, white	½ tsp	
Swiss cheese, grated	3 lb	Sprinkle partially baked shells with Swiss cheese, 4 oz per pie, and bacon or ham, 2 oz per pie.
Bacon, chopped, cooked, and drained, or ham, finely diced	1 lb	Pour egg mixture into shells, 15 oz (approximately 2 cups) per pie.
Parmesan cheese, grated	8 oz	Sprinkle with Parmesan cheese, 2 Tbsp per pie. Bake until custard is set and lightly browned.

Approximate nutritive values per portion

Calories (kcal)	Protein (grams)	Carbohydrate (grams)	Fat (grams)	Cholesterol (mg)	Sodium (mg)	Iron (mg)	Calcium (mg)
473	21 (18%)	18.3 (16%)	34.9 (67%)	189	589	1.5	448

Variations

- **Mushroom Quiche.** Delete bacon or ham and Parmesan cheese. Sprinkle 3 lb sliced fresh mushrooms and 8 oz finely chopped onions sautéed in 4 oz margarine over bottoms of shells, approximately 4 oz per pie.

- **Sausage Quiche.** Substitute 1 lb cooked, drained sausage (1 lb 12 oz AP) for bacon or ham.

- **Seafood Quiche.** In place of bacon, use 3 lb flaked crab meat, shrimp pieces, or other seafood, 1 lb sliced fresh mushrooms, and 12 oz finely chopped onions sautéed in 4 oz margarine. Scale approximately 5 oz per pie. Delete Parmesan cheese.

- **Swiss Spinach Quiche.** Delete bacon or ham and Parmesan cheese. Increase Swiss cheese to 6 lb. Add 3 lb 8 oz chopped spinach, well drained. Add 1 tsp nutmeg.

EGG FOO YUNG

Yield: 50 portions   *Portion:* 4 oz with 1½ oz sauce

Ingredient	Amount	Procedure
Mushrooms, canned Bean sprouts	1 lb 1 No. 10 can	Drain and coarsely chop mushrooms and bean sprouts. Reserve liquid for use in final step.
Onions, shredded Green peppers, shredded	1 lb 8 oz 8 oz	Combine onions and green peppers with mushrooms and bean sprouts.
Vegetable oil	1 cup	Sauté vegetable mixture in hot oil for 2 minutes.
Eggs, beaten Ham, cooked, shredded	40 (4 lb 6 oz) 1 lb	Combine eggs and ham. Add to vegetables and mix.
		Portion with No. 10 dipper onto preheated grill or frying pan. Brown on one side, fold in half. Serve with the following sauce.
Cornstarch Soy sauce Reserved vegetable juice or chicken stock	2 oz 1½ cups 2 qt	Combine cornstarch and soy sauce into a smooth paste. Add to vegetable juice, stirring with a wire whip. Cook until thickened.

Approximate nutritive values per portion

Calories (kcal)	Protein (grams)	Carbohydrate (grams)	Fat (grams)	Cholesterol (mg)	Sodium (mg)	Iron (mg)	Calcium (mg)
157	9.9 (24%)	9.4 (23%)	9.4 (52%)	174	864	1.7	38

Note   ■   Roast pork, chicken, or bacon may be used in place of ham; green onions in place of shredded onions; and bamboo shoots and shredded water chestnuts in place of bean sprouts.

DEVILED EGGS ▪

Yield: 50 portions   *Portion:* 2 halves

Ingredient	Amount	Procedure
Eggs, hard-cooked (p. 308)	50	Peel eggs. Cut in half lengthwise. Remove yolks to mixer bowl. Arrange whites in rows on a tray.
Milk	½ cup	Mash yolks, using flat beater. Add milk and mix until blended.
Mayonnaise or salad dressing	1½ cups	Add remaining ingredients to yolks and mix until smooth. Refill whites with mashed yolks, approximately 1½ Tbsp for each half egg white. Sprinkle with paprika (optional).
Salt	1 Tbsp	
Dry mustard	2 tsp	
Sugar, granulated	1 tsp	
Vinegar, cider	½ cup	

Approximate nutritive values per portion

Calories (kcal)	Protein (grams)	Carbohydrate (grams)	Fat (grams)	Cholesterol (mg)	Sodium (mg)	Iron (mg)	Calcium (mg)
105	6.4 (24%)	3.4 (13%)	7.5 (63%)	215	242	0.8	31

Notes

- Pastry bag may be used to fill egg whites. Yolk mixture should be smooth and creamy. Use plain or rose tip.
- 6 oz finely chopped pimientos may be added to yolk mixture.

Variations

- **Dilled Eggs.** Combine 1¾ qt vinegar, 1¼ qt water, 1 Tbsp dill weed, 1 tsp white pepper, 1 oz (1½ Tbsp) salt, ¼ tsp dry mustard, 1 Tbsp onion juice, and 3 cloves garlic. Pour over peeled, hard-cooked eggs. Cover tightly and refrigerate overnight.

- **Hot Stuffed Eggs.** Proceed as for Deviled Eggs. To mash egg yolks, add 3 oz melted margarine or butter, 2 tsp salt, ⅛ tsp cayenne pepper, 1 Tbsp prepared mustard, 1 lb ham, minced. Arrange stuffed eggs in two 12 × 20 × 2-inch baking pans. Cover with 1 gal white sauce (p. 582), 2 qt per pan. Bake at 325°F for 30 minutes. Sprinkle with chopped parsley. Ham may be added to the white sauce instead of to egg yolks.

- **Pickled Eggs.** Combine 3½ cups beet juice, 3½ cups vinegar, 12 oz granulated sugar, and ¼ tsp salt. Stir until sugar is dissolved. Pour over peeled, hard-cooked eggs. Cover tightly and refrigerate overnight.

- **Smoked Eggs.** Combine ½ cup soy sauce, 1 Tbsp salad oil, 1 tsp liquid smoke, 5 tsp granulated sugar, and 1¼ cups water. Pour over peeled hard-cooked eggs. Marinate for 2–3 hours. Stir eggs occasionally to keep them moistened with marinade.

CHEESE BALLS

Yield: 50 portions or 150 balls   *Portion:* 3 balls
Deep-fat fryer: 360°F   *Fry:* 2–3 minutes

Ingredient	Amount	Procedure
Cheddar cheese, shredded	9 lb	Mix cheese, flour, and seasonings.
Flour, all-purpose	8 oz	
Salt	2 Tbsp	
Pepper, cayenne	few grains	
Egg whites	48 (3 lb 8 oz)	Beat egg whites until stiff. Fold into cheese mixture. Shape into balls 1–1¼ inches in diameter or dip with No. 30 dipper onto trays or baking sheets. Chill.
Eggs, beaten	6 (10 oz)	Combine eggs and milk.
Milk	2 cups	Dip cheese balls in egg mixture, then roll in crumbs.
Bread crumbs	1 lb 8 oz	Chill for several hours. Fry in deep fat for 2–3 minutes.

Approximate nutritive values per portion

Calories (kcal)	Protein (grams)	Carbohydrate (grams)	Fat (grams)	Cholesterol (mg)	Sodium (mg)	Iron (mg)	Calcium (mg)
429	26.9 (25%)	15.3 (14%)	28.7 (60%)	111	927	1.4	624

Notes

- Serve cheese balls in center of hot buttered pineapple rings, three per ring.
- For serving as first-course accompaniment, use half the recipe and shape into balls ½–¾ inch in diameter. Yield: 150 balls.
- For two cheese balls per portion, use No. 24 dipper. Yield: 40 portions.

CHEESE SOUFFLÉ

Yield: 48 portions or 2 pans 12 × 20 × 2 inches   *Portion:* 4 oz
Oven: 300°F   *Bake:* 55–60 minutes

Ingredient	Amount	Procedure
Margarine Flour, all-purpose Salt	1 lb 4 oz 10 oz 1 tsp	Melt margarine. Add flour and salt. Stir until smooth. Cook 5 minutes.
Milk	3 qt	Add milk gradually, stirring constantly with wire whip. Cook until thick.
Egg yolks, beaten	38 (1 lb 8 oz)	Add egg yolks to white sauce, stirring constantly. Cook for 2 minutes.
Cheddar cheese, shredded	1 lb 8 oz	Add cheese to sauce and stir until cheese is melted. Remove from heat.
Egg whites Cream of tartar	38 (2 lb 12 oz) 2 tsp	Add cream of tartar to egg whites. Beat until stiff, but not dry. Fold into cheese mixture.
		Scale mixture into two 12 × 20 × 2-inch baking pans, greased only on the bottoms, 6 lb 12 oz per pan. Bake at 300°F for 55–60 minutes or until set. Cut 4 × 6.

Approximate nutritive values per portion

Calories (kcal)	Protein (grams)	Carbohydrate (grams)	Fat (grams)	Cholesterol (mg)	Sodium (mg)	Iron (mg)	Calcium (mg)
265	11.4 (17%)	8.2 (12%)	20.7 (70%)	205	323	0.9	201

Note   ■ Serve with Cheese Sauce (p. 582), Mushroom Sauce (p. 587), or Shrimp Sauce (p. 583).

Variation   ■ **Mushroom Soufflé.**   Add 1 lb chopped mushrooms and 5 oz chopped green peppers to uncooked mixture. Serve with Béchamel Sauce (p. 584).

CHEESE AND BROCCOLI STRATA

Yield: 56 portions or 2 pans 12 × 20 × 2 inches   *Portion:* 8 oz
Oven: 325°F   *Bake:* 1–1½ hours

Ingredient	Amount	Procedure
Bread slices, dry	2 lb	Cut bread into 1½-inch cubes. Set aside.
Broccoli cuts, frozen	5 lb	Cook broccoli until tender.
Cheddar cheese, shredded	2 lb	Layer as follows in each pan: 8 oz bread cubes 2 lb 8 oz broccoli 1 lb cheese 8 oz bread cubes
Eggs, beaten Milk Salt Prepared mustard Hot pepper sauce	9 doz (12 lb) 1 gal 2 oz 3 oz (6 Tbsp) 1½ tsp	Combine eggs, milk, and seasonings. Pour 1¼ gal into each pan. Smooth down evenly.
Paprika	½ tsp	Sprinkle with paprika, ¼ tsp per pan. Set each pan in another counter pan containing 3 cups hot water. Bake uncovered at 325°F until custard sets, 1–1½ hours. Cut 4 × 7.

Approximate nutritive values per portion

Calories (kcal)	Protein (grams)	Carbohydrate (grams)	Fat (grams)	Cholesterol (mg)	Sodium (mg)	Iron (mg)	Calcium (mg)
305	21.2 (28%)	13.9 (18%)	18.2 (54%)	441	783	2.3	282

Notes   ■ Baking time may be reduced if milk mixture is warmed to 140°F before baking.
  ■ May be served with 1 oz Cheese Sauce (p. 582).

BROCCOLI AND CHEESE CASSEROLE

Yield: 48 portions or 4 pans 12 × 10 × 2 inches   *Portion:* 8 oz
Oven: 350°F   *Bake:* 1 hour 15 minutes

Ingredient	Amount	Procedure
Eggs	3 lb (27)	Beat eggs and flour together, using a wire whip, until smooth.
Flour, all-purpose	12 oz	
Broccoli cuts, thawed, drained	6 lb 4 oz	Drain, then weigh. Fold into the egg-flour mixture.
Cottage cheese, low fat, drained	10 lb	Drain cottage cheese, then weigh. Add cheeses and salt to eggs.
Cheddar cheese, shredded	5 lb 6 oz	
Salt	2 Tbsp	
		Scale mixture into 4 greased 10 × 12 × 2-inch pans, 6 lb per pan. Bake at 350°F for 1 hour 15 minutes or until a knife inserted near the center comes out clean. Let stand 15 minutes. Cut 3 × 4.

Approximate nutritive values per portion

Calories (kcal)	Protein (grams)	Carbohydrate (grams)	Fat (grams)	Cholesterol (mg)	Sodium (mg)	Iron (mg)	Calcium (mg)
374	31.7 (34%)	12.8 (14%)	21.8 (52%)	182	1017	1.7	475

Notes

- May add topping of 3 cups bread crumbs mixed with ⅓ cup melted margarine and 6 oz Parmesan cheese. Add during last 15 minutes of cooking.
- May be garnished with fresh broccoli florets.
- For a vegetable, serve 4 oz portion.

NACHOS

Yield: 50 portions   *Portion:* 3½ oz sauce + 1 oz chips

Ingredient	Amount	Procedure
Shortening	1 oz	Sauté onions in shortening until tender.
Onions, chopped	3 oz	
Green chili peppers, chopped	6 oz	Add chilies and tomatoes to onions. Simmer for 15 minutes.
Tomatoes, diced, canned	1 lb 8 oz	
Chicken Stock (p. 615)	2 qt	Add stock and seasonings. Bring to a boil. Reduce heat to medium.
Cumin, ground	1 Tbsp	
Garlic powder	2 tsp	
Processed cheese, shredded	6 lb 10 oz	Add cheese to hot mixture. Stir until melted.
Cornstarch	3 oz	Combine cornstarch and water to make a smooth paste. Add slowly to cheese mixture, stirring constantly.
Water	½ cup	Cook and stir until mixture thickens. Turn heat to low.
Nacho chips	4 lb	Place 12 nacho chips on dinner plate.
Jalapeño peppers, sliced	8 oz	Using a 4 oz ladle, pour 3½ oz of sauce over chips. Garnish with sliced jalapeño peppers.

Approximate nutritive values per portion							
Calories (kcal)	Protein (grams)	Carbohydrate (grams)	Fat (grams)	Cholesterol (mg)	Sodium (mg)	Iron (mg)	Calcium (mg)
424	16.8 (16%)	26.3 (24%)	28.8 (60%)	58	1264	1	430

Note   ■   The sauce may be thinned with chicken broth.

WELSH RAREBIT

Yield: 50 portions or 6½ qt   *Portion:* ½ cup (4 oz)

Ingredient	Amount	Procedure
Margarine	10 oz	Melt margarine. Add flour and salt. Stir until smooth.
Flour, all-purpose	8 oz	Cook 5 minutes.
Salt	1 oz (1½ Tbsp)	
Milk	1 gal	Add milk gradually, stirring constantly with wire whip. Cook until thickened.
Cheddar cheese, shredded	5 lb	Add cheese and seasonings to sauce. Cook over hot water until cheese is melted.
Dry mustard	2 Tbsp	Serve on toast or toasted buns.
Worcestershire sauce	2 Tbsp	
Pepper, white	½ tsp	

Approximate nutritive values per portion

Calories (kcal)	Protein (grams)	Carbohydrate (grams)	Fat (grams)	Cholesterol (mg)	Sodium (mg)	Iron (mg)	Calcium (mg)
290	14.5 (20%)	8 (11%)	22.4 (69%)	58	571	0.6	427

Variation   ■ **Welsh Rarebit with Bacon.** Serve rarebit over toast, with 2 slices cooked bacon and 2 slices fresh tomato.

7

Fish and Shellfish

FIN FISH

Market Forms

Fish may be purchased fresh or frozen, and some are available canned. Following are the most common market forms:

Aberdeen Cuts   Rhombus-shaped cuts from a block of frozen fish are known as Aberdeen cuts; sides may be squared off or cut with a tapered edge. These usually are breaded or battered. Also called diamond cuts, French cuts.

Bits or Nuggets   Small pieces of fish breaded or coated with batter, weighing less than 1 ounce each, are called bits or nuggets. Shapes may be round, square or irregular. Some are cut from regular blocks of fish; others are cut from frozen blocks of minced fish. Also called bites, cubes, nuggets, petites, tidbits. Generally sold by count per pound, for example, 25–35 per pound.

Boneless Fillet   The pinbones are removed from the fillet. Boneless fillets need not be completely boneless; the U.S. Federal Grade Standards allow for an occasional small bone in Grade A fillets.

Butterfly Fillet   Fish is cut along both sides, with the two pieces remaining joined by a piece of skin and flesh.

TABLE 7.1 **Fin fish buying and cooking guide**

Species	Characteristics	Fat or lean	Usual market forms	Cooking methods
Bass, sea	Flaky, white; rich flavor	Fat	Fillets, steaks; whole, pan-dressed	Fry, broil, bake
Bluefish	Dark, turning light when cooked; mild, soft	Fat	Fillets	Bake, poach
Catfish	Firm flesh, abundant flavor	Lean	Whole, dressed; fillets	Fry
Cod	Mild flavor; soft white meat, flakes easily	Lean	Fillets, steaks; breaded portions	Bake, fry, broil
Dolphin (mahimahi)	Firm, white meat; delicate flavor	Lean	Fillets	Broil, sauté, bake
Flounder	Delicate flavor, white	Lean	Whole, pan-dressed; fillets; breaded	Fry, bake, broil
Grouper	Flaky white, firm; rich flavor	Lean	Whole, steaks, fillets	Fry, bake, poach
Haddock	White meat, mild flavor	Lean	Whole, steaks, fillets, breaded portions	Bake, fry, broil, poach
Halibut	Tender, white; mild flavor	Lean	Drawn, dressed, steaks	Broil, bake, fry, poach
Monkfish	Firm, white flesh; mild lobster-like flavor	Lean	Fillets, tails	Broil, sauté
Orange roughy	Snow-white flesh; delicate flavor, sweet taste	Lean	Fillets	Sauté, broil
Perch, ocean	Firm, white, flaky; mild flavor	Lean	Whole, pan-dressed; fillets; breaded fillets and portions	Pan fry, bake, deep-fat fry
Pike, walleye	Snowy white meat, sweet flavor	Lean	Whole, fillets, round	Pan fry

Drawn Fish Drawn fish have had the entrails, gills, and scales removed.

Fillet A slice of fish flesh of irregular size and shape that is removed from the carcass by a cut made parallel to the backbone, usually 2–12 ounces.

Fingers Fingers are irregular-shaped pieces of fish, similar to a long, thin fillet, breaded or battered, raw or precooked. Weight per piece varies; they are usually available in portions of 1–3 ounces or in bulk.

Fish Sticks Sticks are rectangles of fish cut from a frozen block, usually 2 × 3 inches, weighing 1–2 ounces each, breaded or battered.

Headed and Gutted Head, tails, fins, and viscera have been removed before sale.

Portion Usually a square or rectangle, cut from a block of frozen fish. Weights vary from 1½ ounces to about 6 ounces. May be plain or breaded, raw or precooked.

TABLE 7.1 **Continued**

Species	Characteristics	Fat or lean	Usual market forms	Cooking methods
Pollack	Firm texture, white meat; mild	Lean	Fillets, breaded and precooked sticks and portions	Fry, broil, bake
Pompano	Firm white flesh	Fat	Whole, fillets	Sauté, broil
Redfish	Light firm flesh, sweet flavor	Lean	Whole, fillets	Pan fry, blackened
Red snapper	Firm, white flesh; mild flavor	Lean	Dressed, fillets, portions	Bake, fry, broil
Salmon	Pink to red flesh, rich flavor	Fat	Dressed, steaks, fillets	Bake, poach, broil, pan fry
Shark	Firm, white flesh	Fat	Steaks	Grill, broil
Sole	Firm, white flesh; delicate flavor	Lean	Whole, fillets	Bake, fry, broil, poach
Swordfish	Firm flesh, mild flavor	Fat	Steaks, chunks	Broil, bake, poach
Trout, lake	Firm texture, rich flavor	Fat	Whole, drawn, fillets	Bake, poach, pan fry
Trout, rainbow	Delicate flesh, excellent flavor	Lean	Whole, dressed; boned and breaded fillets	Pan fry, oven fry, broil, bake
Tuna (ahi)	Light flesh, good flavor	Fat	Steaks, drawn, chunks	Bake, broil, sauté
Turbot	Very tender, white, mild flavor	Lean	Fillets	Fry, bake, broil
Whitefish	Rich flavor; tender, white flesh	Fat	Whole, drawn, dressed; fillets	Bake, broil, poach
Whiting	Firm texture, abundant flavor	Lean	Drawn; breaded portions and fillets	Deep-fat fry, broil, sauté

Steaks Slices of dressed fish, smaller than chunks, ready for cooking, are called steaks. Salmon, halibut, swordfish, and other large fish are commonly processed and sold as steaks.

Whole or Round Fish Fish are sold just as they come from the water. They must be dressed before cooking.

The cost per edible pound in terms of both convenience and waste should be considered when deciding which form of fish to buy. Whole or round fish yield about 50 percent edible flesh after they have been eviscerated and scaled and the head, tail, and fins have been removed; dressed fish yield 70 percent, steaks 90 percent, and fillets and portions 100 percent. The U.S. government standard on breaded portions is 25 percent breading and 75 percent fish when raw; 35 percent breading and 65 percent fish when oven finished. Battered portions are typically 50 percent batter and 50 percent fish.

TABLE 7.2   **Methods of cooking fin fish and shellfish**

Type	Baking Temperature (°F)	Baking Time (minutes)	Broiling (3–4 inches from heat) Time (minutes)	Deep-fat frying (350°–375°F) Time (minutes)	Pan frying (moderate heat) Time (minutes)
Fin Fish					
Dressed, 3–4 lb	350–400	40–60			
Pan-dressed, ½–1 lb	350–400	25–30	5–15	4–5	15–20
Steaks, ½–1¼ inch	350–400	25–35	5–15	4–5	15–25
Fillets	350–400	25–35	5–15	4–5	8–10
Portions, 1–6 oz	350–400	30–40		4–5	8–10
Sticks, ¾–1¼ oz	400	15–20		3–5	
Shellfish					
Clams, live, shucked	450	12–15	5–8	2–3	4–5
Crabs, live, soft-shell			8–10	2–4	
Lobsters, live, ¾–1 lb	400	15–20	12–15	2–4	8–10
Spiny lobster tails, frozen, ¼–½ lb	450	20–30	8–12	3–5	8–10
Oysters, live, shucked	450	12–15	5–8	2–3	4–5
Scallops, ocean	350	15–20	6–8	2–3	4–6
Shrimp, headless, raw, peeled	350	15–20	5–8	2–3	8–10

Adapted from *How to Eye and Buy Seafood*, National Marine Fisheries Service, U.S. Department of Commerce; *Seafood, Foodservice Training*, U.S. Department of Commerce, Chicago, IL; and *Seafood, Foodservice Training Manual*, the National Fisheries Institute.

Notes
- See p. 330 for microwave cooking methods.
- A basic guide is to bake or pan fry fish for 20–25 minutes (350°–400°F) per inch of thickness for frozen fish; 10–15 minutes per inch of thickness for thawed or fresh fish.
- For steaming fish or shellfish, see Table 7.3.

Storage

Seafood is perishable and should be handled with great care during storage, thawing, preparation, cooking, and serving. Fresh fish should be delivered packed in crushed ice and stored in the refrigerator at 32°F. Frozen seafood should be delivered hard frozen and stored in the freezer at 0°F to −20°F until it is removed for cooking. Thawed fish should not be held longer than one day before cooking.

Frozen fish need not be thawed prior to cooking if is not to be breaded. Some tempering may be necessary, however, to separate fish portions or cut them into appropriate-size pieces. Breaded fish portions should *not* be thawed before cooking.

Cooking Methods

Fish by nature is tender and free of tough fibers that need to be softened by cooking, and it should be cooked only until the fish flakes easily when tested with a fork. Fish may be cooked in many ways, but the best method is determined by size, fat content, and flavor. Baking and broiling are suitable for fat fish. If lean fish is baked or broiled, fat is added to prevent dryness, and it often is baked in a sauce. Fish cooked in moist heat requires very little cooking time and usually is served with a sauce. Frying is suitable for all types, but those with firm flesh that will not break apart easily are best for deep-fat frying. Table 7.1 suggests cooking methods for specific types of fish. Table 7.2 lists cooking times and temperatures.

Baking

Fish Fillets   Brush frozen fish in melted margarine or dip in fat, then in flour. Place in greased shallow pan or pan lined with parchment paper or aluminum foil; do not cover. Season with spices. A thin slice of lemon may be placed on each piece. See p. 599 for herb seasoning. Bake frozen fish at 350°–400°F for 20–25 minutes per inch of thickness. If fish is thawed or fresh, reduce cooking time to 10–12 minutes per inch of thickness.

Whole Fish for Buffet Display   Rinse and dry fish, then salt inside and out. Bake at 325°F until fish flakes easily, about 2 hours for a 12-pound fish and approximately 3 hours for a 20–24 pound fish. When done, gently remove skin, then garnish, being careful to arrange garnish so that fish can be cut and served easily. See p. 339 for Baked Whole Salmon.

Broiling

Fish fillets or steaks should be as dry as possible and at least 1 inch thick. Brush both sides with melted margarine or basting sauce, then season. See p. 599 for Lemon Herb Seasoning. Place frozen fish on greased broiler rack or pan. If the skin is on, place skin side down. Broil 2–4 inches from preheated heating unit. Broiling time will range from 5 to 20 minutes. Thicker fillets may need to be turned once, halfway through cooking time.

Frying

Pan Frying and Sautéing   To pan fry, season fillets, steaks, or small whole fish with salt and pepper. Dip in milk and roll in flour or cornmeal or a combination of both. To sauté, lightly dust thawed, dry fish with seasoned flour. Cook in a small amount of fat at 360°–375°F. Turn halfway through cooking time to brown each side.

Deep-Fat Frying   Dip frozen fish fillets, steaks, or small whole fish in milk or egg mixture and seasoned crumbs; or purchase breaded or battered product. Fry 4–5 minutes at 360°–375°F (thicker whole fish wll require more time).

Oven Frying   Dip frozen fillets or steaks in seasoned milk; drain, then coat with fine bread crumbs. Place in greased shallow pan or pan lined with parchment paper or aluminum foil. Do not cover. Drizzle melted fat over fish. Bake at 400°F.

Microwave

Primary Cooking Guidelines   The source for the following microwave cooking directions is the *Seafood Foodservice Training Manual,* published by the National Fisheries Institute, Washington, D.C.:

1. Maximum moisture retention and even cooking can be achieved by generously brushing the fish and seafood item with margarine and tightly covering or wrapping the item before cooking. Fish Marinade, p. 604, may be used.
2. If the item is to be browned under a broiler after microwave cooking, it should be cooked to only 75–80 percent doneness in the microwave. Fish will not yet be flaky, and shellfish will be slightly translucent.
3. Microwave individual portions on medium-high setting to retain juices and flavor.
4. Let fish or seafood stand 2–3 minutes prior to serving.
5. Test for doneness: Fish is flaky when lifted gently with a fork near the center. It should be opaque in color; bones should be easily removed from meat. Shellfish will be slightly translucent in center. Let stand for a short period to finish cooking.

Oven Steaming

Place frozen fish on greased aluminum foil. Season and flavor with lemon juice, spices, and thinly sliced vegetables. Wrap securely. Place in shallow baking pan. Bake at 400°F for 20–25 minutes per inch of thickness.

Poaching

Prepare poaching liquid: acidulated water, court bouillon, fish stock, milk, or milk and water. Place fish fillets or thick steaks in a flat, shallow baking pan. Barely cover fish with boiling liquid, then cover with parchment paper or a lid. Cook in a 350°F oven or in a steamer until fish loses its transparent appearance or until fish flakes easily when tested with a fork. See Table 7.3, Timetable for Steaming Fish and Shellfish. Remove fish from liquid and serve with a sauce or garnish.

Acidulated Water   Use 1 Tbsp salt and 3 Tbsp lemon juice or vinegar for each quart of water.

Court Bouillon   Add to 1 gal water ¾ cup each of chopped carrots, chopped onion, and chopped celery; 3 Tbsp salt; ½ cup vinegar; 2 or 3 bay leaves; 6 peppercorns; 9 cloves; and 3 Tbsp margarine or butter. Boil gently for 20–30 minutes. Strain to remove spices and vegetables.

TABLE 7.3 Timetable for steaming fish and shellfish

Type	Amount per pan	Pan size solid	Procedure	Time (minutes)		
				5 PSI	15 PSI	Pressureless
Clams, soft-shell	8–10 servings	12 × 20 × 2½-inch Perforated	Place washed clams in a 2½″ perforated pan inside a 4″ solid pan with 2–3 qt water.	6–8	4–6	6–8
Clams, hard shell	12 each 3 lbs	12 × 20 × 2½-inch	As above.	6–8	4–6	6–8
Crabs	10–16 each	12 × 20 × 2½-inch Perforated	Put live crabs in perforated pan. Steam cook.	16–18	14–16	16–18
Fish fillets (haddock, sole, cod)	5 lbs	12 × 20 × 2½-inch	Place pre-portioned fresh or defrosted fish in pan, skin side down. Season as desired. Time depends on thickness of fish.	4–12	2–8	4–12
Fish steaks	5 lbs	12 × 20 × 2½-inch	Place steaks, fresh or defrosted in shallow pan. Season if desired. Cooking time dependent on thickness.	6–12	4–8	6–12
Lobster (1–1½ lb each)	4–5 each	12 × 20 × 2½-inch Perforated	Put lobsters in perforated pan. Steam cook.	6–8	4½–6	6–8
Lobster (1½–2 lb each)	4 each	12 × 20 × 2½-inch Perforated	Put lobsters in perforated pan. Steam cook.	8–10	7–9	8–10
Oysters	12 each 3 lbs	12 × 20 × 2½-inch Perforated	Put oysters in perforated pan. Steam cook.	4–6	3–4	5–7
Shrimp, cooked and deveined (12–15), frozen	5 lbs	12 × 20 × 2½-inch	Place shrimp in solid pan. Add 1 quart water and seasonings if desired.	4–8	3–6	4–8

From Market Forge Co., *Recipes for Market Forge Steam Cookers*, 1991.

SHELLFISH

Shellfish may be purchased fresh, frozen, and canned. Frozen shellfish should be delivered hard-frozen and stored in the freezer at 0°F to −20°F until it is removed for cooking. Thawed shellfish should not be held longer than one day before cooking. Live shellfish should be delivered at 35°F but not in direct contact with ice or water. Information on buying and cooking shellfish is given below. See Table 7.2 for additional information on cooking.

TABLE 7.4 **Marketing sizes for oysters**

Eastern oysters		Pacific oysters	
Size	Count per gallon	Size	Count per gallon
Counts or extra large	160	Large	fewer than 65
Extra selects or large	161–200	Medium	65–96
Selects or medium (preferred for frying)	201–300	Small	95–114
		Extra small	more than 144
Standards or small	300–400		
Very small	more than 500		

Based on information from the National Fisheries Institute, Washington, D.C.

Clams

Clams are available alive in the shell; shucked, fresh or frozen; and canned, whole or chopped. Frozen clam strips are available for deep-fat frying.

Crabs

Crabs may be purchased alive, but most are marketed cooked and frozen in the shell, as crab legs or claws, or as frozen or canned crabmeat. To cook, simmer hard-shelled crabs for 10–15 minutes in salted water. Cool rapidly in ice water. Break the shells apart and remove meat to be used in cooked dishes and salads. One 2-pound crab yields about 12 ounces of cooked body and leg meat. Soft-shelled crabs usually are parboiled, dipped in Egg and Crumbs (p. 47), pan fried or cooked in deep fat.

Lobsters

Northern lobsters are marketed alive in the shell and as cooked meat, fresh or frozen. A 1-pound lobster will yield about 4 ounces of cooked meat. Rock lobsters are marketed only as lobster tails, usually individually quick frozen (IQF). To prepare frozen lobster tails, follow instructions on the package. Lobster meat, frozen or canned, may be used for salads and in cooked dishes. Live lobsters may be broiled or boiled.

Oysters

Oysters are marketed alive in the shell; shucked, fresh or frozen; and canned. Shucked oysters are in far greater demand in foodservices than those in the shell. Eastern oysters are larger and more readily available than Pacific oysters. Both are graded according to the number per gallon. Sizes of oysters are given in Table 7.4.

Oysters are not ordinarily washed before using. If washing seems necessary, care should be taken to remove the oysters from the water quickly, so that they do not become soaked or waterlogged. Any bits of shell should be removed. Cook oysters just enough to heat through to keep oysters juicy and plump; overcooking shrinks and dries them. To fry, dip oysters in Egg and Crumbs (p. 47) before frying.

Scallops

Scallops are always sold shucked and are available fresh, by the gallon or pound; and frozen, as individually quick frozen (IQF), in 3- to 5-pound units, or frozen in block form in 5-pound units. Frozen breaded scallops for deep-fat frying are typically sold in 2½- to 3-pound units. They may be breaded whole or cut from a frozen block in uniform pieces before breading. Large sea scallops are graded in sizes from 10 to 70 count per pound; bay scallops are smaller, graded in sizes from 70 to 120 per pound. To prepare fresh scallops, wash and remove any shell particles. Drain. To fry, dip in egg and crumbs (p. 47), and fry in deep fat at 350°F for 2–3 minutes.

Shrimp

Shrimp are available raw or cooked, fresh or frozen, shelled or in the shell. Raw shrimp in the shell are called green shrimp. Peeled and deveined (P&D) shrimp have had both the shells and sand veins removed. Peeled, deveined and cooked (P&DC) shrimp have been cooked. Other terms used to specify the method of processing are: butterfly (also called split or fantail), in which the shrimp have been cut along the vein; butterfly breaded, which are split part way through on the vein side and spread open, then breaded; whole breaded, which are headless, usually deveined, and available tail on or off. Shrimp are sold by size or count per pound. The larger the shrimp, the more they cost. The name *prawn* is usually given to large shrimp, those designated jumbo or larger. Count and descriptive names for raw shrimp are given in Table 7.5.

Raw, or green, shrimp should be washed carefully. Cover with water and bring to a boil. Let simmer for 3–5 minutes in water to which has been added 1½ tsp salt to each

TABLE 7.5   **Count and descriptive names for raw shrimp**

Number per pound	Description	Uses	Amount to buy
Less than 10	Extra colossal	Hors d'oeuvres sautéed, cocktails	3–4 oz shelled shrimp per person
10–15	Colossal		
16–20	Extra jumbo		
21–25	Jumbo	Breaded	8 oz per person
26–35	Extra large to large	Breaded	8 oz per person
36–50	Medium large to medium	Salads, with sauces	4–8 oz per person when combined with other foods
51–70	Small to extra small	Dips, canapes, open sandwiches	1 cup cooked, shelled and deveined per person (12 oz raw shrimp in the shell or 7 oz frozen shelled shrimp)
More than 70	Tiny		

Note   ■   Terms used to specify processing method are given on p. 328.

quart, 2 bay leaves, and mixed spices. Drain. Remove shell and sand vein from the center back of each shrimp. Two pounds of raw shrimp in the shells will yield about 1 pound of cooked, shelled, and deveined meat; about 1½ pounds cooked shrimp in the shells are needed to yield 1 pound of shelled meat. To fry, dip peeled and cleaned raw or cooked shrimp in batter or egg and crumb (p. 47). Fry in deep fat at 360°–375°F for 2–3 minutes. Breaded frozen shrimp may be cooked from their hard-frozen state.

FISH AND SHELLFISH RECIPES

BAKED FISH FILLETS

Yield: 50 portions   *Portion:* 5 oz
Oven: 375°F   *Bake:* 25–35 minutes

Ingredient	Amount	Procedure
Frozen fish fillets, 5 oz	50	Dip fish in margarine.
Margarine, melted	1 lb	
Bread crumbs	1 lb 12 oz	Combine bread crumbs, flour, and seasonings.
Flour, all-purpose	12 oz	
Salt	1 Tbsp	
Paprika	1½ Tbsp	
Seasoned salt	1 Tbsp	
Marjoram	1 tsp	
Grated lemon peel, fresh	1 tsp	
		Dredge fish with crumb mixture and place on greased baking pans.
		Bake at 375°F for 25–35 minutes or until fish flakes easily.

Approximate nutritive values per portion

Calories (kcal)	Protein (grams)	Carbohydrate (grams)	Fat (grams)	Cholesterol (mg)	Sodium (mg)	Iron (mg)	Calcium (mg)
281	16.7 (24%)	25 (36%)	12.6 (41%)	49	832	1.1	92

Note   ■ Fish portions or steaks may be substituted for fish fillets.

Variation   ■ **Herbed Marinated Fish Steak.**   Make Fish Marinade (p. 604). Marinate steaks for 3 hours. Grill or broil according to Table 7.2, p. 328.

LEMON BAKED FISH

Yield: 50 portions   *Portion:* 5 oz
Oven: 375°F   *Bake:* 25–35 minutes

Ingredient	Amount	Procedure
Frozen fish fillets, 5 oz	50	Thaw fish and bake, using either Method 1 or Method 2.

Method 1

Margarine	1 lb 8 oz	Place 16 thawed fillets onto each 18 × 26-inch sheet pan.
Salt	1 oz (1½ Tbsp)	Melt margarine. Mix with lemon juice and seasonings.
Paprika	3 Tbsp	Brush generously on each piece of fish.
Lemon juice	⅓ cup	Bake at 375°F for 25–35 minutes or until fish flakes easily with a fork. Transfer to 12 × 10 × 2-inch pans.

Method 2

Shortening, melted	1 lb	Mix shortening, salt, pepper, and lemon juice.
Salt	1 Tbsp	Dip each piece of fish into seasoned fat.
Pepper, white	1 tsp	
Lemon juice	½ cup	
Flour, all-purpose	1 lb	Dredge fish with flour. Place close together in single layer in greased baking pans.
Margarine, melted	2 oz	Mix margarine and milk and drizzle over fish.
Milk	¾ cup	Bake at 375°F for 25–35 minutes or until fish flakes easily. Sprinkle with chopped parsley before serving.

Approximate nutritive values per portion—Method 1

Calories (kcal)	Protein (grams)	Carbohydrate (grams)	Fat (grams)	Cholesterol (mg)	Sodium (mg)	Iron (mg)	Calcium (mg)
213	23.8 (46%)	0.3 (1%)	12.5 (54%)	67	451	0.4	24

Approximate nutritive values per portion—Method 2

Calories (kcal)	Protein (grams)	Carbohydrate (grams)	Fat (grams)	Cholesterol (mg)	Sodium (mg)	Iron (mg)	Calcium (mg)
239	24.7 (42%)	7.3 (13%)	11.7 (45%)	67	244	0.7	25

Variation

■ **Creole Baked Fish.** Make spice mixture of 1 cup dried parsley flakes, ½ cup red pepper flakes, ½ cup black pepper, ½ cup paprika, ¼ cup crushed thyme leaves, ¼ cup crumbled rosemary, 2 Tbsp crumbled oregano, 2 Tbsp crumbled basil. Brush fish fillets with melted margarine. Sprinkle generously with spice mixture. Follow baking directions for Lemon Baked Fish, Method 1.

BREADED FISH FILLETS

Yield: 50 portions   *Portion:* 5 oz
Deep-fat fryer: 360°F   *Fry:* 4–5 minutes

Ingredient	Amount	Procedure
Frozen fish fillets, 5 oz	50	Dredge fish in mixture of flour, salt, and pepper.
Flour, all-purpose	8 oz	
Salt	1 Tbsp	
Pepper, white	1 tsp	
Eggs, beaten	6 (11 oz)	Combine eggs and milk.
Milk	2 cups	
Bread crumbs	1 lb 4 oz	Dip fish in egg mixture, then in crumbs. Fry in deep fat at 360°F for 4–5 minutes or until fish is golden brown. Serve at once or place in uncovered counter pans in 250°F oven until service.

Approximate nutritive values per portion

Calories (kcal)	Protein (grams)	Carbohydrate (grams)	Fat (grams)	Cholesterol (mg)	Sodium (mg)	Iron (mg)	Calcium (mg)
191	26.7 (58%)	12.3 (27%)	3.1 (15%)	94	327	1	48

Note ■ Suggested fish: flounder, sole, haddock, perch, grouper.

Variation ■ **Cornmeal-Breaded Fish Fillets.**   Delete eggs, milk, and bread crumbs. Increase flour to 1 lb. Mix flour, 2 lb 8 oz cornmeal, salt and pepper. Dip fish fillets into cornmeal/flour mixture, thoroughly coating each piece. Fry according to directions.

FILLET OF SOLE AMANDINE

Yield: 50 portions   *Portion:* 5 oz
Oven: 375°F   *Bake:* 15–20 minutes

Ingredient	Amount	Procedure
Fillet of sole, 3 per lb	17 lb	Dredge fish in mixture of flour, salt, and pepper. Place in greased counter pans in single layers.
Flour, all-purpose	8 oz	
Salt	1 Tbsp	
Pepper, white	1 tsp	
Margarine	1 lb 8 oz	Sauté onion and garlic in margarine.
Onion, finely chopped	4 oz	
Garlic, minced	1 clove	
Water	2 cups	Combine water, lemon juice, and seasonings. Add onions and garlic.
Lemon juice	1½ cups	
Salt	1 Tbsp	Heat, but do not boil.
Pepper, white	1 tsp	Just before baking, pour sauce over fish, 1 cup per pan.
Almonds, slivered	8 oz	Sprinkle almonds over fish. Bake at 375°F for 15–20 minutes.

Approximate nutritive values per portion

Calories (kcal)	Protein (grams)	Carbohydrate (grams)	Fat (grams)	Cholesterol (mg)	Sodium (mg)	Iron (mg)	Calcium (mg)
323	38.8 (49%)	5.3 (7%)	15.8 (45%)	104	548	0.9	48

Note

■ Other white fish, such as halibut, haddock, cod, or flounder, may be used. Baking time on thicker fillets or steaks will be 25–35 minutes.

LEMON RICE-STUFFED COD

Yield: 50 portions   *Portion:* 6 oz cod, 2¼ oz rice
Oven: 350°F   *Bake:* 25–30 minutes

Ingredient	Amount	Procedure
Cod fillets, 6 oz	50	Cut cod portions to open like a wallet, hinged in center.
Margarine Celery, diced Onion, chopped	4 oz 12 oz 6 oz	Sauté celery and onions in margarine in steam-jacketed kettle or other large pan.
Water, hot Salt Thyme	1½ qt 1 Tbsp 1 tsp	Add water and seasonings to vegetable mixture.
Rice, uncooked	1 lb 4 oz	Stir in raw rice. Cover and simmer until rice is tender and liquid is absorbed, approximately 15 minutes.
Yogurt, plain Lemon, peeled and diced	1 lb 4 oz	Stir in yogurt and lemon.
		Place No. 16 dipper (2¼ oz) of rice mixture on one side of fish fillet. Fold other half over top to close like a wallet. Place on greased baking sheets or 12 × 20-inch counter pans. Bake uncovered at 350°F for 25–30 minutes. Serve garnished with a slice of lemon.

Approximate nutritive values per portion

Calories (kcal)	Protein (grams)	Carbohydrate (grams)	Fat (grams)	Cholesterol (mg)	Sodium (mg)	Iron (mg)	Calcium (mg)
207	31.4 (64%)	10.5 (21%)	3.3 (15%)	75	253	1.1	50

Notes
- Brown rice or a brown or wild rice mixture may be substituted for white rice.
- Any firm, flaky fish may be substituted for cod: orange roughy, perch, pollack.

BAKED WHOLE SALMON, CHILLED

Yield: 1 salmon or 50 portions
Oven: 350°F   *Bake:* 2 hours

Ingredient	Amount	Procedure
Whole salmon, thawed	1 (approx. 10 lb)	Thoroughly wash fish. Rub inside and outside of fish while running cool, clear water over. Place fish on 12 × 20-inch sheet pan that has been sprayed with vegetable spray or lined with parchment paper. Bake at 350°F for 1 hour.
		Remove from oven and skin fish. Cut skin behind head, down the length of back and halfway down across belly. Remove cut skin. Leave head, fins, and tail on.
Margarine or butter, melted	4 oz	Combine melted butter or margarine and lemon juice. Use to baste fish.
Lemon juice	½ cup (4 oz)	Return fish to oven and bake 1 hour.
		Remove fish from oven. Refrigerate. Fish should be cooked 1 day in advance to be served on cold buffet.

To Serve Whole Baked Salmon:

1. Place fish on attractive tray.

2. Garnish with orange, lemon, and cucumber slices; carrot curls, ripe olives, and shredded cabbage. If mouth is large and open, a fluted orange can be inserted.

Approximate nutritive values per portion

Calories (kcal)	Protein (grams)	Carbohydrate (grams)	Fat (grams)	Cholesterol (mg)	Sodium (mg)	Iron (mg)	Calcium (mg)
100	13 (54%)	0.2 (1%)	4.9 (46%)	16	576	0.6	9

Note   ■   Thaw fish in refrigerator for 1–2 days.

SALMON LOAF

Yield: 50 portions or 5 loaves 5 × 9 inches   *Portion:* 4½ oz
Oven: 325°F   *Bake:* 1–1½ hours

Ingredient	Amount	Procedure
Milk, scalded	3¾ cups	Mix milk and bread cubes.
Bread cubes, soft	1 lb 4 oz	
Eggs, beaten	18 (2 lb)	Add eggs to milk and bread mixture.
Salmon, flaked	10 lb	Add salmon and other ingredients.
Salt	1 oz (1½ Tbsp)	Mix lightly.
Paprika	1 tsp	Scale salmon mixture into 5 greased 5 × 9-inch loaf
Pepper, white	1 tsp	pans, 2 lb 14 oz per pan.
Onions, chopped	3 oz	Bake at 325°F for 1–1½ hours.
Lemon juice	½ cup	

Approximate nutritive values per portion							
Calories (kcal)	Protein (grams)	Carbohydrate (grams)	Fat (grams)	Cholesterol (mg)	Sodium (mg)	Iron (mg)	Calcium (mg)
196	21.8 (46%)	7 (15%)	8.4 (40%)	130	785	1.4	240

Note   ■ For a lighter-textured product, beat egg whites separately and fold into salmon mixture.

Variation   ■ **Tuna Loaf.** Substitute drained tuna for salmon.

SCALLOPED SALMON

Yield: 50 portions or 2 pans 12 × 20 × 2 inches   *Portion:* 6 oz
Oven: 375°F   *Bake:* 25 minutes

Ingredient	Amount	Procedure
Margarine	1 lb	Melt margarine in steam-jacketed or other kettle.
Flour, all-purpose	12 oz	Add flour and stir until smooth.
Salt	1 oz (1½ Tbsp)	Cook 5 minutes.
Pepper, white	½ tsp	
Milk	1 gal	Add milk gradually, stirring constantly with wire whip. Continue cooking until thickened.
Parsley, chopped	¼ cup	Add parsley, onion, and celery salt to sauce.
Onion, chopped	4 oz	
Celery salt	1 tsp	
Salmon, canned	10 lb	Drain salmon. Remove skin and bones. Flake.
Bread crumbs	8 oz	Arrange salmon, sauce, and crumbs in layers in 2 greased 12 × 20 × 2-inch baking pans, 10 lb per pan.
Bread crumbs	4 oz	Combine crumbs and margarine and sprinkle over the top.
Margarine, melted	4 oz	Bake at 375°F for 25 minutes.

Approximate nutritive values per portion

Calories (kcal)	Protein (grams)	Carbohydrate (grams)	Fat (grams)	Cholesterol (mg)	Sodium (mg)	Iron (mg)	Calcium (mg)
308	22.2 (29%)	14.1 (19%)	17.6 (52%)	61	933	1.4	301

Note   ■ Diced hard-cooked eggs and frozen peas are good additions.

Variation   ■ **Scalloped Tuna.** Substitute tuna for salmon.

TUNA AND NOODLES

Yield: 48 portions or 2 pans 12 × 20 × 2 inches   *Portion:* 8 oz
Oven: 350°F   *Bake:* 30–45 minutes

Ingredient	Amount	Procedure
Noodles Water, boiling Salt Vegetable oil	3 lb AP 3 gal 2 oz (3 Tbsp) 2 Tbsp	Cook noodles according to directions on p. 407. Drain. (Should yield 9 lb cooked.)
Tuna	5 lb 8 oz	Flake tuna and add to noodles.
Margarine Onions, chopped Celery, chopped	8 oz 1 lb 8 oz 1 lb 8 oz	Melt margarine in steam-jacketed or other kettle. Add onions and celery. Sauté until tender.
Flour, all-purpose Pepper, black	6 oz ½ tsp	Add flour and pepper to onion mixture. Stir until blended. Cook 5–10 minutes.
Chicken base Water	3 oz 1 gal	Stir in chicken base. Add water gradually, stirring constantly with wire whip. Cook until thickened. Add tuna and noodles to sauce. Stir gently until well blended.
Processed cheese, shredded Paprika	8 oz ½ tsp	Scale noodle mixture into 2 greased 12 × 20 × 2-inch baking pans, 13 lb per pan. Sprinkle with cheese, 4 oz per pan. Sprinkle lightly with paprika. Bake at 350°F until mixture is heated through and cheese is melted, 30–45 minutes.

Approximate nutritive values per portion							
Calories (kcal)	Protein (grams)	Carbohydrate (grams)	Fat (grams)	Cholesterol (mg)	Sodium (mg)	Iron (mg)	Calcium (mg)
245	20.9 (35%)	23.3 (39%)	7.1 (26%)	39	699	3.2	6.5

Note   ■   Two 46-oz cans cream of mushroom or cream of celery soup and 1 qt milk may be substituted for the sauce made from margarine, flour, chicken base, and water.

Variations   ■   **Tuna Macaroni Casserole.**   Substitute macaroni for noodles.

■   **Tuna and Rice.**   Substitute 1 lb 8 oz rice for the noodles. Cook rice according to directions on p. 430.

CREAMED TUNA

Yield: 50 portions or 7½ qt   *Portion:* 4 oz

Ingredient	Amount	Procedure
Eggs, hard-cooked (p. 308)	9	Peel eggs and chop coarsely.
Margarine Flour, all-purpose Salt	12 oz 6 oz 1 Tbsp	Melt margarine in steam-jacketed or other kettle. Add flour and salt. Stir until smooth. Cook 5 minutes.
Milk	1 gal	Add milk gradually, stirring constantly with a wire whip. Cook until thickened.
Green pepper, chopped Pimiento, chopped Worcestershire sauce (optional) Pepper, cayenne	6 oz 6 oz 6 Tbsp ¼ tsp	Add green pepper, pimiento, and seasonings to sauce.
Tuna, flaked	5 lb	Add tuna and eggs to sauce. Reheat to serving temperature. Serve with 4-oz ladle on toast, biscuits, or corn bread.

Approximate nutritive values per portion

Calories (kcal)	Protein (grams)	Carbohydrate (grams)	Fat (grams)	Cholesterol (mg)	Sodium (mg)	Iron (mg)	Calcium (mg)
186	17.6 (37%)	7.1 (15%)	9.3 (44%)	57	422	1.9	109

Note
- Other cooked fish may be substituted for tuna.

Variations
- **Creamed Salmon.** Substitute salmon for tuna.
- **Creamed Tuna and Celery.** Delete hard-cooked eggs and green pepper. Add 1 lb diced cooked celery, 3 oz chopped onion sautéed in margarine, and 3 oz chopped pimiento.
- **Creamed Tuna and Peas.** Delete hard-cooked eggs and green pepper. Add 3 lb frozen peas, cooked until just tender and drained.
- **Tuna Rarebit.** Delete hard-cooked eggs. Add 1 lb 8 oz shredded cheddar cheese.

DEVILED CRAB

Yield: 50 portions   *Portion:* 3 oz
Oven: 400°F   *Bake:* 15 minutes

Ingredient	Amount	Procedure
Crabmeat	6 lb	Separate crabmeat into flakes.
Eggs, beaten	5 (9 oz)	Combine eggs, lemon juice, and seasonings.
Lemon juice	¼ cup	Add to crabmeat. Mix lightly.
Salt	1 oz (1½ Tbsp)	
Pepper	2 tsp	
Pepper, cayenne	few grains	
Worcestershire sauce	1 Tbsp	
Onion juice (optional)	2 Tbsp	
Margarine	12 oz	Melt margarine in steam-jacketed or other kettle.
Flour, all-purpose	8 oz	Add flour and stir until smooth.
		Cook 5 minutes.
Milk	2 qt	Add milk gradually to flour mixture, stirring constantly with wire whip.
		Cook until thick.
Prepared mustard	1½ tsp	Add mustard to sauce. Combine with crab mixture. Mix lightly.
		Fill individual casseroles or shells.
Bread crumbs	8 oz	Combine crumbs and margarine.
Margarine, melted	4 oz	Sprinkle over crab.
		Bake at 400°F for 15 minutes.

Approximate nutritive values per portion

Calories (kcal)	Protein (grams)	Carbohydrate (grams)	Fat (grams)	Cholesterol (mg)	Sodium (mg)	Iron (mg)	Calcium (mg)
186	12.8 (28%)	9.3 (20%)	10.7 (52%)	81	614	1	85

Note   ■   Lobster, shrimp, or imitation crab may be substituted for crabmeat.

SCALLOPED OYSTERS

Yield: 50 portions or 2 pans 12 × 20 × 2 inches   *Portion:* 5 oz
Oven: 400°F   *Bake:* 30 minutes

Ingredient	Amount	Procedure
Oysters	6 qt	Drain oysters, saving liquor.
Cracker crumbs	3 qt	Mix crumbs, margarine, and seasonings.
Margarine, melted	1 lb	Spread a third of the crumbs over bottoms of 2 greased
Salt	1 oz (1½ Tbsp)	12 × 20 × 2-inch baking pans.
Paprika	½ tsp	Cover with half of the oysters; repeat with crumbs and
Pepper, white	½ tsp	oysters.
Milk	1 qt	Mix milk and oyster liquor. Pour over top of oysters.
Oyster liquor (or milk)	3 cups	Cover with remaining crumbs. Bake at 400°F for 30 minutes.

Approximate nutritive values per portion

Calories (kcal)	Protein (grams)	Carbohydrate (grams)	Fat (grams)	Cholesterol (mg)	Sodium (mg)	Iron (mg)	Calcium (mg)
251	11.3 (19%)	19.6 (33%)	13 (49%)	74	670	8.8	102

Note   ■   2 cups finely chopped, partially cooked celery may be added.

CREOLE SHRIMP WITH RICE

Yield: 50 portions   *Portion:* 4 oz creole shrimp + 4 oz rice

Ingredient	Amount	Procedure
Shortening	8 oz	Cook onion, celery, and garlic in shortening until almost tender but not brown.
Onion, finely chopped	10 oz	
Celery, finely chopped	12 oz	
Garlic, minced	1 tsp	
Flour, all-purpose	6 oz	Add flour and seasonings. Stir until smooth. Cook 5 minutes.
Salt	1 oz (1½ Tbsp)	
Pepper, cayenne	¾ tsp	
Tomato juice	2 cups	Add tomato juice, tomatoes, and sugar. Cook 10 minutes.
Tomatoes, canned	2½ qt	
Sugar, granulated	1 Tbsp	
Shrimp, cooked, peeled, and deveined	6 lb EP	Add shrimp and green pepper to sauce. Heat to serving temperature.
Green pepper, chopped	8 oz	
Rice, converted	3 lb 8 oz	Cook rice according to directions on p. 430.
Water, boiling	4¼ qt	Serve shrimp with 4-oz ladle over No. 10 dipper of rice.
Salt	2 Tbsp	
Margarine or vegetable oil	2 Tbsp	

Approximate nutritive values per portion

Calories (kcal)	Protein (grams)	Carbohydrate (grams)	Fat (grams)	Cholesterol (mg)	Sodium (mg)	Iron (mg)	Calcium (mg)
232	12.3 (21%)	31.8 (55%)	6 (23%)	83.6	667	3.3	48

Note   ■   If raw shrimp are used, purchase 12–14 lb. Cook as directed on p. 333.

ORIENTAL SHRIMP AND PASTA

Yield: 50 portions   *Portion:* 6 oz shrimp and sauce + 4 oz pasta

Ingredient	Amount	Procedure
Sugar, granulated	1 oz	Combine in steam-jacketed or other kettle. Blend with wire whip.
Cornstarch	10 oz	
Pepper, white	½ tsp	
Ginger, ground	1½ Tbsp	
Garlic powder	¾ tsp	
Pepper, cayenne	few grains	
Water	1½ gal	Stir into dry ingredients.
Soy sauce	1 cup	Cook and stir with wire whip until thickened and clear.
Soup base, clam	5 oz	
Bamboo shoots, sliced, canned	1 lb	Rinse bamboo shoots and water chestnuts. Drain. Add to sauce.
Water chestnuts, sliced, canned	1 lb	
Broccoli stalks, sliced	1 lb 12 oz	Cook vegetables (p. 643) until tender-crisp. Drain. Add to sauce.
Carrots, julienne	12 oz	
Green onions, cut into ½-inch pieces	8 oz	Add onions and shrimp to sauce.
Shrimp, cooked	2 lb 8 oz	
Fettuccine	5 lb	Cook according to directions on p. 407. Drain. Serve 6 oz shrimp over 4 oz cooked pasta.
Water	5 gal	
Salt	5 oz	
Vegetable oil	3 Tbsp	

Approximate nutritive values per portion

Calories (kcal)	Protein (grams)	Carbohydrate (grams)	Fat (grams)	Cholesterol (mg)	Sodium (mg)	Iron (mg)	Calcium (mg)
160	9 (22%)	16.2 (40%)	6.6 (37%)	45	1357	1.3	39

Meat

PURCHASING AND STORAGE

The quality of cooked meat depends on the quality purchased, the storage and handling of meat after delivery, and cooking methods. All meats marketed in interstate commerce in the United States must meet federal inspection standards for wholesomeness. This requirement covers all processed meat products and fresh and frozen meats. Meat slaughtered, processed, and sold within a given state must be inspected by programs "at least equal to" federal inspection standards.

Quality grading helps predict the palatability of meat. Beef grades are based on two factors: the amount of marbling present and the age of the animal. Quality grades for young cattle include (from best to least) Prime, Choice, Select, and Standard. Each grade denotes a specific level of quality as determined by the USDA. Yield grading is a system that estimates the percentage of boneless and closely trimmed foodservice cuts that can be obtained from a beef carcass. These grades identify carcasses for differences in cutability or yield and are applied by the USDA grading service. Possible yield grades are (best to worst) 1 through 5.

Meat for foodservice use is available in wholesale (primal) cuts, subprimals, and portioned cuts. The chuck, loin, rib, and round are the major wholesale cuts of beef, making up 76 percent of the carcass. Other beef primal cuts are brisket, flank, foreshank, and plate. Pork primal cuts are belly, loin, shoulder, and leg or ham. Subprimals are produced by breaking down the primals into smaller cuts. Portioned cuts are processed from subprimals into individual steaks, chops, and other products. Portion cuts have several advantages for the foodservice operator: Less skilled labor is needed by the operator, the product is more uniform, the actual amount of product needed can be prepared and costs can more easily be controlled, and packaging often allows for safer, more efficient storage. Storing meat in a refrigerator at a cold temperature is necessary to retard bacterial growth and slow the action of muscle enzymes. Fresh meat may be stored unwrapped or loosely covered with waxed paper at a temperature of 28°–32°F, with a relative humidity of 85–90 percent. Meat should be used as soon after purchase as possible, not more than 3–4 days later. Fresh meat stored in vacuum packaging will last several weeks. Vacuum-packaged meat should be stored according to the processor's recommendations. Once removed from the vacuum package, the meat should be used within 3–4 days.

Frozen meat requires a uniform holding temperature of 0°F or below. It should be well-wrapped to exclude air and keep the moisture in. Fresh meat frozen at 0°F may be successfully stored for 6 months, and fresh beef frozen at −10°F for a year. Frozen meat should be kept wrapped while defrosting in a refrigerator at 30°–35°F and should be cooked soon after defrosting. Once thawed, it should not be refrozen. Refreezing will result in some moisture loss and could pose a health risk if the total thawed time exceeds acceptable standards. Cooked meat may be frozen provided it is frozen soon after cooking and cooling.

Cured meats and cured and smoked meats such as ham and bacon, sausages, and dried beef require refrigerator storage. Although ham, bacon, and other cured meats can be frozen, freezing should only be for short periods, since undesirable flavor changes occur because of their salt, spice, and fat content.

COOKING METHODS

Meat is cooked by either dry or moist heat. The method used will depend on the grade and location of the cut. Meat cuts containing relatively small amounts of connective tissue are cooked by dry heat (roasting, broiling, or frying). Moist heat (braising or cooking in liquid) is used for less tender cuts that have larger amounts of connective tissue. Veal, lamb, and pork, all tender meats, often are cooked with moist heat to develop their flavor and to provide variety in menu items. Veal, because of its delicate flavor and low fat content, combines well with sauces and other foods.

Dry-heat cooking does not improve tenderness; under some conditions, it reduces tenderness. Cooking with moist heat tends to soften some connective tissue and to make meat tender. The degree of doneness affects percentage losses, with a smaller loss in rare meat than in medium or well-done meat, provided other factors are the same. Faster cooking rates, complete trimming of external fat, and lengthy postcooking holding periods may substantially increase cooking and holding loss.

Roasting

The term "roasting," which is a dry-heat method, refers to cooking meat in an oven, in an open pan, with no moisture added. Meat cuts must be tender to be roasted. In beef, these are the less-used muscles, or those attached to the backbone. Most veal, pork, and lamb cuts may be cooked by this method.

Meats may be completely or partially defrosted or frozen at the time the cooking process is begun. Research has shown that meat roasted from the frozen state will yield as much meat as roasts partially or completely thawed before cooking. However, when time is a factor, defrosting meat before cooking usually is the accepted method. The additional cooking time required for frozen roasts is from one-third to one-half again the amount of time recommended for cooking a similar cut from the chilled state. Oven temperature should not change. Steps in roasting are as follows:

1. Place the meat, fat side up, on a rack in an open roasting pan. As the fat on top melts and runs down over the meat, it bastes the roast. Basting adds flavor and keeps the surface of the roast from drying out.

2. Insert a meat thermometer in the roast so that the bulb rests in the center of the cut but does not rest on bone or fat. If the meat is frozen, the thermometer is inserted toward the end of the cooking period after the meat has thawed.

3. Season the roast with salt, pepper, and other spices. See p. 599 for Seasoned Salt recipe. Salt penetrates less than an inch during cooking, so it makes little difference whether the roast is seasoned at the beginning of, during, or at the end of cooking.

4. Do not add water and do not cover. If water is added to the pan, the cooking will be by moist heat.

5. Roast at a constant low oven temperature, 250°–325°F, depending on the kind of meat and size of the roast. If cooking in a convection oven, the temperature should be reduced by 50°F to minimize drying of the roast's surface by moving air. Searing the roast initially at a high temperature does not hold in meat juices and may increase cooking losses. A constant low temperature reduces shrinkage and produces a more evenly done roast that is easier to carve and more attractive to serve.

6. Roast to the desired degree of doneness. The length of the cooking period depends on several factors: oven temperature, size and shape of the roast, style of cut (boned or bone in), oven load, quality of meat, and degree of doneness desired. Approximate cooking times and temperatures are given in Tables 8.1 through 8.4. Although approximate total cooking time can be used as a general guide, the interior temperature of the meat as measured by a meat thermometer is a more reliable indicator of doneness. Roasts will continue cooking for a period of time after removal from the oven, and the internal temperature of the roast may rise as much as 5°F. The roast should be allowed to set in a warm place for 15–20 minutes before it is sliced. The roast becomes more firm, retains more of its juices, and is easier to slice. Refrigerating the roast for an extended period of time prior to slicing and service, however, results in loss of flavor. To ensure the highest quality, roasts should be served as soon as possible after cooking and slicing. Table 1.1 provides information on serving yields.

Broiling

Broiling is a dry-heat method of cooking using direct or radiant heat. It is used for small, individualized, tender cuts such as steaks, chops, and patties. Low-temperature cooking methods apply to proper broiling. Broiled meats should not be seared, for searing in-

TABLE 8.1 Timetable for roasting beef

Cut	Approx. weight of single roast (pounds)	Oven temperature (°F)	Interior temperature of roast when removed from oven (°F)	Minutes per pound based on one roast	Approximate total cooking time (hours)
Rib, roast ready No. 109	20–25	250	130 (rare) 140 (medium) 150 (well)	13–15 15–17 17–19	4½–5 5–6 6–6½
Rib, roast ready No. 109	20–25	300	130 (rare) 140 (medium) 150 (well)	10–12 12–14 14–16	4–4½ 4½–5 5–5½
Rib, roast ready No. 109	2 roasts, 28 lb each	300	130 (rare) 140 (medium) 150 (well)	5–6 6 7–8	5–5½ 6 6–7
Ribeye roll No. 112 or No. 112A	4–6	350	140 (rare) 160 (medium) 170 (well)	18–20 20–22 22–24	1⅓–1⅔ 1½–2 1⅔–2¼
Full tenderloin No. 189 or No. 190	4–6	425	140 (rare)		¾–1
Strip loin boneless No. 180	10–12	325	140 (rare)	10	1½–2
Top sirloin butt No. 184	8	300	140 (rare)	25	3.5
Top (inside) round No. 168	10	300	140 (rare) 150 (medium)	18–19 22–23	3–3¼ 3½–4
Top (inside) round No. 168	15	300	140 (rare) 150 (medium)	15 17	3½–4 4–4½
Round, rump and shank off, boneless, tied special No. 165B	50	250	140 (medium) 150 (well)	12 14	10 11–12

From National Live Stock and Meat Board, *Meat in the Foodservice Industry* (Chicago, reviewed 1991, copyright 1977).

creases broiling losses. If marking on a hot broiler rack is desired, the remainder of the broiler time after marking should be at a moderate temperature.

Broiling is most successful for cuts 1–2 inches thick. Veal should not be broiled unless it is fairly mature and well marbled with fat, and then only loin chops or steaks should be used. Broiling is an acceptable cooking method for pork chops, but because pork

TABLE 8.2   Timetable for roasting lamb and veal

Cut	Approximate weight (pounds)	Oven temperature (°F)	Interior temperature of roast when removed from oven (°F)	Minutes per pound based on one roast	Approximate total cooking time (hours)
LAMB					
Leg, shank off, No. 233C	5–9	325	140 (rare)	20–25	2–3
			150 (medium)	25–30	2½–3¾
			160 (well)	30–35	3–4½
Leg, shank off, boneless, No. 233D	4–7	325	140 (rare)	25–30	2–3
			150 (medium)	30–35	2¼–3½
			160 (well)	35–40	2½–4
Shoulder, boneless and tied, No. 208	3½–5	325	140 (rare)	30–35	2–2½
			150 (medium)	35–40	2¼–3
			160 (well)	40–45	2½–3½
Rib rack, No. 204	1½–2	375	140 (rare)	30–35	¾–1
			150 (medium)	35–40	1–1¼
			160 (well)	40–45	1–1½
Rib rack, No. 204	2–3	375	140 (rare)	25–30	1–1¼
			150 (medium)	30–35	1¼–1½
			160 (well)	35–40	1½–1¾
VEAL					
Leg, shank off, oven-prepared, boneless No. 336	3½–7	325	170	25–30	2–3
Loin, two ribs, trimmed, No. 332 or 332A	4–6	325	170	30–35	2½–3

Adapted from National Live Stock and Meat Board, *Meat in the Foodservice Industry* (Chicago, reviewed 1987, 1991, copyright 1977) and from American Lamb Council, American Lamb, Finest for Foodservice (Englewood, CO, 1987).

should be cooked to an internal temperature of 160°F, the temperature should be moderate so the chop does not become charred by the time it is cooked well-done.

Frozen cuts may be successfully broiled, especially those 1½ inches thick or less. They should be broiled at a greater distance from the heat or at a lower temperature than unfrozen cuts to provide more uniform doneness. Although cooking times will vary, a general guideline is that frozen steaks will take nearly twice as long as unfrozen steaks.

Meat may be broiled in an oven broiler or other type of heat-from-above gas or electric broiler, or on an open hearth, which is heated from below. In pan broiling or griddle broiling, the heat is transferred from the pan or grill to the meat being cooked.

TABLE 8.3   **Timetable for roasting pork in conventional oven**

Cut	Weight	Oven temperature (°F)	Food product internal temperature (°F)	Minutes per pound	Approximate total cooking time
Loin, boneless, tied	8–12 lb	325	155	17–20	2½–3½ hr
Fresh ham boneless, tied	10–14 lb	325	155	20–25	3½–4½ hr
Spare ribs (panned flat)	3 lb and down	325	well-done	—	1½ hr
Loin, back ribs (shingled)	1¾–2½ lb	325	well-done	—	1½ hr
Bacon, flat pack	18–22 slices/lb	400	—	—	6–8 min
Sausage	1-oz patties/ links	400	well-done	—	15–20 min
Boneless cured ham, fully cooked	10–12 lb	325	140	15–18	2½–3½ hr
Boneless pork chops	4 oz	425	160	—	18–20 min
Boneless pork chops	5 oz	425	160	—	22–24 min
Boneless pork chops	6 oz	425	160	—	24–26 min
Boneless pork chops	8 oz	425	160	—	25–27 min
Bone-in pork chop	4 oz	425	160	—	10–12 min
Bone-in pork chop	5 oz	425	160	—	12–14 min
Bone-in pork chop	6 oz	425	160	—	15–17 min
Bone-in pork chop	8 oz	425	160	—	25–30 min

From National Pork Producers Council, Today's Pork (copyright 1988).

TABLE 8.4   **Timetable for roasting pork in convection oven**

Cut	Weight	Oven temperature (°F)	Food product internal temperature (°F)	Minutes per pound	Approximate total cooking time
Loin, boneless, tied	8–12 lb	275	155	12–15	2–2½ hr
Fresh ham boneless, tied	10–14 lb	275	155	13–16	3–3½ hr
Whole tenderloin	¾–1 lb	425	155	—	15 min
Spare ribs (panned flat)	3 lb and down	275	well-done	—	60–70 min
Loin, back ribs (shingled)	1¾–2½ lb	275	well-done	—	60–70 min
Bacon, flat pack	18–22 slices/lb	325	—	—	4–6 min
Sausage	1-oz patties/ links	325	well-done	—	10–12 min
Boneless cured ham, fully cooked	10–12 lb	275	140	10–12	2–2½ hr
Boneless pork chops	4 oz	425	160	—	6–8 min
Boneless pork chops	5 oz	425	160	—	8–10 min
Boneless pork chops	6 oz	425	160	—	13–15 min
Boneless pork chops	8 oz	425	160	—	15–17 min
Bone-in pork chop	4 oz	425	160	—	8–10 min
Bone-in pork chop	5 oz	425	160	—	11–13 min
Bone-in pork chop	6 oz	425	160	—	13–15 min
Bone-in pork chop	8 oz	425	160	—	20–22 min

From National Pork Producers Council, Today's Pork (copyright 1988).

TABLE 8.5   **Timetable for broiling meat**

Cut	Approximate thickness or weight (inches/weight)	Approximate total cooking time (minutes)		
		Rare	Medium	Well-done
Beef rib, club, top loin, T-bone, porter-house, tenderloin, or individual servings of sirloin steak	1 1½ 2	15 25 35	20 35 50	
Beef sirloin steak	1 1½	20–25 30–35	30–35 40–45	
Ground beef patties	1 (4 oz)	15	20	
Pork chops (boneless, rib or loin)	4 oz 6 oz 8 oz			8–10 13–15 18–20
Pork chops, smoked (rib or loin)				10–12
Bacon				4–5
Ham slice (cooked)	½ 1			8–10 14–16
Lamb shoulder, rib, loin and sirloin chops or leg chops (steaks)	5 oz 8 oz			10–12 14–16
Ground lamb patties	1 (4 oz)			18–20

Adapted from National Live Stock and Meat Board, *Meat in the Foodservice Industry* (Chicago, reviewed 1991, copyright 1977), and National Pork Producers Council, Today's Pork (copyright 1988).

Following is the standard procedure for broiling:

1. Preheat the broiler. A preheated broiler rack will provide desired markings on the meat.

2. Place the meat on the broiler rack. A distance of 3–5 inches is recommended. If frozen meat is used, increase distance from the heat source.

3. Broil the meat until the side closest to the heat source is attractively browned and the cut is cooked almost half through.

4. Turn meat only once during cooking.

5. Broil second side to desired doneness. Season. See Table 8.5 for approximate time.

Pan Broiling and Griddle Broiling

1. Place meat on a preheated ungreased griddle or heavy frying pan.

2. Cook slowly, turning as necessary. Since the meat is in contact with the hot metal of the pan or griddle, turning more than once may be necessary for even cooking. If the steak is thick, reduce the temperature after browning.

TABLE 8.6   Timetable for griddle-broiling meat (surface 400°–450°F)

Cut	Approximate thickness or weight (inches/weight)	Rare	Medium	Well-done
Beef steaks	¾	4	8	12
	1	6	10	15
	1½	10–12	15–18	20
Ground beef	¾	4–5	8–10	12
patties	1 (4 oz)	6–8	10–12	15
Lamb chops	1		10	15
	1½		15	20–25
Ground lamb	¾		10	12–15
patties	1 (4 oz)		10–15	15–20
Smoked ham slice	½			6–10
Bacon				2–3
Boneless pork chop	4 oz			11–13
	5 oz			12–14
Bone-in pork chop	4 oz			6–8
	6 oz			11–13

Adapted from National Live Stock and Meat Board, *Meat in the Foodservice Industry* (Chicago, reviewed 1991, copyright 1977), and National Pork Producers Council, Today's Pork (copyright 1988).

3. Cook the meat at a moderate temperature. Care should be taken not to puncture the meat while cooking. Use long-handled tongs or a spatula for turning.

4. Do not add additional fat or water. Pour off or scrape away any excess fat as it accumulates.

5. Cook meat to the desired degree of doneness. See Table 8.6 for approximate cooking times.

Frying

Frying, a dry-heat method, is cooking in fat and may be accomplished by pan or griddle frying in a small amount of fat; by deep-fat frying, which uses a large amount of fat; or by stir-frying. Meat for frying generally is cut thinner than that for broiling and may be breaded or tenderized by scoring, cubing, or grinding.

Pan Frying or Griddle Frying

Procedures for pan frying or griddle frying are similar to pan or griddle broiling, but the meat may be dredged with seasoned flour, and a small amount of fat is used for cooking. Confusion often surrounds whether or not to cover the pan. Covering is not recommended for griddle frying, because doing so changes the method from dry-heat to moist-heat cooking.

Pan frying and sautéing are terms sometimes used interchangeably. Generally, sautéing refers to cooking small, thin pieces of meat in a pan with a small amount of fat, usually at a high temperature and for a short period. Following is the standard procedure for pan frying or griddle frying:

1. Dredge the meat with seasoned flour, crumbs, cornmeal, or similar coatings.
2. Brown the meat on both sides in a small amount of fat. Allow the fat to remain on the griddle or in the pan as the meat cooks.
3. Do not cover meat. Cook at moderate temperature until done, turning occasionally.
4. Drain meat and serve at once.

Deep-Fat Frying

In deep-fat frying, the hot fat is in constant contact with the entire surface of the meat, resulting in rapid heat transfer. A portion of the fat will be absorbed and contribute to the flavor of the product. At a low temperature, absorption is much greater, resulting in a greasy, less desirable product that will not fry to an attractive golden-brown color. Overloading the fryer will reduce the temperature of the fat. Following is the procedure for deep-fat frying meat:

1. Coat or bread meat. (See p. 47 for methods of preparing food for deep-fat frying.) Portioned, prebreaded items may be cooked from a frozen state in the deep-fat fryer.
2. Heat the fat to approximately 350°F.
3. Place pieces of meat in the wire basket and carefully lower into the fryer. Do not fill the basket while holding over the fat, because crumbs could fall into the fat.
4. Do not overload the basket or the fryer. An overload drastically reduces the temperature of the fat, thereby increasing fat absorption and inhibiting browning. This is especially true when the product is frozen. A ratio of about 5 to 1 by weight of fat to product is the maximum effective load.
5. Continue cooking until the outside of the product is browned and crisp and the meat reaches the desired doneness. Cooking time depends on the size of the piece, whether it is frozen or chilled, and whether the meat has been precooked.
6. Remove meat from fat and let drain. Do not shake the basket over the fat if the product is coated; shaking will cause particles and crumbs to fall into the fat. The product should not be salted over the fat, either, because salt shortens the life of the fat.

Stir-Frying

Stir-frying consists of cooking sliced or chopped meat and vegetables in a small amount of oil over high heat. Quick cooking helps retain nutrients and enhances the flavor and attractiveness of the food. Following is the standard procedure for stir-frying:

1. Cut meat and vegetables into uniform pieces that cook quickly. Slice meat into thin slices or strips. Partially freezing meat will facilitate slicing.
2. Stir-fry the meat in small batches to avoid the accumulation of moisture in the pan. Drain accumulated drippings after each batch. Continually stir and turn meat strips with a scooping motion. Stir-fry meat until the pink color disappears.

3. If using vegetables, stir-fry separately from meat, then combine.

4. Add liquid (water or broth) and seasonings. Cover and steam for 3 minutes.

5. Add cornstarch mixed with a small amount of cold water (see recipe on p. 688).

6. Cook and stir just until the sauce thickens.

Braising

Braising is a moist-cooking method adapted to the less tender cuts of meat, particularly the much-used muscles and low grades of beef. Certain cuts of veal and thin cuts of pork such as chops and steaks are better if braised, although they are tender. The terms "pot roasting" or "fricasseeing" also apply to this method of cooking. Steps in braising are as follows:

1. Season meat and dredge with flour. Flour increases browning but may be omitted.

2. Brown meat in a small amount of fat. The meat can be browned in its own fat or added fat. Browning develops the aroma, flavor and color of the meat. Large cuts can be browned in a heavy pot on top of the range, in a pan in the oven, or in a steam-jacketed kettle. Smaller individual pieces can be browned in a tilting fry pan, on the grill, in the oven, or in the deep-fat fryer.

3. Add a small amount of water or other liquid. Use additional liquid as needed during the cooking. Braising or pot roasting in a steam-jacketed kettle will require more water than pot roasting in the oven. Other liquid, such as meat stock, tomato juice, or sour cream, may be used.

4. Cover with a tight-fitting lid or aluminum foil. Long, slow cooking in moisture will produce meat that is well-done without being dried out.

5. Cook at low temperature until tender. Simmer in a steam-jacketed kettle or heavy pot on top of the range or in the oven at 300°–325°F. See Table 8.7 for approximate cooking times.

Cooking in Liquid

This method of moist cookery involves cooking meat covered with water or other liquid and is sometimes referred to as simmering, boiling, or stewing. This method is suitable for the least tender cuts, such as shank, neck, and brisket, and for variety meats such as heart and tongue.

Following is the procedure for cooking large cuts in liquid:

1. Cover meat with liquid. Water or meat stock are used and may be hot or cold when added to the meat. If desired, the meat may be browned first, but some cuts such as corned beef, cured and smoked meats, and variety meats generally are not browned.

TABLE 8.7   **Timetable for braising meat**

Cut	Average weight or thickness	Approximate total cooking time (hours)
Pot roast	4–6 lb	3–4
Swiss steak	1–2½ inches	2–3
Short ribs	pieces 2 × 2 × 2 inches	1½–2
Lamb shanks	½ lb each	1–1½
Lamb riblets	¾ × 2½ × 3 inches	1½–2½
Pork chops or steaks	¾–1 inch	¾–1
Spareribs	2–3 lb	1½
Veal cutlets	½ × 3 × 5½ inches	¾–1
Veal steaks or chops	½–¾ inch	¾–1

From National Live Stock and Meat Board, *Meat in the Foodservice Industry* (Chicago, reviewed 1991, copyright 1977).

TABLE 8.8   **Timetable for cooking meat in liquid (large cuts and stews)**

Cut	Average size or weight	Approximate cooking time	
		Minutes per pound	Total hours
Fresh beef	4–8 lb	40–50	3–4
Corned beef	6–8 lb	40–50	4–6
Beef shank crosscuts	¾–1 lb		2½–3½
Lamb or veal for stew	1- to 2-inch cubes		1½–2½
Beef for stew	1- to 2-inch cubes		2–3

From National Live Stock and Meat Board, *Meat in the Foodservice Industry* (Chicago, reviewed 1991, copyright 1977).

2. Season with salt and pepper. Herbs, spices, and vegetables, used wisely, add to the variety and flavor of stewed meats. Suggested seasonings are carrots, celery, onions, bay leaves, thyme, marjoram, and parsley.

3. Cover and cook below boiling point until tender. Cooking may be in a steam-jacketed kettle, tilting fry pan, or a tightly covered heavy utensil on top of the range. See Table 8.8 for approximate cooking times.

BEEF RECIPES

POT ROAST OF BEEF

Yield: 50 portions   *Portion:* 3 oz
Oven: 450°F, then reduce to 300°F   *Bake:* 30 minutes, 3 hours

Ingredient	Amount	Procedure
Beef, boneless, inside round	18 lb	Season meat with salt and pepper. Place in roasting pan and brown at 450°F for about 30 minutes.
Salt	1 oz (1½ Tbsp)	
Pepper, black	½ tsp	
Water	2 qt	When meat is browned, add water. Reduce heat to 300°F. Cover and cook slowly until tender (3 hours). Add water as necessary. When meat is done, remove from pan. Let stand ½ hour before slicing.
Flour, all-purpose	6 oz	Mix flour and cold water, stirring with wire whip until smooth. Add to drippings in pan.
Water, cold	1½ cups	
Water (additional)	as necessary	Remove excess fat if necessary and add water to make 1 gal gravy. Add salt and pepper.
Salt	1 oz (1½ Tbsp)	
Pepper, black	½ tsp	

Approximate nutritive values per portion

Calories (kcal)	Protein (grams)	Carbohydrate (grams)	Fat (grams)	Cholesterol (mg)	Sodium (mg)	Iron (mg)	Calcium (mg)
269	36.9 (57%)	2.6 (4%)	11.2 (39%)	111	500	4.2	10

Notes
- Beef chuck may be used. Increase to 20 lb (AP).
- Meat may be cooked in a steam-jacketed kettle. Brown in a small amount of fat. Add water, salt, and pepper. Cover kettle and cook until tender. Add water as necessary.
- 2 lb carrots, 2 lb celery, and 12 oz onion, cut into chunks, may be added for flavoring during last hour of cooking. See Table 1.3 for amount of vegetables to use if serving vegetables as an accompaniment.

Variations
- **Savory Pot Roast or Brisket.** Place meat in baking pan. Sprinkle with 5 oz dry onion soup mix. Cover tightly with aluminum foil. Bake at 300°F for 5–6 hours. Remove foil and bake ½ hour longer. Use juice for gravy. If brisket is used, increase to 25 lb. Cooked Barbecue Sauce (p. 588) may be added the last half hour of cooking.

- **Smoked Beef Brisket.**   Use 25 lb well-trimmed beef brisket. Combine ⅔ cup liquid smoke, 2 Tbsp salt, 2 Tbsp onion salt, ¼ cup celery salt, ¼ cup garlic salt, ½ cup Worcestershire sauce, and 1 oz black pepper. Spread on brisket. Cover with aluminum foil. Seal. Refrigerate overnight. Bake at 275°F for 4 hours covered. Uncover and spread with Barbecue Sauce (p. 588). Bake 1 hour longer. To serve, slice in thin slices across the grain of the meat.

- **Yankee Pot Roast.**   Add 1½ qt tomato puree and one bay leaf to the water used in cooking the pot roast.

SAUERBRATEN

Yield: 50 portions   *Portion:* 4 oz
Oven: 350°F   *Bake:* 2–2½ hours

Ingredient	Amount	Procedure
Red cooking wine	3 cups	Heat to boiling point. Do not boil.
Red wine vinegar	2½ cups	Cool to room temperature.
Water	2½ cups	
Bay leaves	5	
Juniper berries, whole	14	
Peppercorns, black	18	
Beef, boneless, inside round	20 lb	Rub beef with salt and pepper.
Salt	4 oz	
Pepper, black	2 Tbsp	
Onions, sliced	4 lb EP	Place meat and onions in deep pans.
		Pour marinade over beef. Turn beef to moisten all sides with marinade. Cover tightly.
		Refrigerate 2 or 3 days, turning the meat twice a day if meat is not covered with marinade.
		Strain marinade and reserve to pour over beef.
		Place meat in roasting pan. Pour strained marinade over meat. Cover tightly.
		Roast at 350°F until internal temperature reaches 140°F.
		Remove meat from liquid.
		Reserve liquid for gingersnap sauce.
		Slice beef. Place in two 2-inch counter pans.

Gingersnap Sauce

Liquid from roast	3½ qt	Measure liquid from roast. Add water if needed.
Gingersnaps, crushed	1 lb	Add gingersnaps. Bring to boil, stirring constantly until mixture thickens.
		Ladle gingersnap sauce over beef. Additional sauce may be served with meat.

Approximate nutritive values per portion

Calories (kcal)	Protein (grams)	Carbohydrate (grams)	Fat (grams)	Cholesterol (mg)	Sodium (mg)	Iron (mg)	Calcium (mg)
356	41.7 (48%)	11.5 (13%)	13.1 (34%)	124	99.0	4.9	26

PEPPER STEAK

Yield: 50 portions   *Portion:* 6 oz meat + 4 oz rice

Ingredient	Amount	Procedure
Beef round or sirloin, cut into thin strips	13 lb	Cook meat in shortening in kettle or deep frypan until lightly browned, about 10 minutes.
Shortening	8 oz	
Beef Stock (p. 616)	2 qt	Add stock, tomatoes, onions, and seasonings to meat. Simmer until tender, 1–1½ hours, stirring occasionally.
Tomatoes, canned, diced	1 No. 10 can	
Onions, chopped	1 lb	
Garlic	3 cloves, cut in half	
Salt	2 Tbsp	
Green peppers, thinly sliced in rings	12	Add green pepper and cook until tender but firm.
Cornstarch	3 oz	Combine cornstarch, water, and soy sauce into a smooth paste.
Water, cold	2½ cups	
Soy sauce	⅔ cup	Add to meat-vegetable mixture. Cook 5 minutes.
Rice, converted	3 lb 8 oz	Cook rice according to directions on p. 430. Serve 6 oz meat mixture over 4 oz rice.
Water, boiling	4¼ qt	
Salt	2 Tbsp	
Margarine or vegetable oil	2 Tbsp	

Approximate nutritive values per portion

Calories (kcal)	Protein (grams)	Carbohydrate (grams)	Fat (grams)	Cholesterol (mg)	Sodium (mg)	Iron (mg)	Calcium (mg)
538	61.1 (46%)	34.1 (26%)	16.5 (28%)	80	1171	4.8	64

SWISS STEAK

Yield: 50 portions   *Portion:* 5 oz
Oven: 350°F   *Bake:* 2–2½ hours

Ingredient	Amount	Procedure
Beef round, sliced, ¾ inch thick	17 lb	Cut meat into portions, 3 per lb.
Flour, all-purpose Salt Pepper, black	1 lb 3 oz 2 tsp	Mix flour, salt, and pepper. Pound into meat with mallet or cleaver.
Shortening, hot	1 lb 8 oz	Brown meat in shortening. Place, slightly overlapping, in two 12 × 20 × 2-inch counter pans.
Fat (meat drippings), hot Flour, all-purpose Salt Pepper, black Water or beef stock	6 oz 6 oz 2 tsp ¾ tsp 3 qt	Make gravy according to directions on p. 586. Add 1½ qt gravy to each pan of meat. Cover tightly with aluminum foil. Bake at 350°F for 2–2½ hours.

Approximate nutritive values per portion

Calories (kcal)	Protein (grams)	Carbohydrate (grams)	Fat (grams)	Cholesterol (mg)	Sodium (mg)	Iron (mg)	Calcium (mg)
421	38.7 (37%)	9.8 (9%)	24.3 (53%)	105	829	4.4	15

Note   ■ Portioned steaks, cut 3 per pound, may be substituted for beef round. Reduce cooking time to 1½ hours.

Variations   ■ **Chicken-Fried Steak.**   Dip portioned steaks or beef cutlets into mixture of 6 eggs and 3 cups milk, then into crumb mixture (1 lb 4 oz bread crumbs, 12 oz flour, 3 oz salt, and 2 Tbsp pepper). Brown steaks in hot shortening. Arrange slightly overlapping in lined counter pans. Cover with aluminum foil. Bake at 325°F for 30–45 minutes or until tender.

■ **Country-Fried Steak.**   Use beef round cut ⅜ inch thick. Proceed as for Swiss Steak but do not add gravy. Place steaks on racks in roaster or counter pans. Cover bottom of pan with water, 2 cups per pan. Cover with aluminum foil and bake. Make Cream Gravy (p. 586) to serve with the steaks.

■ **Spanish Steak.**   Substitute Spanish Sauce (p. 592) for gravy.

■ **Steak Smothered with Onions.**   Proceed as for Swiss Steak. Add 3 lb sliced onions slightly browned.

■ **Baked Steak Teriyaki.**   Combine 2 cups pineapple juice, drained from canned sliced pineapple, 1 qt water, 1½ cups soy sauce, ½ tsp garlic powder, ¼ tsp ginger, and ¼ cup honey. Bring to a boil. Thicken with 1½ cups cold water and ½ cup cornstarch, mixed. Pour 2 lb 8 oz mixture over each pan of browned steaks. Cover tightly. Bake at 325°F for 1–1½ hours or until tender. Garnish with green pepper rings and pineapple slices.

- **Swiss Steak with Tomatoes.** Substitute 1 No. 10 can tomatoes for the gravy. Add 8 oz chopped onions.

SALISBURY STEAK

Yield: 50 portions   *Portion:* 5 oz
Oven: 325°F   *Bake:* 25 minutes

Ingredient	Amount	Procedure
Ground beef	12 lb 8 oz	Combine all ingredients and mix on low speed until blended. Do not overmix.
Bread crumbs	1 lb 8 oz	
Eggs	14 (1 lb 8 oz)	
Onions, chopped	8 oz	
Salt	2½ oz	
Pepper, black	½ tsp	
Milk	4½ cups	
		Portion meat with No. 8 dipper onto lightly greased baking sheets.
		Flatten slightly.
		Bake at 325°F for 25 minutes.
		Pour off grease.
Brown Gravy (p. 586)	1 gal	Serve with Brown Gravy.

Approximate nutritive values per portion

Calories (kcal)	Protein (grams)	Carbohydrate (grams)	Fat (grams)	Cholesterol (mg)	Sodium (mg)	Iron (mg)	Calcium (mg)
383	24 (25%)	15.9 (17%)	24.2 (58%)	130	1104	3	69

Notes
- Steaks may be browned on a grill.
- 1 oz (½ cup) dehydrated onions, rehydrated in ¾ cup water, may be substituted for fresh onions (p. 55).

Variation
- **Bacon-Wrapped Beef.** To 15 lb ground beef, add 4 oz chopped green pepper, 8 oz chopped onion, 2½ cups catsup, 2 Tbsp salt, and 1 Tbsp black pepper. Shape as for Salisbury Steak and wrap one slice bacon around each portion. Place on baking sheet. Bake at 350°F for 30–45 minutes.

CHUCK WAGON STEAK

Yield: 50 portions   *Portion:* 6 oz
Oven: 400°F   *Bake:* 10–15 minutes

Ingredient	Amount	Procedure
Ground beef patties, 3 per lb	50	Mix eggs and milk.
Eggs, beaten	6 (10 oz)	Dip meat in egg mixture. Drain.
Milk	1¾ cups	
Bread crumbs, dry	1 lb 3 oz	Combine bread crumbs, flour, and seasonings.
Flour, all-purpose	12 oz	Dredge steaks with crumb mixture and place 3 × 4
Salt	1½ tsp	onto lightly greased 18 × 26-inch baking sheets.
Pepper, black	½ tsp	Brown steaks in 400°F oven for 10–15 minutes.

Approximate nutritive values per portion

Calories (kcal)	Protein (grams)	Carbohydrate (grams)	Fat (grams)	Cholesterol (mg)	Sodium (mg)	Iron (mg)	Calcium (mg)
373	27.5 (30%)	13.5 (15%)	22.4 (55%)	117	239	3.3	39

Variation   ■ **Chuck Wagon Steak on a Bun.**   Serve on steak bun, with lettuce and thick slices of tomato and onion.

STIR-FRIED BEEF WITH SUGAR SNAP PEAS

Yield: 50 portions   *Portion:* 7 oz beef and sauce + 4 oz rice

Ingredient	Amount	Procedure
Sugar, granulated	2 Tbsp	Combine sugar, pepper, and cornstarch in steam-
Cornstarch	8 oz	jacketed or other kettle.
Pepper, white	¾ tsp	
Water, cold	1¼ gal	Add gradually to dry ingredients, stirring constantly
Beef soup base	4 oz	with wire whip.
Molasses	4 oz	Cook and stir until mixture thickens and looks clear.
Soy sauce	8 oz	Reduce heat. Cover and keep warm for use in final step.
Vegetable oil	¼ cup	Pour enough vegetable oil into tilting frypan just to
Tender beef strips	5 lb	cover bottom of pan. Heat to 375°F.
		Add beef strips. Stir-fry until done.
Garlic, minced	1½ oz	Add to beef and stir-fry until peas are tender-crisp.
Sugar snap peas	4 lb	
Water chestnuts, canned, sliced, drained	3 lb	
		Stir in sauce reserved from earlier step. Serve immediately.
Rice, converted	3 lb 8 oz	Cook rice according to directions on p. 430.
Water	4¼ qt	Serve 7 oz beef mixture over 4 oz cooked rice.
Salt	2 Tbsp	
Margarine	2 Tbsp	

Approximate nutritive values per portion

Calories (kcal)	Protein (grams)	Carbohydrate (grams)	Fat (grams)	Cholesterol (mg)	Sodium (mg)	Iron (mg)	Calcium (mg)
314	12.8 (17%)	38.7 (50%)	11.5 (33%)	32	1098	3.5	62

Notes
- Snow peas may be substituted for sugar snap peas.
- Caramel color may be used to darken sauce.

KABOBS

Yield: 50 kabobs   *Portion:* 1 kabob
Oven: 400°F   *Bake:* 15–20 minutes

Ingredient	Amount	Procedure
Beef (tender), cut in 1½-inch cubes	20 lb	Place beef in stainless steel baker's bowl.
Salad oil	2 lb	Combine oil and seasonings.
Soy sauce	2½ cups	Pour over beef cubes to cover completely.
Lemon juice	2 cups	Refrigerate for 24–36 hours.
Worcestershire sauce	1 cup	Drain well.
Prepared mustard	1 cup	
Garlic, fresh, minced	½ oz	
Pepper, black	1 oz (4 Tbsp)	
Green peppers, fresh	1 lb 6 oz	Cut peppers into ¾-inch squares.
Onions, whole, canned	4 lb	Thread beef cubes (5 oz), green pepper, onions, and pineapple alternately on skewer. Do not crowd.
Pineapple, fresh or fresh frozen chunks	2 lb	Place on oiled 18 × 26 × 1-inch baking sheets. Bake at 400°F for 8–10 minutes. Turn. Continue baking for 5–10 minutes more; total
Skewers, bamboo	50	15–20 minutes.
Cherry tomatoes	1 lb 10 oz	Place a cherry tomato on tip of each skewer. Place in 12 × 20 × 2-inch pans with liners. Keep hot.

Approximate nutritive values per portion

Calories (kcal)	Protein (grams)	Carbohydrate (grams)	Fat (grams)	Cholesterol (mg)	Sodium (mg)	Iron (mg)	Calcium (mg)
407	30.1 (30%)	5 (5%)	29.1 (65%)	111	195	3.6	36

Note   ■ Other garnishes may be substituted for those listed in recipe: tomato quarters, mandarin orange sections, carrot chunks (slightly cooked), stuffed olives, button mushrooms. Poultry or shellfish may be substituted for the beef. Marinate only 12–24 hours.

BEEF LIVER WITH SPANISH SAUCE

Yield: 50 portions   *Portion:* 4 oz
Oven: 350°F   *Bake:* 1 hour

Ingredient	Amount	Procedure
Beef liver, sliced, cut 5 per lb	10 lb	Dredge liver with seasoned flour.
Flour, all-purpose	8 oz	
Salt	2 oz (3 Tbsp)	
Pepper, black	2 tsp	
Shortening	1 lb 8 oz	Brown liver in hot shortening. Place in two 12 × 20 × 2-inch baking pans.
Spanish Sauce (p. 592)	1 recipe	Pour sauce over liver, 5 cups per pan. Cover with aluminum foil. Bake at 350°F until tender, about 1 hour.

Approximate nutritive values per portion

Calories (kcal)	Protein (grams)	Carbohydrate (grams)	Fat (grams)	Cholesterol (mg)	Sodium (mg)	Iron (mg)	Calcium (mg)
284	17.1 (24%)	12.4 (17%)	18.5 (59%)	284	723	6	20

Note
- Liver may be soaked in milk before cooking.

Variations
- **Baked Liver and Onions.** Brown liver as above. Sauté 5 lb sliced onions in 8 oz shortening. Arrange liver in 2 counter pans. Spread onions over liver. Cover pans with aluminum foil. Bake 30–40 minutes.
- **Braised Liver.** Brown liver as above. Cover with sauce made of 10 oz shortening, 5 oz flour, 3 qt beef stock, 2 oz salt, and 2 tsp pepper.
- **Grilled Liver and Onions.** Have liver cut ⅜ inch thick. Preheat grill to 350°F. Oil grill slightly. Cook liver quickly, browning on one side, then turning and browning on the other side. Serve immediately with steamed or grilled sliced onions.
- **Liver and Bacon.** Dredge liver with seasoned flour and fry in bacon fat. Top each serving with one slice of crisp bacon.

MEAT LOAF ◼

Yield: 50 portions or 5 loaves 5 × 9-inch   *Portion:* 4 oz
Oven: 325°F   *Bake:* 1½ hours

Ingredient	Amount	Procedure
Ground beef	10 lb	Mix all ingredients on low speed until blended, using flat beater. Do not overmix.
Ground pork	2 lb	
Bread crumbs, soft	12 oz	Press meat mixture into five 5 × 9-inch pans, 3 lb 4 oz per pan.
Milk	1 qt	
Eggs	12 (1 lb 5 oz)	Bake at 325°F for 1½ hours.
Onion, finely chopped	4 oz	Meat loaf may also be made in a 12 × 20 × 4-inch counter pan.
Salt	2 Tbsp	Press mixture into pan. Divide into 2 loaves (Figure 8.1). Increase baking time to 2 hours.
Pepper, black	1 tsp	
Pepper, cayenne	few grains	

Approximate nutritive values per portion

Calories (kcal)	Protein (grams)	Carbohydrate (grams)	Fat (grams)	Cholesterol (mg)	Sodium (mg)	Iron (mg)	Calcium (mg)
276	20.6 (30%)	6.2 (9%)	18.2 (60%)	120	376	2.3	47

Notes
- Ground pork may be omitted. Increase ground beef to 12 lb.
- Topping of 8 oz brown sugar, 2 Tbsp dry mustard, 1¼ cups catsup, and 1 Tbsp nutmeg may be spread over loaves the last ½ hour of cooking.
- ½ oz (¼ cup) dehydrated onions, rehydrated in ½ cup water, may be substituted for fresh onions (p. 55).

Variations
- **Barbecued Meatballs.** Measure with No. 8 dipper and shape into balls. Cover with 1 gal Barbecue Sauce (p. 588).
- **Italian Meatballs.** Omit cayenne pepper. Increase onion to 8 oz. Add ¼ cup minced garlic, 1 cup grated Parmesan cheese, 1 cup grated Romano cheese, 1½ cups chopped fresh parsley, and 4 tsp dried oregano leaves. Proceed as for Swedish Meatballs, p. 373. If adding to Italian Tomato Sauce, cook until partially done. Add to sauce and continue cooking until done.
- **Meatballs.** Measure with No. 8 dipper and shape into balls. Proceed as for Swedish Meatballs (p. 373) or Spaghetti with Meatballs (p. 424).
- **Vegetable Meat Loaf.** Add 2 cups catsup; 8 oz each raw carrots, onions, and celery; and 4 oz green peppers. Grind vegetables. Pour a small amount of tomato juice over loaves before baking.

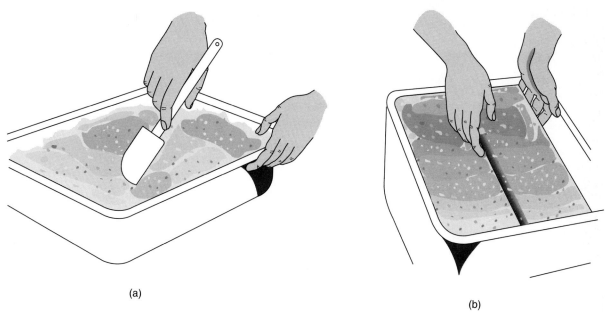

(a)

(b)

FIGURE 8.1   Shaping meat loaf. (a) Press mixture into counter pans, then smooth top. (b) Form into two loaves.

SPANISH MEATBALLS

Yield: 50 portions   *Portion:* 2 3-oz meatballs
Oven: 325°F   *Bake:* 1½ hours

Ingredient	Amount	Procedure
Rice, converted	1 lb 2 oz	Cook rice (p. 430) until slightly underdone.
Water	1¼ qt	Drain off excess liquid.
Salt	1 tsp	
Ground beef	12 lb	Place ground beef in mixer bowl.
Eggs	12 (1 lb 5 oz)	Add cooked rice and other ingredients.
Potatoes, cooked and mashed	1 lb	Mix until blended, using flat beater. Do not overmix.
Onion, grated	4 oz	
Green peppers, chopped	4 oz	
Salt	2 oz (3 Tbsp)	
Pepper, black	1½ Tbsp	
		Form meatballs, using a No. 12 dipper. Place in a single layer on two 12 × 20 × 2-inch baking pans. Bake at 325°F for 1½ hours. Drain off fat.
Chili sauce	3 qt	Mix chili sauce and water.
Water	2 qt	Pour over meatballs. Cover tightly and bake an additional 30 minutes. Add more liquid if necessary.

Approximate nutritive values per portion							
Calories (kcal)	Protein (grams)	Carbohydrate (grams)	Fat (grams)	Cholesterol (mg)	Sodium (mg)	Iron (mg)	Calcium (mg)
348	21.5 (25%)	24.7 (29%)	17.6 (46%)	117	1344	2.9	39

Notes
- Spanish Sauce (p. 592) or tomato puree may be substituted for chili sauce.
- ½ oz (¼ cup) dehydrated onions, rehydrated in ½ cup water, may be substituted for fresh onions (p. 55).

SWEDISH MEATBALLS

Yield: 50 portions   *Portion:* 2 2½-oz meatballs
Oven: 300°F   *Bake:* 1 hour

Ingredient	Amount	Procedure
Bread	2 lb 8 oz	Soak bread in milk for 1 hour.
Milk	1½ qt	
Ground beef	5 lb	Combine meat, potato, onion, and seasonings in mixer
Ground pork	3 lb	bowl.
Potato, raw, grated	1 lb 4 oz	Add bread. Mix to blend, using flat beater. Do not
Onion, minced	12 oz	overmix.
Salt	2 oz	
Pepper, black	2 tsp	
		Form meatballs, using a No. 16 dipper. Place in a single layer on baking pans.
		Brown in hot oven (400°F).
		Transfer to two 12 × 20 × 2-inch counter pans.
Meat drippings	6 oz	Add flour and seasonings to meat drippings and blend.
Flour, all-purpose	6 oz	Add milk gradually, stirring constantly with a wire
Salt	2 tsp	whip.
Pepper, black	¾ tsp	Cook until smooth and thickened.
Milk	3 qt	Pour over meatballs.
		Bake at 300°F for 1 hour.

Approximate nutritive values per portion

Calories (kcal)	Protein (grams)	Carbohydrate (grams)	Fat (grams)	Cholesterol (mg)	Sodium (mg)	Iron (mg)	Calcium (mg)
293	20.3 (28%)	19.9 (27%)	14.7 (45%)	56	768	2.3	134

Notes
- Veal may be substituted for part of beef.
- 1½ oz (¾ cup) dehydrated onions, rehydrated in 1 cup water, may be substituted for fresh onions (p. 55).

BEEF STEW

Yield: 50 portions   *Portion:* 7 oz

Ingredient	Amount	Procedure
Beef, 1-inch cubes	15 lb AP (10 lb EP)	Brown beef in kettle or oven.
Water Salt Pepper, black Worcestershire sauce	2 qt 2 oz (3 Tbsp) 2 tsp ¾ cup	Add water and seasonings to meat. Cover and simmer 2 hours. Add more water as necessary.
Potatoes, cubed Carrots, sliced or cubed Onion, cubed Celery, diced	4 lb 3 lb 1 lb 12 oz	Cook vegetables in steamer or in small amount of water in kettle or oven.
Flour, all-purpose Water	12 oz 1 qt	Mix flour and water until smooth. Add to meat and cook until thickened. Add vegetables.

Approximate nutritive values per portion

Calories (kcal)	Protein (grams)	Carbohydrate (grams)	Fat (grams)	Cholesterol (mg)	Sodium (mg)	Iron (mg)	Calcium (mg)
289	32.3 (46%)	16.7 (24%)	9.5 (30%)	93	550	4.2	29

Note
- One 40-oz package of frozen green peas may be added just before serving. Reheat to serving temperature.

Variations
- **Beef Pot Pie.**   Add one 40-oz package of frozen peas. Place cooked stew in two 12 × 20 × 2-inch counter pans, 13 lb per pan. Make Pastry for One-Crust Pies (p. 254). Roll out 2 lb per pan and place on stew. Bake at 425°F for 20–25 minutes.
- **Beef Stew with Biscuits.**   Place hot stew in two 12 × 20 × 2-inch counter pans. Prepare ½ recipe of Baking Powder Biscuits (p. 118). Cut into 48 2½-inch biscuits. Place on hot stew, 24 per pan. Bake at 425°F for 15–20 minutes.
- **Beef Stew with Dumplings.**   Drop Dumplings (p. 143) on meat mixture and steam 15–18 minutes.
- **Beef Stew with Tomatoes.**   Delete carrots and celery. Add 4 lb diced canned tomatoes and 1 lb 8 oz green pepper strips the last 5 minutes of cooking.

BEEF STROGANOFF

Yield: 50 portions or 2 gal   *Portion:* 6 oz Stroganoff + 4 oz noodles

Ingredient	Amount	Procedure
Beef round, cut in ¼-inch strips	12 lb	Brown meat in shortening. Add onion and seasonings.
Shortening	8 oz	
Onion, chopped	1 lb 4 oz	
Salt	1 Tbsp	
Pepper, black	1 tsp	
Beef stock (p. 616)	2½ qt	Add stock to meat and simmer 35–40 minutes or until meat is tender.
Flour, all-purpose	8 oz	Mix flour, water, and Worcestershire sauce and stir until smooth.
Water, cold	2 cups	
Worcestershire sauce	¾ cup	Add to meat while stirring and cook until thickened.
Mushrooms, fresh, sliced	2 lb 8 oz	Sauté mushrooms in margarine.
Margarine, melted	4 oz	
Sour cream	1 qt	Add sour cream to meat mixture, stirring constantly. Add mushrooms. Heat to serving temperature.
Noodles	4 lb 8 oz	Cook noodles according to directions on p. 407.
Water	4½ gal	Serve 6 oz Stroganoff over 4 oz noodles.
Salt	2 oz	
Vegetable oil	3 Tbsp	

Approximate nutritive values per portion

Calories (kcal)	Protein (grams)	Carbohydrate (grams)	Fat (grams)	Cholesterol (mg)	Sodium (mg)	Iron (mg)	Calcium (mg)
612	70.2 (46%)	35.8 (24%)	20.3 (30%)	119	717	5.4	68

Note
- May be served over rice. Cook 3 lb 8 oz rice in 4¼ qt water, 2 Tbsp salt, and 2 Tbsp oil. See p. 430.

Variation
- **Ground-Beef Stroganoff.** Substitute ground beef for beef round. Add 1 lb 8 oz chopped celery, ¼ cup paprika, ¼ cup Worcestershire sauce, and 2 tsp dry mustard.

SPANISH RICE

Yield: 50 portions or 2 pans 12 × 20 × 2 inches   *Portion:* 8 oz
Oven: 350°F   *Bake:* 1 hour

Ingredient	Amount	Procedure
Rice, converted	2 lb 8 oz	Cook rice according to directions on p. 430.
Water, boiling	3 qt	
Salt	1 oz (1½ Tbsp)	
Vegetable oil	2 Tbsp	
Ground beef	7 lb	Cook beef until meat loses pink color.
Onions, chopped	1 lb 8 oz	Add onion, peppers, and celery to meat.
Green pepper, chopped	8 oz	Cook about 10 minutes.
Celery, chopped	8 oz	
Tomatoes, canned, diced	1 No. 10 can	Add remaining ingredients to meat mixture. Combine with cooked rice.
Chili sauce	3 cups	Scale into two 12 × 20 × 2-inch pans, 15 lb per pan.
Tomato paste	3 cups	Bake at 350°F for 1 hour.
Salt	2 oz (3 Tbsp)	
Pepper, black	¼ tsp	
Pepper, cayenne	few grains	
Sugar, granulated	2 Tbsp	
Water	2 cups	

Approximate nutritive values per portion

Calories (kcal)	Protein (grams)	Carbohydrate (grams)	Fat (grams)	Cholesterol (mg)	Sodium (mg)	Iron (mg)	Calcium (mg)
260	13.5 (21%)	29.7 (46%)	9.7 (33%)	38	1115	2.8	53

Notes

- 3 lb bacon, diced and cooked, may be substituted for the ground beef.
- 3 oz (1½ cups) dehydrated onions, rehydrated in 2 cups water, may be substituted for fresh onions (p. 55).

Variation

- **Stuffed Peppers.**   Wash 25 large green peppers and remove stem end. Cut peppers in half lengthwise. Remove seeds and tough white portion. Place in baking pans and steam or parboil for 3–5 minutes. Place No. 8 dipper of Spanish Rice in each pepper half. Combine 2 50-oz cans tomato soup and 2 qt tomato sauce. Ladle 2 oz over each pepper. Bake at 350°F for 45–60 minutes. Ladle extra sauce over peppers during baking.

CHOP SUEY

Yield: 50 portions   *Portion:* 5 oz chop suey + 4 oz rice

Ingredient	Amount	Procedure
Beef, julienne strips	5 lb	Brown meat in steam-jacketed or other kettle.
Pork, julienne strips	2 lb	
Water	2 qt	Add water and salt to meat.
Salt	2 tsp	Simmer until tender.
Cornstarch	8 oz	Make a smooth paste of cornstarch and water.
Water, cold	1¼ cups	Pour slowly into meat and broth, stirring constantly while pouring. Cook until thickened.
Soy sauce	1 cup	Add soy sauce and Worcestershire sauce. Stir to blend.
Worcestershire sauce	1 cup	
Green peppers, sliced	4 oz	Steam vegetables until tender crisp.
Onions, sliced	1 lb	
Celery, diagonally sliced	2 lb	
Bean sprouts, canned, undrained	3 lb	Add bean sprouts and vegetables to meat mixture just before serving.
Rice, converted	3 lb 8 oz	Cook rice according to directions on p. 430.
Water	4¼ qt	Serve 5 oz chop suey over 4 oz rice.
Salt	2 Tbsp	
Margarine or vegetable oil	2 Tbsp	

Approximate nutritive values per portion

Calories (kcal)	Protein (grams)	Carbohydrate (grams)	Fat (grams)	Cholesterol (mg)	Sodium (mg)	Iron (mg)	Calcium (mg)
252	16.1 (26%)	33.9 (55%)	5.1 (19%)	39	760	3	51

Notes
- 8 oz water chestnuts may be added.
- May be served over 2 oz chow mein noodles (6 lb) instead of rice.

Variation
- **Chicken Chow Mein.** Substitute cubed, cooked chicken or turkey for beef and pork; chicken stock for water. Delete green peppers and add 1 lb sliced mushrooms. Serve over rice or chow mein noodles.

VEGETABLE CHOW MEIN

Yield: 50 portions   *Portion:* 6 oz chow mein + 2 oz noodles

Ingredient	Amount	Procedure
Water	5¼ qt	Combine in steam-jacketed kettle.
Sugar, granulated	2 oz	Heat to a simmer.
Salt	2¼ tsp	
Pepper, white	1 tsp	
Ginger, ground	1 tsp	
Garlic powder	1 tsp	
Soy sauce	1¼ cups	
Cornstarch	10 oz	Blend cornstarch, water, and soup base to a smooth paste.
Water	2¼ cups	Add slowly to broth, stirring constantly.
Chicken base	¾ oz	Cook until thickened and clear.
Bamboo shoots, canned	12 oz	Drain vegetables. Rinse and drain again.
Bean sprouts, canned	1 lb 4 oz	Add to mixture in kettle.
Water chestnuts, canned, sliced	1 lb	
Celery	12 oz	Cut celery into diagonal slices.
Onions	8 oz	Dice onions into ½-inch cubes.
Carrots	1 lb 4 oz	Cut carrots into matchsticks.
		Steam vegetables until tender-crisp.
		Add to mixture.
Pimiento, canned, chopped, drained	4 oz	Add to mixture.
Mushrooms, canned, drained	1 lb	
Broccoli, fresh	1 lb 8 oz	Divide broccoli tops into florets. Cut stalks into ¼-inch slices.
Green peppers	4 oz	Cut green peppers into ½-inch squares.
		Steam until tender-crisp.
		Scale sauce into two 12 × 10 × 6-inch pans, approximately 9 lb per pan.
		Stir 12 oz broccoli and 2 oz peppers into each pan.
Chow mein noodles	6 lb	Ladle 6 oz Chow Mein over 2 oz chow mein noodles.

Approximate nutritive values per portion

Calories (kcal)	Protein (grams)	Carbohydrate (grams)	Fat (grams)	Cholesterol (mg)	Sodium (mg)	Iron (mg)	Calcium (mg)
341	6.3 (7%)	43.4 (48%)	17 (43%)	0	889	3.3	33

Note ■ May be served over rice instead of chow mein noodles. Cook 3 lb 8 oz rice according to directions on p. 430.

CREAMED BEEF

Yield: 50 portions   *Portion:* 6 oz (¾ cup)

Ingredient	Amount	Procedure
Ground beef	13 lb AP	Brown beef and onion.
Onions, chopped	3 oz	Drain off fat.
Margarine	8 oz	Melt margarine. Stir in flour and cook for 5 minutes.
Flour, all-purpose	8 oz	
Beef Stock (p. 616)	2 qt	Add stock and milk to fat-flour mixture while stirring.
Milk	2 qt	Cook until thickened.
Salt	2 oz (3 Tbsp)	Add seasonings and meat. If beef soup base has been
Pepper, black	1½ tsp	used for stock, salt may need to be reduced.
		Serve 6 oz meat over toast, biscuits, or baked potato.

Approximate nutritive values per portion

Calories (kcal)	Protein (grams)	Carbohydrate (grams)	Fat (grams)	Cholesterol (mg)	Sodium (mg)	Iron (mg)	Calcium (mg)
435	54.2 (50%)	7.4 (7%)	20.4 (43%)	83	802	2.5	72

Variation ■ **Sausage Gravy on Biscuits.** In place of ingredients in recipe, substitute the following: 10 lb AP (6 lb EP) sausage, browned and well drained, 6 oz margarine, 8 oz flour, 3 qt milk, and salt and pepper to taste. Serve over Baking Powder Biscuits (p. 118).

CREAMED CHIPPED BEEF

Yield: 50 portions   *Portion:* 4 oz (½ cup)

Ingredient	Amount	Procedure
Chipped beef	2 lb 8 oz	Chop beef coarsely. Sauté in margarine until edges
Margarine or butter	8 oz	curl.
Margarine or butter	1 lb 4 oz	Melt margarine. Stir in flour and pepper. Cook 4–5
Flour, all-purpose	10 oz	minutes.
Pepper, white	1 tsp	
Milk	5 qt	Add milk, stirring constantly. Cook until thickened. Add chipped beef. Serve 4 oz beef over toast, biscuit, or baked potato.

Approximate nutritive values per portion

Calories (kcal)	Protein (grams)	Carbohydrate (grams)	Fat (grams)	Cholesterol (mg)	Sodium (mg)	Iron (mg)	Calcium (mg)
232	10.6 (18%)	9.4 (16%)	17 (66%)	34	985	1.4	123

Variations

- **Chipped Beef and Noodles.** Add 2 lb ground cheddar cheese to white sauce. Combine with 2 lb (AP) noodles, cooked. Top with buttered crumbs. Bake at 350°F for 30 minutes.

- **Creamed Chipped Beef and Peas.** Reduce beef to 2 lb and add 1 40-oz package frozen peas, cooked until peas are tender, before serving.

PIZZA

Yield: 48 portions or 3 pans 18 × 26 × 1 inches or 6 round 14-inch pans   *Portion:* 7 oz
Oven: Baking sheet, 475°F for 10–12 minutes; round, 500°F for 5–8 minutes

Ingredient	Amount	Procedure
Dough		
Flour, all-purpose	5 lb	Place flour, salt, sugar, and dry milk in mixer bowl. Mix
Salt	1½ oz	on low speed, using dough hook.
Sugar, granulated	4 oz	
Nonfat dry milk	2 oz	
Yeast, active dry (see Notes)	1½ oz	Soften yeast in warm water.
Water, warm (110°F)	1½ qt	

Shortening	4 oz	Add softened yeast and shortening to dry ingredients. Mix on low speed to form dough. Continue kneading until smooth and elastic. Cover and let rise until double in bulk, about 2 hours.
		Punch down dough according to directions on p. 146 and let rest 45 minutes.

Pizza Sauce

Onions, chopped	12 oz	Cook onions in fat until transparent.
Shortening or oil	1 oz	Add tomatoes, sugar, and seasonings.
Tomato juice	2 qt	Heat to boiling. Reduce heat and simmer 30–45 minutes. Cool.
Tomato paste	1 qt	
Sugar, granulated	2 oz	Remove bay leaves.
Oregano, dried, crumbled	1 Tbsp	Spread sauce over dough, 1 qt per 18 × 26-inch pan or 1¼ cups per 14-inch round pan.
Basil, dried, crumbled	2 Tbsp	
Garlic powder	1 tsp	
Pepper, black	1 tsp	
Bay leaves	3 leaves	

Seasoned Beef

Ground beef	9 lb	Brown beef in steam-jacketed kettle or pan. Drain well.
Salt	1 Tbsp	Add seasonings, stirring to distribute.
Fennel seed	1 tsp	Sprinkle evenly over tomato sauce, approximately 1 lb 8 oz per 18 × 26 × 1-inch pan, 8 oz per 14-inch round pan.
Paprika	1 tsp	
Pepper, cayenne	½ tsp	
Oregano, dried, crumbled	1 tsp	
Basil, dried, crumbled	1 Tbsp	

Assembly and Baking

If using 18 × 26 × 1-inch baking sheet:

1. Divide dough into three portions, 2 lb 8 oz each. Roll out very thin, stretching to fit three 18 × 26 × 1-inch baking sheets. Allow 1¼ inches to extend up sides of pan.
2. Spread 1 qt sauce over dough.
3. Sprinkle 1 lb 8 oz seasoned beef over sauce.
4. Top each pan with 1 lb 4 oz mozzarella cheese.
5. Bake at 475°F for 10–12 minutes.
6. Cut each pan 2 × 4 and then each of the 8 pieces diagonally, yielding 16 pie-shaped portions per pan (48 slices).

If using 14-inch round pans:

1. Prepare six 14-inch pans by spraying lightly with vegetable spray.
2. Press 1 lb 6 oz dough into pans, allowing 1 inch to extend up sides.
3. Perforate dough with fork or dough docker.
4. Choose pizza topping from the following variations and layer in the order given.
5. Bake at 500°F for 5–8 minutes or until crust is browned, sauce is bubbly and cheese is melted.
6. Cut each pizza into 8 slices, yielding 8 portions per pan (48 slices).

Approximate nutritive values per portion

Calories (kcal)	Protein (grams)	Carbohydrate (grams)	Fat (grams)	Cholesterol (mg)	Sodium (mg)	Iron (mg)	Calcium (mg)
491	30 (25%)	47.4 (39%)	19.8 (37%)	83	884	5.7	57

Notes
- Active dry yeast may be mixed with dry ingredients. See p. 146 for procedure.
- Sausage (4 lb 8 oz) may be substituted for 4 lb 8 oz ground beef. Omit fennel, paprika, cayenne pepper, and garlic.

Variations for Round Pizzas
- **Ground Beef and Mushroom Pizza.**   Layer in the following order: 10 oz sauce; 8 oz shredded mozzarella cheese; 8 oz seasoned ground beef; 3 oz canned sliced mushrooms, drained; and 3 oz shredded mozzarella cheese.
- **Ground Beef Pizza Supreme.**   Layer in the following order: 10 oz sauce; 8 oz shredded mozzarella cheese; 8 oz seasoned beef; 1 oz each of diced onions, chopped green peppers, and sliced ripe olives; and 3 oz shredded mozzarella cheese.
- **Pepperoni Pizza.**   Layer in the following order: 10 oz sauce, 8 oz shredded mozzarella cheese, 2 oz sliced pepperoni (arranged evenly over the top), and 3 oz mozzarella cheese.
- **Triple Cheese Pizza.**   Layer in the following order: 10 oz sauce, 8 oz shredded mozzarella cheese, 4 oz shredded Monterey Jack cheese, and 4 oz shredded cheddar cheese.
- **Garden Pizza.**   Layer in the following order: 10 oz sauce; 6 oz shredded mozzarella cheese; 2 oz shredded cheddar cheese; 1 oz each of diced green peppers, sliced canned mushrooms, diced onion, and sliced ripe olives.

TACO SALAD CASSEROLE

Yield: 48 portions or 3 pans 12 × 20 × 2 inches   *Portion:* 8 oz

Ingredient	Amount	Procedure
Corn chips	2 lb 8 oz	Spread corn chips in bottoms of three 12 × 20 × 2-inch counter pans, 14 oz per pan.

Ground beef	8 lb AP	Brown meat in steam-jacketed kettle. Drain off fat.
Onions, minced Garlic, minced	8 oz 3 cloves	Add onions and garlic to meat. Cook until tender.
Flour, all-purpose Tomato juice	3 oz 1¼ qt	Combine flour and tomato juice and add to meat mixture.
Vinegar, cider Catsup Chili sauce Sugar, granulated Salt Pepper, black Chili powder Pepper, cayenne Hot pepper sauce Worcestershire sauce Red beans, canned	2 Tbsp 1½ cups 1 cup 2 Tbsp 2 Tbsp ½ tsp 2 tsp ¼ tsp ¾ tsp 1 tsp 3 lb 12 oz	Add to meat mixture. Blend. Heat until very hot. Scale 4 lb 5 oz meat sauce over each pan of chips. Keep warm and serve soon after vegetables are layered on top. (See Notes for an alternate assembly method.)
Lettuce, chopped Green peppers, chopped Onions, finely chopped Tomatoes, fresh, diced	4 lb 12 oz 12 oz 2 lb 10 oz	Combine vegetables. Mix gently. Sprinkle over hot meat mixture, 2 lb 8 oz per pan.
Processed cheese, shredded	2 lb 10 oz	Sprinkle 14 oz cheese over each pan. Cut 4 × 4. Serve immediately.

Approximate nutritive values per portion

Calories (kcal)	Protein (grams)	Carbohydrate (grams)	Fat (grams)	Cholesterol (mg)	Sodium (mg)	Iron (mg)	Calcium (mg)
441	24.1 (22%)	30 (27%)	25.3 (51%)	73	1204	3.1	224

Notes
- Chips will become soggy if held for very long. Spread meat on chips only as needed.
- Casserole may be assembled on each plate individually. Place ¾ oz taco chips on plate. Ladle 4 oz hot meat mixture over chips and top with 2½ oz salad mixture and ¾ oz shredded cheese.
- Serve with Salsa Sauce (p. 589) or commercial salsa.
- 1 oz (½ cup) dehydrated onion, rehydrated in ¾ cup water (p. 55), may be substituted for the fresh onions that are added to the ground beef.

CHEESEBURGER PIE

Yield: 48 portions or 2 pans 12 × 20 × 2 inches   *Portion:* 8 oz (6 oz meat)
Oven: 400°F   *Bake:* 30–35 minutes

Ingredient	Amount	Procedure
Ground beef	12 lb AP (8 lb EP)	Brown beef in steam-jacketed or other kettle. Drain off fat.
Onions, chopped	1 lb 4 oz	Add onions and green peppers to meat. Cook until vegetables are tender.
Green peppers, chopped	1 lb 4 oz	
Garlic powder	1 tsp	Add seasonings and tomatoes.
Salt	1 oz (1½ Tbsp)	Simmer 30 minutes or until thick.
Chili powder	3 oz	Scale meat mixture into two 12 × 20 × 2-inch pans,
Cumin, ground	1 tsp	9 lb per pan.
Pepper, cayenne	¼ tsp	
Sugar, brown	1 oz	
Tomatoes, diced, canned	7 lb 12 oz	

Cheese Biscuit Topping

Ingredient	Amount	Procedure
Flour, all-purpose	2 lb 14 oz	Combine dry ingredients in mixer bowl on low speed for 1 minute, using flat beater.
Baking powder	2¾ oz (6 Tbsp)	
Salt	2 Tbsp	
Dry mustard	1 tsp	
Nonfat dry milk	7 oz	
Shortening	12 oz	Cut shortening and cheese into flour on low speed for 1–1½ minutes.
Processed cheese, shredded	10 oz	
Water	1½ qt	Add water to make a thick batter. Mix only until flour is moistened.
		With No. 20 dipper, place topping 4 × 6 over meat mixture just before baking. Bake at 400°F for 30–35 minutes. Cut 4 × 6.

Approximate nutritive values per portion

Calories (kcal)	Protein (grams)	Carbohydrate (grams)	Fat (grams)	Cholesterol (mg)	Sodium (mg)	Iron (mg)	Calcium (mg)
446	27.2 (24%)	29.8 (27%)	24.1 (49%)	80	920	4.2	202

Note   ■   2½ oz (1¼ cups) dehydrated onions, rehydrated in 2 cups water, may be substituted for fresh onions (p. 55).

VEAL RECIPES

VEAL BIRDS

Yield: 50 portions   *Portion:* 4 oz
Oven: 300°F   *Bake:* 2 hours

Ingredient	Amount	Procedure
Margarine	8 oz	Sauté onion and celery in margarine.
Onions, finely chopped	8 oz	
Celery, finely chopped	8 oz	
Beef base	1½ oz	Combine beef base, seasonings, and water. Add to sautéed vegetables.
Salt	1 tsp (see Notes)	
Pepper, black	1½ tsp	
Sage, ground	1 Tbsp	
Water	2 qt	
Bread, dry, cubed	2 lb	Add bread gradually to vegetable mixture, tossing lightly until thoroughly mixed.
Veal cutlets, 4 oz	50	Place No. 16 dipper of bread mixture on each piece of meat. Roll and fasten with a pick.
Flour, all-purpose	8 oz	Combine flour and salt.
Salt	2 oz	Roll each "bird" in flour and brown in hot shortening.
Shortening	1 lb 8 oz	Place in two 12 × 20 × 2-inch counter pans.
Water	1 qt	Add 2 cups water to each pan. Cover with aluminum foil. Bake at 300°F for 2 hours.

Approximate nutritive values per portion

Calories (kcal)	Protein (grams)	Carbohydrate (grams)	Fat (grams)	Cholesterol (mg)	Sodium (mg)	Iron (mg)	Calcium (mg)
351	20 (23%)	17.6 (20%)	22.1 (57%)	71	867	1.7	50

Notes
- Veal round, ¼-inch thick, cut into 4-oz pieces, may be substituted for the cutlets.
- 1 oz (½ cup) dehydrated onion, rehydrated in ¾ cup water, may be substituted for fresh onion (p. 55).
- If beef base is highly salted, reduce or delete salt in recipe.

Variations
- **Beef Birds.**   Make with beef cubed steaks or flank steaks.
- **Pork Birds.**   Make with pork cutlets.
- **Veal Birds with Sausage Stuffing.**   Reduce bread to 2 lb 8 oz. Reduce salt to 1 tsp and sage to 1 Tbsp. Add 2 lb 8 oz sausage, cooked and drained.

BREADED VEAL CUTLETS

Yield: 50 portions   *Portion:* 4 oz
Oven: 325°F   *Bake:* 45–60 minutes

Ingredient	Amount	Procedure
Veal cutlets, 4 oz	12 lb 8 oz	Dredge cutlets with seasoned flour.
Flour, all-purpose	8 oz	
Salt	1 oz (1½ Tbsp)	
Pepper, black	¼ tsp	
Eggs, beaten	7 (12 oz)	Combine eggs and milk.
Milk	1½ cups	Dip cutlets in egg mixture, then roll in crumbs.
Bread crumbs, fine	1 lb	
Shortening	1 lb 8 oz	Brown meat in hot fat.
		Place, slightly overlapping, in two 12 × 20 × 2-inch counter pans.
		Add 2 cups water to each pan. Cover with aluminum foil.
		Bake at 325°F for 45–60 minutes.

Approximate nutritive values per portion

Calories (kcal)	Protein (grams)	Carbohydrate (grams)	Fat (grams)	Cholesterol (mg)	Sodium (mg)	Iron (mg)	Calcium (mg)
418	41.3 (40%)	10.5 (10%)	22.4 (49%)	159	363	2	47

Note
- Veal round, sliced ¼-inch thick and cut into 5-oz portions, may be used.

Variations
- **Veal Cacciatore.** Dredge cutlets with flour. Brown in fat and place in baking pans. Pour over sauce made of 1 lb chopped peppers, 1 lb chopped onions, and ⅛ tsp minced garlic, simmered in margarine or butter for 10 minutes; 1 lb 8 oz sautéed sliced mushrooms; 1½ qt canned tomatoes; ¼ cup vinegar; 2 qt Chicken Stock (p. 615); 1 oz salt; and 1 tsp pepper. Bake 45 minutes.

- **Veal New Orleans.** To 2 qt medium White Sauce (p. 582), add 8 oz chopped onions, 12 oz sliced mushrooms, 2 Tbsp Worcestershire sauce, ¼ tsp salt, ¼ tsp pepper, ¼ tsp paprika, and 3½ cups tomato soup. Arrange browned breaded cutlets in two 12 × 20 × 2-inch counter pans. Pour 1¾ qt sauce over each pan. Cover with aluminum foil and bake at 325°F for 1 hour.

- **Veal Parmesan.** Add 8 oz grated Parmesan cheese to bread crumbs. After cutlets are browned and arranged in baking pans, pour 2 qt Tomato Sauce (p. 591) over them. Top with 1 lb 8 oz grated mozzarella cheese. Bake at 325°F for 1 hour.

- **Veal Piccata.** Flour cutlets and brown in hot shortening. Arrange in two 12 × 20 × 2-inch counter pans. Sauté 1 lb sliced mushrooms and 2 cloves garlic, minced, in 2 Tbsp margarine. Add 2½ cups Beef Stock (p. 616) and 2 Tbsp lemon juice. Bring to a boil. Pour 2 cups over each pan. Sprinkle ¼ cup Parmesan cheese over each pan. Cover with aluminum foil. Bake at 325°F for 1 hour.

- **Veal Scallopini.** Dredge cutlets with seasoned flour and sauté in hot shortening. Arrange in baking pans. Sauté 3 lb fresh mushrooms, sliced, and 1 lb chopped onion in 8 oz margarine. Add 2 qt Chicken Stock (p. 615), 1½ cups lemon juice or vinegar, and 1 tsp each of parsley, rosemary, and oregano or marjoram. Pour over cutlets. Bake at 325°F for 1 hour.

PORK RECIPES

JEWELED PORK LOIN

Yield: 50 portions   *Portion:* 4 oz
Oven: 325°F   *Bake:* Approx. 2–3 hours

Ingredient	Amount	Procedure
Boneless pork loin	20 lb	Rub pepper over all sides of loin.
Pepper, black	1 Tbsp	Cut vertical slits 1-inch deep along top of roasts.
Prunes, pitted, dried	8 oz	Cut dried fruit into medium-size pieces. Push into the slits on top of the loin.
Apricots, dried	8 oz	Roast, uncovered, at 325°F until meat thermometer registers 160°F.
		Remove from oven and cover loosely with aluminum foil. Let stand about 15 minutes before slicing.

Approximate nutritive values per portion

Calories (kcal)	Protein (grams)	Carbohydrate (grams)	Fat (grams)	Cholesterol (mg)	Sodium (mg)	Iron (mg)	Calcium (mg)
253	40.4 (66%)	5.7 (9%)	6.8 (25%)	129	94	2.5	16

Variations

- **Garlic and Peppercorn Pork Loin.** Brush pork loins with olive oil. Cover with approximately 1 cup crushed peppercorns and approximately ¾ cup chopped garlic. Roast as for Jeweled Pork Loin.

- **Herbed Pork Loin.** Combine 1½ oz salt, 2 Tbsp dried whole rosemary, 2 Tbsp dried whole thyme, 3 Tbsp coarse cracked black pepper, ½ cup crushed garlic, ¾ cup fresh lemon juice, and ¾ cup vegetable oil. Rub paste over roasts. Refrigerate for several hours or overnight. Roast as for Jeweled Pork Loin.

- **Teriyaki-Glazed Pork Loin.** Omit pepper and dried fruit. Make marinade by combining 2 cups soy sauce, 1 cup cooking sherry, ¼ cup sugar, 3 Tbsp black pepper, ¼ cup minced garlic, 1½ cup oil. Pour over pork loin roasts. Turn to cover all sides. Marinate in refrigerator a minimum of 8 hours or overnight. Drain marinade. Roast as directed in above recipe.

BREADED PORK CHOPS ▪

Yield: 50 chops   *Portion:* 5 oz
Oven: 400°F, 325°F   *Bake:* 10 minutes, 1 hour

Ingredient	Amount	Procedure
Pork chops, cut 3 per lb	17 lb	Dredge chops with seasoned flour.
Flour, all-purpose	12 oz	
Salt	3 oz	
Pepper, black	2 Tbsp	
Eggs, beaten	6 (10 oz)	Combine eggs and milk.
Milk	3½ cups	Dip chops in egg mixture, then roll in crumbs.
Bread crumbs	1 lb 4 oz	Place in single layer on greased sheet pans.
Shortening, melted	8 oz	Pour melted shortening over top of chops. Bake at 400°F until browned, about 10 minutes.
Water	1 qt	Remove chops from oven and arrange in partially overlapping rows in two 12 × 20 × 2-inch counter pans. Add 2 cups water to each pan. Cover pans. Bake at 325°F until tender, approximately 1 hour.

Approximate nutritive values per portion

Calories (kcal)	Protein (grams)	Carbohydrate (grams)	Fat (grams)	Cholesterol (mg)	Sodium (mg)	Iron (mg)	Calcium (mg)
344	26.9 (32%)	14.5 (17%)	19.2 (51%)	107	822	1.7	50

Variations

- **Baked Pork Chops.** Dredge chops with 1 lb flour, ¼ cup vegetable oil, 2 oz salt, and 1 tsp black pepper, mixed. Place on well-greased sheet pans. Bake at 350°F until thoroughly cooked and browned, approximately 1¼ hours.

- **Baked Pork Chops and Apples.** Brown chops as for Breaded Pork Chops. Place in two greased 12 × 20 × 2-inch baking pans. Pour over 1 qt apple juice, 2 cups per pan. Bake at 350°F for 1 hour. Serve with Buttered Apples (p. 537).

- **Pork Chops and Dressing.** Serve chops with No. 16 dipper of Bread Dressing (p. 474) and ladle of gravy dipped over.

- **Stuffed Pork Chops.** Use 6-oz pork chops and cut a pocket in each chop. Fill with Bread Dressing (use ¼ recipe, p. 474) or Apple Stuffing (p. 474, ½ recipe). Brown chops and place in baking pans. Pour 2 cups water or chicken broth in each pan. Cover and bake at 350°F for 1½ hours.

DEVILED PORK CHOPS

Yield: 50 chops   *Portion:* 5 oz
Oven: 350°F   *Bake:* 1½ hours

Ingredient	Amount	Procedure
Chili sauce	1½ qt	Combine into a sauce.
Water	3 cups	
Dry mustard	1 tsp	
Worcestershire sauce	3 Tbsp	
Lemon juice	3 Tbsp	
Onion, grated	2 tsp	
Pork chops, cut 3 per lb	17 lb	Dip each chop in sauce. Place in single layer on greased sheet pans. Bake at 350°F for 1½ hours.

Approximate nutritive values per portion

Calories (kcal)	Protein (grams)	Carbohydrate (grams)	Fat (grams)	Cholesterol (mg)	Sodium (mg)	Iron (mg)	Calcium (mg)
247	24.3 (40%)	7.4 (12%)	12.9 (48%)	80	458	1	14

Variations

- **Barbecued Pork Chops.** Place chops on greased baking sheets. Brush with melted fat. Sprinkle with salt. Brown chops in 450°F oven for 12–15 minutes. Transfer to counter pans. Pour Barbecue Sauce (p. 588) over chops. Bake at 325°F for 1½ hours or until chops are tender.

- **Chili-Seasoned Pork Chops.** Prepare a spice blend by combining 6 Tbsp chili powder, 2 Tbsp ground cumin, 2 tsp garlic powder, 1 Tbsp onion powder, 1 tsp salt and 2 tsp black pepper. Mix 1 Tbsp of the spice mixture with 1 cup vegetable oil. Cover and store for several hours to blend seasonings with oil. Save the remaining dry spice mixture to sprinkle on top of the chops. To cook chops, oil griddle with seasoned oil, heat to 350°F. Place chops on griddle and cook until browned, turn and brown other side. Sprinkle remaining seasonings lightly over chops. Place in 12 × 10 × 2-inch counter pans. Cover with foil and bake at 350°F for 1 hour.

- **Honey-Glazed Pork Chops.** Marinate pork chops for 4 hours in a mixture of 2 cups soy sauce, 6 oz honey, 1 cup applesauce, 1 oz salt, and 4 oz sugar. Place in single layer on greased baking sheets. Bake at 350°F for 1 hour. Turn and brush with marinade as needed.

- **Pork Chops Supreme.** Arrange chops in single layer in baking pans. Sprinkle with salt. Combine 1 lb brown sugar, 3 cups catsup, and 1 cup lemon juice. Place about 2 Tbsp, No. 30 dipper, on each chop. Cut 4 medium-size onions into thin slices. Place 1 slice on top of each chop. Cover and bake at 350°F for 45 minutes. Uncover and bake 30 minutes longer.

BARBECUED SPARERIBS ◾

Yield: 50 portions   *Portion:* 8 oz
Oven: 350°F   *Bake:* 2½ hours

Ingredient	Amount	Procedure
Pork spareribs or loin back ribs	25 lb	Separate ribs into 8-oz portions. Place in roasting pans. Brown uncovered in oven at 350°F until browned lightly, about 30 minutes. Pour off fat.
Barbecue Sauce (p. 588)	3 qt	Pour sauce over ribs. Cover with aluminum foil. Bake at 350°F until meat is tender, about 1½ hours. Uncover and bake an additional 20–30 minutes.

Approximate nutritive values per portion

Calories (kcal)	Protein (grams)	Carbohydrate (grams)	Fat (grams)	Cholesterol (mg)	Sodium (mg)	Iron (mg)	Calcium (mg)
715	70.7 (41%)	7.7 (4%)	42.2 (55%)	211	621	8.2	36

Note

- For larger portions, use 40 lb spareribs and 1 gal Barbecue Sauce.

Variations

- **Baked Spareribs with Dressing.** Brown ribs as for Barbecued Spareribs. Pour off fat. Spread with mixture of 2 oz salt, 2 tsp pepper, 1½ tsp ground sage, 1 lb chopped apples, 2 tsp caraway seeds, 1 tsp ground cloves, and 12 oz brown sugar. Bake 1½ hours until tender. Baste to keep moist. Serve with Bread Dressing (p. 474).

- **Baked Spareribs with Sauerkraut.** Sprinkle ribs with 2 oz seasoned salt. Brown lightly. Pour off fat. Remove ribs from pan. Add 2 No. 10 cans sauerkraut to baking pan and place ribs on top. Bake for 1 hour.

- **Barbecued Short Ribs.** Substitute beef short ribs for spareribs.

- **Sweet-Sour Spareribs.** Brown spareribs for 30 minutes in 400°F oven, or simmer in water for 1 hour. Drain and cover with Sweet-Sour Sauce (p. 595). Bake at 350°F until meat is done. Serve with Steamed Rice or Fried Rice with Almonds (p. 432).

SWEET-SOUR PORK

Yield: 50 portions   *Portion:* 5 oz pork + 4 oz rice

Ingredient	Amount	Procedure
Pork strips, julienne	10 lb AP (7 lb EP)	Brown pork in steam-jacketed kettle.
Water	2 qt	Add water to pork and simmer until meat is tender.
Vinegar Soy sauce Catsup Sugar, granulated Pineapple juice Pineapple chunks	1¼ qt 1½ cups 1½ cups 2 lb 1 qt 1 lb	Combine and add to pork. Simmer until sugar is dissolved and pineapple is hot, 10–15 minutes.
Cornstarch Water Ginger, ground Garlic powder	8 oz 2 cups 1½ tsp ½ tsp	Combine to make a smooth paste. Pour slowly into pork mixture, stirring constantly. Cook until thickened and clear.
Carrots, fresh, sliced	1 lb 12 oz	Steam carrots until tender-crisp. Add to mixture.
Snow peas	1 lb	Stir in just before serving.
Rice, converted Water, boiling Salt Margarine or vegetable oil	3 lb 8 oz 4¼ qt 2 Tbsp 2 Tbsp	Cook rice according to directions on p. 430. Serve 5 oz pork over 4 oz rice.

Approximate nutritive values per portion

Calories (kcal)	Protein (grams)	Carbohydrate (grams)	Fat (grams)	Cholesterol (mg)	Sodium (mg)	Iron (mg)	Calcium (mg)
354	16 (18%)	58.6 (65%)	6.7 (17%)	41	868	2.4	42

Variations

- **Sweet-Sour Beef.** Substitute beef strips for pork.
- **Sweet-Sour Chicken.** Substitute cooked chicken or turkey for the pork. Do not brown.

GLAZED BAKED HAM

Yield: 50 portions   *Portion:* 3 oz
Oven: 325°F   *Bake:* 2–2½ hours

Ingredient	Amount	Procedure
Ham, boneless, fully cooked	15 lb	Place ham fat side up on a rack in roasting pan. Do not cover. Bake at 325°F for 2–2½ hours.
Cloves, whole	3 Tbsp	Remove ham from oven about 30 minutes before it is done. Drain off drippings. Score ham ¼ inch deep in diamond pattern. Stud with whole cloves. Cover with glaze.

Ham Glaze

Sugar, brown	8 oz	Combine ingredients for glaze.
Cornstarch	2 Tbsp	Spoon over ham. Repeat if heavier glaze is desired.
Corn syrup	¼ cup	Return ham to oven and bake until internal tempera-
Pineapple juice	2 Tbsp	ture reaches 140°F (see timetable, p. 354).

Approximate nutritive values per portion

Calories (kcal)	Protein (grams)	Carbohydrate (grams)	Fat (grams)	Cholesterol (mg)	Sodium (mg)	Iron (mg)	Calcium (mg)
160	22.7 (35%)	17.4 (26%)	11.4 (39%)	57	1931	0.2	6

Note

- If using a whole cured ham, not precooked, increase cooking time to 4–4½ hours; or simmer 3–4 hours in a kettle, then trim, glaze, and complete cooking in the oven.

Glaze Variations

- **Apricot Glaze.**   1 cup apricot jam and ¼ cup fruit juice or enough to cover ham.
- **Brown Sugar Glaze.**   6 oz brown sugar, 1½ tsp dry mustard (or 3 Tbsp prepared mustard), and ¼ cup vinegar.
- **Cranberry Glaze.**   1¼ cups strained cranberry sauce, or enough to cover.
- **Honey Glaze.**   1 cup honey, ½ cup brown sugar, and ¼ cup fruit juice. Baste with fruit juice or ginger ale.
- **Orange Glaze.**   1 cup orange marmalade and ¼ cup orange juice.

HAM LOAF

Yield: 50 portions or 5 pans 5 × 9 inches   *Portion:* 4 oz
Oven: 350°F   *Bake:* 1–1½ hours

Ingredient	Amount	Procedure
Ground cured ham	7 lb	Combine all ingredients in mixer bowl. Mix on low speed, using flat beater, only until ingredients are blended. *Do not overmix.*
Ground fresh lean pork	7 lb	
Onion, finely chopped	4 oz	
Milk	1 qt	
Eggs, beaten	14 (1 lb 8 oz)	
Pepper, black	1 tsp	
Bread crumbs	1 lb	

Press meat mixture into five 5 × 9-inch loaf pans, 3 lb 8 oz per pan.
Bake at 350°F for 1–1½ hours.
If desired, cover tops of loaves with glaze (see Variations) during last 30 minutes of cooking.
Cut 10 slices per pan.

Approximate nutritive values per portion

Calories (kcal)	Protein (grams)	Carbohydrate (grams)	Fat (grams)	Cholesterol (mg)	Sodium (mg)	Iron (mg)	Calcium (mg)
245	23.6 (33%)	13.2 (18%)	15.8 (49%)	121	1017	0.9	44

Notes

- Meat may be baked in 12 × 20 × 4-inch baking or counter pan. Press mixture into pan and divide into 2 loaves. Increase baking time to 1½–2 hours.
- 4 lb ground beef may be substituted for 4 lb fresh pork.
- ½ oz (¼ cup) dehydrated onion, rehydrated in ½ cup water, may be substituted for fresh onion (p. 55).

Variations

- **Glazed Ham Balls.**   Measure with No. 8 dipper and shape into balls. Place on baking sheets. Brush with glaze (below) and bake 1 hour.
- **Glazed Ham Loaf.**   Cover tops of loaves with a mixture of 1 lb 8 oz brown sugar, 1 cup vinegar, and 1½ Tbsp dry mustard.
- **Ham Patties with Cranberries.**   Measure with No. 8 dipper and shape into patties. Spread pan with Cranberry Sauce (p. 538). Place ham patties on sauce and bake 1 hour.
- **Ham Patties with Pineapple.**   Measure with No. 8 dipper and shape into patties. Top each with slice of pineapple and a clove. Pour pineapple juice over patties and bake 1 hour.

CREAMED HAM

Yield: 50 portions or 6¼ qt   *Portion:* 4 oz (½ cup)

Ingredient	Amount	Procedure
Margarine	1 lb	Melt margarine. Add flour and stir until smooth.
Flour, all-purpose	6 oz	Cook 5 minutes.
Milk	1 gal	Add milk gradually, stirring constantly with wire whip. Cook until thickened.
Ham, cooked	6 lb	Cut ham in cubes or grind coarsely.
Salt	To taste	Add to sauce and heat slowly for about 20 minutes.
Pepper, white	½ tsp	Add salt, if needed, and pepper.
		Serve 4 oz ham over biscuits, toast, spoon bread, corn bread, or baked potato.

Approximate nutritive values per portion

Calories (kcal)	Protein (grams)	Carbohydrate (grams)	Fat (grams)	Cholesterol (mg)	Sodium (mg)	Iron (mg)	Calcium (mg)
180	12.1 (22%)	10.9 (20%)	14.5 (59%)	33	938	0.2	97

Note   ■ 1 lb chopped celery or sliced mushrooms or 1 dozen chopped hard-cooked eggs may be added. Reduce ham to 5 lb.

Variation ■ **Plantation Shortcake.**   Substitute 3 lb cooked turkey for 3 lb cooked ham. Substitute Chicken Stock for half of milk in sauce. Add 1 lb grated cheddar cheese. Serve over hot Corn Bread.

OVEN-FRIED BACON

Yield: 50 portions   *Portion:* 2 slices
Oven: 400°F; convection, 325°F   *Bake:* 6–10 minutes; convection 4–6 minutes

Ingredient	Amount	Procedure
Bacon, 17–20 slices per lb	100 slices (5–6 lb)	Arrange bacon slices on baking sheets. Bake at 400°F, without turning, until crisp, about 6–10 minutes. In convection oven, cook 4–6 minutes at 325°F for 4–6 minutes. Pour off accumulating fat as necessary. Drain on paper towels or place in perforated pans for serving.

Approximate nutritive values per portion

Calories (kcal)	Protein (grams)	Carbohydrate (grams)	Fat (grams)	Cholesterol (mg)	Sodium (mg)	Iron (mg)	Calcium (mg)
73	3.8 (21%)	0.1 (0%)	6.2 (78%)	11	202	0.2	1

Note	■	Bacon may be purchased separated and arranged on parchment paper, ready to be placed on baking sheets and baked.
Variation	■	**Oven-Fried Sausage.** Arrange 1-oz sausage patties or links on baking sheets. In conventional oven, bake at 400°F for 15–20 minutes. In convection oven, bake at 325°F for 10–12 minutes.

SCRAPPLE

Yield: 50 portions or 5 loaf pans 5 × 9 inches   *Portion:* 2 slices

Ingredient	Amount	Procedure
Sausage, bulk	8 lb AP	Crumble sausage and cook until done. Do not over-brown. Drain off fat.
Water Salt	1½ gal 1 oz (1½ Tbsp)	Add salt to water. Bring to a boil.
Cornmeal Water, cold	3 lb 2 qt	Mix cornmeal with cold water. Pour gradually into boiling water, stirring constantly. Cook until very thick, 10–15 minutes.
		Add cooked sausage to cornmeal mixture. Scale into 5 greased 5 × 9-inch loaf pans, 4 lb 5 oz per pan. Cover with waxed paper to prevent formation of crust. Chill for 24 hours.
		Cut into ½-inch slices. Cook on greased grill preheated to 350°F. Grill until browned and crisp on both sides. Serve with warm syrup.

Approximate nutritive values per portion

Calories (kcal)	Protein (grams)	Carbohydrate (grams)	Fat (grams)	Cholesterol (mg)	Sodium (mg)	Iron (mg)	Calcium (mg)
262	10.9 (17%)	21.4 (33%)	14.8 (51%)	37	777	1.5	20

Note	■	8 lb fresh pork, simmered until done and chopped finely, may be used in place of the sausage. Increase salt to 2 oz and add 1 Tbsp ground sage.
Variation	■	**Fried Cornmeal Mush.** Delete sausage. Increase cornmeal to 4 lb, salt to 2 oz, boiling water to 2 gal, and cold water to 2½ qt. Proceed as for Scrapple.

CHEESE-STUFFED FRANKFURTERS

Yield: 50 portions   *Portion:* 2 frankfurters
Oven: 350°F   *Bake:* 30 minutes

Ingredient	Amount	Procedure
Frankfurters, 10 per lb	10 lb	Split frankfurters lengthwise, but do not cut completely through.
Cheddar cheese Pickle relish	3 lb 1 qt	Cut cheese into strips about 3½ inches long. Place a strip of cheese and ½ Tbsp relish in each frankfurter.
Bacon, 24–26 slices per lb	100 slices (4–5 lb)	Wrap a slice of bacon around each frankfurter. Secure with a pick. Place on greased baking sheets. Bake at 350°F for 30 minutes.

Approximate nutritive values per portion

Calories (kcal)	Protein (grams)	Carbohydrate (grams)	Fat (grams)	Cholesterol (mg)	Sodium (mg)	Iron (mg)	Calcium (mg)
499	20.9 (17%)	9.1 (7%)	41.7 (76%)	85	1545	1.6	211

Note

■ 8 lb 4 oz wieners, 12 per lb, may be substituted for the frankfurters. With the wieners, 1 slice of bacon may be wrapped around 2 wieners.

Variations

■ **Barbecued Frankfurters.**   Place frankfurters in counter pans. Cover with Barbecue Sauce (p. 588). Bake at 400°F for about 30 minutes. Add more sauce if necessary.

■ **Chili Dog.**   Serve 2 oz Chili Con Carne (p. 622) over a frankfurter or wiener in a hot dog bun. Chili may be made with or without beans.

■ **Frankfurters and Sauerkraut.**   Steam frankfurters or cook in boiling water. Serve with sauerkraut (2 No. 10 cans) that has been heated.

■ **Nacho Dog.**   Serve 2 oz Nacho Sauce (p. 323) over a frankfurter or wiener in a hot dog bun. Sprinkle over the top one or more of the following: chopped green chilies or jalapeño peppers, chopped tomatoes, chopped black olives, or chopped onion.

SAUSAGE ROLLS

Yield: 50 rolls   *Portion:* 1 roll, 2 oz gravy
Oven: 400°F   *Bake:* 20 minutes

Ingredient	Amount	Procedure
Sausages, link	12 lb 8 oz	Partially cook sausages. Remove from fat.
Flour, all-purpose Baking powder Salt Shortening Milk	3 lb 3 oz 3½ tsp 12 oz 1 qt	Make into biscuit dough, according to directions on p. 118.

		Divide biscuit dough into 2 portions.
		Roll each portion to ½-inch thickness and cut into
		  3 × 4-inch rectangles.
		Place 2 sausages in the center of each piece of dough
		  and fold over.
		Place seam side down on greased baking sheets.
		Bake at 400°F for 20 minutes.

Margarine
Flour, all-purpose
Salt
Pepper, black
Water or chicken
  stock
	6 oz
	6 oz
	2 tsp
	½ tsp
	3 qt
		Melt margarine, add flour, and blend. Add salt and
		  pepper. Cook for 5 minutes.
		Add water or stock gradually, stirring constantly. Cook
		  until smooth and thickened.
		Ladle 2 oz of gravy over each sausage roll.

Approximate nutritive values per portion

Calories (kcal)	Protein (grams)	Carbohydrate (grams)	Fat (grams)	Cholesterol (mg)	Sodium (mg)	Iron (mg)	Calcium (mg)
629	26.1 (17%)	26 (17%)	45.8 (66%)	97	1884	2.8	175

Variations

- **Italian Sausage Sandwich.** Grill fifty 5- to 6-inch-long Italian sausages. Serve one sausage in a long bun with 1 oz Sandwich Tomato Sauce (p. 419) ladled on top. May be sprinkled with 1 oz shredded mozzarella cheese.

- **Pigs in Blankets.** Substitute 50 wieners for link sausages. Place each wiener diagonally on dough portion and roll up. Delete gravy. May serve with Cheese Sauce (p. 582).

- **Pigs in Blankets with Cheese.** Wrap 1 oz cheese around each wiener. Proceed as above.

9

Pasta, Rice, and Cereals

The cooking of pasta, rice, and cereals is similar. Water is added, heat is applied, and cooking is continued until the starch granules gelatinize.

PASTA

Pasta is a generic name for a basic dough mixture of durum semolina or other high-protein hard wheat flour and water. With the exception of noodles, which contain eggs, the various pasta products are made from the same basic dough. Flavor variations may include whole wheat, herb, carrot, tomato, and spinach. Pasta comes in many different forms, and an estimated 150 different varieties are available. A few of the more popular types appear in Figures 9.1 and 9.2. Pasta may be purchased fresh, frozen, or dry. Pre-cooked dry pasta is also available in some markets.

Most dry pasta will approximately double in *volume* after cooking (egg noodle volume remains about the same). Thickness varies among pasta shapes, and the volume increase is directly related to this variation. Certain shapes such as ziti, lasagna, and rigatoni have more fluctuation in their volume increase than do spaghetti and macaroni. The *weight* of dry pasta increases, but the amount depends on the type of pasta. See p. 407 for the weight increase of selected pastas.

Pasta is best if cooked uncovered at a fast boil, using plenty of water. A general rule is to allow 1 gallon of water, 1 ounce (1½ tablespoons) salt, and 1½ teaspoons cooking oil for every pound of pasta. Directions for cooking are given on p. 407. Pasta should be cooked until it is tender but firm (*al dente*) then drained to stop the cooking. Overcooking produces a soft, pasty product that breaks easily when combined with sauces or other ingredients.

FIGURE 9.1 Frequently used pasta shapes (see description of pasta shapes in Figure 9.2). Photo courtesy of the National Pasta Association.

FIGURE 9.2   Shapes and descriptions of selected pasta.

Name	Shape	Description
Alphabets		Miniature pasta in letter shapes. Used in soups.
Bow ties		Bow-shaped noodles. Used with entree sauces and also salads.
Capellini	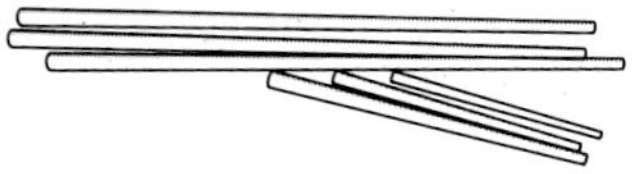	Delicate long thin threads. Used with light sauces.
Conchiglie	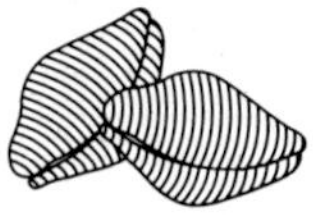	Shell-shaped. Used with sauces; larger shells stuffed, smaller shells used in salads.
Dumplings	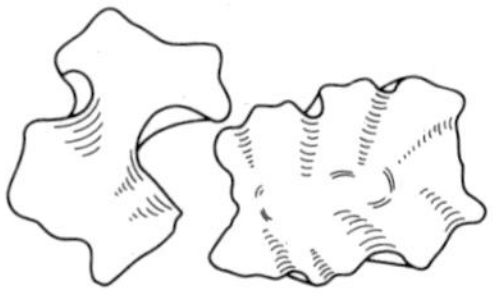	Flat, with rippled edges. Used in soups and baked casseroles.
Fettuccine		Pasta shaped like ribbons, slightly thick. Used with cream or meat sauces.
Fusilli		Long strands of spiraled spaghetti, corkscrew-shaped. Used with thick cream sauces.

FIGURE 9.2 **Continued**

Name	Shape	Description
Kluski		Long narrow egg noodles, with homemade appearance. Used for soups, baked casseroles, and with cream sauces.
Lasagne	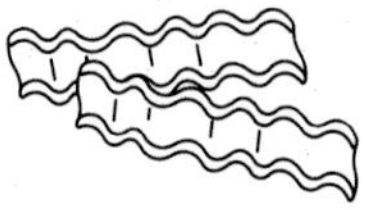	Wide, long, flat noodles with wavy edges. Baked layered with cheese and sauces.
Linguine	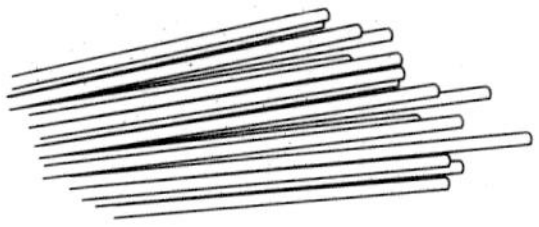	Thin narrow rods, slightly flattened. Used with sauces, especially cream sauces.
Elbow macaroni		Short tubes that are slightly curved. Used in salads and casseroles.
Macaroni	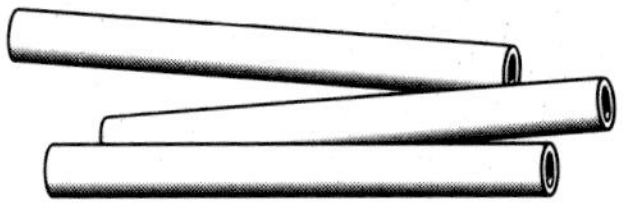	Long hollow round tubes, straight cut ends. Baked in casseroles or with sauces.
Manicotti		Giant pasta tubes. Stuffed with cheese or meat fillings.
Mostaccioli	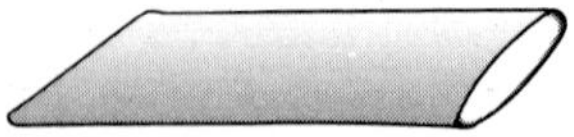	Grooved medium-sized hollow tubes, ends cut diagonally. Used in baked casseroles or with sauces.

FIGURE 9.2 **Continued**

Name	Shape	Description
Noodles	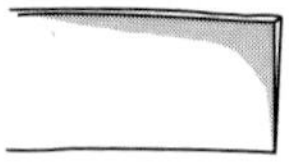 X-Wide Noodles 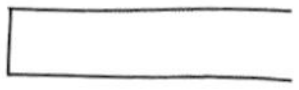 Wide Noodles  Medium Noodles	Narrow flat pasta; typically contains egg. Used in a variety of casseroles, with sauces, and as a side dish.
Pastina (tiny dough) Ditalini	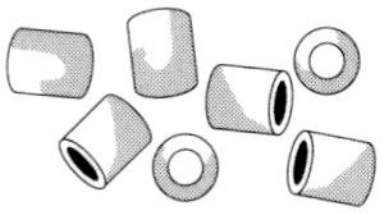	Used in soups and salads. Very short hollow tube.
Orzo		Shaped like rice.
Stelline		Star-shaped.
Acini	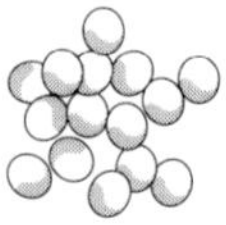	Small round shape.

Radiatore		Frilly shaped pasta,
		  short, thick, and
		  compact.
		Used for salads, casseroles,
		  with sauce, and in soups.

Rigatoni	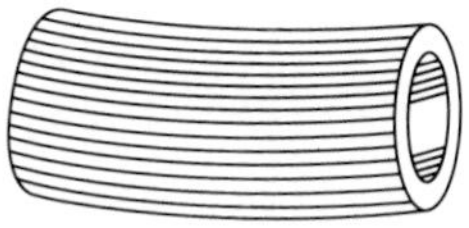	Large ribbed hollow tubes. Used in baked casseroles or with sauces.

FIGURE 9.2   **Continued**

Name	Shape	Description
Rotini		Spiraled pasta. Used in baked casseroles or with salads.
Spaghetti	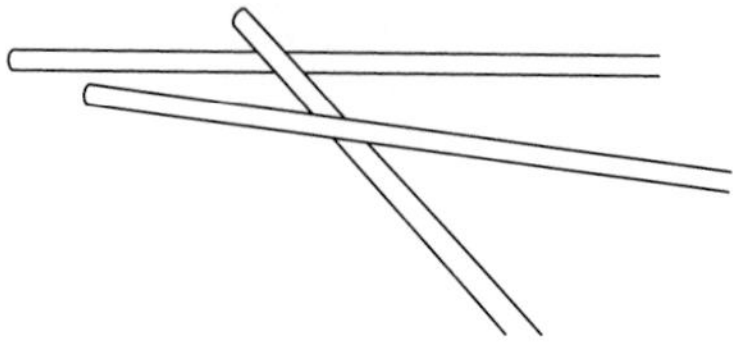	Long round rods. Used with all sauces, especially tomato.
Spaghettini	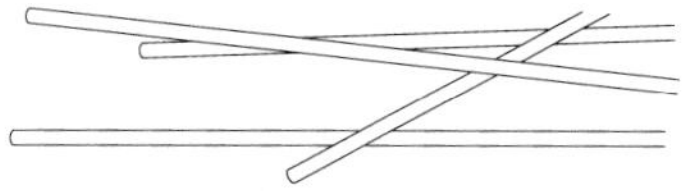	Thin round rods. Used like spaghetti, typically with light sauces.
Vermicelli	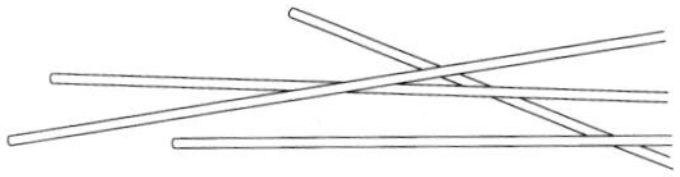	Extra thin spaghetti-like rods. Used with light delicate sauces.
Wagon wheels		Die-cut shape resembling wheels. Used with sauces, in salads and soups.
Ziti	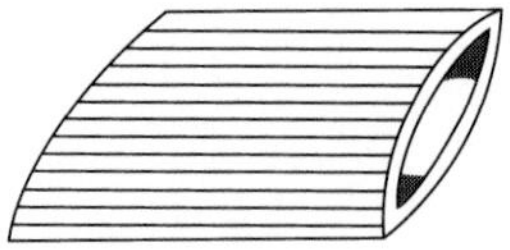	Short hollow round tubes with straight cut ends; resembles large macaroni. Used in baked casseroles or with sauces.

RICE

Rice is used in foodservices as a side or main dish, as an accompaniment to many stir-fried and Oriental foods, and as an ingredient in casseroles and other entrees. Three major types of rice are available.

Long-Grain Rice   Cooked grains are light and fluffy and are inclined to separate; excellent for serving as a side dish, in salads, curries, stew, and in poultry, seafood or meat entrees.

Medium-Grain Rice   Cooked grains are tender and moist, tending to cling together; especially good as a binding and extending agent in meat and fish loaves; also used in puddings and rice molds. Less water is needed to prepare medium-grain than long-grain rice.

Short-Grain Rice   Small, round kernels that become sticky when cooked. Short-grain rice requires considerably less water for preparation than long-grain. Short-grain rice is often used in Asian dishes.

Rice is available with various degrees of milling and processing.

Regular or milled rice has had the outer husk removed, and layers of bran are milled away until the grain is white. Sometimes called polished rice.

Parboiled (converted) rice has been subjected to a special steam/pressure process then dried before milling. After cooking, the grains tend to be more separate and plump. Parboiled rice is noted for its holding quality after cooking.

Precooked (instant) rice has been milled, cooked, and dehydrated. It is slightly higher in cost than parboiled rice but needs merely to be rehydrated to be ready for use. Precooked rice does not hold well after cooking, and the grains quickly lose their shape.

Brown rice is the whole unpolished grain with only the outer husks and a small amount of bran removed. It has a nut-like flavor and a slightly chewy texture. Brown rice is available as short-, medium-, or long-grain rice. Good for use in stuffings, as pilaf, and with chicken or meat in entrees. Shelf life is shortened due to the oil content of the bran.

Many varieties of rice are available, and with increasing frequency, recipes are being developed to use them. Following are some rice varieties often used in foodservice.

Italian short-grain rice has polished white kernels, a little longer than wide. The grain is most commonly represented by the arborio variety. The Italian short-grain rice is used for risotto.

Spanish rice absorbs juices evenly and is lighter in texture than Italian rice and retains an al dente feel. Grana, available in the United States, is often used for paella.

Sticky or glutinous rice, also called *sweet rice,* becomes extremely sticky when cooked. Sticky rice is used almost exclusively for Asian cooking and generally for dessert dishes. The grains become bouncy and full when cooked. Sticky or glutinous rice may be white, brown, or black.

Aromatic rices give off an earthy aroma when cooked. Imported *basmati* requires less water and a shorter cooking time than long-grain rice. American basmati-type rice is

TABLE 9.1   **Basic proportions and yields for converted rice**

Rice	Water	Salt	Approximate volume yield	Approximate number of 4-oz servings
1 lb	1¼ qt	1 Tbsp	2 qt	16
2 lb	2½ qt	2 Tbsp	1 gal	32
3 lb	3¾ qt	3 Tbsp (2 oz)	6¼ qt	50
4 lb	5 qt	¼ cup (2½ oz)	8½ qt	68
5 lb	6¼ qt	⅓ cup (3½ oz)	11 qt	88
8 lb	10 qt	½ cup (5 oz)	18½ qt	148
10 lb	12½ qt	¾ cup (8 oz)	24 qt	192

easier to find than true basmati. It cooks to a dry, fluffy texture with separate grains similar to long-grain rice. *Thai jasmine* rice, an imported aromatic long-grain rice, cooks up soft and tender.

Wild rice is not a rice but a seed of a native grass; it has long, unpolished kernels, an intense nutty flavor and firm, chewy texture. Wild rice is combined with other rices and ingredients for stuffings, entrees, salads, and side dishes. If cooking with white rice, choose a thinner kernel that takes about 25 minutes to cook. To cook with brown rice or alone, choose a plumper grain that will take about 45 minutes to cook.

Long-grain rice is cooked until all of the water is absorbed, so the key to properly cooked rice is the proportion of rice to water and the correct cooking time. Parboiled (converted) long-grain white rice requires slightly more water and a longer cooking time than does regular long-grain or medium-grain rice. Table 9.1 gives basic proportions and yields for converted rice. The cooking time for brown rice is almost double that of white rice. Rice may be cooked in a kettle, steamer, or oven. See p. 430 for cooking directions.

CEREALS

Cereals may be whole, cracked, flaked or rolled, or granular. The amount of water used for cooking determines the volume of the finished product. Cereal swells to the extent of water used until the limit of the grain is reached. As a rule, granular cereals absorb more water than whole or flaked. The fineness of grind of the cereal and the amount of bran or cellulose are factors that determine the length of time a cereal needs to be cooked. Cereals cooked in quantity usually are prepared in a steam-jacketed kettle or steamer but may be cooked in a heavy kettle on top of the range. Directions for cooking breakfast cereals are given on p. 439.

PASTA RECIPES

COOKING PASTA

Yield: 50 portions   *Portion:* 4 oz

Ingredient	Amount	Procedure
Pasta	5 lb	Bring water to a rapid boil. Add salt and oil.
Water	5 gal	Add pasta gradually while stirring.
Salt	5 oz	Return to boiling. Cook uncovered at a fast boil until
Vegetable oil (optional)	3 Tbsp	tender but firm (al dente), 5–10 minutes (see Cooking Times table). Stir occasionally to prevent sticking. Test for doneness. Drain.

Notes

- Weight of cooked pasta will vary, depending on length of time cooked.
- Addition of oil is optional. It helps prevent foaming and sticking.
- If pasta is to be used as an ingredient in a recipe requiring further cooking, under-cook slightly.
- If product is not to be served immediately, drain and rinse quickly with cold water. To keep pasta from becoming sticky or drying out, toss lightly with a little vegetable oil. Cover tightly and store in the refrigerator. To reheat, put pasta in a colander and immerse in rapidly boiling water just long enough to heat through. *Do not continue to cook.* Or, reheat in a microwave oven.
- Pasta can be covered tightly and refrigerated or frozen. Reheat to serving temperature.

APPROXIMATE YIELD AND COOKING TIMES FOR SELECTED PASTAS

Type of pasta	Approximate cooking time (al dente)	Yield of cooked pasta from 1 lb dry pasta
Acini di pepe	8 minutes	3 lb 4 oz
Bow ties	11 minutes	2 lb
Fettucine	8 minutes	2 lb 12 oz
Kluski	15 minutes	2 lb 12 oz
Lasagne noodles	15 minutes	2 lb
Linguine	10 minutes	2 lb 8 oz
Elbow macaroni	6 minutes	2 lb 12 oz
Mostaccioli	10 minutes	2 lb 4 oz
Noodles	6 minutes	2 lb 12 oz
Rigatoni	10 minutes	2 lb
Rotini	8 minutes	2 lb
Shells	9 minutes	2 lb 8 oz
Spaghetti	10 minutes	2 lb 8 oz
Vermicelli	7 minutes	2 lb 8 oz
Wheels	11 minutes	2 lb
Ziti	10 minutes	2 lb 4 oz

MACARONI AND CHEESE

Yield: 48 portions or 2 pans 12 × 20 × 2 inches   *Portion:* 8 oz
Oven: 350°F   *Bake:* 35 minutes

Ingredient	Amount	Procedure
Macaroni Water, boiling Salt Vegetable oil	3 lb 8 oz 3½ gal 2 Tbsp 2 Tbsp	Cook macaroni according to directions on p. 407. Drain.
Margarine Flour, all-purpose Salt Dry mustard Worcestershire sauce	12 oz 8 oz 2 Tbsp 1 Tbsp ¼ cup	Melt margarine. Stir in flour and seasonings. Cook 5–10 minutes.
Milk	1 gal	Add milk gradually, stirring constantly with wire whip. Cook until thickened.
Cheddar cheese, sharp, shredded	4 lb	Add cheese to sauce. Stir until cheese melts. Pour over macaroni and mix carefully. Scale into 2 greased 12 × 20 × 2-inch baking pans, 12 lb per pan.
Bread crumbs Margarine, melted	1 lb 6 oz	Mix crumbs and melted margarine. Sprinkle over macaroni and cheese, 8 oz per pan. Bake at 350°F for about 35 minutes.

Approximate nutritive values per portion

Calories (kcal)	Protein (grams)	Carbohydrate (grams)	Fat (grams)	Cholesterol (mg)	Sodium (mg)	Iron (mg)	Calcium (mg)
450	18.1 (16%)	39.2 (35%)	24.5 (49%)	51	781	1.4	405

Note
- For variety, use rotini, shells, or other shapes of pasta.
- A combination of Swiss and mozzarella cheese may be substituted for some or all of the Cheddar cheese.

Variation
- **Macaroni, Cheese, and Ham.**   Add 3 lb chopped ham, 1 lb 8 oz per pan. Reduce salt to 1 Tbsp.

HERBED FETTUCCINE

Yield: 50 portions   *Portion:* 4 oz

Ingredient	Amount	Procedure
Margarine	1 lb 10 oz	Melt margarine in steam-jacketed or other kettle.
Garlic, minced	6 cloves	Add garlic and cook until golden.
Cream cheese, softened	3 lb 4 oz	Mix cream cheese on medium speed until fluffy, using flat paddle.
Parsley, fresh, minced	½ cup	Blend into cream cheese.
Basil, dried, crumbled	2 Tbsp	
Pepper, black	1 tsp	
Salt	2 tsp	
Water, boiling	1 qt	Add water gradually to cream cheese mixture. Mix until smooth. Add margarine and garlic. Mix until smooth.
Fettuccine	1 lb 12 oz (AP)	Cook fettuccine according to directions on p. 407.
Water, boiling	2 gal	Drain.
Salt	1½ oz	
Vegetable oil	2 Tbsp	
		Place 2 lb 12 oz cooked fettuccine in each of two 12 × 10 × 4-inch counter pans. Stir 3 lb 6 oz cream cheese sauce into each pan of pasta. Cover. Keep hot. Sprinkle with Parmesan cheese and snipped fresh parsley just before serving.

Approximate nutritive values per portion							
Calories (kcal)	Protein (grams)	Carbohydrate (grams)	Fat (grams)	Cholesterol (mg)	Sodium (mg)	Iron (mg)	Calcium (mg)
266	4.4 (7%)	11.5 (17%)	22.9 (76%)	46	364	1.1	4.0

Note   ■   Other fresh herbs may be substituted for parsley.

NOODLES ROMANOFF

Yield: 50 portions or 2 pans 12 × 20 × 2 inches   *Portion:* 5 oz
Oven: 350°F   *Bake:* 45 minutes

Ingredient	Amount	Procedure
Noodles	3 lb	Cook noodles according to directions on p. 407.
Water, boiling	3 gal	Drain.
Salt	3 oz	
Vegetable oil (optional)	1 Tbsp	
Margarine	10 oz	Sauté onions in margarine until tender.
Onions, chopped	6 oz	
Flour, all-purpose	4 oz	Add flour and seasonings to onions, stirring constantly.
Salt	1 oz (1½ Tbsp)	Cook 5–10 minutes.
Garlic powder	¼ tsp	
Milk	1¼ qt	Add milk gradually to flour mixture, stirring constantly. Cook until thickened.
Parmesan cheese, grated	4 oz	Add cheese, sour cream, and paprika to sauce. Combine noodles and sauce.
Cottage cheese	2 lb 8 oz	
Sour cream	2½ cups	
Paprika	1 Tbsp	
Cheddar cheese, shredded	8 oz	Scale pasta mixture into two 12 × 10 × 2-inch counter pans, 8 lb per pan. Sprinkle with cheese, 4 oz per pan. Bake at 350°F for 45 minutes or until heated through.

Approximate nutritive values per portion							
Calories (kcal)	Protein (grams)	Carbohydrate (grams)	Fat (grams)	Cholesterol (mg)	Sodium (mg)	Iron (mg)	Calcium (mg)
238	9.8 (17%)	22.2 (37%)	12.1 (46%)	42	502	1.4	138

Note   ■   Linguine or other pasta may be substituted for the noodles.

PASTA WITH CLAM SAUCE

Yield: 50 portions   *Portion:* 6 oz sauce + 4 oz pasta ■

Ingredient	Amount	Procedure
Margarine	1 lb 8 oz	Melt margarine in a large kettle.
Flour, all-purpose	1 lb	Stir in flour and cook for 5–10 minutes.
Milk, hot	6½ qt	Add milk and seasonings to flour-margarine mixture, while stirring.
Salt	2 oz	
Nutmeg	½ tsp	Heat to boiling.
Light cream (half and half)	1½ qt	Reduce heat. Add cream slowly and continue to cook until thickened.
Minced clams	2 lb	Stir clams into sauce.
Pasta	5 lb	Cook pasta according to directions on p. 407.
Water, boiling	5 gal	Serve 6 oz sauce over 4 oz pasta.
Salt	5 oz	
Vegetable oil (optional)	3 Tbsp	

Approximate nutritive values per portion

Calories (kcal)	Protein (grams)	Carbohydrate (grams)	Fat (grams)	Cholesterol (mg)	Sodium (mg)	Iron (mg)	Calcium (mg)
449	16.6 (15%)	50.2 (45%)	20 (40%)	40	895	7.2	224

Notes
- Clam sauce is excellent served on whole-wheat pasta.
- 2 oz chopped green onion tops, 2 oz chopped chives, or 6 oz sliced mushrooms may be added for variety and color.

Variations
- **Pasta with Cheese Sauce.** Delete salt, nutmeg, and clams. Reduce margarine to 1 lb, flour to 12 oz, milk to 5 qt, and cream to 1 qt. Stir in 4 oz chicken base. Add 2 oz Parmesan cheese, 8 oz provolone cheese, and 4 oz shredded Swiss cheese, and stir until melted. Thin with hot milk if sauce becomes too thick.
- **Pasta with Shrimp Sauce.** Substitute 4 lb cooked salad shrimp for the clams.

PASTA PRIMAVERA

Yield: 50 portions   *Portion:* 5 oz sauce + 4 oz pasta

Ingredient	Amount	Procedure
Carrots, fresh	1 lb	Cut carrots into thin julienne strips 1½ inches long. Steam until tender-crisp. Drain. Save for later step.
Broccoli cuts	1 lb	Steam broccoli until tender-crisp. Drain. Save for later step.
Margarine, melted	12 oz	Add onion and garlic to melted margarine.
Onion, chopped	4 oz	Cook until onions are tender.
Garlic, minced	4 cloves	
Flour, all-purpose	12 oz	Add flour. Stir with wire whip until flour is mixed in. Cook for 5 minutes, stirring often.
Water	2¾ qt	Combine water, milk, and chicken base and gradually add to roux, stirring with wire whip.
Milk	2½ qt	
Chicken base	4 oz	Cook, stirring often, until no starchy flavor remains.
Parsley, fresh, snipped	2½ cups	Add to sauce.
Basil, dried, crumbled	½ cup	Add carrots and broccoli cuts. Keep hot. Thin as needed with warm milk or chicken stock.
Ham, diced, ½-inch cubes	1 lb 8 oz	
Frozen peas	10 oz	
Mushrooms, sliced	8 oz	
Pasta	5 lb	Cook pasta according to directions on p. 407.
Water, boiling	5 gal	Drain.
Salt	5 oz	Serve 5 oz sauce over 4 oz pasta, accompanied by Parmesan cheese.
Vegetable oil	3 Tbsp	

Approximate nutritive values per portion

Calories (kcal)	Protein (grams)	Carbohydrate (grams)	Fat (grams)	Cholesterol (mg)	Sodium (mg)	Iron (mg)	Calcium (mg)
320	12.7 (16%)	40.5 (51%)	11.8 (33%)	55	681	2.5	98

Note   ■   ½ oz (¼ cup) dehydrated onion, rehydrated in ½ cup water, may be substituted for fresh onion (p. 55).

SWISS BROCCOLI PASTA

Yield: 50 portions   *Portion:* 4 oz sauce + 4 oz pasta

Ingredient	Amount	Procedure
Broccoli cuts	1 lb 12 oz	Steam broccoli until tender-crisp. Drain. Save for later step.
Margarine, melted Flour, all-purpose	8 oz 8 oz	Combine melted margarine and flour in steam-jacketed or other kettle. Stir and cook until smooth (5–10 minutes).
Milk	3¼ qt	Add milk gradually. Cook over low heat, stirring constantly, until thick. Do not boil. Turn off heat.
Swiss cheese, shredded Nutmeg, ground	3 lb 4 oz ¼ tsp	Add cheese and stir until melted. Stir in nutmeg.
Mushrooms, sliced, canned, drained	1 lb	Stir in mushrooms and broccoli.
Pasta Water, boiling Salt Vegetable oil	5 lb 5 gal 5 oz 3 Tbsp	Cook pasta according to directions on p. 407. Drain. Serve 4 oz sauce over 4 oz pasta. Thin sauce as necessary with hot milk.

Approximate nutritive values per portion

Calories (kcal)	Protein (grams)	Carbohydrate (grams)	Fat (grams)	Cholesterol (mg)	Sodium (mg)	Iron (mg)	Calcium (mg)
382	17.5 (18%)	43.8 (46%)	15 (35%)	36	426	2.2	387

Variation   ■ **Ham and Swiss Broccoli Pasta.** Omit nutmeg. Reduce cheese to 2 lb 8 oz, broccoli to 1 lb, and mushrooms to 8 oz. Add 2 lb diced ham and 8 oz diced green pepper.

SPINACH LASAGNE (DEEP DISH)

Yield: 64 portions or 2 pans 12 × 20 × 4 inches   *Portion:* 10 oz
Oven: 350°F   *Bake:* 1½–2 hours

Ingredient	Amount	Procedure
Onions, chopped	1 lb 8 oz	Sauté vegetables in hot oil.
Green pepper, chopped	12 oz	
Garlic, minced	2 oz	
Vegetable oil	½ cup	
Tomatoes, diced, canned	8 lb	Stir tomato and seasonings into sautéed vegetables. Simmer uncovered for about 20 minutes. Remove bay leaves. Use sauce in layering steps.
Tomato juice	3 qt	
Tomato paste	2 lb 8 oz	
Parsley, chopped	3 oz	
Oregano, dried, crumbled	1 Tbsp	
Basil, dried, crumbled	1 Tbsp	
Bay leaves	2	
Spinach, chopped	3 lb	Cook spinach. Drain.
Cottage cheese	5 lb	Mix. Add to spinach.
Parmesan cheese, grated	1 lb	
Eggs, beaten	5 (8 oz)	
Salt	1 Tbsp	
Pepper, black	2 tsp	
Lasagne noodles, dry	5 lb	See the following directions for layering.
Mozzarella cheese, shredded	3 lb 12 oz	

Layer ingredients in each of two 12 × 20 × 4-inch pans as follows:

1. Tomato sauce, 3 lb 4 oz
2. Dry noodles, 13 oz
3. Spinach-cheese mixture, 2 lb 5 oz
4. Mozzarella cheese, 11 oz
5. Repeat layers 1 through 4
6. Dry noodles, 13 oz
7. Tomato sauce, 3 lb 4 oz
8. Mozzarella cheese, 8 oz

Bake at 350°F covered with aluminum foil for 1 hour. Remove foil and bake an additional 30–60 min utes or until hot and bubbly. If browning too fast, cover again with foil. Let set for 15–20 minutes before cutting. Cut 4 × 8.

Approximate nutritive values per portion

Calories (kcal)	Protein (grams)	Carbohydrate (grams)	Fat (grams)	Cholesterol (mg)	Sodium (mg)	Iron (mg)	Calcium (mg)
333	19.8 (23%)	35 (41%)	13.3 (35%)	77	901	3.6	323

Notes

- Frozen lasagne noodle sheets may be used. Reduce diced tomatoes to 5 lb 8 oz, tomato juice to 2¼ qt, and tomato paste to 2 lb. Replace dry noodles with 6 lb frozen lasagne sheets, using 3 lb per pan.

- 3¾ oz (1¾ cups) dehydrated onions, rehydrated in 3 cups water, may be substituted for fresh onions (p. 55).

LASAGNE ■

Yield: 48 portions or 2 pans 12 × 20 × 2 inches   *Portion:* 6 oz
Oven: 350°F   *Bake:* 40–45 minutes

Ingredient	Amount	Procedure
Ground beef	5 lb AP	Cook beef, onion, and garlic until meat has lost pink color.
Onions, finely chopped	12 oz	Drain off fat.
Garlic, minced	2 cloves	
Tomato sauce	3 qt	Add tomato and seasonings to meat.
Tomato paste	1 qt	Continue cooking for about 30 minutes, stirring occasionally.
Pepper, black	1 tsp	
Basil, dried, crumbled	1 tsp	
Oregano, dried, crumbled	1 Tbsp	
Noodles, lasagne	2 lb 8 oz	Cook noodles according to directions on p. 407.
Water, boiling	2 gal	Store in cold water to keep noodles from sticking.
Salt	2 oz	Drain when ready to use.
Vegetable oil	2 Tbsp	
Mozzarella cheese, shredded	2 lb 8 oz	Combine cheeses.
Parmesan cheese, grated	6 oz	Arrange in two greased 12 × 20 × 2-inch counter pans in layers in the following order: Meat sauce, 1 qt
Ricotta cheese or cottage cheese, dry or drained	2 lb 8 oz	Noodles, overlapping, 1 lb 12 oz Cheeses, 1 lb 4 oz Repeat sauce, noodles, and cheeses. Spoon remainder of meat sauce on top. Bake at 350°F for 40–45 minutes. Cut 4 × 6.

Approximate nutritive values per portion

Calories (kcal)	Protein (grams)	Carbohydrate (grams)	Fat (grams)	Cholesterol (mg)	Sodium (mg)	Iron (mg)	Calcium (mg)
338	21.4 (25%)	26 (30%)	16.8 (44%)	81	840	3.1	254

Note   ■   1½ oz (¾ cup) dehydrated onions, rehydrated in 1 cup water, may be substituted for fresh onions (p. 55).

BAKED ZITI WITH FOUR CHEESES

Yield: 48 portions or 2 pans 12 × 20 × 4 inches   *Portion:* 8 oz
Oven: 350°F   *Bake:* 20–25 minutes

Ingredient	Amount	Procedure
Tomatoes, canned, crushed	5½ qt	Combine tomatoes and seasonings in steam-jacketed kettle.
Tomato puree	1 qt	Cover and simmer about 10 minutes.
Onion, finely chopped	3 oz	Turn off heat.
Basil, dried, crumbled	1 Tbsp	
Oregano, dried, crumbled	2 tsp	
Parsley, fresh, minced	4 oz	
Pepper, black	½ tsp	
Salt	1 oz (1½ Tbsp)	
Ziti	3 lb	Cook according to directions on p. 407. Drain.
Water	3 gal	Cooked yield should be about 6 lb 6 oz.
Salt	3 oz	
Vegetable oil	2 Tbsp	
Cottage cheese	3 lb	Layer as follows into 2 12 × 20 × 4-inch pans:
Mozzarella cheese, shredded	1 lb 8 oz	1. 2 lb sauce
		2. 1 lb 10 oz cooked ziti
Swiss cheese, shredded	1 lb 8 oz	3. 12 oz cottage cheese
		4. 6 oz mozzarella cheese
		5. 6 oz Swiss cheese
		Repeat steps 1–5.
		Smooth 2 lb sauce over top.
Parsley, fresh, minced	4 oz	Sprinkle 2 oz parsley over sauce.
		Sprinkle 8 oz provolone cheese over parsley.
Provolone cheese, shredded	1 lb	Cover. Bake at 350°F for 20–25 minutes or until hot and cheese melts.

Approximate nutritive values per portion

Calories (kcal)	Protein (grams)	Carbohydrate (grams)	Fat (grams)	Cholesterol (mg)	Sodium (mg)	Iron (mg)	Calcium (mg)
299	17.9 (24%)	31 (41%)	11.8 (35%)	34.9	794	2.4	350

PASTA WITH VEGETABLE SAUCE

Yield: 50 portions or 2½ gal sauce   *Portion:* 6 oz sauce + 4 oz pasta

Ingredient	Amount	Procedure
Onions, chopped	2 lb	Sauté onion in oil until tender, using a steam-jacketed
Olive oil	1 cup	or other large kettle.
Oregano, dried, crumbled	¼ cup	Add spices to onion. Mix well.
Basil, dried, crumbled	½ oz (½ cup)	
Pepper, black	1 Tbsp	
Garlic powder	1 Tbsp	
Salt	1 oz (1½ Tbsp)	
Bay leaves	2	
Tomato juice	5 46-oz cans	Add tomato juice and paste to spices and onion. Heat to boiling.
Tomato paste	1 lb 12 oz	Reduce heat and simmer uncovered for 15–20 minutes. Remove bay leaves.
Zucchini, sliced	2 lb 8 oz	Add zucchini and mushrooms just before serving. Cook
Mushrooms, sliced	1 lb 8 oz	only until zucchini is tender.
Pasta	5 lb	Cook pasta according to directions on p. 407.
Water, boiling	5 gal	Serve 6 oz sauce over 4 oz pasta.
Salt	5 oz	
Vegetable oil (optional)	3 Tbsp	

Approximate nutritive values per portion

Calories (kcal)	Protein (grams)	Carbohydrate (grams)	Fat (grams)	Cholesterol (mg)	Sodium (mg)	Iron (mg)	Calcium (mg)
265	8.2 (12%)	46.8 (69%)	5.7 (19%)	0	1023	3.4	47

Notes
- 2 cups finely chopped fresh basil may be substituted for dried basil.
- 4 oz (2 cups) dehydrated onions, rehydrated in 3 cups water, may be substituted for fresh onions (p. 55).

Variations
- **Italian Sausage Pasta.**   Delete olive oil, salt, and zucchini. Brown 5 lb bulk Italian sausage in steam-jacketed kettle. Drain. Add onions to sausage and continue to cook until onions are tender. Add spices, tomato juice, and tomato paste. Simmer for 15–20 minutes. Add meat sauce to 6 lb 8 oz cooked pasta (approximately 3 lb AP) and mix gently. Be careful not to overcook pasta. Scale 12 lb per 12 × 20 × 2-inch pan. Sprinkle 1 lb shredded mozzarella cheese over each pan and place in low oven until cheese is melted. Suggested pasta combination: 1 lb (AP) rotini, 1 lb (AP) bow ties, 1 lb (AP) rigatoni.
- **Pizza Sauce.**   Reduce olive oil to 4 oz. Delete zucchini and mushrooms. Increase

tomato paste to 5 lb 8 oz and decrease tomato juice to 5¼ qt. Add 1 tsp fennel seed, 2 Tbsp sugar, 1 tsp paprika, and ¼ tsp cayenne. Spread 1 qt sauce on top of 18 × 26-inch pizza dough before adding toppings.

- **Sandwich Tomato Sauce.**   Delete salt, zucchini, and mushrooms. Add 1 Tbsp sugar. Reduce olive oil to 1 Tbsp, onions to ½ cup, oregano to 1 tsp, basil to 1 Tbsp, pepper to ½ tsp, garlic powder to ½ tsp, bay leaf to 1, tomato juice to 1¼ qt, and tomato paste 1½ cups. Yield: 50 1-oz servings.

PASTA WHEELS AND VEGETABLES

Yield: 50 portions   *Portion:* 4 oz

Ingredient	Amount	Procedure
Pasta wheels	5 lb	Cook according to directions on p. 407. Drain. (Should yield 10 lb cooked pasta.)
Water	5 gal	
Salt	5 oz	Scale 3 lb 5 oz into each of three 12 × 10 × 4-inch counter pans.
Vegetable oil	3 Tbsp	
Margarine, melted	1 lb	Combine margarine and basil. Ladle 5 oz over each pan of pasta. Toss to coat. Keep hot.
Basil, crumbled, dried	3 Tbsp	
Broccoli florets	1 lb	Steam vegetables separately until tender crisp.
Sweet red pepper strips	1 lb	To each pan of pasta, add 5 oz broccoli, 5 oz red peppers, and 2 oz carrots.
Carrot sticks, matchstick	6 oz	Toss. Keep warm.

Approximate nutritive values per portion

Calories (kcal)	Protein (grams)	Carbohydrate (grams)	Fat (grams)	Cholesterol (mg)	Sodium (mg)	Iron (mg)	Calcium (mg)
242	6.3 (10%)	35.5 (59%)	8.3 (31%)	0	324	2	31

Notes
- Other vegetables and pasta may be substituted. Suggested vegetables: zucchini, summer squash, asparagus, bell peppers (green, yellow, or red). Suggested pasta: shells, mostaccioli, bow ties.
- May be served as a side dish with poultry or pork or, sprinkled with Parmesan or Romano cheese, as an entree.

Variations
- **Fettucine with Herbed Butter Sauce.**   Substitute fettucine for pasta wheels. Omit vegetables. To the melted margarine, add 3 Tbsp dried basil leaves, 1 Tbsp dried thyme leaves, 1 cup snipped parsley, and ½ cup chopped chives. Toss pasta in margarine sauce. Serve hot.
- **Fettucine with Pesto Sauce.**   Cook and drain fettucine. Toss with pesto sauce (2 oz pesto to 6 oz cooked pasta). If necessary, thin sauce with small amount of pasta water. Serve at once. May sprinkle with freshly grated Parmesan or Romano cheese and cracked black pepper.

CREOLE SPAGHETTI

Yield: 50 portions or 2 pans 12 × 20 × 2 inches   *Portion:* 8 oz
Oven: 325°F   *Bake:* 30 minutes

Ingredient	Amount	Procedure
Ground beef	7 lb (AP) (4 lb 10 oz EP)	Cook beef in steam-jacketed or other kettle until meat loses its red color. Drain off fat.
Onion, chopped	8 oz	Add onion and green pepper to meat.
Green pepper, chopped	5 oz	Cook until vegetables are tender.
Water	2 qt	Add water, tomatoes, sauce, and puree to meat.
Tomatoes, canned, diced	2 qt	
Tomato puree	2 qt	
Tomato paste	1 qt	
Salt	2 Tbsp	Add seasonings to meat mixture. Stir to blend.
Sugar, granulated	1 Tbsp	Simmer for 15 minutes.
Pepper, cayenne	1 tsp	Remove bay leaves.
Garlic, fresh, minced	2 cloves	
Worcestershire sauce	¼ cup	
Bay leaves	4	
Thyme, ground	1 tsp	
Oregano, crumbled, dried	1 Tbsp	
Spaghetti	2 lb AP (6 lb cooked)	Cook spaghetti according to directions on p. 407. Do not overcook.
Water, boiling	3 gal	
Salt	3 oz	
Vegetable oil (optional)	2 Tbsp	
Cheddar cheese, shredded	1 lb 4 oz	Combine sauce and cooked spaghetti. Pour into two 12 × 20 × 2-inch baking pans, 13 lb 12 oz per pan. Sprinkle cheese over top. Bake at 325°F for 30 minutes.

Approximate nutritive values per portion

Calories (kcal)	Protein (grams)	Carbohydrate (grams)	Fat (grams)	Cholesterol (mg)	Sodium (mg)	Iron (mg)	Calcium (mg)
272	18.1 (26%)	23.4 (34%)	12.5 (40%)	53	766	3.1	122

Note   ■ 1 oz (½ cup) dehydrated onions, rehydrated in ¾ cup water, may be substituted for fresh onions (p. 55).

VEGETARIAN SPAGHETTI

Yield: 50 portions or 1 pan 12 × 20 × 4 inches   *Portion:* 8 oz

Ingredient	Amount	Procedure
Margarine, melted Flour, all-purpose	1 lb 12 oz	Combine margarine and flour in steam-jacketed kettle. Cook and stir until smooth. Cook 5 minutes, stirring frequently.
Milk	1 gal	Add milk gradually. Cook over low heat until thick, stirring constantly. Turn off heat.
Salt American cheese, shredded	1 Tbsp 1 lb 6 oz	Add salt and cheese to sauce. Stir until cheese melts.
Carrots, sliced Green peppers, chopped Celery, chopped Broccoli, cut	1 lb 12 oz 8 oz 1 lb 1 lb	Steam vegetables until tender. Drain. Combine with cheese sauce.
Mushrooms, pieces and stems, canned	3 lb	Add mushrooms to sauce.
Spaghetti Water, boiling Salt Vegetable oil	2 lb 12 oz 2¾ gal 3 oz 2 Tbsp	Cook spaghetti according to directions on p. 407. Drain. Combine cooked spaghetti gently with cheese sauce.

Approximate nutritive values per portion

Calories (kcal)	Protein (grams)	Carbohydrate (grams)	Fat (grams)	Cholesterol (mg)	Sodium (mg)	Iron (mg)	Calcium (mg)
303	10.5 (14%)	33.2 (43%)	14.6 (43%)	22	684	1.9	200

Variations

- **Garden Pasta.** Substitute 3 lb rotini for spaghetti. Omit green peppers and salt. Reduce mushrooms to 2 lb. Increase milk to 1¼ gal and cheese to 2 lb. Add 4 oz chicken base. Add 1 lb 8 oz cauliflower florets, steamed only until tender-crisp.

- **Spaghetti with Vegetarian Sauce.** Ladle 4 oz of sauce over 4 oz cooked spaghetti. Increase spaghetti to 5 lb AP for 50 servings.

SPAGHETTI WITH CHICKEN SAUCE

Yield: 50 portions   *Portion:* 6 oz sauce + 4 oz spaghetti

Ingredient	Amount	Procedure
Margarine	7 oz	Sauté vegetables in margarine until tender crisp.
Celery, chopped	1 lb 8 oz	
Onions, chopped	1 lb 8 oz	
Green peppers, chopped	2 oz	
Flour, all-purpose	10 oz	Stir in flour. Cook over low heat for 10 minutes.
Chicken Stock (p. 615)	4¾ qt	Add stock to vegetable mixture, stirring constantly. Cook until thickened.
Salt	2 tsp	Season with salt and pepper.
Pepper, white	1 tsp	
Chicken, cooked, cubed	7 lb	Fold in chicken and pimiento.
Pimiento, chopped	2 oz	
Spaghetti	5 lb	Cook spaghetti according to directions on p. 407. Serve 6 oz sauce over 4 oz spaghetti.
Water, boiling	5 gal	
Salt	5 oz	
Vegetable oil (optional)	3 Tbsp	

Approximate nutritive values per portion							
Calories (kcal)	Protein (grams)	Carbohydrate (grams)	Fat (grams)	Cholesterol (mg)	Sodium (mg)	Iron (mg)	Calcium (mg)
322	19.1 (24%)	42.8 (54%)	7.6 (21%)	29	687	2.8	37

Notes
- Sauce may be combined with spaghetti and served as a casserole.
- 3 oz (1½ cups) dehydrated onions, rehydrated in 2¼ cups water, may be substituted for fresh onions (p. 55).

SPAGHETTI WITH MEAT SAUCE

Yield: 50 portions   *Portion:* 6 oz sauce + 4 oz spaghetti

Ingredient	Amount	Procedure
Ground beef	8 lb AP	Brown beef. Drain off fat.
Tomato puree (or tomatoes)	5 qt	Add remaining sauce ingredients to cooked beef.
Water	1 qt	Cook slowly, stirring frequently, until thickened, approximately ½ hour.
Tomato sauce	1¾ qt	
Onions, chopped	1 lb	Remove bay leaves before serving.
Bay leaves	2	
Thyme, ground	1 tsp	
Garlic, minced	1 clove	
Oregano, dried, crumbled	1 Tbsp	
Basil, dried, crumbled	1 Tbsp	
Sugar, granulated	1 oz (2 Tbsp)	
Worcestershire sauce	¼ cup	
Pepper, cayenne	1 tsp	
Salt	1 oz (1½ Tbsp)	
Spaghetti	5 lb	Cook spaghetti according to directions on p. 407.
Water, boiling	5 gal	Serve 6 oz sauce over 4 oz spaghetti.
Salt	5 oz	
Vegetable oil	3 Tbsp	

Approximate nutritive values per portion

Calories (kcal)	Protein (grams)	Carbohydrate (grams)	Fat (grams)	Cholesterol (mg)	Sodium (mg)	Iron (mg)	Calcium (mg)
377	21.4 (22%)	50.4 (53%)	10.4 (24%)	47	1088	4.5	52

Notes
- Grated Parmesan cheese may be sprinkled over top of each serving.
- 2 oz (1 cup) dehydrated onions, rehydrated in 1½ cups water, may be substituted for fresh onions (p. 55).

SPAGHETTI WITH MEATBALLS

Yield: 50 portions   *Portion:* 3 2-oz or 2 3-oz meatballs + 4 oz spaghetti
Oven: 400°F, 350°F   *Bake:* 15, 30 minutes

Ingredient	Amount	Procedure
Meatballs		
Ground beef	15 lb AP	Mix meat, bread crumbs, eggs, milk, and seasonings on low speed. Do not overmix.
Bread crumbs, dry	8 oz	
Eggs	16 (1 lb 10 oz)	Portion meat with No. 20 dipper onto baking sheets for 150 2-oz balls; use No. 12 dipper for 100 3-oz balls.
Milk	3¾ cups	
Salt	3 oz	Brown in 400°F oven for 15–20 minutes.
Pepper, black	4 tsp	Remove to 12 × 20 × 4-inch counter pan or roasting pan.
Basil, dried, crumbled	4 Tbsp	
Garlic, minced	6 cloves	
Parsley, fresh, chopped (optional)	3 cups	
Sauce		
Italian Tomato Sauce	2 gal (1 recipe)	Make sauce according to directions on p. 591. Pour over browned meatballs. Cover and cook in 350°F oven for about 30 minutes.
Pasta		
Spaghetti	5 lb	Cook spaghetti according to directions on p. 407.
Water, boiling	5 gal	Serve 2 or 3 meatballs and 5 oz sauce over 4 oz spaghetti.
Salt	5 oz	
Vegetable oil	3 Tbsp	

Approximate nutritive values per portion

Calories (kcal)	Protein (grams)	Carbohydrate (grams)	Fat (grams)	Cholesterol (mg)	Sodium (mg)	Iron (mg)	Calcium (mg)
557	33.3 (24%)	52.6 (38%)	23.6 (38%)	148	1960	6.1	102

Note
- If desired, mix the cooked spaghetti with the tomato sauce. Place in 2 counter pans, arrange meatballs over top, and bake at 375°F for 20–30 minutes.

HUNGARIAN GOULASH

Yield: 50 portions   *Portion:* 6 oz goulash + 4 oz noodles

Ingredient	Amount	Procedure
Beef, cubed	10 lb AP	Brown beef and vegetables in shortening in steam-jacketed kettle or tilting frypan.
Onion, chopped	1 lb 8 oz	
Garlic, finely chopped	1 clove	
Shortening	8 oz	
Sugar, brown	5 oz	Combine sugar, seasonings, and liquid ingredients. Add to browned meat. Cover container and simmer 2½–3 hours or until meat is tender.
Mustard, dry	1 Tbsp	
Paprika	1 oz (¼ cup)	
Pepper, cayenne	⅛ tsp	
Salt	2½ oz	
Worcestershire sauce	1½ cups	
Vinegar, cider	2 Tbsp	
Catsup	1 qt	
Water	3 qt	
Flour, all-purpose	1 lb 4 oz	Mix flour and water until smooth.
Water, cold	1 qt	Add gradually to hot mixture and cook until thickened.
Noodles	4 lb 8 oz	Cook noodles according to directions on p. 407. Serve 6 oz goulash over 4 oz noodles.
Water, boiling	4½ gal	
Salt	2 oz	
Vegetable oil	3 Tbsp	

Approximate nutritive values per portion

Calories (kcal)	Protein (grams)	Carbohydrate (grams)	Fat (grams)	Cholesterol (mg)	Sodium (mg)	Iron (mg)	Calcium (mg)
410	26.9 (27%)	45.9 (45%)	12.7 (28%)	97	1098	5.3	49

Notes

- Beef may be browned in a roasting pan in 450°F oven.
- 3 lb 8 oz dry rice, cooked, may be substituted for the noodles. See p. 430 for directions for cooking.
- 3 oz (1½ cups) dehydrated onions, rehydrated in 2¼ cups water, may be substituted for fresh onions (p. 55).

CHICKEN TETRAZZINI

Yield: 50 portions or 2 pans 12 × 20 × 2 inches   *Portion:* 8 oz
Oven: 350°F   *Bake:* 30–40 minutes

Ingredient	Amount	Procedure
Cooked chicken	6 lb	Dice chicken.
Pimiento, chopped	4 oz	Add pimiento and parsley.
Parsley, chopped	2 Tbsp	
Spaghetti	3 lb AP (9 lb cooked)	Cook spaghetti according to directions on p. 407. Drain.
Water, boiling	3 gal	
Salt	1 oz (1½ Tbsp)	
Vegetable oil (optional)	2 Tbsp	
Margarine	6 oz	Sauté vegetables in margarine.
Onions, finely chopped	1 lb	
Green peppers, chopped	4 oz	
Mushrooms, sliced	1 lb 8 oz	
Flour, all-purpose	9 oz	Blend flour and seasonings into sautéed vegetables. Stir in chicken base. Cook 5 minutes.
Salt	1 tsp	
Pepper, black	1 tsp	
Chicken base	3 oz	
Water	1 gal	Add water, stirring constantly. Cook until thickened. Combine cooked spaghetti, chicken, and sauce. Scale into 2 greased 12 × 20 × 2-inch baking pans, 10 lb per pan.
Processed cheese, shredded	1 lb	Sprinkle 8 oz cheese over top of each pan. Bake at 350°F for 30–40 minutes or until heated through and cheese is bubbly.

Approximate nutritive values per portion							
Calories (kcal)	Protein (grams)	Carbohydrate (grams)	Fat (grams)	Cholesterol (mg)	Sodium (mg)	Iron (mg)	Calcium (mg)
284	22.4 (31%)	24.8 (34%)	10.4 (32%)	54	500	2.1	8.2

Notes

- 18–20 lb chickens AP will yield approximately 6 lb cooked meat.
- 2 oz (1 cup) dehydrated onions, rehydrated in 1½ cups water, may be substituted for fresh onions (p. 55).

Variations

- **Tuna Tetrazzini.**   Substitute tuna for chicken.
- **Turkey Tetrazzini.**   Substitute turkey for chicken.

PASTA, BEEF, AND TOMATO CASSEROLE

Yield: 50 portions   *Portion:* 8 oz

Ingredient	Amount	Procedure
Ground beef	10 lb AP (7 lb EP)	Cook meat in kettle. Stir often to prevent lumps from forming. Drain off fat.
Onions, chopped	6 oz	Add onions and celery to meat.
Celery, chopped	3 oz	Cook until tender.
Tomatoes, canned, diced	1½ gal	Add tomatoes and seasonings to meat mixture. Simmer 45–60 minutes.
Tomato puree	2 cups	
Chili sauce	3 cups	
Salt	2 oz (3 Tbsp)	
Pepper, black	1½ tsp	
Sugar, granulated	2 Tbsp	
Macaroni, elbow	2 lb 8 oz	Cook macaroni according to directions on p. 407.
Water, boiling	2½ gal	Fold into tomato-meat mixture.
Salt	2 oz	Simmer until hot.
Vegetable oil	2 Tbsp	

Approximate nutritive values per portion

Calories (kcal)	Protein (grams)	Carbohydrate (grams)	Fat (grams)	Cholesterol (mg)	Sodium (mg)	Iron (mg)	Calcium (mg)
315	21.8 (28%)	27.9 (36%)	12.8 (37%)	62	981	3.5	56

Notes

- Other pasta shapes may be substituted for macaroni.
- ¾ oz (⅓ cup) dehydrated onions, rehydrated in ¾ cup water, may be substituted for fresh onions (p. 55).

BEEF, PORK, AND NOODLE CASSEROLE

Yield: 50 portions or 2 pans 12 × 20 × 2 inches   *Portion:* 6 oz
Oven: 325°F   *Bake:* 30 minutes

Ingredient	Amount	Procedure
Ground beef	4 lb AP	Brown meat and onion.
Ground pork	4 lb AP	Drain off fat.
Onion, finely chopped	1 lb	
Tomato soup	1½ qt	Mix soup, water, and seasonings. Add to meat.
Water	1½ qt	
Salt	1 Tbsp	
Pepper, black	1 tsp	
Noodles	1 lb 12 oz	Cook noodles according to directions on p. 407. Drain.
Water, boiling	1¼ gal	
Salt	2 Tbsp	
Vegetable oil (optional)	1 Tbsp	
Cheddar cheese, grated or ground	2 lb	Combine noodles, meat mixture, and cheese. Scale into two 12 × 20 × 2-inch pans, 8 lb 4 oz per pan.
Bread crumbs	1 lb 2 oz	Combine crumbs and margarine.
Margarine, melted	5 oz	Sprinkle over meat and noodle mixture, 10 oz per pan. Bake at 325°F for 30 minutes.

Approximate nutritive values per portion

Calories (kcal)	Protein (grams)	Carbohydrate (grams)	Fat (grams)	Cholesterol (mg)	Sodium (mg)	Iron (mg)	Calcium (mg)
339	21.1 (25%)	20.8 (25%)	18.8 (50%)	79	583	2.7	163

Note   ■ 2 oz (1 cup) dehydrated onions, rehydrated in 1½ cups water, may be substituted for fresh onions (p. 55).

BEEF ON NOODLES

Yield: 50 portions   *Portion:* 6 oz meat and sauce + 4 oz noodles

Ingredient	Amount	Procedure
Beef, cubed	15 lb AP (10 lb EP)	Brown beef in steam-jacketed or other kettle.
Onions, chopped Celery, chopped	2 lb 8 oz 1 lb 8 oz	Add onions and celery to meat. Sauteé until vegetables are tender.
Water Pepper, black Worcestershire sauce	2 qt 1 Tbsp ½ cup	Add water and seasonings to meat-vegetable mixture. Simmer until beef is tender.
Flour, all-purpose Water Beef base	12 oz 1½ qt 5 oz	Make a smooth paste of flour, water, and beef base. Add to meat mixture to make a gravy. Cook until thickened.
Noodles Water, boiling Salt Vegetable oil	4 lb AP (12 lb cooked) 4 gal 4 oz 2 Tbsp	Cook noodles according to directions on p. 407. Drain. Serve 6 oz beef and sauce over 4 oz cooked noodles.

Approximate nutritive values per portion

Calories (kcal)	Protein (grams)	Carbohydrate (grams)	Fat (grams)	Cholesterol (mg)	Sodium (mg)	Iron (mg)	Calcium (mg)
382	36.4 (39%)	31.8 (34%)	11.1 (27%)	124	239	5.5	39

Note   ■ 5 oz (2½ cups) dehydrated onions, rehydrated in 3¼ cups water, may be substituted for fresh onions (p. 55).

RICE RECIPES

COOKING RICE

Yield: 50 portions   *Portion:* 4 oz

Ingredient	Amount	Procedure
Rice, converted	3 lb 8 oz	Cook in steamer, oven, or in a stockpot or steam-jacketed kettle, according to directions that follow.
Salt	2 Tbsp	
Margarine or vegetable oil	2 Tbsp	
Water, hot	4¼ qt	

Steamer

Weigh rice into a 12 × 20 × 2-inch counter pan. Add salt and margarine.
Pour boiling water over rice. Stir.
Steam uncovered for 30–40 minutes.
Fluff with fork.

Oven

Weigh rice into a 12 × 20 × 2-inch counter pan. Add salt and margarine.
Pour boiling water over rice. Stir.
Cover pans tightly with aluminum foil.
Bake at 350°F for one hour.
Remove from oven and let stand covered for 5 minutes.
Fluff with fork.

Stockpot or Steam-Jacketed Kettle (Boiled Rice)

Bring water to a boil in steam-jacketed kettle or other large kettle.
Add salt, rice, and margarine. Stir. Cover tightly.
Cook on low heat until rice is tender and all water is absorbed, about 15–20 minutes.
Remove from heat and let stand covered 5–10 minutes.
Fluff with fork.

Approximate nutritive values per portion

Calories (kcal)	Protein (grams)	Carbohydrate (grams)	Fat (grams)	Cholesterol (mg)	Sodium (mg)	Iron (mg)	Calcium (mg)
123	2.2 (7%)	25.9 (87%)	0.7 (5%)	0	260	1.1	22

Notes
- If using regular white rice in place of converted rice, the cooking time may need to be reduced.
- For brown rice, increase cooking time to 50–60 minutes for steamed rice, to 1½ hours for baked rice, and to 40–50 minutes for boiled rice.

- For buttered rice, add 5 oz butter or margarine. Add to dry rice in counter pan. Add salt and hot water.
- 1 lb uncooked rice yields 2 qt cooked rice.
- Suggested spices to use with rice: allspice, basil, coriander, curry powder, ginger, marjoram, mint, oregano, rosemary, tarragon, thyme.

GINGER RICE STIR-FRY

Yield: 50 portions   *Portion:* 3 oz
Griddle: 300°F

Ingredient	Amount	Procedure
Rice, converted Water	3 lb 4 oz 3⅓ cups	Place 1 lb 10 oz rice and 1⅔ cups water in each of two 12 × 4 × 10-inch pans. Steam uncovered for 15 minutes or until all of the liquid has been absorbed. Rice will be firm.
Soy sauce Sugar, granulated Garlic powder Pepper, white Ginger, ground	1 cup 1 Tbsp 1 tsp 1 tsp 1 tsp	Mix together soy sauce and spices. Set aside.
Eggs Green onions, chopped	1 lb 12 oz 1 lb 8 oz	Grease griddle lightly with cooking oil. Preheat to 300°F. Place eggs on griddle. Spread thin, scramble, and chop into small pieces. Add chopped onions and continue to cook 3–4 minutes until onions are tender. Add steamed rice and blend well. Drizzle soy sauce mixture over rice. Cook, turning frequently until mixture reaches 160°F. Place in 12 × 10 × 4-inch pan. Serve 3 oz with No. 12 dipper.

Approximate nutritive values per portion

Calories (kcal)	Protein (grams)	Carbohydrate (grams)	Fat (grams)	Cholesterol (mg)	Sodium (mg)	Iron (mg)	Calcium (mg)
142	4.5 (13%)	26 (75%)	1.8 (12%)	68	353	1.6	36

Note

- If griddle is small, prepare in 2 batches. Use ½ cup soy sauce, 14 oz eggs, and 12 oz green onions for each pan of cooked rice.

FRIED RICE

Yield: 50 portions   *Portion:* 4 oz

Ingredient	Amount	Procedure
Rice	2 lb 8 oz	Cook rice according to directions on p. 430.
Water	3 qt	Do not overcook. Let cool.
Salt	2 tsp	
Frozen peas	1 lb 8 oz	Cook peas and drain. Set aside.
Eggs	6 (11 oz)	Break eggs into bowl and stir until yolks and whites are mixed. Add salt.
Salt	2 tsp	
Vegetable oil	2 Tbsp	Cook eggs in oil, stirring to break into small pieces. Set aside.
Onions, chopped	1 lb	Sauté onions and carrots in oil until tender.
Carrots, shredded	8 oz	Add rice and cook until heated.
Vegetable oil	¾ cup	
Soy sauce	1 cup	Add soy sauce to rice mixture, stirring to mix evenly. Stir in peas and eggs. Serve at once.

Approximate nutritive values per portion

Calories (kcal)	Protein (grams)	Carbohydrate (grams)	Fat (grams)	Cholesterol (mg)	Sodium (mg)	Iron (mg)	Calcium (mg)
147	3.4 (10%)	22.3 (62%)	4.6 (29%)	27	513	1.3	26

Variations

■ **Fried Rice with Almonds.** Cook 3 lb rice according to directions on p. 430. Sauté 4 oz chopped onions and 4 oz chopped green peppers in 1 cup vegetable oil. Add cooked rice, 1 Tbsp pepper, 1 tsp garlic salt, ½ cup soy sauce, and 2 lb slivered almonds. Add salt if needed. Bake until heated.

■ **Fried Rice with Ham.** Delete peas. Reduce chopped onions to 4 oz. Increase carrots to 12 oz. Add 4 oz sliced green onions, 12 oz sliced celery, and 1 lb chopped ham.

■ **Pork Fried Rice.** Delete peas. Add 4 lb cubed, cooked pork. Fry 1 lb bacon. Use bacon fat for sautéing vegetables and rice. Crumble bacon and add.

■ **Rice and Black-Eyed Peas (Hoppin' John).** Cook 1 lb rice according to directions on p. 430. Cook 3 lb 8 oz frozen black-eyed peas according to directions on p. 643. Sauté 8 oz onion in ¼ cup vegetable oil. Add hot rice and black-eyed peas. Stir to combine. Add 1 tsp ground allspice, 1 Tbsp dried whole thyme, and 2 tsp coarse ground black pepper. Heat until very hot. Stir in 4 lb fresh tomatoes (peeled, seeded, and diced), 2 cups chopped fresh parsley, and 1 lb shredded cheddar cheese.

■ **Shrimp Fried Rice.** Add 1 lb 8 oz cooked shrimp.

RICE PILAF

Yield: 50 portions or 1 pan 12 × 20 × 4 inches   *Portion:* 4 oz
Oven: 350°F   *Bake:* 45 minutes

Ingredient	Amount	Procedure
Onions, finely chopped	1 lb 8 oz	Sauté onion in margarine until it begins to soften. Do not brown.
Margarine, melted	8 oz	
Rice, converted	3 lb	Add uncooked rice to onions and stir over heat until completely coated with the margarine.
Salt	1 tsp	Place rice in a 12 × 20 × 4-inch counter pan.
Pepper, white	¼ tsp	Add seasonings and Chicken Stock.
Bay leaf	1	Stir to combine.
Chicken Stock (p. 615)	1 gal	Cover tightly with aluminum foil. Bake at 350°F for 45 minutes; or steam uncovered for 30 minutes. Stir before serving.

Approximate nutritive values per portion

Calories (kcal)	Protein (grams)	Carbohydrate (grams)	Fat (grams)	Cholesterol (mg)	Sodium (mg)	Iron (mg)	Calcium (mg)
151	3.6 (10%)	23.7 (64%)	4.3 (26%)	0	336	1.2	24

Notes

- Suggested additions for variety: chopped green pepper, pimiento, tomato, or nuts; sliced mushrooms or water chestnuts; ground or diced ham.
- 3 oz (1½ cups) dehydrated onions, rehydrated in 2¼ cups water, may be substituted for fresh onions (p. 55).

Variations

- **Curried Rice.** Add 3 Tbsp curry powder.
- **Mexican Rice.** Sauté 14 oz chopped onion, 10 oz chopped green pepper, and 3 oz chopped celery in ⅓ cup vegetable oil. Add uncooked rice and stir 2–3 minutes until grains are coated with oil. Stir in 3 Tbsp salt, 2 oz chili powder, and 1 tsp garlic powder. Place in a 12 × 20 × 4-inch counter pan. Pour a mixture of 2½ qt tomato juice and 1¾ qt Beef Stock (p. 616) over rice. Steam 25–35 minutes. Stir before serving.
- **Mushroom Rice Pilaf.** Reduce rice to 1 lb 12 oz and chicken stock to 2½ qt. Delete bay leaf and add 1½ tsp thyme. Add 2 lb mushroom pieces and stems and 1 lb 8 oz chopped celery.
- **Toasted Herb Rice.** Measure uncooked rice into 12 × 2 × 4-inch pan. Bake at 325°F for 20 minutes or until rice is toasted and golden. Proceed as for Rice Pilaf. Add 2 Tbsp crumbled dried basil or tarragon.

SICILIAN RICE AND VEGETABLES

Yield: 48 portions   *Portion:* 8 oz
Oven: 325°F   *Bake:* 10–15 minutes

Ingredient	Amount	Procedure
Brown rice	1 lb 4 oz	Cook rice according to directions on p. 430. Should yield 4 lb 8 oz cooked rice. Save for later step.
Water	1½ qt	
Salt	1 Tbsp	
Onions, sliced	1 lb	Sauté onions and garlic in oil until tender.
Garlic, minced	4 cloves	
Olive oil	½ cup	
Oregano, dried, crumbled	2 Tbsp	Add seasonings and brown sugar to onion. Mix well.
Sweet basil, dried, crumbled	3 Tbsp	
Salt	2 Tbsp (3 oz)	
Pepper, black	1 tsp	
Bay leaves	4	
Parsley, fresh, chopped	2 cups	
Sugar, brown	¼ cup (1½ oz)	
Tomato juice	3 qt (2 46-oz cans)	Combine tomato, paste, and juice, spices, and onion. Reduce heat and simmer uncovered for 15–20 minutes. Remove bay leaves. Add cooked rice from first step.
Tomato paste	12 oz	
Diced tomatoes, canned	1½ qt	
Broccoli stalks, sliced	2 lb	Add broccoli, carrots, and mushrooms to sauce and cook for 5 minutes.
Carrots, julienne cut	1 lb	
Mushrooms, fresh, sliced	1 lb 8 oz	
Squash, yellow summer	3 lb	Quarter squash lengthwise, then slice ½ inch thick. Carefully stir squash into sauce. Cook for 5 minutes. Scale into four 12 × 10 × 2-inch pans, 6 lb per pan.
Squash, zucchini	3 lb	
Mozzarella cheese, shredded	2 lb	Sprinkle 8 oz cheese over each pan. Place in 325°F oven to melt cheese.

Approximate nutritive values per portion

Calories (kcal)	Protein (grams)	Carbohydrate (grams)	Fat (grams)	Cholesterol (mg)	Sodium (mg)	Iron (mg)	Calcium (mg)
170	7.1 (16%)	21.6 (48%)	7.1 (36%)	15	808	2	157

Notes
- Mixture may be scaled into pan after the raw vegetables are added, then baked at 350°F for approximately 30 minutes. Sprinkle with cheese the last 2–3 minutes of baking.
- Other vegetables may be substituted, or ratio of vegetables changed, for those listed in the recipe. Use a total of 10 lb 8 oz vegetables for 50 servings. Suggested substitutes: eggplant, Japanese eggplant, celery, onion, frozen green beans, peas.

RICE PRIMAVERA

Yield: 50 portions   *Portion:* 4 oz

Ingredient	Amount	Procedure
Rice, converted	2 lb	Cook rice according to directions on p. 430. Save for later step. (Should yield 6 lb 8 oz cooked rice.)
Water	2½ qt	
Salt	2 Tbsp	
Yogurt, plain	1½ cups	Combine in steam-jacketed kettle.
Milk, skim	2½ cups	Heat over low heat.
Parmesan cheese	6 oz	Add rice. Toss to coat.
Salt	1 oz (1½ Tbsp)	
Pepper, white	1 tsp	
Garlic powder	¼ tsp	
Broccoli florets	12 oz	Cook vegetables until tender crisp (p. 643). Drain.
Zucchini, sliced	1 lb 8 oz	Add to rice mixture. Toss to coat.
Mushrooms, fresh, sliced	8 oz	Heat.
Carrots, julienne	1 lb	
Parsley, fresh, minced	1¼ cups	Stir in. Put in 12 × 10 × 4-inch pans. Cover and keep hot.

Approximate nutritive values per portion

Calories (kcal)	Protein (grams)	Carbohydrate (grams)	Fat (grams)	Cholesterol (mg)	Sodium (mg)	Iron (mg)	Calcium (mg)
101	3.8 (15%)	17.9 (72%)	1.4 (13%)	4	531	1	95

BLACK BEANS AND HAM ON RICE

Yield: 50 portions   *Portion:* 6 oz ham and beans + 4 oz rice

Ingredient	Amount	Procedure
Black turtle beans	3 lb	Rinse beans with cold running water.
Water	1¼ gal	Discard any stones and other foreign material or shriveled beans.
		Add water and bring to a boil. Boil for 2 minutes.
		Cover. Turn off heat and allow to stand for 1 hour.
Cumin, ground	1 Tbsp	Add seasonings to beans. Simmer until almost tender, about 45 minutes.
Hot pepper sauce	1½ tsp	
Pepper, black	1 tsp	If beans become too thick, add some tomato juice
Thyme, crumbled, dried	1 Tbsp	drained from the diced tomatoes used in a later step.
Oregano, crumbled, dried	1 Tbsp	
Onions, chopped	12 oz	Add to beans. Simmer until beans are tender, about 30 minutes.
Garlic cloves, minced	3	
Salt	1½ oz	Add tomato juice from later step or a small amount of
Ham, diced	2 lb 8 oz	water if necessary to keep beans from becoming too thick.
Tomatoes, diced, canned	3 lb 8 oz	Add tomatoes with juice and peppers.
Green peppers, ¾-inch chunks	12 oz	Simmer for 15 minutes.
Rice, converted	3 lb 8 oz	Cook rice according to directions on p. 430.
Water, boiling	4½ qt	
Salt	2 Tbsp	
Vegetable oil	2 Tbsp	
Parsley, fresh, chopped	4 oz	Serve 6 oz ham and beans over 4 oz cooked rice. Garnish plate by sprinkling with 1 Tbsp chopped parsley.

Approximate nutritive values per portion

Calories (kcal)	Protein (grams)	Carbohydrate (grams)	Fat (grams)	Cholesterol (mg)	Sodium (mg)	Iron (mg)	Calcium (mg)
212	10.2 (20%)	35.2 (67%)	3.1 (13%)	13	987	2.6	54

Note   ■   Anaheim chilies may be substituted for green peppers.

Variations

- **Black Beans and Andouille Sausage.**   Reduce hot sauce to ½ tsp. Omit ham. Add 3 lb cooked andouille sausage cut diagonally into ¾-inch pieces.

- **Black Beans over Rice.**   Delete ham. Increase salt to 2 oz. Chicken broth may be substituted for the water to enhance flavor.

- **Black Bean Soup.**   Follow recipe for Black Beans and Ham on Rice but make the following changes: Increase beans to 4 lb, water to 2¼ gal, onions to 1 lb, and salt to 2 oz. Decrease ham to 2 lb, tomatoes to 2 lb, and green pepper to 6 oz. Delete rice.

BROCCOLI RICE AU GRATIN ▪

Yield: 50 portions   *Portion:* 4 oz

Ingredient	Amount	Procedure
Rice, converted	1 lb 4 oz	Cook rice according to directions on p. 430. Reserve for later step.
Water	1½ qt	
Salt	1 Tbsp	Should yield 4 lb 4 oz cooked rice.
Margarine, melted	5 oz	Sauté onions in margarine in steam-jacketed kettle until transparent. Do not brown.
Onions, fresh, minced	3 oz	
Flour, all-purpose	8 oz	Add flour and seasonings to onions. Stir with wire whip. Cook 15–20 minutes to make a roux. Stir often.
Seasoned salt	2 tsp	
Pepper, white	½ tsp	
Milk	2 qt	Add milk to roux gradually, blending with wire whip. Cook until thickened, 10–20 minutes.
American cheese, shredded	12 oz	Add cheeses and cooked rice. Heat until cheese melts.
Cheddar cheese, shredded	12 oz	
Broccoli cuts, frozen	3 lb	Steam broccoli (p. 643) until tender-crisp. Do not drain. Add to sauce. Stir gently. Put in 12 × 10 × 4-inch pans. Keep hot.

Approximate nutritive values per portion							
Calories (kcal)	Protein (grams)	Carbohydrate (grams)	Fat (grams)	Cholesterol (mg)	Sodium (mg)	Iron (mg)	Calcium (mg)
164	6.6 (16%)	16.3 (40%)	8.2 (45%)	19	386	0.9	160

Variations

■ **Cauliflower Rice au Gratin.**   Substitute cauliflower for broccoli. Sprinkle each pan with chopped fresh parsley.

■ **Green Rice.**   To 2 lb rice, cooked, add 4 lb finely chopped raw or frozen spinach, 2 Tbsp chopped onion, and 1¼ qt medium White Sauce (p. 582). Place in one 12 × 20 × 2-inch counter pan. Bake at 325°F for 30–40 minutes.

■ **Jalapeño Rice.**   Cook 2 lb 8 oz rice (p. 430). Combine in mixer bowl the cooked rice, 4 oz chopped jalapeño peppers, 1 cup chopped chives, 7 oz chopped green chili peppers, 3 lb 6 oz sour cream, 1 tsp salt, and 3 lb shredded American cheese. Scale 5 lb 12 oz into each of three 12 × 10 × 2-inch half counter pans. Sprinkle 4 oz shredded processed cheese over each pan. Bake uncovered at 250°F for 1–1½ hours. Cut 4 × 4.

CEREAL RECIPES

COOKED BREAKFAST CEREALS

Yield: 50 portions   *Portion:* 6 oz

Ingredient	Amount	Procedure
Water Salt	2–2¼ gal 2 oz (3 Tbsp)	Measure water into steam-jacketed kettle or heavy stock pot. Add salt and bring to a rolling boil.
Cereal, granular or flaked	2 lb	Stir dry cereal gradually into boiling water, using wire whip. Stir until some thickening is apparent. Reduce heat and cook until cereal reaches desired consistency and raw starch taste has disappeared. Cereal should be thick and creamy but not sticky.

Approximate nutritive values per portion

Calories (kcal)	Protein (grams)	Carbohydrate (grams)	Fat (grams)	Cholesterol (mg)	Sodium (mg)	Iron (mg)	Calcium (mg)
70	2.9 (17%)	12.1 (69%)	1.1 (15%)	0	390	0.8	15

Notes
- Granular cereals may be mixed with cold water to separate particles and prevent formation of lumps.
- Do not stir excessively; overstirring or overcooking produces a sticky, gummy product.
- 1 lb raisins may be added to cereal the last 2 minutes of cooking.

Variation
- **Rice and Raisins.**   Cook 8 oz rice (2 lb cooked) according to directions on p. 430. Heat 1 gal milk. Add cooked rice, 8 oz softened raisins, 12 oz granulated sugar, and 2 Tbsp cinnamon.

BAKED CHEESE GRITS

Yield: 48 portions or 3 pans 12 × 10 × 2 inches   *Portion:* 6 oz
Oven: 350°F   *Bake:* 30–40 minutes

Ingredient	Amount	Procedure
Water	1¾ gal	Bring water to a brisk boil in steam-jacketed kettle.
Grits, quick Salt	2 lb 4 oz 2 tsp	Stir in grits quickly with wire whip. Reduce heat to medium. Cook 5–7 minutes or until thickened.
Eggs	1 lb (9)	Stir a small amount of cooked grits into eggs. Add to remainder of grits in kettle, stirring constantly.
Cheddar cheese, shredded Margarine Garlic powder Worcestershire sauce	2 lb 4 oz 1 lb 1 tsp ¼ cup	Add to grits. Cook over low heat until cheese is melted. Scale into 3 greased 12 × 10 × 2-inch pans, 6 lb per pan.
Paprika	1 tsp	Sprinkle lightly over grits. Bake at 350°F for 30–40 minutes or until top is set and slightly puffed. Let stand 5 minutes before serving. To serve, cut 4 × 4.

Approximate nutritive values per portion

Calories (kcal)	Protein (grams)	Carbohydrate (grams)	Fat (grams)	Cholesterol (mg)	Sodium (mg)	Iron (mg)	Calcium (mg)
248	8.5 (14%)	17.7 (29%)	15.9 (58%)	63	338	1.2	166

VEGETABLE COUSCOUS

Yield: 50 portions   *Portion:* 4 oz

Ingredient	Amount	Procedure
Margarine, melted	10 oz	Sauté vegetables in margarine in steam-jacketed kettle or stock pot until tender crisp.
Zucchini, julienne	1 lb	
Green onions, sliced	3 oz	
Carrots, julienne	8 oz	
Chicken base	3 oz	Mix chicken base with water. Add to vegetables. Bring to a rolling boil.
Water	3¼ qt	
Couscous	4 lb	Add couscous to vegetables and stir. Cover. Turn off heat. Let stand 5 minutes. Stir to fluff. Place in 12 × 10 × 4-inch pans. Cover tightly and keep hot.

Approximate nutritive values per portion

Calories (kcal)	Protein (grams)	Carbohydrate (grams)	Fat (grams)	Cholesterol (mg)	Sodium (mg)	Iron (mg)	Calcium (mg)
185	5.1 (11%)	29.2 (64%)	5.1 (25%)	0	378	0.5	18

BARLEY CASSEROLE

■

Yield: 50 portions or 1 pan 12 × 20 × 2 inches   *Portion:* 4 oz
Oven: 350°F   *Bake:* 1½ hours

Ingredient	Amount	Procedure
Margarine	6 oz	Sauté barley and vegetables in margarine.
Pearl barley	2 lb 6 oz	
Onions, chopped	1 lb 4 oz	
Mushroom pieces and stems, canned	1 lb 11 oz	
Chicken Stock (p. 615)	3½ qt	Add chicken stock to barley mixture. Pour into a 12 × 20 × 2-inch counter pan. Bake at 350°F for 1½ hours. Serve with No. 10 dipper.

Approximate nutritive values per portion

Calories (kcal)	Protein (grams)	Carbohydrate (grams)	Fat (grams)	Cholesterol (mg)	Sodium (mg)	Iron (mg)	Calcium (mg)
119	3.9 (13%)	18.7 (62%)	3.4 (25%)	0	317	0.8	14

Note   ■   2½ oz (1¼ cups) dehydrated onions, rehydrated in 2 cups water, may be substituted for fresh onions (p. 55).

Variations   ■   **Chicken Barley Casserole.**   Increase chicken stock to 1 gal. Stir in 6 lb cooked cubed chicken. Turkey may be substituted for chicken.

■   **Mediterranean Barley Pilaf.**   Add 1 lb 8 oz golden raisins, 1 lb chopped pecans, and 1 tsp dried thyme.

10

Poultry

PURCHASING AND STORAGE

Poultry is used extensively in all types of foodservices. It is available ready to cook, either fresh or frozen, whole or cut in pieces, and in a variety of other forms. Common forms include the following:

- *Whole birds:* broilers (2½–4 lb), roasters (4–8 lb), capon (9 lb approximately), Cornish hens (1½ lb or less), turkeys (4–24 lb or more), ducks (3–7 lb), and geese (6–12 lb).

- *Pieces:* halves, quarters, breasts, split breasts, thighs, drumsticks, wings, drumettes. See Figure 10.1 for instructions on how to cut serving pieces from raw turkey breasts.

- *Other forms:* cooked breasts, rolled breasts, pieces (cooked and uncooked), cold cuts, hot dogs, sausage links and patties.

All poultry is highly perishable, and caution regarding cleanliness should be exercised in preparing, cooking, cooling, storing, and serving poultry products. Fresh-chilled poultry should be kept at a temperature of 28°–32°F and used within one to two days. Frozen poultry should be kept hard-frozen at 0°F until it is removed from storage for thawing and cooking.

Poultry should be defrosted in a refrigerator. Place covered or wrapped poultry on trays to catch any drippings and arrange on refrigerator shelves so that air can circulate. Never thaw poultry in a manner that will contaminate cooked foods or foods ready to

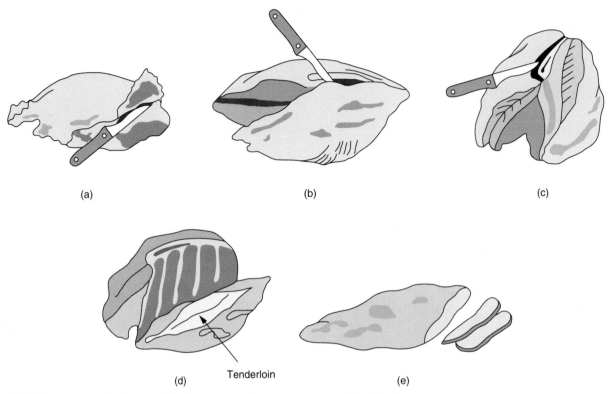

(a)   (b)   (c)

(d)   Tenderloin   (e)

FIGURE 10.1   Skinning and boning a turkey breast. Courtesy of National
Turkey Federation.

eat with drippings from the raw birds. Allow thawing time of one to two days for whole
chickens and turkey roasts, and one day or less for cut-up chicken or small poultry pieces.
Whole turkeys require approximately 5 hours' thawing time for every pound of bird.
Once thawed, poultry may be kept safely no longer than 24 hours at 32°F before cooking.
Poultry should never be refrozen.

COOKING METHODS

Most frozen poultry, except breaded and precooked products, is thawed prior to cooking. If
frozen poultry is cooked, it will take approximately 1½ times longer than thawed poultry.

Poultry should be cooked at moderate heat (325°–350°F) for optimum tenderness
and juiciness. Recommended cooking methods for various classes of poultry are given in
Table 10.1.

Poultry is easily flavored by imaginative use of herbs and spices. Possible spice choices
for poultry include celery salt, curry, dill weed, fennel seed, garlic, marjoram, ground
mustard, oregano, paprika, parsley, poultry seasoning, rosemary, saffron, savory, sesame
seeds, sweet basil, tarragon, and thyme. A recipe for salt-free seasoning is on p. 599.

TABLE 10.1   **Cooking methods for poultry**

Kind of poultry	Class	Average ready-to-cook weight (pounds)	Cookery method	Per-person allowance, ready-to-cook weight (ounces)
Chicken	Broiler-fryer	2–4	Fry, broil, grill, roast	¼–½ bird
	Roaster	3–5	Roast	12–16
	Breast, boneless		Grill, broil	5–6
Turkey	Whole	8–24	Roast	12–16
	Roast, boned and tied	12	Roast	5–6
	Roll, ready to cook	3–6	Roast	5–6
	Cutlet		Grill, broil	
	Steaks	¼–½	Grill, broil	
	Tenderloin		Grill, broil	
	Wings		Roast, broil	
	Drumsticks		Roast, broil	
Duck		3–7	Roast	12–16
Goose		6–12	Roast	12–16

Notes

- For cooked yields for chicken and turkey, see p. 19.
- For additional information on amounts of poultry to purchase, see Table 1.1, p. 11.
- For roasting times see Table 10.2. For broiling and grilling times, see Broiling or Grilling, p. 450.

Broiling or Grilling

Most cuts of chicken and some turkey products may be cooked by broiling or grilling. Choose from half and quarter chickens, bone-in parts, and boneless chicken or turkey cuts such as breasts, breast or thigh steaks, and tenderloins. The procedure for broiling poultry follows:

- Use poultry that has been marinated, or brush with melted fat. Season as appropriate.
- Place rack 6–8 inches from heat source, grease lightly. Place poultry on broiler, skin side down if skin is left on. Turn larger pieces often so they cook and brown evenly. Thin steaks and breasts should be turned only once. For chicken breasts or turkey breast steaks, cook 4–7 minutes per side; for cutlets, 2–3 minutes per side; and 8–12 minutes per side for turkey tenderloin.

Poultry browns very quickly and larger pieces may become too dark before they are cooked through. If the poultry is browning too quickly it may be placed in an oven on sheet pans or racks to complete cooking.

Deep-Fat Frying

Broiler-fryer pieces and many breaded patties, cutlets, and steaks may be cooked by submerging in hot fat—deep-fat frying. Pressure frying (deep-fat frying in a covered fryer that allows steam to build up and cook the product under pressure) is also a common way to cook poultry.

Poultry products usually are breaded before deep-fat frying or are purchased with a batter or breaded coating. The recipe for coating chicken is on p. 47. Figure 10.2 shows the technique for breading. Guidelines for deep-fat frying raw broiler fryer pieces are as follows:

- Fry at 350°–375°F for regular deep-fat frying, 345°–350°F for pressure frying.
- Fill baskets so that hot fat can circulate around pieces. Do not overload.
- Use a good-quality fat with a high smoke point.
- 15–20 percent fresh fat should be added after each daily use. Old fat should be discarded.
- Cook until chicken reaches an internal temperature of 185°F.

Cooking time will vary because of size differences. Approximate frying times for raw chicken pieces are 15–20 minutes for regular deep-fat frying and 14–18 minutes for pressure frying. If cooked or partially cooked pieces are being used, refer to manufacturer's directions.

Pan Frying

Pan-fried chicken pieces are usually coated with flour or breading before cooking. See recipe on p. 455 and description of breading technique (Figure 10.2). Chicken may be purchased breaded and ready to pan fry. Follow these guidelines for pan frying raw chicken pieces:

- Heat ½ inch of fat to 350°F. Arrange breaded chicken in hot fat skin side down. Brown on all sides.
- Reduce temperature to 325°F and cook slowly until tender, usually 40–60 minutes, or until internal temperature reaches 180°F. Cooking time depends on size of pieces. Turn as necessary to assure even browning and doneness.

Sautéing thin slices of poultry in a small amount of fat is popular for many poultry dishes. Large pieces may require pan sautéing for browning, then finishing by another method, such as braising or baking.

Arrange work station in the order shown in the diagram.

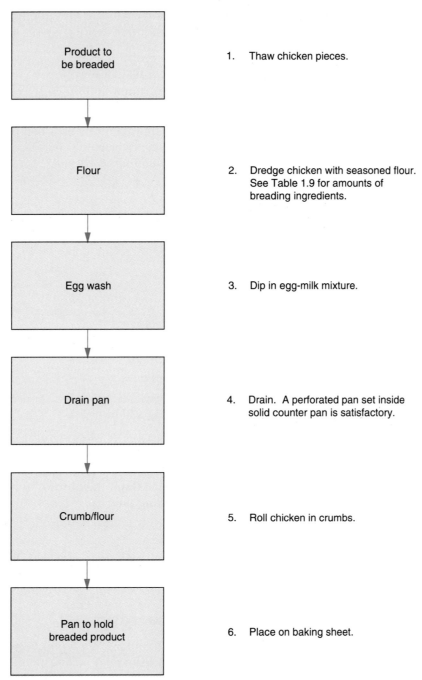

1. Thaw chicken pieces.

2. Dredge chicken with seasoned flour. See Table 1.9 for amounts of breading ingredients.

3. Dip in egg-milk mixture.

4. Drain. A perforated pan set inside solid counter pan is satisfactory.

5. Roll chicken in crumbs.

6. Place on baking sheet.

FIGURE 10.2   Breading techniques for poultry.

Oven Frying

Oven frying is a satisfactory method for producing fried chicken without large quantities of fat. When properly cooked, the finished product is tender, moist, and crispy. The following guidelines are for oven frying chicken:

- Dredge chicken in seasoned flour, then roll in melted fat.
- Place on sheet pans and bake approximately 1 hour at 350°–375°F or until internal temperature reaches 185°F.

This method of cooking chicken should result in a nicely browned product with no turning. See recipe on p. 456. Turkey drumsticks and drumettes may be oven fried using the same procedure. Cooking time will vary depending on the size.

Braising

Braising—cooking meat slowly in a closely covered pan with a small amount of moisture—is often required for mature, less tender poultry. Guidelines for braising whole and cut-up poultry follow:

Braising Whole Poultry

- Preheat oven to 450°F for young poultry, 325°F for more mature birds.
- Season and brush ready-to-cook poultry with fat.
- Place poultry in a heavy pan and cover tightly.
- Poultry is done when internal temperature reaches 185°F, 1–2 hours. Uncovering the poultry for the last 30 minutes of cooking will brown it.

Braising Cut-up Poultry

- Roll serving-size pieces of poultry in seasoned flour, then brown in fat in a heavy frypan. Drain off fat. Place chicken in a baking pan.
- Add a small amount of hot water. Cover tightly and cook in a 325°F oven. Add more water as necessary to prevent sticking.
- Remove cover during the final 30 minutes of cooking to brown. Total cooking time will be 1½–2½ hours, depending on size of the pieces and maturity of the bird.

Stewing or Simmering and Poaching

Stewing or simmering and poaching all refers to cooking in a liquid. Stewing or simmering requires that the temperature be kept just below the boiling point, bubbling very gently. Poaching temperature is slightly lower and less liquid is used. This moist-heat method of stewing and simmering is used for larger, older, and tougher birds that require longer cooking times to soften. Poaching is used to gently cook tender poultry and develop a delicate subtle flavor. Guidelines are as follows:

Stewing or Simmering

- Barely cover poultry with seasoned boiling water.
- Simmer until tender, approximately 2½ hours.
- For cooking in a steamer, place whole or parts of birds in a solid steamer pan. Cook until tender.

Poaching

- Place tender poultry product in a pan.
- Pour cold liquid, usually stock, in the pan to cover poultry part way up. Cover the pan.
- Heat gently on the range top or in the oven at 325°F until internal temperature reaches 185°F.
- Drain poultry well after cooking. Liquid may be used for making a sauce.

When stewed or simmered poultry meat is to be used in salads or creamed dishes, the following may be added to the cooking water for additional flavor: 1 carrot, 1 medium onion, 1 celery stalk, and 2 whole peppercorns for each bird.

Cooked poultry must be cooled immediately if prepared for use at a later time. Remove from broth and place on sheet pans. When poultry is cool enough to handle, remove meat from bones, place in shallow pans and store in the refrigerator at 38°F or below. Broth should be cooled rapidly by stirring frequently during cooling.

Roasting

For large-quantity cookery, it is recommended that poultry be roasted unstuffed and that dressing be baked separately. If turkey is to be stuffed, mix the stuffing just before it is needed. Do not prepare the dressing or stuff the bird in advance. Follow this order of procedure in roasting poultry:

1. Prepare bird. Remove giblets and neck from body and neck cavities. Rinse bird well inside and out. Tuck wing tips under back of bird.
2. Season inside and outside of bird.
3. Brush with vegetable oil or soft fat (optional).
4. Place bird on rack in shallow baking pan, breast up. If bird will not be carved for show, bake breast side down.

TABLE 10.2 **Roasting guide for poultry (defrosted)**

Kind of poultry	Ready-to-cook weight (pounds)	Approximate total roasting time at 325°F	Internal temperature of poultry when done (°F)
Chicken, whole roasters	2½–4	1–1½ hr	185
Ducks	3–7	1–2 hr	180
Geese	6–8	2½–3½ hr	180
	8–12	3½–4½ hr	180
Turkeys, whole	6–8	2¼–3¼ hr	180–185
	8–12	3–4 hr	180–185
	12–16	3½–4½ hr	180–185
	16–20	4–5 hr	180–185
	20–24	4½–5½ hr	180–185
Turkey, breast and breast portions		15–20 min per pound	180
Turkey roast, boneless	3–10	35–45 min per pound	180
Turkey tenderloin		18–30 min at 400°F	180–185
Turkey wings, drumsticks, wing drumettes, thigh		1–1¾ hr	180–185

Note

■ Thermometer is inserted in thigh muscle of whole turkeys and in center of turkey roasts. The thermometer should not touch bone.

5. Baste with pan drippings or vegetable oil (optional).

6. Roast at 325°F to an internal temperature of 180°–185°F. Insert thermometer in center of inside thigh muscle, being careful not to touch the bone with the stem (see Table 10.2 for roasting guide). If thermometer is not available, test doneness by moving drumstick. It moves easily at the thigh joint when done. Juices should be clear when meat is pierced in the deepest part with a long-tined fork.

7. Whole turkeys and larger roasts should be allowed to stand 20 minutes before carving. See Figure 10.3 for carving instructions.

The yield of cooked meat from poultry is influenced by the size of the bird, the amount of bone, the method of preparation and service, and the size of portions desired. Whole, ready-to-cook turkey will yield approximately 47 percent edible cooked meat without skin, neck meat, or giblets; turkey roast or roll will yield about 66 percent. Large fryers will yield approximately 35–40 percent usable cooked meat.

Carving Dark Meat

1

2

3

4

1. Remove drumstick and thigh by pulling leg away from body. Joint connecting leg to backbone will often snap free or may be severed easily with knife point. Cut dark meat from body by following body contour carefully with knife.
2. Place drumstick and thigh on cutting surface and cut through connecting joint.
3. Tilt drumstick to convenient angle, slicing down toward cutting surface.
4. Hold thigh firmly on cutting surface with fork. Cut slices evenly and parallel to bone.

Carving White Meat

1

2

Traditional Method
1. Hold turkey breast firmly on cutting surface with fork. Place knife parallel and as close to wing as possible. Make deep cut into breast cutting toward ribs. This makes a base cut. Each breast slice will stop at this horizontal base cut.
2. Slice breast by carving downward, ending at base cut. Keep slices thin and even.

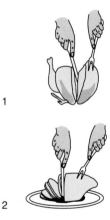

1

2

Kitchen Method
1. Hold turkey breast firmly on cutting surface with fork. Using a sharp knife, carve each breast half away from ribs by cutting along keel bone and rib cage.
2. On cutting surface, carve each breast half into thin, even slices against grain of meat.

FIGURE 10.3   Carving a turkey. Courtesy of National Turkey Federation.

POULTRY RECIPES

FRICASSEE OF CHICKEN

Yield: 50 portions   *Portion:* 3 oz cooked meat
Oven: 325°F   *Bake:* 1½–2 hours

Ingredient	Amount	Procedure
Chicken	35 lb AP (13 2½–3 lb fryers)	Cut chickens into pieces of desired serving size. Mix flour and seasonings. Dredge chicken with seasoned flour.
Flour, all-purpose	12 oz	
Salt	2 Tbsp	
Pepper, white	1 tsp	
Shortening	1 lb	Brown chicken in hot shortening. Remove to roasting pan and cover with boiling water. Bake at 325°F, adding more water if necessary, until chicken is tender, 1½–2 hours.
Margarine	10 oz	When tender, remove chicken from stock.
Flour, all-purpose	6 oz	Make gravy, using liquid in which chicken was cooked
Chicken broth	3½ qt	(see p. 586). Serve over chicken.

Approximate nutritive values per portion

Calories (kcal)	Protein (grams)	Carbohydrate (grams)	Fat (grams)	Cholesterol (mg)	Sodium (mg)	Iron (mg)	Calcium (mg)
609	52.9 (36%)	13.8 (9%)	36.5 (55%)	154	893	3.1	38

Variations

- **White Fricassee of Chicken.**   Do not brown chicken. Simmer until tender. Remove from liquid. Boil liquid until concentrated. Add milk or cream to make 1½ gal; thicken to make a Medium White Sauce (p. 582). Beat constantly with wire whip while pouring sauce gradually over 10 beaten egg yolks. Season to taste. Add chicken.

- **Chicken with Black Olives.**   Brown floured chicken. Place in baking pans. Cover with chicken gravy. Bake 1–1½ hours. Prior to serving, sprinkle with sliced ripe olives and sautéed fresh mushrooms.

- **Chicken Tahitian.**   Cut chickens into quarters. Melt 12 oz shortening in baking pans. Arrange chicken in pans in single layer. Brown in 425°F oven for 30 minutes. Brush chicken with mixture of 2 12-oz cans undiluted frozen orange juice, 1 lb melted margarine, 2 Tbsp ground ginger, and 2 Tbsp soy sauce. Bake at 325°F for 30–40 minutes, basting as needed until chicken is glazed. Serve with Steamed Rice (p. 430) and garnish with slivered almonds and avocado wedges.

GRILLED CHICKEN BREAST

Yield: 50   *Portion:* 6 oz
Grill: 350°F

Ingredient	Amount	Procedure
Chicken breasts, skinless, boneless, 6 oz	50	Grill chicken breasts on preheated, well-oiled grill preheated to 350°F, for 3–5 minutes, or until done.
Seasonings (see Variations, or salt and pepper to taste)		

Approximate nutritive values per portion							
Calories (kcal)	Protein (grams)	Carbohydrate (grams)	Fat (grams)	Cholesterol (mg)	Sodium (mg)	Iron (mg)	Calcium (mg)
181	32.4 (75%)	0 (0%)	4.7 (25%)	89	80	1.1	1.6

Variations

- **Chicken Breast Dijon.** In baker's bowl mix 2⅔ cups honey, 2 cups Dijon mustard, 1½ cups fresh or reconstituted frozen lemon juice, 1½ tsp dried tarragon leaves, and ¾ cup Worcestershire sauce. Brush glaze over chicken breasts during last few minutes of grilling.

- **Chicken Breast with Grilled Tomato Sauce.** Sauté 2 Tbsp minced garlic in 1½ cups vegetable oil until fragrant but not browned. Add 5 lb 12 oz firm tomatoes, diced, and 1½ Tbsp granulated sugar. Sauté 2 minutes until heated. Add ⅓ cup red wine vinegar, 1½ Tbsp salt, 2 Tbsp cracked black pepper, and ½ cup snipped fresh parsley. Toss lightly. Ladle 2 oz sauce over cooked chicken breast.

- **Curried Chicken Breast.** In baker's bowl blend 1 qt vegetable oil, 2⅔ cups fresh or reconstituted frozen lemon juice, 6 oz curry powder, 3 oz minced garlic, ½ tsp cayenne, and ½ tsp ground cumin. Place chicken breasts in marinade and turn so all surfaces are covered. Cover and refrigerate for several hours or overnight. Drain. Grill as for Grilled Chicken Breast.

- **Herb-Marinated Chicken Breast.** In baker's bowl, mix 2½ cups red wine vinegar, 2 tsp dried rosemary leaves, ¼ tsp ground thyme, 3 Tbsp minced garlic, 2 Tbsp salt, and 1 qt vegetable oil. Place chicken breasts in marinade and turn so all surfaces are covered. Cover and refrigerate for several hours or overnight. Drain. Grill as for Grilled Chicken Breast.

- **Sesame Mustard Chicken.** Prepare sauce by combining in steam-jacketed kettle or saucepan 1½ qt water, 2¾ cups cider vinegar, ¼ cup cooking sherry, 1 lb 4 oz granulated sugar, ¾ cup soy sauce, 2 oz dry mustard, 1 tsp turmeric, 1 oz toasted sesame seeds, 2 oz cornstarch, and 5 tsp sesame oil. Heat to boiling, stirring constantly, until thickened. Ladle 2 oz sauce over cooked chicken breast.

- **Tarragon Chicken.** Follow recipe for Tarragon Turkey Steaks, p. 472. Substitute chicken breasts for turkey. Grill as for Grilled Chicken Breast.

CHEESE-STUFFED CHICKEN BREAST

Yield: 50 portions   *Portion:* 5–7 oz
Oven: 375°F   *Bake:* 15 minutes, 30 minutes

Ingredient	Amount	Procedure
Chicken breasts, boneless and skinless 4–6 oz	50	Flatten chicken breasts and sprinkle with salt and pepper.
Salt	2 Tbsp	
Pepper, black	2 Tbsp	
Butter or margarine, softened	1 lb 8 oz	Mix together butter and seasonings. Spread each chicken breast with 1 tsp seasoned butter (save remaining seasoned butter for later step).
Oregano, dried, crumbled	2½ tsp	
Marjoram, dried, crumbled	1 Tbsp	
Parsley, fresh, chopped	½ oz	
Swiss cheese	1 lb 8 oz	Cut cheese into ½ oz strips and roll inside each piece of chicken.
Flour, all-purpose	12 oz	Roll each chicken breast in flour, then egg, then crumbs.
Eggs, beaten	9 (1 lb)	Place in 12 × 20 × 2-inch pans.
Bread crumbs, dry	1 lb 8 oz	Bake at 375° for 15 minutes.
Dry white wine	3 cups	Heat wine with butter reserved from earlier step. Pour over chicken and bake 30 minutes. Baste occasionally.

Approximate nutritive values per portion

Calories (kcal)	Protein (grams)	Carbohydrate (grams)	Fat (grams)	Cholesterol (mg)	Sodium (mg)	Iron (mg)	Calcium (mg)
402	30.5 (31%)	16.1 (16%)	22.5 (51%)	146	571	2	173

Note   ■ Monterey Jack cheese may be substituted for Swiss.

Variation   ■ **Cheese-Stuffed Chicken with Tomato Basil Sauce.**   Sauté 8 oz chopped onion and 3 Tbsp minced garlic in ½ cup olive oil. Add 2 cups white wine and cook to reduce, approximately 5 minutes. Add 8 lb (EP) fresh tomatoes that have been peeled, seeded, and diced, along with 4 oz chopped fresh green onion, 1½ oz chopped fresh basil, and ½ tsp salt. Stir gently and briefly, 2–3 minutes. A mixture of chopped fresh herbs may be used. Choose from basil, marjoram, tarragon, thyme and fennel. Serve 3 oz sauce over cooked chicken breast. Chicken and sauce may be served with pasta, rice, or couscous.

PAN-FRIED CHICKEN

Yield: 50 portions   *Portion:* 8–12 oz AP

Ingredient	Amount	Procedure
Chicken fryers, 2–3 lb	13	Cut chickens into pieces of desired serving size.
Flour, all-purpose	1 lb	Mix flour and seasonings.
Salt	2 Tbsp	Dredge chicken pieces with seasoned flour.
Paprika or poultry seasoning	1 Tbsp	
Pepper, black	1 tsp	
Shortening	1 lb	Brown chicken in hot shortening, ½ inch deep in pan. Reduce heat and cook slowly until tender, 45–60 minutes. Turn for even browning.

Approximate nutritive values per portion

Calories (kcal)	Protein (grams)	Carbohydrate (grams)	Fat (grams)	Cholesterol (mg)	Sodium (mg)	Iron (mg)	Calcium (mg)
644	63.7 (41%)	12.9 (8%)	35.7 (51%)	191	432	3.3	39

Notes
- Chicken portions (quarters, thighs, or breasts) may be used.
- Chicken may be browned in a skillet, then placed in counter pans or baking pans, skin side up, and finished in the oven at 325°F for 20–30 minutes.

Variations
- **Chicken Cantonese.**   Flour chicken and brown as above. Place in 12 × 20 × 2-inch counter pans. Cover with aluminum foil. Bake at 350°F for approximately 1 hour. Before serving, cover with sauce made of 3 qt pineapple juice, 3 qt orange juice, 12 oz flour, 3 lb pineapple cubes, 12 oranges peeled and diced, 1 lb 4 oz almonds slivered and browned, 2 tsp nutmeg, and 2 tsp salt. Combine juice and flour; cook until thickened. Add seasonings, fruit, and almonds. Pour over chicken. Bake uncovered about 10 minutes. Serve with cooked rice.

- **Chicken Cacciatore.**   Brown chicken as above. Arrange in two 12 × 20 × 4-inch counter pans. Sauté 1 lb 8 oz coarsely diced onions and 2 cloves garlic, minced, in 5 oz margarine. Add 1 lb 8 oz green peppers cut into strips, 2 lb sliced mushrooms, 1 No. 10 can diced tomatoes with juice, ½ tsp oregano, ½ tsp thyme, and 1 qt Chicken Stock. Thicken with 4 oz flour mixed with 2 cups cold water. Pour over chicken, 3½ qt per pan. Cover with aluminum foil. Bake at 325°F for 1 hour.

- **Deep-Fat Fried Chicken.**   Use 1¾ to 2-lb broiler-fryers, cut in serving pieces, or chicken quarters. Dredge in seasoned flour as for Pan-fried Chicken; or dredge in flour, dip in egg and milk mixture (3 eggs to 1 cup milk), and roll in crumbs (12 oz); or dip in batter (p. 47). Fry in deep fat at 325°F for 12–15 minutes or until golden brown and cooked through. For larger fryers, brown in deep fat, drain, then place in baking pans and finish in the oven at 325°F for 20–30 minutes.

OVEN-FRIED CHICKEN

Yield: 50 portions   *Portion:* 1 chicken quarter or 2 pieces
Oven: 350°F   *Bake:* 1 hour

Ingredient	Amount	Procedure
Chicken quarters *or*	50	Mix flour and seasonings.
chicken breasts	100	Dredge chicken with seasoned flour.
and thighs		Place in single layer on greased or parchment-lined
Flour, all-purpose	1 lb	baking sheets.
Nonfat dry milk	8 oz	
Salt	2 Tbsp	
Paprika	1 Tbsp	
Pepper, black	1 tsp	
Margarine, melted	1 lb	Brush chicken with melted margarine.
		Bake at 350°F for 1 hour or until chicken is browned and tender.

Approximate nutritive values per portion							
Calories (kcal)	Protein (grams)	Carbohydrate (grams)	Fat (grams)	Cholesterol (mg)	Sodium (mg)	Iron (mg)	Calcium (mg)
574	51.3 (37%)	14.8 (11%)	32.9 (53%)	154	510	2.8	91

Note
- Chicken may be breaded. See Table 1.9 for coating and Figure 10.2 for procedures.

Variations
- **Barbecued Chicken.**   Brown chicken at 425°F for 20–30 minutes. Reduce heat to 325°F. Pour 1½ gal Cooked Barbecue Sauce (p. 588) over chicken. Bake 40–45 minutes.

- **Chicken Parmesan.**   Combine 1 lb flour, 1 oz salt, ½ tsp pepper, and ¾ cup Parmesan cheese. Dredge chicken pieces in flour mixture, then dip in mixture of 12 (1 lb 5 oz) eggs and 1 qt milk, then back into flour mixture. Arrange chicken on greased or parchment-paper-lined baking sheets. Drizzle lemon butter (8 oz melted butter or margarine and ¼ cup lemon or lime juice) over chicken. Bake at 325°F for 1 hour. Use drippings from baking sheets for gravy.

- **Chicken Teriyaki.**   Marinate chicken overnight in a marinade of 3 cups soy sauce, 10 oz brown sugar, 1½ Tbsp garlic powder, and 1½ Tbsp ground ginger. Arrange chicken pieces in single layer on greased or parchment-paper-lined baking sheets. Bake at 350°F for 30 minutes. Remove from oven. Brush chicken with remaining marinade and bake until tender, about 30 minutes. 1 cup orange juice or pineapple juice may be added to the marinade.

- **Herb Baked Chicken.**   Combine 1 lb 8 oz dry bread crumbs, 8 oz flour, 1½ oz salt, 1 Tbsp paprika, 1½ tsp onion salt, 1 tsp garlic salt, 1 Tbsp rosemary, and ¾ cup vegetable oil. Dredge chicken with crumb mixture. Place on parchment-paper-lined 18 × 26 × 1-inch baking sheets. Bake at 350°F for 1 hour.

- **Italian Baked Chicken.**   Melt 3 lb butter. Dip chicken in melted margarine, then roll in coating mixture of 3 lb dry bread crumbs, 1 cup chopped parsley, 2 Tbsp paprika, 1 Tbsp salt, 3 Tbsp garlic salt, 2 Tbsp crumbled dried oregano, 1½ tsp crumbled dried basil, 1 tsp black pepper, and 12 oz grated Parmesan cheese. Place in shallow baking pans with skin side up. Bake at 350°F for 1 hour.

ORANGE GLAZED CORNISH GAME HENS

Yield: 50   *Portion:* 16 oz (1 hen)
Oven: 325°F   *Bake:* 1½–1¾ hours

Ingredient	Amount	Procedure
Cornish game hens	50 hens	Wash hens inside and out. Remove packaged giblets. Place 4 × 4 in 18 × 26 × 2-inch pans.
Butter or margarine, melted	1 lb 8 oz	Brush hens with melted butter. Bake at 325°F for 1½–1¾ hours; follow glazing instructions that follow.
Orange juice, frozen, undiluted	2 cups	Blend together juice concentrate, syrup, and marmalade.
Corn syrup, light	2¼ cups	Brush over poultry 30 minutes before end of roasting time and again 15 minutes before end of roasting time.
Orange marmalade	12 oz	

Approximate nutritive values per portion

Calories (kcal)	Protein (grams)	Carbohydrate (grams)	Fat (grams)	Cholesterol (mg)	Sodium (mg)	Iron (mg)	Calcium (mg)
720	83.4 (48%)	19.2 (11%)	32.3 (41%)	286	372	4.2	57

Note   ■   Other glazes may be substituted for orange glaze. See p. 392 for apricot, brown sugar, and honey glazes.

CHICKEN AND SNOW PEAS OVER RICE

◼

Yield: 50 portions   *Portion:* 4 oz sauce + 4 oz rice

Ingredient	Amount	Procedure
Sugar, granulated	2 Tbsp	Combine in steam-jacketed kettle or saucepan.
Cornstarch	8 oz	
Pepper, black	1¼ tsp	
Ground ginger	1¼ tsp	
Garlic powder	¼ tsp	
Water	1¼ gal	Stir in water, soy sauce, and chicken base.
Soy sauce	¾ cup	Cook until clear and thickened.
Chicken base	4 oz	Turn off heat. Cover and keep warm.
Chicken strips or cubes, uncooked	12 lb 8 oz	Stir-fry chicken in hot oil until lightly browned and cooked through. Drain off any liquid.
Green onions, sliced	6 oz	Add chicken and vegetables to reserved sauce.
Mushrooms, canned, drained	1 lb 10 oz	Cook for about 1 minute until snow peas are hot.
Snow peas, frozen	2 lb 12 oz	
Rice, converted	3 lb 8 oz	Cook rice according to directions on p. 430.
Water	4¼ qt	Serve 4 oz sauce over 4 oz cooked rice.
Salt	2 Tbsp	
Margarine	2 Tbsp	

Approximate nutritive values per portion							
Calories (kcal)	Protein (grams)	Carbohydrate (grams)	Fat (grams)	Cholesterol (mg)	Sodium (mg)	Iron (mg)	Calcium (mg)
275	22.4 (34%)	36.3 (54%)	3.6 (12%)	49	1044	2.4	49

CHICKEN AND VEGETABLE STIR-FRY

Yield: 50 portions   *Portion:* 6 oz chicken and vegetables + 4 oz rice

Ingredient	Amount	Procedure
Water	1 qt	Combine. Set aside.
Chicken base	2 oz	
Soy sauce	2 cups	
Cornstarch	6 oz	
Ginger, ground	1 Tbsp	
Garlic, fresh, minced	2 Tbsp	
Red pepper, crushed	½ tsp	
Vegetable oil	½ cup	
Sesame seed oil	¼ cup	
Chicken breast, cut in strips	6 lb 4 oz	Lightly coat bottom of fry pan with oil. Heat to 375°F. Add chicken. Stir-fry until lightly brown and cooked (about 3 minutes).
Broccoli florets and sliced stems	3 lb 8 oz	Add vegetables to chicken. Stir fry 3–4 minutes until tender crisp. Add sauce from first step. Cook, stirring constantly until mixture is thickened and thoroughly heated.
Carrots, sliced diagonally	3 lb	
Mushrooms, fresh, sliced	1 lb 4 oz	
Green onions, sliced in 1-inch lengths	12 oz	
Water chestnuts, canned sliced, drained	3 lb	
Rice, converted	3 lb 8 oz	Cook rice according to directions on p. 430.
Water, boiling	4¼ qt	
Salt	2 Tbsp	
Margarine	2 Tbsp	

Approximate nutritive values per portion

Calories (kcal)	Protein (grams)	Carbohydrate (grams)	Fat (grams)	Cholesterol (mg)	Sodium (mg)	Iron (mg)	Calcium (mg)
247	14.2 (23%)	39.7 (64%)	3.5 (13%)	25	1178	2.7	58

Variations
- **Pork Stir-Fry.** Substitute pork loin for chicken.
- **Vegetable Stir-Fry.** Delete chicken. Increase vegetables to 6 lb total. May use summer squash, zucchini, celery, cauliflower, snow peas, or sweet peppers.
- **Beef and Broccoli Stir-Fry.** Delete carrots. Increase broccoli to 6 lb 8 oz. Substitute beef base for chicken base and beef strips for chicken breast.

SZECHWAN CHICKEN WITH CASHEWS

Yield: 50 portions   *Portion:* 6 oz chicken + 4 oz rice

Ingredient	Amount	Procedure
Vegetable oil	1 qt	Add ginger root and garlic to oil in stock pot.
Ginger root, fresh, sliced	½ oz	Heat, then remove ginger root and garlic and discard.
Garlic	3 cloves	
Chicken, uncooked, cut in cubes	6 lb	Add chicken to hot oil. Stir fry until chicken turns white, 3–5 minutes.
Green onions	1 lb 10 oz	Cut onions into 1-inch lengths.
Green peppers	4 lb	Cut peppers into 1-inch squares. Add to chicken mixture.
Mushrooms, pieces and stems, canned	4 lb	Add and stir fry 1–2 minutes.
Water chestnuts, sliced	1 lb	
Mushroom liquid plus water	1¾ qt	Combine and mix until smooth. Stir into chicken mixture. Cook and stir until thickened, 1–2 minutes.
Chicken base	1 oz	
Soy sauce	¼ cup	
Cornstarch	5 oz	
Pepper, cayenne	1 Tbsp	
Cashew nuts	1 lb	Stir in nuts and pimiento.
Pimiento, chopped	2 oz	
Rice, converted	3 lb 8 oz	Cook rice according to directions on p. 430.
Water, boiling	4¼ qt	Serve 6 oz chicken over 4 oz rice.
Salt	2 Tbsp	
Margarine or vegetable oil	2 Tbsp	

Approximate nutritive values per portion							
Calories (kcal)	Protein (grams)	Carbohydrate (grams)	Fat (grams)	Cholesterol (mg)	Sodium (mg)	Iron (mg)	Calcium (mg)
499	14.2 (11%)	38.2 (30%)	32.6 (58%)	44	654	3	53

CHICKEN CREPES

Yield: 50 portions   *Portion:* 2 crepes
Oven: 325°F   *Bake:* 10 minutes

Ingredient	Amount	Procedure
Margarine	1 lb 8 oz	Melt margarine in steam-jacketed or other large kettle.
Flour, all-purpose	12 oz	Add flour and salt. Blend and cook for 5 minutes.
Salt	1 oz (1½ Tbsp)	
Chicken Stock (p. 615) or milk	1½ gal	Gradually add stock, stirring constantly with wire whip.
Cooked chicken, diced	10 lb	Combine chicken, mushrooms, and seasonings.
		Add enough sauce to hold chicken together (1–2 qt).
Mushrooms, chopped	2 8-oz cans	Reserve remaining sauce to pour over crepes.
Worcestershire sauce	2 Tbsp	
Curry powder	2 Tbsp	
Salt	To taste	
Crepes (p. 141)	1 recipe	Make batter. Fry on lightly greased griddle, using No. 20 dipper (1¾ oz) of batter.
		Brown lightly on one side.
		Turn and cook to set batter.
		Place Crepes on trays, with waxed paper between layers. Hold for next step.
		Portion No. 20 dipper of chicken mixture onto each crepe; roll and place on baking sheets.
		Heat in 325°F oven for 10 minutes.
		Serve with remaining sauce, ladled on top.

Approximate nutritive values per portion							
Calories (kcal)	Protein (grams)	Carbohydrate (grams)	Fat (grams)	Cholesterol (mg)	Sodium (mg)	Iron (mg)	Calcium (mg)
411	27.4 (27%)	26.6 (26%)	21 (47%)	154	1055	2.7	102

Note ▪ 1 lb sautéed mushrooms may be added to sauce that is ladled over crepes.

Variations ▪ **Fruit Cheese Crepes.** Fill Crepes (recipe on p. 141) with 1½ Tbsp of the following mixture: 2 lb cream cheese, whipped and combined with 2 cups sour cream. Serve with frozen strawberries or raspberries, thickened slightly, or with prepared fruit pie filling, heated.

▪ **Spinach Crepes.** Omit chicken and sauce. Fill crepes with cooked Spinach Soufflé (p. 683). Serve with Cheese Sauce (p. 582) or Swiss Cheese and Mushroom Sauce (p. 583).

CHICKEN À LA KING

Yield: 50 portions   *Portion:* 6 oz (¾ cup)

Ingredient	Amount	Procedure
Cooked chicken	6 lb	Dice chicken.
Margarine Onions, minced	1 lb 12 oz 4 oz	Melt margarine in steam-jacketed or other large kettle. Add onions and sauté until tender.
Flour, all-purpose Salt Pepper, white	1 lb 4 oz 1 oz (1½ Tbsp) 1 tsp	Add flour and seasonings to onions. Stir and cook for 5 minutes.
Chicken Stock (p. 615) Milk	3 qt 2¼ qt	Add stock and milk, stirring constantly with wire whip. Cook until thickened.
Green pepper, chopped Pimiento, shredded Mushrooms, sliced, sautéed	4 oz 4 oz 1 lb	Add to sauce.
		Fold chicken gently into sauce. Check seasoning. Heat to serving temperature. Serve over biscuits, toast, or rice.

Approximate nutritive values per portion

Calories (kcal)	Protein (grams)	Carbohydrate (grams)	Fat (grams)	Cholesterol (mg)	Sodium (mg)	Iron (mg)	Calcium (mg)
283	19 (27%)	11.3 (16%)	17.6 (57%)	50	586	1.3	69

Notes
- 18–20 lb of chicken (AP) will yield approximately 6 lb cooked meat.
- ½ oz (¼ cup) dehydrated onions, rehydrated in ½ cup water, may be substituted for fresh onions (p. 55).

Variations
- **Creamed Chicken.**   Delete green pepper, pimiento and mushrooms.
- **Tuna à la King.**   Substitute tuna for chicken. Stir carefully to avoid breaking up tuna pieces.
- **Turkey à la King.**   Substitute turkey for chicken.

HOT CHICKEN SALAD

Yield: 56 portions or 2 pans 12 × 20 × 2 inches or 50 individual casseroles   *Portion:* 5 oz
Oven: 350°F   *Bake:* 25–30 minutes

Ingredient	Amount	Procedure
Cooked chicken	6 lb	Dice chicken.
Celery, diced	4 lb	Combine and add to chicken. Mix lightly.
Onion, chopped	3 oz	Scale mixture into two 12 × 20 × 2-inch counter pans,
Almonds, browned and chopped coarsely	1 lb	7 lb per pan. If using individual casseroles, portion with No. 8 dipper.
Lemon juice	½ cup	
Lemon peel, grated	3 Tbsp	
Pepper, white	1 tsp	
Salt	1 Tbsp	
Mayonnaise	1½ qt	
Cheddar cheese, shredded	3 lb	Sprinkle cheese over top of salad mixture.
Potato chips, crushed	12 oz	Distribute potato chips uniformly over cheese. Bake at 350°F for 25–30 minutes, or until bubbly. Cut 4 × 7 or serve with No. 8 dipper.

Approximate nutritive values per portion

Calories (kcal)	Protein (grams)	Carbohydrate (grams)	Fat (grams)	Cholesterol (mg)	Sodium (mg)	Iron (mg)	Calcium (mg)
440	21.9 (20%)	7.3 (7%)	36.6 (74%)	80	491	1.4	223

Notes

- 18–20 lb of chicken (AP) will yield approximately 6 lb cooked meat.
- Swiss cheese may be substituted for cheddar cheese.
- 2 lb of the cheese may be added to the chicken mixture and 1 lb sprinkled on top.
- Should be served as soon as possible after preparation.

Variation

- **Hot Turkey Salad.**   Substitute turkey for chicken. A 16- to 18-lb turkey AP will yield approximately 6 lb cooked meat.

SCALLOPED CHICKEN

Yield: 48 portions or 2 pans 12 × 20 × 2 inches   *Portion:* 8 oz
Oven: 350°F   *Bake:* 30–40 minutes

Ingredient	Amount	Procedure
Cooked chicken	6 lb	Cut chicken into ½-inch pieces. Save for layering step.
Margarine Flour, all-purpose Chicken base	1 lb 8 oz 3 oz	Melt margarine in steam-jacketed or other kettle. Stir in flour and chicken base. Cook 5 minutes.
Water	1 gal	Add water to roux, while stirring with wire whip. Cook until thickened.
Eggs, beaten	12 (1 lb 5 oz)	When sauce is thick, add small amount of hot mixture to eggs, then stir into remainder of sauce. Save for layering step.
Dry bread, cubed Salt Pepper, black Sage, ground, or poultry seasoning	2 lb 6 oz 1 tsp 2 tsp 1½ tsp	Add seasonings to bread. Mix to distribute seasonings.
Margarine Celery, chopped Onion, chopped Chicken base	10 oz 8 oz 8 oz 2 oz	Sauté celery and onion in melted margarine. Stir in chicken base. Add to bread.
Water	2½ qt	Add water to bread. Toss lightly. Do not overmix.
		Place dressing, sauce, and chicken in 2 greased 12 × 20 × 2-inch counter pans, layered in each pan as follows: ■ 4 lb 8 oz dressing ■ 1¼ qt sauce ■ 3 lb chicken ■ 1¼ qt sauce
Cracker crumbs, coarse Margarine, melted	6 oz 3 oz	Mix crumbs and margarine and sprinkle on mixture, 4 oz per pan. Bake at 350°F for 30–40 minutes. Cut 4 × 6.

Approximate nutritive values per portion

Calories (kcal)	Protein (grams)	Carbohydrate (grams)	Fat (grams)	Cholesterol (mg)	Sodium (mg)	Iron (mg)	Calcium (mg)
335	21 (25%)	17.8 (21%)	19.8 (53%)	100	1007	2	48

Notes	■ Scalloped Turkey or Chicken may be made by preparing one recipe of Bread Dressing (p. 474) and scaling it in the following manner in each of two 12 × 20 × 2-inch pans. Scale 4 lb dressing into pans and spread evenly. Arrange 3 lb cooked turkey or chicken over dressing. Scale 4 lb dressing over turkey, spreading evenly. Bake at 325°F for 1 hour 15 minutes. Serve with Chicken Gravy (p. 586).

■ 1 oz (½ cup) dehydrated onions, rehydrated in ¾ cup water, may be substituted for fresh onions (p. 55).

Variation	■ **Scalloped Turkey.** Substitute turkey for chicken.

BRUNSWICK STEW

Yield: 50 portions or 3 gal   *Portion:* 8 oz (1 cup)

Ingredient	Amount	Procedure
Cubed fresh pork	2 lb AP	Brown pork. Drain off fat.
Cooked chicken	7 lb 8 oz	Cube chicken.
Celery, diced Carrots, diced Potatoes, diced Onions, finely 　chopped	1 lb 8 oz 2 lb 4 oz 2 lb 10 oz	Cook vegetables until partially done.
Margarine Flour, all-purpose	8 oz 8 oz	Melt margarine in steam-jacketed or other large kettle. Add flour and stir until smooth.
Chicken Stock 　(p. 615) Salt Pepper, white	1 gal 1 Tbsp 1½ tsp	Add stock gradually, stirring constantly with wire whip. Add chicken, pork, and vegetables. Simmer until vegetables are tender. Do not overcook.
Green peas, frozen	1 lb	Add peas. Cook an additional 5 minutes. Stew should be fairly thick. Serve in soup bowls or deep plates.

Approximate nutritive values per portion

Calories (kcal)	Protein (grams)	Carbohydrate (grams)	Fat (grams)	Cholesterol (mg)	Sodium (mg)	Iron (mg)	Calcium (mg)
252	24.5 (40%)	12.2 (20%)	11.1 (41%)	66	494	1.6	31

Note	■ If large fryers are used, cook 15 lb AP. Remove meat from bones and cube. Save broth for sauce.

SINGAPORE CURRY

Yield: 50 portions   *Portion:* 8 oz curry + 6 oz rice

Ingredient	Amount	Procedure
Cooked chicken	15 lb	Cut chicken into ¾-inch pieces. Reserve for later step.
Margarine Flour, all-purpose	1 lb 1 lb 4 oz	Melt margarine in steam-jacketed or other large kettle. Add flour and stir until smooth. Cook 5 minutes.

Chicken Stock
(p. 615)
Salt
Pepper, white
Curry powder
	5 qt
	
	1 tsp
	½ tsp
	2 oz
		Add stock gradually, stirring constantly with wire whip.
		    Cook until thickened.
		Add salt, pepper, and curry powder.
		Add chicken and stir gently to prevent breaking of
		    chicken pieces.
		Taste and add more seasonings as the chicken takes up
		    the curry flavor. It should be quite yellow and have a
		    distinct curry flavor.

Rice, converted Salt Water, boiling Margarine or vegeta- ble oil	5 lb 3 oz 6¼ qt 3 Tbsp	Cook rice according to directions on p. 430. This amount of rice will allow very generous servings.
French fried onion rings Tomatoes, fresh, sliced Bananas, cut in thick slices or chunks Pineapple chunks, drained Coconut, shredded or flaked Salted peanuts Chutney	50 servings 10 lb 10 lb 1 No. 10 can 1 lb 8 oz 1 lb 3 1-lb jars	Serve curried chicken over rice, with accompaniments. See directions for serving in Notes.

Approximate nutritive values per portion

Calories (kcal)	Protein (grams)	Carbohydrate (grams)	Fat (grams)	Cholesterol (mg)	Sodium (mg)	Iron (mg)	Calcium (mg)
881	48.8 (22%)	103 (47%)	31 (31%)	113	1334	5.9	100

Notes   ■ Shrimp, veal, lamb, or a combination of chicken and pork may be used, allowing 6 oz cooked meat per person.

■ For a Singapore Curry dinner, arrange foods on a buffet table in the following order: rice, curried chicken or other meat, and accompaniments in the order listed in the recipe. Each guest serves rice in the center of the plate, dips a generous serving of curried meat over the rice, and then adds accompaniments as desired.

CHICKEN POT PIE

Yield: 50 portions or 2 pans 12 × 20 × 2 inches   *Portion:* 8 oz
Oven: 400°F   *Bake:* 20–25 minutes

Ingredient	Amount	Procedure
Margarine Onions, chopped	12 oz 14 oz	Sauté onions in margarine in steam-jacketed or other large kettle.
Flour, all-purpose Pepper, black	1 lb 6 oz ½ tsp	Add flour and pepper to onions. Stir until blended. Cook 30 minutes.
Chicken Stock (p. 615)	1¼ gal	Add stock, stirring constantly with wire whip. Cook until thickened, stirring often. Check for seasoning. Add salt if necessary.
Cooked chicken	6 lb	Cut chicken into ½- to ¾-inch pieces. Add to sauce.
Celery, sliced Carrots, sliced	1 lb 8 oz 2 lb	Cook celery and carrots until partially done. Drain. Fold into sauce.
Green peas, frozen	2 lb	Add peas (uncooked) to chicken mixture. Mix carefully. Scale chicken into two 12 × 20 × 2-inch counter pans, 12 lb per pan.
Pastry (p. 254)	3 lb	Roll out 1 lb 8 oz Pastry to fit each pan. Place on chicken mixture and seal edges to pan. Bake at 400°F for 20–25 minutes or until crust is done.

Approximate nutritive values per portion

Calories (kcal)	Protein (grams)	Carbohydrate (grams)	Fat (grams)	Cholesterol (mg)	Sodium (mg)	Iron (mg)	Calcium (mg)
370	20.9 (23%)	26.1 (28%)	19.9 (49%)	45	590	2.5	34

Notes
■ 18–20 lb of chicken AP will yield approximately 6 lb cooked meat.
■ Chicken mixture may be topped with Baking Powder Biscuits (p. 118).
■ 1¾ oz (¾ cup) dehydrated onions, rehydrated in 1¼ cups water, may be substituted for fresh onions (p. 55).

Variation
■ **Turkey Pie.** Substitute turkey for chicken.

CHICKEN AND NOODLES

Yield: 50 portions or 2 pans 12 × 20 × 2 inches   *Portion:* 8 oz
Oven: 350°F   *Bake:* 30 minutes

Ingredient	Amount	Procedure
Cooked chicken	7 lb 8 oz	Cut chicken into ½-inch pieces.
Noodles Water, boiling Salt Vegetable oil	3 lb 3 gal 3 oz 1 Tbsp	Cook noodles according to directions on p. 407. Drain.
Margarine Onions, chopped	12 oz 2 oz	Melt margarine in a steam-jacketed or other large kettle. Add onions and sauté until tender.
Flour, all-purpose Salt	7 oz 1 Tbsp	Add flour and salt to onions. Stir until blended. Cook 5 minutes.
Milk or chicken stock (p. 615)	3½ qt	Add stock or milk gradually, stirring constantly with wire whip. Cook until thickened.
		Combine chicken, cooked noodles, and sauce. Scale into two 12 × 20 × 2-inch counter pans, 11 lb 12 oz per pan. Bake at 350°F for 30 minutes.

Approximate nutritive values per portion

Calories (kcal)	Protein (grams)	Carbohydrate (grams)	Fat (grams)	Cholesterol (mg)	Sodium (mg)	Iron (mg)	Calcium (mg)
331	25.1 (31%)	25.7 (32%)	13.6 (38%)	91	414	2.3	108

Notes

- 20–22 lb of chicken AP will yield approximately 7 lb 8 oz cooked meat.
- ¼ oz (2 Tbsp) dehydrated onion, rehydrated in ¼ cup water, may be substituted for fresh onions (p. 55).

Variations

- **Chicken and Noodles with Mushrooms.**   Add 2 lb sliced mushrooms, sautéed with the onions.
- **Pork and Noodle Casserole.**   Substitute 10 lb pork, diced and cooked, for chicken.
- **Turkey and Noodle Casserole.**   Substitute cooked turkey for chicken (cook 18- to 20-lb turkey).

CHICKEN AND RICE CASSEROLE

Yield: 50 portions or 2 pans 12 × 20 × 2 inches   *Portion:* 8 oz
Oven: 350°F   *Bake:* 1 hour

Ingredient	Amount	Procedure
Cooked chicken	6 lb	Dice chicken.
Rice, converted Water, boiling Salt Margarine or vegetable oil	2 lb 8 oz 2 qt 2 Tbsp 2 Tbsp	Cook rice according to directions on p. 430.
Margarine, melted Onion, chopped Celery, chopped Mushrooms, sliced	6 oz 3 oz 8 oz 1 lb	Sauté onion, celery, and mushrooms in margarine.
Flour, all-purpose	8 oz	Add flour to vegetables and stir to blend.
Milk Chicken Stock (p. 615) Pepper, white	1½ qt 2 qt ¼ tsp	Add milk and stock, stirring constantly with wire whip. Cook until thickened. Add pepper. Add salt if needed.
Almonds, slivered Pimiento, chopped	6 oz 3 oz	Add almonds, pimiento, and chicken to sauce. Combine carefully. Scale into two lightly greased 12 × 20 × 2-inch baking pans, 10 lb 8 oz per pan.
Bread crumbs Margarine, melted Cheddar cheese, shredded	9 oz 3 oz 6 oz	Combine bread crumbs, margarine, and cheese. Sprinkle over mixture in pans, 9 oz per pan. Bake at 350°F for 1 hour or until heated through.

Approximate nutritive values per portion

Calories (kcal)	Protein (grams)	Carbohydrate (grams)	Fat (grams)	Cholesterol (mg)	Sodium (mg)	Iron (mg)	Calcium (mg)
320	21.1 (26%)	28.9 (36%)	12.9 (36%)	53	585	2.2	105

Notes

- 18–20 lb of chicken AP will yield approximately 6 lb cooked meat.
- Sliced water chestnuts may be substituted for almonds.
- Chopped parsley may be sprinkled over the baked product just before serving.
- ¼ oz (2 Tbsp) dehydrated onions, rehydrated in ¼ cup water, may be substituted for fresh onions (p. 55).

TURKEY AND DUMPLINGS ◼

Yield: 48 portions or 2 pans 12 × 20 × 2 inches   *Portion:* 8 oz

Ingredient	Amount	Procedure
Margarine Onions, chopped	14 oz 1 lb	Melt margarine in steam-jacketed or other kettle. Sauté onions under tender.
Flour, all-purpose Pepper, black	1 lb 8 oz 1½ tsp	Stir flour and pepper into onions. Cook for 5–10 minutes, stirring often.
Water Chicken base	1½ gal 6 oz	Add water and chicken base to mixture in kettle. Cook until thickened, stirring often.
Turkey, cooked	6 lb 10 oz	Cut turkey into ½-inch cubes. Add to sauce.
Celery, chopped Carrots, sliced	1 lb 10 oz 2 lb 4 oz	Steam celery and carrots until tender-crisp. Fold into turkey mixture. Scale into two 12 × 20 × 2-inch pans, 13 lb per pan.

Steamed Dumplings

Flour, all-purpose Baking powder Salt	2 lb 4 oz 3 oz 2 Tbsp	Combine flour, baking powder, and salt in mixer bowl. Mix until blended.
Eggs, beaten Milk Parsley, fresh, chopped Poultry seasoning	5 (9 oz) 1½ qt 1 oz 2 tsp	Combine eggs, milk, and seasonings. Add to dry ingredients and mix only until blended. Portion 4 × 6 with No. 24 dipper onto turkey and gravy. Steam for 20 minutes.

Approximate nutritive values per portion

Calories (kcal)	Protein (grams)	Carbohydrate (grams)	Fat (grams)	Cholesterol (mg)	Sodium (mg)	Iron (mg)	Calcium (mg)
336	12.8 (21%)	34.7 (42%)	13.5 (37%)	62	1593	2.9	205

Notes

- Steam as soon as dumplings are portioned onto gravy. Product holds well after cooking.
- 2 oz (1 cup) dehydrated onions, rehydrated in 1½ cups water, may be substituted for fresh onions (p. 55).

TURKEY DIVAN

Yield: 50 portions   *Portion:* 3 oz broccoli + 2 oz turkey
Oven: 350°F   *Bake:* 15 minutes

Ingredient	Amount	Procedure
Broccoli spears, fresh or frozen	10 lb EP	Cook broccoli according to directions on p. 643. Arrange in 3-oz portions in two 12 × 20 × 2-inch counter pans.
Margarine, melted	8 oz	Pour margarine over broccoli.
Salt Pepper, black Parmesan cheese, grated	1 oz (1½ Tbsp) ½ tsp 9 oz	Sprinkle broccoli with salt, pepper, and cheese.
Cooked turkey breast	7 lb	Slice turkey in 2-oz portions. Arrange turkey slices over broccoli. Serving will be easier if edges of turkey slices are tucked under the broccoli portions.
Margarine Flour, all-purpose Salt	12 oz 6 oz 1 oz (1½ Tbsp)	Melt margarine. Add flour and salt. Stir until blended. Cook 5 minutes.
Milk	3 qt	Add milk, stirring constantly with wire whip. Cook until thickened.
Egg yolks, slightly beaten	1 cup	Add egg yolks to sauce. Stir until blended. Pour sauce over turkey and broccoli. Bake at 350°F for 15 minutes or until bubbly and golden brown.

Approximate nutritive values per portion

Calories (kcal)	Protein (grams)	Carbohydrate (grams)	Fat (grams)	Cholesterol (mg)	Sodium (mg)	Iron (mg)	Calcium (mg)
289	19.6 (27%)	11.9 (16%)	18.7 (57%)	105	1009	1.8	219

Note   ■   Turkey or Chicken Stock may be substituted for part of milk in sauce; salt may then need to be reduced.

LIME TARRAGON TURKEY STEAK ■

Yield: 50 steaks   *Portion:* 6 oz
Grill: 350°F   *Grill:* 4–7 minutes per side

Ingredient	Amount	Procedure
Turkey steaks, 6-oz	50	
Vegetable oil	3½ cups	Combine oil, liquids and spices in stainless steel container.
Lime juice, frozen, reconstituted	1 qt	Pour over turkey steaks and refrigerate for several hours or overnight. Turn if necessary to make sure both sides of turkey are coated.
Cooking sherry	2 cups	
Garlic cloves, minced	4 oz	
Chives, chopped	3 oz	
Tarragon, dried whole leaves	½ cup	
Salt	2½ oz	
Pepper, black	5 tsp	
Dry mustard	1 tsp	
Worcestershire sauce	¼ cup	
Water	2 cups	

Drain marinade from turkey steaks.
Preheat grill to 350°F.
Grill steaks until done, 4–7 minutes per side.

Approximate nutritive values per portion							
Calories (kcal)	Protein (grams)	Carbohydrate (grams)	Fat (grams)	Cholesterol (mg)	Sodium (mg)	Iron (mg)	Calcium (mg)
217	32.5 (62%)	1.9 (4%)	7.9 (34%)	74	207	1.9	38

Variation   ■ **Creole Turkey Steaks.** Prepare Creole Spice Mixture, p. 335 (Creole Baked Fish). Dip turkey steaks in melted margarine, then sprinkle generously with spice mixture. Grill steaks until done, 4–7 minutes per side.

CORN BREAD DRESSING

Yield: 50 portions or 1 pan 12 × 20 × 2 inches *Portion:* 4 oz
Oven: 375°F *Bake:* 20–30 minutes

Ingredient	Amount	Procedure
Corn Bread (p. 132) ⅓ recipe	3 lb 10 oz	Prepare Corn Bread. Crumble.
Bread, cubed or torn	1 lb 12 oz	Crumble bread. Add to Corn Bread.
Margarine Onions, chopped Celery, chopped	4 oz 1 lb 1 lb 8 oz	Melt margarine in steam-jacketed or other kettle. Add onions and celery. Sauté until vegetables are tender. Add bread.
Chicken base Water, hot Salt (see Note) Poultry seasoning Pepper, black	2 oz 3 qt 1 tsp 1 Tbsp 1 tsp	Combine chicken base, water, and seasonings. Pour over bread mixture. Stir to moisten.
		Scale mixture (12 lb) into lightly greased 12 × 20 × 2-inch pan. Bake at 375°F for 20–30 minutes or until hot. Serve with No. 12 dipper.

Approximate nutritive values per portion

Calories (kcal)	Protein (grams)	Carbohydrate (grams)	Fat (grams)	Cholesterol (mg)	Sodium (mg)	Iron (mg)	Calcium (mg)
157	3.8 (10%)	22.9 (58%)	5.7 (32%)	15	546	1.2	87

Note ■ If chicken base is highly salted, reduce or delete salt in recipe.

BREAD DRESSING (OR STUFFING)

■

Yield: 50 portions or 1 pan 12 × 20 × 2 inches   *Portion:* 4½ oz
Oven: 325°F   *Bake:* 1 hour 15 minutes

Ingredient	Amount	Procedure
Onion, chopped	1 lb	Sauté onion and celery in margarine until lightly browned.
Celery, chopped (optional)	1 lb	
Margarine	1 lb	
Water (see Notes)	1 gal	Add water, chicken base, and seasonings to sautéed vegetables. Heat until hot.
Chicken base	3 oz	
Salt (see Notes)	1 Tbsp	
Pepper, black	1 Tbsp	
Poultry seasoning (see Notes)	1 Tbsp	
Thyme, ground	1 Tbsp	
Dry bread, cubed	3 lb 12 oz	Add bread gradually to vegetable mixture, tossing lightly until thoroughly mixed. Avoid overmixing, which causes dressing to be soggy and compact.
		Scale dressing (15 lb) into lightly greased 12 × 20 × 2-inch pan. Bake at 325°F for 1 hour 15 minutes. Serve with No. 10 dipper.

Approximate nutritive values per portion

Calories (kcal)	Protein (grams)	Carbohydrate (grams)	Fat (grams)	Cholesterol (mg)	Sodium (mg)	Iron (mg)	Calcium (mg)
159	3.8 (9%)	17.1 (41%)	9.1 (49%)	0	757	1.4	41

Notes
- The amount of liquid will depend on the dryness of the bread.
- If chicken base is highly salted, reduce or delete salt in recipe.
- Sage may be used for part or all of the poultry seasoning.

Variations
- **Apple Stuffing.** Add 1 lb finely chopped apples. Reduce bread cubes to 3 lb 4 oz.
- **Chestnut Stuffing.** Add 1 lb 4 oz cooked chestnuts, chopped. Reduce bread to 3 lb 8 oz. Substitute 2 qt milk for 2 qt water.
- **Mushroom Stuffing.** Reduce celery and onions to 8 oz each. Sauté 2 lb fresh mushrooms with the vegetables.

- **Nut Stuffing.**   Add 2 cups chopped almonds or pecans that have been browned lightly in 4 oz melted margarine. Substitute 1 qt milk for 1 qt water.
- **Oyster Stuffing.**   Add 1 lb 8 oz oysters.
- **Raisin Stuffing.**   Add 1 lb seedless raisins.
- **Sausage Stuffing.**   Reduce bread cubes to 3 lb 4 oz. Add 2 lb sausage, cooked and drained, and 1 lb tart apples, peeled and chopped.

11

Salads and Salad Dressings

SALADS

Salads are popular menu items, versatile enough to be served in a variety of ways. Appetizer salads are served as a first course and play an important role in stimulating the appetite and creating a sense of anticipation for the remainder of the meal. The visual appearance as well as taste and flavor combinations must be considered.

Accompaniment salads are considered side dishes to the entree. These salads should be selected carefully so that the flavor and food group characteristics will be in harmony. Many accompaniment salads have traditional significance: turkey and cranberries, pork and applesauce, sandwiches and pasta or potato salad, and fish and cole slaw.

Entree salads offer an upscale approach to dining, particularly at the noon meal and among the health-conscious patron. Other than bread or crackers and a beverage, the salad is generally the only menu item, making the ingredient selections especially important. Entree salads should be substantial in the amount of food provided, and they may include at least one ingredient that is a source of protein. The salad should be fresh in appearance and attractive in design.

A salad course is occasionally offered after the entree. The objective is to "cleanse the palate" in preparation for dessert. The salad served as a separate course should be light and refreshing. Fruit salads or lightly dressed greens are appropriate choices.

With the exception of separate course salads, which are always served, the presentation of salads may be either individually placed and served or self-service from a buffet line or salad bar. The choice of method will depend on the clientele's expectations and objectives of the foodservice.

ARRANGED SALADS

Arranged salads may be served to the patron either after they have been seated, on the table as for some banquets and catered functions, or à la carte from a cafeteria counter. Regardless of the serving method, the principles of placed salad construction are the same:

- Select plates or bowls that are appropriately sized and will add to the salad's attractiveness.
- Place salad green underliners on the dish. The curly edge should be at the back and top of the salad and should not extend over the edge of the plate. Tossed green salads may not include an underliner but are decorated with an attractive garnish.
- To gain height, place chopped lettuce on the underliner and under salad ingredients.
- Place the main salad ingredients neatly on the plate. They should be prepared and arranged attractively with careful consideration given to color and balance.
- Garnish appropriately to give accent in color and flavor.
- Keep salad chilled and sprinkle with dressing just before serving or pass dressings for individual service.

TABLE 11.1   Basic salad bar components

Item	Number of choices	Ideas for choices
Greens	1 bowl	Combine 2–3 different greens. See p. 480 for types of greens.
Fresh vegetables	2–3 containers	Alfalfa sprouts, broccoli, cabbage (red or green), carrots, cauliflower, celery, cucumber, green onions, mushrooms, peppers (red, green, yellow), radishes, snow peas, tomatoes, zucchini
Toppings	1–2 containers	Bacon bits, garbanzo beans, croutons, pickles, olives, peanuts, raisins, sesame seeds, sunflower seeds
Gelatin	1–2 molds	Fruit or vegetable gelatin salads
Fruit, pasta, and vegetable salads	2–3 containers	Rice salads, potato salad, pasta salad, ambrosia, applesauce, other fruit or marinated vegetable salads
Protein	1–2 containers	Chopped hard-cooked eggs, egg salad, meat salad, cottage cheese, shredded cheese
Crackers and bread	1 basket	Variety crackers, warm breads
Dressings	3–4 containers	Blue cheese, buttermilk, French, Italian, oil and vinegar, Thousand Island

Notes	■ More choices are appropriate if the salad bar or buffet serving area can accommodate the variety.
	■ Select salads that will retain quality during the serving period.

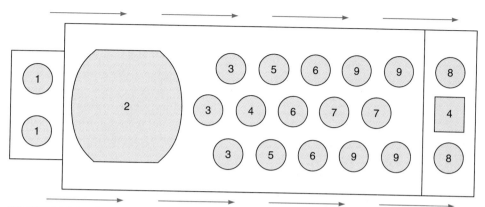

FIGURE 11.1   Suggested salad bar arrangement: (1) plates and bowls; (2) greens; (3) fresh vegetables; (4) toppings; (5) gelatins; (6) fruit, pasta, and vegetable salads; (7) protein salads; (8) crackers and breads; (9) dressings.

SALAD BARS

Salad bars have expanded the selection of items available and are very popular in many types of foodservices. For a salad bar to be successful, enough variety must be offered so patrons will enjoy creating their own salad. See Table 11.1 for components of a basic salad bar and Figure 11.1 for a suggested salad bar arrangement. Basic rules for salad bars are as follows:

- The salad bar should be equipped with a sneeze guard, and standards of good sanitation should be maintained. A clean plate should be used each time a patron visits the salad bar. Serving utensils should facilitate sanitary service.

- A salad bar should look well-supplied throughout the serving period. This purpose can be accomplished by selecting appropriate-size containers and resupplying them when one-half to two-thirds empty. Avoid arranging too few food items on plates that will look empty after only a few servings are taken.

- Spills, drips, and misplaced food items should be cleaned up regularly. Arranging food containers so spills are reduced is important, and items that could become unsightly should be placed where they will be easy to reach without spilling onto other food. Correct serving utensils will help eliminate untidiness.

- The selections should be varied and creative enough to appeal to many different people. The variety of items offered should be changed periodically when serving repeat customers.

SALAD INGREDIENTS AND THEIR PREPARATION

Many salad ingredients may be purchased that have some or all of the preliminary preparation completed. Torn salad greens, prepared grapefruit sections, and diced or chopped vegetables are examples. In many foodservices, however, salad ingredients are prepared on the premises. Information about the most commonly used salad ingredients and their preparation is provided in the following sections.

Salad Greens

Many types of greens may be used for salads. The most common ones are described here and shown in Figure 11.2.

Arugula   Narrow, bright-green leaves with a spicy, peppery taste. Small leaves are the mildest. Combines well with mild greens. Sometimes used as an underliner garnish.

Belgian or French Endive   An upright, thin, elongated stock resembling a spear. Off-white or pale green color. Served typically as a small, separate course salad after a meal or as a decorative component of an arranged salad.

Bibb Lettuce   Small cup-shaped lettuce with a deep rich green color that blends into whitish green near the core. Flavor is buttery and sweet, texture delicate and tender.

Boston Lettuce   Soft, pliable leaf and delicate sweet flavor. Not as tender or sweet as Bibb lettuce. Deep green outside blending to light yellow near the core.

Cabbage   *Green:* Pale green tough crisp leaves generally used in slaws. *Red:* Purple crisp leaves; may be used with other greens to add color. *Chinese:* Very light green, crinkly leaves with a delicate cabbage flavor. May be used sparingly in a tossed green salad.

Cress   A hot peppery leaf that resembles radish leaves. Mix sparingly with mild greens.

Curly Endive   A bunchy head with narrow, ragged-edge leaves. Mild center leaves, slightly bitter outer leaves. Used sparingly in combination salads. Primary use for underliners and garnishing.

Escarole   A variety of endive with broad leaves that do not curl at the tips. Texture is coarse and slightly tough, flavor somewhat bitter. May be mixed sparingly with other greens or served alone.

Iceberg Lettuce (Head Lettuce)   The most popular lettuce used in green salads. Firm, round heads ranging in color from bright to light green. Mild in flavor; combines well with other greens.

FIGURE 11.2 Salad greens. Photo courtesy of the United Fresh Fruit and Vegetable Association.

Kale   A hardy dark green, curly leaf. Often used as a garnish for salad bars, or may be cooked.

Leaf Lettuce   Most varieties have soft, fragile leaves with curly edges. Color varies by variety but may be all green or various shades of red. May be mixed with other greens in a combination salad or used as an underliner or garnish.

Mâche   Spoon-shaped leaves, sweet, nutty flavor. Mix with other young tender greens, Belgian endive, or serve alone.

Radicchio   Brilliant, ruby-colored leaves with a bitter peppery taste. Combine with mild tender greens, Belgian endive, or arugula.

Romaine or Cos   Long, loaf-shaped head and long, narrow leaves. Tender, sweet and tasty. Coarse dark green outer leaves and golden-yellow inner ones. Used in combination salads.

Spinach   Curly, dark green, flat leaves, with a bold flavor. Very young tender leaves are often served fresh, more mature leaves cooked.

Watercress   Dark green, glossy leaves with a spicy flavor. Used as a garnish or mixed with tender leaf greens.

Preparation

Greens should be clean, crisp, chilled, and well drained. It may be necessary to separate leaves for thorough washing. Wash in a spray of water or in a large container of tepid water. Repeat if necessary until all grit disappears. Shake off excess water, drain thoroughly, and refrigerate. Draining in a colander or on a rack placed on a baking sheet will

 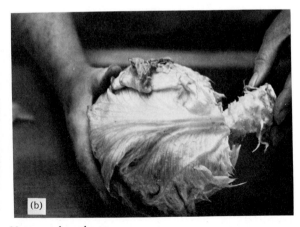

FIGURE 11.3   Coring head lettuce. (a) Hit stem end of lettuce sharply on flat surface. (b) Remove loosened core.

FIGURE 11.4   Preparing leaf lettuce. (a) Wash lettuce under cold running water. (b) Remove stem end by cutting with a sharp knife. (c) Place leaf end up in a perforated pan to drain. Chill 2 to 3 hours to crisp.

keep the greens from standing in water while chilling. Cover with a clean damp cloth or plastic to prevent dehydration.

When preparing head lettuce for garnish, remove stem end or core (Figure 11.3). Hold inverted head under cold, running water to loosen tightly wrapped leaves. Do not soak. Turn heads open-side down to drain. Separate the leaves and stack 6 or 7 leaves to a nest. Invert and pack in a covered container or plastic bag. Refrigerate 2 hours or more to complete crisping.

Leaf lettuce is convenient to use for salad liners. Wash lettuce thoroughly (Figure 11.4). Cut stem end and place in perforated pan to drain. Chill 2 to 3 hours for crisping.

Spinach should be carefully examined, removing veins and tough stems. Discard all dry, yellow, wilted, or decayed leaves. Wash first in tepid water, then in cold, as many times as necessary to remove sand.

Herbs

Today, there is much interest by the public in foods, not only from the standpoint of their nutritive values but also in their texture, flavor, color, and design. People have become more discerning about the aroma and flavors of prepared dishes. Fresh herbs, now in season year-round, awaken the senses and create exciting new taste sensations.

A wide variety of fresh herbs is available, as shown in Figure 11.5. Most herbs can be purchased also as dried leaves, seeds, or ground. Descriptions of the most common fresh herbs follow.

Basil   Used to season poultry, seafood, and most Italian dishes. Basil is one of the few herbs that enhances in flavor when heated. Varieties include sweet basil, dark opal, and lemon basil.

Chervil   Delicate herb with subtle celery-licorice taste. Essential for fines herbes.

Chives   Delicate herb with mild onion or garlic taste. Used for decorative purposes or chopped for use in food products.

Cilantro   Also known as Chinese parsley, cilantro is spicy and used in Chinese and Mexican cooking. Coriander is the seed of the cilantro plant.

Dill   A feathery leaf herb used often as an attractive garnish.

Lemon Balm   Herb with sweet lemon flavor. Used in mild soups and summer salads.

Lemon Grass   Straw-like stalk with a lemony flavor. Used often with fish, shellfish, chicken, and vinaigrettes.

Marjoram   An herb similar to oregano but with a more delicate flavor. Used with fish, poultry, and with vegetable dishes.

Oregano   Used to season Italian foods, it has a sharp flavor, tasting somewhat like thyme.

Parsley   Crisp herb with a strong flavor. Available in two common varieties, the stronger Italian flat leaf and curly leaf. Curly parsley is used most often for garnishing.

Rosemary   A very fragrant herb. Imparts a subtle sweet and savory flavor.

Sage   Silver green leaf herb with a musky flavor. Used often as a garnish when fresh.

Tarragon   Fresh tarragon is multibranched with narrow, twisted leaves. Has a slight licorice flavor.

Thyme   A very aromatic herb with minty tea-like flavor. Varieties include lemon, orange, English and French thyme. Popular for creole and poultry dishes.

See Appendix B for information on dried herbs.

FIGURE 11.5   Fresh herbs. Photo courtesy of United Fresh Fruit and Vegetable Association.

Salad Vegetables

Whether vegetables are used raw or cooked, strive to preserve their shape, color, flavor, and crispness. Marinating in a well-seasoned French dressing adds flavor. Following are preparation instructions for salad vegetables.

Artichokes   Wash. Cut 1 inch off tops. Cut off stem and bottom leaves. Trim the outer leaves if necessary. With a melon ball cutter or spoon, remove and discard the fuzzy center core (choke). Dip in lemon juice immediately.

Asparagus   Break or cut off tough end of stems. Thoroughly wash remaining portions. Lower scales may harbor sand; remove if necessary. Lower stalks may be peeled. Blanch asparagus by immersing in boiling water for 2 minutes. Remove quickly and dip in cold water. Drain.

FIGURE 11.6   Cruciferous vegetables. Clockwise from lower right are Brussels sprouts, kohlrabi, red cabbage, turnips, broccoli, cauliflower, and nappas. Photo courtesy of the United Fresh Fruit and Vegetable Association.

Broccoli   Wash. If insects are present, soak in salt water for 15–20 minutes (1 oz salt per 1 gal water). Trim blemished outer leaves and stalks. Discard tough stalk end. Cut florets from flower end. Stem may need to be sliced or split.

Cabbage   Remove outer leaves. Wash heads and cut into 4–6 pieces. Remove center core. Shred remaining portions as desired with a long sharp knife or shredder. Crisp in ice water 15–30 minutes, drain well.

Carrots   Peel and remove blemishes. Cut into wedges, rounds, or strips. For *curls* cut long, paper-thin slices. Roll each strip around finger, fasten with pick, and chill in ice water for several hours.

Cauliflower   Remove all leaves and cut away dark spots. Separate into florets, leaving 1-inch stem. If insects are present, soak in salt water (1 oz salt or $\frac{1}{3}$ cup vinegar per gal of water). See Figure 11.6.

Celery   Separate outer stalks from the heart. (Outer stalks may be used for soup.) Wash, trim, and remove bruised and blemished parts and strings. To dice, cut lengthwise. Several stalks may be cut at one time. Place on board and cut crosswise with a French knife. For celery *curls* or fans, cut celery into 2½ inch lengths. Make lengthwise cuts ⅛ inch apart about 1 inch in length on one or both ends of celery strips. Place in ice water for about 2 hours before serving. For celery *rings,* cut celery into 2 inch lengths and then into pieces ⅛ inch thick. Place in ice water for several hours. Each strip of celery will form a ring.

Cucumbers   Wash and peel, or score lengthwise with a fork. Crisp and let stand in salted ice water 15 minutes. Cut into slices or wedges.

Garlic   Separate cloves from bulb. Trim root end and peel cloves.

Jicama   See Figure 11.7. Peel and cut into strips, slices, or cubes.

Mushrooms   Do not soak in water or scrub. Trim bottoms of stems. Rinse quickly in cold water just before serving. Adding a small amount of acid to the water will help keep mushrooms white. See Figure 11.8 for common types of mushrooms.

Onions   Pour water over onions to cover. Under water, remove outer layer of the bulb, firm root end, and all bruised or decayed parts. See Figure 11.9 for common types of onions.

Peppers (Green, Red, Yellow)   Wash. Remove seeds, membrane, and stems. Cut into desired shapes. To make *rings,* cut into thin crosswise slices. To make *sticks,* cut peppers lengthwise into narrow strips.

Potatoes   Peel. Remove eyes and blemishes. Cut into cubes and cook; or wash, cook with skins on, peel, and dice.

FIGURE 11.7   Less commonly used produce adds variety to the menu.
Photo courtesy of the United Fresh Fruit and Vegetable Association.

Agaricus bisporus   The most popular, all-purpose mushroom, with a delicate flavor and firm texture. Ranges in color from brown to cream to snow white and varies in size from tiny button to medium and large. Serve the entire mushroom (cap and stem) raw in salads or as a garnish. The natural cup-like configuration of large mushroom caps makes them ideal for stuffing. Bake, fry, sauté, stir-fry, grill, or broil.

Italian brown (Cremini)   Dense, earthy flavor distinguishes this mushroom from its close relation, the Agaricus bisporus. Preparation methods remain the same as the Agaricus bisporus.

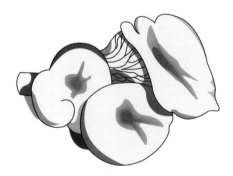

Oyster   An oyster-like tasting mushroom with a silky consistency and graceful appearance. Serve whole. The flavor of the mushroom is enhanced by sautéing in butter. In preparations calling for extensive cooking, such as soups, sauces, and stews, add this mushroom toward the end to preserve its delicate texture.

Shiitake   The distinctive woodsy or smoky flavor of this popular cultivated "exotic" mushroom complements red meats, sauces, soups, and oriental sir-fry dishes. Use only the spongy, full-bodied caps, and discard the fibrous, tough stems.

FIGURE 11.8   Common types of mushrooms. Courtesy of Monterey Mushrooms, Inc. and The American Mushroom Institute.

FIGURE 11.9   Types of onions used in food production. Photo courtesy of the United Fresh Fruit and Vegetable Association.

Radishes   Cut off root and stem end with a sharp knife. Wash. To make *accordions*, cut long radishes not quite through into 10–12 narrow slices. Place in ice water. Slices will fan out accordion-style. To make *roses*, leave an inch or two of the green stem. Cut 4 or 5 petal-shaped slices around the radish from cut tip to center. Place radishes in ice water, and petals will open.

Tomatoes   Wash, remove core, stem and flower end. If peeling, place in wire basket and dip in boiling water 10–20 seconds or until skins begin to loosen. Dip in ice water immediately and remove skins and core. Chill.

Fresh Fruits

Apples   Wash, pare, core, remove bruises and spots. If the skins are tender and the desired color, do not pare.

To dice, cut into rings and dice with sectional cutter. Drop diced pieces into salad dressing, lemon, pineapple, or other acid fruit juice to prevent discoloration. If diced apple is placed in fruit juice, drain before using in a salad.

To section, cut into uniform pieces, with the widest part of the section not more than ½ inch thick. Remove core from each section. If the peeling has not been removed, score it in several places to facilitate cutting when it is served. Prevent discoloration by the same method as for diced apples, only do not use salad dressing.

Apricots   Cut into halves or sections and remove seed. Remove skins if desired.

Avocados   If hard, ripen at room temperature. Peel shortly before serving, cut into halves or quarters, and remove seed. Slice, dice, or cut into balls. Dip into French dressing or lemon juice to prevent discoloration.

Bananas   Remove skins and bruised or discolored parts. Cut into strips, sections, wedges, or slices. Dip each piece into pineapple juice, other acid fruit juice, or salad dressings to prevent discoloration.

Cantaloupes and Other Melons   Pare, dice, and cut into balls, or cut into uniform wedges or strips (Figure 11.10).

Cherries and Grapes   Wash, drain, halve, and remove seeds. To frost, brush with slightly beaten egg white. Sprinkle with sugar. Let dry before using.

Grapefruit   For sections, select large grapefruit, wash and dry. Cut off a thick layer of skin from the top and bottom. Place grapefruit on cutting board, start at the top, and cut toward the board (Figure 11.11). Always cut with a downward stroke and deeply enough to remove all the white membrane. Turn grapefruit while cutting. When paring is completed and pulp is exposed, remove sections by cutting along the membrane of one section to the center of the fruit.

Kiwi   Remove fuzzy skin with a very sharp paring knife. Slice, chop, dice, or cut into wedges.

FIGURE 11.10   Melons are available in many varieties. (clockwise from top left): watermelon, casaba, Persian, Crenshaw, cantaloupe, honeydew, and Santa Claus. Photo courtesy of the United Fresh Fruit and Vegetable Association.

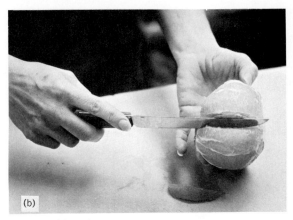

FIGURE 11.11   Peeling and sectioning grapefruit: (a) Cut layer of peel from top and bottom of grapefruit. Using a sharp knife, remove peel. Cut with a downward stroke and deeply enough to remove all the white membrane. (b) Section grapefruit by cutting along membrane of one section to the center of the fruit. Turn the knife and force the blade along the membrane of the next section.

Mango   Cut in half and remove the seed carefully. Scoop the flesh out of the shell. For chunks, peel back the skin from each mango half and cut as desired.

Melons   Melons may be peeled or served with the peel on. Remove seeds from the center of the melon using a spoon. Remove watermelon seeds with a sharp tipped knife or fork.

Oranges   Peel, section as grapefruit, or slice or dice (Figure 11.11).

Papaya   Cut papaya in half lengthwise, remove the seeds and scoop out of shell. For rings, slice the papaya into circles and neatly cut out seeds at the center of each ring.

Peaches   Remove skins only a short time before using. Peel or submerge in boiling water for a few seconds and remove skins. Chill. Cut into halves, wedges, or slice. Drop into acid fruit juice to prevent discoloration.

Pears   Peel and remove core and seeds a short time before serving. Cut into halves, wedges, or slices. Dipping in lemon juice or other acid fruit juice will prevent oxidation and discoloration.

Pineapple   Remove crown by holding pineapple in one hand and crown in the other, then twisting in opposite directions (Figure 11.12). Trim top of pineapple and cut off base. Using a sharp knife, remove peel by using a downward cutting motion. Remove eyes by making narrow wedge-shaped grooves into the pineapple. Cut diagonally around the fruit, following the pattern of the eyes. Cut away as little of the fruit as possible. Cut pineapple vertically into eighths, then cut hard center core from each spear. To make pineapple chunks, cut each spear into pieces of the desired size.

FIGURE 11.12   Preparing fresh pineapple: (a) Remove crown by holding pineapple in one hand and crown in the other, then twisting in opposite directions. (b) Trim top of pineapple and cut off base. Using a sharp knife, remove peel by using a downward cutting motion. (c) Remove eyes by making narrow wedge-shaped grooves into the pineapple. Cut diagonally around the fruit, following the pattern of the eyes. Cut away as little of the fruit as possible. (d) Cut pineapple vertically into eighths, then cut the hard center core from each spear. To make pineapple chunks, cut each spear into pieces of the desired size.

Pomegranates   Cut open and remove seeds. Discard peeling and white membrane.

Star Fruit (Carambola)   Wash and slice. Use for garnish.

Canned Fruit

Select whole pieces uniform in size and shape and with a firm appearance. Drain. If cubes or sections are desired, cut into pieces uniform in size and shape with well-defined edges. Pieces should not be too small.

Other Foods

Almonds, Blanched   To blanch almonds, cover with boiling water and let stand until skins will slip. Drain. Cover with cold water and rub off skins. Place skinned almonds between dry clean towels to remove water.

Almonds, Toasted   Spread blanched almonds in a shallow pan in a thin layer. Heat at 250°F, stirring occasionally until nuts are light brown in color.

Cheese   Grate, shred, or cut in tiny cubes; or soften and put through a pastry tube.

Chicken or Turkey   Cook, remove skin, gristle, and bone. Cut into ⅓-inch cubes. Marinate if desired. Mix with dressing and other ingredients just before serving.

Eggs   Hard-cook (p. 308). Use whole, halved, sliced, or sectioned. Slice or mince whites. Force yolks through ricer.

Fish   Cook, remove skin and bones. Flake. Marinate if desired. Mix with dressing just before serving. See p. 332 for preparation of crab, lobster, and shrimp.

Flowers   Edible flowers are commonly used for garnish. See Appendix A for color information.

Meat   Cut cooked meat into ⅓-inch cubes. Marinate with French or Italian dressing. Mix just before serving.

Nuts   Heat in hot oven to freshen if desired. Use whole, shredded, or chopped.

SALAD DRESSINGS

A salad dressing's function is to "dress" or accent the salad; it should not mask the flavor of the other ingredients. Care should be taken to choose an appropriate dressing to match the salad.

The basic ingredients of a salad dressing are oil combined with vinegar or another acid liquid such as lemon juice. Cooking oils such as canola, corn, safflower, soybean, and sesame seed are often used for salad dressing. Other oils that are commonly used include avocado, nut, olive, and oils flavored with herbs, peppers, or other seasonings. Variation in the vinegar will change the salad dressing flavor. Types of vinegars that may be used for making salad dressings include:

balsamic—a sweet tart vinegar with a dark color and intense flavor, imported from Modena, Italy

cider—caramel colored and made from apples

distilled—a strong vinegar made from grains

fruit—white wine or cider vinegar with added fruit such as blueberries, cranberries, limes, raspberries, or strawberries

herb—wine or cider vinegar that has been flavored with herbs such as basil, tarragon, thyme, rosemary, or dill

wine—a mild vinegar made from red or white wine.

Added to the basic ingredients are emulsifiers or binding agents. Temporary emulsifiers may be herbs, spices, sugar, and salt. More permanent emulsifiers include egg yolk, as in mayonnaise, or a starch paste and egg mixture, as in a cooked dressing.

Salad dressings should be stored in glass, plastic, or stainless steel containers with tight-fitting lids at 40°F.

VEGETABLE AND PASTA SALAD RECIPES

BASIC MIXED GREEN SALAD

Yield: 50 portions or 10 lb   *Portion:* 3 oz

Ingredient	Amount	Procedure
Head lettuce (iceberg)	7 lb	Cut or tear lettuce and other greens into bite-sized pieces. (Use sharp steel-bladed knife if greens are cut.)
Leaf lettuce, Bibb or romaine	3 lb	
French dressing, oil and vinegar, or Italian dressing	1¼ qt	Just before serving, toss lightly with dressing, or portion greens into individual salad bowls, 3 oz per bowl, and serve with choice of dressings.

Approximate nutritive values per portion

Calories (kcal)	Protein (grams)	Carbohydrate (grams)	Fat (grams)	Cholesterol (mg)	Sodium (mg)	Iron (mg)	Calcium (mg)
125	1 (3%)	2.9 (9%)	12.7 (88%)	0	8	0.7	31

Notes

- Any combination of salad greens may be used. For contrast, mix dark greens with light, crisp with tender, and smooth leaves with curly. With pale iceberg lettuce, use dark green spinach, romaine, curly endive, or red-tipped leaf lettuce. See p. 480 for major types of salad greens.

- If serving on a salad bar, place greens in a large bowl and offer choice of dressing and garnishes (see p. 478).

Variations

- **Hawaiian Tossed Salad.** To 7 lb mixed greens, add sections from 8 grapefruit, 8 oranges, 4 avocados, and 1 fresh pineapple, cubed. Serve with Honey French Dressing, p. 548.

- **Salad Greens with Grapefruit.** Place 3 oz greens in each bowl. Garnish each with 3 sections of pink grapefruit. Serve with Poppy Seed Dressing (p. 551) or French Dressing (p. 547).

- **Spinach Salad.**   Use 4 lb lettuce and 6 lb fresh spinach, 2 bunches green onions, sliced, and 12 eggs, hard-cooked and sliced. To serve, toss lightly with French Dressing (p. 547) or Dijon Mustard Vinaigrette Dressing (p. 549) and portion into bowls. Sprinkle with bacon (1 lb) that has been diced, cooked until crisp, and drained.
- **Spinach Mushroom Salad.**   Use 10 lb fresh spinach (may be part lettuce), 4 lb fresh mushrooms, sliced, and 2 bunches green onions, sliced. Toss lightly with French Dressing (p. 547) just before serving. Sprinkle with cooked crumbled bacon if desired.

TOSSED VEGETABLE SALAD

Yield: 50 portions or 10 lb   *Portion:* 3 oz

Ingredient	Amount	Procedure
Salad greens (see Notes)	7 lb	Wash greens thoroughly and drain. Tear into bite-sized pieces.
Salad ingredients (see Notes)	3 lb	Add salad ingredients to greens. Toss lightly. Portion into individual salad bowls or plates, 3 oz per portion.
Garnish (see Notes)	As needed	Garnish salads if desired.
Salad dressing (see Notes)	1¼ qt	Serve with choice of dressings. If preferred, French, Italian, or oil-and-vinegar dressing may be added to the salad just before serving.

Notes

- **Salad Greens.**   Select one or more: iceberg, leaf, Bibb, Boston, or romaine lettuce, endive, spinach, escarole, celery cabbage, watercress. See Figure 11.2 for kinds of lettuce and p. 480 for types of salad greens.
- **Salad Ingredients.**   Select one or more: diagonally sliced asparagus, sliced Jerusalem artichokes, artichoke hearts, sliced avocado, bean sprouts, garbanzo beans, broccoli florets or sliced broccoli stems, chopped or shredded red cabbage, shredded or thinly sliced carrots, sliced cauliflower florets, sliced or diced celery, sliced or diced cucumbers, sliced green onions or scallions, diced green peppers, sliced fresh mushrooms, cooked green peas, sliced radishes, halved cherry tomatoes, fresh tomato wedges, sliced water chestnuts, sliced zucchini.
- **Garnishes.**   Alfalfa sprouts, crumbled crisp-cooked bacon, crumbled blue cheese, shredded cheddar cheese, cheese strips or cubes, seasoned croutons, sliced or quartered hard-cooked eggs, sliced olives, onion rings (fresh or French fried), parsley sprig, green pepper rings or strips, sunflower seeds, cherry tomatoes, tomato wedges, toasted wheat germ.
- **Salad Dressings.**   French, Italian, Oil and Vinegar, Roquefort, Thousand Island, Buttermilk, Horseradish Cream, Green Peppercorn Cream, Sour Cream Basil.

TENDER GREENS AND FRUIT SALAD

Yield: 50 portions   *Portion:* 3 oz greens + 1 oz fruit

Ingredient	Amount	Procedure
Tender greens (see Notes)	10 lb	Toss greens with fruit. Sprinkle garnish on top. Serve with dressing to the side.
Fruit (see Notes)	4 lb	
Garnish (see Notes)	1 lb–1 lb 8 oz	
Salad dressing (see Notes)	1¾ qt	

Approximate nutritive values per portion							
Calories (kcal)	Protein (grams)	Carbohydrate (grams)	Fat (grams)	Cholesterol (mg)	Sodium (mg)	Iron (mg)	Calcium (mg)
275	4.7 (7%)	21.6 (30%)	20.2 (63%)	10	412	1.3	111

Notes
- **Greens:** Bibb lettuce, heart of romaine, tiny spinach leaves.
- **Fruit:** Blueberries, strawberries, raspberries, fresh pineapple, apples.
- **Garnish:** Blue cheese, feta cheese, walnuts, pecans.
- **Dressing:** Sweet Sesame Vinaigrette (p. 550), Golden Fruit Dressing (p. 551).

CARRIFRUIT SALAD

Yield: 50 portions or 4½ qt   *Portion:* ⅓ cup (3 oz)

Ingredient	Amount	Procedure
Carrots, shredded	4 lb 8 oz	Combine ingredients. Mix lightly.
Pineapple tidbits, drained	2 lb 12 oz	
Flaked coconut	8 oz	
Miniature marshmallows	9 oz	
Mayonnaise	2¼ cups	Mix mayonnaise and cream.
Light cream (half-and-half)	¾ cup	Add to salad ingredients. Mix carefully. Serve with No. 12 dipper.

Approximate nutritive values per portion							
Calories (kcal)	Protein (grams)	Carbohydrate (grams)	Fat (grams)	Cholesterol (mg)	Sodium (mg)	Iron (mg)	Calcium (mg)
143	1.1 (3%)	13.9 (37%)	9.9 (60%)	7	75	0.5	21

Notes
- 8 oz raisins may be added.
- Best when served the same day it is prepared.

CARROT RAISIN SALAD

Yield: 50 portions or 4¼ qt   *Portion:* ⅓ cup (2½ oz)

Ingredient	Amount	Procedure
Raisins	8 oz	Soften raisins in steamer or simmer in a small amount of water for about 3 minutes.
Carrots, raw	7 lb AP	Peel carrots. Shred or grind coarsely. Combine with raisins.
Mayonnaise Salad dressing Salt	2 cups 2 cups 1 Tbsp	Mix mayonnaise, salad dressing, and salt. Add to carrot-raisin mixture. Mix lightly. Serve with No. 12 dipper.

Approximate nutritive values per portion

Calories (kcal)	Protein (grams)	Carbohydrate (grams)	Fat (grams)	Cholesterol (mg)	Sodium (mg)	Iron (mg)	Calcium (mg)
141	1 (3%)	13.4 (36%)	10.3 (62%)	8	267	0.5	22

Variations

- **Carrot Celery Salad.** Omit raisins. Use 5 lb ground carrots. Add 2 lb chopped celery and 2 oz sugar.

- **Carrot-Apple-Celery Salad.** Substitute 3 lb diced apples for 2 lb carrots.

- **Carrot-Celery-Cucumber Salad.** Use 4 lb 8 oz shredded carrots, 1 lb 8 oz chopped celery, and 1 lb 8 oz chopped cucumber.

- **Carrot Coconut Salad.** Substitute 1 lb toasted coconut for raisins.

TRIPLE BEAN SALAD

Yield: 50 portions or 6 qt   *Portion:* ½ cup (4 oz)

Ingredient	Amount	Procedure
Green beans, French style or cut, canned	3 lb 8 oz (1 No. 10 can)	Drain green and wax beans thoroughly.
Wax beans, cut, canned	2 lb 8 oz	
Kidney beans, canned	3 lb	Rinse kidney beans. Drain.
Onion, thinly sliced	1 lb 8 oz	Add onion, green pepper, and seasonings to beans. Cover. Marinate overnight in the refrigerator.
Green pepper, diced	6 oz	
Vinegar, cider	3 cups	
Sugar, granulated	1 lb 8 oz	
Salt	1 Tbsp	
Pepper, black	1 Tbsp	
Celery seed	1 Tbsp	
Salad oil	1 cup	Just before serving, drain vegetables well. Add oil and toss lightly. Serve with No. 12 dipper.

Approximate nutritive values per portion

Calories (kcal)	Protein (grams)	Carbohydrate (grams)	Fat (grams)	Cholesterol (mg)	Sodium (mg)	Iron (mg)	Calcium (mg)
166	4.3 (10%)	29.2 (66%)	4.8 (24%)	0	276	1.2	41

Variations   ■ **Cauliflower Bean Salad.**   Delete kidney beans and add 3 lb cauliflower florets, slightly cooked.

■ **Oriental Bean Salad.**   Delete kidney beans. Add 1 lb 8 oz cooked red beans, drained and rinsed, and 1 lb 8 oz bean sprouts.

BROWN BEAN SALAD

Yield: 50 portions or 6 qt   *Portion:* ½ cup (4 oz)

Ingredient	Amount	Procedure
Eggs, hard-cooked (p. 308)	12	Peel and dice eggs.
Brown or kidney beans	1½ No. 10 cans	Rinse beans with cold water. Drain.
Celery, diced	12 oz	Combine with beans. Add eggs.
Green pepper, chopped	3 oz	
Onion, minced	3 oz	
Pickle relish	10 oz	
Salad dressing or mayonnaise	3 cups	Combine and add to bean mixture. Mix lightly.
Salt	2 Tbsp	
Vinegar, cider	¾ cup	

Approximate nutritive values per portion

Calories (kcal)	Protein (grams)	Carbohydrate (grams)	Fat (grams)	Cholesterol (mg)	Sodium (mg)	Iron (mg)	Calcium (mg)
203	7 (13%)	17.7 (34%)	12.1 (52%)	59	688	2	40

Notes

- 4 lb dried beans, cooked according to directions on p. 646, may be substituted for canned beans.
- Great Northern or pinto beans may be substituted for half of the kidney beans.

GARBANZO BEAN SALAD

Yield: 50 portions or 4½ qt   *Portion:* ⅓ cup (3 oz)

Ingredient	Amount	Procedure
Garbanzo beans, canned	2 lb 8 oz	Rinse beans with cold water. Drain.
Red beans, canned	1 lb 8 oz	
Pinto beans, canned	2 lb	
Celery, sliced	1 lb	Combine with beans.
Cucumbers, peeled and sliced	12 oz	
Green onions, sliced	5 oz	
Radishes, sliced	8 oz	
Black olives, sliced	4 oz	
French Dressing (p. 547)	1 cup	Pour dressing over bean mixture. Toss lightly. Marinate for 2 hours.

Approximate nutritive values per portion

Calories (kcal)	Protein (grams)	Carbohydrate (grams)	Fat (grams)	Cholesterol (mg)	Sodium (mg)	Iron (mg)	Calcium (mg)
80	2.9 (14%)	9.7 (47%)	3.7 (40%)	0	260	1.3	29

Notes
- Cooked Great Northern beans may be substituted for garbanzo beans.
- Vegetable Marinade (p. 605) may be substituted for French Dressing.

Variation
- **Garbanzo Pasta Salad.** Delete pinto beans. Cook 8 oz shell marcaroni to the *al dente* stage. Combine with other ingredients.

COLE SLAW

Yield: 50 portions or 4½ qt   *Portion:* ⅓ cup (2½ oz)

Ingredient	Amount	Procedure
Cabbage	7 lb EP (9 lb AP)	Shred or chop cabbage.
Vinegar, cider	3 cups	Combine vinegar, sugar, and seasonings.
Sugar, granulated	1 lb 8 oz	Add to cabbage. Mix lightly.
Salt	1 oz (1½ Tbsp)	
Celery seed	1 Tbsp	

Approximate nutritive values per portion

Calories (kcal)	Protein (grams)	Carbohydrate (grams)	Fat (grams)	Cholesterol (mg)	Sodium (mg)	Iron (mg)	Calcium (mg)
67	0.8 (4%)	18 (94%)	0.1 (2%)	0	204	0.5	34

Note
- Red cabbage may be substituted for part or all of green cabbage.

Variations
- **Cauliflower Broccoli Salad.** Substitute 3 lb 8 oz EP each of cauliflower and broccoli florets for the cabbage. Add 3 oz chopped onion. Serve soon after preparing.
- **Green Pepper Slaw.** Add 4 oz chopped green pepper, 2 oz chopped onion, and 4 Tbsp celery seed.
- **Oriental Cole Slaw.** Substitute ⅓ recipe Sesame Seed Dressing (p. 547) for dressing given in recipe.

CREAMY COLE SLAW

Yield: 50 portions or 4¼ qt   *Portion:* ⅓ cup (2½ oz)

Ingredient	Amount	Procedure
Cabbage	7 lb EP (9 lb AP)	Shred or chop cabbage.
Mayonnaise or salad dressing	2 cups	Combine and add to cabbage. Mix lightly. Serve with No. 12 dipper.
Light cream, half-and-half	2 cups	
Vinegar, cider	½ cup	
Sugar, granulated	4 oz	
Salt	1 oz (1½ Tbsp)	
Pepper, white	½ tsp	

Approximate nutritive values per portion

Calories (kcal)	Protein (grams)	Carbohydrate (grams)	Fat (grams)	Cholesterol (mg)	Sodium (mg)	Iron (mg)	Calcium (mg)
100	1.2 (5%)	6.5 (25%)	8.3 (71%)	9	257	0.4	43

Variations
- **Cabbage Apple Salad.** See p. 518.
- **Cabbage Carrot Slaw.** Reduce cabbage to 5 lb. Add 1 lb shredded or chopped carrots, 8 oz chopped green pepper, and 4 oz chopped onion.
- **Cabbage-Pineapple-Marshmallow Salad.** To 4 lb shredded or chopped cabbage, add 2 lb pineapple tidbits, drained, 1 lb miniature marshmallows, and a dressing made of 2 cups mayonnaise or salad dressing and 2 cups cream, whipped.
- **Creamy Cauliflower-Broccoli Salad.** Substitute 3 lb 8 oz EP each of cauliflower and broccoli for the cabbage. Add 3 oz chopped green onion. Garnish with cherry tomatoes.

SLICED CUCUMBER AND ONION IN SOUR CREAM

Yield: 50 portions or 4¼ qt   *Portion:* ⅓ cup (2½ oz)

Ingredient	Amount	Procedure
Cucumbers	5 lb	Cut cucumbers and onions in thin slices.
Onions	8 oz	
Sour cream	3 cups	Blend rest of ingredients to form a thin cream dressing.
Mayonnaise	3 cups	Pour over cucumbers and onions. Mix lightly.
Salt	1½ tsp	
Sugar, granulated	3 Tbsp	
Vinegar, cider	¾ cup	

Approximate nutritive values per portion							
Calories (kcal)	Protein (grams)	Carbohydrate (grams)	Fat (grams)	Cholesterol (mg)	Sodium (mg)	Iron (mg)	Calcium (mg)
135	0.9 (3%)	3.6 (10%)	13.5 (87%)	14	148	0.3	26

Note   ■   This cream dressing may be used as a dressing for lettuce.

Variation   ■   **German Cucumbers.**   Reduce onions to 4 oz. Delete cream dressing. Pour mixture of 1 cup vinegar, ½ cup water, 1 Tbsp salt, and 8 oz sugar over cucumbers and onions. Marinate at least 1 hour.

MARINATED MUSHROOMS

Yield: 50 portions   *Portion:* 2¾ oz

Ingredient	Amount	Procedure
Mushrooms, fresh, small	6 lb	Clean mushrooms and trim ends. Leave whole.
Water	1 qt	Combine water and lemon juice.
Lemon juice	½ cup	Bring to a boil. Add mushrooms and blanch for 1–3 minutes. Drain and immerse in cold water. Drain.
Vegetable Marinade (p. 605)	1½ qt	Pour marinade over mushrooms. Refrigerate for 2–3 hours. Drain off most of the marinade before serving.

Approximate nutritive values per portion							
Calories (kcal)	Protein (grams)	Carbohydrate (grams)	Fat (grams)	Cholesterol (mg)	Sodium (mg)	Iron (mg)	Calcium (mg)
21	1.2 (18%)	3.1 (45%)	0.8 (27%)	0	30	0.8	6

Note	■	Before serving, mushrooms may be tossed with fresh minced parsley or other fresh herb.
Variations	■	**Marinated Asparagus.** Blanch fresh asparagus spears (see above). Marinate. To serve, drain and arrange 3–5 spears on plate with Bibb lettuce liner. Garnish with lemon twist or pimiento strip.
	■	**Marinated Green Beans.** Cover whole green beans with marinade. If fresh green beans are used, cook until tender-crisp.
	■	**Vegetable Collage.** Pour 3 cups Italian Salad Dressing (p. 547) or Vegetable Marinade (p. 605) over: 2 lb broccoli florets, 2 lb cauliflower florets, 12 oz sliced celery, 1 lb 8 oz cherry tomatoes cut in half, 2 lb sliced zucchini, 1 lb sliced green onions, 6 oz sliced carrots, and 1 lb 8 oz sliced black olives. Marinate in refrigerator for 4 hours, but if salad is to be held longer than that, add broccoli shortly before serving. Add 1 lb cooked crumbled bacon and toss.

MARINATED TOMATOES

Yield: 50 portions   *Portion:* 2 slices

Ingredient	Amount	Procedure
Tomatoes, fresh, peeled	6 lb	Cut peeled tomatoes into ½-inch slices. Place in bottom of 12 × 20 × 2-inch pan.
Onion, chopped	¾ cup	Combine. Pour over tomato slices.
Garlic, minced	3 cloves	Cover tightly. Refrigerate if storing for later use.
Parsley, chopped	⅓ cup	
Basil, crumbled, dried	1 Tbsp	
Sugar, granulated	1 Tbsp	
Salt	2 tsp	
Pepper, black	1½ tsp	
Olive oil	2 cups	
Vinegar, red wine or balsamic	1½ cups	

Approximate nutritive values per portion

Calories (kcal)	Protein (grams)	Carbohydrate (grams)	Fat (grams)	Cholesterol (mg)	Sodium (mg)	Iron (mg)	Calcium (mg)
97	0.6 (2%)	4.6 (18%)	8.9 (79%)	0	175	0.7	17

Notes	■	⅓ cup fresh basil may be substituted for dried.
	■	Salad oil may be substituted for olive oil.
Variation	■	**Fresh Tomato Relish.** Cut peeled tomatoes in half and squeeze out most of the seeds. Chop coarsely and stir into the marinade.

MARINATED CARROTS

Yield: 50 portions   *Portion:* ⅓ cup (3 oz)

Ingredient	Amount	Procedure
Carrots, fresh, cut in ¼-inch slices	5 lb	Cook carrots until tender-crisp. Drain.
Tomato soup	2 cups	Combine and heat to boiling point.
Sugar, granulated	1 lb	Pour over warm carrots.
Salad oil	½ cup	Marinate for at least 4 hours.
Vinegar, cider	1½ cups	
Salt	2 tsp	
Pepper, black	1 tsp	
Prepared mustard	1 Tbsp	
Worcestershire sauce	1 Tbsp	
Onions, chopped	12 oz	
Green pepper, chopped	3 oz	

Approximate nutritive values per portion							
Calories (kcal)	Protein (grams)	Carbohydrate (grams)	Fat (grams)	Cholesterol (mg)	Sodium (mg)	Iron (mg)	Calcium (mg)
80	0.7 (3%)	15.6 (72%)	2.4 (25%)	0	143	0.4	16

Notes
- Frozen crinkle-sliced carrots, cooked until tender-crisp, may be substituted for fresh carrots.
- Marinated carrots will keep in the refrigerator for a week.

MARINATED GARDEN SALAD

Yield: 50 portions or 8 lb   *Portion:* ⅓ cup (2½ oz)

Ingredient	Amount	Procedure
Carrots, sliced	1 lb EP	Steam carrots just until tender-crisp. Drain.
Cauliflower, fresh	2 lb EP	Cut cauliflower into florets.
Broccoli spears	2 lb EP	Cut broccoli into florets and slice stems.
Mushrooms, fresh	1 lb	Clean mushrooms. Cut large mushrooms in half. Combine all vegetables.

French Dressing (p. 547)	1½ qt	Combine dressing and seasonings.
		Pour over vegetables.
Dill weed	¼ oz	Marinate at least 2 hours.
Basil, dried, crumbled	1 Tbsp	
Oregano, dried, crumbled	1 tsp	

Approximate nutritive values per portion

Calories (kcal)	Protein (grams)	Carbohydrate (grams)	Fat (grams)	Cholesterol (mg)	Sodium (mg)	Iron (mg)	Calcium (mg)
145	1.4 (4%)	8.5 (23%)	12.4 (74%)	3.7	461	0.7	25

Note   ■ Peel broccoli stems before slicing if they appear tough.

SPINACH CHEESE SALAD

Yield: 50 portions   *Portion:* 3 oz

Ingredient	Amount	Procedure
Spinach, chopped, frozen	3 lb	Thaw spinach. Squeeze out excess moisture and drain.
Eggs, hard-cooked (p. 308)	10	Peel and chop eggs coarsely.
Onion, chopped	6 oz	Add onions, celery, cheese, and eggs to spinach. Mix lightly.
Celery, chopped	8 oz	
Cheddar cheese, shredded	1 lb	
Mayonnaise or salad dressing	1¼ qt	Combine mayonnaise and seasonings.
		Pour over spinach mixture. Mix lightly.
Salt	2 tsp	Refrigerate for 2 hours.
Hot pepper sauce	2 tsp	Serve with No. 12 dipper.
Vinegar, cider	2 Tbsp	
Horseradish	⅔ cup	

Approximate nutritive values per portion

Calories (kcal)	Protein (grams)	Carbohydrate (grams)	Fat (grams)	Cholesterol (mg)	Sodium (mg)	Iron (mg)	Calcium (mg)
221	4.8 (8%)	3.1 (6%)	21.7 (86%)	65	343	0.8	118

BASIC PASTA SALAD

Yield: 50 portions   *Portion:* 4 oz

Ingredient	Amount	Procedure
Pasta	3 lb 8 oz (AP)	Cook pasta according to directions on p. 407. Do not overcook. Pasta should be *al dente*.
Water, boiling	3½ gal	
Salt	3 oz	There should be approximately 9 lb cooked pasta. Information on cooked weights of pasta is given on p. 407.
Vegetable oil	2 Tbsp	
Dressing	1½–1¾ qt	Add dressing and toss gently to mix.
Vegetables and/or other ingredients	1 lb 8 oz–2 lb	Fold in other ingredients. Chill.

Suggested Ingredients

- **Pasta:** Rotini, rigatoni, shell macaroni, elbow macaroni, radiatore, wheels. See p. 401 for other pasta choices.

- **Dressing:** Vinaigrette and variations (p. 549), Lemon Basil (p. 549), Lime Salad Dressing (p. 549), Pepper Cream (p. 543), Green Peppercorn (p. 543), Thousand Island (p. 543), Italian (p. 547), Sour Cream Basil (p. 543).

- **Vegetables (cooked until tender crisp):** Asparagus cuts, broccoli florets, carrot coins, Italian green beans, snow peas, sugar snap peas.

- **Vegetables (raw):** Avocado slices or chunks, broccoli, cauliflower, chives, cucumbers, green peppers, red onion rings, parsley, radishes, summer squash slices, tomatoes, water chestnuts, zucchini slices or strips.

- **Other:** Chicken strips, beef strips, pepperoni slices, ham, crabmeat, scallops, shrimp, turkey, olives, pickles, cheese.

Note

- Yield for this recipe may vary, depending on the shape of the pasta used and the amount of vegetable and other ingredients added.

MACARONI SALAD

Yield: 50 portions or 6 qt   *Portion:* ½ cup (4 oz)

Ingredient	Amount	Procedure
Elbow macaroni	2 lb 8 oz	Cook macaroni according to directions on p. 407.
Water, boiling	2½ gal	Rinse in cold water. Drain well after rinsing.
Salt	2 Tbsp	(Should be 6 lb 10 oz cooked macaroni.)
Vegetable oil	1 Tbsp	
French Dressing (p. 547)	2 cups	Combine. Pour over macaroni and let marinate overnight.
Salt	¾ tsp	
Vinegar, cider	½ cup	
Eggs, hard-cooked (p. 308)	12	Peel and coarsely chop eggs.
Green peppers, chopped	6 oz	Add vegetables, cheese, and eggs to marinated macaroni.
Celery, chopped	1 lb 4 oz	
Onions, chopped	6 oz	
Pimiento, chopped and drained	3 oz	
Cheddar cheese, diced or shredded	1 lb	
Salad dressing	1 lb	Combine dressing and relish.
Sweet pickle relish, drained	10 oz	Pour over macaroni mixture. Mix carefully to combine. Serve with No. 10 dipper.

Approximate nutritive values per portion							
Calories (kcal)	Protein (grams)	Carbohydrate (grams)	Fat (grams)	Cholesterol (mg)	Sodium (mg)	Iron (mg)	Calcium (mg)
234	7 (12%)	25.6 (42%)	12.1 (44%)	64	623	1.3	90

Note   ■ Other types of pasta may be substituted for elbow macaroni. (See p. 401.)

Variations   ■ **Chicken and Pasta Salad.**   Delete cheese, pickle relish, and eggs. Cook 2 lb 8 oz fettuccine or other type of pasta according to directions on p. 407. Add 3 lb cooked chicken, diced.

■ **Ham and Pasta Salad.**   Delete eggs. Add 2 lb cooked ham, diced.

ITALIAN PASTA SALAD

■

Yield: 50 portions   *Portion:* ½ cup (4 oz)

Ingredient	Amount	Procedure
Rotini or other pasta	2 lb 8 oz	Cook pasta according to directions on p. 407.
Water, boiling	2½ gal	Rinse in cold water. Drain.
Salt	2 Tbsp	
Vegetable oil	1 Tbsp	
Thousand Island Dressing (p. 543)	1¾ qt	Combine dressing and seasonings. Pour over pasta. Mix gently.
Basil, dried, crumbled	1 Tbsp	Chill.
Salt	1 Tbsp	
Garbanzo beans, canned	8 oz	Drain and rinse beans. Add to pasta mixture.
Tomatoes, fresh, cut in wedges	1 lb 8 oz	Add vegetables and olives to pasta mixture. Toss gently. Refrigerate until served.
Cucumbers, peeled and sliced	1 lb	
Cauliflower, fresh, sliced	8 oz	
Black olives, large, pitted	4 oz	

Approximate nutritive values per portion							
Calories (kcal)	Protein (grams)	Carbohydrate (grams)	Fat (grams)	Cholesterol (mg)	Sodium (mg)	Iron (mg)	Calcium (mg)
164	1,5 (4%)	11.4 (27%)	13 (70%)	11	418	0.8	19

Note   ■   An oil-base dressing may be substituted for Thousand Island Dressing.

CHILLED FETTUCCINE VINAIGRETTE

Yield: 50 portions   *Portion:* 5 oz

Ingredient	Amount	Procedure
Fettuccine	3 lb 6 oz	Cook fettuccine according to directions on p. 407.
Water	3½ gal	Drain.
Salt	2 Tbsp	There should be 10 lb cooked fettuccine.
Vegetable oil	2 Tbsp	
Yogurt, plain, nonfat	2 lb	Blend yogurt and vinaigrette well.
Vinaigrette dressing	2 qt	Pour over hot fettuccine. Toss, using tongs, until all pasta is coated with dressing. Cover and chill until service.

Approximate nutritive values per portion

Calories (kcal)	Protein (grams)	Carbohydrate (grams)	Fat (grams)	Cholesterol (mg)	Sodium (mg)	Iron (mg)	Calcium (mg)
336	5.2 (6%)	26.8 (31%)	23.6 (62%)	1	438	1.4	53

Notes

- Serve Fettuccine Vinaigrette as an accompaniment to a chilled poultry breast. Add a colorful fruit garnish.

- Bottled Italian salad dressing may be substituted for vinaigrette dressing.

Variation

- **Marinated Fettuccine.**   Prepare as for Chilled Fettuccine Vinaigrette. After the yogurt and dressing are added, heat in oven. Serve hot.

POTATO SALAD

■

Yield: 50 portions or 7 qt   *Portion:* ½ cup (4 oz)

Ingredient	Amount	Procedure
Potatoes, peeled	10 lb EP (12 lb AP)	Cook potatoes until tender. Dice while warm.
Salad oil Vinegar, cider Lemon juice Prepared mustard Sugar, granulated Salt Hot pepper sauce	½ cup ½ cup 1 Tbsp 2 Tbsp 3 oz 1 Tbsp Few drops	Make a marinade of oil, vinegar, lemon juice, and seasonings. Add to warm potatoes and mix gently. Marinate until cold.
Eggs, hard-cooked (p. 308), diced Celery, diced Onion, finely chopped Pepper, black	12 1 lb 8 oz ½ tsp	Add eggs, celery, onion, and pepper to marinated potatoes. Mix lightly.
Mayonnaise	2 cups	Add mayonnaise. Mix carefully to blend. Chill at least 1 hour before serving. Serve with No. 10 dipper.

Approximate nutritive values per portion

Calories (kcal)	Protein (grams)	Carbohydrate (grams)	Fat (grams)	Cholesterol (mg)	Sodium (mg)	Iron (mg)	Calcium (mg)
189	3.3 (7%)	21.2 (44%)	10.6 (49%)	56	214	0.6	20

Notes

- 2 cups French Dressing may be substituted for the marinade given in the recipe.
- Sour cream or yogurt may be substituted for half of the mayonnaise.
- Potatoes may be cooked with skins on, then peeled. Use 12 lb AP.
- 4 oz pickle relish, chopped pimiento, or chopped green pepper may be added.

Variation

- **Sour Cream Potato Salad.**   Reduce eggs to 8 and mayonnaise to 1 cup. Add 2 cups sour cream, 1 tsp celery seed, and 12 oz peeled, sliced cucumbers.

HOT POTATO SALAD

Yield: 50 portions   *Portion:* ⅔ cup (6 oz)

Ingredient	Amount	Procedure
Potatoes	12 lb EP (15 lb AP)	Wash potatoes and trim as necessary. Steam until just tender, about 30 minutes. Peel and slice.
Bacon	1 lb	Dice bacon. Cook until crisp. Drain. Reserve fat.
Onion, chopped	8 oz	Sauté onion in bacon fat.
Flour, all-purpose	4 oz	Add flour to onions and stir until well mixed. Cook 5 minutes.
Sugar, granulated	1 lb	Mix sugar, spices, vinegar, and water. Boil 1 minute.
Salt	2½ oz	Add to fat-flour mixture gradually while stirring.
Pepper, black	2 tsp	Cook until slightly thickened.
Celery seed	1 Tbsp	
Vinegar, cider	3 cups	
Water	1 qt	
		Add hot dressing to warm potatoes and bacon. Mix lightly. Serve hot.

Approximate nutritive values per portion

Calories (kcal)	Protein (grams)	Carbohydrate (grams)	Fat (grams)	Cholesterol (mg)	Sodium (mg)	Iron (mg)	Calcium (mg)
204	3 (6%)	34 (64%)	7.1 (30%)	8	597	0.7	17

Notes
- 12 hard-cooked eggs, sliced or diced, may be added.
- Mayonnaise or a combination of mayonnaise and salad dressing may be used in place of the hot vinegar dressing. Add to potato mixture and heat to serving temperature.

GELATIN SALAD RECIPES

FRUIT GELATIN SALAD ◼

Yield: 40 or 48 portions or 1 pan 12 × 20 × 2 inches   *Portion:* 2¼ × 2½ or 2 × 2½ inches

Ingredient	Amount	Procedure
Gelatin, flavored Water, boiling	1 lb 8 oz 2 qt	Pour boiling water over gelatin. Stir until dissolved.
Fruit juice or water, cold	2 qt	Add to hot liquid. Chill.
Fruit, drained	4 lb	Place fruit in counter pan. When gelatin begins to congeal, pour over fruit. Place in refrigerator to congeal. Cut 5 × 8 for 40 portions. Cut 6 × 8 for 48 portions.

Approximate nutritive values per portion

Calories (kcal)	Protein (grams)	Carbohydrate (grams)	Fat (grams)	Cholesterol (mg)	Sodium (mg)	Iron (mg)	Calcium (mg)
98	1.3 (5%)	23.4 (95%)	0.1 (0%)	0	27	0	7

Notes

- For quick preparation, dissolve 1 lb 8 oz flavored gelatin in 1½ qt boiling water. Measure 2½ qt chipped or finely crushed ice, then add enough cold water or fruit juice to cover ice. Add to gelatin and stir constantly until ice is melted. Gelatin will begin to congeal at once. Speed of congealing depends on proportion of ice to water and size of ice particles.

- One or more canned, frozen, or fresh fruits, cut into desired shapes and sizes, may be used. Fresh or frozen pineapple must be cooked before adding to gelatin salad.

- Fruit juice may be used for part or all of the liquid. Not more than 50 percent of heavy syrup, however, should be substituted for water.

- If unflavored granulated gelatin is used, sprinkle 2½ oz over 2 cups cold water and let stand for 10 minutes. Add 3½ qt boiling fruit juice and 1 lb sugar.

Variations

- **Apple Cinnamon Swirl.**   Heat 1¼ qt water to boiling. Add 1 lb lemon gelatin and 10 oz cinnamon candies (red-hots). Stir until dissolved. Stir in 3 lb (1½ qt) applesauce, ¼ cup lemon juice, and 1 Tbsp salt. Pour into a 12 × 20 × 2-inch pan and chill until partially set. Fold in 8 oz coarsely chopped walnuts. Beat 10 oz cream cheese, ½ cup milk, ¼ cup mayonnaise until smooth. Spoon mixture (2 cups) on top of gelatin. Swirl through gelatin with rubber spatula to marble.

- **Applesauce Gelatin Salad.**   Heat 6 lb 10 oz (1 No. 10 can) applesauce, 8 oz granulated sugar, 1 Tbsp ground cinnamon, and 2 tsp ground nutmeg, stirring frequently. Add 1 lb 8 oz strawberry gelatin and stir until dissolved. Add 2 qt cold water and ⅓ cup lemon juice.

- **Arabian Peach Salad.** Drain 1 No. 10 can sliced peaches, saving juice. Combine peach juice, 1½ cups white vinegar, 1 lb 12 oz granulated sugar, 1 oz stick cinnamon, and 2 tsp whole cloves. Simmer 10 minutes. Strain, and add enough hot water to make 1 gal liquid. Add to 1 lb 8 oz orange gelatin and stir until dissolved. When slightly thickened, add peaches. Apricot halves may be substituted for peaches.

- **Autumn Salad.** Dissolve 1 lb 8 oz orange gelatin in 2 qt boiling water. Add 2 qt cold liquid, 2 lb 8 oz sliced fresh peaches, and 3 lb 8 oz fresh pears.

- **Blueberry Gelatin Salad.** Make in two layers. First layer: Drain 1 No. 10 can blueberries. Add water to juice if necessary to make 1 qt and heat to boiling. Add 12 oz raspberry gelatin and stir until dissolved. Pour into 12 × 20 × 2-inch pan and chill. Second layer: Drain 1 No. 10 can crushed pineapple. Add water if necessary to make 1 qt liquid. Heat to boiling and add 12 oz lemon gelatin. Stir until dissolved. Stir in the crushed pineapple and 1 qt sour cream. Cool. Pour over first layer and chill.

- **Boysenberry Mold.** Thaw 2 lb 12 oz frozen boysenberries in a colander. Reserve juice. Heat juice plus water if needed to make 2 qt. Add 1 lb 8 oz raspberry gelatin and stir until dissolved. Stir in 1½ cups cold water. Chill until gelatin is the consistency of egg whites. Whip 1¼ qt whipped topping until soft peaks form. Fold in the thickened gelatin mixture and boysenberries. Pour into molds and refrigerate until firm.

- **Cranberry Apple Salad.** Dissolve 1 lb 8 oz cherry or raspberry gelatin in 2 qt boiling water. Add 3 lb fresh or frozen cranberry relish, 1 lb chopped apples, and 1 lb crushed pineapple. One No. 10 can whole cranberry sauce and 4 oranges, ground, may be used in place of the relish. Delete pineapple.

- **Cranberry Mold.** Drain 3½ cups crushed pineapple (2½ cups drained). Heat juice, plus enough water to make 3¼ cups, to boiling. Add 1 lb raspberry gelatin and stir until dissolved. Stir in 1½ qt cranberry relish. Chill until consistency of unbeaten egg whites. Fold in 3 cups mandarin oranges, drained and chopped, and 3¼ cups whipped topping whipped until stiff (6½ cups whipped). Spread in oiled gelatin molds.

- **Cucumber Soufflé Salad.** Dissolve 1 lb 8 oz lime or lemon gelatin in 1½ qt boiling water. Add 2 qt ice and cold water. Chill until partially set. Whip until fluffy. Add 3 cups mayonnaise and ⅓ cup lemon juice. Fold in 5 lb cucumbers, chopped.

- **Frosted Cherry Salad.** Dissolve 1 lb 8 oz cherry gelatin in 2 qt boiling water. Add 2 qt cold fruit juice, 2 lb drained, pitted red cherries, and 2 lb crushed pineapple. When congealed, frost with whipped cream cheese and chopped toasted almonds.

- **Frosted Lime Mold.** Dissolve 1 lb 8 oz lime gelatin in 2 qt boiling water. Add 2 qt cold fruit juice and, when mixture begins to congeal, add 4 lb crushed pineapple, drained, 2 lb 8 oz cottage cheese, 8 oz diced celery, 4 oz chopped pimiento, and 4 oz chopped nuts. When congealed, frost with mixture of 4 lb cream cheese blended with ½ cup mayonnaise.

- **Jellied Waldorf Salad.** Dissolve 1 lb 8 oz raspberry or cherry gelatin in 2 qt boiling water. Add 1 cup red cinnamon candies (ret-hots) and stir until dissolved. Add

2 qt cold water or fruit juice. When mixture begins to congeal, add 2 lb diced apple, 12 oz finely diced celery, and 8 oz chopped pecans or walnuts.

- **Lemon Cream Mold.** Dissolve 1 lb 8 oz lemon gelatin in 1 qt boiling water. Stir in 1 qt cold water, ¾ cup vinegar, and ¼ tsp salt. Cool to room temperature. Add to 3 lb 12 oz sour cream and mix until smooth. Garnish with very thin slices of lemon and cucumber.

- **Molded Pineapple Cheese Salad.** Dissolve 1 lb 8 oz lemon gelatin in 2 qt boiling water. Add 2 qt cold fruit juice, 1 lb grated cheddar cheese, 3 lb drained crushed pineapple, 3 oz chopped green pepper or pimiento, and 4 oz finely chopped celery.

- **Ribbon Gelatin Salad.** Dissolve 1 lb 8 oz raspberry gelatin in 1 gal boiling water. Divide into three equal parts. Pour one-third into one 12 × 20 × 2-inch pan and chill. Add 1 lb cream cheese to another third and whip to blend; pour on the first part when it is congealed. Return it to the refrigerator until it, too, is congealed, then top with remaining portion.

- **Sunshine Salad.** Dissolve 1 lb 8 oz lemon gelatin in 2 qt boiling water. Add 2 qt cold fruit juice, 3 lb drained crushed pineapple, and 8 oz grated raw carrot.

- **Swedish Green-Top Salad.** Dissolve 12 oz lime gelatin in 2 qt boiling water. Pour into a 12 × 10 × 2-inch pan. Dissolve 12 oz orange gelatin in 2 qt boiling water. While still hot, add 1 lb 8 oz marshmallows and stir until melted. When cool, add 12 oz cream cheese, 1½ cups mayonnaise, and ½ tsp salt, blended together. Fold in 1 pt cream, whipped. Pour over congealed lime gelatin and return to the refrigerator to chill. To serve, invert so that green portion is on top.

- **Under-the-Sea Salad.** Dissolve 1 lb 8 oz lime gelatin in 1 gal boiling water. Divide into two parts. Pour one part into a 12 × 20 × 2-inch pan and chill. When it begins to congeal, add 12 oz drained crushed pineapple or sliced pears. To the remaining gelatin mixture, add 1 lb cream cheese and whip until smooth. Pour over first portion.

PERFECTION SALAD

Yield: 40 or 48 portions or 1 pan 12 × 20 × 2 inches   *Portion:* 2¼ × 2½ or 2 × 2½ inches

Ingredient	Amount	Procedure
Gelatin, unflavored	3 oz	Sprinkle gelatin over cold water.
Water, cold	2 cups	Let stand 10 minutes.
Water, boiling	3 qt	Add boiling water to gelatin.
		Stir until gelatin is dissolved.
Vinegar, cider	1 cup	Add to gelatin mixture. Stir until sugar is dissolved.
Lemon juice	1 cup	Chill.
Salt	1 oz (1½ Tbsp)	
Sugar, granulated	1 lb	

Cabbage, chopped	1 lb 8 oz	When liquid begins to congeal, add vegetables.
Celery, chopped	10 oz	Pour into a 12 × 20 × 2-inch counter pan. Place in
Pimiento, chopped	4 oz	the refrigerator to congeal.
Green pepper, chopped	4 oz	Cut 5 × 8 for 40 portions.
Paprika	1 Tbsp	Cut 6 × 8 for 48 portions.

Approximate nutritive values per portion

Calories (kcal)	Protein (grams)	Carbohydrate (grams)	Fat (grams)	Cholesterol (mg)	Sodium (mg)	Iron (mg)	Calcium (mg)
49	1.8 (12%)	11.4 (75%)	0.1 (1%)	0	213	0.3	13

TOMATO ASPIC

Yield: 40 or 48 portions or 1 pan 12 × 20 × 2 inches   *Portion:* 2¼ × 2½ or 2 × 2½ inches

Ingredient	Amount	Procedure
Gelatin, unflavored	4 oz	Sprinkle gelatin over cold water.
Water, cold	1 qt	Let stand 10 minutes.
Tomato juice	1 gal	Combine tomato juice and seasonings.
Onions, small, sliced	2	Boil 5 minutes. Strain.
Bay leaf	1	Add gelatin. Stir until dissolved.
Celery stalks	4	
Cloves, whole	8	
Dry mustard	2 tsp	
Sugar, granulated	14 oz	
Salt	1 Tbsp	
Vinegar or lemon juice	2 cups	Add vinegar or lemon juice. Pour into a 12 × 20 × 2-inch counter pan. Place in refrigerator to congeal. Cut 5 × 8 for 40 portions. Cut 6 × 8 for 48 portions.

Approximate nutritive values per portion

Calories (kcal)	Protein (grams)	Carbohydrate (grams)	Fat (grams)	Cholesterol (mg)	Sodium (mg)	Iron (mg)	Calcium (mg)
57	2.8 (18%)	12.6 (81%)	0.1 (2%)	0	436	0.7	11

FRUIT SALAD RECIPES

WALDORF SALAD

Yield: 50 portions or 6 qt   *Portion:* ⅓ cup (3 oz)

Ingredient	Amount	Procedure
Cream, whipping (optional)	½ cup	Whip cream. Combine with mayonnaise.
Mayonnaise or salad dressing	2 cups	
Apples, tart (peeled or unpeeled)	8 lb EP	Dice apples into fruit juice to prevent apples from turning dark. Drain and stir into salad dressing.
Celery, chopped	2 lb EP	Add celery, seasonings, and nuts to apples.
Salt	1 oz (1½ Tbsp)	Mix lightly until all ingredients are coated with dressing.
Sugar, granulated (optional)	6 oz	Serve with No. 12 dipper.
Walnuts, coarsely chopped	8 oz	

Approximate nutritive values per portion

Calories (kcal)	Protein (grams)	Carbohydrate (grams)	Fat (grams)	Cholesterol (mg)	Sodium (mg)	Iron (mg)	Calcium (mg)
158	1.1 (3%)	16.3 (39%)	10.9 (58%)	8	260	0.4	21

Notes
- Add walnuts only to salad that will be used immediately, as nuts will cause the salad to become gray.
- Fruit Salad Dressing (p. 551) may be substituted for mayonnaise.

Variations
- **Apple Cabbage Salad.**   Use 6 lb diced apples and 4 lb crisp shredded cabbage. Omit celery. Sour cream or plain yogurt may be substituted for half the mayonnaise.
- **Apple Carrot Salad.**   Use 6 lb diced apples, 3 lb shredded carrots, and only 1 lb chopped celery.
- **Apple Celery Salad.**   Delete walnuts. Add 8 oz marshmallows.
- **Apple Date Salad.**   Substitute 2 lb cut dates for celery.
- **Apple Fruit Salad.**   Substitute 4 lb fresh fruit in season for half the apples.

ACINI DE PEPE FRUIT SALAD

Yield: 50 portions   *Portion:* 4 oz

Ingredient	Amount	Procedure
Acini de pepe Water, boiling Salt	2 lb 6 oz (AP) 2 gal 1 oz (1½ Tbsp)	Cook pasta according to directions on p. 407. Drain and cool slightly. There should be 7 lb 8 oz cooked product. Save for later step.
Sugar, granulated Flour, all-purpose Salt	7 oz 2 Tbsp 1 tsp	Combine sugar, flour, and salt in steam-jacketed kettle.
Pineapple juice drained from pineapple	1½ cups	Pour juice slowly into mixture while stirring with wire whip. Cook over moderate heat, stirring until slightly thickened.
Eggs, beaten	2 (3 oz)	Stir a small amount of the hot mixture into eggs, then stir eggs into the hot mixture. Cook and stir until thickened.
Lemon juice	1 Tbsp	Add lemon juice. Cool to room temperature. Combine with cooked pasta. Mix lightly. Chill.
Mandarin oranges, drained Crushed pineapple, drained Pineapple tidbits, drained	1 lb 1 lb 12 oz 1 lb 12 oz	Add fruit to pasta mixture. Mix lightly but thoroughly.
Whipped topping	1¼ cups	Whip topping to stiff peaks. There should be 2½ cups whipped. Fold into salad. Chill until served. Serve with No. 8 dipper.

Approximate nutritive values per portion

Calories (kcal)	Protein (grams)	Carbohydrate (grams)	Fat (grams)	Cholesterol (mg)	Sodium (mg)	Iron (mg)	Calcium (mg)
139	3.3 (9%)	26.6 (75%)	2.4 (15%)	14	96	1	21

AMBROSIA FRUIT SALAD

Yield: 50 portions   *Portion:* 2½ oz

Ingredient	Amount	Procedure
Mandarin oranges, canned, drained	3 lb	Combine fruits, marshmallows, and coconut.
Pineapple tidbits, canned, drained	3 lb 8 oz	
Miniature marshmallows	12 oz	
Shredded coconut	6 oz	
Sour cream	12 oz	Add sour cream to fruit. Toss lightly to combine. Serve with No. 12 dipper.

Calories (kcal)	Protein (grams)	Carbohydrate (grams)	Fat (grams)	Cholesterol (mg)	Sodium (mg)	Iron (mg)	Calcium (mg)
82	0.9 (4%)	14.7 (69%)	2.6 (27%)	3	17	0.3	25

Approximate nutritive value per portion

Note
- Salad does not hold well and is best when served soon after mixing.
- Plain unflavored yogurt may be substituted for sour cream.

GRAPEFRUIT ORANGE SALAD

Yield: 50 portions   *Portion:* 2 orange, 3 grapefruit sections

Ingredient	Amount	Procedure
Grapefruit, medium	16	Peel and section fruit according to directions on p. 493.
Oranges, large	17	For each salad, arrange 3 grapefruit sections and 2 orange sections alternately on lettuce or other salad greens.
		Serve with Celery Seed Fruit Dressing (p. 550) or Honey French Dressing (p. 548).

Calories (kcal)	Protein (grams)	Carbohydrate (grams)	Fat (grams)	Cholesterol (mg)	Sodium (mg)	Iron (mg)	Calcium (mg)
45	0.9 (7%)	11.2 (91%)	0.1 (2%)	0	0	0.1	29

Approximate nutritive values per portion

Variations
- **Citrus Pomegranate Salad.**   Arrange grapefruit and orange sections on curly endive. Sprinkle pomegranate seeds over fruit. Serve with Celery Seed Dressing (p. 550).

- **Fresh Fruit Salad Bowl.**   Place chopped lettuce or other salad greens in individual salad bowls, 2 oz per bowl. Arrange wedges of cantaloupe, honeydew melon, and avocado, and sections of orange or grapefruit on the lettuce. Garnish with green grapes, Bing cherries, or fresh strawberries. Fresh pineapple, peaches, or apricots are good also in this salad. Serve with Celery Seed Fruit Dressing (p. 550) or Honey French Dressing (p. 548).
- **Grapefruit Apple Salad.**   Substitute wedges of unpeeled red apples for oranges.
- **Grapefruit-Orange-Avocado Salad.**   Place avocado wedges between grapefruit and orange sections. Garnish with fresh strawberries.
- **Grapefruit-Orange-Pear Salad.**   Alternate slices of fresh pear with grapefruit and orange sections.

SPICED APPLE SALAD

Yield: 50 portions   *Portion:* 1 apple

Ingredient	Amount	Procedure
Sugar, granulated	6 lb	Combine sugar, water, and flavorings.
Water	2 qt	Boil for about 5 minutes to form a thin syrup.
Vinegar, cider	1 cup	Set aside for next step.
Red coloring	½ tsp	
Whole cloves	1 oz	
Cinnamon sticks	1 oz	
Apples, fresh	50	Core and peel apples. Leave apples whole unless they are large; then cut in half crosswise. Place apples in a flat pan. Pour syrup over apples. Cook on top of range or in oven until tender. Turn while cooking. Cool.
Celery, chopped	8 oz	Combine celery and nuts.
Nuts, chopped	4 oz	Add mayonnaise and salt.
Mayonnaise	¾ cup	Fill centers of cooked apples with this mixture.
Salt	½ tsp	

Approximate nutritive value per portion

Calories (kcal)	Protein (grams)	Carbohydrate (grams)	Fat (grams)	Cholesterol (mg)	Sodium (mg)	Iron (mg)	Calcium (mg)
182	0.6 (1%)	38.3 (78%)	4.5 (21%)	2	46	0.3	16

Notes
- Select apples that will hold their shape when cooked, such as Jonathan, Rome Beauty, or Winesap. Approximately 12 lb will be needed.
- 8 oz softened cream cheese may be substituted for mayonnaise.

FROZEN FRUIT SALAD

Yield: 48 portions or 1 pan 12 × 20 × 2 inches   *Portion:* 4 oz

Ingredient	Amount	Procedure
Gelatin, unflavored	1 oz	Sprinkle gelatin over cold water.
Water, cold	½ cup	Let stand 10 minutes.
Orange juice	1¾ cups	Combine juices and heat to boiling point.
Pineapple juice	1¾ cups	Add gelatin and stir to dissolve.
		Cool until slightly congealed.
Cream, whipping	2 cups	Whip cream. Combine with mayonnaise.
Mayonnaise	1 cup	Fold into the slightly congealed gelatin mixture.
Pineapple chunks, drained	1 lb 12 oz	Fold fruit into gelatin mixture.
Orange sections, cut in halves	1 lb 8 oz	Pour into a 12 × 20 × 2-inch counter pan or into molds.
Peaches, sliced, drained	1 lb 8 oz	Freeze. Cut 6 × 8.
Bananas, diced	2 lb	
Pecans, chopped	12 oz	
Maraschino cherries	8 oz	
Miniature marshmallows	8 oz	

Approximate nutritive values per portion							
Calories (kcal)	Protein (grams)	Carbohydrate (grams)	Fat (grams)	Cholesterol (mg)	Sodium (mg)	Iron (mg)	Calcium (mg)
178	2.1 (5%)	18.6 (39%)	11.7 (56%)	14	33	0.5	24

Notes
- Whipped topping may be used in place of whipped cream.
- Other combinations of fruit (a total of 8 lb) may be used.

ENTREE SALAD RECIPES

CHEF'S SALAD BOWL

Yield: 50 portions   *Portion:* 7 oz

Ingredient	Amount	Procedure
Head lettuce or mixed greens	12 lb	Cut or tear lettuce into bite-sized pieces. Portion into individual salad bowls, 4 oz per bowl.
Cooked turkey	6 lb	Cut meat and cheese into thin strips.
Cooked ham	3 lb	Arrange on top of lettuce, 2 oz turkey, 1 oz ham, 1 oz
Cheddar cheese or Swiss cheese	3 lb	cheese per bowl.
Green pepper rings	50 (8 lb AP)	Garnish with 1 green pepper ring, 2 tomato wedges,
Tomatoes, cut into wedges	6 lb AP	and 2 egg quarters.
Eggs, hard-cooked, quartered (p. 308)	25	
Salad dressing (see Note)	1½–2 qt	Serve salad with choice of dressings.

Approximate nutritive values per portion

Calories (kcal)	Protein (grams)	Carbohydrate (grams)	Fat (grams)	Cholesterol (mg)	Sodium (mg)	Iron (mg)	Calcium (mg)
458	34.9 (30%)	15.5 (13%)	28.8 (56%)	200	903	3	256

Note
- Suggested salad dressings: Mayonnaise, Thousand Island, Roquefort, Creamy French, or Ranch.

Variations
- **Chicken and Bacon Salad.**   Delete ham and turkey. Cut 6 lb cooked chicken or turkey into strips or cubes and mix with salad greens. Sprinkle 4 lb chopped, crisply cooked bacon over top of salads, 1 oz per salad.
- **Seafood Chef Salad.**   Delete turkey and ham. Substitute 1 oz salmon, drained and broken into small chunks, 1 oz shrimp pieces or 2 whole shrimp for each salad.
- **Taco Salad.**   Fry fifty 10-inch flour tortillas by forming in basket shape around a large dipper or can. Submerge tortillas in hot fat, while still formed around dipper or can, for 20–30 seconds. Remove from fat and drain on paper towel. Prepare ground beef mixture (p. 382). Chill. Prepare lettuce mixture (p. 382). In bottom of shell basket, place 2½ oz lettuce mixture, then 4 oz cold ground beef mixture on top of lettuce. Sprinkle with sliced black olives and Cheddar cheese. Serve with Salsa (p. 589).

CHICKEN SALAD

Yield: 50 portions or 6¼ qt   *Portion:* ½ cup (4 oz)

Ingredient	Amount	Procedure
Cooked chicken	8 lb	Cut chicken into ½-inch cubes.
Eggs, hard-cooked (p. 308)	12	Peel and dice eggs.
Celery, diced	3 lb	Combine all ingredients. Mix lightly. Chill.
Onion, minced	2 Tbsp	Serve with No. 8 dipper.
Salt	2 Tbsp	
Pepper, white	1 tsp	
Mayonnaise	1 qt	
Lemon juice	4 tsp	

Approximate nutritive values per portion

Calories (kcal)	Protein (grams)	Carbohydrate (grams)	Fat (grams)	Cholesterol (mg)	Sodium (mg)	Iron (mg)	Calcium (mg)
227	13.7 (24%)	1.7 (3%)	18.4 (73%)	94	423	0.8	27

Notes
- 24–25 lb of chicken (AP) will yield approximately 8 lb cooked meat.
- Cubed chicken may be marinated for 2 hours in ⅔ cup French Dressing.

Variations
- **Chicken-Avocado-Orange Salad.** Delete eggs. Gently stir into chicken mixture 1 qt diced orange segments, drained, 12 oz broken or slivered toasted almonds, and 6 oz chopped pimiento. Just before serving, add 6 avocados, diced.
- **Crunchy Chicken Salad.** Add 8 oz sliced water chestnuts or toasted slivered almonds or walnuts.
- **Curried Chicken Salad.** Add 1 Tbsp curry powder to mayonnaise.
- **Fruited Chicken Salad.** Just before serving add 2 lb 8 oz seedless grapes or pineapple chunks, drained, and 8 oz sunflower seeds.
- **Mandarin Chicken Salad.** Delete eggs and pepper. Reduce mayonnaise to 2 cups. Add 2 cups sour cream. Substitute 2 Tbsp lime juice for lemon juice. Gently fold in 1 No. 10 can mandarin oranges and 1 No. 10 can pineapple tidbits, well drained.
- **Turkey Salad.** Substitute turkey for chicken.

MARINATED CHICKEN AND FRESH FRUIT SALAD

Yield: 50 portions   *Portion:* 3 oz chicken + 3 oz greens + 3 oz fruit + 2 oz dressing

Ingredient	Amount	Procedure
Chicken breasts, 3 oz	50	Prepare and grill chicken according to Tarragon Chicken recipe, p. 453.
Head lettuce (iceberg)	7 lb	Cut or tear lettuce into bite-size pieces.
Leaf lettuce, Bibb or romaine	3 lb	
Fresh fruit in season (see Note)	10–12 lb	Prepare fruit. Peel if necessary and cut into wedges, medium-sized chunks, or clusters.
Leaf lettuce	2 lb	For plate liners.
Golden Fruit Dressing, p. 551.	3 qt	Serve to the side.

To Assemble:

1. Line 50 9-inch luncheon plates with leaf lettuce.
2. Arrange 3 oz greens on each plate.
3. Place 3 oz grilled chicken strips in center of plate.
4. Arrange 3 oz fruit around the chicken.
5. In a side dish, serve Golden Fruit Dressing, p. 551.

Approximate nutritive values per portion							
Calories (kcal)	Protein (grams)	Carbohydrate (grams)	Fat (grams)	Cholesterol (mg)	Sodium (mg)	Iron (mg)	Calcium (mg)
460	16 (14%)	33.9 (29%)	30.7 (58%)	39	431	2	66

Note   ■ Choose at least 3 kinds of fruit that complement each other. Suggested fruits: cantaloupe wedges, watermelon chunks, fresh pineapple spears or chunks, whole fresh strawberries, papaya pieces, mango slices, green or red grapes.

CHICKEN AND PASTA SALAD PLATE

Yield: 50 portions   *Portion:* 7 oz

Ingredient	Amount	Procedure
Rotini	1 lb 2 oz AP (2 lb 8 oz cooked)	Cook according to directions on p. 407. Drain.
Water, boiling	1 gal	
Salt	1 Tbsp	
Vinegar, cider	2¾ cups	Combine in mixer bowl.
Lemon juice	⅓ cup	
Prepared mustard	3 Tbsp	
Garlic, minced	3 cloves	
Salt	2 Tbsp	
Oregano, dried, crumbled	1 tsp	
Pepper, black	2 tsp	
Sugar, granulated	2 tsp	
Salad oil	3½ cups	Add oil very gradually while mixing on medium speed with wire whip attachment.
Cooked chicken, cut in 1-inch pieces	8 lb 8 oz	Add chicken to dressing. Toss to coat well. Add cooked rotini and mix well. Chill overnight.
Broccoli florets	1 lb 4 oz	Steam broccoli until tender-crisp. Add to marinated mixture shortly before serving.
Cherry tomatoes, cut in half	3 lb	Add to marinated mixture shortly before serving.
Zucchini, fresh, cut in julienne strips	2 lb 4 oz	
Carrots, shredded	10 oz	
Green onions, chopped	8 oz	
Leaf lettuce	2 lb	Cover plate with leaf lettuce.
Hard rolls	50	Portion 7 oz salad onto lettuce. Place one hard roll on each salad plate shortly before service.

Approximate nutritive values per portion

Calories (kcal)	Protein (grams)	Carbohydrate (grams)	Fat (grams)	Cholesterol (mg)	Sodium (mg)	Iron (mg)	Calcium (mg)
486	28.6 (23%)	42.8 (35%)	22.9 (42%)	64	711	3.3	69

Note   ■   Salad may be served in a bowl or on a plate with a bed of shredded lettuce.

SHRIMP TORTELLINI SALAD PLATE

Yield: 50 portions   *Portion:* 6 oz salad mixture

Ingredient	Amount	Procedure
Spinach tortellini, cheese-stuffed, frozen	4 lb AP (6 lb cooked)	Cook tortellini in boiling water for 3–5 minutes. Drain. Place in bowl.
Italian Dressing (p. 547)	2¼ qt	Pour dressing over pasta and toss gently to coat.
Salad shrimp, cooked, frozen	5 lb	Thaw shrimp under cold running water. Drain well and add to pasta.
Celery, thinly sliced	1 lb 10 oz	Add to pasta mixture. Toss well.
Carrots, cut into ¾-inch-long thin julienne strips	12 oz	Cover. Refrigerate until thoroughly chilled.
Green onions, thinly sliced	10 oz	
Water chestnuts, sliced, drained	1 lb 6 oz	
Leaf lettuce	2 lb 12 oz	Cover plate with leaf lettuce. Portion 6 oz salad onto lettuce.
Black olives	1 lb	Garnish plate with 3 black olives and 1 cherry tomato.
Cherry tomatoes	1 lb	Serve with 2 breadsticks.
Bread sticks	100	

Approximate nutritive values per portion

Calories (kcal)	Protein (grams)	Carbohydrate (grams)	Fat (grams)	Cholesterol (mg)	Sodium (mg)	Iron (mg)	Calcium (mg)
704	24.3 (14%)	88.2 (50%)	27.9 (36%)	89	1850	5	128

CRAB SALAD

Yield: 50 portions or 6 qt   *Portion:* ½ cup (4 oz)

Ingredient	Amount	Procedure
Eggs, hard-cooked (p. 308)	30	Peel and chop eggs coarsely.
Crabmeat, flaked	5 lb	Add eggs and other ingredients to crabmeat.
Almonds, blanched, slivered (optional)	1 lb	Mix lightly. Chill.
Black olives, sliced	1 lb	Serve with No. 10 dipper.
Lemon juice	⅓ cup	
Mayonnaise	1 qt	

Approximate nutritive values per portion							
Calories (kcal)	Protein (grams)	Carbohydrate (grams)	Fat (grams)	Cholesterol (mg)	Sodium (mg)	Iron (mg)	Calcium (mg)
281	13.9 (20%)	3.8 (5%)	23.9 (75%)	183	445	1.6	71

Notes
- Olives may be deleted and 1 lb diced cucumbers added.
- If desired, omit mayonnaise and marinate with French Dressing (p. 547).

Variation
- **Lobster Salad.**   Substitute lobster for crab.

PASTA AND CRAB SALAD

Yield: 50 portions   *Portion:* 2½ oz

Ingredient	Amount	Procedure
Radiatore	1 lb 8 oz	Cook pasta according to directions on p. 407.
Water	1½ gal	Drain. Yield should be 3 lb cooked radiatore.
Salt	1 oz (1½ Tbsp)	
Lemon Basil Dressing (p. 549)	3¾ cups	Add dressing. Toss to coat pasta.
Onions, green, finely chopped	2 oz	Add onions and snow peas. Toss.
Snow peas, thawed, uncooked	1 lb 4 oz	
Crabmeat, diced	2 lb	Add crabmeat. Toss. Keep chilled.

Approximate nutritive values per portion							
Calories (kcal)	Protein (grams)	Carbohydrate (grams)	Fat (grams)	Cholesterol (mg)	Sodium (mg)	Iron (mg)	Calcium (mg)
139	5.3 (15%)	13.5 (39%)	7.2 (46%)	18	267	1	20

Note   ■ Cooked shrimp, cooked scallops, or lobster may be substituted for crabmeat.

SHRIMP SALAD

Yield: 50 portions or 6¼ qt   *Portion:* ½ cup (4 oz)   ■

Ingredient	Amount	Procedure
Cooked shrimp (see Notes)	6 lb	Cut shrimp into ½-inch pieces. Place in bowl.
Celery, diced	2 lb	Add vegetables to shrimp.
Cucumber, diced	1 lb	
Lettuce, chopped (optional)	1 head	
Mayonnaise	1 qt	Combine mayonnaise and seasonings. Add to shrimp mixture. Mix lightly. Chill. Serve with No. 10 dipper.
Lemon juice	2 Tbsp	
Salt	2 tsp	
Paprika	1 tsp	
Prepared mustard	2 tsp	

Approximate nutritive values per portion							
Calories (kcal)	Protein (grams)	Carbohydrate (grams)	Fat (grams)	Cholesterol (mg)	Sodium (mg)	Iron (mg)	Calcium (mg)
187	12 (26%)	1.7 (4%)	14.8 (7%)	117	327	2	35

Notes
- ■ 12 lb raw shrimp in shell or 10 lb raw, peeled, and deveined shrimp will yield the 6 lb cooked shrimp needed. Cook according to directions on p. 331.
- ■ 1 dozen hard-cooked eggs (p. 308), coarsely chopped, may be added. Reduce shrimp to 5 lb.
- ■ Salad may be garnished with tomato wedges or served in a tomato cup.

SHRIMP RICE SALAD

Yield: 50 portions   *Portion:* ½ cup (4 oz)

Ingredient	Amount	Procedure
Rice, converted	1 lb	Cook rice according to directions on p. 430.
Water	1¼ qt	Chill.
Salt	1 Tbsp	
Margarine or vegetable oil	1 Tbsp	
Celery	1 lb 8 oz	Cut celery in thin slices crosswise.
Green peppers	1 lb	Slice green peppers in thin strips.
Cooked shrimp, chilled	5 lb	Combine shrimp, rice, and vegetables.
Vinegar, cider	1 cup	Combine and pour over shrimp-rice mixture.
Salad oil	½ cup	Marinate at least 3 hours.
Worcestershire sauce	2 Tbsp	
Sugar, granulated	2 Tbsp	
Salt	1 Tbsp	
Curry powder	2 tsp	
Ginger, ground	¾ tsp	
Pepper, black	½ tsp	
Pineapple chunks, canned or frozen, drained	3 lb	Just before serving, add pineapple. Serve with No. 8 dipper.

Approximate nutritive values per portion

Calories (kcal)	Protein (grams)	Carbohydrate (grams)	Fat (grams)	Cholesterol (mg)	Sodium (mg)	Iron (mg)	Calcium (mg)
122	10.4 (34%)	13.1 (43%)	3.1 (23%)	89	377	2	37

TUNA PASTA SALAD PLATE

Yield: 50 portions   *Portion:* 3½ oz salad mixture

Ingredient	Amount	Procedure
Shell macaroni	2 lb AP (6 lb cooked)	Cook macaroni according to directions on p. 407. Drain. Place in bowl.
Water, boiling	2 gal	
Salt	2 oz	
Vegetable oil	2 Tbsp	
Italian Dressing (p. 547)	1 qt	Pour dressing over cooked macaroni. Stir to coat evenly. Cover and refrigerate overnight.
Canned tuna	2 lb	Drain tuna. Carefully fold into macaroni.
Green peppers	1 lb 6 oz	Cut peppers into strips approximately 1 inch long. Add to macaroni mixture.
Stuffed green olives, chopped	4 oz	Add chopped olives to macaroni mixture.
Lettuce leaves	1 lb 8 oz	Place 1 lettuce leaf off center on dinner plate. Place 3½ oz (¾ cup) salad on lettuce.
Eggs, hard-cooked (p. 308)	25	Place half an egg on one side of macaroni salad.
Fresh tomatoes	6 lb	Cut each tomato into 8 wedges.
Hard rolls	50	Place 2 wedges on other side of salad. Place one hard roll on plate shortly before serving.

Approximate nutritive values per portion

Calories (kcal)	Protein (grams)	Carbohydrate (grams)	Fat (grams)	Cholesterol (mg)	Sodium (mg)	Iron (mg)	Calcium (mg)
392	16.6 (17%)	49.6 (50%)	14.7 (33%)	110	657	3.3	61

TUNA SALAD

Yield: 50 portions or 6¼ qt   *Portion:* ½ cup (4 oz)

Ingredient	Amount	Procedure
Eggs, hard-cooked (p. 308)	12	Peel and dice eggs.
Tuna, flaked	7 lb	Add vegetables, relish, and eggs to tuna. Mix lightly.
Celery, chopped	1 lb	
Cucumber, diced	1 lb	
Onion, minced	2 oz	
Pickle relish, drained	8 oz	
Mayonnaise	1 qt	Add mayonnaise to tuna mixture. Mix lightly to blend. Chill. Serve with No. 8 dipper.

Approximate nutritive values per portion

Calories (kcal)	Protein (grams)	Carbohydrate (grams)	Fat (grams)	Cholesterol (mg)	Sodium (mg)	Iron (mg)	Calcium (mg)
237	20.6 (35%)	2.8 (5%)	15.6 (60%)	73	387	2.4	22

Variations
- **Salmon Salad.**   Substitute salmon for tuna.
- **Tuna Apple Salad.**   Substitute tart, diced apples for cucumbers. Omit pickle relish.
- **Tuna Pea Salad.**   Delete eggs and minced onion. Substitute 5 cups sour cream mixed with ½ cup lemon juice for the mayonnaise. Add 2 lb frozen green peas, thawed, 8 oz green pepper, and 8 oz sliced green onions.

STUFFED TOMATO SALAD

Yield: 50 portions   *Portion:* 1 tomato

Ingredient	Amount	Procedure
Tomatoes, medium size	50	Place tomatoes in a wire basket and dip in boiling water. Let stand for 1 minute. Dip in cold water. Remove skins. Chill.
Chicken, crab, shrimp, tuna, or egg salad	10 lb	Turn tomato stem end down. Cut, not quite through, into fourths. Fill with No. 12 dipper of salad.

Approximate nutritive values per portion

Calories (kcal)	Protein (grams)	Carbohydrate (grams)	Fat (grams)	Cholesterol (mg)	Sodium (mg)	Iron (mg)	Calcium (mg)
248	12.5 (20%)	13.4 (21%)	16.4 (59%)	0	628	0.6	6

Note
- 50 medium-sized tomatoes will weigh approximately 12 lb.

Variations
- **Tomato Cabbage Salad.** Combine 1 lb cabbage and 1 lb celery, finely chopped, 1 Tbsp salt, and 1 cup mayonnaise for salad mixture. Fill tomato cup, using a No. 40 dipper.
- **Tomato Cottage Cheese Salad.** Substitute 6 lb cottage cheese for salad mixture. Fill tomato cups, using No. 20 dipper.

COTTAGE CHEESE SALAD

Yield: 50 portions or 6 qt   *Portion:* ½ cup (4 oz)

Ingredient	Amount	Procedure
Tomatoes, fresh, peeled and diced	3 lb	Prepare vegetables.
Green peppers, chopped	4 oz	
Celery, diced	1 lb	
Cucumber, diced	1 lb	
Radishes, sliced	8 oz	
Cottage cheese, dry curd (see Note)	6 lb	Just before serving, add vegetables and mix all ingredients gently.
Salt	2 oz (3 Tbsp)	
Mayonnaise	3 cups	

Approximate nutritive values per portion

Calories (kcal)	Protein (grams)	Carbohydrate (grams)	Fat (grams)	Cholesterol (mg)	Sodium (mg)	Iron (mg)	Calcium (mg)
98	7.3 (29%)	3.8 (15%)	6.1 (56%)	11	257	0.3	41

Note
- If creamed cottage cheese is used, reduce mayonnaise to 1 cup and omit salt.

DELI PLATE ■

Yield: 50 portions   *Portion:* 2½ oz salad + 2 oz meat and cheese

Ingredient	Amount	Procedure
Pasta Salad (p. 508) or Potato Salad (p. 512) or Macaroni Salad (p. 509)	9 lb	Prepare salad.
Pastrami, corned beef, or other cold cuts	3 lb	Wafer slice meat.
Lettuce leaves Swiss cheese, sliced	1 lb 8 oz 3 lb	Place lettuce leaf on dinner plate. Place one 1-oz cheese slice on lettuce. Portion 1 oz pastrami on cheese. Place No. 16 dipper pasta, potato, or macaroni salad on plate.
Tomatoes, sliced Dill pickle spears, drained Black olives	6 lb 8 oz (EP) 1 lb 8 oz 6 oz	Arrange on plate: 2 tomato slices 1 dill pickle spear 1 black olive
Rye bread	100 slices	Place alongside meat on plates.

Suggestions for variation

■ Ham rolls or slices, sliced turkey, deviled or hard-cooked egg, green pepper ring, green onion, cucumber slices, onion slices, cherry tomato, or marinated mushrooms may be used.

TURKEY CROISSANT SALAD PLATE

Yield: 50 portions   *Portion:* 2½ oz turkey

Ingredient	Amount	Procedure
Spinach, fresh, raw	2 lb EP	Prepare vegetables and fruits.
Tomatoes, fresh, sliced	7 lb	
Oranges, navel, fresh, unpeeled, sliced	3 lb 3 oz	
Grapes, red seedless	6 lb	
Alfalfa sprouts	2 oz	
Smoked turkey, wafer-sliced	8 lb	
Croissants	50 (2½-oz size)	Assemble plates according to directions given below.

To Assemble Turkey Croissant Plates:

1. Line three-fourths of plate with ¾ oz spinach.
2. Place 2 tomato slices on spinach leaves.
3. Cut orange slices in half. Place beside tomato slices.
4. Place 2½ oz turkey beside orange slices.
5. Place 1 Tbsp alfalfa sprouts beside turkey.
6. Place a 2-oz cluster of grapes beside sprouts.
7. Place 1 croissant on plate.

Approximate nutritive values per portion							
Calories (kcal)	Protein (grams)	Carbohydrate (grams)	Fat (grams)	Cholesterol (mg)	Sodium (mg)	Iron (mg)	Calcium (mg)
304	16.9 (21%)	31.5 (39%)	14.4 (40%)	0	116	3.1	162

Note
■ Chicken salad, crab salad, shrimp salad, or other wafer-sliced deli meats may be substituted for smoked turkey. If substituting salad meat for solid meat, omit tomato slices and add another fruit (e.g., apples or plums).

FRUIT SALAD PLATE

Yield: 50 portions   *Portion:* 6 oz fruit + 4 oz salad or sherbet

Ingredient	Amount	Procedure
Fruit in season (3–4 selections from fruits listed in Note)	20 lb EP	Prepare fruit.
Cottage cheese, Chicken Salad (p. 524), or sherbet	12 lb	Prepare salad according to recipe.
Nut bread sandwiches or muffins	50–100	
Lettuce	1 lb 8 oz	Prepare lettuce. Place lettuce leaf on dinner plate. Arrange fruit, salad, and bread on lettuce.

Note   ■   Choose a combination that offers contrast in shape, color, and flavor from the following lists:

Fruit suggestions
Apple wedges
Avocado wedges, slices, or halves
Bananas, cut in strips or chunks,
    rolled in chopped nuts
Cherries, sweet
Grape clusters, red or green
Grapefruit sections
Kiwi fruit
Mangoes
Melon: cantaloupe, honeydew,
    watermelon; cut in wedges,
    rings, or balls
Orange slices, half slices, sections
Papayas
Peach halves or slices: cream
    cheese filling, cranberry sauce,
    or
    cottage cheese in halves
Pear halves, filled, or slices
Pineapple chunks, spears, rings
Plums
Strawberries

Salad suggestions
Cheese strips or slices
Cottage cheese
Chicken salad
Sliced chicken or turkey
Ham roll

Bread suggestions
Hard roll
Muffin
Finger sandwich: chicken, tuna
Nut bread sandwich
Raisin bread–cream cheese sandwich

Garnishes
Coconut
Lemon or lime wedge
Pomegranate seeds
Stuffed prune

RELISH RECIPES

BUTTERED APPLES

Yield: 50 portions or 7 qt   *Portion:* ½ cup (4 oz)

Ingredient	Amount	Procedure
Apples, fresh	13 lb EP (16 lb AP)	Wash apples and cut into sections. Remove cores. Arrange in pan.
Margarine, melted	8 oz	Mix remaining ingredients and pour over apples.
Water, hot	2 cups	Cover and simmer until apples are tender, approximately 1 hour.
Sugar, granulated	1 lb 8 oz	
Salt	1 Tbsp	

Approximate nutritive values per portion

Calories (kcal)	Protein (grams)	Carbohydrate (grams)	Fat (grams)	Cholesterol (mg)	Sodium (mg)	Iron (mg)	Calcium (mg)
169	0.3 (1%)	35.8 (79%)	4.2 (21%)	0	171	0.3	13

Notes
- Select apples that will hold their shape when cooked, such as Jonathan, Rome Beauty, or Winesap.
- Apple sections may be arranged in a counter pan and steamed until tender. Sprinkle margarine and sugar over the top and bake for 15–20 minutes.
- Hot buttered apples often are served in place of a vegetable.
- Frozen or canned apples may be used.

Variations
- **Apple Rings.**   Cut rings of unpared apples, steam until tender. Add sugar and margarine and bake 15 minutes.
- **Cinnamon Apples.**   Cut pared apples into rings. Add cinnamon drops (red-hots) for flavor and color. Proceed as for Buttered Apples but reduce sugar to 12 oz.
- **Fried Apples.**   Melt 1 lb margarine or butter in frying pan. Add sliced apples. Add 8 oz brown sugar, 1 tsp salt, and 1 tsp cinnamon. Cook apples, turning occasionally, until apples are lightly browned and just tender. Frozen apple slices, thawed and drained, may be used.

CRANBERRY RELISH (RAW)

Yield: 50 portions or 5 qt   *Portion:* ⅓ cup (3 oz)

Ingredient	Amount	Procedure
Oranges, unpeeled	3 (size 72)	Wash and quarter oranges and apples.
Apples, cored	5 lb	Sort and wash cranberries.
Cranberries, raw	3 lb	Put fruit through chopper or grinder.
Sugar, granulated	2 lb 4 oz	Add sugar to fruit and blend.
		Chill for 24 hours.
		Serve with No. 16 dipper as a relish or salad.

Approximate nutritive values per portion

Calories (kcal)	Protein (grams)	Carbohydrate (grams)	Fat (grams)	Cholesterol (mg)	Sodium (mg)	Iron (mg)	Calcium (mg)
120	0.3 (1%)	31.8 (98%)	0.2 (2%)	0	0	0.1	8

Variation   ■ **Cranberry Orange Relish.**   Delete apples. Increase oranges to 6 and sugar to 3 lb. Add ¼ cup lemon juice.

CRANBERRY SAUCE

Yield: 50 portions or 5 qt   *Portion:* ⅓ cup

Ingredient	Amount	Procedure
Cranberries	4 lb AP	Wash cranberries. Discard soft berries.
Sugar, granulated	4 lb	Combine sugar and water. Bring to a boil.
Water	1 qt	Add cranberries and boil gently until skins burst. Do not overcook. Chill.
		Serve with No. 12 dipper.

Approximate nutritive values per portion

Calories (kcal)	Protein (grams)	Carbohydrate (grams)	Fat (grams)	Cholesterol (mg)	Sodium (mg)	Iron (mg)	Calcium (mg)
154	0.1 (0%)	40.9 (99%)	0.1 (0%)	0	1	0.1	3

Note   ■ Make sauce at least 24 hours before using.

Variations   ■ **Baked Cranberry Relish.**   Wash and drain 4 lb cranberries. Stir in 2 lb 12 oz granulated sugar, ⅓ cup water, and 1 tsp cinnamon. Place berries in glass chafing dishes or other baking pan suitable for serving. Mix together 2½ cups chopped pecans, ½ cup grated fresh lemon rind, and 4 cups orange marmalade. Spread on top of berries. Bake at 350°F for 45 minutes. Serve warm.

- **Pureed Cranberry Sauce.**   Add water to cranberries and cook until skins burst. Puree cranberries and add sugar. Cook until sugar is dissolved.
- **Royal Cranberry Sauce.**   Make half of cranberry sauce recipe. When cool add 3 oranges, chopped; 1 lb apples, chopped; 1 lb white grapes, seeded; 1 lb pineapple, diced; and 4 oz coarsely chopped pecans. Serve with No. 24 dipper as a relish. Yield: 1 gal.

CORN RELISH

Yield: 50 portions   *Portion:* 3 oz

Ingredient	Amount	Procedure
Sugar, granulated	1 lb	Mix sugar, flour, and salt in steam-jacketed kettle or stockpot until well blended.
Flour, all-purpose	2 oz (½ cup)	
Salt	1 oz	
Water	1½ cups	Add to dry ingredients in kettle. Stir until smooth. Cook until thickened, stirring constantly.
Vinegar, cider	1⅔ cups	
Prepared mustard	6 Tbsp	
Corn, whole kernel, frozen, thawed	6 lb	Place corn and seasonings in baker's bowl. Pour hot dressing over corn and mix lightly. Serve chilled.
Celery seed	1½ tsp	
Pimiento, chopped, drained	3 oz	
Onions, fresh, finely chopped	2 oz	
Green peppers, chopped	3 oz	

Approximate nutritive values per portion							
Calories (kcal)	Protein (grams)	Carbohydrate (grams)	Fat (grams)	Cholesterol (mg)	Sodium (mg)	Iron (mg)	Calcium (mg)
90	1.8 (7%)	22.6 (85%)	0.5 (4%)	0	246	0.5	7

Variation   ■   **Black Bean and Corn Relish.**   Substitute 2 lb cooked black beans for 2 lb corn.

SAUERKRAUT RELISH

Yield: 50 portions   *Portion:* ⅓ cup (3 oz)

Ingredient	Amount	Procedure
Sauerkraut	1 No. 10 can	Combine all ingredients.
Carrots, shredded	1 lb	Refrigerate for at least 12 hours.
Celery, chopped	12 oz	
Onion, chopped	8 oz	
Green pepper, chopped	1 lb	
Sugar, granulated	1 lb 8 oz	

Approximate nutritive values per portion

Calories (kcal)	Protein (grams)	Carbohydrate (grams)	Fat (grams)	Cholesterol (mg)	Sodium (mg)	Iron (mg)	Calcium (mg)
71	0.8 (4%)	18.3 (94%)	0.1 (2%)	0	400	1	25

Note ■ Sauerkraut may be chopped before combining with other ingredients.

PICKLED BEETS

Yield: 50 portions or 2 gal   *Portion:* 3 oz

Ingredient	Amount	Procedure
Beets, canned, sliced or whole	2 No. 10 cans	Drain beets. Reserve 1 cup juice for next step.
Vinegar, cider	2 qt	Mix vinegar, sugars, spices, and liquid from beets.
Sugar, brown	1 lb	Heat to boiling point. Boil 5 minutes.
Sugar, granulated	8 oz	Pour hot mixture over beets.
Salt	1 tsp	Chill 24 hours before serving.
Pepper, black	½ tsp	
Cinnamon sticks	2	
Cloves, whole	1 tsp	
Allspice, whole	1 tsp	

Approximate nutritive values per portion

Calories (kcal)	Protein (grams)	Carbohydrate (grams)	Fat (grams)	Cholesterol (mg)	Sodium (mg)	Iron (mg)	Calcium (mg)
63	1.1 (6%)	16.5 (92%)	0.2 (2%)	0	345	2.4	28

Notes ■ If using fresh beets, cook 14 lb (AP) according to directions on p. 655. Peel and slice, then proceed as in the recipe. Substitute 1 cup water for beet juice.

■ Sliced onions, separated into rings, may be added.

■ Granulated sugar may be substituted for brown sugar.

MINTED TABOULI

Yield: 50 portions   *Portion:* 2 oz

Ingredient	Amount	Procedure
Bulgur (cracked wheat)	8 oz	Combine bulgur and water in large mixing bowl. Let stand at least 2 hours.
Water	1¼ qt	Drain well.
Tomatoes, fresh, seeded and diced	1 lb	Add to bulgur.
Cucumbers, peeled and chopped	6 oz	
Red onions, finely chopped	6 oz	
Parsley, fresh, chopped	2 oz	
Mint leaves, coarsely chopped	½ oz	
Lemon juice, fresh	1¼ cups	Blend lemon juice, oil, and spices.
Olive oil	½ cup	Pour over bulgur mixture. Toss to blend. Cover.
Salt	2¼ tsp	Refrigerate for at least 12 hours before serving. Keeps
Pepper, black	1 tsp	well.
Sugar, granulated	1½ tsp	

Approximate nutritive values per portion

Calories (kcal)	Protein (grams)	Carbohydrate (grams)	Fat (grams)	Cholesterol (mg)	Sodium (mg)	Iron (mg)	Calcium (mg)
41	0.7 (7%)	5.1 (46%)	2.3 (47%)	0	100	0.3	7

Note   ■ Salad oil may be substituted for olive oil. Mint leaves may be omitted for plain Tabouli.

SALAD DRESSING RECIPES

MAYONNAISE ■

Yield: 1 gal

Ingredient	Amount	Procedure
Egg yolks (see Notes) Salt Paprika Dry mustard	8 (5 oz) 2 oz (3 Tbsp) 2 tsp 2 Tbsp	Place egg yolks and seasonings in mixer bowl. Mix thoroughly, using wire whip attachment.
Vinegar, cider	¼ cup	Add vinegar and blend.
Salad oil	2 qt	Add oil very slowly, beating steadily on high speed until an emulsion is formed. Oil may then be added, ½ cup at a time and later 1 cup at a time, beating well after each addition.
Vinegar, cider	¼ cup	Add vinegar. Beat well.
Salad oil	2 qt	Continue beating and adding oil until all oil has been added and emulsified.

Approximate nutritive values per ounce

Calories (kcal)	Protein (grams)	Carbohydrate (grams)	Fat (grams)	Cholesterol (mg)	Sodium (mg)	Iron (mg)	Calcium (mg)
221	0.2 (0%)	0.1 (0%)	24.9 (99%)	13	136	0.1	3

Notes
- The use of pasteurized frozen egg yolks is recommended.
- The addition of oil too rapidly or insufficient beating may cause the oil to separate from the other ingredients, resulting in a curdled appearance. Curdled or broken mayonnaise may be reformed by adding it (a small amount at a time) to 2 well-beaten egg yolks or eggs and beating well after each addition. It also may be reformed by adding it to a small portion of uncurdled mayonnaise.

Variations   To make approximately 2 qt dressing:
- **Buttermilk Dressing.**   To 1 qt mayonnaise, add 1 qt buttermilk, 2 tsp basil, ½ tsp oregano, 1 Tbsp finely chopped fresh parsley, 1 clove garlic, minced, 2 tsp black pepper, 2 oz chopped onion, and 1 tsp tarragon.
- **Campus Dressing.**   To 2 qt mayonnaise, add ⅓ cup chopped fresh parsley, ¼ cup chopped green pepper, and ½ cup finely chopped celery.

- **Chantilly Dressing.** To 1½ qt mayonnaise, fold in 1½ cups cream, whipped.
- **Creamy Blue Cheese Dressing.** To 1 qt mayonnaise, add 2 cups (1 lb) sour cream, ¼ cup lemon juice, 1 Tbsp grated onion, 1 tsp salt, and 8 oz finely crumbled blue cheese.
- **Dilly Dressing.** To 1½ qt mayonnaise, add 2 cups evaporated milk or buttermilk, 1 Tbsp seasoned salt, 1 tsp garlic powder, and ¼ cup chopped dill weed.
- **Egg and Green Pepper Dressing.** To 1¾ qt mayonnaise, add 12 chopped hard-cooked eggs, ¼ cup finely chopped green pepper, 2 Tbsp onion juice, and a few grains cayenne pepper.
- **Garden Dressing.** Combine 3 cups mayonnaise and 1½ qt (3 lb) sour cream. Add 3 oz granulated sugar, 2 tsp salt, and 1 tsp black pepper. Fold in 12 oz thinly sliced green onions, 8 oz thinly sliced radishes, 8 oz chopped cucumbers, and 8 oz minced green pepper. This may be used for a vegetable dip also.
- **Green Peppercorn Cream Dressing.** To 1 cup mayonnaise, add 1¼ qt (2 lb 8 oz) sour cream, 1 cup Dijon-style mustard, ⅓ cup finely crushed and drained green peppercorns, ¼ cup white wine vinegar, and ⅔ cup chopped parsley (optional).
- **Honey Cream Dressing.** Blend together 4 oz cream cheese, 1⅓ cups honey, 1 cup lemon or pineapple juice, and ¼ tsp salt; then fold into 1½ qt mayonnaise.
- **Honey Yogurt Dressing.** To 1 cup mayonnaise, add 1½ qt unflavored yogurt, ⅓ cup honey, ¼ cup raspberry vinegar, 2 Tbsp lemon juice, and 1 Tbsp grated fresh orange peel.
- **Horseradish Cream Dressing.** To 1 cup mayonnaise, add 1½ qt (3 lb) sour cream, 2 Tbsp lemon juice, 2 tsp curry powder, 5 oz horseradish, 1 tsp salt, and 1 tsp paprika.
- **Pepper Cream Dressing.** To 1½ qt mayonnaise, add 1 oz grated Parmesan cheese, 1 clove garlic, minced, 1 Tbsp monosodium glutamate, 2 Tbsp freshly ground black pepper, 1 Tbsp lemon juice, 1½ Tbsp onion juice, 1½ tsp hot pepper sauce, 1 Tbsp cider vinegar, and ¾ cup water.
- **Roquefort Dressing.** To 1½ qt mayonnaise, add 2 cups French dressing, 8 oz crumbled Roquefort cheese, and 2 tsp Worcestershire sauce.
- **Russian Dressing.** To 2 qt mayonnaise, add 2 cups chili sauce, 2 Tbsp Worcestershire sauce, 2 tsp onion juice, and a few grains of cayenne.
- **Sour Cream Basil Dressing.** To 1 cup mayonnaise, add ¾ cup vinegar, 1½ qt (3 lb) sour cream, 1 oz granulated sugar, 1½ oz salt, 1½ Tbsp celery seed, and 2 Tbsp basil leaves.
- **Thousand Island Dressing.** To 1½ qt mayonnaise, add 1½ oz minced onion, 3 oz chopped pimiento, 1 cup chili sauce, 8 chopped hard-cooked eggs, 1 tsp salt, ¼ cup pickle relish, and a few grains of cayenne.

COOKED SALAD DRESSING

Yield: 3 gal

Ingredient	Amount	Procedure
Sugar, granulated Flour, all-purpose Salt Dry mustard	3 lb 1 lb 8 oz 6 oz 3 oz	Combine dry ingredients in a steam-jacketed kettle or stockpot.
Water, cold	1 qt	Add water to dry ingredients and stir with wire whip until a smooth paste is formed.
Milk, hot Water, hot	1 gal 2 qt	Add hot milk and water, stirring continuously while adding. Cook 20 minutes, or until thickened.
Margarine Vinegar, cider, hot	1 lb 3 qt	Stir in margarine and vinegar.
Egg yolks, beaten (see Note)	50 (2 lb)	Add cooked mixture slowly to egg yolks, stirring briskly. Cook 7–10 minutes. Remove from heat and cool.

Approximate nutritive values per ounce

Calories (kcal)	Protein (grams)	Carbohydrate (grams)	Fat (grams)	Cholesterol (mg)	Sodium (mg)	Iron (mg)	Calcium (mg)
44	1 (8%)	6 (51%)	2.1 (40%)	32	189	0.2	19

Note	■ 25 whole eggs may be substituted for egg yolks, and hot water for hot milk.
Variations	■ **Chantilly Dressing.** Combine 1 qt Cooked Salad Dressing and 2 cups cream, whipped.
	■ **Combination Dressing.** Combine 1 qt Cooked Salad Dressing and 1 qt mayonnaise.

BACON DRESSING

Yield: 2 qt

Ingredient	Amount	Procedure
Bacon, sliced, cut into 1-inch pieces	12 oz	Fry bacon until crisp. Remove from fat.
Onions, finely chopped	4 oz	Sauté onions in bacon fat.

Sugar, granulated	8 oz	Add sugar, vinegar, and water to sautéed onions.
Vinegar, cider	¼ cup	Bring to boiling point.
Water	1½ cups	Cool.
Mayonnaise (p. 542)	3 cups	Place Mayonnaise in mixer bowl. Add cooled onion-vinegar mixture slowly, beating on low speed until smooth. Stir in bacon pieces. Serve with tossed green salad.

Approximate nutritive values per ounce

Calories (kcal)	Protein (grams)	Carbohydrate (grams)	Fat (grams)	Cholesterol (mg)	Sodium (mg)	Iron (mg)	Calcium (mg)
97	0.6 (2%)	4.1 (16%)	9 (81%)	7	83	0.1	2

SOUR CREAM DRESSING

Yield: 3 qt

Ingredient	Amount	Procedure
Eggs, beaten	16 (1 lb 12 oz)	Mix eggs and sour cream.
Sour cream	1 qt	
Sugar, granulated	2 lb	Combine sugar and flour.
Flour, all-purpose	1½ oz	Add water and mix only until smooth.
Water, cold	1 cup	Add to the cream and egg mixture.
Vinegar, cider	2 cups	Add vinegar and cook until thick. Stir as necessary. Chill.

Approximate nutritive values per ounce

Calories (kcal)	Protein (grams)	Carbohydrate (grams)	Fat (grams)	Cholesterol (mg)	Sodium (mg)	Iron (mg)	Calcium (mg)
65	1.3 (8%)	9.8 (58%)	2.6 (35%)	36	14	0.2	15

Note   ■   2 cups cream, whipped, may be added before serving.

CHILEAN DRESSING

Yield: 1½ qt

Ingredient	Amount	Procedure
Salad oil	2 cups	Combine all ingredients.
Vinegar, cider	1 cup	Beat on low speed until well blended.
Sugar, granulated	4 oz	Store in covered container.
Salt	2 tsp	Shake or beat well before serving.
Onion, finely chopped	2 oz	
Chili sauce	2 cups	
Catsup	1 cup	

Approximate nutritive values per ounce

Calories (kcal)	Protein (grams)	Carbohydrate (grams)	Fat (grams)	Cholesterol (mg)	Sodium (mg)	Iron (mg)	Calcium (mg)
105	0.3 (1%)	6.6 (24%)	9.1 (75%)	0	275	0.1	4

FRENCH DRESSING (THICK)

Yield: 2 qt

Ingredient	Amount	Procedure
Sugar, granulated	2 lb	Combine sugar and seasonings in mixer bowl, using
Paprika	2 Tbsp	wire whip attachment.
Dry mustard	4 tsp	
Salt	2 Tbsp	
Onion juice	1½ tsp	
Vinegar, cider	1½ cups	Add vinegar. Mix well.
Salad oil	1 qt	Add oil gradually in small amounts. Beat well after each addition.

Approximate nutritive values per ounce

Calories (kcal)	Protein (grams)	Carbohydrate (grams)	Fat (grams)	Cholesterol (mg)	Sodium (mg)	Iron (mg)	Calcium (mg)
160	0.1 (0%)	13.5 (32%)	12.3 (68%)	0	183	0.1	3

Note   ■ If a French Dressing of usual consistency is desired, use only 8 oz of sugar.

Variations ■ **Celery Seed Dressing.** Add 2 oz celery seed.

■ **Poppy Seed Dressing.** Add 1 oz poppy seed.

FRENCH DRESSING

Yield: 3 qt

Ingredient	Amount	Procedure
Salt	2 oz (3 Tbsp)	Combine dry ingredients in mixer bowl.
Dry mustard	2 Tbsp	
Paprika	2 Tbsp	
Pepper, black	1 Tbsp	
Vinegar, cider	1 qt	Add vinegar and onion juice to dry ingredients.
Onion juice	4 tsp	Add salad oil slowly. Beat on high speed until thick and blended.
Salad oil	2 qt	This is a temporary emulsion that separates rapidly. Beat well or pour into a jar and shake vigorously just before serving.

Approximate nutritive values per ounce							
Calories (kcal)	Protein (grams)	Carbohydrate (grams)	Fat (grams)	Cholesterol (mg)	Sodium (mg)	Iron (mg)	Calcium (mg)
161	0 (0%)	0.8 (2%)	18.2 (98%)	0	204	0.1	3

Variations Prepare by adding the following to 3 qt (1 recipe) French Dressing:

- **Chiffonade Dressing.** Add ⅓ cup chopped fresh parsley, 4 oz chopped onion, 6 oz chopped green pepper, 4 oz chopped red pepper or pimiento, and 16 chopped hard-cooked eggs.

- **Italian Dressing.** Delete paprika. Add 2 tsp oregano, ¼ tsp garlic powder, and 1 Tbsp basil.

- **Mexican Dressing.** Add 3 cups chili sauce, 10 oz chopped green pepper, 2 oz chopped onion, and 1 Tbsp cilantro.

- **Oil and Vinegar.** Delete mustard, paprika, and onion juice.

- **Roquefort Cheese Dressing.** Add French Dressing slowly, while whipping, to 1 lb finely crumbled Roquefort cheese. 1 qt cream may be mixed with cheese before it is added to the dressing.

- **Sesame Seed Dressing.** Delete salt, paprika, pepper, and onion juice. Increase mustard to ¼ cup and vinegar to 5½ cups. Add 3½ cups granulated sugar, 1¼ cups soy sauce, and ½ cup toasted sesame seeds.

- **Tarragon Dressing.** Use tarragon vinegar in place of cider vinegar.

- **Tomato Dressing.** Add 1 lb granulated sugar, 1½ qt tomato soup, and ¼ cup celery or poppy seeds. Increase onion juice to 2 Tbsp.

HONEY FRENCH DRESSING ▪

Yield: 2 qt

Ingredient	Amount	Procedure
Dry mustard	4 tsp	Mix mustard, salt, and celery seed in large mixing
Salt	1 tsp	bowl.
Celery seed or poppy seed	4 tsp	
Honey	2 cups	While mixing, add remaining ingredients in order
Vinegar, cider	1¼ cups	listed.
Lemon juice	¼ cup	
Onion, grated	1 Tbsp	
Salad oil	1 qt	

Approximate nutritive values per ounce

Calories (kcal)	Protein (grams)	Carbohydrate (grams)	Fat (grams)	Cholesterol (mg)	Sodium (mg)	Iron (mg)	Calcium (mg)
155	0 (0%)	9 (23%)	13.7 (77%)	0	34	0.2	4

BASIL VINAIGRETTE DRESSING ▪

Yield: 1½ qt

Ingredient	Amount	Procedure
Vinegar, cider	2 cups	Combine in mixer bowl, using wire whip.
Water	¾ cup	
Sugar, granulated	2 oz	
Garlic, fresh, minced	1½ Tbsp	
Salt	2 oz	
Basil, dried, crumbled	⅔ cup	
Salad oil	2 cups	Add oil very gradually while mixing.
Olive oil	½ cup	Store covered in the refrigerator. Stir before serving.

Approximate nutritive values per ounce

Calories (kcal)	Protein (grams)	Carbohydrate (grams)	Fat (grams)	Cholesterol (mg)	Sodium (mg)	Iron (mg)	Calcium (mg)
108	0 (0%)	2.1 (7%)	11.6 (92%)	0	468	0.2	9

VINAIGRETTE DRESSING

Yield: 2 qt

Ingredient	Amount	Procedure
Vinegar, cider	2 cups	Combine in mixer bowl.
Salt	1½ oz	
Pepper, white	2 tsp	
Pepper, cayenne	¼ tsp	
Salad oil	2½ cups	Combine oils. Add very slowly to vinegar mixture, mixing on low speed until oil is blended in.
Olive oil	2¾ cups	
Parsley, fresh, chopped	½ cup	Add to dressing. Mix. Store in refrigerator.
Garlic, minced	5 cloves	Stir or shake before serving.
Chives, frozen	½ cup	
Capers	4 oz	

Approximate nutritive values per ounce

Calories (kcal)	Protein (grams)	Carbohydrate (grams)	Fat (grams)	Cholesterol (mg)	Sodium (mg)	Iron (mg)	Calcium (mg)
156	0 (0%)	0.7 (2%)	17.5 (98%)	0	254	0.1	4

Variations

- **Dijon Mustard Vinaigrette.**   Combine 2½ cups red wine vinegar, ¾ oz chopped chives, ¾ cup Dijon mustard, and 1 oz (1½ Tbsp) salt in mixer bowl. Slowly add 4¾ cups salad oil while mixing on medium speed, using wire whip. Mix until oil is blended in. Makes approximately 2 qt.

- **Lemon Basil Dressing.**   Combine 2 cups cider vinegar, 1½ cups lemon juice, 6 oz granulated sugar, 2½ oz salt, and 4½ Tbsp dried basil leaves. Gradually add 3 cups salad oil.

- **Lime Salad Dressing.**   Combine in mixer bowl 2½ cups frozen reconstituted lime juice, 1¼ cups sugar, 2 oz salt, 1 tsp white pepper, ¾ tsp red pepper, and 1½ tsp celery salt. Add 4½ cups salad oil very slowly, mixing on medium speed until oil is blended in. Makes approximately 2 qt dressing.

- **Pimiento Vinaigrette Dressing.**   Substitute 4 oz diced pimiento for capers.

SWEET SESAME VINAIGRETTE DRESSING

Yield: 2 qt

Ingredient	Amount	Procedure
Sugar, granulated	1 lb 10 oz	Combine in mixer bowl.
Sesame seeds	4 oz	
Poppy seeds	2 oz	
Paprika	1½ tsp	
Onion, minced	3 Tbsp	
Worcestershire sauce	1½ tsp	
Salad oil	3 cups	Using a whip attachment to mix, add vinegar and oil in a slow stream.
Vinegar, cider	1⅔ cups	Whip for at least 1 minute and make sure sugar is dissolved.

Approximate nutritive values per ounce							
Calories (kcal)	Protein (grams)	Carbohydrate (grams)	Fat (grams)	Cholesterol (mg)	Sodium (mg)	Iron (mg)	Calcium (mg)
112	0.4 (1%)	9.6 (33%)	8.6 (66%)	0	1	0.3	24

Note   ■   Serve over fresh greens and fruit.

CELERY SEED FRUIT DRESSING

Yield: 2 qt

Ingredient	Amount	Procedure
Sugar, granulated	1 lb 8 oz	Mix dry ingredients in kettle.
Cornstarch	⅓ cup	
Dry mustard	2 Tbsp	
Salt	2 Tbsp	
Paprika	2 Tbsp	
Vinegar, cider	2 cups	Add vinegar to dry ingredients. Stir and cook until thickened and clear.
Onion juice	1 tsp	Add onion juice. Cool to room temperature.
Salad oil	1 qt	Add oil slowly to cooked mixture while beating on high speed.
Celery seed	2 Tbsp	Add celery seed. Serve with any fruit salad combination.

Approximate nutritive values per ounce							
Calories (kcal)	Protein (grams)	Carbohydrate (grams)	Fat (grams)	Cholesterol (mg)	Sodium (mg)	Iron (mg)	Calcium (mg)
166	0.1 (0%)	12 (28%)	13.8 (72%)	0	200	0.2	7

Variations
- **Poppy Seed Dressing.** Add poppy seed in place of celery seed.
- **Golden Fruit Dressing.** Add 1½–2 Tbsp prepared mustard after mixture has cooked.

FRUIT SALAD DRESSING

Yield: 4½ qt

Ingredient	Amount	Procedure
Pineapple juice	1 qt	Combine juices. Heat to boiling point.
Orange juice	3 cups	
Lemon juice	2 cups	
Sugar, granulated	2 lb	Mix sugar and cornstarch.
Cornstarch	5 oz	Add to hot mixture while stirring with a wire whip.
Eggs, beaten	16 (1 lb 12 oz)	Add eggs to hot mixture while stirring. Cook until thickened. Chill.
Cream, whipping	2 cups	Whip cream and fold into dressing just before serving. Serve with fruit salads.

Approximate nutritive values per ounce							
Calories (kcal)	Protein (grams)	Carbohydrate (grams)	Fat (grams)	Cholesterol (mg)	Sodium (mg)	Iron (mg)	Calcium (mg)
52	0.8 (6%)	9.1 (67%)	1.6 (27%)	27	9	0.1	7

YOGURT HERB DRESSING

Yield: 3½ qt

Ingredient	Amount	Procedure
Yogurt, plain	6 lb	Blend in mixer bowl, using flat beater.
Salad dressing	1 lb	
Prepared horse-radish	4 oz	
Basil, dried, crumbled	1 Tbsp	Add seasonings. Blend well.
Tarragon, dried, crumbled	1 Tbsp	Store in refrigerator in covered containers.
Thyme, ground	½ tsp	
Celery seed	1 Tbsp	
Pepper, black, cracked	1 Tbsp	

Approximate nutritive values per ounce

Calories (kcal)	Protein (grams)	Carbohydrate (grams)	Fat (grams)	Cholesterol (mg)	Sodium (mg)	Iron (mg)	Calcium (mg)
30	0.9 (11%)	2.6 (32%)	2.1 (58%)	4	49	0.1	31

Note   ▪ May be used as a dip for fresh vegetables.

YOGURT ORANGE DRESSING

Yield: 3½ qt

Ingredient	Amount	Procedure
Yogurt, plain	6 lb	Measure all ingredients into mixer bowl. Blend together, using wire whip.
Honey	1¼ cups	
Orange juice concentrate, thawed	6 oz	Refrigerate covered until chilled. Serve over fruit.
Cinnamon, ground	1½ tsp	
Nutmeg, ground	1 tsp	

Approximate nutritive values per ounce

Calories (kcal)	Protein (grams)	Carbohydrate (grams)	Fat (grams)	Cholesterol (mg)	Sodium (mg)	Iron (mg)	Calcium (mg)
29	0.9 (12%)	4.7 (64%)	0.8 (24%)	3	11	0.1	30

Note   ▪ May be used as a dip for fresh fruit.

CUCUMBER YOGURT DRESSING

Yield: 2½ qt

Ingredient	Amount	Procedure
Salad dressing	2 cups	Combine in mixer bowl.
Sour cream	12 oz	
Garlic, fresh, minced	1 Tbsp	
Chives, frozen	½ cup	
Salt	1½ tsp	
Pepper, black	⅛ tsp	
Cucumbers, fresh	1 lb 8 oz AP	Peel and seed cucumbers. Chop finely. Add to sour cream mixture.
Yogurt, plain	3½ cups	Fold in. Chill.

Approximate nutritive values per ounce

Calories (kcal)	Protein (grams)	Carbohydrate (grams)	Fat (grams)	Cholesterol (mg)	Sodium (mg)	Iron (mg)	Calcium (mg)
39	0.6 (6%)	2.9 (27%)	3.2 (67%)	5	88	0.1	19

12

Sandwiches

Sandwiches continue to be favorite choices for the noon and evening meals. They have become popular, too, at breakfast or any meal throughout the day where a fast, flavorful meal is desired. Sandwiches are popular also as hors d'oeuvres or buffet foods. Sandwiches may be closed or open-faced and may be served hot or cold. Nutritional requirements are easily satisfied by choosing breads and fillings that are high in fiber, low in fat, and low in cholesterol.

PREPARATION OF INGREDIENTS

Sandwich ingredients include bread, spread, filling, and vegetable accompaniments. Many ingredient variations are possible, but the basic procedures for preparing ingredients are the same.

Breads

Different breads and rolls add variety in flavor, texture, size, and shape. Bread should be kept fresh during and after preparation. Keep bread tightly wrapped until used. French bread or other crusty breads, however, should not be wrapped because the crust will soften. They should be used the day they are baked. Bread should not be refrigerated, because it will become stale faster than if kept at room temperature. If bread must be kept longer than one or two days, it may be frozen. Defrost frozen bread without unwrapping.

Spreads

Bread for sandwiches is first spread with plain or seasoned margarine or butter, mayonnaise, or a Sandwich Spread (p. 559). Covering bread evenly with a spread helps keep the sandwich from becoming soggy. Margarine or butter may be softened by letting it stand at room temperature, or it may be whipped for easy spreading (see p. 559). Allow 1 tsp of spread per slice of bread.

Fillings

Slice meat and cheese into even slices. Tender meats may be sliced thicker than less tender ones. A serving of thinly sliced or wafer-sliced meats usually appears larger than an equal weight of thicker slices. Since sliced meats and cheeses dry out quickly, they should be sliced only as needed and kept covered. Mixed fillings should be prepared the day they are served and kept chilled.

Vegetable Accompaniments

Prepare greens, tomato and onion slices, and pickles or other vegetable accompaniments. Ingredients should be fresh, crisp, and attractive. See pp. 480–491 for preparing vegetable accompaniments.

PREPARATION OF SANDWICHES

Closed Sandwiches

1. Prepare filling and spread.
2. Arrange fresh bread in rows on a baking sheet or a worktable. Four rows of ten slices each is a manageable number.
3. Spread all bread slices to the edges with softened margarine or butter or other spread.
4. Portion filling with dipper or spoon on alternate rows of bread and spread to the edges, or arrange sliced filling to fit the sandwich.
5. If lettuce or other vegetable accompaniment is used, arrange on filling. If sandwiches are to be held for some time, vegetable accompaniments should be omitted.
6. Place plain buttered (or spread) slices of bread on the filled slices.
7. If the sandwiches are to be cut in half or in fourths, stack two or three together and cut with a sharp knife, being careful not to mash bread.
8. To keep sandwiches fresh, place in sandwich bags or plastic wrap. Avoid stacking sandwiches more than three high, because stacking insulates the filling and prevents it from reaching the desired temperature as quickly as it should.

9. Refrigerate until served. If freezing sandwiches for later use, see precautions on p. 558.

10. Handle bread and fillings as little as possible during preparation. Use plastic gloves or tongs when picking up food.

Grilled and Toasted Sandwiches

1. For a grilled sandwich, place filling between two slices of bread. Fillings may be sliced cheese, meat, or poultry; chopped fillings as in salads; or a combination of fillings as in a Reuben Sandwich (p. 573).

2. Brush the outside with melted margarine or butter. For large quantities, a brush or roller dipped in the melted spread may be used. The steps for this method are: (a) Place parchment paper in bottom of baking sheet. (b) Place bread slices directly on coated paper. Add filling to all slices in pan. (c) Top with slices of bread.

3. Brown sandwich on a griddle, in a hot oven, or under a broiler.

4. For a toasted sandwich, toast the bread before filling.

Open-Faced Hot Sandwiches

1. Place buttered or unbuttered bread on a serving plate.

2. Cover with hot meat or other filling.

3. Top with gravy, sauce, or other topping.

4. For a hot sandwich that is to be broiled, arrange slices of bread on a baking sheet. Cover with slices of cheese or other topping. Broil just before serving.

Canapés

1. Remove crusts from bread.

2. Cut into desired shapes.

3. Spread with softened margarine or butter.

4. Cover with filling.

5. Decorate with parsley, sliced olives, sliced radishes, pimiento pieces, chopped hard-cooked eggs, or other garnish.

Ribbon Sandwiches

1. Remove crusts from two kinds of bread, being careful to have all slices the same size.

2. Spread one or more fillings on slices of bread.

3. Make stacks of five slices of bread, alternating kinds of bread.

4. Press together firmly.

5. Arrange stacks in shallow pan; cover with plastic wrap, plastic bag, or waxed paper.

6. Chill for several hours.

7. To serve, cut each slice into thirds, halves, or triangles.

Checkerboard Sandwiches

1. Spread slices of white and whole wheat bread with desired filling.
2. Make stacks of ribbon sandwiches by alternating two slices of white and two slices of whole wheat bread. Trim and cut each stack into ½-inch slices.
3. Using butter or smooth spread as a filling, stack three slices together so that white and whole wheat squares alternate to give a checkerboard effect.
4. Chill for several hours.
5. Remove from refrigerator and, with sharp knife, slice into checkerboard slices, ½ inch thick.

Rolled Sandwiches

1. Remove crusts from three sides of a loaf of unsliced bread.
2. With crust at left, cut loaf into lengthwise slices ⅛–¼ inch thick.
3. Run rolling pin the length of each slice to make it easier to handle.
4. Spread with softened margarine or butter.
5. Spread with desired smooth filling.
6. Place olives, watercress, or other foods across the end.
7. Starting at end with garnish, roll tightly, being careful to keep sides straight. Tight rolling makes for easier slicing.
8. Wrap rolls individually in waxed paper or aluminum foil, twisting ends securely.
9. Chill several hours or overnight. Rolls may be made ahead of time, then wrapped and frozen. Let thaw about 45 minutes before slicing.
10. Cut chilled rolls into ¼–⅓ inch slices.

FREEZING SANDWICHES

When making sandwiches to be frozen for later use, certain precautions should be taken.

1. Spread bread with margarine or butter instead of mayonnaise or salad dressing.
2. Do not use fillings containing mayonnaise, egg white, or some vegetables such as tomatoes and parsley. Chicken, meat, fish, cheese, and peanut butter freeze well.
3. Place large closed sandwiches individually in a sandwich bag or wrap individually in plastic wrap.
4. Pack tea-sized closed sandwiches in layers, separated by waxed paper or plastic wrap, in freezer boxes; or place in any suitable box and overwrap with moisture-proof material.
5. Place open-faced sandwiches on trays, wrap as for closed sandwiches.

6. Wrap ribbon, closed, or other loaf sandwiches uncut.

7. Allow 1–2 hours for sandwiches to defrost. Do not remove outer wrapping until sandwiches are partly thawed.

8. If sandwiches are not served immediately after thawing, refrigerate until serving time.

SANDWICH RECIPES

WHIPPED MARGARINE OR BUTTER

Yield: spread for 50 sandwiches   *Portion:* 1 tsp per slice

Ingredient	Amount	Procedure
Margarine or butter	1 lb	Place in mixer bowl. Let stand at room temperature until soft enough to mix.
Milk or boiling water (optional)	½ cup	Add milk or water while whipping. Mix on low speed, gradually increasing to high speed. Whip until fluffy.

Variations
- **Honey Butter.**   Cream 1 lb butter or margarine until light and fluffy. Add 8 oz honey gradually, beating on medium speed until mixture is light. Serve with hot biscuits or other hot bread.
- **Savory Spread.**   Add minced cucumber, onion, or pimiento; chopped chives or parsley; horseradish; or prepared mustard to whipped butter or margarine.

SANDWICH SPREAD

Yield: spread for 100 sandwiches   *Portion:* 1 tsp per slice

Ingredient	Amount	Procedure
Margarine or butter	8 oz	Whip margarine on high speed until light and fluffy.
Light cream (half-and-half)	¼ cup	Add cream and mix.
Prepared mustard	1½ tsp	Fold in remaining ingredients.
Mayonnaise	3 cups	Use as a spread for meat or cheese sandwiches.
Pickle relish	½ cup	

CHEESE SALAD SANDWICH

Yield: 50 sandwiches

Ingredient	Amount	Procedure
Cheddar cheese	3 lb 8 oz	Grind or shred cheese.
Salad dressing or cream	2 cups	Combine with cheese.
Salt	2 tsp	
Pepper, cayenne	Few grains	
Margarine, softened	4 oz	
Bread	100 slices	Assemble filling and bread (p. 556). Portion filling with No. 20 dipper.

Approximate nutritive values per portion

Calories (kcal)	Protein (grams)	Carbohydrate (grams)	Fat (grams)	Cholesterol (mg)	Sodium (mg)	Iron (mg)	Calcium (mg)
318	13.4 (16%)	29 (35%)	17.9 (49%)	36	726	2.1	272

Variation   ■ **Pimiento Cheese Sandwich.**   Add 6 oz chopped pimiento.

EGG SALAD SANDWICH

Yield: 50 sandwiches   *Portion:* 2 oz filling

Ingredient	Amount	Procedure
Eggs, hard-cooked (p. 308)	36	Peel eggs and chop coarsely.
Mayonnaise or salad dressing	2½ cups	Combine and add to eggs. Mix lightly.
Pickle relish	1 cup	
Salt	2 tsp	
Pepper, white	¼ tsp	
Onion juice	1 tsp	
Pimiento, chopped	4 oz	
Bread	100 slices	Assemble filling, bread, and lettuce (p. 556). Portion filling with No. 20 dipper.
Lettuce, iceburg or leaf	2–3 heads	

Approximate nutritive values per portion							
Calories (kcal)	Protein (grams)	Carbohydrate (grams)	Fat (grams)	Cholesterol (mg)	Sodium (mg)	Iron (mg)	Calcium (mg)
248	10.3 (15%)	31.9 (48%)	10.2 (34%)	156	611	2.6	66

Notes
- 1 lb chopped celery may be substituted for pickle relish.
- 2 Tbsp prepared mustard may be added.

HAM SALAD SANDWICH

Yield: 50 sandwiches   *Portion:* 2 oz filling

Ingredient	*Amount*	*Procedure*
Cooked ham	4 lb	Grind ham coarsely.
Eggs, hard-cooked (p. 308)	6	Peel eggs and chop coarsely.
Onion, finely chopped	4 oz	Combine all ingredients. Mix lightly.
Pickle relish	8 oz	
Mayonnaise or salad dressing	2–2½ cups	
Bread	100 slices	Assemble filling, bread, and lettuce (p. 556).
Lettuce, iceberg or leaf	2–3 heads	Portion filling with No. 20 dipper.

Approximate nutritive values per portion							
Calories (kcal)	Protein (grams)	Carbohydrate (grams)	Fat (grams)	Cholesterol (mg)	Sodium (mg)	Iron (mg)	Calcium (mg)
257	14.7 (22%)	30.8 (46%)	9.5 (32%)	49	1014	2.6	53

Variations
- **Ham and Cheese Sandwich.**   Delete eggs. Reduce ham to 3 lb. Add 1 lb 8 oz cheddar or Swiss cheese, ground.
- **Meat Salad Sandwich.**   Substitute ground cooked beef or pork for ham. Add 4 oz finely chopped celery. Check for seasoning and add salt and pepper if needed.

CHICKEN SALAD SANDWICH

Yield: 50 sandwiches   *Portion:* 2 oz filling

Ingredient	Amount	Procedure
Cooked chicken	5 lb	Chop chicken coarsely.
Salt	2 tsp	Add remaining ingredients. Mix to blend.
Pepper, white	½ tsp	
Celery, finely chopped	8 oz	
Lemon juice or cider vinegar	¼ cup	
Mayonnaise or salad dressing	2–2½ cups	
Bread	100 slices	Assemble filling, bread, and lettuce (p. 556).
Lettuce, iceberg or leaf	2–3 heads	Portion filling with No. 20 dipper.

Calories (kcal)	Protein (grams)	Carbohydrate (grams)	Fat (grams)	Cholesterol (mg)	Sodium (mg)	Iron (mg)	Calcium (mg)
258	18.1 (27%)	29.3 (44%)	8.7 (29%)	40	546	2.6	55

Approximate nutritive values per portion

Notes
- 4 oz chopped, toasted almonds may be added.
- Alfalfa sprouts may be placed on top of filling for variety.

TUNA SALAD SANDWICH

Yield: 50 sandwiches   *Portion:* 2 oz filling

Ingredient	Amount	Procedure
Eggs, hard-cooked (p. 308)	7	Peel eggs and chop coarsely.
Tuna, flaked	4 lb	Combine all filling ingredients.
Celery, chopped	4 oz	
Lemon juice	¼ cup	
Onion juice	1 tsp	
Mayonnaise or salad dressing	1½ cups	
Bread	100 slices	Assemble filling, bread, and lettuce (p. 556).
Lettuce, iceberg or leaf	2–3 heads	Portion filling with No. 20 dipper.

Calories (kcal)	Protein (grams)	Carbohydrate (grams)	Fat (grams)	Cholesterol (mg)	Sodium (mg)	Iron (mg)	Calcium (mg)
251	17.2 (26%)	28.4 (44%)	8.6 (30%)	38	547	2.6	55

Approximate nutritive values per portion

Note
- 1 cup pickle relish may be substituted for celery.

Variations
- **Grilled Tuna Salad Sandwich.**   Brush both sides of sandwiches with melted margarine or butter. Grill until golden brown.
- **Salmon Salad Sandwich.**   Substitute salmon for tuna.

BACON, LETTUCE, AND TOMATO SANDWICH

Yield: 50 sandwiches

Ingredient	Amount	Procedure
Tomatoes, fresh	7 lb	Wash tomatoes. Peel, if desired, and cut into thin slices.
Lettuce, iceberg or leaf	2–3 heads or 2 lb leaf	Wash lettuce and separate leaves. Drain.
Bacon	150 slices (7 lb)	Cook bacon according to directions on p. 394. Drain.
Bread (white or whole wheat)	100 slices	Spread 50 slices of bread with mayonnaise.
Mayonnaise	1 cup	Place 3 cooked bacon slices, 2 tomato slices, and a lettuce leaf on each.
Whipped margarine or butter (p. 559)	8 oz	Top with remaining 50 slices of bread, which have been spread with Whipped Margarine or Butter.

Approximate nutritive values per portion

Calories (kcal)	Protein (grams)	Carbohydrate (grams)	Fat (grams)	Cholesterol (mg)	Sodium (mg)	Iron (mg)	Calcium (mg)
286	11.6 (16%)	28.9 (39%)	14.9 (45%)	17	671	2.6	49

Variations
- **Club Sandwich.**   Use 150 thin slices white bread toasted. Spread with mayonnaise. Place on first slice 1 lettuce leaf, 2 tomato slices, and 2 strips of bacon. Place second slice of toast on top, spread side down. Spread top with mayonnaise, then add 2 oz thinly sliced turkey or chicken breast and lettuce leaf. Top with third slice of toast, spread side down. Secure with 4 picks. Cut into quarters to serve.
- **Sliced Ham and Cheese Sandwich.**   Substitute 6 lb 8 oz wafer-sliced ham and 3 lb 2 oz (1 oz slices) cheese for bacon.
- **Turkey Club Hoagie.**   Reduce bacon to 2 lb. Substitute 7-inch hoagie buns for sliced bread. Use 6 lb 8 oz cooked turkey breast (approximately 10 lb AP), wafer-sliced. Each sandwich includes choice of sandwich spread, 2 oz sliced turkey, 1 bacon slice, 1 lettuce leaf, and 2 tomato slices. Garnish plate with dill pickle spear.

SUBMARINE SANDWICH

Yield: 50 sandwiches   *Portion:* 3 oz meat + 1 oz cheese

Ingredient	Amount	Procedure
Buns, submarine or hoagie, 4–5 inches	50	Slice buns in half lengthwise. Spread both sides of bun with Sandwich Spread.
Sandwich Spread (p. 559)	½ recipe	
Salami, 1-oz slices	3 lb 2 oz	Cut slices of meat and cheese in half.
Luncheon meat, 1-oz slices	3 lb 2 oz	Arrange 1 oz of each kind of meat and 1 oz cheese on bottom half of each bun.
Ham, pullman, 1-oz slices	3 lb 2 oz	Alternate meat and cheese and arrange so that full length of each bun is covered.
Cheese, processed, American or Swiss, 1-oz slices	3 lb 2 oz	
Tomatoes, fresh, sliced	24	Place 2 slices tomato, ½ oz shredded lettuce, and 2 dill pickle slices on each sandwich.
Dill pickle slices, well drained (optional)	1 qt	Cover with top half of bun. To serve, cut each sandwich in half.
Shredded head lettuce	1 lb 9 oz	

Approximate nutritive values per portion

Calories (kcal)	Protein (grams)	Carbohydrate (grams)	Fat (grams)	Cholesterol (mg)	Sodium (mg)	Iron (mg)	Calcium (mg)
789	32.2 (16%)	80.5 (41%)	37 (43%)	80	2557	4.8	252

Notes
- Other meats such as turkey, corned beef, pastrami, or roast beef may be used.
- Shredded red or green cabbage, alfalfa sprouts, or leaf lettuce may be substituted for shredded head lettuce.
- Mayonnaise or Italian dressing may be substituted for sandwich spread.

Variations
- **Buffet Submarine.**   Use 12 long, thin buns, approximately 18 inches. Arrange 4 oz each of meats and cheese on each bun. Garnish with 2 tomatoes, sliced, ⅓ cup pickle slices, and 1–2 oz shredded lettuce. Secure with long picks. Portion as served into 4–5-inch sections.
- **Ring Submarine.**   Use bread shaped in a ring. See p. 147 for Sandwich Ring recipe.

GRILLED SANDWICHES

Yield: 50 portions   *Portion:* 1 sandwich
Griddle: 350°F

Ingredient	Amount	Procedure
Bread (white, whole wheat, or rye)	100 slices	See following procedures for preparing sandwiches.
Meat and/or cheese	6 lb 4 oz	
Margarine	1 lb	Grill sandwiches at 350°F on griddle until both sides are delicately brown.

Procedure No. 1

1. Melt margarine. Pour into 2-inch counter pan.
2. Pick up two slices of bread, one in each hand. Dip one side of one slice in melted margarine. Press dipped slice against second slice.
3. Place buttered side of one slice on 18 × 26-inch baking sheet lined with parchment or waxed paper. Place 24 slices 4 × 6.
4. Top each slice with 2 oz meat and/or cheese.
5. Top meat and/or cheese with buttered bread (from Step 2), buttered side up.
6. Cover layer with parchment or waxed paper.
7. Repeat for a second layer or use another baking sheet. Cover tightly with plastic wrap if the sandwiches are not to be grilled immediately.

Procedure No. 2

1. Place meat and/or cheese between two slices of bread.
2. Brush sandwiches with melted margarine; or in large quantities, use a roller dipped in melted margarine.
3. Place sandwiches on baking sheet and cover with plastic wrap until grilled.

Variations
- **Grilled Cheese.**   Use processed American cheese, 2 1-oz slices per sandwich.
- **Grilled Corned Beef and Swiss on Rye.**   Substitute corned beef for ham in variation No. 3. Use Swiss cheese and rye bread.
- **Grilled Ham and Cheese.**   Use 1½ oz ham and 1 oz cheese per sandwich. 4 lb 12 oz wafer-sliced ham and 3 lb 2 oz (1-oz slices) will be needed.
- **Grilled Turkey and Swiss on Whole Wheat.**   Use 1½ oz turkey and 1 oz Swiss cheese per sandwich. 4 lb 12 oz wafer-sliced turkey and 3 lb 2 oz cheese (1-oz slices) will be needed.
- **Hot Tuna Grill.**   Use No. 10 dipper of Tuna Salad Sandwich filling (p. 562) for each sandwich. Other salad sandwich fillings may be used.

BIEROCKS   ■

Yield: 50 sandwiches
Oven: 400 °F   *Bake:* 25–30 minutes, 5 minutes

Ingredient	Amount	Procedure
Dough		
Yeast, active dry	1¼ oz	Sprinkle yeast over water. Let stand 5 minutes.
Water, warm (110°F)	2 qt	
Sugar, granulated	14 oz	Add sugar, salt, and flour to yeast.
Salt	1 oz (1½ Tbsp)	Mix on medium speed, until mixture is smooth, using
Flour, all-purpose	2 lb 6 oz	dough arm or flat beater.
Eggs	8 (14 oz)	Add eggs and shortening. Continue beating.
Shortening, melted	5 oz	
Flour, all-purpose	5 lb 8 oz	Add flour on low speed to make a soft dough. Knead 5 minutes.
		Cover and let rise until double in bulk.
		When dough has doubled, punch down and divide into 4 or 5 portions.
		Roll dough to ¼-inch thickness.
		Cut into 4 × 6-inch rectangles.
		Place on each piece of dough a No. 8 dipper of filling (recipe follows).
		Fold lengthwise and pinch edges of dough securely to seal.
		Place on baking sheets with sealed edges down.
		Bake at 400°F for 25–30 minutes.
Egg yolk	1	Brush with egg and water mixture.
Water	2 Tbsp	Return to oven for 5 minutes.
Filling		
Ground beef	10 lb AP (7 lb EP)	Brown beef. Drain.
Cabbage, chopped	2 lb 8 oz	Steam cabbage and onion until slightly underdone.
Onion, chopped	3 lb	
Worcestershire sauce	⅓ cup	Add seasonings and vegetables to beef.
Salt	2½ oz	
Pepper, black	1½ tsp	
Savory, ground	1 tsp	
Chili powder	1½ tsp	

Approximate nutritive values per portion

Calories (kcal)	Protein (grams)	Carbohydrate (grams)	Fat (grams)	Cholesterol (mg)	Sodium (mg)	Iron (mg)	Calcium (mg)
529	26.5 (20%)	66.8 (51%)	16.6 (29%)	100	834	5.6	47

Variation   ■ **Bierock Pockets.** Scale 3 lb dough onto 18 × 26 × 1-inch greased pans. Cut dough in half lengthwise. Spread 2 lb beef mixture evenly onto each strip of dough. Roll jelly roll fashion and seal tightly. Place seam side down on greased 18 × 26 × 1-inch pan. Bake at 350°F for 30–35 minutes or until done. Cut each roll into 8 portions, 16 per pan.

HOT MEAT AND CHEESE SANDWICH

Yield: 50 portions   *Portion:* 2½ oz meat + 1½ oz sauce

Ingredient	Amount	Procedure
Ham, roast beef, or corned beef	8 lb	Wafer-slice meat into 12 × 10 × 2-inch pans. Cover and heat.
Hamburger buns	50	To serve, place open bun on plate. Portion 2½ oz meat on bottom half of bun.
Cheese Sandwich Sauce, American or Cheddar (p. 583) or Swiss (p. 583)	3 qt	Ladle 1½ oz (No. 30 dipper) sauce over meat.

Approximate nutritive values per portion

Calories (kcal)	Protein (grams)	Carbohydrate (grams)	Fat (grams)	Cholesterol (mg)	Sodium (mg)	Iron (mg)	Calcium (mg)
383	26.3 (28%)	25.2 (27%)	19.1 (45%)	67	1604	2.6	245

TUNA MELT

■

Yield: 50   *Portion:* 1 sandwich
Griddle: 350°F

Ingredient	Amount	Procedure
Tuna, drained	3 lb 4 oz	Mix drained tuna and drained pickle with celery and salad dressing.
Pickle relish, drained	12 oz	
Celery, finely chopped	1 lb	
Salad dressing	1 lb 8 oz	
Wheat bread, pull-man	100 slices	Assemble and cook sandwiches as described next.
Swiss cheese, ½ oz slices	3 lb 2 oz	
Margarine, melted	1 lb	

To Assemble:

1. Preheat griddle to 350°F.

2. Assemble sandwiches on greased griddle as follows:
   1 slice wheat bread
   1 slice Swiss cheese
   1 No. 24 (2 oz) dipper tuna mixture (preceding recipe)
   1 slice Swiss cheese
   1 slice wheat bread

3. When bread has browned (approximately 10 minutes), pour small amount of melted margarine on empty portion of grill.

4. Flip the sandwiches onto empty portion of grill. Cook until browned.

5. Place cooked sandwiches in 12 × 20 × 2-inch pans. Serve within 15 minutes.

6. Serve cut in half diagonally and garnish with tomato wedge on parsley sprig.

Approximate nutritive values per portion							
Calories (kcal)	Protein (grams)	Carbohydrate (grams)	Fat (grams)	Cholesterol (mg)	Sodium (mg)	Iron (mg)	Calcium (mg)
409	21.9 (21%)	33.6 (32%)	22.2 (47%)	34	774	3	325

Variation ■ **Patty Melt.** Substitute grilled ground beef patty for tuna mixture. Place 1 oz grilled onions on top of patty before last slice of cheese is added. Rye bread may be substituted for wheat bread and cheddar or American cheese for Swiss cheese.

HOT ROAST BEEF SANDWICH

Yield: 50 sandwiches   *Portion:* 3 oz meat + ¼ cup gravy

Ingredient	Amount	Procedure
Beef roast	10 lb EP (15 lb AP)	Roast beef according to directions on p. 352. Slice into 3-oz portions. Place in two 12 × 20 × 2-inch counter pans.
Beef Stock (p. 616)	1½ qt	Heat stock. Pour over meat. Cover with aluminum foil and place in oven to keep warm.
Bread	50 slices	Place 3 oz meat on each slice of bread.
Mashed Potatoes (p. 671)	12 lb 8 oz	Serve No. 12 dipper of Mashed Potatoes on the plate beside the bread.
Gravy (p. 586)	1 gal	Cover meat and potato with Gravy, using 2-oz ladle.

Approximate nutritive values per portion

Calories (kcal)	Protein (grams)	Carbohydrate (grams)	Fat (grams)	Cholesterol (mg)	Sodium (mg)	Iron (mg)	Calcium (mg)
468	36.9 (31%)	35.2 (40%)	20.1 (39%)	100	1034	5	63

Notes
- A tender cut of meat should be used.
- Meat may be covered with additional slice of bread if desired. Omit mashed potatoes. Cover entire sandwich with gravy.

Variations
- **Barbecued Beef Sandwich.**   Place thinly sliced beef roast in 2 counter pans and keep warm. Heat 1½ qt Barbecue Sauce (p. 588) and pour 3 cups over each pan of meat. Toss together until sauce is evenly distributed. Serve in warm hamburger buns.
- **French Dip Sandwich.**   Slice roast beef wafer thin. Place in 12 × 20 × 2-inch counter pan. Pour 1 cup Beef Stock (p. 616) over meat. Cover with aluminum foil and keep warm. To serve, place 3 oz beef on hard roll. Serve with side cup of hot seasoned broth for dipping.
- **Hot Roast Pork Sandwich.**   Substitute roast pork for beef.
- **Hot Turkey Dip.**   Follow directions for French Dip Sandwich, but substitute wafer-sliced turkey for beef and chicken broth for beef broth. Season chicken stock with poultry seasoning.
- **Hot Turkey Sandwich.**   Substitute roast turkey or turkey roll for beef. Use Chicken Stock (p. 615) in place of Beef Stock.
- **Meatloaf Sandwich.**   Prepare Meatloaf (p. 370). Substitute Meatloaf for roast beef.

FAJITAS

Yield: 50 portions   *Portion:* 1 fajita, 2 oz meat + 2 oz vegetable

Ingredient	Amount	Procedure
Pureed jalapeño peppers, with juice	4 oz	Combine in bowl to make a marinade.
Lemon juice	1½ cups	
Pineapple juice	1½ cups	
Salt	1 Tbsp	
Pepper, black	2 Tbsp	
Meat tenderizer	2 oz	
Water	3 cups	
Beef, round or flank steak	10 lb AP	Cut beef into 1 × 5-inch strips, ¼-inch thick (see Notes). Pour marinade over meat. Stir to coat meat. Cover and marinate for 24 hours.
		Drain meat in colander. Discard marinade. Stir-fry in frying pan with a small amount of oil until cooked.
Onions, sliced, separated in rings	2 lb 8 oz	Add onions and green peppers to meat. Stir-fry until tender-crisp.
Green pepper strips	1 lb 8 oz	Transfer to 12 × 10 × 4-inch pan.
Tomatoes, fresh	2 lb 8 oz	Cut tomatoes into thin wedges. Combine carefully with beef. Gently lift beef and vegetables from juice into 12 × 20 × 2-inch counter pan.
Tortillas, flour, 10-inch	50	Heat tortillas to soften. Keep covered. Do not allow to dry out. Serve 1 tortilla on plate and 4 oz beef and vegetables in center of tortilla. Tortilla may be rolled or folded in half.
		Serve with condiments: Guacamole (p. 88), shredded Monterey Jack cheese, shredded lettuce, sour cream, Salsa (p. 589), sliced black olives, sliced jalapeños.

Approximate nutritive values per portion							
Calories (kcal)	Protein (grams)	Carbohydrate (grams)	Fat (grams)	Cholesterol (mg)	Sodium (mg)	Iron (mg)	Calcium (mg)
262	23.5 (36%)	23 (35%)	8.2 (28%)	62	199	3.7	61

Notes
- Meat will slice more easily if it is partially frozen.
- Fajita meat can be made spicier by substituting additional pureed jalapeños for equal parts of water. More water in proportion to less jalapeños may be used for a less spicy Fajita.
- Beef strips may be purchased frozen, seasoned or unseasoned.
- Commercial Fajita marinade mix may be substituted for marinade in the recipe.

Variation
- **Chicken Fajitas.**   Delete meat tenderizer. Increase salt to 2 Tbsp. Substitute chicken breasts for beef.

WESTERN SANDWICH

Yield: 50 sandwiches   *Portion:* 3 oz

Ingredient	Amount	Procedure
Ground beef	10 lb AP	Brown beef and onion. Drain off fat.
Onion, chopped	1 lb	
Tomato puree	3 cups	Add remaining filling ingredients to meat.
Catsup	3 cups	Simmer 15–20 minutes.
Water	1 cup	
Salt	1 Tbsp	
Paprika	2 tsp	
Dry mustard	2 tsp	
Worcestershire sauce	2 Tbsp	
Chili powder	1 Tbsp	
Hamburger buns	50	Serve with No. 12 dipper of filling on buns.

Approximate nutritive values per portion

Calories (kcal)	Protein (grams)	Carbohydrate (grams)	Fat (grams)	Cholesterol (mg)	Sodium (mg)	Iron (mg)	Calcium (mg)
179	7.5 (17%)	26.5 (59%)	4.8 (24%)	13	599	1.9	65

Notes
- If mixture becomes dry, add a small amount of water.
- 2 oz (1 cup) dehydrated onions, rehydrated in 1½ cups water, may be substituted for fresh onions (p. 55).

Variation
- **Pizzaburger.**   Delete paprika and chili powder. Add 1 Tbsp oregano, 1½ tsp basil, and 8 oz sliced mushrooms. Serve meat on bun and sprinkle with 1 lb 8 oz grated mozzarella cheese, ½ oz per serving.

TACOS

Yield: 50 portions   *Portion:* 2 tacos

Ingredient	Amount	Procedure
Ground beef, round	13 lb AP (9 lb EP)	Brown beef in steam-jacketed or other kettle. Drain off fat.
Onion, chopped	1 lb	Add onions and cook until softened.
Cornstarch	3 Tbsp	Combine cornstarch and seasonings in a bowl.
Chili powder	½ cup	Add to ground beef and onions. Mix well.
Garlic powder	1¾ Tbsp	
Salt	3 Tbsp	
Oregano, leaf	1 Tbsp	
Cumin, ground	2 Tbsp	
Pepper, cayenne	1 Tbsp	
Water	1½ qt	Add water to meat mixture. Mix. Simmer 45 minutes, stirring frequently.
Taco shells	100	Place shells in counter pans. Heat in oven until warm and crisp. To serve, fill each taco shell with No. 24 dipper of meat mixture 1½ oz each.

Topping

Head lettuce, chopped	4 lb EP	Cover meat mixture with lettuce, then tomato, and top with shredded cheese.
Tomatoes, fresh, diced	3 lb EP	Serve with Salsa (p. 589) to spoon on top.
Processed cheese, shredded	2 lb	

Approximate nutritive values per portion							
Calories (kcal)	Protein (grams)	Carbohydrate (grams)	Fat (grams)	Cholesterol (mg)	Sodium (mg)	Iron (mg)	Calcium (mg)
428	29.5 (27%)	19.1 (18%)	26.3 (55%)	99	591	3.6	193

Notes
- Commercial salsa may be substituted for Salsa recipe.
- Commercial taco seasoning mix may be substituted for spices. Follow manufacturer's directions for amount to use.
- 2 oz (1 cup) dehydrated onions, rehydrated in 1½ cups water, may be substituted for fresh onions (p. 55).

Variations
- **Nacho Tostadas.**   Place ¾ oz (about 6 large) round unsalted nacho chips on serving plate. Place No. 12 dipper (3 oz) taco meat on top of chips. Ladle 2 oz Nacho Sauce (p. 323) over meat. Place approximately 1½ oz shredded head lettuce and ¾ oz diced fresh tomatoes on top of meat. Serve with condiments: Guacamole (p. 88), sour cream, and Salsa (p. 589).
- **Tostadas.**   Fry fifty 10-inch flour or corn tortillas in hot oil, 20–30 seconds on each side, until crisp and golden brown. Drain on paper towel. Keep warm. To serve, spread each tortilla with No. 20 dipper Refried Beans (p. 654), then one No. 12 dipper of meat (3 oz). Top with 1½ oz chopped head lettuce, ¾ oz chopped fresh tomatoes, and 1 oz shredded cheese. Serve with condiments: Guacamole (p. 88), sour cream, Salsa (p. 589), chopped green onions, chopped green chilies, and sliced ripe olives.
- **Turkey Tacos.**   Substitute ground turkey for ground beef.

REUBEN SANDWICH

Yield: 50 sandwiches   *Portion:* 3 oz

Ingredient	Amount	Procedure
Cooked corned beef	4 lb 8 oz	Cut corned beef into very thin slices.
Rye bread Mayonnaise or Sandwich Spread (p. 559)	100 slices 2 cups	Spread No. 100 dipper (scant 2 tsp) dressing on bread.
Sauerkraut, well drained Swiss cheese, 1-oz slices	1½ qt 3 lb 2 oz	Place filling on bread, in order given: —1½ oz corned beef —2 Tbsp sauerkraut —1 oz cheese Cover with top slice of bread.
Margarine, melted	1 lb	Brush sandwiches with melted margarine. Preheat grill to 325°F. Grill sandwiches on both sides until delicately browned.

Approximate nutritive values per portion

Calories (kcal)	Protein (grams)	Carbohydrate (grams)	Fat (grams)	Cholesterol (mg)	Sodium (mg)	Iron (mg)	Calcium (mg)
447	23.7 (21%)	29.6 (26%)	26.2 (52%)	63	1172	2.7	332

CHIMICHANGA

Yield: 50 portions   *Portion:* 4 oz
Deep-Fat Fryer: 350°F

Ingredient	Amount	Procedure
Ground beef	10 lb 12 oz AP	Brown meat in steam-jacketed kettle. Drain.
Onions, chopped Green chili peppers, chopped	1 lb 10 oz 8 oz	Add onions and chili peppers to meat. Cook until tender.
Flour, all-purpose Garlic powder Cumin, ground Chili powder	4 oz ½ tsp 2 tsp 1 Tbsp	Stir flour and seasonings into meat mixture.
Salsa (see Notes) Beef base Water	1 lb 14 oz ¾ oz 1 qt	Add Salsa, beef base, and water. Cook 15–20 minutes or until very thick. The filling may be prepared the day before and refrigerated.
Flour tortillas, 10-inch	5 lb 8 oz	Separate tortillas and place slightly overlapping in counter pans. Cover tightly and heat a few at a time for about 5 minutes or just until soft.
Water, cold Cornstarch	2¼ cups 2 oz	Mix water and cornstarch.

To assemble:

1. Brush edges of tortillas with water-cornstarch mixture (Figure 12.1).
2. Place No. 12 dipper or 4 oz meat mixture slightly below center of each tortilla.
3. Fold bottom edge over filling.
4. Fold sides in, then roll into a cylinder. If necessary, brush on more water-cornstarch mixture to help seal edges.
5. Place seam side down on baking sheets until ready to fry. Cover.
6. Fry at 350°F until golden brown and crisp. Internal temperature should be 160°F.
7. Place in counter pans with liners. Do not cover.
8. Serve with topping (recipe follows).

Topping

Lettuce, shredded	3 lb 8 oz	Serve each Chimichanga with 1 oz each of shredded lettuce, chopped tomato, Guacamole, sour cream, and olives; 2 oz Salsa. See Notes.
Tomato, chopped	3 lb 8 oz	
Guacamole (p. 88)	3 lb 8 oz	
Sour cream	3 lb 8 oz	
Black olives, chopped	3 lb 8 oz	
Salsa (p. 589) or Spanish Sauce (p. 592)	3 qt	

Approximate nutritive values per portion

Calories (kcal)	Protein (grams)	Carbohydrate (grams)	Fat (grams)	Cholesterol (mg)	Sodium (mg)	Iron (mg)	Calcium (mg)
576	27 (18%)	47.1 (31%)	35.4 (52%)	76	910	5.4	180

Notes

- Salsa (p. 589) or commercial salsa may be used.
- 7 lb shredded cooked beef may be substituted for ground beef. Omit browning the beef and sauté onions and peppers in a little shortening.
- 3 oz (1½ cups) dehydrated onions, rehydrated in 2½ cups water, may be substituted for fresh onions (p. 55).

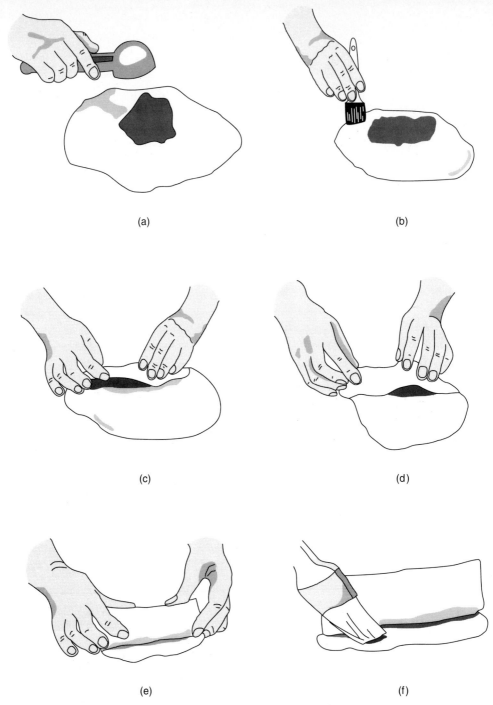

FIGURE 12.1 Preparing Chimichangas: (a) Portion meat mixture onto flour tortilla. (b) Shape meat mixture into elongated form. Brush tortilla edges with water-cornstarch mixture. (c) Fold bottom edge over filling. (d) Fold in sides of tortilla. (e) Roll into a cylinder shape. (f) Brush water-cornstarch mixture on the top edge to help seal. Place seam side down on baking sheets and cover until ready to fry.

OVEN-BAKED HAMBURGERS

Yield: 50 portions   *Portion:* 4 oz
Oven: 400°F   *Bake:* 15–20 minutes

Ingredient	Amount	Procedure
Ground beef	12 lb AP	Place meat in mixer bowl.
Eggs, beaten Milk	3 (5 oz) 2 cups	Combine eggs and milk and add to meat.
Bread crumbs, soft Onion, chopped Salt Pepper, black	4 oz 4 oz 2 Tbsp 2 tsp	Add crumbs and seasonings. Blend on low speed for approximately 1 minute, using flat beater.
		Portion meat mixture with No. 10 dipper onto lightly greased baking sheets. Flatten into patties. Bake at 400°F for 15–20 minutes.
Hamburger buns	50	Serve patties on warm buns.

Approximate nutritive values per portion

Calories (kcal)	Protein (grams)	Carbohydrate (grams)	Fat (grams)	Cholesterol (mg)	Sodium (mg)	Iron (mg)	Calcium (mg)
350	21.9 (25%)	21.9 (26%)	18.8 (49%)	80	563	3.2	80

Note
- ½ oz (¼ cup) dehydrated onions, rehydrated in ½ cup water, may be substituted for fresh onions (p. 55).

Variations
- **Barbecued Hamburgers.**   Place browned hamburgers in baking pans. Pour Barbecue Sauce (p. 588) over patties. Cover with aluminum foil and bake at 325°F until hot, about 10–20 minutes.
- **Grilled Hamburgers and Accompaniments.**   Cook 4-oz hamburger patties on the grill only until they are no longer pink. Place on bun and serve with accompaniments: mayonnaise, mustard, catsup, sliced dill pickles, sliced or chopped onions, sliced tomato, and leaf lettuce.

CROISSANT WITH SAUTÉED GARDEN VEGETABLES

Yield: 50 portions   *Portion:* 1 sandwich
Oven: 350°F   *Heat:* 5–10 minutes

Ingredient	Amount	Procedure
Green peppers, sliced	2 lb 6 oz	Toss together.
Onions, sliced	2 lb 6 oz	
Mushrooms, fresh, sliced	2 lb 6 oz	
Margarine	14 oz	Melt margarine in steam-jacketed kettle. Add vegetables. Sauté until tender-crisp. Drain.
Croissants, cut in half lengthwise	50 (2½ oz size)	Assemble sandwiches in 12 × 20 × 2-inch pans:
Swiss cheese, ⅔ oz slices	4 lb 3 oz (100 slices)	1. bottom of croissant 2. ⅔ oz Swiss cheese slice
Ripe olives, sliced, drained	1 lb 6 oz	3. 2 oz sautéed vegetables 4. ½ oz sliced olives
Tomatoes, sliced	2 lb	5. 2 tomato slices 6. ⅔ oz Swiss cheese slice 7. top of croissant

Heat at 350°F just long enough to melt cheese, 5–10 minutes. Do not hold over 15 minutes before serving.

Approximate nutritive values per portion							
Calories (kcal)	Protein (grams)	Carbohydrate (grams)	Fat (grams)	Cholesterol (mg)	Sodium (mg)	Iron (mg)	Calcium (mg)
346	14.3 (16%)	18.5 (21%)	24.4 (63%)	34.8	516	1.9	399

13

Sauces

A sauce serves to complement an entree, vegetable, or dessert. It may be used as a binding agent to hold foods together or as a topping. Sauces add richness, moistness, color, and form to foods and may enhance or offer contrast in flavor or color to foods they accompany.

ENTREE AND VEGETABLE SAUCES

Basic to many sauces is a roux, which is a cooked mixture of fat and flour, usually equal parts by weight. A roux may range from white, in which the fat and flour are cooked only for a short time, to brown, cooked until it is light brown in color and has a nutty aroma. The amount of browning will influence both the flavor and color characteristics of the sauce. Calories may be lowered by eliminating the fat and making the sauce with a starch thickener, such as flour or cornstarch, mixed with a cold liquid (stock or milk).

Other starch thickening agents commonly used in sauces are arrowroot, cornstarch, pregelatinized or instant starch, and waxy maize. Waxy maize is preferred for sauces that will be frozen because it will not break and separate as easily as other starches. When reheated, products containing waxy maize are smoother than those with cornstarch. Egg yolks have a slight thickening power and are used for some sauces. When egg yolks are cooked to too high a temperature, the egg protein will coagulate and cause a curdled effect. When using egg yolks to thicken, care must be exercised to keep the sauce temperature below 158°F and to minimize the holding time.

Most meat and vegetable sauces are modifications of the basic recipes: white sauce, blond sauce, brown sauce, red sauce, and butter sauces.

- *White Sauce* (p. 582), made with a roux of fat and flour and with milk as the liquid, has many uses in quantity food preparation, as a sauce with vegetables, eggs, and fish and as an ingredient in many casseroles. A White Sauce Mix (p. 581), combining flour, fat, and nonfat dry milk, may be made and stored in the refrigerator until needed. Water and seasonings are added when the mixture is to be used. Béchamel Sauce (p. 584) is a white sauce that uses milk and chicken stock as the liquid and, with its variations, usually is served with poultry, seafood, eggs, or vegetables.

- *Blond sauces* are made from a roux that is cooked a little longer than the white sauce, just until the roux begins to brown. Velouté Sauce (p. 584) is a blond sauce that uses chicken, veal, or fish broth as its liquid.

- *Brown Sauce* (p. 586) is made with a well-browned roux, and beef stock as the liquid. Brown Sauce is used with meat.

- *Red sauces* (pp. 588–592) include tomato as a primary ingredient. These sauces are generally used with meat and pasta.

- *Butter sauces* (p. 600) are used with vegetables, fish, meats, and egg dishes.

Some sauces use chicken or beef stock as part or all of the liquid. Recipes for stocks are on pp. 615 and 616. A broth made with a high-quality commercial stock base can be substituted for the chicken or beef stock called for in sauces, but the salt in the recipe may need to be adjusted if the base is highly seasoned.

Sauces made from concentrated canned soups are time-saving and may be used effectively in many items. Undiluted canned cream soups such as chicken, mushroom, celery, and cheese, or tomato soup may be used alone or in combination. If the soup is too thick, a small amount of milk or chicken or meat stock may be added. Two soups may be combined for a special flavor effect, or pimiento, green pepper, almonds, curry powder, or other ingredients may be added for variety.

Marinades are used to flavor and tenderize meats and poultry and to flavor raw or cooked vegetables. The less-tender cuts of meat should be marinated at least two hours; pork, chicken, and the more tender cuts of beef often are basted before and during cooking but do not need to stand in the marinade.

DESSERT SAUCES

Sauces serve as both a garnish and a basic ingredient for many desserts. The choice of sauce should complement the dessert in both color and flavor. Most dessert sauces are added shortly before serving.

ENTREE AND VEGETABLE SAUCE RECIPES

WHITE SAUCE MIX

■

Yield: 13 lb 8 oz mix

Ingredient	Amount	Procedure
Flour, all-purpose Nonfat dry milk	3 lb 6 lb	Blend flour and milk in 60-qt mixer bowl.
Shortening Margarine	2 lb 4 oz 2 lb 4 oz	Using pastry knife or flat beater, blend fats with dry ingredients until mixture is crumbly, scraping sides of bowl occasionally. Store in covered containers in the refrigerator.
To Prepare 1 Gallon of White Sauce		
Water Salt	3¼ qt 1 oz (1½ Tbsp)	Heat water and salt to boiling point.

White sauce mix
  Thin
  Medium
  Thick
	
	1 lb 12 oz
	2 lb 4 oz
	2 lb 14 oz
		Add mix for sauce of desired thickness. Stirring with wire whip, continue cooking until thickened.

WHITE SAUCE

Yield: 1 gal

		Ingredients			
Consistency	*Milk*	*Flour, all-purpose*	*Margarine or butter*	*Salt*	*Uses*
Thin	4 qt	6 oz	6 oz	1 oz	Cream soups
Medium	4 qt	8 oz	8 oz	1 oz	Creamed foods, gravy
Thick	4 qt	12 oz	12 oz	1 oz	Soufflés

Notes

- 1 lb nonfat dry milk and 3¾ qt cool water may be substituted for fluid milk. Combine dry milk and water and whip until smooth. Heat to scalding (185°F). Add, while stirring, roux made of margarine and flour. Cook on low heat, stirring as necessary, until thickened.

- 1 oz salt equals 1½ Tbsp.

- **Method 1.**   Melt margarine, remove from heat. Add flour and salt. Stir until smooth. Cook 5–10 minutes. Add milk gradually, stirring constantly with wire whip. Cook and stir as necessary until smooth and thick, about 15 minutes.

- **Method 2.**   This method is used for making quantities larger than 4 qt. Make a roux by melting margarine, adding flour, and cooking and stirring until smooth. Add one-fourth of the milk and beat with wire whip until smooth. Gradually add remaining milk while stirring. Cook until smooth and thickened, about 15 minutes.

- **Method 3.**   Combine flour with one-fourth of the milk. Heat remaining milk. Add milk-flour paste, using wire whip. Cook to desired consistency, then add margarine and salt.

- **Method 4.**   This method uses a steamer. Make a paste of flour and margarine. Add cold milk until mixture is the consistency of cream. Heat remaining milk. Add flour and margarine mixture, stirring constantly with wire whip. Place in steamer until flour is cooked; if necessary, stir once during cooking.

Variations

To be used with 1 gallon medium white sauce:
- **À la King Sauce.**   Add 12 oz chopped green pepper, 12 oz sliced mushrooms, sautéed, and 1 lb chopped pimiento. Combine with cubed chicken, meats, seafood, vegetables, or hard-cooked eggs.

- **Bacon Sauce.**   Add 1 lb 8 oz cooked chopped bacon. Use bacon fat in making the sauce. Combine with eggs or vegetables in scalloped dishes.

- **Cheese Sauce.**   Add 3 lb sharp cheddar cheese, shredded or ground, 2 Tbsp Worcestershire sauce, and a few grains of cayenne pepper. Serve on fish, egg dishes, soufflés, and vegetables. Worcestershire sauce and cayenne pepper may be omitted for a milder sauce.

- **Cheese Sandwich Sauce (American or Cheddar).**   Prepare 2 qt (half recipe) Thick White Sauce. Add ¼ cup dry mustard and 1 tsp white pepper with the flour. When sauce has thickened, stir in 2 lb shredded sharp cheese and ½ tsp hot pepper sauce. Ladle 1½ oz sauce over meat in sandwich.

- **Cheese Sandwich Sauce (Swiss).**   Prepare 2 qt (half recipe) Medium White Sauce. Reduce margarine to 6 oz. After sauce has thickened, add 2 lb shredded Swiss cheese and stir until melted. Serve 1½ oz sauce ladled over meat in sandwich.

- **Egg Sauce.**   Add 20 chopped hard-cooked eggs and 2 Tbsp prepared mustard. Serve over salmon or other fish loaf.

- **Golden Sauce.**   Add 2 cups slightly beaten egg yolks. Serve on fish, chicken, or vegetables.

- **Mushroom Sauce.**   Add 1 lb 8 oz sliced mushrooms and 4 oz minced onion, sautéed in 4 oz margarine or butter. Serve over egg, meat, poultry dishes, or vegetables.

- **Pimiento Sauce.**   Add 1 lb 4 oz finely chopped pimiento and 2 cups finely chopped parsley. Serve with poached fish, croquettes, or egg dishes.

- **Shrimp Sauce.**   Add 4 lb cooked shrimp, 2 Tbsp prepared mustard, and 2 Tbsp Worcestershire sauce. Serve with fish, eggs, or cheese soufflé.

- **Swiss Cheese and Mushroom Sauce.**   Prepare 2 qt (half recipe) Medium White Sauce. Sauté 8 oz chopped onions, 2 oz chopped green peppers, and 8 oz sliced mushrooms in 6 oz margarine. Stir in 6 oz flour. Cook 10–15 minutes. Add slowly, while stirring, 2 qt milk and heat to 170°F. Add 2 lb 8 oz shredded Swiss cheese and stir until melted.

BÉCHAMEL SAUCE

Yield: 2 qt   *Portion:* 3 Tbsp (1½ oz)

Ingredient	Amount	Procedure
Chicken Stock (p. 615)	1½ qt	Cook stock and seasonings together for 20 minutes. Strain.
Onion slices	4	Save liquid for preparation of sauce. There should be 1 qt liquid.
Peppercorns, black	2 Tbsp	
Carrots, chopped	3 oz	
Bay leaf	1	
Margarine	8 oz	Melt margarine. Add flour and stir until smooth. Cook 5–10 minutes.
Flour, all-purpose	4 oz	
Seasoned stock (prepared above)	1 qt	Add liquids gradually, stirring constantly with wire whip.
Milk, hot	1 qt	Cook until smooth and thickened.
Salt	½ tsp	Add seasonings.
Pepper, white	½ tsp	Serve with 2-oz ladle (scant) on chicken or meat entrees.
Pepper, cayenne	Few grains	

Approximate nutritive values per ounce

Calories (kcal)	Protein (grams)	Carbohydrate (grams)	Fat (grams)	Cholesterol (mg)	Sodium (mg)	Iron (mg)	Calcium (mg)
38	0.9 (9%)	2.1 (22%)	2.9 (69%)	2	90	0.2	18

Variations:

- **Mornay Sauce.** Add gradually to hot Béchamel Sauce 4 oz each of grated Parmesan and Swiss cheese. Let sauce remain over heat until cheese is melted, then remove and gradually beat in 8 oz margarine or butter. Serve with fish or egg entrees.

- **Velouté Sauce.** Cook the margarine and flour (roux) until slightly brown in color. Substitute Chicken Stock for milk. Serve on chicken entrees. For Fish Velouté, substitute fish stock for milk. Serve on fish.

SAVORY CREAM GRAVY

Yield: 1 gal

Ingredient	Amount	Procedure
Chicken Stock (p. 615)	1¾ qt	Combine.
Water	2 cups	
Soy sauce	¾ cup	
Light cream (half-and-half)	2 cups	
Margarine, melted	8 oz	Sauté vegetables in margarine.
Celery leaves, fresh, coarsely chopped	4 oz	
Green onions, finely chopped	4 oz	
Garlic, minced	2 cloves	
Basil leaves, dried, crumbled	2 Tbsp	Blend spices and flour into vegetables, while stirring with a wire whip.
Nutmeg, ground	1½ tsp	Slowly add combined liquids, stirring constantly until mixture thickens.
Flour, all-purpose	7 oz	
Sour cream	2½ cups	Blend in sour cream. Do not boil. Keep warm.

Approximate nutritive values per ounce							
Calories (kcal)	Protein (grams)	Carbohydrate (grams)	Fat (grams)	Cholesterol (mg)	Sodium (mg)	Iron (mg)	Calcium (mg)
37	0.8 (9%)	1.9 (21%)	2.9 (71%)	3	161	0.2	13

Note   ■   Ladle over poultry or meat.

PAN GRAVY

Yield: 1 gal   *Portion:* ⅓ cup (2½ oz)

Ingredient	Amount	Procedure
Fat, hot (meat drippings)	8 oz	Add flour to fat and blend.
Flour, all-purpose	8 oz	
Salt	1 Tbsp	Stir in salt and pepper. Cook 5 minutes.
Pepper, black	1 tsp	
Meat or Chicken Stock (pp. 616, 615)	1 gal	Add stock gradually, stirring constantly with wire whip. Cook until smooth and thickened.

Approximate nutritive value per ounce							
Calories (kcal)	Protein (grams)	Carbohydrate (grams)	Fat (grams)	Cholesterol (mg)	Sodium (mg)	Iron (mg)	Calcium (mg)
25	0.5 (9%)	1.4 (23%)	1.9 (69%)	2	148	0.1	2

Note
- If beef or chicken base is used for stock, delete or reduce salt.

Variations
- **Brown Gravy.** Use 10 oz flour and brown in the fat.
- **Chicken Gravy.** Use chicken drippings for fat and chicken stock for liquid.
- **Cream Gravy.** Substitute milk for water or stock.
- **Giblet Gravy.** Use chicken drippings for fat and chicken stock for liquid. Add 1 qt cooked giblets, chopped.
- **Onion Gravy.** Lightly brown 1 lb thinly sliced onions in fat before adding flour.
- **Vegetable Gravy.** Add 1 lb diced carrots, 4 oz chopped celery, and 12 oz chopped onion, cooked in water or meat stock.

BROWN SAUCE

Yield: 2 qt   *Portion:* 3 Tbsp (1½ oz)

Ingredient	Amount	Procedure
Beef Stock (p. 616)	2 qt	Add onions and seasonings to meat stock. If soup base has been used to make stock, taste before adding salt.
Onion, thinly sliced	4 oz	
Salt	2 tsp	Simmer about 10 minutes.
Pepper, black	¼ tsp	Strain.
Shortening	8 oz	Heat shortening and blend with flour. Cook about 10 minutes until it becomes uniformly brown in color. Add hot stock while stirring with wire whip. Cook until thickened.
Flour, all-purpose	5 oz	

Approximate nutritive values per ounce							
Calories (kcal)	Protein (grams)	Carbohydrate (grams)	Fat (grams)	Cholesterol (mg)	Sodium (mg)	Iron (mg)	Calcium (mg)
39	0.5 (6%)	1.7 (18%)	3.3 (77%)	0	150	0.1	3

Variations

- **Jelly Sauce.**   Add 2 cups currant jelly, beaten until soft, 2 Tbsp tarragon vinegar, and 4 oz sautéed minced onions. Serve with lamb or game.

- **Mushroom Sauce.**   Add 1 lb sliced mushrooms and 2 oz minced onions, sautéed. Serve with steak.

- **Olive Sauce.**   Add 6 oz chopped stuffed olives. Serve with meat or duck.

- **Piquant Sauce.**   Add 2 oz minced onions, 2 oz capers, ½ cup vinegar, 4 oz sugar, ¼ tsp salt, ¼ tsp paprika, and ½ cup chili sauce or chopped sweet pickle. Serve with meats.

- **Savory Mustard Sauce.**   Add ½ cup prepared mustard and ½ cup horseradish. Serve with meats.

FRESH MUSHROOM SAUCE

Yield: 1 gal   *Portion:* 2½ oz

Ingredient	Amount	Procedure
Mushrooms, fresh	4 lb	Clean, trim, and slice mushrooms.
Margarine Onions, minced	8 oz 2 oz	Melt margarine. Sauté onions and mushrooms.
Flour, all-purpose	4 oz	Add flour and blend. Cook 5 minutes.
Chicken Stock, hot (p. 615) Milk or cream Salt	2 qt 2 cups To taste	Add stock and milk while stirring with wire whip. Cook until thickened. Taste for seasoning. Add salt if needed.

Approximate nutritive values per ounce							
Calories (kcal)	Protein (grams)	Carbohydrate (grams)	Fat (grams)	Cholesterol (mg)	Sodium (mg)	Iron (mg)	Calcium (mg)
21	0.7 (13%)	1.4 (26%)	1.5 (61%)	1	58	0.2	6

Note

- Canned, drained mushrooms may be substituted for fresh mushrooms. Stir into prepared sauce.

Variations

- **Mushroom and Almond Sauce.**   Add 1 lb slivered almonds. Serve over rice as an entree.

- **Mushroom and Cheese Sauce.**   Add 1 lb shredded cheese. Serve over asparagus or broccoli.

BARBECUE SAUCE (COOKED)

Yield: 1½ gal

Ingredient	Amount	Procedure
Catsup	1 No. 10 can	Combine all ingredients.
Water	3 qt	Simmer 10 minutes.
Vinegar, cider	2 cups	Baste chicken or meat with sauce during cooking.
Salt	2 Tbsp	
Pepper, black	1 tsp	
Sugar, granulated	4 oz	
Chili powder	1 tsp	
Worcestershire sauce	¼ cup	
Hot pepper sauce	1 Tbsp	
Onion, grated	4 oz	

Approximate nutritive values per ounce							
Calories (kcal)	Protein (grams)	Carbohydrate (grams)	Fat (grams)	Cholesterol (mg)	Sodium (mg)	Iron (mg)	Calcium (mg)
17	0 (0%)	4.5 (100%)	0 (0%)	0	211	0.1	4

Note   ■   ½ oz (¼ cup) dehydrated onion may be substituted for the fresh onion.

BARBECUE SAUCE (UNCOOKED)

Yield: 1 gal

Ingredient	Amount	Procedure
Catsup	1 No. 10 can	Mix all ingredients.
Vinegar, cider	3 cups	Pour over meat or chicken.
Sugar, granulated	12 oz	Follow cooking directions for meat or poultry.
Salt	4 oz	
Onion, grated	4 oz	

Approximate nutritive values per ounce							
Calories (kcal)	Protein (grams)	Carbohydrate (grams)	Fat (grams)	Cholesterol (mg)	Sodium (mg)	Iron (mg)	Calcium (mg)
33	0 (0%)	9.3 (100%)	0 (0%)	0	583	0.2	7

Note   ■   ½ oz (¼ cup) dehydrated onion may be substituted for the fresh onion.

SALSA

Yield: 1 gal

Ingredient	Amount	Procedure
Tomatoes, canned, crushed	3 lb 10 oz	Combine all ingredients in stainless steel or glass container.
Tomato juice	3 lb 6 oz	Mix well.
Green pepper, dried, chopped	1 oz	Store covered in refrigerator.
Onion, fresh, chopped	8 oz	May be heated before service.
Garlic powder	¼ tsp	
Peppers, green chilies	8 oz	
Peppers, jalapeño, canned, chopped	10 oz	
Vinegar, cider	¾ cup	
Salt	2 tsp	
Sugar, granulated	1 Tbsp	
Hot pepper sauce	1 Tbsp	
Oregano, dried, crumbled	½ tsp	
Pepper, cayenne	¾ tsp	
Cumin, ground	¾ tsp	

Approximate nutritive values per ounce

Calories (kcal)	Protein (grams)	Carbohydrate (grams)	Fat (grams)	Cholesterol (mg)	Sodium (mg)	Iron (mg)	Calcium (mg)
6	0.2 (13%)	1.5 (80%)	0.1 (7%)	0	133	0.2	5

Note   ■   May be served as a condiment with Tacos, Tostadas, Chimichangas, or other Mexican entrees.

MARINARA SAUCE

Yield: 2 gal   *Portion:* 4 oz

Ingredient	Amount	Procedure
Onion, chopped Garlic, minced Olive oil	1 lb 8 cloves ¾ cup	Sauté onion and garlic in oil until tender and golden in color.
Plum tomatoes, canned, undrained	20 lb (2½ gal)	Add tomatoes to onion/garlic mixture. Break tomatoes into small pieces.
Parsley, fresh, chopped Basil, dried, crumbled Salt Pepper, black	3 oz 3 Tbsp 2 Tbsp 1½ tsp	Stir in seasonings. Cover and simmer for 2 hours, stirring occasionally. Cook until sauce reaches desired consistency.

Approximate nutritive values per ounce

Calories (kcal)	Protein (grams)	Carbohydrate (grams)	Fat (grams)	Cholesterol (mg)	Sodium (mg)	Iron (mg)	Calcium (mg)
14	0.4 (10%)	1.7 (47%)	0.7 (44%)	0	108	0.2	11

Notes
- Serve over pasta, meats, or poultry. Sprinkle with Parmesan cheese.
- 3 Tbsp brown sugar may be added for a sweeter sauce.
- Vegetable oil may be substituted for olive oil.
- 2 oz finely chopped sweet red bell pepper may be added along with parsley and spices.
- Diced tomatoes may be substituted for plum tomatoes. Drain some of the juice before adding or cook longer until the liquid evaporates and sauce thickens.
- To make a thicker sauce requiring less cooking time substitute 6 lb of tomato puree for 6 lb of tomatoes.

Variations
- **Marinara Sauce with Olives.**   Add to sauce 2 lb 8 oz sliced black olives, drained; 2 Tbsp oregano, dried, leaf; and 2 tsp red pepper flakes. Small whole olives may be substituted for sliced olives. 8 oz capers may be added.
- **Tomato Zucchini Sauce.**   Follow recipe for Marinara Sauce with Olives. Add 3 lb sliced zucchini just before serving and heat to serving temperature. Serve with grated Romano or Parmesan cheese.

ITALIAN TOMATO SAUCE

Yield: 1½ gal   *Portion:* 4 oz

Ingredient	Amount	Procedure
Margarine, melted	3 oz	Sauté peppers and onion in margarine until trans-
Onions, chopped	1 lb 6 oz	parent.
Green peppers, chopped	8 oz	
Tomato juice	2½ qt	Add tomato juice, paste and puree, water, and spices.
Tomato paste	3½ cups	Stir well to combine.
Tomato puree	3 cups	Heat to boiling. Reduce heat and simmer 20–30 min-
Water	2 qt	utes or until desired consistency is reached.
Salt	1 Tbsp	Remove bay leaves.
Pepper, black	1 Tbsp	
Sugar, granulated	2 Tbsp	
Oregano, dried, leaf	1 Tbsp	
Basil, dried, leaf	¼ cup	
Garlic powder	4 tsp	
Thyme, ground	1 tsp	
Parsley, dried	1 Tbsp	
Bay leaves	2	

Approximate nutritive values per ounce

Calories (kcal)	Protein (grams)	Carbohydrate (grams)	Fat (grams)	Cholesterol (mg)	Sodium (mg)	Iron (mg)	Calcium (mg)
14	0.4 (11%)	2.5 (64%)	0.4 (25%)	0	122	0.3	7

Notes

- Serve over pasta or as a base for Italian sauces.
- Olive oil may be substituted for margarine.
- 3 Tbsp granulated sugar may be added for a sweeter sauce.

SPANISH SAUCE

Yield: 3 qt   *Portion:* 3 Tbsp (2 oz)

Ingredient	Amount	Procedure
Onion, chopped	4 oz	Sauté onion in shortening.
Shortening	4 oz	
Tomatoes, canned, diced	2 qt	Add remaining ingredients. Simmer until vegetables are tender.
Celery, diced	1 lb	
Green pepper, chopped	8 oz	
Pimiento, chopped	6 oz	
Salt	1 Tbsp	
Pepper, black	½ tsp	
Pepper, cayenne	Few grains	

Approximate nutritive values per ounce

Calories (kcal)	Protein (grams)	Carbohydrate (grams)	Fat (grams)	Cholesterol (mg)	Sodium (mg)	Iron (mg)	Calcium (mg)
17	0.3 (5%)	1.4 (24%)	1.3 (49%)	0	104	0.2	8

Notes
- Serve with meat, fish, cheese, or Mexican entrees.
- ½ oz (¼ cup) dehydrated onions, rehydrated in ½ cup water, may be substituted for fresh onions (p. 55).
- 1 tsp cilantro may be added.

HORSERADISH SAUCE

Yield: 5 cups   *Portion:* 1½ Tbsp (½ oz)

Ingredient	Amount	Procedure
Horseradish, drained	8 oz	Combine.
Prepared mustard	2 Tbsp	
Salt	½ tsp	
Paprika	¼ tsp	
Pepper, cayenne	⅛ tsp	
Vinegar, cider	⅓ cup	
Cream, whipping	2 cups	Whip cream. Fold in horseradish mixture. Chill.

Approximate nutritive values per ounce							
Calories (kcal)	Protein (grams)	Carbohydrate (grams)	Fat (grams)	Cholesterol (mg)	Sodium (mg)	Iron (mg)	Calcium (mg)
54	0.6 (4%)	1.4 (10%)	5.3 (86%)	19	61	0.1	15

Note   ■ Serve with ham or roast beef.

COCKTAIL SAUCE

Yield: 2 qt   *Portion:* 2½ Tbsp (1½ oz)

Ingredient	Amount	Procedure
Chili sauce	1 qt	Mix all ingredients. Chill.
Catsup	2 cups	
Lemon juice	1 cup	
Onion juice	2 Tbsp	
Celery, finely chopped	10 oz	
Worcestershire sauce	5 tsp	
Horseradish	3 oz	
Hot pepper sauce	Few drops	

Approximate nutritive values per ounce							
Calories (kcal)	Protein (grams)	Carbohydrate (grams)	Fat (grams)	Cholesterol (mg)	Sodium (mg)	Iron (mg)	Calcium (mg)
26	0.5 (7%)	6.3 (92%)	0 (1%)	0	288	0.2	7

Note   ■ Serve with clam, crab, lobster, oyster, or shrimp.

MUSTARD SAUCE (COLD)

Yield: 3 cups   *Portion:* 1 Tbsp

Ingredient	Amount	Procedure
Sugar, granulated Salt Dry mustard	2 Tbsp ½ tsp 2 tsp	Mix dry ingredients.
Water Vinegar, cider Eggs, beaten	2 Tbsp ¼ cup 2 (3 oz)	Add water, vinegar, and eggs to dry ingredients. Cook until thick.
Margarine	1 oz	Add margarine. Stir until melted. Cool.
Cream, whipping	2 cups	Whip cream and fold into cooked mixture.

Approximate nutritive values per ounce							
Calories (kcal)	Protein (grams)	Carbohydrate (grams)	Fat (grams)	Cholesterol (mg)	Sodium (mg)	Iron (mg)	Calcium (mg)
76	0.9 (5%)	1.8 (9%)	7.5 (86%)	37	72	0	17

Note   ■   Serve cold with ham, pork, or beef roast.

Variation   ■   **Hot Chinese Mustard.**   Combine 8 oz dry mustard, ⅓ cup salad oil, and 1 oz (1½ Tbsp) salt. Add 2 cups boiling water. Stir until smooth. Serve with egg rolls.

MUSTARD SAUCE (HOT)

Yield: 2 qt   *Portion:* 2 Tbsp (1 oz)

Ingredient	Amount	Procedure
Beef Stock (p. 616)	2 qt	Heat stock to boiling point.
Cornstarch Sugar, granulated Salt Pepper, white Water, cold	5 oz 2 Tbsp 2 tsp ½ tsp ½ cup	Blend dry ingredients with cold water. Add gradually to hot stock. Cook and stir until thickened.
Prepared mustard Horseradish Vinegar, cider Margarine	2 oz 4 oz 2 Tbsp 1 oz	Add remaining ingredients. Stir until blended.

Approximate nutritive values per ounce

Calories (kcal)	Protein (grams)	Carbohydrate (grams)	Fat (grams)	Cholesterol (mg)	Sodium (mg)	Iron (mg)	Calcium (mg)
14	0.3 (10%)	2.2 (65%)	0.4 (25%)	0	155	0.1	3

Note   ■   Serve hot with fresh or cured ham or fish.

SWEET-SOUR SAUCE

Yield: 1¼ qt   *Portion:* 1½ Tbsp

Ingredient	Amount	Procedure
Sugar, granulated Cornstarch	10 oz ¼ cup	Combine sugar and cornstarch in kettle.
Vinegar, cider Water Soy sauce	1 cup 2½ cups ¼ cup	Add vinegar, water, and soy sauce to dry ingredients and stir until smooth.
Catsup	¾ cup	Stir catsup into mixture in kettle. Cook until translucent, stirring constantly. Serve as a condiment with egg rolls or chicken nuggets.

Approximate nutritive values per ounce

Calories (kcal)	Protein (grams)	Carbohydrate (grams)	Fat (grams)	Cholesterol (mg)	Sodium (mg)	Iron (mg)	Calcium (mg)
23	0.1 (1%)	6.7 (99%)	0 (0%)	0	106	0.1	2

RAISIN SAUCE

Yield: 1½ qt   *Portion:* 2 Tbsp

Ingredient	Amount	Procedure
Seedless raisins	1 lb	Steam raisins or simmer in small amount of water for 3–5 minutes.
Sugar, granulated	4 oz	Mix sugar and water, and heat to boiling point.
Water	2 cups	
Currant jelly	1 lb	Add cooked raisins, currant jelly, and remaining ingredients.
Vinegar, cider	⅓ cup	dients.
Margarine	2 oz	Simmer 5 minutes or until jelly is melted.
Worcestershire sauce	1 Tbsp	
Salt	1 tsp	
Pepper, white	¼ tsp	
Cloves, ground	½ tsp	
Mace	⅛ tsp	
Red food coloring (optional)	Few drops	

Approximate nutritive values per ounce							
Calories (kcal)	Protein (grams)	Carbohydrate (grams)	Fat (grams)	Cholesterol (mg)	Sodium (mg)	Iron (mg)	Calcium (mg)
66	0.3 (2%)	15.3 (87%)	0.9 (12%)	0	56	0.4	7

Note   ■   Serve with baked ham.

CUCUMBER SAUCE

Yield: 3 cups   *Portion:* 1 Tbsp (½ oz)

Ingredient	Amount	Procedure
Cucumbers	1 lb	Peel cucumbers; remove seeds. Grate or chop finely.
Sour cream	1 cup	Combine remaining ingredients and add to cucumber. Chill.
Onion, grated	1 Tbsp	
Vinegar, cider	1 Tbsp	
Lemon juice	1½ Tbsp	
Salt	½ tsp	
Pepper, cayenne	Few grains	

Approximate nutritive values per ounce							
Calories (kcal)	Protein (grams)	Carbohydrate (grams)	Fat (grams)	Cholesterol (mg)	Sodium (mg)	Iron (mg)	Calcium (mg)
23	0.4 (7%)	1.1 (18%)	2 (75%)	4	50	0.1	14

Note   ■   Serve with fish.

TARTAR SAUCE

Yield: 1¾ qt   *Portion:* 2 Tbsp (1 oz)

Ingredient	Amount	Procedure
Mayonnaise	1 qt	Mix all ingredients.
Pickle relish	6 oz	
Green pepper, chopped	¼ cup	
Parsley, chopped	¼ cup	
Green olives, chopped	6 oz	
Onion, minced	1 Tbsp	
Pimiento, chopped	2 oz	
Vinegar or lemon juice	½ cup	
Worcestershire sauce	Few drops	
Hot pepper sauce	Few drops	

Approximate nutritive values per ounce							
Calories (kcal)	Protein (grams)	Carbohydrate (grams)	Fat (grams)	Cholesterol (mg)	Sodium (mg)	Iron (mg)	Calcium (mg)
136	0.4 (1%)	2 (6%)	14.5 (91%)	10	198	0.2	6

Note   ■   Serve with fish.

HOLLANDAISE SAUCE

Yield: 12 portions   *Portion:* 1½ Tbsp (¾ oz)

Ingredient	Amount	Procedure
Butter	2 oz	Place butter, lemon juice, and egg yolks over hot (not
Lemon juice	1½ Tbsp	boiling) water.
Egg yolks	3	Cook slowly, beating constantly.
Butter	2 oz	When first portion of butter is melted, add second portion and beat until mixture thickens.
Butter	2 oz	Add third portion of butter and seasonings.
Salt	Few grains	Beat until thickened.
Pepper, cayenne	Few grains	Serve immediately.

Approximate nutritive values per ounce

Calories (kcal)	Protein (grams)	Carbohydrate (grams)	Fat (grams)	Cholesterol (mg)	Sodium (mg)	Iron (mg)	Calcium (mg)
176	1.2 (3%)	0.3 (1%)	19.2 (97%)	127	180	0.3	14

Notes
- Serve with fish or green vegetables such as asparagus or broccoli.
- If sauce tends to curdle, add hot water, a teaspoon at a time, stirring vigorously.
- It is recommended that this sauce be made only in small quantity.

MOCK HOLLANDAISE SAUCE

Yield: 2 qt   *Portion:* 2½ Tbsp (1½ oz)

Ingredient	Amount	Procedure
Butter or margarine	6 oz	Melt butter. Add flour and stir until smooth.
Flour, all-purpose	3 oz	Cook 3–5 minutes.
Milk	1½ qt	Add milk gradually, stirring constantly with wire whip. Cook until smooth and thickened.
Salt	1 tsp	Add seasonings.
Pepper, white	½ tsp	
Pepper, cayenne	Few grains	
Egg yolks, unbeaten	12 (8 oz)	Add 1 egg yolk at a time, a little butter, and a little lemon juice until all are added.
Butter, cut in pieces	1 lb	
Lemon juice	½ cup	Beat well.

Approximate nutritive values per ounce

Calories (kcal)	Protein (grams)	Carbohydrate (grams)	Fat (grams)	Cholesterol (mg)	Sodium (mg)	Iron (mg)	Calcium (mg)
82	1.3 (6%)	1.8 (9%)	7.8 (85%)	51	104	0.2	28

LEMON HERB SEASONING

Yield: Approximately 2 cups

Ingredient	Amount	Procedure
Lemons	8	Finely shred lemon peel. Spread on baking pan. Dry in 300°F oven for about 10 minutes. Stir occasionally. Cool.
Basil, dried, leaves	5 Tbsp	Crush herbs. Mix with dry lemon peel.
Marjoram, dried, leaves	5 Tbsp	Store in airtight container.
Sage, dried, leaves	2 Tbsp	
Savory, dried, leaves	5 Tbsp	
Parsley, dried, leaves	3 Tbsp	
Thyme, dried, leaves	5 Tbsp	

Notes
- Use Lemon Herb Seasoning sparingly to season soups, stews, meats, fish, poultry, and vegetables.
- To substitute fresh herbs for dried herbs, use three times more fresh than dried. If using ground herbs, use only one-fourth as much as dried.
- Variation in flavor may be made by using different combinations of herbs. The following herbs may be substituted for those in the recipe: celery flakes, cilantro, dill weed, oregano, rosemary, or tarragon.

SEASONED SALT

Yield: Approximately 2 cups

Ingredient	Amount	Procedure
Salt	1 lb	Mix all ingredients together thoroughly.
Celery salt	2 oz	Store covered.
Onion powder	2 oz	
Garlic powder	1 oz	
Paprika	1 Tbsp	
Chili powder	4 Tbsp	

Note
- Can be used to season meats, salads, or vegetables.

MEUNIÈRE SAUCE ■

Yield: 3 cups

Ingredient	Amount	Procedure
Margarine	1 lb 4 oz	Heat margarine until lightly browned.
Onion, minced	2 oz	Add onion and brown slightly.
Lemon juice	½ cup	Add juice and seasonings.
Worcestershire sauce	1 Tbsp	Serve hot over broccoli, brussels sprouts, green beans,
Lemon peel, grated	1 Tbsp	spinach, or cabbage.
Salt	1 tsp	

Approximate nutritive values per ounce							
Calories (kcal)	Protein (grams)	Carbohydrate (grams)	Fat (grams)	Cholesterol (mg)	Sodium (mg)	Iron (mg)	Calcium (mg)
180	0.3 (1%)	0.9 (2%)	19.9 (97%)	0	333	0.1	1.0

Note   ■   3 oz toasted sliced almonds may be sprinkled over top of vegetable.

DRAWN BUTTER SAUCE ■

Yield: 2 qt   *Portion:* 3 Tbsp (1½ oz)

Ingredient	Amount	Procedure
Butter	2 oz	Melt butter. Add flour and blend.
Flour, all-purpose	4 oz	
Water, hot	2 qt	Gradually add hot water, while stirring with wire whip. Cook 5 minutes.
Salt	1 tsp	When ready to serve, add salt and butter. Beat until blended.
Butter, cut into pieces	6 oz	

Approximate nutritive values per ounce							
Calories (kcal)	Protein (grams)	Carbohydrate (grams)	Fat (grams)	Cholesterol (mg)	Sodium (mg)	Iron (mg)	Calcium (mg)
29	0.2 (3%)	1.2 (17%)	2.7 (81%)	7	58	0.1	2

Note   ■   Serve with green vegetables, fried or broiled fish, or egg dishes.

Variations   ■   **Almond Butter Sauce.**   Add ¼ cup lemon juice and 6 oz toasted slivered almonds just before serving.

- **Lemon Butter Sauce.** Add 1 Tbsp grated lemon peel and ¼ cup lemon juice just before serving. Serve with fish, new potatoes, broccoli, or asparagus.
- **Maître d'Hôtel Sauce.** Add ¼ cup lemon juice, ¼ cup chopped parsley, and 8 egg yolks, well beaten.
- **Parsley Butter Sauce.** Add 1½ cups minced parsley just before serving. Serve with fish, potatoes, or other vegetables.

COMPOUND BUTTERS

Yield: 2 lb

Ingredient	Amount	Procedure
Butter, unsalted, softened	2 lb	Mix flavoring with softened butter.
		Form into ¾-inch diameter logs or cube.
Flavoring	see Variations	Refrigerate until firm enough to slice.
		Use for meats, pasta, rice, vegetables, and breads. A ¼-inch slice equals 1 tsp; a ¾-inch slice equals 1 Tbsp.

Note
- Compound butter may be tightly wrapped in foil and frozen.

Variations
- **Basil Butter.** Add 4 cups fresh basil leaves; 3 cloves garlic, minced; and ¼ cup lemon juice.
- **Lemon Butter.** Add 1 cup lemon juice, 2 tsp lemon zest, and ¼ cup Dijon-style mustard (optional).
- **Herb Butter.** Add 1 cup finely chopped chives, 1 cup finely chopped fresh parsley, ¼ cup fresh tarragon, and 1 tsp lemon juice.
- **Parsley Butter.** Add 2 cups finely chopped fresh parsley. Use on potatoes and other vegetables, rice, fish, soups, and sauces.
- **Dill Butter.** Add 2 cups minced dill or ½ cup dried dill weed and ¼ cup lemon juice. Use on potatoes and other cooked vegetables, rice, and fish.
- **Garlic Butter.** Add 16 cloves garlic, crushed. Use on potatoes and other cooked vegetables, pasta, and pasta sauce.
- **Red Pepper Butter.** Add 1 cup sweet red pepper, finely chopped; 1 cup yellow onion, finely chopped; and 8 cloves garlic, finely minced.

HERB BUTTER SEASONING

Yield: 1 qt

Ingredient	Amount	Procedure
Butter	2 lb	Place butter in mixer bowl. Let stand at room temperature until soft enough to mix.
Lemon juice Seasonings	2 tsp See next step	Add lemon juice and seasonings to butter. Mix on low speed, using flat beater, until all ingredients are mixed thoroughly.
For vegetables:		
Basil leaves, dried, crushed	1 Tbsp	
Marjoram, ground	2 tsp	
Savory leaves, dried, crushed	1 Tbsp	
For meats:		
Marjoram, ground	2 tsp	
Dry mustard	4 tsp	
Tarragon leaves, dried, crushed	1 Tbsp	
Rosemary leaves, dried, crushed	1 Tbsp	

Notes
- Other spices and herbs may be substituted for those listed in the recipe. See Appendix B for Use of Herbs and Spices in Cooking.
- White, cider, or wine vinegar may be substituted for part or all of the lemon juice.
- Unsalted butter may be substituted for salted butter.

Variations
- **Curry Butter.**   Omit seasonings. Add 1 Tbsp curry powder.
- **Dill Butter.**   Omit seasonings. Add 1 Tbsp dill weed.
- **Lemon Butter.**   Omit seasonings. Increase lemon juice to 1 cup and add 3 Tbsp freshly grated lemon peel.
- **Onion Butter.**   Omit seasonings and lemon juice. Blend in 2 oz onion soup mix.
- **Tarragon Butter.**   Omit seasonings. Add 4 Tbsp tarragon leaves.

HOT BACON SAUCE

Yield: 2½ qt

Ingredient	Amount	Procedure
Bacon	1 lb	Dice bacon. Fry until crisp.
Flour, all-purpose	4 oz	Add flour and stir until smooth.
Sugar, granulated Salt Vinegar, cider Water	1 lb 4 oz ¼ cup 3 cups 3 cups	Mix sugar, salt, vinegar, and water. Boil 1 minute. Add to fat-flour mixture gradually while stirring. Cook until slightly thickened.

Approximate nutritive values per ounce							
Calories (kcal)	Protein (grams)	Carbohydrate (grams)	Fat (grams)	Cholesterol (mg)	Sodium (mg)	Iron (mg)	Calcium (mg)
64	1.9 (11%)	8.8 (52%)	2.8 (37%)	5	411	0.2	4

Note   ■   Use to wilt lettuce or spinach; or with hot potato salad or shredded cabbage.

MEAT MARINADE

Yield: 2 qt

Ingredient	Amount	Procedure
Salad oil Worcestershire sauce Liquid smoke Soy sauce Vinegar, cider Garlic, minced Celery salt Dry mustard Ginger, ground Sugar, brown	1 qt ¼ cup ¼ cup 2 cups ¼ cup 4 cloves ¼ cup ¼ cup ¼ cup 1 cup	Combine ingredients, mixing well. Pour over meat. Marinate in the refrigerator 6 hours or longer.

Note   ■   Pour over pork or beef.

DRY MARINADE FOR MEAT OR POULTRY

Yield: 10 oz dry spice

Ingredient	Amount	Procedure
Salt	2 oz	Mix spices. Store in sealed glass jar.
Cracked black pepper	1 Tbsp	Use as needed for marinade (follows).
Paprika	4 oz	
Oregano, dried, crumbled	1 oz	
Thyme, dried, crumbled	2 oz	
Cumin, ground	2 Tbsp	

Marinade for 20 lb of Meat:

Ingredient	Amount	Procedure
Spice blend (above)	4 oz (1 cup)	Mix spices with onion, garlic, oil, and lemon juice. May be prepared in food processor.
Onion, very finely chopped	1 lb	Rub over meat or poultry. Marinate several hours or overnight in the refrigerator.
Garlic cloves, minced	2 oz	Grill or roast meat or poultry as per recipe instructions.
Vegetable oil	½ cup	
Lemon juice	½ cup	

FISH MARINADE

Yield: 2½ qt

Ingredient	Amount	Procedure
Vegetable oil	1 qt	Combine ingredients, mixing well.
Olive oil	3 cups	Place fish in marinade.
Lemon juice, fresh	3 cups	Refrigerate for 3 hours. Remove fish from marinade and grill or broil.
Oregano, dried, crumbled	¼ cup	
Parsley, dried	¼ cup	
Basil, dried, crumbled	¼ cup	
Garlic powder	1 Tbsp	
Salt	1 Tbsp	
Pepper, black	1 tsp	

VEGETABLE MARINADE

Yield: 1½ qt   ■

Ingredient	Amount	Procedure
Lemon juice	2½ Tbsp	Combine.
Vinegar, white	⅓ cup	
Salad oil	1 cup	
Worcestershire sauce	1 Tbsp	
Water	⅓ cup	
Onion, finely chopped	3 oz	Add and mix.
Garlic, crushed	2 cloves	
Pimiento, chopped	¼ cup	
Parsley, finely chopped	¼ cup	
Salt	1½ Tbsp	Blend in and mix.
Sugar, granulated	1 Tbsp	Pour over fresh vegetables and marinate 6 hours or longer.
Pepper, black	⅛ tsp	
Tarragon	1 Tbsp	

Note   ■   Pour over fresh mushrooms or other fresh vegetables or pasta.

DESSERT SAUCE RECIPES

BUTTERSCOTCH SAUCE

Yield: 1¼ qt   *Portion:* 1½ Tbsp (1 oz)   ■

Ingredient	Amount	Procedure
Sugar, brown	1 lb	Combine and cook to soft-ball stage (240°F). Remove from heat.
Corn syrup, light	1⅓ cups	
Water	⅔ cup	
Margarine	6 oz	Add margarine and marshmallows. Stir until melted. Cool.
Marshmallows	2 oz	
Evaporated milk	1⅓ cups	When cool, add milk.

Approximate nutritive values per ounce

Calories (kcal)	Protein (grams)	Carbohydrate (grams)	Fat (grams)	Cholesterol (mg)	Sodium (mg)	Iron (mg)	Calcium (mg)
96	0.5 (2%)	16.8 (68%)	3.2 (30%)	2	49	0.7	30

CARAMEL SAUCE

Yield: 2 qt   *Portion:* 2½ Tbsp (1½ oz)

Ingredient	Amount	Procedure
Sugar, brown	1 lb	Mix sugars and flour. Stir in water.
Sugar, granulated	1 lb	Boil until thickened.
Flour, all-purpose	2 oz	
Water	1 qt	
Margarine	8 oz	Stir in margarine and vanilla.
Vanilla	1 Tbsp	

Approximate nutritive values per ounce

Calories (kcal)	Protein (grams)	Carbohydrate (grams)	Fat (grams)	Cholesterol (mg)	Sodium (mg)	Iron (mg)	Calcium (mg)
81	0.1 (1%)	14.5 (69%)	2.8 (30%)	0	3.6	0.3	7

Note   ■ Serve warm or cold over ice cream or apple desserts.

CHOCOLATE SAUCE

Yield: 1½ qt   *Portion:* 2 Tbsp (1 oz)

Ingredient	Amount	Procedure
Sugar, granulated	12 oz	Mix dry ingredients.
Cornstarch	2 oz	
Salt	1 tsp	
Cocoa	3 oz	
Water, cold	1 cup	Add cold water gradually to form a smooth paste.
Water, boiling	3½ cups	Add boiling water slowly while stirring. Boil for 5 minutes or until thickened. Remove from heat.
Margarine	6 oz	Add margarine and vanilla. Stir to blend.
Vanilla	1 tsp	

Approximate nutritive values per ounce

Calories (kcal)	Protein (grams)	Carbohydrate (grams)	Fat (grams)	Cholesterol (mg)	Sodium (mg)	Iron (mg)	Calcium (mg)
58	0.4 (2%)	8.9 (56%)	2.9 (41%)	0	77	0.6	4

Note   ■ Serve warm or cold on puddings, cake, cream puffs, or ice cream.

HOT FUDGE SAUCE

Yield: 1½ qt   *Portion:* 2 Tbsp (1 oz)

Ingredient	Amount	Procedure
Margarine, soft	8 oz	Combine margarine, sugar, and milk over hot water.
Sugar, powdered	1 lb 8 oz	Stir and cook slowly for 30 minutes.
Evaporated milk	1 13-oz can	
Unsweetened choco- late, chipped or melted	8 oz	Add chocolate and stir until blended.

Approximate nutritive values per ounce

Calories (kcal)	Protein (grams)	Carbohydrate (grams)	Fat (grams)	Cholesterol (mg)	Sodium (mg)	Iron (mg)	Calcium (mg)
133	1.2 (3%)	18 (50%)	7.5 (47%)	2	58	0.4	28

Notes
- Serve hot over ice cream.
- This sauce may be stored in the refrigerator. Heat over hot water before serving. If too thick or grainy, add evaporated milk before heating.

CUSTARD SAUCE

Yield: 1 gal   *Portion:* ⅓ cup (2½ oz)

Ingredient	Amount	Procedure
Sugar, granulated	14 oz	Mix dry ingredients.
Cornstarch	2 oz	
Salt	½ tsp	
Milk, cold	2 cups	Add cold milk and mix until smooth.
Milk, hot	3 qt	Add cold mixture to hot milk gradually while stirring.
Egg yolks, beaten	10 (6 oz)	Stir in egg yolks gradually. Cook over hot water until thickened, about 5 minutes.
Vanilla	2 Tbsp	Remove from heat and add vanilla. Cool.

Approximate nutritive values per ounce

Calories (kcal)	Protein (grams)	Carbohydrate (grams)	Fat (grams)	Cholesterol (mg)	Sodium (mg)	Iron (mg)	Calcium (mg)
35	1.1 (12%)	4.8 (55%)	1.3 (33%)	21	22	0.1	34

Note
- Serve over cake-type puddings.

FLUFFY ORANGE SAUCE

Yield: 3 qt   *Portion:* 3 Tbsp (1½ oz)

Ingredient	Amount	Procedure
Margarine	1 lb 5 oz	Melt margarine. Gradually add sugar.
Sugar, powdered	2 lb 2 oz	Beat with wire whip until it resembles whipped cream.
Eggs, beaten	10 (1 lb 2 oz)	Add eggs slowly, beating constantly.
Orange juice	1¾ cup	Slowly blend in orange juice and peel. Heat 10–15 minutes.
Orange peel, grated	1½ Tbsp	Beat again.

Approximate nutritive values per ounce

Calories (kcal)	Protein (grams)	Carbohydrate (grams)	Fat (grams)	Cholesterol (mg)	Sodium (mg)	Iron (mg)	Calcium (mg)
109	0.9 (3%)	12.4 (45%)	6.5 (52%)	27	77	0.1	6

LEMON SAUCE

Yield: 3 qt   *Portion:* 3 Tbsp (2 oz)

Ingredient	Amount	Procedure
Sugar, granulated	2 lb	Mix dry ingredients.
Cornstarch	3 oz	
Salt	½ tsp	
Water, boiling	2 qt	Add boiling water. Cook until clear.
Lemon juice	⅔ cup	Add lemon juice and margarine.
Margarine	1 oz (2 Tbsp)	

Approximate nutritive values per ounce

Calories (kcal)	Protein (grams)	Carbohydrate (grams)	Fat (grams)	Cholesterol (mg)	Sodium (mg)	Iron (mg)	Calcium (mg)
47	0 (0%)	11.7 (95%)	0.3 (5%)	0	17	0	1

Note
- Serve hot with Steamed Pudding (p. 290), Bread Pudding (p. 288), or Rice Custard (p. 288).

Variations
- **Nutmeg Sauce.** Omit lemon juice. Add 1 tsp nutmeg. Increase margarine to 4 oz.
- **Orange Sauce.** Substitute orange juice for lemon juice. Add 1 tsp freshly grated orange peel.
- **Vanilla Sauce.** Omit lemon juice and reduce sugar to 1 lb 4 oz. Add 2 Tbsp vanilla.

HARD SAUCE

Yield: 3⅓ cups   *Portion:* 1 Tbsp (½ oz)

Ingredient	Amount	Procedure
Butter	8 oz	Cream butter on medium speed until soft and fluffy.
Water, boiling	2 Tbsp	Add water and continue to cream until very light.
Sugar, powdered	1 lb 3 oz	Add sugar gradually. Continue creaming.
Lemon juice	½ tsp	Add lemon juice. Place in refrigerator to harden.

Approximate nutritive values per ounce							
Calories (kcal)	Protein (grams)	Carbohydrate (grams)	Fat (grams)	Cholesterol (mg)	Sodium (mg)	Iron (mg)	Calcium (mg)
143	0.1 (0%)	20.7 (56%)	7.1 (43%)	19	73	0	2

Note
- Serve with Christmas Pudding (p. 290), Baked Apples (p. 295), or Peach Cobbler (p. 299).

Variations
- **Cherry Hard Sauce.** Add ½ cup chopped maraschino cherries.
- **Strawberry Hard Sauce.** Omit lemon juice and water. Add ¾ cup fresh or frozen strawberries, chopped.

BROWN SUGAR HARD SAUCE

Yield: 1 qt   *Portion:* 1 Tbsp (½ oz)

Ingredient	Amount	Procedure
Butter	12 oz	Cream butter on medium speed until light.
Sugar, light brown	1 lb 4 oz	Add sugar gradually while creaming.
Vanilla	2 tsp	Add vanilla. Cream until fluffy.
Cream, whipping	¾ cup	Whip cream. Fold into sugar mixture. Chill.

Approximate nutritive values per ounce							
Calories (kcal)	Protein (grams)	Carbohydrate (grams)	Fat (grams)	Cholesterol (mg)	Sodium (mg)	Iron (mg)	Calcium (mg)
160	0.2 (1%)	17.3 (42%)	10.4 (57%)	30	95	0.6	21

Note
- Serve with Christmas Pudding (p. 290).

PEANUT BUTTER SAUCE

Yield: 2 qt   *Portion:* 2½ Tbsp (1½ oz)

Ingredient	Amount	Procedure
Sugar, granulated	12 oz	Combine sugar, syrup, and water.
Corn syrup, light	1⅓ cups	Cook to 228°F and turn off heat or remove from
Water, hot	¾ cup	burner.
Margarine	6 oz	Add margarine and marshmallows.
Marshmallows, miniature	3 oz	Stir until melted. Cool. Place in mixer bowl.
Evaporated milk	12 oz	Add milk and peanut butter.
Peanut butter	8 oz	Beat until well blended. Refrigerate.

Approximate nutritive values per ounce

Calories (kcal)	Protein (grams)	Carbohydrate (grams)	Fat (grams)	Cholesterol (mg)	Sodium (mg)	Iron (mg)	Calcium (mg)
108	1.6 (6%)	15.2 (53%)	5.2 (41%)	2	59	0.1	20

Note   ■   Serve over ice cream.

RASPBERRY SAUCE

Yield: 3 qt   *Portion:* 3 Tbsp (2 oz)

Ingredient	Amount	Procedure
Red raspberries, frozen	5 lb	Defrost berries. Do not drain.
Sugar, granulated	2 oz	Combine sugar and cornstarch and add to berries.
Cornstarch	1 oz	Cook until clear.
Currant jelly	1 lb 8 oz	Add jelly. Stir until melted. Cool.

Approximate nutritive values per ounce

Calories (kcal)	Protein (grams)	Carbohydrate (grams)	Fat (grams)	Cholesterol (mg)	Sodium (mg)	Iron (mg)	Calcium (mg)
47	0.2 (1%)	12.2 (98%)	0 (1%)	0	1	0.3	5

Notes	■	Serve over vanilla ice cream or raspberry, lemon, or lime sherbet.
	■	Raspberries may be strained before thickening.
Variations	■	**Fresh Strawberry Sauce.** Substitute 5 lb fresh strawberries, cleaned and hulled, for raspberries. Mash berries, add 2½ cups water, and strain to remove seeds. Combine 1¼ cups sugar and ⅓ cup cornstarch with juice. Heat to boiling, stirring constantly. Cook until thickened and clear. Chill. Serve over ice cream or other desserts.
	■	**Peach Melba.** Pour 3 Tbsp Raspberry Sauce over a scoop of vanilla ice cream placed in the center of a canned, fresh, or frozen peach half.

BROWN SUGAR SYRUP

Yield: 2 gal

Ingredient	Amount	Procedure
Sugar, brown	5 lb	Combine all ingredients.
Sugar, granulated	5 lb 8 oz	Stir and heat until sugar is dissolved.
Corn syrup	1 cup	
Water	2½ qt	
Margarine	4 oz	

Approximate nutritive values per ounce

Calories (kcal)	Protein (grams)	Carbohydrate (grams)	Fat (grams)	Cholesterol (mg)	Sodium (mg)	Iron (mg)	Calcium (mg)
75	0 (0%)	18.8 (96%)	0.4 (4%)	0	8	0.4	9

Notes	■	Serve warm or cold on pancakes, fritters, or waffles.
	■	½ tsp maple flavoring may be added.
Variation	■	**Blueberry Syrup.** Combine 1½ qt water, 12 oz granulated sugar, 1 tsp salt, and ⅓ cup lemon juice. Heat to boiling. Mix 4 oz waxy maize starch and 1½ cups cold water to make a paste. Add slowly to sugar mixture, stirring constantly. Cook until thickened and clear. Fold in 3 lb 8 oz individually quick frozen (IQF) blueberries. Serve warm over pancakes, French toast, or ice cream.

14

Soups

Homemade soups are popular and versatile menu items that may be served as an appetizer or as a center-of-the-plate entree. The type of soup served should complement the other menu items or be hearty enough for the entree. Hot soups should be heated to 180°F and cold soups served chilled.

TYPES OF SOUPS

Soups may be clear and thin or thick and hearty. Stock or broth, the basic ingredient of many soups, is made by simmering meat and/or meat, fish, or poultry bones, and/or vegetables in water to extract their flavor. The most frequently used stocks are brown (made from beef that has been browned before simmering) and white or light (made from veal and/or chicken). See pp. 615–616 for stock recipes.

Mirepoix, a mixture of chopped vegetables—usually in the proportion of 50 percent onions, 25 percent carrots, and 25 percent celery—is used in flavoring soup stock. Flavorings commonly used are bay leaves, peppercorns, whole cloves, and parsley stems.

For a clear soup, the stock should be clarified. Clarifying removes flecks that are too small to be strained out with cheesecloth, but that will cloud a soup's appearance. Stock is highly perishable. If it is not to be used immediately, it may be reduced in volume by boiling to one-half or one-fourth its volume and frozen for later use. Recipes for beef and chicken stocks and directions for clarifying stock are given on pp. 615 and 616.

Clear soups are made from a clear, seasoned stock or broth and include:

- *Bouillon,* made from beef broth that may or may not be clarified.

- *Consommé,* a strong, concentrated stock or broth.

- *Vegetable soup,* a clear seasoned stock or broth, with the addition of vegetables and sometimes meat or poultry products.

Thick soups are opaque rather than transparent. They are thickened either by a roux, which is a mixture of melted fat and flour slightly browned, or a puree of one of the ingredients. Examples are:

- *Cream soups,* made with a thin or medium white sauce combined with either mashed, strained, or finely chopped vegetables or meat, chicken, or fish. Chicken stock may be used to replace part of the milk in the sauce to enhance the flavor. If a stock base is used, it may be added to the margarine-flour roux or may be added to water and used as part of the liquid.

- *Chowders,* unstrained, chunky, hearty soups prepared from meat, poultry, seafood, and/or vegetables. Most chowders contain potatoes and milk or cream.

- *Purees,* thick soups made by pressing cooked vegetables or fish through a sieve into their own stock.

COMMERCIAL SOUP BASES

Because preparation of soups, especially those made from stock, is time-consuming, commercial food or soup bases are often used. The amount of meat concentrate in commercial soup bases varies, so the choice of base should be made carefully to ensure a desirable, full-flavored stock. A high-quality base is a concentrate of cooked meat, poultry, seafood, or vegetables that includes the concentrated cooking juices and seasonings. It has a puree- or paste-like consistency and may require refrigeration. One pound of soup base produces an average of 5 gallons of ready-to-use-stock. Most granulated soup bases and many paste products are highly salted. When using these products, the salt listed in the recipe should be deleted or reduced. Soup bases also can be used to prepare sauces, gravies, and stuffings.

SERVING AND HOLDING SOUPS

Hot soup cools off quickly in serving bowls. It is important that soup be very hot when served. Using a heated bowl helps hot soups retain their heat. Soups should be prepared in batches small enough for ingredients to retain their texture throughout the serving period. Cream soups will curdle if kept at too high a temperature or held for too long a time. For this reason, the milk may be added just before serving and the mixture reheated to serving temperature (180°F). Cold soups should be served in chilled bowls at 40°F.

STOCK SOUP RECIPES

CHICKEN STOCK

Yield: 3 gal

Ingredient	Amount	Procedure
Chicken, uncooked	20 lb AP	Cut up chicken and place in large kettle or steam-jacketed kettle.
Water, cold	5 gal	Add water.
Onions, quartered	8 oz	Add vegetables and seasonings. Bring to boiling point.
Celery, with leaves, chopped	8 oz	Reduce heat and simmer until chicken is tender.
Salt	3 oz	
Peppercorns	1 Tbsp	
Bay leaves	2	
Marjoram	2 tsp	
		Remove chicken and strain broth. Refrigerate.
		Remove chicken from bones. Cut up for soup or reserve for later use.
		When broth is cold, fat will congeal on top; skim off.
Egg shells, washed and crushed	3	If a clear broth is desired, clarify it by adding egg shells and whites to broth.
Egg whites, beaten	3	Bring to boiling point and simmer for 15 minutes.
		Strain through cheesecloth or fine strainer.

Variations

- **Chicken Stock with Soup Base.** Add 8 oz concentrated chicken base to 2½ gal water. Exact proportion may vary with different manufacturers. If soup base is used for sauces and casseroles, delete or reduce amount of salt specified in recipe.
- **White Stock.** Substitute knuckle of veal for part of chicken.

BEEF STOCK

Yield: 3 gal

Ingredient	Amount	Procedure
Beef shank, lean	15 lb	Pour water over beef shanks in large kettle or steam-jacketed kettle.
Water, cold	5 gal	
Onions, quartered	8 oz	Add vegetables and seasonings.
Celery with leaves, chopped	8 oz	Bring to boiling point.
Carrots, chopped	8 oz	Reduce heat and simmer until meat leaves bone, about 4 hours.
Peppercorns	1 Tbsp	
Bay leaves	2	
Salt	3 oz	
		Remove meat, strain broth, and refrigerate for several hours.
		Skim congealed fat off top.

Variations

- **Beef Stock with Soup Base.**   Add 8 oz concentrated beef base to 2½ gal water. Exact proportion may vary with different manufacturers. If soup base is used for sauces and casseroles, delete or reduce amount of salt specified in recipe.

- **Brown Stock.**   Allow 10 lb beef shank to stand 30 minutes in cold water. Heat slowly to boiling point. Simmer 2 hours. Add vegetables that have been browned with remaining meat. Add seasonings. Simmer 3 hours.

BOUILLON

Yield: 3 gal   *Portion:* 1 cup (8 oz)

Ingredient	Amount	Procedure
Beef, lean	8 lb	Sear beef. Add bone and water.
Beef bone, cracked	4 lb	Simmer for 3–4 hours. Replace water as necessary.
Water, cold	4 gal	
Carrots, diced	8 oz	Add vegetables and seasonings.
Celery, chopped	8 oz	Cook 1 hour. Strain.
Onions, quartered	8 oz	Chill overnight.
Bay leaves	4	Remove congealed fat from broth.
Peppercorns	1 Tbsp	
Salt	¼ cup	

To clarify:		Add egg shells and whites to clarify the broth.
Egg shells, washed and crushed	3	Bring slowly to boiling point, stirring constantly. Boil 15–20 minutes without stirring.
Egg whites, beaten	3	Strain through a fine strainer.

Variations

■ **Chicken Bouillon.** Substitute 20 lb chicken, cut up, for the beef and bone. Do not sear chicken.

■ **Tomato Bouillon.** To 1½ gal Bouillon, add four 46-oz cans tomato juice, 2 oz chopped onion, 2 oz sugar, 2 oz salt (amount will vary), ½ tsp pepper, and 2 bay leaves.

BEEF BARLEY SOUP

Yield: 50 portions or 3 gal   *Portion:* 1 cup (8 oz)

Ingredient	Amount	Procedure
Beef, cubed	3 lb	Brown beef cubes in kettle. Drain off fat.
Celery, chopped	1 lb 6 oz	Add celery and onions. Sauté until tender.
Onions, chopped	1 lb 6 oz	
Beef Stock (p. 616)	3 gal	Add remaining ingredients. Bring to a boil.
Pepper, black	1 tsp	Lower heat and simmer for 1 hour.
Salt	1 tsp	Taste for seasoning and add salt if needed.
Bay leaf	1	
Carrots, diced	1 lb 6 oz	
Pearl barley	10 oz	

Approximate nutritive values per portion

Calories (kcal)	Protein (grams)	Carbohydrate (grams)	Fat (grams)	Cholesterol (mg)	Sodium (mg)	Iron (mg)	Calcium (mg)
91	9.7 (43%)	7.3 (32%)	2.5 (25%)	19	819	1.4	28

Note

■ 2¾ oz (1⅓ cups) dehydrated onions may be substituted for fresh onions (p. 55).

VEGETABLE BEEF SOUP

Yield: 50 portions or 3 gal   *Portion:* 1 cup (8 oz)

Ingredient	Amount	Procedure
Beef Stock (p. 616)	2 gal	Heat stock in kettle.
Carrots, cubed	8 oz	Add vegetables and seasonings.
Celery, chopped	1 lb	Cover and simmer about an hour. Replace water as
Onions, chopped	1 lb 8 oz	necessary.
Potatoes, cubed	1 lb	Taste for seasoning. Add additional salt if needed.
Salt	1 Tbsp	
Pepper, black	1 tsp	
Tomatoes, diced, canned	1 No. 10 can	
Cooked beef, chopped	2 lb	Add chopped beef. Heat to serving temperature.

Approximate nutritive values per portion

Calories (kcal)	Protein (grams)	Carbohydrate (grams)	Fat (grams)	Cholesterol (mg)	Sodium (mg)	Iron (mg)	Calcium (mg)
80	8.7 (43%)	6.4 (31%)	2.3 (26%)	18	747	1.4	35

Notes
- 8 oz raw rice or 4 oz dry noodles may be substituted for the potatoes.
- Browned beef cubes may be substituted for cooked beef. Brown in kettle before stock is added.
- 3 oz (1½ cups) dehydrated onions may be substituted for fresh onions (p. 55).

Variations
- **Julienne Soup.** Cut carrots, celery, and potatoes in long, thin strips.
- **Mexican Beef Soup.** Omit carrots and celery. Add 12 oz whole-kernel corn, 4 oz green peppers, chopped, 1 lb 8 oz sliced zucchini, and 3 Tbsp ground cumin.
- **Vegetable Soup.** Delete beef. Increase carrots and celery to 1 lb 8 oz each.

HEARTY BEEF VEGETABLE SOUP

Yield: 50 portions or 3 gal   *Portion:* 1 cup (8 oz)

Ingredient	Amount	Procedure
Ground beef	8 lb AP	Brown meat. Drain off fat.
Onions, chopped	1 lb	Add onions to meat and cook until tender.
Margarine Flour, all-purpose	9 oz 9 oz	Melt margarine and stir in flour. Cook for 5 minutes.
Beef Stock (p. 616) Salt Pepper, black	1¼ gal 1 Tbsp ½ tsp	Add stock and seasonings, stirring constantly. Cook until mixture boils and has thickened. Add browned meat and onions.
Carrots, fresh, diced Celery, sliced	12 oz 10 oz	Cook vegetables until barely tender. Drain. (Vegetables should be crunchy.)
Mixed vegetables, frozen	4 lb	Cook mixed vegetables until partially done. Add, with other vegetables, to the soup. Stir carefully to blend.
Tomatoes, diced, canned	2 lb 8 oz	Add tomatoes. Heat to serving temperature.

Approximate nutritive values per portion

Calories (kcal)	Protein (grams)	Carbohydrate (grams)	Fat (grams)	Cholesterol (mg)	Sodium (mg)	Iron (mg)	Calcium (mg)
235	16.3 (28%)	11.4 (19%)	13.8 (53%)	48	593	2.2	36

Note

■ 2 oz (1 cup) dehydrated onions may be substituted for fresh onions (p. 55).

BEEF NOODLE SOUP

Yield: 50 portions or 3 gal   *Portion:* 1 cup (8 oz)

Ingredient	Amount	Procedure
Vegetable oil Beef, fresh, cubed Salt Pepper, black	½ cup 2 lb 2 tsp ½ tsp	Heat oil in kettle. Add beef cubes and seasonings and cook until lightly browned. Drain off fat.
Onions, chopped Celery, chopped	8 oz 12 oz	Add onions and celery, and sauté.
Beef Stock (p. 616)	2¾ gal	Add stock. Simmer for one hour.
Noodles	12 oz	Add noodles and simmer until tender, 5–10 minutes. Add salt if needed.

Approximate nutritive values per portion

Calories (kcal)	Protein (grams)	Carbohydrate (grams)	Fat (grams)	Cholesterol (mg)	Sodium (mg)	Iron (mg)	Calcium (mg)
91	7.5 (33%)	5.6 (25%)	4.2 (42%)	19	787	1.2	20

Note
- 1 oz (½ cup) dehydrated onions may be substituted for fresh onions (p. 55).

Variations
- **Alphabet Soup.** Use alphabet noodles.
- **Beef Rice Soup.** Substitute 1 lb 8 oz rice for noodles.
- **Creole Soup.** Reduce Beef Stock to 2¼ gal. Add 1 No. 10 can tomatoes, 8 oz shredded green peppers, 1 lb sliced okra, and 4 bay leaves. Substitute rice for noodles.

CHICKEN NOODLE SOUP

Yield: 50 portions or 3 gal   *Portion:* 1 cup (8 oz)

Ingredient	Amount	Procedure
Chicken Stock (p. 615) Onion, chopped Celery, chopped	3 gal 8 oz 8 oz	Bring stock to a boil. Add onion and celery. Cook until tender.
Noodles	1 lb	Add noodles. Cook for about 15 minutes or until noodles are tender.

Margarine, melted	8 oz	Blend margarine and flour.
Flour, all-purpose	4 oz	Add to soup, stirring until slightly thickened.
Salt	1 tsp	Add seasonings.
Pepper, white	½ tsp	
Cooked chicken, diced	1 lb 8 oz	Add chicken and simmer for 5 minutes.

Approximate nutritive values per portion

Calories (kcal)	Protein (grams)	Carbohydrate (grams)	Fat (grams)	Cholesterol (mg)	Sodium (mg)	Iron (mg)	Calcium (mg)
140	10.1 (30%)	9.7 (28%)	6.3 (42%)	20	846	1.2	18

Note ■ 1 oz (½ cup) dehydrated onions may be substituted for fresh onions (p. 55).

Variation ■ **Chicken Rice Soup.** Substitute 12 oz rice for the noodles.

TURKEY VEGETABLE SOUP

Yield: 50 portions   *Portion:* 1 cup (8 oz)

Ingredient	Amount	Procedure
Carrots, fresh	1 lb	Cut carrots into thin julienne strips.
Potatoes, red	2 lb	Do not peel potatoes. Dice into ½-inch cubes.
Onions, minced	12 oz	Combine in steam-jacketed kettle.
Celery, chopped	10 oz	Add carrots and potatoes.
Mushrooms, sliced	8 oz	Simmer 20 minutes or until vegetables are tender.
Chicken Stock (p. 615)	2½ gal	
Sage, rubbed	⅛ tsp	Add seasonings to soup.
Thyme, ground	¼ tsp	
Pepper, black	¼ tsp	
Cooked turkey, chopped	2 lb	Add turkey and parsley. Heat to 180°F.
Parsley, fresh, chopped	2 oz	

Approximate nutritive values per portion

Calories (kcal)	Protein (grams)	Carbohydrate (grams)	Fat (grams)	Cholesterol (mg)	Sodium (mg)	Iron (mg)	Calcium (mg)
88	9.9 (47%)	6.7 (31%)	2.1 (22%)	14	644	1	21

Note ■ 1½ oz (¾ cup) dehydrated onions may be substituted for fresh onions (p. 55).

CHILI CON CARNE ▪

Yield: 3 gal   *Portion:* 1 cup (8 oz)

Ingredient	Amount	Procedure
Ground beef	10 lb AP	Cook beef, onions, and garlic in steam-jacketed kettle until meat loses pink color.
Onions, chopped	8 oz	
Garlic, minced	1 clove	
Tomatoes, canned, diced	2½ qt	Mix tomato and seasonings. Add to beef. Cook until blended.
Tomato puree	2 qt	
Water	1 qt	
Chili powder	3 oz	
Cumin seed, ground	1½ Tbsp	
Salt	1 oz (1½ Tbsp)	
Pepper, black	½ tsp	
Sugar, granulated	2 oz	
Beans, pinto, kidney, or red, canned	9 lb 8 oz	Add beans to meat mixture. Cover and simmer for 1 hour. Add water if chili becomes too thick.

Approximate nutritive values per portion

Calories (kcal)	Protein (grams)	Carbohydrate (grams)	Fat (grams)	Cholesterol (mg)	Sodium (mg)	Iron (mg)	Calcium (mg)
299	23.7 (31%)	23.8 (31%)	12.7 (38%)	61	660	4.4	63

Notes

- If dried beans are used, substitute 3 lb for canned beans. Wash and prepare according to directions on p. 646.
- If desired, thicken chili by mixing 5 oz flour and 2 cups cold water. Add to chili mixture and heat until flour is cooked.
- 1 oz (½ cup) dehydrated onions, rehydrated in ¾ cup water, may be substituted for fresh onions (p. 55).

Variations

- **Chili and Cheese.** Sprinkle grated cheddar or Monterey Jack cheese over chili, 1 Tbsp per bowl.
- **Chili Spaghetti.** Use only 7 lb ground beef. Cook 1 lb 8 oz spaghetti according to directions on p. 407. Add to chili mixture just before serving. Macaroni or other pasta shapes may be used also.
- **Chili Buffet.** Serve chili with accompaniments: chopped onions, tomatoes, and green peppers; sliced black olives; shredded cheese; and sliced jalapeño peppers.
- **Turkey Chili.** Substitute 8 lb ground turkey for ground beef.

GARDEN CHILI

Yield: 50 portions   *Portion:* 8 oz

Ingredient	Amount	Procedure
Vegetable oil	¾ cup	Heat oil. Add onions and garlic and sauté until transparent.
Onions, chopped	3 lb 12 oz	
Garlic, minced	1½ Tbsp	
Celery, chopped	2 lb 4 oz	Add celery, carrots, and seasonings to onions.
Carrots, chopped finely	1 lb	Cook until tender-crisp.
Oregano, dried, crumbled	2 tsp	
Cumin, ground	2 Tbsp	
Chili powder	2 Tbsp	
Salt	1 oz (1½ Tbsp)	
Pepper, black	1 Tbsp	
Green peppers, chopped	1 lb	Add to onion mixture.
Zucchini, chopped	2 lb	Heat thoroughly.
Mushrooms and stems, canned	1 lb 8 oz	
Tomatoes, diced, canned	5 lb 6 oz	
Water	1 qt	
Red beans, canned	5 lb 6 oz	
Lemon juice, frozen, reconstituted	⅓ cup	
Cheddar cheese, shredded	1 lb 8 oz	To serve, ladle chili into soup bowls. Sprinkle ½ oz cheese over each portion.

Approximate nutritive values per portion

Calories (kcal)	Protein (grams)	Carbohydrate (grams)	Fat (grams)	Cholesterol (mg)	Sodium (mg)	Iron (mg)	Calcium (mg)
169	7.9 (18%)	17.3 (39%)	8.4 (43%)	14	599	2	154

WHITE CHILI

Yield: 50 portions   *Portion:* 8 oz

Ingredient	Amount	Procedure
Great Northern beans	3 lb	Sort and wash beans. Cover with water to 2 inches above beans. Let soak overnight.
		Drain beans. Place in steam-jacketed kettle.
Water Chicken soup base Onion, chopped Garlic, minced Salt	2 gal 6 oz 2 lb 1 oz 1½ tsp	Add to beans. Bring to a boil. Cover. Reduce heat and simmer for 2 hours, stirring occasionally.
Chicken or turkey, white meat, diced Green chilies, canned, diced Cumin, ground Oregano, dried, crumbled Pepper, cayenne Cloves, ground Cilantro, dried, crumbled	3 lb 1 lb 8 oz 2 Tbsp 1½ Tbsp 1½ tsp ½ tsp 1 Tbsp	Add to beans. Cover and cook 30 minutes.
Monterey Jack cheese, shredded (optional)	1 lb 12 oz	Sprinkle ½ oz cheese over each portion as it is served.

Approximate nutritive values per portion

Calories (kcal)	Protein (grams)	Carbohydrate (grams)	Fat (grams)	Cholesterol (mg)	Sodium (mg)	Iron (mg)	Calcium (mg)
209	18.2 (35%)	19.6 (37%)	6.6 (28%)	35	859	2.3	187

Note   ■   If a highly salted chicken base is used, check for seasoning before adding salt.

MINESTRONE SOUP

Yield: 50 portions or 3 gal   *Portion:* 1 cup (8 oz)

Ingredient	Amount	Procedure
Bacon, diced	1 lb	Fry bacon until crisp. Drain.
Onions, chopped	12 oz	Sauté onion and garlic in a little bacon fat until tender.
Garlic, minced	2 cloves	Place, with bacon, in a large kettle.
Beef Stock (p. 616)	2 gal	Add stock and seasonings. Heat to boiling.
Bay leaves	2	
Pepper, black	1 tsp	
Cabbage, chopped	12 oz	Add vegetables and spaghetti. Simmer 45 minutes.
Carrots, fresh, diced	12 oz	
Potatoes, raw, chopped	12 oz	
Celery, chopped	12 oz	
Spinach, fresh, chopped	3 oz	
Green beans, cut, canned	12 oz	
Tomatoes, canned, diced	2 lb	
Red beans, canned	1 lb 12 oz	
Spaghetti, long	2 oz	
Flour, all-purpose	3 oz	Make a smooth paste of the flour and water.
Water, cold	1 cup	Stir into soup. Cook 10 minutes longer.
Parsley, chopped	¼ cup	Add parsley just before serving.

Approximate nutritive values per portion

Calories (kcal)	Protein (grams)	Carbohydrate (grams)	Fat (grams)	Cholesterol (mg)	Sodium (mg)	Iron (mg)	Calcium (mg)
70	4.5 (25%)	9.3 (52%)	1.8 (23%)	2	634	1	33

Note   ■   1½ oz (¾ cup) dehydrated onions may be substituted for fresh onions (p. 55).

NAVY BEAN SOUP

Yield: 50 portions or 3 gal   *Portion:* 1 cup (8 oz)

Ingredient	Amount	Procedure
Navy beans, dry	4 lb	Wash beans. Add boiling water. Cover and let stand
Water, boiling	3 gal	1 hour or longer.
		Simmer beans for about 1 hour.
Ham cubes	3 lb	Add ham and seasonings to beans.
Onion, chopped	12 oz	Cook until beans are tender, 1–1½ hours.
Celery, diced	8 oz	Add water to make volume of 3¼ gal.
Pepper, black	1 Tbsp	Check seasoning. Add salt if needed. Heat to serving
Water	(see procedure)	temperature.

Approximate nutritive values per portion

Calories (kcal)	Protein (grams)	Carbohydrate (grams)	Fat (grams)	Cholesterol (mg)	Sodium (mg)	Iron (mg)	Calcium (mg)
93	9 (39%)	8.3 (36%)	2.6 (25%)	16	582	1.1	27

Notes
- Great Northern beans may be substituted for navy beans.
- Ham base may be added for additional flavor.
- 1½ oz (¾ cup) dehydrated onions may be substituted for fresh onions (p. 55).

SPLIT PEA SOUP

Yield: 50 portions or 3 gal   *Portion:* 1 cup (8 oz)

Ingredient	Amount	Procedure
Split peas	3 lb	Wash peas. Add water and bring to a boil.
Water	2 gal	Boil for 2 minutes, then turn off heat.
		Cover and let stand for 1 hour.
Ham cubes	2 lb	Add ham, onions, carrots, and potatoes.
Onions, chopped	1 lb	Cook for 1 hour or until peas are soft.
Carrots, fresh, chopped	1 lb 8 oz	
Potatoes, raw, chopped	2 lb	
Margarine	4 oz	Melt margarine and add flour. Stir until smooth. Cook
Flour, all-purpose	2 oz	5 minutes.
Chicken Stock (p. 615)	2 qt	Add stock, while stirring, and cook until thickened. Add to peas.
Pepper, black	1 tsp	Taste for seasoning. Add pepper and salt if needed.

Approximate nutritive values per portion

Calories (kcal)	Protein (grams)	Carbohydrate (grams)	Fat (grams)	Cholesterol (mg)	Sodium (mg)	Iron (mg)	Calcium (mg)
176	12.3 (27%)	23.3 (52%)	4.1 (20%)	11	432	1.7	2.8

Notes

- If soup becomes too thick, add hot water to bring to desired consistency. If a smoother soup is desired, cook and puree peas before adding ham and vegetables.
- 1 lb chopped celery may be substituted for 1 lb potatoes.
- 3 lb sliced Polish sausage may be added to soup before serving. Reduce ham to 1 lb.
- 2 oz (1 cup) dehydrated onions may be substituted for fresh onion (p. 55).

Variations

- **Lentil Soup.**   Substitute lentils for split peas.
- **Yellow Split Pea Soup.**   Substitute yellow split peas for green split peas.

TOMATO RICE SOUP

Yield: 50 portions or 3 gal   *Portion:* 1 cup (8 oz)

Ingredient	Amount	Procedure
Beef or Chicken Stock (pp. 616, 615)	2 gal	Heat stock and puree to boiling point.
Tomato puree	1 gal	
Onion, chopped	2 oz	Add vegetables and rice. Cook until rice is tender.
Green pepper, chopped	4 oz	
Rice, converted	8 oz	
Margarine	6 oz	Melt margarine and add flour. Mix until smooth.
Flour, all-purpose	3 oz	Add to soup while stirring. Add salt to taste.

Approximate nutritive values per portion

Calories (kcal)	Protein (grams)	Carbohydrate (grams)	Fat (grams)	Cholesterol (mg)	Sodium (mg)	Iron (mg)	Calcium (mg)
92	3.6 (15%)	13.4 (55%)	3.2 (30%)	0	852	1.3	25

Note

- ¼ oz (2 Tbsp) dehydrated onions may be substituted for fresh onions (p. 55).

Variation

- **Tomato Barley Soup.**   Add 1 lb barley in place of rice.

PEPPER POT SOUP

Yield: 50 portions or 3 gal   *Portion:* 1 cup (8 oz)

Ingredient	Amount	Procedure
Margarine	12 oz	Sauté vegetables in margarine until lightly browned, about 15 minutes.
Onion, finely chopped	8 oz	
Green peppers, finely chopped	8 oz	
Celery, thinly sliced	6 oz	
Potatoes, diced	3 lb 8 oz	
Flour, all-purpose	5 oz	Add flour to vegetables and stir until well blended.
Beef or Chicken Stock (pp. 616, 615)	2¼ gal	Combine stock and milk. Add to vegetable mixture, while stirring. If soup base is used for the stock, taste before adding salt.
Milk, hot	1 qt	
Salt	1 oz (1½ Tbsp)	
Pimiento, chopped	2 Tbsp	Add pimiento. Keep just below boiling point for 30 minutes, stirring frequently.

Approximate nutritive values per portion

Calories (kcal)	Protein (grams)	Carbohydrate (grams)	Fat (grams)	Cholesterol (mg)	Sodium (mg)	Iron (mg)	Calcium (mg)
116	3.7 (12%)	10.9 (37%)	6.6 (50%)	3	834	0.6	42

Notes
- This soup is good served with Spaetzles (p. 143). Prepare 1 recipe for 50 servings.
- 1 oz (½ cup) dehydrated onions may be substituted for fresh onions (p. 55).

FRENCH ONION SOUP

Yield: 50 portions or 3 gal   *Portion:* 1 cup (8 oz)

Ingredient	Amount	Procedure
Onions, fresh	8 lb	Cut onions in thin slices.
Margarine or short-ening	12 oz	Sauté in margarine in large kettle.
Flour, all-purpose	3 oz	Add flour and pepper. Cook for 10 minutes.
Pepper, black	1 tsp	
Beef Stock (p. 616)	3 gal	Add stock and Worcestershire sauce.
Worcestershire sauce	3 Tbsp	Cook until onions are tender.
Salt	1 tsp (if needed)	
Croutons	12 oz	To serve, ladle soup over croutons or toasted bread.
Parmesan cheese, grated, or Swiss cheese, shredded	2 oz	Sprinkle with cheese.

Approximate nutritive values per portion

Calories (kcal)	Protein (grams)	Carbohydrate (grams)	Fat (grams)	Cholesterol (mg)	Sodium (mg)	Iron (mg)	Calcium (mg)
127	5.1 (16%)	12.5 (39%)	6.5 (45%)	1	974	1	48

CREAM SOUP RECIPES

BASIC SAUCE FOR CREAM SOUP

Yield: 2½ gals basic sauce

Ingredient	Amount	Procedure
Margarine Onions, finely chopped	8 oz 2 oz	Melt margarine. Add onions and sauté until tender.
Flour, all-purpose Chicken base Pepper, white	12 oz 3 oz ½ tsp	Add flour, chicken base, and pepper to onions. Stir until blended. Cook for 5 minutes.
Water	2 qt	Add water and stir until mixture thickens. Add vegetables and seasonings as suggested in Variations to make a variety of cream soups.
Milk, hot	2 gal	Stir in milk. Heat to 180°F.

Notes
- Chicken base may be omitted. Omit the water and use 2½ gal milk. Add 2 oz salt.
- ¼ oz (2 Tbsp) dehydrated onions, rehydrated in ¼ cup water, may be substituted for fresh onions (p. 55).

Variations
- To make 3 gallons of soup (50–60 one-cup, 8-oz portions), use 1 recipe Basic Sauce for Cream Soup plus additions suggested below.
- **Cream of Asparagus Soup.**   Add 6 lb cooked, chopped (or pureed) asparagus.
- **Cream of Broccoli Soup.**   Add 6 lb cooked, chopped broccoli.
- **Cream of Cauliflower Soup.**   Increase onion to 1 lb 8 oz and water to 1 gal. Reduce milk to 1½ gal. Add 6 lb cauliflower, cut into small florets, and 1 Tbsp Worcestershire sauce. Stir in 1 lb 8 oz processed American cheese, shredded. Stir until melted. Sprinkle with chopped chives.
- **Cream of Celery Soup.**   Increase onions to 8 oz. Add 2 lb 8 oz cooked chopped celery and 1 lb cooked diced carrots.
- **Cream of Mushroom Soup.**   Increase onion to 8 oz. Add 3 lb mushrooms, sliced or chopped, sautéed with the onion in margarine.
- **Mushroom Barley Soup.**   Reduce milk to 3 qt and increase water to 1¾ gal. Increase margarine to 1 lb, onions to 1 lb, and chicken base to 8 oz. Add 3 lb sliced mushrooms, ½ tsp garlic powder, and 1 lb barley after water has been added. Simmer about 30 minutes, then add milk slowly and heat to 180°F. Sprinkle with chopped parsley.

- **Cream of Potato Soup.**   Increase onions to 12 oz. Add 8 lb cooked diced potatoes and 1 lb cooked chopped celery. Increase chicken base to 5 oz. Potatoes may be mashed or pureed if desired.
- **Cream of Spinach Soup.**   Increase onion to 8 oz. Add 3 lb chopped spinach, cooked.
- **Cream of Vegetable Soup.**   Increase onion to 1 lb. Add 1 lb cooked chopped celery, 1 lb 8 oz cooked died carrots, and 2 lb cooked diced potatoes.

CREAM OF CHICKEN SOUP

Yield: 50 portions or 3 gal   *Portion:* 1 cup (8 oz)

Ingredient	Amount	Procedure
Margarine	8 oz	Melt margarine. Sauté celery until tender.
Celery, chopped	1 lb	
Flour, all-purpose	8 oz	Add flour and salt. Stir until blended.
Salt	1 oz (1½ Tbsp)	Cook for 5 minutes.
Chicken Stock (p. 615)	2 gal	Add stock and seasonings. Cook over low heat until it has the consistency of thin white sauce. If chicken base is used for stock, taste before adding celery salt.
Celery salt	2 tsp	
Pepper, white	½ tsp	
Milk	1 gal	Add milk while stirring.
Cooked chicken, chopped	3 lb	Add chicken. Heat to 180°F.

Approximate nutritive values per portion

Calories (kcal)	Protein (grams)	Carbohydrate (grams)	Fat (grams)	Cholesterol (mg)	Sodium (mg)	Iron (mg)	Calcium (mg)
172	13.7 (33%)	8.1 (19%)	9 (48%)	33	839	0.9	111

Note   ■   1 lb cooked rice or noodles may be added. Reduce margarine and flour to 4 oz each.

Variation   ■   **Chicken Velvet Soup.**   Substitute 2 qt light cream (half-and-half) for 2 qt milk. Increase flour to 12 oz.

CHEESE SOUP

Yield: 50 portions or 3 gal   *Portion:* 1 cup (8 oz)

Ingredient	Amount	Procedure
Margarine	8 oz	Sauté onion in margarine until lightly browned.
Onions, chopped	8 oz	
Flour, all-purpose	4 oz	Add flour and cornstarch. Blend.
Cornstarch	2 oz	Cook for 5 minutes.
Paprika	1 tsp	Add seasonings and blend.
Salt	2 Tbsp	Add milk and stock slowly, while stirring.
Pepper, white	1 tsp	Cook until thickened.
Milk	1 gal	
Chicken Stock (p. 615)	1½ gal	
Carrots, finely diced	1 lb	Cook carrots and celery until tender but slightly crisp.
Celery, finely diced	12 oz	Add to soup.
Cheddar cheese, sharp, shredded	1 lb	Add cheese and blend at low temperature.
Parsley, fresh, chopped	½ cup	Garnish with chopped parsley.

Approximate nutritive values per portion							
Calories (kcal)	Protein (grams)	Carbohydrate (grams)	Fat (grams)	Cholesterol (mg)	Sodium (mg)	Iron (mg)	Calcium (mg)
156	7.7 (20%)	8.7 (22%)	10 (58%)	20	775	0.6	173

Note   ■ 1 oz (½ cup) dehydrated onions, rehydrated in ¾ cup water, may be substituted for fresh onions (p. 55).

BROCCOLI AND CHEESE SOUP

Yield: 50 portions or 3 gal   *Portion:* 1 cup (8 oz)

Ingredient	Amount	Procedure
Margarine	10 oz	Melt margarine in steam-jacketed or other large kettle.
Onions, finely chopped	10 oz	Add onions and sauté until tender.
Flour, all-purpose	12 oz	Add flour and seasonings. Stir until blended.
Salt	1 Tbsp	Cook for 5 minutes, stirring often.
Pepper, black	1 tsp	
Chicken base	3 oz	Stir in chicken base, then add water and milk, stirring constantly.
Water	3 qt	
Milk	1½ gal	Reduce heat and cook until thickened, stirring often.
Processed cheese, coarsely shredded	2 lb 8 oz	Add cheese and stir until melted.
Broccoli cuts, frozen	4 lb	Steam broccoli until just tender. Chop, if necessary. Add to cheese mixture and heat to serving temperature.

Approximate nutritive values per portion

Calories (kcal)	Protein (grams)	Carbohydrate (grams)	Fat (grams)	Cholesterol (mg)	Sodium (mg)	Iron (mg)	Calcium (mg)
239	11.1 (18%)	13.8 (23%)	15.9 (59%)	38	890	0.7	306

Note   ■   1¼ oz (⅔ cup) dehydrated onions, rehydrated in 1 cup water, may be substituted for fresh onions (p. 55).

CHOWDER RECIPES

CORN CHOWDER

Yield: 50 portions or 3 gal   *Portion:* 1 cup (8 oz)

Ingredient	Amount	Procedure
Potatoes, diced	2 lb	Cook potatoes. Drain. Save for later step.
Margarine, melted Onions, finely chopped Celery, chopped	8 oz 4 oz 6 oz	Sauté onions and celery in margarine until tender.
Flour, all-purpose Pepper, white Chicken base	12 oz 1 tsp 3 oz	Add flour, pepper, and chicken base to onions. Stir until well blended. Cook for 5 minutes.
Water	1½ gal	Add water, stirring constantly. Cook until mixture thickens.
Corn, cream style Chives, frozen	1 No. 10 can 1 cup	Add corn, chives, and potatoes. Heat until hot.
Milk	2½ qt	Stir milk into soup. Heat to 180°F.

Approximate nutritive values per portion

Calories (kcal)	Protein (grams)	Carbohydrate (grams)	Fat (grams)	Cholesterol (mg)	Sodium (mg)	Iron (mg)	Calcium (mg)
154	4.1 (10%)	22.8 (57%)	5.8 (33%)	6.8	392	0.7	72

Notes
- ½ oz (¼ cup) dehydrated onions, rehydrated in ½ cup water, may be substituted for fresh onions (p. 55).
- 1 lb bacon, diced and cooked until crisp, may be added before serving.

Variations
- **Potato Chowder.**   Omit corn and increase potatoes to 8 lb.
- **Vegetable Chowder.**   Substitute 3 lb whole kernel corn for cream style corn. Add 4 oz chopped green pepper and 1 lb cooked, diced carrots.

NEW ENGLAND CLAM CHOWDER

Yield: 50 portions or 3 gal   *Portion:* 1 cup (8 oz)

Ingredient	Amount	Procedure
Potatoes, cubed	6 lb	Cook potatoes until tender. Drain.
Water	1 qt	Reserve potatoes to add in last step.
Salt	1 Tbsp	
Bacon, finely diced	4 oz	Sauté bacon, onion, and celery in steam-jacketed or
Onion, chopped	8 oz	other large kettle for 5 minutes, or until lightly
Celery, chopped	12 oz	browned.
Margarine	8 oz	Add margarine to onion and stir until melted.
Flour, all-purpose	8 oz	Add flour, seasonings, and chicken base. Stir until
Pepper, white	1 tsp	blended.
Chicken base	4 oz	Cook for 5 minutes.
Milk	2 gal	Add milk gradually while stirring. Cook until thickened.
Minced clams, undrained	4 lb	Add clams and potatoes. Heat to serving temperature.

Approximate nutritive values per portion

Calories (kcal)	Protein (grams)	Carbohydrate (grams)	Fat (grams)	Cholesterol (mg)	Sodium (mg)	Iron (mg)	Calcium (mg)
235	12.1 (20%)	24.6 (42%)	10 (38%)	34	709	5.6	217

Notes

- 1 gal fresh clams may be used. Clean and steam until tender. Drain and chop. Save juice.

- Garnish with fresh or frozen chives, chopped.

- 1 oz (½ cup) dehydrated onions, rehydrated in ¾ cup water, may be substituted for fresh onions (p. 55).

Variation

- **Fish Chowder.**   Delete clams. Add 1 tsp thyme, 1 tsp crushed rosemary, 2 tsp Worcestershire sauce, ½ tsp hot pepper sauce, and 3 lb flaked white fish, or 1 lb shrimp and 2 lb minced clams.

HEARTY POTATO HAM CHOWDER

Yield: 50 portions or 3 gal   *Portion:* 1 cup (8 oz)

Ingredient	Amount	Procedure
Margarine	3 oz	Melt margarine in steam-jacketed or other large kettle.
Onion, green, finely chopped	8 oz	Add onion and green pepper and sauté until tender.
Green pepper, chopped	12 oz	
Flour, all-purpose	3 oz	Add flour and seasonings. Stir until blended.
Pepper, white	½ tsp	Cook for 5 minutes, stirring often.
Paprika	1 tsp	
Chicken Stock (p. 615)	3 qt	Add stock and stir until smooth. Cook until mixture begins to thicken.
Ham, coarsely chopped	2 lb 8 oz	Add ham, potatoes, and corn. Heat.
Potatoes, cooked, cubed	5 lb 8 oz	
Corn, whole kernel	3 lb 12 oz	
Milk	2¾ qt	Add milk and mix well. Heat to serving temperature.
Parsley, fresh, chopped	½ cup	Sprinkle parsley over chowder before serving.

Calories (kcal)	Protein (grams)	Carbohydrate (grams)	Fat (grams)	Cholesterol (mg)	Sodium (mg)	Iron (mg)	Calcium (mg)
Approximate nutritive values per portion							
276	12.6 (18%)	41 (59%)	7.2 (23%)	21	584	1.7	76

Note   ▪ 1 oz (½ cup) dehydrated onions, rehydrated in ¾ cup water, may be substituted for fresh onions (p. 55).

OYSTER STEW

Yield: 50 portions or 3 gal   *Portion:* 1 cup (8 oz)

Ingredient	Amount	Procedure
Milk	2½ gal	Scald milk by heating to point just below boiling.
Oysters	2½ qt	Heat undrained oysters and butter only until edges of
Butter or margarine	8 oz	oysters begin to curl.

| Salt | 2 oz (3 Tbsp) | About 10 minutes before serving, add oysters, with the oyster liquid, and seasonings to scalded milk. Serve immediately to avoid curdling. |
| Pepper | ½ tsp | |

Approximate nutritive values per portion

Calories (kcal)	Protein (grams)	Carbohydrate (grams)	Fat (grams)	Cholesterol (mg)	Sodium (mg)	Iron (mg)	Calcium (mg)
203	11.6 (23%)	11.9 (24%)	12 (53%)	76	599	5	269

MANHATTAN FISH OR CLAM CHOWDER

Yield: 50 portions or 3 gal   *Portion:* 1 cup (8 oz)

Ingredient	Amount	Procedure
Bacon, diced	1 lb	Cook bacon until crisp. Drain off excess fat.
Onion, chopped	1 lb 6 oz	Add onion and sauté until tender. Place onion and bacon in large kettle.
Water	3 qt	Add water, vegetables, and spices. Bring to a boil.
Tomatoes, diced, canned	1 No. 10 can	Reduce heat. Simmer 40–45 minutes or until vegetables are tender.
Potatoes, chopped	3 lb	Remove bay leaves before serving.
Carrots, fresh, diced	1 lb 4 oz	
Celery, chopped	1 lb 4 oz	
Catsup	2 cups	
Worcestershire sauce	⅓ cup	
Salt	2 Tbsp	
Pepper, black	1 tsp	
Bay leaves	2	
Thyme, ground	1 tsp	
Fish, boneless, cooked and flaked, or minced clams	3 lb 8 oz	Add fish. Cover and simmer 5–10 minutes.
Parsley, fresh, chopped	¼ cup	Sprinkle parsley over soup before serving.

Approximate nutritive values per portion

Calories (kcal)	Protein (grams)	Carbohydrate (grams)	Fat (grams)	Cholesterol (mg)	Sodium (mg)	Iron (mg)	Calcium (mg)
98	6.3 (25%)	14.8 (59%)	1.8 (16%)	13	543	5.3	49

Note   ■   2¾ oz (1½ cups) dehydrated onions, rehydrated in 2¼ cups water, may be substituted for fresh onions (p. 55).

CHILLED SOUP RECIPES

GAZPACHO (SPANISH CHILLED SOUP)

Yield: 50 portions or 1¾ gal   *Portion:* ½ cup (4 oz)

Ingredient	Amount	Procedure
Mushrooms, fresh, chopped	4 oz	Sauté mushrooms in olive oil until light brown.
Olive oil	½ cup	
Garlic	3 cloves	Crush garlic in salt.
Salt	2 Tbsp	
Tomatoes, fresh, finely chopped	3 lb	Combine remaining ingredients in a stainless steel or glass container.
Green peppers, finely chopped	1 lb 4 oz	Add mushrooms and garlic.
		If too thick, add more tomato juice.
Celery, finely chopped	12 oz	Cover and chill.
Cucumbers, finely chopped	1 lb	
Onion, finely chopped	1 lb 8 oz	
Chives, chopped	2 Tbsp	
Parsley, chopped	3 Tbsp	
Pepper, black	1 Tbsp	
Worcestershire sauce	1 Tbsp	
Tarragon vinegar	1½ cups	
Hot pepper sauce	1 tsp	
Tomato juice	2½ qt	

Approximate nutritive values per portion

Calories (kcal)	Protein (grams)	Carbohydrate (grams)	Fat (grams)	Cholesterol (mg)	Sodium (mg)	Iron (mg)	Calcium (mg)
45	1.1 (8%)	6.5 (50%)	2.4 (41%)	0	487	0.7	23

VICHYSSOISE (CHILLED POTATO SOUP)

Yield: 50 portions or 3 gal   *Portion:* 1 cup (8 oz)

Ingredient	Amount	Procedure
Chicken Stock (p. 615)	1 gal	Combine stock and onions. Cook until onions are tender.
Onions, chopped	3 lb	Strain.
Potatoes, diced	6 lb	Steam potatoes until tender. Mash.
Salt	1 Tbsp	Add seasonings and chicken stock to potatoes. If soup base is used in stock, salt may need to be reduced.
Celery salt	2 tsp	
Garlic salt	1 tsp	
Pepper, white	½ tsp	
Light cream (half-and-half)	1¼ gal	Add cream and mix well. Chill thoroughly.
Parsley, chives, or green onion tops, chopped	⅓ cup	Garnish chilled soup with chopped parsley, chives, or green onion tops.

Approximate nutritive values per portion

Calories (kcal)	Protein (grams)	Carbohydrate (grams)	Fat (grams)	Cholesterol (mg)	Sodium (mg)	Iron (mg)	Calcium (mg)
200	5.8 (12%)	18.6 (37%)	11.7 (52%)	36	545	0.5	115

15

Vegetables

With the increased interest in nutrition, the place of the vegetable in today's foodservice menu has assumed new importance. A wide array of fresh vegetables is available year-round, as is a variety of frozen and canned vegetables. Proper preparation and cooking are essential to preserving the nutritive value, color, and palatability of fresh vegetables, and the addition of herbs and spices enhances the vegetables without the addition of salt and fat.

Frozen and canned vegetables require less labor to prepare than fresh vegetables and have more predictable yields, but fresh vegetables, especially those that are not too time-consuming to prepare, should be considered when they are in season.

The quantity of vegetables to buy depends on the portion size and the method of preparation. One No. 10 can or 5 pounds of most frozen vegetables will yield 25 3-oz portions. For fresh vegetables, the loss in preparation must be considered in determining the amount to purchase. Table 1.1 suggests amounts to buy and Table 1.2 gives the approximate yield in the preparation of fresh vegetables.

FRESH AND FROZEN VEGETABLES

Fresh or frozen vegetables may be cooked by boiling, steaming, baking, or frying. The method used depends largely on the type of product, the amount to be cooked, and the equipment available. Fresh vegetables should be washed, trimmed, peeled if necessary, and cut into even-sized pieces for cooking. Detailed instructions are given for individual recipes in this section. (Salad vegetables and their preparation are discussed in Chapter 11.) Preparing fresh vegetables too far in advance causes them to discolor. Covering prepared vegetables with cold water helps retain color but reduces their nutritive value if they are held too long.

A small steam-jacketed kettle is satisfactory for cooking both fresh and frozen vegetables. It should be large enough to prevent crowding and to allow the water to return to the boiling point quickly after vegetables are added. A tilting frypan also may be used successfully.

Vegetables may be cooked in a steamer if cooked in small quantities and arranged in thin layers in shallow pans. The time and temperature must be controlled carefully. Cooking in a high-pressure or zero-pressure steamer is especially successful. One advantage of steam cooking is that vegetables may be weighed and placed in serving pans, then cooked and served from the same pans.

When steam equipment is not available, top-of-range cooking may be used. Vegetables should be cooked in as small an amount of water as is practicable and as quickly as possible.

Whatever the method used, vegetables should be cooked only until tender. *Do not overcook.* Vegetables should be cooked in as small a quantity at one time as is feasible for the type of service. The needs of most foodservices can be met by the continuous cooking of vegetables in small quantities. Vegetables should be served as soon as possible after cooking for optimum quality and should be handled carefully to prevent breaking or mashing. Appearance is important to customer acceptance of vegetables, as is the seasoning. Individual recipes recommend the amount of salt for 50 portions and suggest seasonings appropriate to that vegetable.

Directions for Boiling

1. Prepare vegetables. See pp. 486–491 for directions for preparing fresh vegetables. Frozen vegetables should not be thawed before cooking except for solid pack frozen vegetables, which should be thawed only long enough to break apart easily.

2. Add prepared vegetables to boiling salted water in steam-jacketed kettle or stockpot. Cook in lots no larger than 10 lb. Use 1 oz (1½ Tbsp) salt to the amount of water specified in Table 15.1, except for corn. Add salt and/or sugar after cooking to prevent toughening and discoloring of corn kernels.

   The amount of water used in cooking all vegetables is important for retention of nutrients. The less water used, the more nutrients retained. Addition of baking soda to the water also causes loss of vitamins. Mature root vegetables that need longer cooking require more water than young, tender vegetables. Spinach and other greens need only the water clinging to their leaves from washing.

3. Cover and bring water quickly back to the boiling point. Green vegetables retain their color better if the lid is removed just before boiling begins; strong-flavored vegetables, such as cabbage, cauliflower, and brussels sprouts, should be cooked uncovered to prevent development of unpleasant flavors.

4. Start timing when water returns to the boiling point. Use Table 15.1 as a guide. Stir greens occasionally while boiling.

TABLE 15.1   Timetable for boiling or steaming fresh and frozen vegetables

	Boiling— approximate cooking time[a] (minutes)	Steaming—Approximate cooking time[b,c] for 1–3 pans (minutes)		
		5–6 psi[d]	12–15 psi[d]	Zero pressure
Asparagus, fresh, frozen	10–15	10–12	4–8	6–13
Beans, black-eyed beans or peas, frozen	30–45	20–25	10–20	25–35
Beans, green or wax, fresh	20–30	15–20	4–10	10–20
Beans, green or wax, frozen	10–12	10–12	7–11	6–13
Beans, lima, frozen	12–14	10–12	6–10	6–13
Beets, whole, fresh	40–50	40–50	25–35	40–50
Broccoli, cuts or spears, fresh, frozen	10–15	10–15	4–8	5–15
Brussels sprouts, fresh, frozen	10–15	10–12	6–10	9–14
Cabbage, cored, cut	10–12	14–16	7–14	14–18
Carrots, fresh	10–20	18–20	6–15	18–20
Carrots, frozen	10–20	9–10	5–9	7–12
Cauliflower, fresh, frozen	12	10–15	5–10	7–15
Celery, fresh	10–15	10–15	5–10	10–15
Corn, whole kernel, frozen	6–8	9–10	5–9	5–10
Corn on the cob, fresh, frozen	15–20	10–12	5–10	8–12
Eggplant, fresh	15–20	10–15	4–8	5–15
Greens, collard, fresh	30–40	10–15	8–10	12–15
Kale, fresh	15–20	10–15	8–10	12–15
Okra, fresh, frozen	8–15	10–12	6–10	10–12
Onions, fresh	20–30	15–20	5–10	10–15
Parsnips, fresh	20–40	15–20	6–15	18–20
Peas, green, fresh, frozen	10–12	6–7	2–6	3–10
Potatoes, fresh, whole	25–40	20–25	13–25	35–40
Rutabagas, fresh	20–35	25–30	10–20	25–30
Spinach, fresh	3–5	3–5	1–3	3–5
Spinach, frozen, thawed	3–5	8–10	4–8	8–10
Squash, summer, fresh, frozen	5–10	8–12	5–8	7–10
Squash, winter, fresh	30–40	15–20	7–9	15–20
Sweet potatoes, fresh	30–40	20–30	13–25	30–40
Turnips, fresh	20–40	25–30	10–20	25–30
Vegetables, mixed, frozen	12–15	10	5–9	5–10

[a]Figures calculated for boiling 10–12 lb of vegetables in 1–3 qt water. Greens require the addition of no extra water; the water clinging to their leaves is sufficient.
[b]Figures calculated for steaming 5–6 lb vegetables per batch. A steamer filled to less than capacity will need the cooking time reduced slightly. An overloaded steamer may require a longer cooking time.
[c]Wherever possible, use 2½-inch-deep perforated steamer pans. For best results, break up frozen vegetables to speed cooking.
[d]Pounds per square inch.

Note   ■ Canned vegetables require the following cooking times: 5 psi, 3–5 minutes; 15 psi, 3–4 minutes; 0 psi, 5–10 minutes.

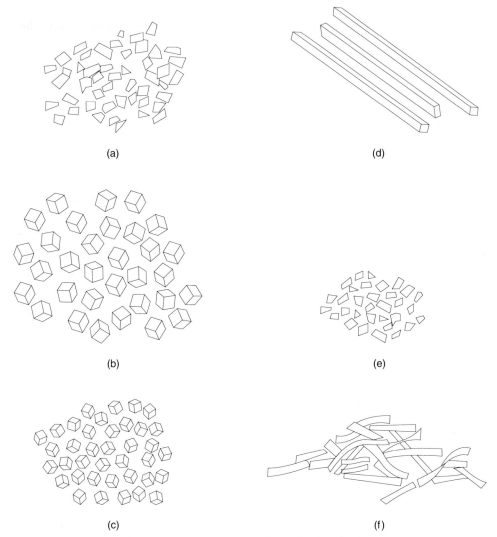

FIGURE 15.1   Terminology for cutting vegetables and other foods:
(a) chopped, (b) cubed, (c) diced, (d) julienne, (e) minced, (f) shredded.

5.   Drain cooked vegetables and place in serving pans. Add 4–8 oz melted margarine or butter to each 50 portions.

6.   Adjust seasonings.

Directions for Steaming

1.   Place prepared vegetables not more than 3–4 inches deep in stainless steel inset pans. Perforated pans provide the best circulation, but if cooking liquid needs to be

retained, use solid pans. When cooking winter squash or sweet potatoes, cover with a lid or aluminum foil to prevent water from accumulating in the pan.

2. Steam, using Table 15.1 as a guide. Begin timing when steamer reaches proper cooking pressure.

3. Add 2–4 oz melted margarine or butter and 2 tsp salt to each 5 lb of drained vegetables.

Directions for Stir-Frying

1. Select vegetables for color, texture, shape, and flavor.

2. Cut or dice diagonally into small uniform pieces (see Figure 15.1).

3. Heat a small amount of oil or seasoned oil in a pan, steam-jacketed kettle, or tilting frypan. Prepare seasoned oil for stir-frying by adding ½ oz sliced ginger root and ½ oz fresh peeled garlic to 2 cups salad oil. Let stand at room temperature for several days. Strain before using.

4. Stir in vegetables, starting with those that take longer to cook (carrots, onions, turnips). Continue to stir for one minute until vegetables are coated with oil.

5. Add liquid (water or broth) and seasonings to vegetables. Cover and steam for 3 minutes or until vegetables are tender but crisp.

6. Add cornstarch mixed with a small amount of cold water. (See recipe on p. 688.) Cook and stir just until the sauce thickens and vegetables are glazed.

CANNED VEGETABLES

Heating of canned vegetables should be scheduled so they will be served soon after heating. Prepare 1–2 No. 10 cans at a time, with approximately 25 portions in each can.

Directions for Heating

Stockpot or Steam-Jacketed Kettle

1. Drain off half the liquid; use for soups, gravies, and sauces.

2. Heat vegetables and remaining liquid in a stockpot or steam-jacketed kettle. Heat only long enough to bring to 160°F.

3. Drain vegetables and place in counter pans. Add 4–8 oz melted margarine or butter.

Steamer or Oven

1. Drain off half the liquid; use for soups, gravies, and sauces.

2. Transfer vegetables and remaining liquid to steamer pans and cover. A 12 × 20 × 2-inch pan will hold contents of 2 No. 10 cans, or 50 portions of most vegetables.

3. Heat in steamer at 5–6 lb pressure for one minute, or in a 350°F oven until 160°F is reached.

4. Drain vegetables and add 4–8 oz melted margarine or butter for each lot of vegetables.

DRIED VEGETABLES

Among the many kinds of dried legumes available today are dried peas (whole green or split green, yellow split, and black-eyed); beans (navy, black, fava, red kidney, brown, pinto, butter beans, and garbanzo, also known as chick peas); lentils (brown and red). High in protein and fiber, legumes are an important factor in meatless dishes and health-conscious menus.

Directions for Cooking

1. Sort, discarding any stones or other foreign material and shriveled vegetables. Rinse with cold water.

2. Heat water to boiling in steam-jacketed or other kettle.

3. Add vegetable and boil for 3 minutes.

4. Turn off steam and allow to stand for 1 hour.

5. Add salt and cook slowly until vegetables are tender (1–1½ hours). Add more water if needed.

6. Vegetable may be covered with cold water and soaked overnight, drained, then cooked.

VEGETABLE RECIPES

SEASONED FRESH ASPARAGUS

Yield: 50 portions   *Portion:* 3 oz

Ingredient	Amount	Procedure
Asparagus, fresh	18–20 lb AP (10 lb EP)	Break or cut off tough stems. Wash and thoroughly clean remaining portions. Arrange spears in steamer pans with tips in one direction. Sprinkle with salt. Steam (p. 643). Asparagus may be cut into 1-inch pieces and steamed or placed in a kettle and boiled (p. 643).
Margarine, melted Salt	4 oz 1 oz (1½ Tbsp)	Pour margarine over cooked asparagus. If boiling asparagus, add salt to cooking water.

Approximate nutritive values per portion

Calories (kcal)	Protein (grams)	Carbohydrate (grams)	Fat (grams)	Cholesterol (mg)	Sodium (mg)	Iron (mg)	Calcium (mg)
58	4.5 (26%)	7.3 (43%)	2.4 (31%)	0	232	1.3	36

Notes
- For frozen asparagus, use 10 lb. See p. 643 for cooking instructions.
- Seasonings for asparagus: sesame seeds, lemon juice, browned butter, crumb butter.

Variations
- **Asparagus with Cheese Sauce.**   Serve 5 or 6 stalks of cooked asparagus with 2 Tbsp Cheese Sauce (p. 582). Make 2 qt sauce.
- **Asparagus Vinaigrette.**   Blanch asparagus (see p. 486). Marinate in 1½ qt Vinaigrette Dressing (p. 549) or Vegetable Marinade (p. 605).
- **Creamed Asparagus.**   Add 1 gal Medium White Sauce (p. 582) to 10 lb asparagus cut in 2-inch lengths and cooked.
- **Fresh Asparagus with Hollandaise Sauce.**   Serve 1 Tbsp Hollandaise Sauce (p. 598) over cooked asparagus spears.

SEASONED FRESH GREEN OR WAX BEANS

Yield: 50 portions   *Portion:* 3 oz

Ingredient	Amount	Procedure
Green or wax beans, fresh	11–12 lb AP (10 lb EP)	Wash beans. Trim ends. Cut or break into 1-inch pieces. Steam or boil (p. 643).
Margarine, melted Salt	4 oz 1 oz (1½ Tbsp)	Pour margarine over cooked beans and sprinkle with salt. If boiling the beans, add salt to cooking water.

Approximate nutritive values per portion

Calories (kcal)	Protein (grams)	Carbohydrate (grams)	Fat (grams)	Cholesterol (mg)	Sodium (mg)	Iron (mg)	Calcium (mg)
51	1.9 (13%)	7.9 (54%)	2.1 (33%)	0	216	1.3	48

Notes

- For frozen beans, use 10 lb. See p. 643 for cooking.
- For canned beans, use 2 No. 10 cans. See p. 645 for heating.
- Seasonings for green beans: basil, dill, marjoram, oregano, savory, tarragon, thyme, onion, chives, mushrooms, bacon.

Variations

- **French Green Beans.** Cook 10 lb frozen French cut green beans. Drain and season with 1 cup mayonnaise, ¾ cup sour cream, 2 Tbsp vinegar, 2 oz chopped onion sautéed in 2 oz margarine, and salt and pepper to taste.
- **Green Beans Amandine.** Add 8 oz slivered almonds lightly browned in 8 oz margarine.
- **Green Beans and Mushrooms.** Add 2 lb sliced mushrooms that have been sautéed in 8 oz margarine.
- **Green Beans Provincial.** Season green beans with 8 oz Onion Butter (p. 602), 2 cloves garlic, minced, 3 Tbsp chopped parsley, and 2 tsp dried crumbled thyme.
- **Herbed Green Beans.** Season 10 lb frozen green beans, cooked, or 2 No. 10 cans green beans with 1 lb chopped onions, 8 oz chopped celery, and 1 tsp minced garlic sautéed in 8 oz margarine, 2 tsp dried crumbled basil, and 2 tsp dried rosemary.
- **Southern-Style Green Beans.** Cut 1 lb 8 oz bacon into small pieces. Add 6 oz chopped onion and sauté until onion is lightly browned. Add to hot, drained green beans. Good served with ham and Corn Bread (p. 132).

GREEN BEAN CASSEROLE

Yield: 50 portions or 1 pan 12 × 20 × 2 inches   *Portion:* 4 oz
Oven: 350°F   *Bake:* 30–40 minutes

Ingredient	Amount	Procedure
Green beans, frozen, French cut or cut	7 lb 8 oz	Cook green beans (p. 643). Drain.
Mushrooms, fresh Margarine, melted	10 oz 3 oz	Clean mushrooms and slice. Sauté in margarine.
Cream of mushroom soup, undiluted Milk Pepper, black Onion powder Soy sauce	1 qt 1 cup ½ tsp 1 tsp 1 Tbsp	Blend soup, milk, and seasonings.
Water chestnuts, sliced, drained	1 lb	Combine soup mixture, mushrooms, and water chestnuts. Add to green beans. Mix lightly. Pour into one 12 × 20 × 2-inch pan.
Swiss cheese, shredded	8 oz	Sprinkle cheese over beans. Bake at 350°F for 25 minutes.
Bread crumbs Margarine, melted	4 oz 4 oz	Combine crumbs and margarine and sprinkle over bean mixture. Bake 5–10 minutes.

Approximate nutritive values per portion

Calories (kcal)	Protein (grams)	Carbohydrate (grams)	Fat (grams)	Cholesterol (mg)	Sodium (mg)	Iron (mg)	Calcium (mg)
108	3.3 (12%)	10.2 (37%)	6.4 (51%)	5	262	0.9	91

Notes

- Two No. 10 cans cut green beans may be substituted for frozen beans. Drain before using.
- 8 oz crumbled French fried onion rings (canned) may be sprinkled over the top during the last 10 minutes of baking.

SPANISH GREEN BEANS

Yield: 50 portions   *Portion:* 3 oz

Ingredient	Amount	Procedure

Bacon, diced
Onion, chopped
Green pepper,
  chopped
	8 oz
	6 oz
	4 oz
		Sauté bacon, onion, and green pepper until lightly
		  browned.

Flour, all-purpose	4 oz	Add flour and stir until smooth.
Tomatoes, canned Salt	2 qt 1 Tbsp	Chop tomatoes and heat. Add salt. Add gradually to bacon-vegetable mixture. Stir and cook until thickened.

Green beans,
  drained
	2 No. 10 cans	Gently stir tomato sauce into the green beans.
		Simmer 20–30 minutes or until beans are heated to
		  160°F.

Approximate nutritive values per portion

Calories (kcal)	Protein (grams)	Carbohydrate (grams)	Fat (grams)	Cholesterol (mg)	Sodium (mg)	Iron (mg)	Calcium (mg)
47	2.4 (18%)	9.1 (68%)	0.9 (15%)	1	213	1.4	40

Note   ■ 8 lb fresh or frozen green beans may be substituted for canned beans. Cook before combining with tomato sauce.

Variations   ■ **Creole Green Beans.**   Omit bacon. Sauté onion, green pepper, and 8 oz chopped celery in 2 oz margarine. Add 2 oz sugar to tomatoes.

■ **Green Beans with Dill.**   Delete bacon and onion. Sauté the green pepper in 5 oz margarine. Add 1 tsp pepper and 1 Tbsp dill seeds. Simmer slowly for 10–15 minutes. Tomato may be increased to one No. 10 can.

■ **Hacienda Green Beans.**   Add 1 oz sugar, 1½ Tbsp chili powder, and ½ tsp garlic powder.

SEASONED LIMA BEANS

Yield: 50 portions   *Portion:* 3 oz

Ingredient	Amount	Procedure
Lima beans, baby or fordhook, frozen	10 lb	Steam or boil beans (p. 643).
Margarine, melted Salt	4 oz 1 oz (1½ Tbsp)	Pour margarine over beans and sprinkle with salt. If boiling the beans, add salt to cooking water.

Approximate nutritive values per portion							
Calories (kcal)	Protein (grams)	Carbohydrate (grams)	Fat (grams)	Cholesterol (mg)	Sodium (mg)	Iron (mg)	Calcium (mg)
130	7.3 (22%)	21.2 (63%)	2.2 (15%)	0	216	2.2	28

Note
- Seasonings for lima beans: basil, marjoram, oregano, sage, savory, tarragon, thyme, pimiento, mushrooms, onion butter, sour cream.

Variations
- **Baked Lima Beans and Peas.**   Thaw 5 lb frozen baby lima beans and 5 lb frozen peas. Combine with 2 Tbsp dried basil, 1 oz (1½ Tbsp) salt, ½ tsp cracked black pepper, and 16 green onions, sliced. Place in baking pan. Sprinkle with 1 cup water and dot with 4–6 oz margarine. Cover and bake at 325°F for 45 minutes. Stir occasionally.

- **Succotash.**   Use 5 lb lima beans and 5 lb frozen or canned whole kernel corn. Season with 4 oz margarine.

BAKED LIMA BEANS

Yield: 50 portions or 2 pans 12 × 20 × 2 inches   *Portion:* 5 oz
Oven: 350°F   *Bake:* 1 hour

Ingredient	Amount	Procedure
Lima beans, dry, large	6 lb AP	Wash beans (p. 646). Add boiling water. Cover. Let stand 1 hour or longer.
Water, boiling	1 gal	Cook beans in the same water until tender, about 1 hour.
Pimiento, chopped	4 oz	Add seasonings to beans.
Salt	1 oz (1½ Tbsp)	Scale into two 12 × 20 × 2-inch pans, 8 lb 6 oz per
Molasses	1 cup	pan.
Bacon, sliced	1 lb 8 oz	Place bacon on top of beans. Bake at 350°F until top is brown, about 1 hour.

Approximate nutritive values per portion							
Calories (kcal)	Protein (grams)	Carbohydrate (grams)	Fat (grams)	Cholesterol (mg)	Sodium (mg)	Iron (mg)	Calcium (mg)
80	3.9 (18%)	11.8 (54%)	2 (20%)	3	444	2.1	58

Variations
- **Baked Lima Beans and Sausage.**   Omit bacon. Place 6 lb link sausages on top of beans.
- **Boiled Lima Beans and Ham.**   Omit bacon and seasonings. Add 5 lb diced ham to beans and simmer until tender.

RANCH STYLE BEANS

Yield: 50 portions or 1 pan 12 × 20 × 4 inches   *Portion:* 5 oz
Oven: 300°F   *Bake:* 3–4 hours

Ingredient	Amount	Procedure
Beans, red or pinto, dried	5 lb	Wash beans (p. 646). Add boiling water. Cover and let stand for 1 hour or longer.
Water, boiling	1½ gal	
Bacon, 1-inch cubes	2 lb 8 oz	Add bacon to beans.
Water, cold	to cover	Add additional water to cover. Cook slowly until tender, about 1 hour.
Chili peppers	3–4 pods	Soak chili peppers in warm water. Remove and discard seeds. Add pods to beans.
Tomatoes, canned	2 qt	Add tomatoes and other seasonings.
Onions, sliced	8 oz	Cook slowly in kettle an additional 2 hours, or pour
Garlic, chopped	2 cloves	into a 12 × 20 × 4-inch baking pan and bake at
Salt	1 oz (1½ Tbsp)	300°F for 2–3 hours.
Pepper, black	1 Tbsp	
Pepper, cayenne	Few grains	

Approximate nutritive values per portion

Calories (kcal)	Protein (grams)	Carbohydrate (grams)	Fat (grams)	Cholesterol (mg)	Sodium (mg)	Iron (mg)	Calcium (mg)
171	9.8 (22%)	25.5 (58%)	3.7 (19%)	5	361	2.8	59

Notes
- If chili peppers are not available, 1 oz chili powder may be substituted.
- 2 No. 10 cans red beans may be substituted for dry beans. Reduce baking time to 1–2 hours.

BAKED BEANS

Yield: 50 portions or 1 pan 12 × 20 × 4 inches   *Portion:* 5 oz
Oven: 350°F   *Bake:* 3–4 hours

Ingredient	Amount	Procedure
Beans, navy or Great Northern, dried	5 lb AP	Wash beans (p. 646). Add boiling water and let stand 1 hour.
Water, boiling	1½ gal	Cook in same water until tender, about 1 hour. Add more water as necessary.
Salt	4 oz	Add remaining ingredients to beans.
Sugar, brown	6 oz	Pour into one 12 × 20 × 4-inch baking pan.
Dry mustard	1 tsp	Cover and bake at 350°F for 3–4 hours. Add more water if needed during baking.
Vinegar, cider	2 Tbsp	Uncover during last half hour of baking.
Molasses	1 cup	
Catsup	2½ cups	
Bacon, cubed	1 lb	
Onion, chopped	3 oz	

Approximate nutritive values per portion

Calories (kcal)	Protein (grams)	Carbohydrate (grams)	Fat (grams)	Cholesterol (mg)	Sodium (mg)	Iron (mg)	Calcium (mg)
108	4.4 (16%)	19.8 (72%)	1.5 (12%)	2	1059	2.5	81

Variations

- **Baked Pork and Beans.** Use 2 No. 10 cans pork and beans. Fry 1 lb diced bacon until partially cooked. Add 4 oz chopped onion and cook until onions are tender. Pour off fat. Add bacon and onions to pork and beans. Stir in 1 cup catsup, ¼ cup vinegar, 4 oz brown sugar, and 1 Tbsp prepared mustard. Bake at 350°F for 1–2 hours.

- **Boston Baked Beans.** Omit catsup.

- **Trio Baked Beans.** Fry 2 lb diced bacon until partially cooked. Drain. Steam 1 lb 12 oz frozen lima beans. Add to bacon. Add 8 oz chopped onion, 2 lb 8 oz canned red beans, 2 lb 12 oz pork and beans, ½ cup molasses, 6 oz brown sugar, 3 cups catsup, ¼ cup vinegar, and 1 Tbsp liquid smoke. Mix gently to blend. Scale into two 12 × 10 × 2-inch counter pans. Bake at 225°F for 3½ hours.

REFRIED BEANS

Yield: 50 portions   *Portion:* 4 oz

Ingredient	Amount	Procedure
Beans, pinto, dried Water, boiling	5 lb 1 gal	Wash beans. Add boiling water. Cover and let stand 1 hour or longer. Cook beans in the same water until tender, about 1 hour. Add more water if necessary.
		When beans are done, drain, reserving liquid for later step. Place cooked beans in mixer bowl and mash thoroughly.
Vegetable oil Onions, chopped	1½ cups 6 oz	Heat oil in frying pan. Add chopped onion. Cook until tender.
Chili powder Garlic powder Salt Hot pepper sauce	2 Tbsp 1 tsp 2 tsp Few drops	Add seasonings to onion and mix thoroughly.
Beef Stock (p. 616)	1 qt	Add beef stock and mix well. Add mashed beans, mixing until well-blended. Turn mixture constantly to keep from burning. Bean liquid in small amounts may be added if mixture becomes too thick. Cook bean mixture for 45–60 minutes or until dry.

Approximate nutritive values per portion

Calories (kcal)	Protein (grams)	Carbohydrate (grams)	Fat (grams)	Cholesterol (mg)	Sodium (mg)	Iron (mg)	Calcium (mg)
132	4.5 (13%)	13.7 (41%)	6.9 (46%)	0	528	1.5	37

Note	■	10 lb canned pinto beans may be substituted for dried beans. Drain beans and reserve liquid for later step.
Variation	■	**Spicy Black Beans.** Use 3 lb dried black beans. Combine 1½ lb beans and 1½ qt water in each of two 12 × 10 × 4-inch pans. Into each pan measure 1 Tbsp cumin, 1 tsp garlic powder, 1 tsp salt, and 1½ Tbsp chili powder. Stir to mix into the beans. Steam for 50–60 minutes or until beans are tender but not mushy. Beans may also be cooked with seasonings in steam-jacketed kettle.

SEASONED FRESH BEETS

Yield: 50 portions   *Portion:* 3 oz

Ingredient	Amount	Procedure
Beets, fresh	14 lb AP (11 lb EP)	Cut off all but 2 inches of the beet tops. Wash beets and leave whole, with root ends attached. Boil or steam until tender (p. 643). Drain. Run cold water over beets. Slip off skins and remove root ends. Slice, dice, or cut into shoestring pieces.
Margarine, melted Salt	4 oz 1 oz (1½ Tbsp)	Pour margarine over cooked beets and sprinkle with salt. Heat to serving temperature.

Approximate nutritive values per portion

Calories (kcal)	Protein (grams)	Carbohydrate (grams)	Fat (grams)	Cholesterol (mg)	Sodium (mg)	Iron (mg)	Calcium (mg)
56	1.4 (10%)	8.5 (60%)	1.9 (30%)	0	276	0.8	16

Notes

- For canned beets, use two No. 10 cans. See p. 645 for heating directions.
- Seasonings for beets: allspice, bay leaves, caraway seed, cloves, dill, ginger, mint, marjoram, mustard seed, basil, nutmeg, onion, orange, sour cream, vinegar.

Variations

- **Beets in Sour Cream.**   Grate fresh cooked beets and season with a mixture of 1½ cups lemon juice, 1½ Tbsp onion juice, 2 tsp salt, and 10 oz sugar. Toss lightly. Serve with a spoonful of sour cream on each portion.
- **Julienne Beets.**   Cut 8 lb cooked beets into julienne strips. Season with a mixture of 4 oz margarine, 4 oz sugar, 4 tsp salt, and 1 cup lemon juice.
- **Pickled Beets.**   See p. 540.

HARVARD BEETS

Yield: 50 portions   *Portion:* 3 oz

Ingredient	Amount	Procedure
Beets, sliced or diced	2 No. 10 cans	Drain beets. Reserve juice for sauce.
Beet juice Bay leaf Cloves, whole	1½ qt 1 1 tsp	Add bay leaf and cloves to beet juice. Heat to boiling point. Remove bay leaf.
Sugar, granulated Salt Cornstarch	12 oz 1 oz (1½ Tbsp) 6 oz	Combine dry ingredients. Add to beet juice while stirring briskly. Cook until thickened and clear.
Margarine Vinegar, cider	4 oz 2 cups	Add margarine and vinegar. Stir until mixed and margarine is melted. Heat beets. Add sauce.

Approximate nutritive values per portion

Calories (kcal)	Protein (grams)	Carbohydrate (grams)	Fat (grams)	Cholesterol (mg)	Sodium (mg)	Iron (mg)	Calcium (mg)
91	1.3 (5%)	18.5 (77%)	1.9 (18%)	0	272	0.8	1.5

Note   ■ For fresh beets, use 10 lb EP (13 lb AP). See p. 643 for cooking procedure.

Variations   ■ **Beets with Orange Sauce.**   Omit bay leaf, cloves, and vinegar. Add 2 cups orange juice and ½ cup lemon juice.

■ **Hot Spiced Beets.**   Drain juice from two No. 10 cans sliced beets and add 1 Tbsp whole cloves, 1½ Tbsp salt, ½ tsp cinnamon, 1 lb brown sugar, 8 oz granulated sugar, and 1 qt cider vinegar. Cook 10 minutes. Pour sauce over beets and heat to serving temperature.

SEASONED BROCCOLI

Yield: 50 portions   *Portion:* 3 oz

Ingredient	Amount	Procedure
Broccoli, fresh	16–20 lb AP (10 lb EP)	Wash broccoli and remove outer leaves and tough part of stocks. Cut broccoli stalks lengthwise into uniform spears, following branching lines. Steam or boil broccoli spears (p. 643).
Margarine, melted Salt	4 oz 1 oz (1½ Tbsp)	Pour margarine over cooked broccoli and sprinkle with salt. If boiling the broccoli, add salt to cooking water.

Calories (kcal)	Protein (grams)	Carbohydrate (grams)	Fat (grams)	Cholesterol (mg)	Sodium (mg)	Iron (mg)	Calcium (mg)
41	2.7 (22%)	4.8 (39%)	2.1 (39%)	0	238	0.8	45

Approximate nutritive values per portion

Notes
- For frozen broccoli, use 12 lb spears or 10 lb chopped.
- Seasonings for broccoli: caraway, dill, or mustard seed, tarragon, lemon, almond, pimiento, onion butter.

Variations
- **Almond Buttered Broccoli.** Brown slivered almonds in margarine and pour over cooked, drained broccoli.
- **Broccoli with Cheese Sauce.** Prepare 2 qt Cheese Sauce (p. 582). Serve 2 Tbsp (1 oz) sauce over each portion of cooked broccoli.
- **Broccoli with Hollandaise Sauce or Lemon Butter.** Serve cooked spears or chopped broccoli with 1 Tbsp Hollandaise Sauce (p. 598) or 1 tsp Lemon Butter (p. 601).

SEASONED BRUSSELS SPROUTS

Yield: 50 portions   *Portion:* 3 oz

Ingredient	Amount	Procedure
Brussels sprouts, fresh	14 lb AP (11 lb EP)	Trim stem end of brussels sprouts. Discard wilted outside leaves. Steam or boil (p. 643) until just tender.
Margarine, melted Salt	4 oz 1 oz (1½ Tbsp)	Pour margarine over brussels sprouts and sprinkle with salt. If boiling the vegetable, add salt to the cooking water.

Calories (kcal)	Protein (grams)	Carbohydrate (grams)	Fat (grams)	Cholesterol (mg)	Sodium (mg)	Iron (mg)	Calcium (mg)
55	2.6 (16%)	8.7 (53%)	2.3 (32%)	0	235	1.2	38

Approximate nutritive values per portion

Note
- Seasonings for brussels sprouts: dill, celery seed, fennel, lemon.

SEASONED CABBAGE

Yield: 50 portions   *Portion:* 3 oz

Ingredient	Amount	Procedure
Cabbage, fresh	14 lb AP (12 lb EP)	Remove wilted outer leaves and wash cabbage. Crisp in cold water if wilted. Cut into wedges and remove center core; or shred coarsely. Steam or boil (p. 643). Drain.
Margarine, melted Salt	4 oz 1 oz (1½ Tbsp)	Pour margarine over cabbage and sprinkle with salt. If boiling cabbage, add salt to the cooking water.

Approximate nutritive values per portion

Calories (kcal)	Protein (grams)	Carbohydrate (grams)	Fat (grams)	Cholesterol (mg)	Sodium (mg)	Iron (mg)	Calcium (mg)
41	1.3 (11%)	5.8 (50%)	2 (39%)	0	232	0.6	52

Note   ■ Seasonings for cabbage: basil, caraway seed, celery seed, curry powder, dill, nutmeg.

Variations   ■ **Cabbage au Gratin.**   Reduce cabbage to 7 lb. Alternate layers of cooked coarsely shredded cabbage, white sauce, and grated sharp cheese in a 12 × 20 × 2-inch baking pan. (Use 2½ qt white sauce, 1 lb cheddar cheese.) Combine 6 oz bread crumbs and 3 oz melted margarine and sprinkle on top. Bake at 350°F for about 25 minutes.

■ **Cabbage Polannaise.**   Arrange cabbage wedges, partially cooked, in baking pans. Cover with 3 qt medium white sauce. Sprinkle with buttered bread crumbs. Bake at 350°F for about 25 minutes.

■ **Creamed Cabbage.**   Omit margarine. Pour 2 qt medium white sauce over shredded, cooked, drained cabbage.

■ **Fried Cabbage.**   Melt 6 oz margarine in frying pan. Add 6 lb EP (7 lb AP) shredded cabbage, 12 oz sliced onions, 12 oz diagonally sliced celery. Stir gently while cooking 6–10 minutes. Just before serving, add 4 lb fresh tomatoes, diced in ½-inch cubes.

■ **Scalloped Cabbage.**   Omit margarine or butter. Pour 2 qt medium white sauce over chopped, cooked, drained cabbage. Cover with buttered crumbs. Bake at 400°F for 15–20 minutes. Shredded cheese may be added.

HOT CABBAGE SLAW

Yield: 50 portions or 1¼ gal   *Portion:* 3 oz

Ingredient	Amount	Procedure
Cabbage, fresh	7 lb 8 oz AP (6 lb EP)	Remove outside leaves and wash cabbage. Shred coarsely.
Sugar, granulated Salt Flour, all-purpose Dry mustard	12 oz 2 tsp 3 oz 1 tsp	Mix dry ingredients in a sauce pan or kettle.
Milk, hot Water, hot	2½ cups 3 cups	Add milk and water while stirring. Cook until thickened.
Eggs, beaten	5 (9 oz)	Add eggs gradually while stirring briskly. Cook for 2–3 minutes.
Vinegar, cider, hot	1½ cups	Add vinegar.
Celery seed	2½ tsp	Pour hot sauce over cabbage just before serving. Add celery seed and mix lightly.

Approximate nutritive values per portion

Calories (kcal)	Protein (grams)	Carbohydrate (grams)	Fat (grams)	Cholesterol (mg)	Sodium (mg)	Iron (mg)	Calcium (mg)
60	1.9 (11%)	12.2 (74%)	1.1 (14%)	23.4	109	0.6	45

PARSLEY BUTTERED CARROTS

Yield: 50 portions   *Portion:* 3 oz

Ingredient	Amount	Procedure
Carrots, fresh	14 lb AP (10 lb EP)	Wash, trim, and peel carrots. Cut into desired shapes (slices, strips, cubes, or quarters). Steam or boil until just tender (p. 643).
Margarine, melted Salt Parsley, chopped	4 oz 1 oz (1½ Tbsp) 1 oz	Pour margarine over carrots and sprinkle with salt and parsley. If boiling carrots, add salt to the cooking water.

Approximate nutritive values per portion

Calories (kcal)	Protein (grams)	Carbohydrate (grams)	Fat (grams)	Cholesterol (mg)	Sodium (mg)	Iron (mg)	Calcium (mg)
56	1 (7%)	9.3 (63%)	2 (31%)	0	245	0.5	27

Note
- Seasonings for carrots: allspice, basil, caraway seed, cloves, curry powder, dill, fennel, ginger, mace, marjoram, mint, nutmeg, thyme, parsley.

Variations
- **Candied Carrots.** Cut carrots into 1-inch pieces. Cook until tender but not soft. Melt 8 oz margarine. Add 8 oz sugar and 1½ tsp salt. Add to carrots. Bake at 400°F for 15–20 minutes. Turn frequently. Carrots may be prepared, using a skillet instead of the oven. Melt butter, sugar, and salt in a skillet. Add carrots and cook until slightly browned and glazed.

- **Candied Carrots and Parsnips.** Use half carrots and half parsnips. Cook as for Candied Carrots. Season lightly with ground ginger.

- **Glazed Parsnips.** Peel parsnips. If parsnip cores are hard and woody, remove the core. Cut in strips and proceed as for Candied Carrots.

- **Lyonnaise Carrots.** Arrange cooked carrot strips in baking pan. Add 3 lb chopped onion that has been cooked until tender in 4 oz margarine. Bake at 350°F for 10–15 minutes or until vegetables are lightly browned. Just before serving, sprinkle with chopped parsley.

- **Marinated Carrots.** See p. 506.

- **Mint-Glazed Carrots.** Cut carrots into quarters lengthwise. Cook until almost tender. Drain. Melt 8 oz margarine, 8 oz sugar, 1½ tsp salt, and 1 cup mint jelly. Blend. Add carrots and simmer 5–10 minutes.

- **Savory Carrots.** Cook carrots in beef or chicken stock. When done, season with 4 oz melted margarine, salt and pepper, and ¼ cup lemon juice. Sprinkle with chopped parsley.

- **Sweet-Sour Carrots.** Add to cooked carrots a sauce made of 1½ qt vinegar, 2 lb 4 oz sugar, 2 Tbsp salt, and 12 oz melted margarine. Bake at 350°F for 15–20 minutes, or simmer until carrots and sauce are thoroughly heated.

CELERY AND CARROTS AMANDINE

Yield: 50 portions   *Portion:* 3 oz

Ingredient	Amount	Procedure
Celery	7 lb AP (5 lb EP)	Wash and trim celery. Cut into diagonal slices. Steam or boil (p. 643).
Salt	2 tsp	Sprinkle with salt. If boiling the celery, add salt to cooking water.
Carrots, fresh	7 lb AP (5 lb EP)	Wash and peel carrots. Cut into strips. Steam or boil until tender but crisp. Drain.
Salt	2 tsp	Sprinkle with salt. If boiling the carrots, add salt to the cooking water.
Margarine	8 oz	Heat margarine in frying pan.
Almonds, blanched, slivered	8 oz	Add almonds and brown lightly.
Lemon juice	⅓ cup	Remove almonds from heat. Add lemon juice. Combine vegetables. Pour almond mixture over and stir carefully to mix seasoning with vegetables.

Approximate nutritive values per portion

Calories (kcal)	Protein (grams)	Carbohydrate (grams)	Fat (grams)	Cholesterol (mg)	Sodium (mg)	Iron (mg)	Calcium (mg)
87	1.8 (8%)	7.3 (32%)	6.2 (60%)	0	269	0.6	45

Note ■ Seasonings for celery: fresh basil, parsley, thyme.

Variation ■ **Creole Celery.**   Cook 5 lb diced celery until partially done. Add 1 lb chopped onions and 4 oz chopped green pepper that have been sautéed in 6 oz margarine. Add 2 No. 10 cans tomatoes and 1½ tsp salt. Cook until tender.

SEASONED CAULIFLOWER

Yield: 50 portions   *Portion:* 3 oz

Ingredient	Amount	Procedure
Cauliflower, fresh	16 lb AP (10 lb EP)	Wash cauliflower. Remove outer leaves and woody stem. Break into florets. Steam or boil cauliflower (p. 643).
Margarine, melted Salt	4 oz 1 oz (1½ Tbsp)	Pour margarine over cooked cauliflower and sprinkle with salt. If boiling the cauliflower, add salt to the cooking water.

Approximate nutritive values per portion

Calories (kcal)	Protein (grams)	Carbohydrate (grams)	Fat (grams)	Cholesterol (mg)	Sodium (mg)	Iron (mg)	Calcium (mg)
48	2.5 (19%)	6.2 (46%)	2.1 (35%)	0	221	0.6	38

Note

- Seasonings for cauliflower: caraway seed, celery salt, dill, mace, tarragon, buttered crumbs, cheese.

Variations

- **Cauliflower with Almond Butter.** Season freshly cooked cauliflower with 12 oz slivered almonds that have been browned in 8 oz margarine.
- **Cauliflower with Cheese Sauce.** Pour 3 qt Cheese Sauce (p. 582) over cooked fresh cauliflower.
- **Cauliflower with Peas.** Combine 6 lb freshly cooked cauliflower with 4 lb cooked frozen peas. Season with 4 oz melted margarine.
- **Creamed Cauliflower.** Pour 3 qt white sauce over cooked cauliflower.
- **French Fried Cauliflower.** See p. 668.

SEASONED WHOLE KERNEL CORN

Yield: 50 portions   *Portion:* 3 oz

Ingredient	Amount	Procedure
Whole kernel corn, frozen	10 lb	Steam or boil corn (p. 643). Do not add salt until after cooking to prevent toughening and discoloring of corn kernels.
Margarine, melted Salt	4 oz 1 oz (1½ Tbsp)	Pour margarine over corn. Stir in salt.

Approximate nutritive values per portion

Calories (kcal)	Protein (grams)	Carbohydrate (grams)	Fat (grams)	Cholesterol (mg)	Sodium (mg)	Iron (mg)	Calcium (mg)
347	8.5 (10%)	67.2 (75%)	6.1 (15%)	0	245	2.4	8

Note
- For canned corn, use two No. 10 cans. See p. 645 for heating instructions.

Variations
- **Corn in Cream.**   Add 1¼ qt light cream (half-and-half), 6 oz margarine or butter, 1½ Tbsp salt, and 1 Tbsp white pepper to cooked corn. Bring just to boiling point and serve immediately.
- **Corn O'Brien.**   Add 1 lb chopped bacon, 12 oz chopped green pepper, and 12 oz chopped onion that have been cooked together. Just before serving, add 3 oz chopped pimiento, salt, and pepper.
- **Creamed Whole Kernel Corn.**   Combine 2 cups whipping cream, 2 oz granulated sugar, and 1 oz (1½ Tbsp) salt. Bring to a boil. Add 1 cup whipping cream and 1½ oz cornstarch, which have been mixed with a wire whip until smooth. Stir and cook until thick and bubbly. Cook 2 minutes longer. Stir into 10 lb cooked frozen whole kernel corn.

SCALLOPED CORN

Yield: 50 portions or 2 pans 12 × 20 × 2 inches   *Portion:* 4 oz
Oven: 350°F   *Bake:* 35–40 minutes

Ingredient	Amount	Procedure
Corn, cream style	2 No. 10 cans	Mix corn, milk, and seasonings.
Milk	1 qt	
Salt	1 Tbsp	
Pepper, black	½ tsp	
Cracker crumbs	14 oz	Combine crumbs and margarine.
Margarine, melted	12 oz	Place alternate layers of buttered crumbs and corn mixture in two 12 × 20 × 2-inch baking pans. Bake at 350°F for 35–40 minutes.

Approximate nutritive values per portion

Calories (kcal)	Protein (grams)	Carbohydrate (grams)	Fat (grams)	Cholesterol (mg)	Sodium (mg)	Iron (mg)	Calcium (mg)
183	3.5 (7%)	28.1 (58%)	7.4 (34%)	5	644	0.8	31

Note
- 6 oz chopped green pepper and 6 oz chopped pimiento may be added.

CORN PUDDING

◾

Yield: 50 portions or 2 pans 12 × 20 × 2 inches   *Portion:* 5 oz
Oven: 325°F   *Bake:* 40–45 minutes

Ingredient	Amount	Procedure
Corn, whole kernel, frozen	9 lb	Thaw corn.
Egg yolks, beaten Milk Margarine, melted Salt Pepper, white	24 (1 lb) 3 qt 6 oz 2 Tbsp 1 tsp	Combine corn and all ingredients except egg whites.
Egg whites	24 (1 lb 10 oz)	Beat egg whites until stiff but not dry. Fold into corn mixture. Pour into two 12 × 20 × 2-inch baking pans. Place in pans of hot water. Bake at 325°F for 40–45 minutes.

Approximate nutritive values per portion							
Calories (kcal)	Protein (grams)	Carbohydrate (grams)	Fat (grams)	Cholesterol (mg)	Sodium (mg)	Iron (mg)	Calcium (mg)
398	12.7 (12%)	63.6 (62%)	11.4 (25%)	124	373	2.6	92

BAKED EGGPLANT

Yield: 50 portions   *Portion:* 3 oz
Oven: 375°F   *Bake:* 30 minutes

Ingredient	Amount	Procedure
Eggplant	12 lb AP (10 lb EP)	Peel eggplant and cut into ½-inch slices. Sprinkle with salt and let stand for 30 minutes. Rinse, drain, and pat dry with paper towels.
Eggs, beaten Milk	6 (10 oz) 2 cups	Combine beaten eggs and milk.
Flour, all-purpose Bread crumbs	1 lb 1 lb 8 oz	Dip eggplant slices in flour, then in egg mixture. Roll in crumbs.
Margarine, melted	8 oz	Place on greased baking sheets. Sprinkle with melted margarine. Bake at 375°F for 30 minutes.

Approximate nutritive values per portion

Calories (kcal)	Protein (grams)	Carbohydrate (grams)	Fat (grams)	Cholesterol (mg)	Sodium (mg)	Iron (mg)	Calcium (mg)
154	4.4 (11%)	22.3 (57%)	5.5 (32%)	25	157	1.3	38

Note   ■   Seasonings for eggplant: basil, garlic, marjoram, onion, oregano, cheese, tomato.

Variations   ■   **Eggplant Parmesan.**   Prepare Italian Tomato Sauce (p. 591). Prepare 10 lb AP eggplant (yield 8 lb EP) and cook as directed for Baked Eggplant. (Frozen eggplant cutlets may be substituted for fresh eggplant.) Cheeses needed: 5 lb shredded mozzarella and 1 lb 4 oz grated Parmesan. Layer eggplant, sauce, and cheeses as follows into each of four 12 × 10 × 2-inch baking pans:

1½ cups sauce
1 lb cooked eggplant cutlets
8 oz shredded mozzarella cheese
2 oz Parmesan cheese
2½ cups sauce
1 lb cooked eggplant cutlets
8 oz shredded mozzarella cheese
3 oz Parmesan cheese
2½ cups sauce
4 oz shredded mozzarella cheese

Bake at 350°F for 25–30 minutes or until heated through. To serve, cut 4 × 3.

■   **Sautéed Eggplant.**   Prepare eggplant as in recipe. Sauté in margarine until tender.

CREOLE EGGPLANT

Yield: 50 portions or 2 pans 12 × 20 × 2 inches   *Portion:* 3 oz
Oven: 350°F   *Bake:* 30 minutes

Ingredient	Amount	Procedure
Eggplant	10 lb AP (8 lb EP)	Peel eggplant and cut into 1-inch cubes. Sprinkle with salt and let stand for 30 minutes.
Water, boiling	1½ gal	Rinse and drain.
Salt	2 Tbsp	Steam or boil (p. 643).
Margarine, melted	1 lb	Cook onion, green pepper, and celery in margarine until tender.
Onion, chopped	1 lb 8 oz	
Green pepper, coarsely chopped	12 oz	
Celery, coarsely chopped	1 lb	
Tomatoes, diced, canned	1 No. 10 can	Combine tomatoes and seasonings with eggplant and other ingredients.
Salt	2 Tbsp	Pour into two 12 × 20 × 2-inch baking pans.
Pepper, black	2 tsp	
Sugar, granulated	2 Tbsp	
Bread crumbs	12 oz	Top with buttered crumbs.
Margarine, melted	8 oz	Bake at 350°F for 30 minutes.

Approximate nutritive values per portion

Calories (kcal)	Protein (grams)	Carbohydrate (grams)	Fat (grams)	Cholesterol (mg)	Sodium (mg)	Iron (mg)	Calcium (mg)
163	2.3 (6%)	14 (33%)	11.6 (62%)	0	800	0.9	44

Variation ■ **Eggplant Tomato Bake.** Peel eggplant and slice 1 inch thick. Steam or parboil until fork-tender. Place on baking sheets in a single layer. Sprinkle with salt and pepper. Cook 1 lb 8 oz chopped onion and 3 cloves garlic, minced, in 1½ cups vegetable oil and 12 oz margarine. Add to 5 lb peeled chopped fresh tomatoes, 1 cup chopped parsley, ¼ tsp oregano, ½ tsp thyme, 1 tsp basil, and 1 lb bread crumbs. Pile mixture on individual slices of eggplant. Sprinkle grated Swiss cheese (2 lb) over top. Bake at 350°F until eggplant is hot and cheese is melted.

BAKED ONIONS

Yield: 50 portions   *Portion:* 1 4-oz onion
Oven: 400°F   *Bake:* 20–30 minutes

Ingredient	Amount	Procedure
Onions, 4 oz, Bermuda or Spanish	50 (15 lb AP)	Peel onions and steam (p. 643) until tender. Place in greased baking pans.
Salt Bread crumbs Margarine, melted	1 Tbsp 8 oz 8 oz	Sprinkle salt and buttered crumbs on onions.
Beef or Chicken Stock (pp. 616, 615)	1 qt	Pour stock around onions. Bake at 400°F for 20–30 minutes.

Approximate nutritive values per portion

Calories (kcal)	Protein (grams)	Carbohydrate (grams)	Fat (grams)	Cholesterol (mg)	Sodium (mg)	Iron (mg)	Calcium (mg)
103	2.4 (9%)	15.1 (56%)	4.1 (35%)	0	271	0.5	36

Notes
- Onions may be cut into thick slices.
- Seasonings for onions: basil, caraway seed, marjoram, oregano, rosemary, sage, or thyme.

Variations
- **Creamed Pearl Onions.** Cook 12 lb 8 oz small unpeeled white onions (p. 643), then peel. Add 2 qt Medium-White Sauce (p. 582) to which 4 oz additional margarine has been added. Garnish with paprika.
- **Glazed Onions.** Mix 1 lb 12 oz brown sugar, 2 cups water, 8 oz margarine, and ½ tsp salt. Pour over cooked onions and bake.
- **Onion Casserole.** Cook 10 lb small pearl onions (p. 643). Combine with 10 oz chopped walnuts, 8 oz pimiento strips, and eight 10½-oz cans cream of mushroom or cream of chicken soup. Cover with 6 oz shredded cheddar or Swiss cheese. Bake at 400°F for approximately 30 minutes.

FRENCH FRIED ONION RINGS

Yield: 50 portions   *Portion:* 3 oz
Deep-fat fryer: 350°F   *Fry:* 3–4 minutes

Ingredient	Amount	Procedure
Onions, large round	10 lb AP (8 lb EP)	Peel onions and cut crosswise into ¼-inch slices. Separate into rings.
Eggs, beaten Milk	6 (10 oz) 2 cups	Combine eggs and milk.
Flour, all-purpose Baking powder Salt	12 oz 2 tsp 1½ tsp	Combine dry ingredients. Add to egg-milk mixture to make a batter. Dip onion rings in batter and fry in deep fat for 3–4 minutes. Drain.

Approximate nutritive values per portion

Calories (kcal)	Protein (grams)	Carbohydrate (grams)	Fat (grams)	Cholesterol (mg)	Sodium (mg)	Iron (mg)	Calcium (mg)
144	2.6 (7%)	12 (33%)	9.8 (60%)	25	90	0.6	38

Variations

- **Deep-Fat Fried Bananas.** Cut peeled bananas into 2-inch pieces. Sprinkle with lemon juice and powdered sugar. Let stand 30 minutes. Dip in batter and fry at 370°F for 1–3 minutes.

- **French Fried Cauliflower.** Dip 10 lb cold cooked cauliflower into batter and fry at 370°F for 3–4 minutes.

- **French Fried Eggplant.** Peel and cut 13 lb AP eggplant as for French Fried Potatoes (p. 672). Dip in batter and fry at 370°F for 5–7 minutes. Eggplant may be dipped in egg and crumb mixture (p. 47) and fried. Eggplant discolors quickly, so it should be placed in cold water if not breaded immediately.

- **French Fried Mushrooms.** Clean small, uniform-sized mushrooms by brushing or rinsing. Do not soak. Dip in batter and fry at 370°F for 4–6 minutes.

- **French Fried Zucchini Sticks.** Cut unpeeled zucchini lengthwise into strips about ½ inch thick. Dip in batter and fry at 370°F for 4–6 minutes.

SEASONED PEAS

Yield: 50 portions   *Portion:* 3 oz

Ingredient	Amount	Procedure
Peas, frozen	10 lb	Steam or boil peas (p. 643).
Margarine, melted Salt	4 oz 1 oz (1½ Tbsp)	Pour margarine over cooked peas and sprinkle with salt. If boiling the peas, add salt to the cooking water.

Approximate nutritive values per portion

Calories (kcal)	Protein (grams)	Carbohydrate (grams)	Fat (grams)	Cholesterol (mg)	Sodium (mg)	Iron (mg)	Calcium (mg)
78	4.1 (21%)	11.4 (57%)	2 (23%)	0	283	1.2	21

Notes
- If using canned peas, heat 2 No. 10 cans. See p. 645.
- For fresh peas, use 25 lb AP. Shell and rinse. Steam or boil (p. 643).
- Seasonings for peas: basil, dill, marjoram, mint, oregano, rosemary, sage, savory, mushrooms, water chestnuts, onions.

Variations
- **Creamed Peas with New Potatoes.**   Combine 7 lb freshly cooked new potatoes and 5 lb cooked frozen peas with 3 qt Medium White Sauce (p. 582).
- **Green Peas and Sliced New Turnips.**   Combine 5 lb frozen peas, cooked, with 3 lb new turnips, sliced and cooked. Add 4 oz melted margarine and salt to taste.
- **Green Peas with Pearl Onions.**   Combine 7 lb 8 oz frozen peas, cooked, and 3 lb pearl onions, cooked. Add 4 oz melted margarine or 2 qt Medium White Sauce (p. 582).
- **Green Peas with Mushrooms.**   Add 2 lb fresh mushrooms, sliced and sautéed in 8 oz margarine, to 10 lb cooked frozen peas.
- **Green Peas with Lemon-Mint Butter.**   Cream 1 lb butter or margarine, ¼ cup lemon juice, and 1 tsp grated lemon peel. Add ½ cup finely chopped fresh mint. The lemon-mint butter can be made ahead and stored in the refrigerator. When ready to use, melt and pour over hot peas.

BAKED POTATOES

Yield: 50 portions   *Portion:* 1 potato
Oven: 400°F   *Bake:* 1–1½ hours

Ingredient	Amount	Procedure
Baking potatoes, uniform size	50	Scrub potatoes and remove blemishes.
Shortening	4 oz	Rub or brush lightly with shortening. Place on baking sheets.
		Bake at 400°F for 1–1½ hours or until tender.

Approximate nutritive values per portion

Calories (kcal)	Protein (grams)	Carbohydrate (grams)	Fat (grams)	Cholesterol (mg)	Sodium (mg)	Iron (mg)	Calcium (mg)
165	3 (7%)	33.6 (80%)	2.4 (13%)	0	8	0.5	8

Note ■ Select a long, mealy type potato, such as russet.

Variations ■ **Baked Potato with Toppings.**   Prepare potatoes and bake. (See recipe.) Serve with one of the following toppings and one or more of the accompaniments: *Toppings* include Cheese Sauce (p. 582), 3 oz; Chili con Carne (p. 622), 3 oz; Creamed Chicken (p. 462), Ham (p. 394), or Beef (p. 379), 3 oz; Nacho Sauce (p. 323), 3 oz; sour cream, 1 oz. *Accompaniments* include Guacamole (p. 88), chopped broccoli, shredded cheese, sliced mushrooms, chopped green onions, chopped chives, sliced black olives, chopped ham or chicken, chopped lettuce, chopped tomatoes, crumbled cooked bacon, slivered almonds.

■ **Broccoli Cheese–Topped Potato.**   See p. 582 for Broccoli Cheese Sauce. Serve over baked potato.

■ **Cheese-Topped Potato.**   Whip 1 lb softened margarine. Add 2 lb sour cream and mix thoroughly. Fold in 1 lb finely shredded American cheese and 6 oz finely chopped green onions. Serve over baked potato.

■ **Stuffed Baked Potato.**   Cut hot baked potatoes into halves lengthwise. If potatoes are small, cut a slice from one side. Scoop out contents. Mash, season with 2 Tbsp salt, 1 tsp white pepper, 8 oz melted margarine, and 3–4 cups hot milk. Beat until light and fluffy. Pile lightly into shells, leaving tops rough. Sprinkle with paprika or Parmesan cheese, if desired. Bake at 425°F until potatoes are hot and lightly browned, about 30 minutes.

MASHED POTATOES

Yield: 50 portions   *Portion:* 5 oz

Ingredient	Amount	Procedure
Potatoes	15 lb AP (12 lb EP)	Peel and eye potatoes. Cut into uniform-sized pieces. Steam or boil (p. 643). When done, drain and place in mixer bowl. Mash, using wire whip attachment, on low speed until there are no lumps. Whip on high speed about 2 minutes.
Milk, hot Margarine Salt	2–2½ qt 8 oz 2 oz (3 Tbsp)	Add hot milk, margarine, and salt. Whip on high speed until light and creamy.

Approximate nutritive values per portion

Calories (kcal)	Protein (grams)	Carbohydrate (grams)	Fat (grams)	Cholesterol (mg)	Sodium (mg)	Iron (mg)	Calcium (mg)
158	3.5 (9%)	25.3 (63%)	5.1 (28%)	5	451	0.4	56

Notes

- A low-moisture white potato must be used to produce a fluffy product.
- Potato water may be substituted for part of the milk.
- 8 oz nonfat dry milk and 2–2½ qt water may be substituted for the liquid milk. Sprinkle dry milk over potatoes before mashing.
- Dehydrated potatoes (2–2½ lb) may be substituted for the raw potatoes. Follow processor's instructions for preparation.
- Seasonings for mashed potatoes: chives, garlic, ground horseradish, nutmeg.

Variations

- **Duchess Potatoes.**   Add 18 eggs (2 lb), beaten, to mashed potatoes. Add additional milk if necessary. Pile lightly into baking pans. Bake at 350°F for 20–30 minutes, or until set.
- **Mashed Potato Casserole.**   Add ½ cup chopped chives, ½ cup crisp, cooked, crumbled bacon, 12 oz cream cheese, 1 tsp white pepper and ¼ tsp garlic powder. Mix until blended. Place in baking pans. Sprinkle lightly with grated Parmesan cheese and paprika. Brush lightly with melted margarine. Bake at 375°F for 30 minutes or until light brown.
- **Potato Croquettes.**   Add 18 egg yolks, well beaten. Shape into croquettes and dip in egg-milk mixture and crumbs (p. 47). Chill. Fry in deep fat at 360°F for 5–8 minutes.
- **Potato Rosettes.**   Force Duchess Potatoes through a pastry tube, forming rosettes. Bake at 350°F until lightly browned. Use as a garnish for planked steak.
- **Whipped Rutabagas and Potatoes.**   Peel 10 lb (AP) rutabagas and 5 lb potatoes. Cut into uniform size pieces and steam or boil (p. 643). Mash and season as for potatoes. 1 tsp nutmeg may be added.

FRENCH FRIED POTATOES

Yield: 50 portions   *Portion:* 3 oz
Deep-fat fryer: 365°F   *Fry:* 6–8 minutes

Ingredient	Amount	Procedure
Potatoes, white	18 lb AP (15 lb EP)	Peel and cut potatoes into uniform strips ¼–⅜ inch thick.
		Cover with cold water to keep potatoes from darkening.
		Just before frying, drain potatoes and dry with paper towels.
		Fill fryer basket about one-third full of potatoes.
		Fry according to Method 1 or 2.

Method 1

Half fill fryer with fat. Preheat to 365°F. Fry potatoes for 6–8 minutes. Drain. Sprinkle with salt. Serve immediately.

Method 2

Blanching: Heat fat to 360°F. Place drained potato strips in hot fat, using an 8 to 1 ratio of fat to potatoes, by weight, as a guide for filling fryer basket. Fry 3–5 minutes depending on thickness of potato. (The potatoes should not brown.) Drain. Turn out on sheet pans. Refrigerate for later browning.
Browning: Reheat fat to 375°F. Place about twice as many potato strips in the kettle as for first-stage frying. Fry 2–3 minutes or until golden brown. Drain. Sprinkle with salt if desired. Serve immediately.

Approximate nutritive values per portion

Calories (kcal)	Protein (grams)	Carbohydrate (grams)	Fat (grams)	Cholesterol (mg)	Sodium (mg)	Iron (mg)	Calcium (mg)
269	3.4 (5%)	33.7 (49%)	14 (46%)	0	184	0.6	16

Notes
- Select a long, mealy potato, such as a russet.
- To cook frozen French Fried Potatoes, use 12 lb for 50 3-oz portions. Fry at 375°F for 3–5 minutes or until golden brown.

Variations
- **Deep-Fat Browned Potatoes.**   Partially cook peeled whole or half potatoes. Fry in deep fat at 365°F for 5–7 minutes. Transfer to serving pan. Sprinkle with salt.
- **Lattice Potatoes.**   Cut potatoes with lattice slicer. Fry at 365°F for 3–10 minutes. Transfer to serving pan. Sprinkle with salt.
- **Potato Chips.**   Cut potatoes into very thin slices. Fry at 365°F for 3–6 minutes. Transfer to serving pan. Sprinkle with salt.
- **Shoestring Potatoes.**   Cut potatoes into ⅛-inch strips. Fry at 365°F for 3–6 minutes. Transfer to serving pan. Sprinkle with salt.

PARSLEY BUTTERED NEW POTATOES

Yield: 50 portions   *Portion:* 3 oz

Ingredient	Amount	Procedure
New potatoes	15 lb AP (10 lb EP)	Wash and peel potatoes, removing eyes. (See Note.) Cut potatoes into 1½-inch cubes, or leave whole. If
Salt	1 oz (1½ Tbsp)	whole potatoes, cut as necessary to be of uniform size. Sprinkle with salt. If boiling the potatoes, add salt to the cooking water. Steam or boil (p. 643) until tender.
Margarine, melted	8 oz	Distribute margarine uniformly over cooked potatoes.
Fresh parsley, chopped	1 oz	Sprinkle with parsley.

Approximate nutritive values per portion

Calories (kcal)	Protein (grams)	Carbohydrate (grams)	Fat (grams)	Cholesterol (mg)	Sodium (mg)	Iron (mg)	Calcium (mg)
110	1.6 (6%)	18 (64%)	3.7 (30%)	0	239	0.3	11

Note
- New potatoes may be peeled after cooking. If skins are thin they may be served unpeeled.

Variations
- **Creamed New Potatoes.**   Add 3 qt Medium White Sauce (p. 582) to cooked potatoes.
- **Creamed New Potatoes and Peas.**   See p. 669.
- **Lemon-Seasoned New Potatoes.**   Peel and cook uniform, small new potatoes. Pour over them a mixture of ¼ cup lemon juice 8 oz melted margarine, then roll in minced parsley.
- **New Potatoes in Mustard.**   Add ¾ cup Dijon mustard and 2 Tbsp dried chervil to the melted margarine.
- **New Potatoes Parmesan.**   Scrub small uniform-sized new potatoes. Remove 1 inch of peeling from around the center of each potato. Steam or boil (p. 643) until just done. Roll potatoes in melted margarine. Place in baking pans. Sprinkle with Parmesan cheese. Bake at 350°F for 20–25 minutes. Canned small whole potatoes may be substituted for fresh potatoes.
- **Paprika-Seasoned New Potatoes.**   Delete parsley. Sprinkle potatoes with 1 Tbsp paprika. Stir lightly to mix seasoning.

AU GRATIN POTATOES

Yield: 50 portions or 2 pans 12 × 10 × 2 inches   *Portion:* 5 oz
Oven: 350°F   *Bake:* 25–30 minutes

Ingredient	Amount	Procedure
Potatoes	10 lb AP (8 lb EP)	Peel and dice potatoes (or dice before cooking). Steam or boil (p. 643) until just tender.
Salt	1 Tbsp	Sprinkle with salt. If boiling the potatoes, add salt to the cooking water.
Margarine	12 oz	Melt margarine. Add flour and salt.
Flour, all-purpose	6 oz	Stir until smooth. Cook 5–10 minutes.
Salt	1 Tbsp	
Milk	3 qt	Add milk gradually while stirring. Cook until thickened.
Cheddar cheese, shredded	1 lb 8 oz	Add cheese to sauce and stir until cheese is melted. Pour over potatoes. Scale into two 12 × 20 × 2-inch baking pans, 8 lb per pan.
Bread crumbs	12 oz	Combine crumbs and margarine.
Margarine, melted	8 oz	Sprinkle over top of potatoes, 10 oz per pan. Bake at 350°F for 25–30 minutes.

Approximate nutritive values per portion

Calories (kcal)	Protein (grams)	Carbohydrate (grams)	Fat (grams)	Cholesterol (mg)	Sodium (mg)	Iron (mg)	Calcium (mg)
279	8.1 (11%)	26.2 (37%)	16.1 (51%)	22	530	0.8	185

Note   ■ 1 lb 10 oz sliced dehydrated potatoes, reconstituted in 5 qt boiling water, and 1½ oz salt may be substituted for fresh potatoes.

COTTAGE FRIED POTATOES

Yield: 50 portions   *Portion:* 4 oz

Ingredient	Amount	Procedure
Potatoes	18 lb AP (15 lb EP)	Peel potatoes. Steam or boil until tender (p. 643).
Fat, hot	As needed	Slice cooked potatoes.
Salt	1 oz (1½ Tbsp)	Add to hot fat in frying pan. Add salt and pepper.
Pepper, black	1 tsp	Turn potatoes as needed and fry until browned.

Approximate nutritive values per portion

Calories (kcal)	Protein (grams)	Carbohydrate (grams)	Fat (grams)	Cholesterol (mg)	Sodium (mg)	Iron (mg)	Calcium (mg)
192	2.8 (6%)	29.4 (60%)	7.4 (34%)	0	284	0.5	11

Variations

- **American Fried Potatoes.**   Add raw sliced potatoes to hot fat. Fry until potatoes are brown and tender. Add additional fat as needed.

- **Hashed Brown Potatoes.**   Add finely chopped boiled potatoes to hot fat in frying pan. Add salt and pepper. Stir occasionally and fry until browned.

- **Lyonnaise Potatoes.**   Cook 2 lb chopped onion slowly in fat without browning. Add seasoned cut, boiled potatoes and cook until browned.

- **O'Brien Potatoes.**   Cook cubed potatoes in a small amount of fat with chopped onion and pimiento.

- **Oven-Fried Potatoes.**   Prepare potatoes as for French Fried Potatoes. Place in greased shallow pans in a thin layer and brush with melted fat, turning to cover all sides. Bake at 450°F for 20–30 minutes, or until browned, turning occasionally. Drain on absorbent paper and sprinkle with salt.

POTATO PANCAKES

Yield: 50 portions or 100 cakes   *Portion:* 2 2-oz cakes

Ingredient	Amount	Procedure
Potatoes	15 lb AP (12 lb EP)	Peel potatoes and onions. Grind. Drain.
Onions	1 lb 8 oz	
Eggs, beaten	8 (14 oz)	Combine and add to potatoes and onion.
Flour, all-purpose	8 oz	
Salt	2 oz (3 Tbsp)	
Baking powder	1 tsp	
Milk	¾ cup	
		Drop potato mixture with No. 20 dipper on hot greased griddle. Fry, turning once, until golden brown on both sides. Serve with applesauce.

Approximate nutritive values per portion

Calories (kcal)	Protein (grams)	Carbohydrate (grams)	Fat (grams)	Cholesterol (mg)	Sodium (mg)	Iron (mg)	Calcium (mg)
128	3.6 (11%)	26.5 (81%)	1.1 (8%)	34	407	0.7	27

SCALLOPED POTATOES

Yield: 50 portions or 2 pans 12 × 20 × 2 inches   *Portion:* 6 oz
Oven: 350°F   *Bake:* 1½–2 hours

Ingredient	Amount	Procedure
Potatoes	15 lb AP (12 lb EP)	Peel and eye potatoes. Slice and place in 2 greased 12 × 20 × 2-inch baking pans, 6 lb per pan.
Salt	2 oz (3 Tbsp)	Sprinkle with salt.
Margarine	8 oz	Melt margarine. Add flour and salt.
Flour, all-purpose	4 oz	Stir until smooth. Cook 5 minutes.
Salt	1 oz (1½ Tbsp)	
Milk	1 gal	Add milk gradually, stirring with wire whip. Cook until thickened. Pour over potatoes.
Bread crumbs	6 oz	Combine crumbs and margarine.
Margarine, melted	2 oz	Sprinkle over potatoes. Bake at 350°F for 1½–2 hours.

Approximate nutritive values per portion

Calories (kcal)	Protein (grams)	Carbohydrate (grams)	Fat (grams)	Cholesterol (mg)	Sodium (mg)	Iron (mg)	Calcium (mg)
211	5.4 (10%)	31.4 (58%)	7.5 (31%)	11	698	0.7	109

Notes

- Potatoes may be partially cooked and hot White Sauce added to shorten baking time.
- Dehydrated sliced potatoes may be substituted for fresh. Reconstitute according to package directions.

Variations

- **Scalloped Potatoes with Ham.**   Add 5 lb cubed ham to White Sauce. Cut salt to 1 Tbsp.
- **Scalloped Potatoes with Onions.**   Before baking, cover potatoes with onion rings. About 5 minutes before removing from oven, cover potatoes with shredded cheese.

SOUR CREAM POTATOES

Yield: 50 portions or 3 pans 12 × 10 × 2 inches   *Portion:* 5 oz
Oven: 350°F   *Bake:* 35–45 minutes

Ingredient	Amount	Procedure
Frozen hashed brown potatoes	10 lb	Thaw potatoes. Steam for 10–15 minutes. Hold for later step.
Margarine Onions, chopped	4 oz 1 lb	Melt margarine in steam-jacketed or other kettle. Add onions and sauté until transparent.
Sour cream Salt (see Notes) Pepper, black Eggs, beaten slightly Chicken base Water	2 lb 12 oz 1 oz 1 Tbsp 6 (10 oz) 1 Tbsp 2 cups	Add to onions and mix well.
		Add potatoes to onion mixture. Mix lightly. Scale into 3 greased 12 × 10 × 2-inch pans, 5 lb 5 oz per pan.
Cornflake crumbs Margarine, melted	3 oz ⅓ cup	Combine crumbs and margarine in mixer bowl, using flat paddle. Mix until crumbly. Sprinkle 2 oz over each pan of potatoes. Bake at 350°F for 35–45 minutes. To serve, spoon into 50 5-oz portions or cut each pan 4 × 4 for 48 servings.

Approximate nutritive values per portion

Calories (kcal)	Protein (grams)	Carbohydrate (grams)	Fat (grams)	Cholesterol (mg)	Sodium (mg)	Iron (mg)	Calcium (mg)
297	4.7 (6%)	29 (38%)	19.2 (56%)	35	377	1.6	51

Notes
- Undiluted cream of mushroom, cream of celery, or cream of chicken soup may be substituted for sour cream. Delete salt and chicken base.
- If a highly salted chicken base is used, delete or reduce salt.
- 2 oz (1 cup) dehydrated onions, rehydrated in 1½ cups water, may be substituted for fresh onions (p. 55).

POTATOES ROMANOFF

Yield: 60 portions or 2 pans 12 × 20 × 2 inches   *Portion:* 6 oz
Oven: 350°F   *Bake:* 35–45 minutes

Ingredient	Amount	Procedure
Frozen hashed brown potatoes	16 lb	Thaw potatoes. Steam for 15 minutes.
Sour cream Green onions, sliced Salt Pepper, black Cheddar cheese, shredded	4 lb 4 oz 6 oz 1½ oz 1 Tbsp 12 oz	Combine in mixer bowl and blend on low speed.
Paprika	½ tsp	Add cooked potatoes to sour cream mixture. Mix well. Scale into two greased 12 × 20 × 2-inch pans, 10 lb per pan. Sprinkle lightly with paprika. Bake uncovered at 350°F for 35–45 minutes. Cut 6 × 5.

Approximate nutritive values per portion

Calories (kcal)	Protein (grams)	Carbohydrate (grams)	Fat (grams)	Cholesterol (mg)	Sodium (mg)	Iron (mg)	Calcium (mg)
356	6.3 (7%)	35.7 (39%)	22.5 (55%)	20	369	2	101

OVEN-BROWNED OR RISSOLÉ POTATOES

Yield: 50 portions   *Portion:* 1 potato
Oven: 450°F   *Bake:* 1 hour

Ingredient	Amount	Procedure
Potatoes, baking variety	50	Peel potatoes and partially cook by boiling or steaming, about 10 minutes.
Margarine, melted Salt	1 lb 1 oz (1½ Tbsp)	Place potatoes on well-greased baking sheets. Pour melted margarine over potatoes. Sprinkle with salt. Bake at 450°F for 1 hour or until tender. Baste every 15 minutes with margarine from pan. Turn potatoes once during baking to ensure uniform browning.

Approximate nutritive values per portion

Calories (kcal)	Protein (grams)	Carbohydrate (grams)	Fat (grams)	Cholesterol (mg)	Sodium (mg)	Iron (mg)	Calcium (mg)
210	3.1 (6%)	33.7 (63%)	7.5 (31%)	0	285	0.6	12

Variations

- **Franconia Potatoes.**   Cook peeled uniform-sized potatoes approximately 15 minutes. Drain and place in pan in which meat is roasting. Bake approximately 40 minutes or until tender and lightly browned, basting with drippings in pan or turning occasionally to brown all sides. Serve with roast.

- **French Baked Potatoes.**   Select small, uniform potatoes and peel. Roll potatoes in melted margarine or shortening, then in cracker crumbs or crushed cornflakes. Place in shallow pans and bake.

- **Herbed Potato Bake.**   Peel baking potatoes and cut into ½-inch slices. Place in greased baking pans. Combine 1½ cups melted margarine, 3½ oz dehydrated onion soup mix, and 2 Tbsp rosemary. Sprinkle over potatoes and toss lightly. Bake at 325°F for 1½ hours or until potatoes are tender.

GLAZED OR CANDIED SWEET POTATOES

Yield: 50 portions   *Portion:* 4 oz
Oven: 400°F   *Bake:* 20–30 minutes

Ingredient	Amount	Procedure
Sweet potatoes or yams	16 lb AP (13 lb EP)	Scrub potatoes. Steam or boil in skins until tender (p. 643). When potatoes are cool enough to handle, peel and cut into halves lengthwise. Arrange in shallow pans.
Sugar, brown Water Margarine Salt	1 lb 12 oz 2 cups 8 oz ½ tsp	Mix sugar, water, margarine, and salt. Heat to boiling point. Pour over potatoes. Bake at 400°F for 20–30 minutes.

Approximate nutritive values per portion

Calories (kcal)	Protein (grams)	Carbohydrate (grams)	Fat (grams)	Cholesterol (mg)	Sodium (mg)	Iron (mg)	Calcium (mg)
214	2.1 (4%)	44 (81%)	3.8 (16%)	0	82	1	48

Notes
- Three No. 10 cans of sweet potatoes may be substituted for fresh sweet potatoes.
- Seasonings for sweet potatoes: allspice, cardamom, cinnamon, cloves, or nutmeg.

Variations
- **Baked Sweet Potatoes.**   Select small even-sized sweet potatoes or yams. Scrub. Bake at 425°F for 40–45 minutes, or until tender.
- **Candied Sweet Potatoes with Almonds.**   Proceed as for Glazed Sweet Potatoes. Increase margarine to 12 oz and reduce brown sugar to 1 lb 8 oz. Add 1 cup dark corn syrup and 2 tsp mace. When partially glazed, sprinkle top with chopped almonds and continue cooking until almonds are toasted.
- **Glazed Sweet Potatoes with Orange Slices.**   Add ¼ cup grated orange peel to syrup. Cut 5 oranges into thin slices; add to sweet potatoes when syrup is added.
- **Mashed Sweet Potatoes.**   Cook and mash sweet potatoes or yams (p. 643), following procedure on p. 671. Add 1½ oz salt, ⅓ tsp nutmeg, 1 oz margarine, melted, and 1¼ qt hot milk.
- **Sweet Potatoes and Apples.**   Reduce sweet potatoes to 9 lb, cooked, peeled, and sliced. Peel and slice 5 lb tart apples. Place alternate layers of sweet potatoes and apples in baking pans. Pour hot syrup (see recipe for Glazed Sweet Potatoes) over potatoes and apples. Bake at 350°F for 45 minutes.

SWEET POTATO SOUFFLÉ

Yield: 50 portions or 1 pan 12 × 20 × 2 inches   *Portion:* 4 oz
Oven: 375°F   *Bake:* 30 minutes

Ingredient	Amount	Procedure
Frozen sweet pota-toes	8 lb	Steam potatoes for 25 minutes. Place in mixer bowl and whip on low, medium, and high speeds for 1 minute each, or until smooth.
Margarine, melted Sugar, brown Cinnamon, ground Mace, ground Ginger, ground Cloves, ground Milk Eggs	12 oz 1 lb 8 oz 1 Tbsp 1 Tbsp 1 tsp ¼ tsp 1 cup 9 (1 lb)	Add to sweet potatoes. Mix until thoroughly blended. Begin on low speed and progress to high speed for a total of approximately 5 minutes or until mixture is fluffy.
Miniature marshmal-lows	6 oz	Fold marshmallows into potato mixture. Scale into greased 12 × 20 × 2-inch pan. Bake at 350°F for 30 minutes or until hot.
Miniature marshmal-lows	4 oz	Sprinkle marshmallows over sweet potatoes. Return to oven long enough for marshmallows to puff and brown slightly.

Approximate nutritive values per portion							
Calories (kcal)	Protein (grams)	Carbohydrate (grams)	Fat (grams)	Cholesterol (mg)	Sodium (mg)	Iron (mg)	Calcium (mg)
211	2.8 (5%)	35.9 (67%)	6.8 (28%)	39	94	1.2	42

SEASONED FRESH SPINACH AND OTHER GREENS

Yield: 50 portions　　*Portion:* 3 oz

Ingredient	Amount	Procedure
Spinach or other greens, fresh	12 lb AP (10 lb EP)	Sort and trim greens. Remove veins, coarse stems, and roots. Wash leaves thoroughly, lifting out of water after each washing. Steam or boil (p. 643).
Margarine, melted Salt	4 oz 1 oz (1½ Tbsp)	Pour margarine over greens and sprinkle with salt. If boiling the greens, add salt to the cooking water.

Approximate nutritive values per portion

Calories (kcal)	Protein (grams)	Carbohydrate (grams)	Fat (grams)	Cholesterol (mg)	Sodium (mg)	Iron (mg)	Calcium (mg)
36	2.6 (25%)	3.2 (30%)	2.2 (45%)	0	285	2.5	93

Notes

- Beet greens, chard, collards, kale, mustard greens, or turnip greens may be used. For kale, strip leaves from coarse stems.
- For frozen spinach, use 10 lb. See p. 643 for cooking.
- Greens may be garnished with 12 hard-cooked eggs, chopped, and 1 lb 8 oz crisp-cooked bacon, crumbled.
- Seasonings for spinach: basil, mace, marjoram, nutmeg, oregano, mushrooms, bacon, cheese, hard-cooked eggs, vinegar.

Variations

- **Creamed Spinach.**　Cook spinach. Drain. Chop coarsely. Add 2 qt White Sauce (p. 582). Season with salt, pepper, and nutmeg.
- **Wilted Spinach or Lettuce.**　To 10 lb chopped raw spinach or lettuce, or a combination of the two, add 2 qt Hot Bacon Sauce (p. 603) just before serving.

SPINACH SOUFFLÉ

Yield: 48 portions or 2 pans 12 × 20 × 2 inches   *Portion:* 4 oz
Oven: 350°F   *Bake:* 40 minutes

Ingredient	Amount	Procedure
Margarine	1 lb 4 oz	Melt margarine. Add flour and salt.
Flour, all-purpose	8 oz	Stir until smooth and cook 5 minutes.
Salt	2½ Tbsp	
Milk	1¼ qt	Add milk and sour cream. Blend over low heat until smooth, stirring constantly.
Sour cream	1¼ qt	Remove from heat.
Spinach, chopped, frozen	6 lb	Thaw spinach. Drain.
Onion, finely chopped	8 oz	Add spinach, onion, nutmeg, and egg yolks to sauce. Mix.
Nutmeg	1½ Tbsp	
Egg yolks, beaten	18 (12 oz)	
Egg whites	18 (1 lb 5 oz)	Beat egg whites until stiff. Fold into spinach mixture.
		Lightly grease two 12 × 20 × 2-inch counter pans on the bottom only. Scale 7 lb 8 oz of the mixture into each pan.
		Set in pans of hot water.
		Bake at 350°F for 40 minutes or until soufflé is set.
		Cut 4 × 6.

Approximate nutritive values per portion

Calories (kcal)	Protein (grams)	Carbohydrate (grams)	Fat (grams)	Cholesterol (mg)	Sodium (mg)	Iron (mg)	Calcium (mg)
219	6.5 (12%)	9.7 (17%)	17.8 (71%)	105	542	1.4	159

Note   ■   1 oz (½ cup) dehydrated onions, rehydrated in 1½ cups water, may be substituted for fresh onions (p. 55).

BAKED ACORN SQUASH

Yield: 50 portions   *Portion:* ½ squash
Oven: 350°F   *Bake:* 30–40 minutes

Ingredient	Amount	Procedure
Acorn squash	25	Wash squash and cut in half lengthwise. Scrape out seeds. Place cut side down in shallow pans with a small amount of water. Bake at 350°F for 20–25 minutes, or until just tender. (Squash may be steamed for 20 minutes).
Margarine, melted Salt Sugar, brown	8 oz 1 oz (1½ Tbsp) 12 oz	Place squash hollow side up. Sprinkle cavities with margarine, salt, and brown sugar. Bake until sugar is melted, about 10–15 minutes.

Approximate nutritive values per portion

Calories (kcal)	Protein (grams)	Carbohydrate (grams)	Fat (grams)	Cholesterol (mg)	Sodium (mg)	Iron (mg)	Calcium (mg)
134	1.8 (5%)	26.6 (72%)	3.8 (23%)	0	244	1.4	86

Variations

- **Acorn Squash with Sausage.** Place 4-oz sausage patty or 2 link sausages, partially cooked, in each cooked squash half. Continue baking until meat is done.

- **Spaghetti Squash.** Prepare and cook as for acorn squash. When tender, scrape vegetable with a fork, carefully separating vegetable into pasta-like strands. Add melted margarine or butter and desired seasonings.

- **Stuffed Acorn Squash.** Fill cooked squash half with No. 12 dipper of the following mixture: 5 qt cooked rice, 4 lb chopped cooked meat, and 4 oz minced onion, sautéed in margarine and moistened with meat stock.

MASHED WINTER SQUASH

Yield: 50 portions   *Portion:* 3 oz

Ingredient	Amount	Procedure
Winter squash	15 lb AP (10 lb EP)	Peel squash and cut into pieces. Steam or boil until tender (p. 643).
Milk, hot Margarine, melted Salt Sugar, brown	1½ qt 8 oz 2 Tbsp 8 oz	Mash squash. Add milk and seasonings. Whip until light. May be garnished with toasted slivered almonds.

Approximate nutritive values per portion

Calories (kcal)	Protein (grams)	Carbohydrate (grams)	Fat (grams)	Cholesterol (mg)	Sodium (mg)	Iron (mg)	Calcium (mg)
102	1.8 (7%)	13.7 (50%)	5.2 (43%)	4	316	0.5	64

Notes

- Acorn, buttercup, butternut, hubbard, turbin or another winter squash variety may be used.

- Seasonings for squash: allspice, basil, cinnamon, cloves, fennel, ginger, marjoram, nutmeg, oregano, rosemary, savory.

Variations

- **Baked Whipped Squash.**   Mix cooked squash until smooth. Add 12 oz margarine, melted, 1 lb brown sugar, 1 Tbsp ground cinnamon, 1 tsp ground allspice, ½ tsp ground cloves, and 1 oz (1½ Tbsp) salt. Mix thoroughly. Scale into 12 × 20 × 2-inch pan. Bake in 350°F oven for 1 hour or until heated through. Cover with 12 oz miniature marshmallows and heat until marshmallows have browned slightly.

- **Butternut Squash–Apple Casserole.**   Cook 8 lb peeled, cored, and sliced apples, 12 oz margarine or butter, and 12 oz sugar until barely tender. Arrange in baking pans. Cover with mashed butternut squash (use 10 lb). Top with mixture of crushed cornflakes, chopped pecans, melted margarine, and brown sugar. Bake at 350°F for 30–40 minutes.

SEASONED ZUCCHINI OR SUMMER SQUASH ■

Yield: 50 portions   *Portion:* 3 oz

Ingredient	Amount	Procedure
Zucchini or other summer squash	11–12 lb AP (10 lb EP)	Wash squash and remove ends. Do not pare. Cut into slices or spears. Steam or simmer until tender (p. 643).
Margarine, melted	4 oz	Pour margarine over squash and sprinkle with salt and pepper.
Salt	1 Tbsp	
Pepper, white	1 tsp	

Approximate nutritive values per portion							
Calories (kcal)	Protein (grams)	Carbohydrate (grams)	Fat (grams)	Cholesterol (mg)	Sodium (mg)	Iron (mg)	Calcium (mg)
30	1.1 (13%)	2.7 (33%)	2 (54%)	0	151	0.4	16

Notes
- 1 tsp garlic or onion salt may be substituted for part of salt.
- ½ cup Parmesan cheese may be sprinkled over zucchini before serving.

Variations
- **French Fried Zucchini.**   See p. 668.
- **Zucchini Casserole.**   Steam or parboil 8 lb sliced zucchini until tender-crisp. Drain. Combine one 46-oz can cream of chicken soup, 3 cups sour cream, 1 cup chopped green onions, and 1 oz shredded carrots. Combine with zucchini. Mix 1 lb 12 oz herb-seasoned bread crumbs and 8 oz melted margarine and spread half in a 12 × 20 × 2-inch counter pan. Pour zucchini mixture over crumbs. Top with remaining crumbs. Bake at 350°F for 30–40 minutes or until heated through. Other vegetables such as broccoli, asparagus, cauliflower, or French cut green beans may be used in this casserole.
- **Zucchini and Summer Squash.**   Wash and slice 5 lb zucchini and 5 lb yellow summer squash. Cook until just tender. Season with 8 oz melted margarine, salt and pepper to taste. Add 2 lb cherry tomatoes just before serving.
- **Zucchini and Tomato Casserole.**   In 12 × 20 × 2-inch counter pan, layer 7 lb zucchini, 3 lb fresh tomatoes, peeled and chopped, and 1 lb chopped onion. Salt and pepper lightly. Sprinkle 1 lb grated cheddar cheese and 1 lb bacon, cooked and crumbled, over top. Cover with buttered bread crumbs. Bake covered at 400°F for about 1 hour, uncovered for the last 20 minutes.

BAKED TOMATOES

Yield: 50 portions   *Portion:* ½ tomato
Oven: 400°F   *Bake:* 10–12 minutes

Ingredient	Amount	Procedure
Tomatoes, fresh (5 oz each)	25	Wash tomatoes. Cut in halves.
Salt	1 tsp	Sprinkle each tomato with salt and pepper or seasoned salt.
Pepper, black	1 tsp	
Margarine, melted	6 oz	Combine margarine, bread crumbs, and onion.
Bread crumbs	2 oz	Place 2 tsp mixture on each tomato half.
Onion, finely chopped	6 oz	Bake at 400°F for 10–12 minutes.

Approximate nutritive values per portion							
Calories (kcal)	Protein (grams)	Carbohydrate (grams)	Fat (grams)	Cholesterol (mg)	Sodium (mg)	Iron (mg)	Calcium (mg)
45	0.8 (7%)	4.5 (37%)	3 (56%)	0	90	0.4	7

Note
- Seasonings for tomatoes: basil, bay leaf, chili powder, garlic, oregano, rosemary, thyme.

Variations
- **Mushroom-Stuffed Tomatoes.** Add 2 lb sautéed mushrooms, sliced or chopped, to crumb mixture.
- **Broiled Tomato Slices.** Cut tomatoes in ½-inch slices. Salt, dot with margarine, and broil.
- **Spinach-Stuffed Tomatoes.** Wash medium-size fresh tomatoes. Remove core and part of the tomato pulp. Fill center with 2 oz Spinach Soufflé (p. 683). Sprinkle with buttered crumbs and Parmesan cheese. Bake at 350°F for about 1 hour.

STIR-FRIED VEGETABLES

Yield: 50 portions   *Portion:* 3 oz

Ingredient	Amount	Procedure
Cornstarch	2 oz	Combine cornstarch and water. Set aside for last step.
Water	1 cup	
Assorted vegetables (see Notes for suggestions)	5 lb 8 oz EP	Cut vegetables into uniform-sized thin slices, strips, or diagonal slices to ensure quick cooking. Pat dry before frying.
Cooking oil	1 cup	Combine oil, garlic, and ginger root in frying pan.
Garlic, minced	2 cloves	Heat to 350°F and cook slightly.
Ginger root, fresh, sliced	½ tsp	Remove ginger root and discard.
Water chestnuts, sliced, drained	8 oz	Add water chestnuts and prepared vegetables to heated oil. Stir with long spatulas in a folding motion. Cook until vegetables are tender-crisp.
Chicken Stock (p. 615)	3 cups	Combine stock and soy sauce. Mix quickly into vegetables. Reduce heat.
Soy sauce	½ cup	Pour cornstarch mixture over vegetables. Cook and stir just until sauce thickens and vegetables are glazed.

Approximate nutritive values per portion

Calories (kcal)	Protein (grams)	Carbohydrate (grams)	Fat (grams)	Cholesterol (mg)	Sodium (mg)	Iron (mg)	Calcium (mg)
64	1.6 (10%)	4.8 (29%)	4.6 (62%)	0	239	0.7	22

Notes

- Select vegetables for contrast in color, shape, texture, and flavor. At least three vegetables should be selected. Cut vegetables into small enough pieces to cook quickly. Frozen vegetables should be thawed before stir-frying.

- Suggested vegetables: asparagus cut diagonally, broccoli or cauliflower florets, green beans, carrot strips or diagonal slices, celery slices, sliced fresh mushrooms, snow peas, onion rings, pepper strips (red, green, or yellow), zucchini or summer squash slices or sticks.

- Suggested combinations (total of 5 lb 8 oz): 1 lb 8 oz sliced carrots, 1 lb 8 oz broccoli florets, 1 lb 8 oz celery sticks, 8 oz mushroom slices, and 8 oz sliced onion; 1 lb 8 oz asparagus cut diagonally, 1 lb 8 oz zucchini slices, 1 lb 8 oz cauliflower florets, 8 oz sliced onions, and 8 oz fresh mushrooms; 1 lb 8 oz sliced celery, 1 lb 8 oz pea pods, 1 lb 8 oz julienne carrots, 8 oz green pepper strips, and 8 oz sliced fresh mushrooms.

RATATOUILLE

Yield: 50 portions   *Portion:* 4 oz
Oven: 300°F   *Heat:* 5 minutes

Ingredient	Amount	Procedure
Vegetable oil	⅓ cup	Heat oil in tilting frypan.
Onion, cut in wedges	8 oz	Add onion and garlic. Cook until tender crisp.
Garlic, minced	1 clove	
Eggplant, peeled, 1-inch cubes	2 lb 8 oz	Add eggplant. Sauté 2 minutes.
Zucchini	2 lb	Add squash and peppers. Sauté 5 minutes or until vegetables are still crisp and brightly colored.
Green peppers, fresh, 1½-inch strips	2 lb	
Tomatoes, canned, diced	6 lb	Add to vegetable mixture. Simmer for 5 minutes. Scale into two 12 × 10 × 2-inch pans, 6 lb per pan.
Salt	2½ tsp	
Pepper, black	1½ tsp	
Basil, dried, crumbled	1 tsp	
Oregano, dried, crumbled	1 tsp	
Monterey Jack cheese, shredded	1 lb	Sprinkle 8 oz cheese over each pan. Heat in 300°F oven for 5 minutes to melt the cheese. Do not cover. Serve with a spoon.

Approximate nutritive values per portion

Calories (kcal)	Protein (grams)	Carbohydrate (grams)	Fat (grams)	Cholesterol (mg)	Sodium (mg)	Iron (mg)	Calcium (mg)
72	3.2 (17%)	5.8 (31%)	4.4 (52%)	8	245	0.6	90

Notes
- Sliced Japanese eggplant may be substituted for all or part of the cubed eggplant.
- Yellow summer squash may be substituted for some or all of the eggplant.

VEGETABLE TIMBALE

Yield: 40 portions or 1 pan 12 × 20 × 2 inches   *Portion:* 3 oz
Oven: 300°F   *Bake:* 2 hours

Ingredient	Amount	Procedure
Eggs	16 (1 lb 9 oz)	Beat eggs.
Salt Margarine, melted Milk	2 Tbsp 5 oz 1½ qt	Add salt, margarine, and milk.
Spinach, chopped, frozen	3 lb	Cook spinach (p. 643). Drain well. Add to egg mixture. Mix until well blended.
		Pour into greased 12 × 20 × 2-inch pan. Set into another pan with 3 cups hot water in it. Bake at 300°F for 2 hours. Test with a silver knife as for custard. Cut 5 × 8. Serve with 1 oz Cheese Sauce (p. 582).

Approximate nutritive values per portion							
Calories (kcal)	Protein (grams)	Carbohydrate (grams)	Fat (grams)	Cholesterol (mg)	Sodium (mg)	Iron (mg)	Calcium (mg)
84	4.5 (21%)	3.8 (17%)	5.9 (62%)	80	423	0.8	105

Note ▪ Spinach, broccoli, brussels sprouts, asparagus, or any combination of these vegetables may be used.

Variation ▪ **Chicken Timbale.**   Use 32 eggs (3 lb 8 oz), 1 oz salt, 1 lb margarine, melted, 1 tsp white pepper, 12 oz bread crumbs, and 6 lb chopped cooked chicken. Mix melted margarine, bread crumbs, and milk. Cook for 5 minutes. Add beaten eggs, seasonings, and chicken. Bake as for Vegetable Timbale. Cut 6 × 8. Serve with Béchamel Sauce (p. 584).

Part Three

Planning the Menu and Special Events ■

16

Menu Planning

Food eaten outside the home has become an integral part of the American life-style. Patrons expect to have food choices that are creative, exciting, and nutritious. Menu writers are challenged to plan innovative menus that support both the goals of the organization and that cater to customer preferences.

A well-planned menu is the cornerstone of a successful foodservice and the focal point from which many activities start. An understanding of menu types, factors affecting menu planning, and planning procedures is important before menu writing can begin.

TYPES OF MENUS

The menu is an outline of food items to be included in each meal or, in a broader sense, a total list of food items offered by a foodservice. Types of menus used in foodservices may be classified as static or set, cycle, or single-use. Menus may be further categorized according to the degree of choice as selective, or nonselective, and by the method of pricing.

Static or *set menus* include the same menu items every day, but with a variety of choices, the exact number depending on the type of foodservice. Most commercial foodservices use this type of menu, and an increasing number of hospitals have adopted the static or restaurant type menu.

Single-use menus are planned for a specific day or event and are not usually repeated in exactly the same form. This type of menu is often used for holidays, special functions, or catering events.

A *cycle menu* is a carefully planned series of menus that offer different items from day to day for one week, two weeks, or other time period, after which the menus are repeated. The length of the cycle depends on the type of foodservice. A short cycle is

TABLE 16.1 Types of menu patterns

	Nonselective menu pattern	
Breakfast	*Lunch*	*Dinner*
Fruit	Soup (optional)	Soup (optional)
Cereal	Entree	Entree
Protein item	Salad and/or vegetable	Two vegetables (one may be potato or starchy food)
Bread, butter or margarine	Bread, butter or margarine	Salad
Beverage	Fruit or other light dessert	Bread, butter or margarine
	Beverage	Dessert
		Beverage

	Selective menu pattern[a]
Breakfast	*Lunch and dinner*
Fruits: 2 or more juices, fresh fruit in season	Soups: 1 cream, 1 broth
Cereals: cooked, choice of cold cereals	Entrees: at least 2 meats, 1 meatless, 1 meat extender, poultry or fish, and a cold plate.
Entrees: eggs, bacon, ham, or sausage, potatoes, breakfast casserole	Sandwiches: 1 hot, 1 or more cold
Breads: toast, white and whole grain; one or more hot breads	Rice or pasta: in addition to or as alternative to potatoes
Beverages: coffee, decaffeinated coffee, tea, milk (whole and lowfat)	Vegetables: 3 or 4, including potatoes in some form
	Salads: 4 to 10, including entree, tossed green, vegetable, gelatin, fruit, cottage cheese, relishes
	Breads: 2 to 3, including white and whole grain, 1 hot bread
	Desserts: 4 to 8, including 2-crust pie, soft pie, cake and/or cookies, pudding, yogurt, ice cream or sherbet, fruit
	Beverages: coffee, decaffeinated coffee, tea, milk (whole and lowfat), fruit juice or fruit flavored drinks.

	Menu pattern for a normal hospital diet	
Breakfast	*Lunch*	*Dinner*
Fruit or juice	Cream soup *or*	Soup (optional)
Cereal with milk	Main dish (made with meat, fish, poultry, egg, or cheese)	Meat, poultry, or fish
Egg		Potato or alternate starchy vegetable
Bread or toast	Vegetable or salad	Green or yellow vegetable
Butter or margarine	Bread with butter or margarine	Salad: fruit or vegetable
Beverage	Fruit or other simple dessert	Bread with butter or margarine
	Beverage	Dessert
		Beverage

[a]Menu variety may be increased or decreased to fit the demands of the foodservice.

appropriate for foodservices having a frequent clientele turnover, such as hospitals. If a short cycle is used for patient meals, a longer cycle is necessary for the employees' and visitors' foodservice. In extended care facilities the cycle usually is four to six weeks. Using a cycle with numbers of days not divisible by seven ensures that the same menu is not served on the same day of the week. Restaurants may prefer to use monthly or seasonal cycles or may use the same menu throughout the year. Many foodservices recognize seasonal changes by having spring, summer, autumn, and winter cycles.

Cycle menus save time for the planner and are effective tools for food and labor cost control, forecasting, and purchasing. Repetition of the same or nearly the same menu helps standardize preparation procedures and gives the employees an opportunity to become more efficient through repeated use of familiar recipes. Menus can become monotonous and repetitious if not carefully planned, however. Regardless of the cycle length, menus should be constantly reviewed and updated. Each day's menus should be analyzed shortly after service, and any production problems or adverse reactions by the clientele should be noted and corrected before the next cycle. The menu planner must allow flexibility for changes resulting from holidays, special occasions, leftover food, and inability to obtain specific food items for production.

Selective menus offer two or more items within each category. Foods from which the individual patron may choose a well-balanced meal should be included. Most commercial and noncommercial foodservices use this type of menu extensively. Table 16.1 gives a suggested pattern for a selective menu, using the same format for lunch and dinner.

Nonselective menus have a single item in each menu category. To assure nutritional adequacy, foods from each of the basic food groups should be included. Table 16.1 gives a general pattern for a nonselective menu. A nonselective menu may be modified to include a limited selection; for example, two entrees may be offered or a choice of two vegetables may be given. A soup and salad may be offered as an alternative to an entree and vegetable for those who wish a lighter meal.

Menus may also be classified by method of pricing. *À la carte menus* price food items separately; the customer chooses menu items individually. *Table d'hôte menus* include the complete meal at a fixed price, and *du jour menus* are planned, written, and priced daily.

FACTORS AFFECTING MENU PLANNING

The production and service of food begins with the menu, which determines the foods to be purchased, the personnel needed and their work schedules, and the equipment necessary for production and service of the food. The menu is closely tied to financial management and marketing and, in a new foodservice, influences the design of the kitchen and selection of equipment. The menu, however, must be one that meets clientele expectations and that can be produced within facility constraints and demands. A number of factors must be considered when planning a menu.

Clientele

The menu planner must consider the makeup of the group to be served—age, gender, nutritional needs, food habits, and individual preferences. This is especially important if the foodservice offers a limited choice of food, as in some extended care facilities, child care centers, and retirement complexes. Menus for this type of foodservice are planned to meet the needs of the majority of patrons, with enough flexibility to satisfy everyone. Planning menus for foodservices with a static population requires strict attention to the complete nutritional needs of the group. Such menus also must offer enough variety to minimize monotony.

The emphasis today is on good nutrition and healthful eating styles, so providing nutritionally adequate food selections that parallel customer expectations is necessary. Menus must reflect foods that allow clientele to follow the Dietary Guidelines for Americans established by U.S. Department of Agriculture and U.S. Department of Health and Human Services: (1) eat a variety of foods; (2) maintain desirable weight; (3) avoid too much fat, saturated fat, and cholesterol; (4) eat foods with adequate starch and fiber; (5) avoid too much sugar; (6) avoid too much sodium; and (7) if you drink alcoholic beverages, do so in moderation.

Clients are increasingly more knowledgeable about new and different foods and desire greater variety and an opportunity to select foods representing new culinary styles. Ethnic, meatless, and regional foods also are popular, and menus should incorporate choices from these categories.

Planning acceptable menus requires the menu planner to be aware of food preferences and periodically evaluate acceptance of foods and food combinations. Plate waste analysis, customer preference surveys, food usage data, meal census information, and informal interactions with clients are a few ways to assess menu acceptability.

Type of Foodservice

Today, the type of foodservice is not as much of a limiting factor for the menu planner, since differences among various kinds of facilities is becoming less evident. For example, most college foodservices offer menu choices similar to commercial restaurants. Hospital menus for general diet patients may be no different than those from any other segment of the foodservice industry. School foodservice menus reflect offerings similar to foods available in the commercial market. Philosophy and specific limitations of individual foodservices provide direction for the menu writer more than the type of foodservice.

Financial Limitations

The budget plays a critical role in planning menus. The costs of food, labor, and supplies for menu items must be considered in relation to projected income and expenses. In some foodservices, a raw food cost allowance per meal or per day may be determined. Although the daily food cost may fluctuate, the cumulative average for a week or a month must stay within the daily allowance. Offering a high-priced item along with a popular low-cost item will help balance costs. This is especially true when served on a buffet or when amounts are not restricted.

In commercial foodservices, the amount of money that can be spent on food is based on projected income from the sale of food. Food and labor costs are used in establishing the selling price, which often must be within a predetermined range, thus making the choice of menu items important. Forecasted need and menu mix in relation to cost must be considered.

Production Capabilities

Available Equipment

The type, size, and amount of food preparation, holding and transporting equipment available is an important factor in planning menus that can be produced. Special attention should be given to oven capacity, number of grills or fryers, refrigerator and freezer facilities, number and size of steam-jacketed kettles and steamers, and availability and capacity of mixers. Certain combinations of menu items often must be avoided because of lack of production equipment or serving pans and dishes.

Number and Experience of Employees

The person-hours of labor available and the efficiency and skill of employees are important factors to consider when deciding on the variety and complexity of the menu. Understanding the relationship between menu and personnel will help the planner develop menus that can be prepared with the available staff.

Distribution of Work

Menus should be planned to distribute the work evenly among the different areas of preparation. In determining a day's work load, the menu planner should consider not only one day's menu but also any preparation necessary for meals for the following day. Care should be exercised so menus are not planned that create an excessive work load for employees one day and underutilize them the next. To introduce variety in the menu, a limited number of foods requiring time-consuming processes may be included if combined with other food items that require minimum preparation. Some foods require last-minute cooking to ensure high quality. To avoid confusion and delayed meal service, the menu should be planned to balance items that may be prepared early and those that must be cooked just prior to serving.

MENU PLANNING PROCEDURES

Menu planning follows no absolute rules as long as the menu writer satisfies the needs and demands of the clientele and the policies of the foodservice. It is suggested that menu planning be done without interruptions and that the following materials be available:

1. Menu forms as dictated by type and needs of the foodservice.
2. Standardized recipe file.
3. Current trade periodicals and other foodservice publications.
4. Menu suggestions lists (Appendix A).
5. Previous menus (if available).
6. Summaries of menu evaluation data.

Key Points in Menu Planning

Plan for Variety and Good Nutrition

1. Include a wide variety of foods from day to day to ensure adequate nutrients. Unless you provide a choice, avoid the same form of food on consecutive days; for example, meat loaf on one day and spaghetti and meatballs the next
2. Include foods that will allow clientele to meet the Dietary Guidelines for Americans as established by the U.S. Department of Agriculture and the U.S. Department of Health and Human Services. See p. 696 for guidelines.
3. Avoid repeating the same food on the same day of the week. For this reason, a short cycle where the days are divisible by seven is undesirable.
4. Vary the method of preparation. For example, serve vegetables raw or cooked, seasoned, stir-fried, marinated, or with a sauce.
5. Introduce new foods regularly and, on a selective menu, pair a new food with a familiar well-liked food.

Plan for Eye Appeal

1. Try to visualize the appearance of the food on the plate.
2. Use at least one or two colorful foods on each menu.
3. Use colorful foods in combination with foods having little color.

Plan for Contrast in Texture and Flavor

1. Offer crisp foods with soft foods.
2. Use strong- and mild-flavored foods together.
3. Balance light and heavy foods; for example, in a nonselective menu pair light desserts with hearty entrees.

Plan for Consumer Acceptance

1. Include food combinations most acceptable to the clientele.
2. The completed menu should, if possible, have a predominance of familiar and

well-accepted menu items, with the introduction of new or less well-liked foods spaced throughout the menu period.

3. In nonselective menus, it is important that the less popular foods be accompanied by some that are well-liked by the majority of the clientele.

4. Periodically assess the food preferences of the consumers.

Plan for Financial, Production, and Service Limitations

1. Include food combinations that can be prepared with available personnel and equipment.

2. Select menu items that will keep food costs within the budget allowance.

Steps in Menu Planning

Determine a Time Period

Plan menus for at least a week at a time, preferably longer. If a cycle menu is being planned, decide on the length of the cycle.

Proceed Systematically

Select menu items systematically. Entrees are selected first because they are the central focus of a meal and form the framework of the menu plan. Other foods are then chosen that complement the entree.

Entrees   Select meat and other entrees for the entire cycle or length of time for which menus are being planned. If planning a week's menus only, choose entrees for a month or longer, then complete the menus as needed. In this way, an entree cycle can be developed that would simplify planning each week's menus. Since entrees usually are the most expensive food on the menu, cost can be controlled to a great extent through careful planning at this point. A balance between high- and low-priced items will average out the cost over the week or period covered by the cycle.

On a selective menu, offer at least one meat and a meatless entree, along with poultry and fish to complete the number of entrees required.

Be specific about method of preparation when recording the menu; for example, show pork chops as baked, stuffed, barbecued, breaded, or whatever method of preparation is desired.

Soups and Sandwiches   Plan soups and sandwiches at the same time as entrees if they are to be offered as a main dish in lieu of meat or other entree. On a selective menu, offer a cream soup and a stock soup. In a cafeteria, a variety of sandwiches may be offered, and these may not change from day to day.

Vegetables   Select vegetables that are compatible with the entrees. Potatoes, rice, or pasta may be included as one choice. On a selective menu, pair a popular vegetable with one that is less well-liked.

Salads   If only one salad is to be offered, select one that complements or is a contrast in texture to the other menu items. On a selective menu, include a green salad and fruit, vegetable, and gelatin salads to complete the desired number. Certain salad items may be offered daily such as tossed salad, cottage cheese, or cabbage slaw; or a salad bar may be a standard menu feature. See p. 478 for salad bar suggestions.

Breads   Vary the kinds of breads offered or provide a choice of white or whole grain bread and a hot bread.

Desserts   If no choice is offered, plan a light dessert with a hearty meal and a rich dessert when the rest of the meal is not too heavy. On a selective menu, include a two-crust pie, a soft pie, cake, pudding, and gelatin dessert. Ice cream, yogurt, baked custard, and fruit may be offered daily.

Breakfast Items   Certain breakfast foods such as cooked and cold cereal, toast, and fruit juices may be standard. Variety may be introduced through a choice of entrees, hot breads, and fresh fruits.

Beverages   A choice of beverages usually is provided. Coffee, decaffeinated coffee, tea, and milk, including lowfat, usually are offered. Lemonade, soft drinks, fruit punch, and a variety of juices may be included also.

Evaluate the Completed Menu

After the menu has been planned, check carefully to see if it has met the established criteria. Evaluate the menu again after the meals have been served. Make notations of satisfactory menus and difficulties encountered in production and service of the meals. If the cycle is to be repeated, desired alterations should be noted.

The responsibility of the menu planner does not end with the writing of the menu. The task is completed only when the food has been prepared and served and the reaction of the consumer noted.

MENU PLANNING FOR DIFFERENT TYPES OF FOODSERVICES

Elementary and Secondary Schools

National School Lunch Program

The National School Lunch Program (NSLP) is designed to provide nutritious, reasonably priced lunches to children in schools and residential child care centers, to contribute to a better understanding of good nutrition, and to foster good food habits. School foodservice is an integral part of the child's education.

The nutrition goal of the NSLP is to provide approximately one-third of the Recommended Dietary Allowances (RDA) by age and grade categories. In the years since passage of the School Lunch Act, choices and greater flexibility in meal patterns have been incorporated. Portion sizes are adjusted for age groups. Schools are encouraged to incorporate the Dietary Guidelines for Americans, p. 696, into their menu planning. The School Lunch Patterns for the various age groups are found in Table 16.2. To qualify for reimbursement, a school is required to use this framework and to meet the minimum requirements, but other foods may be added to help improve acceptability and to satisfy students' appetites.

An "offer versus serve" provision allows students to choose less than all the food items within the lunch pattern. Students must be offered all five food items of the school lunch, and the student must choose at least three of these items for the lunch to be reimbursed. Schools are required to implement the "offer versus serve" provision for senior high school students. The implementation of this provision in middle, junior high, and elementary schools is left to the discretion of the local school food authorities.

The cycle menu is used to some extent in school foodservices, and many schools are using selective menus in which students may select from two items of comparable nutritional value for part of the menu; for example, a student may have a choice of two vegetables and two fruits. Some schools offer multiple menus in which more than one complete menu that meets federal requirements is offered, such as a chef's salad or soup and sandwich meal. À la carte items are also provided in many schools. The more menu choices provided to students, the better their participation in the school foodservice programs.

Many foods on the Suggested Menu Items listed in Appendix A are suitable for school lunches. Keep in mind the nutrition requirements, cost, labor and equipment restraints, and food preferences of the age group served. Adding options such as salad bars, special day celebrations, or ethnic and international food promotions allow the school foodservice operation to compete with the commercial food industry.

School Breakfast Program

Eating a nutritious breakfast is a great start for the day. Breakfast furnishes fuel for the morning, when students do most of their learning. In 1975, Congress passed an amendment which made the School Breakfast Program (SBP) a permanent part of the Child Nutrition Act. All public and nonprofit private schools may participate in the SBP.

The School Breakfast Pattern for the various age groups is found in Table 16.3. To qualify for reimbursement, a school is required to use this framework and to meet the minimum requirements, but other foods may be added to help improve acceptability and to satisfy students' appetites. Offer versus serve is also available to any school in the SBP, whereby students can refuse any one of the four food items comprising a school breakfast. School breakfast can be an easy way to serve a meal that requires little additional labor from the school foodservice operation.

Child and Adult Care Food Program

The Child and Adult Care Food Program (CACFP) is designed to provide nutritious meals for children twelve years of age and younger. Children need well-balanced meals

TABLE 16.2   **School lunch patterns for various age/grade groups**

| Components | Minimum quantities | | | | Recommended quantities[b] | Specific requirements |
| | Preschool | | Grades K–3 | Grades 4–12[a] | Grades 7–12 | |
	Ages 1–2 (Group I)	Ages 3–4 (Group II)	Ages 5–8 (Group III)	Age 9 & over (Group IV)	Age 12 & over (Group V)	
MEAT OR MEAT ALTERNATE A serving of one of the following or a combination to give an equivalent quantity:						■ Must be served in the main dish or the main dish and one other menu item. ■ Textured vegetable protein products, cheese alternate products, and enriched macaroni with fortified protein may be used to meet part of the meat/meat alternate requirement. Fact sheets on each of these alternate foods give detailed instructions for use. ■ No more than 50 percent of the requirement shall be met with nuts or seeds. Amounts shown on the chart provide 50 percent of the minimum requirement. To fulfill the requirement, these items must be served with another meat/meat alternate.
■ Lean meat, poultry, or fish (edible portion as served)	1 oz	1½ oz	1½ oz	2 oz	3 oz	
■ Cheese	1 oz	1½ oz	1½ oz	2 oz	3 oz	
■ Large egg(s)	½	¾	¾	1	1½	
■ Cooked dry beans or peas	¼ cup	⅜ cup	⅜ cup	½ cup	¾ cup	
■ Peanut butter or other nut or seed butters	2 Tbsp	3 Tbsp	3 Tbsp	4 Tbsp	6 Tbsp	
■ Peanuts, soynuts, tree nuts or seeds[c]	½ oz	¾ oz	¾ oz	1 oz	1½ oz	
VEGETABLE AND/OR FRUIT Two or more servings of vegetable or fruit or both to total	½ cup	½ cup	½ cup	¾ cup	¾ cup	■ No more than one-half of the total requirement may be met with full-strength fruit or vegetable juice. ■ Cooked dry beans or peas may be used as a meat alternate or as a vegetable but not as both in the same meal.

[a]Group IV is the one meal pattern which will satisfy all requirements if no portion size adjustments are made.
[b]Group V specifies recommended, not required, quantities for students 12 years and older. These students may request smaller portions, but not smaller than those specified in Group IV.
[c]Amounts shown provide 50 percent of the minimum requirement.

TABLE 16.2 **Continued**

Components	Minimum quantities				Recommended quantities[b]	Specific requirements
	Preschool		Grades K–3	Grades 4–12[a]	Grades 7–12	
	Ages 1–2 (Group I)	Ages 3–4 (Group II)	Ages 5–8 (Group III)	Age 9 & over (Group IV)	Age 12 & over (Group V)	
VEGETABLE AND/OR FRUIT CONTINUED						■ When potatoes are served, at least ½ cup of other fruits and/or vegetables must be offered.
BREAD OR BREAD ALTERNATE						
Servings of bread or bread alternate	5 per week	8 per week	8 per week	8 per week	10 per week	■ At least ½ serving of bread or an equivalent quantity of bread alternate for Group I, and 1 serving for Groups II–V, must be served daily.
A serving is: ■ 1 slice of whole-grain or enriched bread ■ A whole-grain or enriched biscuit, roll, muffin, etc. ■ ½ cup of cooked whole-grain or enriched rice, macaroni, noodles, whole-grain or enriched pasta products, or other cereal grains such as bulgur or corn grits ■ A combination of any of the above						■ Enriched macaroni with fortified protein may be used as a meat alternate or as a bread alternate but not as both in the same meal. Note: *Food Buying Guide for School Food Service*, PA-1257 (1980), provides the information for the minimum weight of a serving.
MILK						
A serving of fluid milk	¾ cup (6 fl oz)	¾ cup (6 fl oz)	½ pint (8 fl oz)	½ pint (8 fl oz)	½ pint (8 fl oz)	The following forms of milk must be offered: ■ Whole milk, flavored or unflavored, and ■ Unflavored lowfat milk, ½, 1, 1½, or 2 percent Note: Flavored milk may be offered in addition to the two types of milk listed above.

Source: U.S. Department of Agriculture, national school lunch program.

TABLE 16.3 School breakfast meal pattern requirements

Food components/items	Minimum required quantities		
	Ages 1–2	Ages 3, 4, 5	Age 6 & up
Fluid milk			
As a beverage, on cereal, or both	½ cup	¾ cup	½ pint
Fruit/vegetable/juice[a]			
Fruit and/or vegetable or full-strength fruit juice or vegetable juice	¼ cup	½ cup	½ cup

SELECT *ONE* SERVING FROM EACH OF THE FOLLOWING
COMPONENTS OR *TWO* SERVINGS FROM ONE COMPONENT

	Ages 1–2	Ages 3, 4, 5	Age 6 & up
Bread/bread alternates[b]			
One of the following or an equivalent combination:			
■ Whole-grain or enriched bread	½ slice	½ slice	1 slice
■ Whole-grain or enriched biscuit, roll, muffin, etc.	½ serving	½ serving	1 serving
■ Whole-grain, enriched, or fortified cereal	¼ cup or ⅓ ounce	⅓ cup or ½ ounce	¾ cup or 1 ounce
Meat/meat alternates			
One of the following or an equivalent combination:			
■ Lean meat, poultry, or fish	½ ounce	½ ounce	1 ounce
■ Cheese	½ ounce	½ ounce	1 ounce
■ Large egg	½	½	½
■ Peanut butter or other nut or seed butters	1 Tbsp	1 Tbsp	2 Tbsp
■ Cooked dry beans and peas	2 Tbsp	2 Tbsp	4 Tbsp
■ Nuts and/or seeds (As listed in program guidance)[c]	½ ounce	½ ounce	1 ounce

Source: U.S. Department of Agriculture, school breakfast program.

[a]Recommended daily: a citrus or a juice or fruit or vegetable that is a good source of vitamin C.
[b]See Food Buying Guide, PA-1331, for serving sizes.
[c]No more than 1 ounce of nuts and/or seeds may be served in any one meal.

to meet their daily energy and nutritional requirements. To meet the nutritional needs, specified meal patterns are followed. Required quantities vary according to the age of the children. CACFP Meal Pattern requirements can be found in Table 16.4.

In planning food for children, their total daily food requirements should be considered. The combination of meals and snacks will vary according to the age group, their time of arrival at the center, and their length of stay. It is important that the planner consider the nutritional needs of the children, their food preferences, regional food habits, equipment, personnel, and other management functions.

Young children need nutritious foods at frequent intervals, but it is important to schedule the service of food to allow sufficient time between meals and supplements. Young children enjoy food they can handle easily. Finger food, snacks, and bite-sized

TABLE 16.4   Child and adult care food program U.S. Department of Agriculture food chart

	Age		
	1–2	*3–5*	*6–12* *Adults*
BREAKFAST			
Fluid milk	½ cup	¾ cup	1 cup
Juice or fruit or vegetable	¼ cup	½ cup	½ cup
Bread or bread alternate	½ slice[a]	½ slice[a]	½ slice[a]
	(or ½ oz)	(or ½ oz)	(or ½ oz)
or cold dry cereal	¼ cup	⅓ cup	¾ cup
	(or ⅓ oz)	(or ½ oz)	(or 1 oz)
or cooked cereal	¼ cup	¼ cup	½ cup
SNACK: Select two of the following four components[b]			
Fluid milk	½ cup	½ cup	1 cup
Juice or fruit or vegetable	½ cup	½ cup	¾ cup
Meat or meat alternate	½ oz	½ oz	1 oz
or yogurt	2 oz	2 oz	4 oz
	(or ¼ cup)	(or ¼ cup)	(or ½ cup)
Bread, bread alternate, or cereal	½ slice[a]	½ slice[a]	1 slice[a]
LUNCH/SUPPER			
Fluid milk	½ cup	¾ cup	1 cup
Meat or poultry or fish	1 oz	1½ oz	2 oz
or cheese	1 oz	1½ oz	2 oz
or cottage cheese, cheese food, or cheese spread	2 oz (¼ cup)	3 oz (⅜ cup)	4 oz (½ cup)
or egg	1	1	1
or cooked dry beans or peas	¼ cup	⅜ cup	½ cup
or peanut butter, soynuts, tree nuts or seeds	2 Tbsp	3 Tbsp	4 Tbsp
or an equivalent quantity of any combination of the above meat/meat alternates	½ oz = 50%	¾ oz = 50%	1 oz = 50%
Vegetables and/or fruits (2 or more)	¼ cup total	½ cup total	¾ cup total
Bread or bread alternate	½ slice[a]	½ slice[a]	1 slice[a]

Adapted from material supplied by the Kansas State Board of Education Nutrition Services.

[a]Or an equivalent serving of an acceptable bread alternate such as corn bread, biscuits, rolls, muffins, etc., made of whole-grain or enriched meal or flour, or a serving of cooked enriched or whole-grain rice or macaroni or other pasta products.

[b]For snack, juice may not be served when milk is served as the only other component.

pieces are most popular. Banana slices, berries, dried peaches or pears, fresh fruit wedges, carrot and celery sticks, cheese cubes, and crackers are examples of finger foods.

Those responsible for foodservice in child care centers should provide the opportunity for children to learn about the foods they eat so they can begin to make wise, nutritious choices.

Colleges and Universities

College and university foodservice menus are representative of the marked change in the college foodservice industry over the last decade. The college customer on most campuses has several menu options: board plan cafeterias, snack bars, specialty shops, food courts, convenience stores, vending operations, cash cafeterias, and fine dining restaurants. Commonplace, too, are catering operations that support social, athletic, and university events both on and off campus.

More than one menu type may be appropriate for these varied functions because the menu must support many objectives. For example, a serving area may provide traditional board, cash meals, and carry-out food options from a single location. The success of these complex operations is closely linked to the menu design and the ability of the menu writer to satisfy both facility and customer objectives.

The selective menu pattern in Table 16.1 may be used for designing a traditional cycle menu. With today's campus diner, however, the most successful menus offer extensive variety daily. Menus must be exciting and creative and reflect choices that parallel student preferences. Basing menu decisions on accurate food trend data is necessary.

Consideration for good nutrition is important for all menu writers but offers a special challenge when the customer is generally from a healthy population and often between 18 and 28 years old. Customers of this age are more apt to make choices based on impulse preference than are clientele from a population having health and dietary concerns. The menu, to be successful, must allow for customer satisfaction and at the same time reflect the principles of sound nutrition and quality nutritious food. Customer input is necessary for designing menus that allow this to happen. See p. 696 for the Dietary Guidelines for Americans.

The following section, "Commercial Foodservices," includes additional information appropriate to the college and university market.

Commercial Foodservices

Menu planning for commercial foodservices varies according to the type and size of operation, its goals and the expected check average. Menus range from the fast-food concept of a limited menu for high volume and quick service to the table d'hôte menu of a formal seated-service restaurant.

The basic rules of menu planning apply to commercial foodservices. Type of foodservice must be determined, financial goals decided, production and service capabilities analyzed, and labor needs addressed. Assessing clientele wants is especially important and should be assessed accurately, using proven research procedures.

Commercial customers make choices daily on what and where to eat and the amount of money they will spend. It is often not enough for the menu planner to follow all the rules that make production and service possible without special consideration for the role the menu plays in making the commercial foodservice operation successful. A few guidelines that should be followed in designing the commercial menu are:

■ Decide what to serve and what to charge. Market research is necessary to assess accurately what customers will purchase.

■ Design the presentation of the menu suitable to the operation. The layout and overall design should be readable and attractive, and should support marketing goals.

■ Determine the sequence of food items on the menu. A generally accepted sequence is appetizers or foods eaten first, then soups, entrees, and desserts. Within this order, salads, side orders, and beverages must be placed. Foods listed first within each category are selected most often so consideration should be given to this placement.

■ Write the menu names to describe the foods offered accurately and to merchandise the food item and the operation. The importance of the menu to create atmosphere and serve as a marketing and advertising tool cannot be overemphasized.

Hospitals

Although hospital menus may be more complex, the principles of meal planning for health care facilities are the same as those for other types of foodservices. Foods must be provided for many kinds of diets, ranging from liquid, ground, soft, or regular, to bland, low sodium, low carbohydrate, or fat restricted, with a wide range in caloric requirements. In addition, a cafeteria generally is available for hospital personnel and visitors.

Like college and university foodservices, hospitals are adopting more characteristics of the commercial foodservice. More emphasis is being placed on developing innovative menus and on offering new and creative food items. Many hospitals use catering and other services as revenue centers.

Cycle menus are widely used in health care facilities. The length of patient stay is an important factor in determining the length of the cycle. In an acute care hospital, where the average length of stay may be three to five days, a short cycle could be used. In an extended care facility, as discussed on p. 708, a longer cycle would be more satisfactory. If a short cycle is used for patient meals, a longer cycle would be required for the employee cafeteria.

When developing a hospital meal pattern, the first step is to plan a regular or normal diet that will supply all food essentials necessary for good nutrition. This pattern then becomes the foundation for most diets required for therapeutic purposes and is the core of all meal planning in a hospital of any type or size. Patients requiring other than a normal diet will receive various modifications of the regular diet to fit their particular needs.

In planning a normal or regular diet, meals should be planned for each day as a unit. Each day's menu then can be checked to be sure that all essential foods have been included. A suggested three-meal-a-day menu pattern for a normal diet is given in Table 16.1.

The selective menu adds much to the satisfaction of patients and also helps to prevent waste. Choices that appeal to various patients usually can be made available with little extra work, if careful planning is used in pairing items on the menu. The main items on the selective menu are the same as those on the general menu. Some items, such as the choice of meat and vegetables, may be the same as foods prepared for one of the modified diets or for the cafeteria. Other choices may be soup or fruit juice, or fruit or ice cream in place of a prepared dessert. On the dinner menu, choices of light or more hearty foods may do much to promote patient acceptance. Some hospitals have adopted a selective menu similar to the table d'hôte menu of the commercial sector. The same menu is offered daily but with a wide enough variety of choices that the patient can select a different meal each day. Patients may order any food item on the menu unless it is restricted on their diets.

Extended Care Facilities and Retirement Communities

For people residing in extended health care facilities and retirement communities, food satisfies basic emotional and physical needs.

Those persons planning meals for older adults should be aware of the problems peculiar to this age group. Their fixed habits and food preferences developed through many years may influence but should not determine entirely the meals planned for them. Healthy adults, regardless of age, need a well-balanced diet and, in planning the day's food, the basic pattern for the normal diet should be followed. Individual problems of the group members, such as difficulty in chewing, special dietary requirements, and their limited mobility and activity, must also be considered.

At least three well-planned meals should be served daily, with a hot food at each meal. The menu pattern is similar to that of the regular hospital diet (p. 694), with adjustments in portions and some modification for residents with individual eating problems. The caloric intake or quantity of food eaten usually is smaller because of lessened activity.

The daily food plan should include the following:

1. At least one food of good-quality protein at each meal—fish, poultry, lean meat, eggs, or cheese.
2. Milk offered at mealtime, with at least two cups a day for each person.
3. Four or more servings of fruits and vegetables, including a green leafy or yellow vegetable and a citrus fruit, such as grapefruit, orange, or some other good source of vitamin C. Although chewing may be difficult for some, raw vegetables or fruits should be included.
4. Four or more servings from the bread/cereal group, which includes bread, break-fast cereals, pasta, rice, and baked goods made with whole grain or enriched flour.

Additional foods containing fat, sweets, and flavoring add to the acceptance of meals.

If a nonselective menu is used, some modification will add to the residents' acceptance of the food. Choice may be provided by offering certain menu items daily in addition to a set menu or through a choice of two items in each menu category for the dinner meal. Foodservice in this type of long-term facility offers opportunity for use of the eight-week or longer cycle.

17

Planning Special Meals and Receptions

Foodservices, for a variety of reasons from producing income to fulfilling educational or social obligations, are often responsible for planning special meals. The types of functions may include coffees, teas, receptions, brunches, buffets, banquets, and catered events on and off the premises. Regardless of the type of service provided, considerable planning is required to ensure a successful foodservice event.

PLANNING RESPONSIBILITIES

Careful advance planning is important to the success of any special function. Some foods may be prepared ahead and refrigerated or frozen. The other meals on the day of the special function may need to be simplified to avoid work overloads. Extra service personnel, if needed and if inexperienced, should be provided with detailed instructions.

The major responsibilities of the foodservice staff in charge of a special meal or other function are as follows:

1. Confer with representatives of the group to be served to determine the type of function, time and place, number to be served, service desired, and financial arrangements. Program arrangements and responsibility for table decorations also should be discussed.

2. Plan menu with the organization's representative. Duplicate copies of the menu plans should be signed and kept by the group's representative and the food director. This procedure confirms the agreement and may prevent a misunderstanding of details and avoid last-minute changes.

3. Determine quantity and estimated cost of food to be served.

4. Place food orders. It is important that orders for special or unusual foods be made early enough to ensure delivery.

5. Check the dish and equipment list and make arrangements for obtaining any additional items needed. A list including the amount and kind of linen, dishes, silverware, glassware, serving utensils, and tables and chairs required should be compiled by the manager and arrangements made for assembling these at least one day before they are to be used.

6. Prepare work schedules. A detailed work schedule includes prepreparation, cooking, serving, and cleanup assignments. If workers are inexperienced, the schedule should indicate time for each task, detailed procedures, and other special instructions. For a seated service luncheon or dinner, assign personnel to the serving counter from which the plates will be filled. Assign and instruct servers for dining room service. See pp. 717–722 for directions for table setting and service.

7. Supervise the preparation and service of food.

8. Supervise the dishwashing and cleanup of preparation and service areas.

9. Prepare, and keep on file, a detailed report including information concerning menu, numbers served, income and expenses, and useful comments for service of similar meals in the future.

RECEPTIONS AND TEAS

Receptions and teas may vary in degree of formality and may accommodate a few or many guests. The menu may be simple or elaborate and should be planned according to the type of event, the time of day, the number to be served, and the money and labor available.

One or two beverages usually are offered, coffee and tea or coffee and punch. The menu may be limited to an attractive dessert, with nuts and mints, or it may include several kinds of sandwiches, cookies, or cakes. The following are suggested choices for a reception or tea:

Beverages   Coffee, tea, hot spiced tea or cider, punch, wine.
See Tables 17.1 and 17.2 for wine purchasing and selection guides. See p. 110 for nonalcoholic cocktails suggestions.

Breads   Open-face sandwiches spread with a variety of fillings and decorated attractively.
Rolled, ribbon, checkerboard, or pinwheel sandwiches.
Nut bread or fruit bread sandwiches with cream cheese or marmalade filling, cut in squares, triangles, round, or oblong shapes.
Cheese wafers or cheese straws.
Miniature cream puffs filled with chicken or fish salad.
Petite biscuits with sliced meat or salad filling.

Dips	Dips with cheese, cream cheese, yogurt, or sour cream base. Served with crisp raw vegetables, fruits, and/or crackers and chips.
Cakes, cookies, and tarts	Petits fours or small decorated cupcakes. Meringue shells with whipped cream and fruit fillings. Small pecan or fruit tarts. Small tea cookies that offer a variety of shapes, flavors, and colors.
Nuts and candies	Salted, toasted, or spiced nuts. Candied orange or grapefruit peel. Mints in pastel colors.

Figure 17.1 suggests a table arrangement for a reception or tea, using two lines of service and set up so that a guest may start by placing a beverage cup on a plate, then selecting food items. The silverware and napkin usually are last. Placing the cup on the plate first ensures adequate space for both food and beverage. If only one or two food selections are offered, beverages may be served last. Use the same directions as in Figure 17.1 but start with plates and end with the beverage or beverages.

The table covering, centerpiece, tea service, silverware, and serving dishes should be attractive, and the food should be colorful and interestingly arranged. To prevent a crowded appearance, there should be a limited amount of silverware, china, napkins, and food on the table when the serving begins. A small serving table with extra china and silverware near the tea table is a convenience. Replacements of small dishes and

TABLE 17.1   Wine selection guide

Wine	*Temperature*	*To accompany*
Champagne	Chilled (40°F)	Appetizers or main course
Dessert wines	Cool room temperature (65°F)	Desserts
Cream sherry		
Marsala		
Muscatel		
Port		
Sweet champagne		
Red wine	Slightly cool (60°F)	Hearty entrees
Burgundy		
Claret		
Rosé	Slightly cool (60°F)	Any entree
Sherry, port	Chilled or room temperature (50°–65°F)	Appetizers
White wine	Chilled (50°F)	Light entrees
Chablis		
Rhine		
Riesling		
Sauterne		

TABLE 17.2   **Wine purchasing guide**

		Servings per container[a]	
Size	Volume (ounces)	Dinner	Cocktail
375 milliliters	12.7	4	4–6
750 milliliters	25.4	8	8–12
1 liter	33.8	11	12–14
1.5 liters	50.7	16	20–25
3 liters	101.4	32	40–50
4 liters	135.2	43	52–64

[a]Number of servings per container is based on dinner portion size 3–3½ oz, cocktail portion size 2–2½ oz. If larger glasses are used, adjustment in the servings per container will need to be made.

appointments are brought on trays from the kitchen. If two beverages are served, they are placed at either end of the table. Cookies, sandwiches, and other foods should be arranged so they do not appear crowded. It is best to use small serving plates and replace them frequently so there is an assortment of food at all times. Arrangements should be made for people to pour the beverages, and employees or hostesses should be assigned to replenish the tea table and to take empty plates from guests.

COFFEES AND BRUNCHES

Coffees and brunches are easy and popular ways to entertain a few or many guests. An ample supply of hot, fresh coffee is necessary, and an alternate choice of tea and/or decaffeinated coffee may be offered. Flavored coffees and teas are popular beverage choices. One or more hot breads are served, and the menu may be expanded to include fresh fruit or juice. A fruit tray, with bite-sized pieces of fresh fruit arranged on a silver or other appropriate tray, is an attractive centerpiece and an interesting addition to a coffee hour or brunch.

Brunch, a meal combining breakfast and lunch, usually includes a wider variety of food than does a coffee. The menu may be made up of foods normally served at breakfast or may resemble a luncheon menu, depending partly on the hour of service. It may be quite simple, consisting of fruits, hot breads, and coffee, or it may be a more substantial meal that will replace lunch. The food usually is placed on a buffet table for self-service but may be served to guests seated at tables. Brunch often starts with fruit juice or sparkling wines served to guests before they go to the buffet table. The main entree may be one or several that are typical of breakfast, such as eggs in some form, bacon, ham, sausage, or a breakfast casserole; or a luncheon-type entree of chicken, turkey, or fish. An assortment of breads usually is offered. A dessert may be served if the meal is sched-

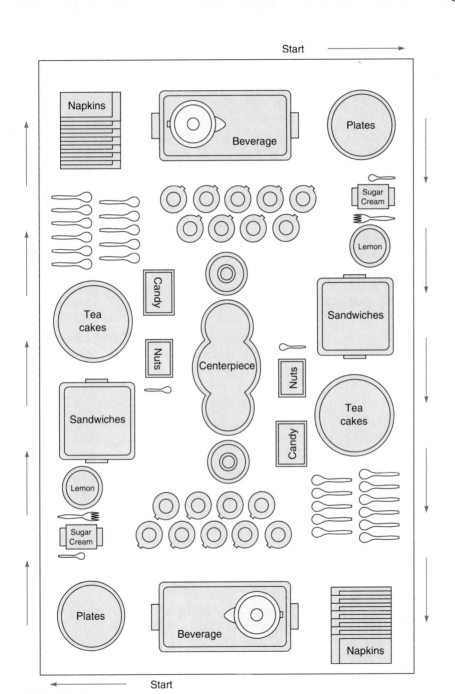

FIGURE 17.1   Table arrangement for a reception or tea.

uled late in the morning, but it should be light. Suggested foods for coffee hours and brunches are as follows:

Fruits and juices	Orange, pineapple, or tomato juice. Fresh fruit cup or fresh berries. Melon wedges, fruit kebobs. Orange juice champagne punch.
Fruit trays	Fresh pineapple chunks, banana wedges, orange sections, fresh strawberries, kiwi fruit, mangos, carambola (star fruit). Apple slices, honeydew melon wedges, kiwi fruit, and frosted grapes. Plums or bing cherries, pear slices, cantaloupe wedges, green grapes, and cheese cubes.
Entrees	Canadian bacon, grilled ham, sausage patties on apple rings. Small biscuits with ham slice. Scrambled eggs, egg and sausage casserole, omelets. Cheese and broccoli strata, quiche, cheese soufflé, crepes, broiled or grilled chicken breast on rice or pasta, chicken divan.
Breads	Small pecan or orange rolls, scones, kolaches, toasted English muffins or bagels with marmalade and/or cream cheese. Coffee cake, Danish pastry. Small doughnuts or doughnut holes, cinnamon puffs. Small nut or fruit bread sandwiches.
Desserts	Fresh pineapple and berries, ambrosia, sherbet. Strawberry-sour cream crepes, fruit and cheese platters. Cookies or small cakes.

BUFFET DINNERS AND LUNCHEONS

Buffet dinners and luncheons provide a means of serving relatively large groups of people with a minimum of service personnel. An assortment of hors d'oeuvres and a beverage may be offered to guests before the buffet is served.

A greater variety of food generally is included in a buffet menu than can be offered at table d'hôte meals, although the extent of the variety will depend on preparation time and space on the buffet table, among other factors. The menu may be built around two or three entrees, one or two vegetables, two or three salads or a salad bar, relishes, hot bread, dessert, and beverage.

In planning a buffet menu, consideration should be given to contrasts in colors, shapes, and sizes of food and to ease of serving and eating, as well as to pleasing flavor combinations. An assortment of breads adds interest and variety to the buffet table. Desserts served on the buffet table usually are "finger foods" such as cookies, small cakes or tarts, or a fresh fruit and cheese tray. If the dessert is to be served to the guests, however, only one is planned, and it might be pie, cake, ice cream, or a baked dessert. Foods appropriate for buffets may be selected from the Suggested Menu Items, pp. 723–731.

Certain precautions should be observed in planning a buffet:

1. Keep the service as simple as possible (i.e., avoid foods difficult to serve or that are soft or runny on the plate). Foods that require extra silverware, such as bread and butter spreaders and salad or cocktail forks, usually are not served.

2. Include a few attractively decorated foods, assorted salads, and an assortment of relishes. Attractive garnishing of the food and serving pans and platters is important.

3. Plan hot food that holds well and serves easily. A hot counter, chafing dishes, or heated trays are essential if hot food is to be served.

4. Plan the arrangement of the table at the same time the menu is planned to be sure of adequate table space and suitable serving dishes.

5. Plan enough food so that the last person in the buffet line will have a choice and will see an attractive display. This can be accomplished partly by not having the serving dishes or pans too large and therefore requiring that they be replenished often. The amount of each food to prepare will depend to a great extent on the variety of foods being offered. Unless there is a limited choice, most people will take smaller servings than normal, and some may select only a few items.

6. Plan plate size to accommodate the foods offered. Plate size will affect the amount of food used and the guests' enjoyment of the meal. Cutting some entree portions in half, when appropriate, may encourage guests to try several items and reduce waste.

The success of a buffet meal depends not only on the quality of food but also on the attractiveness of the buffet table. Interesting colors may be introduced in the table covering, the serving dishes, the food, and the decorations. Visual appearance may be heightened by placing the centerpiece and some foods at different levels. Using mirrors under the centerpiece adds dimension and helps complete a tastefully decorated buffet table.

Food for a buffet may be arranged in several ways. Figure 17.2 illustrates a typical buffet arrangement with a single service line used for small groups. A double line, as shown in Figure 17.3, will speed service but requires more space and duplicate serving dishes. Figure 17.4 illustrates a straight-line buffet arrangement used when larger groups serve themselves from both sides of the table. Deciding whether to serve the entree first or last requires using some judgement. Guests generally take less of the entree and the entree stays hotter if served last. Serving the entree first insures that the guest will have room on the plate for accompaniment foods. An 11-inch plate is generally satisfactory. If a smaller plate is used, consider placing salad plates alongside the salads.

Desserts may be placed on a separate table from which the guests will later serve themselves. If the guests are seated, dishes from the first course usually are removed and the desserts brought to the guests by service personnel.

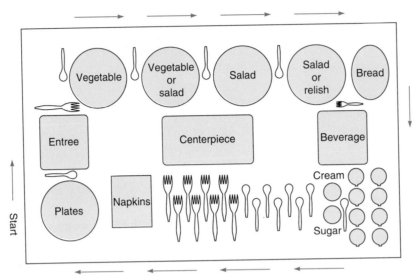

FIGURE 17.2   Table arrangement for buffet service, single line. Beverages may be served at tables. Desserts may be served from a dessert table or to guests at the individual tables. Suitable for serving very small numbers.

The type of service depends largely on the equipment available. If ample table space is provided, places may be set with covers, rolls, and water, and provisions may be made for the beverage to be served by employees. If table room for all is not available, each guest may be given an individual tray on which to place silverware, napkin, water glass, and the plate containing the assembled food. Hot beverages and rolls are served.

BANQUET SERVICE

Although table service for banquets in hotels and many other commercial foodservices may be elaborate, a simplified service may be the most practical for foodservices in which only an occasional banquet is served. The discussion of table setting and plate service that follows is intended primarily for this type of facility.

Preparation of the Dining Room

Tables and chairs should be arranged to allow adequate space for serving after the guests are seated. Chairs should be placed so that the front edge of each touches or is just below the tablecloth. If there is to be a head table, it should be placed so that it is easily seen by the guests, with a podium and microphone available for the program. Audiovisual equipment, if needed, should be properly placed and adjusted. Serving stands, conveniently placed, facilitate service. Such provisions are especially important when the distance to the kitchen is great.

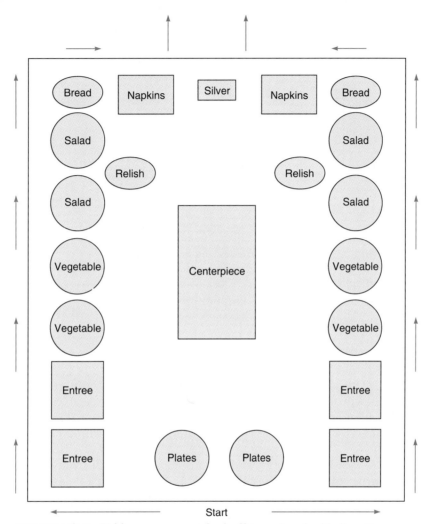

FIGURE 17.3   Table arrangement for buffet service, double line. Beverages may be served at tables. Desserts may be served from a dessert table or to guests at the individual tables. Suitable for serving small numbers.

Setting the Tables

Tablecloth   Tablecloths generally are used for banquets, although place mats make an attractive table setting when the finish of the table top permits and the meal is informal. Place the cloth on the table so that the center lengthwise fold falls exactly in the middle of the table and the four corners are an equal distance from the floor. The cloth should extend over the table top 6–12 inches and should not touch the chair seat.

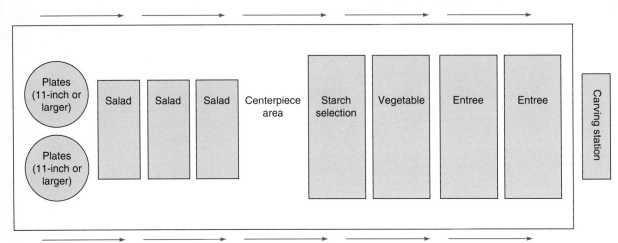

FIGURE 17.4   Double straight-line service for a buffet serving large numbers. Guests serve themselves from either side of a single line of food items. Napkins, silverware, bread and butter, and beverages are usually placed at each table. Desserts may be served at a separate table or individually to each guest.

The Cover   The plate, silverware, glasses, and napkin to be used by each person are known as the cover (see Figure 17.5). Consider 20 inches of table space as the smallest permissible allowance for each cover; 25–30 inches is better. Place all silverware and dishes required for one cover as close together as possible without crowding.

Silverware   Place knives, forks, and spoons about one inch from the edge of the table and in the order of their use (see Figure 17.5). Some prefer to place the salad or dessert fork next to the plate as the menu dictates. If the menu requires no knife, omit it from the cover. When cocktail forks are used, they are placed at the extreme right of the cover. If a butter spreader is used, lay it across the upper right side of the bread and butter plate, with the cutting edge toward the center of the plate. It may be placed straight across the top of the plate or with the handle at a convenient angle. Dessert silverware often is not placed on the table when the cover is laid, except when the amount of silver required for the entire meal is small or when it is necessary to simplify the service. If a dessert fork is used, it is sometimes placed in the area above the dinner plate so the guest will use it for the final course.

Napkin   Place the napkin at the left of the fork with the loose corner at the lower right and the open edges next to the edge of the table and the plate. It may be placed between the knife and fork if space is limited, and it may be folded into an accordion shape and placed upright.

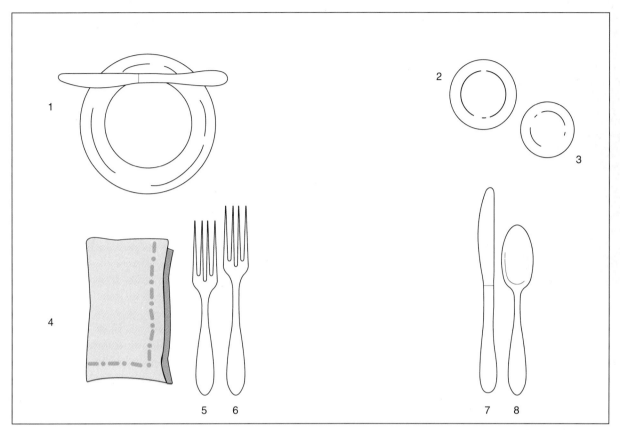

FIGURE 17.5   Cover for a served meal: (1) bread and butter plate, with butter knife; (2) water glass; (3) wine glass; (4) napkin; (5) salad fork; (6) dinner fork; (7) knife; (8) teaspoon.

Glasses   Place the water glass at the tip of the knife or slightly to the right. Goblets and footed tumblers often are preferred for luncheon or dinner and should be used for a formal dinner. Wine glasses are placed to the right of and slightly below the water glass.

Bread and Butter Plate   Place the bread and butter plate at the tip of the fork or slightly to the left.

Salt and Pepper   Salt and pepper shakers should be provided for every six covers. They should be placed parallel to the edge of the table and in line with sugar bowls and creamers.

Decorations   Some attractive decorations should be provided for the center of the table. A centerpiece should be low so the view across the table will not be obstructed. Candles should not be used in the daytime unless the lighting is inadequate or the day is dark. When used, they should be the sole source of light. Do not mix candlelight and daylight or candlelight and electric light. Tall candles in low holders should be high enough so that the flame is not on a level with the eyes of the guests. If place cards are used, they are set on the napkin or above the cover.

Seating Arrangement

The guest of honor, if a woman, usually is seated to the right of the host; if a man, to the right of the hostess. At banquets and public dinners, a man is seated to the left of his partner.

Service Counter Setup for Served Meals

Food should be served from hot counters or, if these are not available, the pans containing food should be placed in hot water. Some provision also must be made for keeping plates and cups hot. For serving 50 plates or less, the plan should provide one person to serve each food item. Such an arrangement for serving is termed a setup. For 60–100 persons, two setups should be provided to hasten service. For more than 100 persons, it is well to provide additional setups.

Food is placed on the hot counter in the following order: meat, potato or substitute, vegetables, sauces, and garnish. The supervisor should demonstrate the size of portions to be given and their arrangement on the plate. There should be a checker at the end of the line to remove with a damp cloth any food spots from the plate and to check the plate for completeness, arrangement, and uniformity of servings. The importance of standardized servings and food arrangement can hardly be overemphasized; these factors can determine the enjoyment of the guests and the financial success or failure of a meal.

Table Service

1. Service personnel should report to the supervisor to receive final instructions at least 15 minutes before the time set for serving the banquet.

2. If the salad is to be on the table when the guests arrive, it should be placed there by the service personnel not more than 15 minutes before serving time. It should be placed to the left of the fork (Figure 17.6). If space does not permit this arrangement, place the salad plate at the tip of the fork and the bread and butter plate, if used, directly above the dinner plate between the water glass and the salad plate. If the salad is to be served as a separate course, it is placed between the knife and the fork, then removed before the main course is served.

3. Place creamer beside the sugar bowl.

4. Place relishes on the table, if desired.

5. For small dinners, the first course may be placed on the table before dinner is announced. For large banquets, however, it is best to wait until the guests are seated.

FIGURE 17.6   Placement of food and cover for a served meal: (1) bread and butter plate; (2) water glass; (3) wine glass; (4) salad plate; (5) dinner plate; (6) cup and saucer. The salad is placed at the left of the fork when salad and beverage are both served with the main course. If space does not permit, place salad plate at tip of fork and bread and butter plate, if used, above the dinner plate.

Hot soups or plated appetizers are served after the guests are seated. A first course of beverages and appetizers may be offered as the guests arrive in the reception area.

6. Place butter on the right side of the bread and butter plate. If no bread and butter plate is used and the salad is to be on the table when guests arrive, place the butter on the side of the salad plate. This procedure is often necessary where dishes and table space are limited.

7. Place glasses filled with ice water on the table just before guests are seated.

8. When the guests are seated, service personnel line up in the kitchen for trays containing the first course. It is helpful if two persons work together, one carrying the

tray and the other placing the food. Place the cocktail glasses, soup dishes, or canapé plates on the service plates, which are already on the table.

9. Place and remove all dishes from the left with the left hand, except those containing beverages, which are placed and removed from the right with the right hand.

10. Serve the head table first, progressing in order to the other tables. To minimize the disruption of guests, it is preferable to have the head table the one farthest from the kitchen entrance.

11. When the guests have finished the first course, service personnel remove the dishes, following the same order used in serving.

12. For the main course, plates may be brought to the dining room on plate carriers or on trays holding several plates and set on tray stands. Each worker serves the plates to a specified group of guests.

    An alternate method often is used in serving large groups. A tray of filled plates is brought from the kitchen by bus personnel to a particular station in the dining room, from which the plates are served. The dining room service personnel remain at their stations during the serving period.

13. Place the plate 1 inch from the edge of the table with the meat nearest the guest.

14. As soon as a table has been served with dinner plates and salad, specially appointed workers should follow immediately with rolls. Coffee may be served at this time or with dessert.

15. Place the coffee cups at the right of the spoons with the handles toward the right at about the 5 o'clock position. If the coffee is served with the main course, the cup and saucer may be placed on the table with the rest of the cover. If it is served with the dessert only, the cups are not placed on the table until the dessert is served.

16. Serve rolls at least twice. Offer them from the left at a convenient height and distance. Plates or baskets of rolls may be placed on the table to be passed by the guests.

17. Refill water glasses as necessary. If the tables are crowded, it may be necessary to remove the glasses from the table to fill them. Handle the glass near the base.

18. Refill coffee cups as necessary. Do not remove cups from table when filling.

19. Ash trays, if placed on tables, should be changed as soon as possible after they have been used. Ash trays should be covered before removing from the table.

20. At the end of the course, remove all dishes and food belonging to that course. Remove dishes from the left of the guest.

21. If the silverware for the dessert was not placed on the table when the table was set, take in on a tray and place at the right of the cover.

22. Serve desserts two at a time and in the same order that the plates were served. When pie is served, place it with the point toward the guest.

23. If possible, the table should be cleared except for decorations before the program begins. The handling of dishes should cease before the start of the program.

Appendix A

Suggested Menu Items .

APPETIZERS

See p. 83.

ENTREES

Meat

Beef

Roast
  Chuck
  Corned beef
  Pot roast
  Ribeye
  Standing rib
  Sauerbraten
  Smoked beef brisket
Steak
  Broiled or grilled
    Club
    Filet mignon
    Sirloin
    T-Bone
  Chicken-fried steak

Country-fried steak
Pepper steak
Spanish steak
Steak teriyaki
Ground beef
  Bacon-wrapped beef
  Cheeseburger pie
  Chuck wagon steak
  Salisbury steak
  Meat loaf
  Meatballs
    Italian
    Swedish
    Spanish
    With spaghetti
  Beef with pasta or rice
  Beef on noodles
  Beef, pork, and
    noodle casserole

Beef stroganoff on
  noodles
Chipped beef and
  noodles
Chop suey on rice
Creole spaghetti
Hungarian goulash
Pasta, beef, and
  tomato casserole
Spaghetti and meat
  balls
Spanish rice
Other beef entrees
  Beef birds
  Beef liver, braised
    Grilled with onions
    With bacon
  Beef pot pie
  Beef stew

With vegetables
With biscuits
Chili con carne
Creamed beef on
  biscuits or baked
  potato
Creamed chipped
  beef on toast or
  baked potato
Kabobs
Lasagne
Pizza
Stir-fried beef
  With broccoli
  With sugar snap
    peas
Stuffed peppers
Taco salad casserole

Veal

Veal birds
Veal cacciatore
Breaded veal cutlets
Veal New Orleans
Veal Parmesan
Veal piccata
Veal scallopine

Lamb

Roast leg of lamb
Broiled lamb chops
Lamb stew
Curried lamb with rice

Pork

Pork chops
  Breaded
  Baked
  Barbecued
  Chili seasoned
  Deviled
  With dressing
  Stuffed
Pork cutlets, breaded
Pork roast, loin
  Garlic and
    peppercorn
  Herbed
  Jeweled
  Teriyaki glazed
  With dressing
Pork roast, fresh ham
Spareribs
  Barbecued
  Sweet-sour
  With dressing
  With sauerkraut
Other pork entrees
  Stir-fried pork
  Sweet and sour pork
  Pork and noodle
    casserole

Pork (cured)
  Bacon
  Frankfurters
    Barbecued
    Cheese-stuffed
  Ham
    Baked glazed
    Grilled slices
    Ham balls
    Ham loaf
    Ham patties
      With cranberries
      With pineapple
    Creamed ham on
      spoonbread or
      biscuits
    Plantation shortcake
    Black beans and
      ham on rice
    Egg foo yung
    Ham and cheese
      quiche
    Scalloped potatoes
      and ham
  Sausage
    Gravy on biscuits
    Patties or links
    With acorn squash
    And egg bake
    Rolls
    Scrapple

Poultry

Chicken (quarters or pieces)

Barbecued
Cantonese
Cacciatore
Fricassee
Fried
  Deep-fat
  Oven-fried
  Pan-fried

Herb baked
Italian baked
Parmesan
Poached
Stewed
  With dumplings
Tahitian

Chicken Breast (grilled or broiled)

Cheese-stuffed
  With tomato basil
    sauce
Curried
Dijon
Herb marinated
Sesame mustard
Tarragon
With tomato sauce

Chicken (using diced meat)

Brunswick stew
Chicken à la king or
  creamed
  On biscuits
  On chow mein
    noodles
  On spoonbread
  In patty shell
Chicken crepes
Chicken pot pie
Chow mein
Hot chicken salad
Chicken and noodles
Chicken rice casserole
Chicken and snow peas
  on rice
Chicken tetrazzini
Chicken and vegetable
  stir-fry
Scalloped chicken
Singapore curry

Spaghetti with chicken
  sauce
Sweet-sour chicken
Szchewan chicken
Cornish game hens,
  orange glazed

Turkey

Roast, with dressing
Steaks, grilled
  Lime tarragon
Scalloped turkey
Turkey à la king
Turkey divan
Turkey with dumplings
Turkey tetrazzini

Fish and Shellfish

Fin Fish

Fillets
  Baked
  Breaded
  Deep-fat fried
  Grilled
  Lemon baked
  Poached
Fillet of sole amandine
Herb marinated fish
  steak
Lemon rice-stuffed cod
Salmon
  Baked (whole)
  Loaf
  Scalloped
Tuna
  À la king
  And noodles
  Scalloped

Shellfish

Deviled crab
Scalloped oysters

Creole shrimp
Oriental shrimp and
    pasta
Pasta with clam sauce
Pasta with shrimp
    sauce
Seafood quiche
Shrimp fried rice
See also Entree Salads

Meatless Entrees

Vegetable

Broccoli and cheese
    casserole
Broccoli rice au gratin
Cheese and broccoli
    strata
Mushroom soufflé
Quiche
  Mushroom
  Spinach
Sicilian rice and
    vegetables
Spinach cheese crepes
Spinach lasagne
Spinach soufflé
Vegetable chow mein
Vegetable stir-fry
Vegetable timbale

Pasta and Rice

Baked ziti with four
    cheeses
Garden pasta
Jalapeño rice
Macaroni and cheese
Pasta primavera
Pasta with vegetable
    sauce
Swiss broccoli pasta
Vegetarian spaghetti

Cheese and Eggs

Cheese balls on
    pineapple slice
Cheese and broccoli
    strata
Cheese soufflé
  With cheese sauce
  With mushroom sauce
Eggs à la king
Goldenrod eggs
Hot stuffed eggs
Nachos
Omelet
  Baked
  Chinese
  Mushroom and
    cheese
  Spanish
Scotch woodcock

Sandwich Entrees

Cold Sandwiches

Bacon, lettuce, tomato
Cheese salad
Chicken salad
Club sandwich
Egg salad
Ham
  With cheese
Ham salad
Sliced turkey
Submarine
Tuna salad
Turkey club hoagy

Hot Sandwiches

Bacon and tomato on
    bun
  With cheese sauce
Beef
  Barbecued

French dip
  Roast beef
Bierocks
Chicken cutlet
Chili dog
Chimichangas
Crab salad
Croissant with sautéed
    garden vegetables
Fajitas
Grilled sandwiches
  Cheese
  Corned beef and
    Swiss on rye
Ham and cheese
Hamburgers
  Barbecued
  With cheese
Hot meat and cheese
Hot tuna grill
Meat loaf
Nacho dog
Patty melt
Roast pork
Tacos
Tuna melt
Turkey, hot
  And Swiss on whole
    wheat
Western

Salad Entrees

Chef's salad bowl
  Seafood chef salad
Chicken or turkey salad
  Crunchy
  Curried
  Fruited
  Mandarin
  And bacon
  With orange-avocado
Chicken and pasta
    salad

Cottage cheese salad
Crab salad
Pasta salad
  Italian pasta salad
Pasta and crab salad
Salad plates
  Chicken and pasta
    salad plate
  Deli plate
  Fruit salad plate
  Marinated chicken
    and fresh fruit
  Shrimp tortellini salad
    plate
  Tuna pasta salad plate
Shrimp salad
  Rice
  Tortellini
Stuffed tomato salad
Taco salad
Tomato cottage cheese
    salad
Tuna salad

ENTREE ACCOMPANIMENTS

Pasta, Rice, and Cereals

Baked cheese grits
Barley casserole
Broccoli and cheese
  casserole
Broccoli rice au gratin
Fettuccine
  With pesto sauce
  Grilled vinaigrette
  Herbed
Noodles
  Buttered
  Romanoff
Pasta wheels with
  vegetables
Rice
  With black-eyed peas
  Buttered
  Curried
  Fried
   With almonds
  Ginger rice stir-fry
  Green
  Mexican
  Pilaf
  Primavera

Silician with
  vegetables
Toasted herb
See also Meatless
  Entrees

Potatoes

White Potatoes

Au gratin
Baked
  With toppings
  French
  Herbed
  Lyonnaise
  Stuffed
Creamed
Croquettes
Duchess
Fried
French fried
Hashed brown
Lyonnaise
Mashed
New potatoes
  Buttered
  Creamed

Creamed with peas
Lemon seasoned
In mustard
Paprika seasoned
Parmesan
O'Brien
Oven-browned
Potato pancakes
  With applesauce
Potato salad, hot or
  cold
Rissole
Romanoff
Rosettes
Scalloped
  With onion
Shoestring
Sour cream

Sweet Potatoes

Baked
Candied or glazed
  With almonds
  With apples
Mashed
Soufflé

Starchy Vegetables

Corn

On the cob
Creamed
O'Brien
Pudding
Scalloped
Succotash

Beans

Baked beans
Lima beans
  Baked
  Seasoned
Ranch style beans
Spicy black beans

Squash

Baked acorn
Mashed butternut or
  hubbard
  With apples
Seasoned spaghetti
  squash

VEGETABLES

Green Vegetables

Asparagus

Seasoned
Creamed
With cheese or
  hollandaise
  sauce
Vinaigrette

Broccoli

Seasoned
  With almonds
  With crumb butter
  With lemon butter
With cheese sauce
With hollandaise sauce

Brussels Sprouts

Seasoned

Cabbage

Seasoned
Au gratin
Hot slaw
Polonaise
Scalloped

Celery

Seasoned
Creamed with almonds

Creole
With carrots amandine

Green Beans

Seasoned
  With almonds
  With dill
  With mushrooms
Casserole
Creole

Herbed
Southern style
Spanish

Peas

Seasoned
  With almonds
  With lemon-mint
    butter
  With mushrooms
With carrots
With cauliflower
With new potatoes
With pearl onions
With turnips

Spinach

Seasoned
  With egg or bacon
Creamed
Soufflé
Wilted

Zucchini

Seasoned
Casserole
  With tomato

Other Vegetables

Beets

Seasoned
  Julienne
Harvard
Hot spiced
  With orange sauce
In sour cream
Pickled

Carrots

Seasoned
  With parsley
Candied or glazed
Mint glazed
Lyonnaise
Marinated
Savory
Sweet-sour
With celery
With peas

Cauliflower

Seasoned
  With almonds
Creamed
French fried
With cheese sauce
With peas

Eggplant

Baked
Creole
French fried
Parmesan
Ratatouille
Sautéed
Tomato bake

Mushrooms

Broiled
French fried
Marinated
Sautéed

Onions

Seasoned
Au gratin
Baked
Casserole
Creamed
French fried

Parsnips

Seasoned
Browned
Glazed
  With carrots

Rutabagas

Seasoned
Mashed
  With potatoes

Summer Squash

Seasoned
With zucchini

Tomatoes

Baked
Broiled
Stewed
Stuffed
  With mushrooms
  With spinach

Turnips

Seasoned
Mashed
With peas
See p. 459 for
  suggested
  combinations for
  stir-fried
  vegetables.

SALADS AND RELISHES

Vegetable Salads

Salad bar
Mixed green
Tossed vegetable
Tossed greens and fruit
Hawaiian tossed
Marinated garden salad
Vegetable collage

Asparagus

Marinated

Beans

Brown been
Garbanzo bean
  With pasta
Triple bean

Cauliflower bean
Oriental bean

Cabbage

Cole slaw
Creamy cole slaw
Green pepper slaw

Carrots

Carrifruit
Carrot celery
Carrot raisin
Marinated carrots

Cauliflower

Cauliflower-broccoli
Creamy cauliflower

Cucumbers

Sliced cucumbers and
    onions
German cucumbers

Green Beans

Marinated green beans

Potatoes

Potato salad
Sour cream potato
    salad
Hot potato salad

Spinach

Spinach-cheese
Spinach-mushroom

Tomatoes

Marinated
Sliced

Fruit Salads

Acini de pepe
Ambrosia fruit
Waldorf

Apple-cabbage
Apple-carrot
Spiced apple
Grapefruit orange
    With apple
    With avocado
Frozen fruit
Tossed greens with
    fruit

Gelatin Salads

Perfection
Tomato aspic
Applesauce
Apple cinnamon swirl
Arabian peach
Autumn salad
Blueberry
Boysenberry mold
Cranberry apple
Cranberry mold
Cucumber soufflé
Frosted cherry
Frosted lime
Jellied Waldorf
Lemon cream
Pineapple cheese
Ribbon gelatin
Sunshine

Swedish green top
Under-the-sea

Pasta and Rice Salads

Garbanzo and pasta
Dilled rice
Macaroni
Italian pasta
See also Salad Entrees

Relishes

Fruit

Buttered apples
Cantaloupe or
    watermelon chunks
Cranberry relish
Cranberry sauce
  Baked
Grapes, green or red
Pineapple, broiled
  Spears
Spiced fruit
  Apples
  Crabapples
  Pears
  Peaches

Vegetables

Broccoli florets
Carrot curls or sticks
Marinated carrots
Cauliflower florets
Celery sticks
Stuffed celery
Cherry tomatoes
Green pepper rings or
    sticks
Marinated mushrooms
Radishes
Tomato slices or
    wedges
Turnip sticks or slices
Zucchini sticks or slices

Miscellaneous

Olives, green, ripe,
    stuffed
Pickles
  Beet
  Corn relish
  Dill
  Sweet
  Watermelon

SOUPS

Stock Soups

Beef alphabet
Beef barley
Beef noodle
Beef rice
Creole beef
French onion
Hearty beef vegetable

Mexican beef
Minestrone
Vegetable beef
  Julienne
Vegetable
Brunswick stew
Chicken bouillon
Chicken gumbo
Chicken noodle

Chicken rice
Chicken with spaetzle
Pepper pot
Turkey vegetable
Tomato barley
Tomato bouillon
Tomato rice
Manhattan clam or fish
    chowder

Cream Soups

Broccoli cheese soup
Cheese soup
Chicken velvet
Cream of:
  Asparagus
  Broccoli
  Cauliflower

Celery
Chicken
Mushroom
Mushroom barley
Potato
Spinach
Tomato
Vegetable

Chowders

Clam (New England)
Corn
Fish
Potato
Vegetable
Oyster stew

Bean and Lentil Soups

Black bean
Navy bean
Chili con carne
  Chili spaghetti
  Garden chili
  White chili

Lentil soup
Split pea soup

Chilled Soups

Gazpacho
Vichyssoise

DESSERTS

Cakes

Angel food
  Chocolate
  Frozen filled
  Yellow
Chiffon
  Cocoa
  Orange
  Walnut
Cupcakes
White, with variations
Yellow, with variations
Applesauce
Banana
Boston cream pie
Burnt sugar
Carrot
Chocolate
Coconut lime
Dutch apple
Fruit cake
Fudge
German chocolate
Lady Baltimore
Lazy daisy
Marble
Pineapple cashew
Pineapple upside-down
Poppy seed
Pound cake

Praline
Pumpkin
Jelly roll
Chocolate roll
Ice cream roll
Pumpkin cake roll
Gingerbread

Cookies

Drop Cookies

Butterscotch
Butterscotch pecan
Chocolate
Coconut macaroons
Chocolate chip
Jumbo chunk chocolate
Molasses
Oatmeal
Peanut butter
Peanut
Snickerdoodles
Sugar
Whole wheat sugar

Bar Cookies

Brownies
Butterscotch squares
Coconut pecan bars
Date bars

Dreamland bars
Oatmeal date bars
Marshmallow krispie
  squares

Pressed, Molded, and Rolled Cookies

Butterscotch
  refrigerator cookies
Butter tea cookies
Chocolate tea cookies
Christmas wreath
  cookies
Coconut cookies
Crisp ginger cookies
Filled cookies
Frosty date balls
Oatmeal crispies
Pinwheel cookies
Rolled sugar cookies
Sandies
Thimble cookies

Pies

Fruit Pies

Apple
  Crumb
  Sour cream
Apricot

Berry
Cherry
Gooseberry
Peach
Pineapple
Raisin
Rhubarb
  Custard

Soft Pies

Chiffon
  Chocolate
  Lemon
  Strawberry
Cream
  Banana
  Butterscotch
  Chocolate
  Coconut
  Date
  Fruit-glazed
  Nut cream
  Pineapple
Custard
  Coconut
Frozen mocha almond
Ice cream
Lemon
Pumpkin
  Praline

Pecan
  Cream cheese

Frozen Desserts

Sundaes and Parfaits

Caramel sundae
Hot fudge sundae
Peanut butter sundae
Strawberry sundae
Chocolate parfait
Strawberry parfait

Ice Cream

Butter brickle
Chocolate
Chocolate chip
Chocolate almond
Coffee
Lemon custard
Peach

Pecan
Peppermint
Pistachio
Strawberry
Toffee
Vanilla
Frozen yogurt

Sherbet

Cranberry
Lemon
Lime
Orange
Pineapple
Raspberry

Puddings and Other Desserts

Cream puddings
  Banana

Butterscotch
Chocolate
Coconut
Pineapple
Tapioca
Vanilla
Custard, baked
  Caramel
  Rice
  Bread pudding
  Floating island
Baked date pudding
Lemon cake pudding
Christmas pudding
  (steamed)
Cream puffs
Eclairs
Ice cream puff
Orange cream puffs
  with chocolate
  filling
Baked apples

Apple dumplings
Apple crisp
Fruit crisp
Fruit cobbler
  Apple
  Apricot
  Cherry
  Peach
  Plum
Fruit and cheese
Strawberry shortcake
Bavarian creams
  Apricot
  Pineapple
  Strawberry
Russian cream
Cheese cake
  With fruit glaze

GARNISHES

Yellow-Orange

Cheese and Eggs

Cheese, grated, strips
Egg, hard-cooked or
  sections
Deviled egg halves
Riced egg yolk

Fruit

Apricot halves
Cantaloupe balls
Lemon wedges, slices
Orange sections, slices
Peach slices
Peach halves with jelly
Spiced peaches

Vegetables

Carrots, rings,
  shredded, strips
Banana peppers

Sweets

Peanut brittle, crushed
Sugar, yellow or orange

Miscellaneous

Coconut, tinted

Flowers

Daisies
Dandelion

Marigold
Nasturtium
Pansies
Rose petals
Snapdragons
Squashblossoms

Red

Fruit

Cherries
Cinnamon apples
Cranberries
Plums
Pomegranate seeds
Red raspberries
Maraschino cherries

Strawberries
Watermelon cubes,
  balls

Vegetables

Beets, pickled, julienne
Beet relish
Red cabbage
Red peppers, rings,
  strips, shredded
Pimiento, chopped,
  strips
Red radishes, sliced,
  roses
Cherry tomatoes
Tomato wedges, slices,
  broiled

Sweets

Red jelly: currant,
cherry, loganberry,
raspberry
Red sugar

Miscellaneous

Paprika
Tinted coconut
Stuffed olives
Cinnamon drops (red
hots)

Flowers

Geranium
Rose petals

Green

Fruit

Avocado
Frosted grapes
Green plums
Honeydew melon
Kiwi fruit
Lime slices or wedges
Maraschino cherries
Mint jelly

Vegetables

Broccoli florets
Celery
Endive

Green pepper strips,
chopped
Green onions
Lettuce cups
Lettuce, shredded
Mint leaves
Parsley, sprig, chopped
Spinach leaves
Watercress
Zucchini sticks, slices

Miscellaneous

Capers
Coconut, tinted
Olives
Pickles, burr gherkins,
strips, fans, rings
Sunflower seeds
Pistachios

White

Fruit

Apple rings
Grapefruit sections

Vegetables

Cauliflower florets
Celery cabbage
Celery curls, hearts,
strips
Cucumber rings, strips,
wedges, cups

Mashed potato rosettes
Onion rings
Onions, pickled
White radishes

Miscellaneous

Almonds
Popcorn
Sliced hard-cooked egg
white
Parmesan cheese
Shredded coconut
Marshmallows
Powdered sugar
Whipped cream

Flowers

Daisies
Geranium
Pansies
Rose petals
Violets

Brown/Tan

Breads

Croustades
Croutons

Miscellaneous

Chocolate, shredded or
shaved
Cinnamon

Dates
French-fried
cauliflower
Mushrooms
Nutmeats
Nut-covered cheese
balls
Potato chips
Toasted coconut

Flowers

Pansies

Black

Caviar
Prunes
Spiced prunes
Raisins, currants
Ripe olives
Rye croutons
Truffles

Blue/Purple

Chive flowers
Chrysanthemum
Pansies
Violets

Appendix B

Use of Herbs and Spices in Cooking ▪

Herb or Spice	Use	Equivalents (tsp per oz)
Allspice, ground or whole	Pot roast, baked products, fruits, puddings, squash, sweet potatoes	14.9
Anise seed	Cookies, cakes, poultry	13.5
Basil, ground	Roasted meat and poultry, stews, fish, pasta, green salads, salad dressings, vegetables	20.2
Bay leaf	Beef, fish, chicken, soups, stews, marinades	47.2 (crumbled)
Caraway seed	Rye bread, apples, beets, cabbage, cheese spreads	13.5
Cardamom, ground	Coffee cakes, Danish pastry, curries, soups	14.2
Cayenne (red) pepper	Meats, fish, sauces, Mexican dishes	15.7
Celery salt, seeds, flakes	Meat, poultry, eggs, soups, salads (if celery salt is used, reduce amount of salt in recipe)	14.2 (seed)
Chervil, dried	Salads, sauces, eggs, stuffings	47.2
Chili powder	Chili, Mexican dishes, eggs, meat sauces, dips	10.9
Cilantro	Guacamole, chili, dips, salsa	47.2
Cinnamon, ground	Baked products, apples, peaches, beverages, squash	12.3
Cloves, ground	Pork, lamb, marinades, squash, sweet potatoes	13.5
Cloves, whole	To stud ham, fruit, glazed pork, or onions	
Coriander seed, whole, ground	Curries, baked products	15.7
Cumin seed	Chili, curries, stews	13.5
Cumin, ground	Chili, curries, stews	12.6
Curry powder	Chicken, lamb, pork, fish, eggs, rice	14.2
Dill seed	Meat, fish, sauces, salads	13.5
Dill weed	Salads, fish, sandwich fillings	28.3
Fennel seed	Italian and Swedish cookery	14.2

Herb or Spice	Use	Equivalents (tsp per oz)
Ginger, ground	Meats, fish, poultry, baked goods, carrots, sweet potatoes	15.7
Mace, ground	Meats, poultry, fish, baked products	16.7
Marjoram, dried	Meats, poultry, fish, soups, stews, tomato dishes, vegetables	47.2
Mint leaves	Lamb, veal, iced tea, sauces, carrots, peas	
Mustard, ground	Meat, poultry, eggs, cheese, salad dressings, sauces	
Mustard seed, yellow	Pickles, cooked beets, cabbage, or sauerkraut	8.6
Nutmeg, ground	Meatballs, veal, chicken, seafood, baked products, carrots, spinach, sweet potatoes, eggnog, custards	12.9
Oregano, ground	Meat, poultry, seafood, eggs, cheese, soups, stews, pizza, chili, pasta sauces, barbecue sauce, tomatoes, green beans, zucchini	18.9
Oregano, leaf	see Oregano, ground	48.9
Paprika	Veal, chicken, fish, salad dressings, garnish	13.5
Parsley flakes	Meat, poultry, fish, soups, eggs, cheese	94.5
Pepper, black	Meat, vegetables, sauces	13.5
Pepper, red (cayenne)	Meats, fish, sauces, Mexican dishes	15.7
Pepper, white	Meat, vegetables, sauces	11.8
Poppy seed	Cakes, cookies, bread toppings, fruit salad dressing, sprinkled on noodles, sweet roll fillings	10.1
Poultry seasoning	Poultry, meat, and fish stuffings, meat loaf	18.9
Pumpkin pie spice	Sweet baked goods, mashed root vegetables	16.7
Rosemary, dried	Roasted meat and poultry, baked or broiled fish, eggs, soups, stews, vegetables	23.6
Saffron	Veal, poultry, rice, soups	40.5
Sage, leaf, or ground	Meats, poultry, stuffings, chowders	40.5 (ground)
Savory, ground	Meats, poultry, fish, eggs, soups, stews, green vegetable salads, rice	20.2
Sesame seed	Bread, rolls, salads, Asian cooking	10.5
Tarragon, ground	Poultry, seafood, eggs, tomatoes, green salads, salad dressings	17.7
Thyme, ground	Meat, poultry, fish, eggs, soups, stews, vegetables	20.2
Turmeric, ground	Ingredient of curry powder, coloring for condiments	12.9

Notes

- Spices should be stored in cool (68°F) and dry (humidity 60% or less) environment. Cold storage (32°–45°F) is recommended for paprika, red pepper, chili powder, allspice, cloves, parsley flakes, dill, marjoram, and cumin. Generally, spices should not be held for longer than three months. All spices should be kept tightly closed and measured with dry utensils and away from steam.

- Spices and herbs can be creatively combined to enhance the flavor of foods. The art of skillfully adding the right amount of seasonings is basic to successful cookery. Both low-sodium and low-calorie foods can be made more interesting by the addition of spices and herbs. Experimentation, using this chart, may add to patron satisfaction.

Glossary of Menu and Cooking Terms .

à la (ah lah) French In the manner of.

à la carte (ah lah cart′) French On the menu, but not part of a meal, usually prepared as ordered and individually priced.

à la king French Served in cream sauce containing green pepper, pimiento, and mushrooms.

à la mode (ah lah mohd′) French When applied to desserts, means with ice cream. *À la mode, boeuf,* a well-larded piece of beef cooked slowly in water with vegetables, similar to braised beef.

al dente (al den′ tay) Italian The point in cooking pasta at which it is still fairly firm to the bite. The term is sometimes used interchangeably with tender crisp when referring to vegetables.

allemande (ahl mahnd′) French A smooth yellow sauce consisting of white sauce with the addition of cream, egg yolk, and lemon juice.

amandine Served with almonds.

antipasto (ahn tee pahs′ toe) Italian Appetizer; a course consisting of relishes, vegetables, fish, or cold cuts.

AP As purchased weight. The weight of an item before trimming or other preparation (as opposed to edible portion weight, or EP).

arroz (ah ros′) The Spanish/American word for rice.

aspic A jellied meat juice or liquid held together with gelatin.

au gratin (oh grah′ ton) French Made with crumbs, scalloped. Often refers to dishes made with cheese sauce.

au jus (oh zhu′) French Meat served in its natural juices or gravy.

bake To cook in the oven by dry heat.

barbecue To cook on a grill or spit over hot coals, or in an oven, basting intermittently with a highly seasoned sauce.

bar-le-duc (bahr luh dük′) French A preserve made of currants and honey. It frequently forms a part of the cheese course.

baron Double sirloin of beef.

baste To moisten meat while roasting to add flavor and to prevent drying of the surface. Melted fat or meat drippings may be used for basting.

batch cooking Dividing the estimated amount needed into smaller quantities and cooking as required to meet the demand.

batter Flour and liquid mixture, usually combined with other ingredients, thin enough to pour or drop from a spoon.

béarnaise (bay ar nayz') French Sauce of clarified butter, egg yolks, vinegar, onion, and spices.

beat To mix ingredients with a rotating motion, using spoon, wire whip, or paddle attachment to mixer.

béchamel (bay sha mel') French A cream sauce made with equal parts of chicken stock and cream or milk.

beurre (buhr) French Butter. *Au beurre noire* (oh buhr nwor), with butter sauce browned in a pan. *Beurre manie* (buhr mah nee), French. Well-blended mixture of butter and flour used to thicken hot soups and sauces.

bisque (bisk) French A thick soup usually made from fish or shellfish. Also a frozen dessert. Sometimes defined as ice cream to which finely chopped nuts are added.

blanch To dip briefly in boiling water.

blanquette (blang ket') French A white stew usually made with veal, lamb, or chicken.

blend To thoroughly mix two or more ingredients.

bleu (bluh) French Blue.

boeuf (buff) French Beef. *Boeuf à la jardinière* (buff a lah zhar de nyoyr), braised beef with vegetables; *boeuf roti* (buff rotee), roast beef.

boil To cook foods in water or a liquid in which the bubbles are breaking on the surface and steam is given off.

bombe (bahm) French A frozen dessert made of a combination of two or more frozen mixtures packed in a round or melon-shaped mold.

bordelaise (bor d'layz') French Of Bordeaux. *Sauce bordelaise,* a sauce with Bordeaux wine as its foundation, with various seasonings added.

borscht (borscht) Russian A soup made with beets and served with thick sour cream.

bouillabaisse (boo yah bes') French A highly seasoned fish soup made with two or more kinds of fish.

bouillon (boo yon') French Clear meat stock.

bouquet (boo kay') Volatile oils that give aroma.

bouquet garni (boo kay' garnee') French Herbs and spices tied in a cloth bag, used for flavoring soups, stews, and sauces, then removed after cooking is completed.

bourguignon (bohr ghee n'yang') French In the Burgundy style, especially a beef stew made with red wine (for which Burgundy is noted), mushrooms, salt pork, and onions.

braise (brays) French To brown in a small amount of fat, cover, add a small amount of liquid, and cook slowly.

bread To coat food with an egg-milk mixture and then bread crumbs before frying.

brew To cook in liquid to extract flavor, as with beverages.

brioche (bree ohsh') French A slightly sweetened rich bread used for rolls or babas.

brochette, à la (bro shet') French Food arranged on a skewer and broiled.

broil To cook over or under direct heat, as in a broiler or over live coals.

broth   A flavorful liquid obtained from the simmering of meats and/or vegetables.

brunoise   (broo noyz) French   Finely diced (⅛ inch) vegetables, such as celery, carrots, leeks, and turnips for soups and sauces.

buffet   (boo fay′) French   A table displaying a variety of foods.

cacciatore   (ca chi a tor′ ee) Italian   Stewed with tomatoes, onion, and garlic.

café au lait   (ca fay′ oh lay′) French   Coffee with hot milk.

café noir   (ca fay′ nwar) French   Black coffee, after-dinner coffee.

canapé   (can ah pay′) French   An appetizer of meat, fish, egg, or cheese arranged on a bread base.

candy   To preserve or cook with heavy syrup.

caper   (kay′ per)   Small pickled bud from wild caper bush; used in salads and sauces.

caramelize   To heat sugar until a brown color and a characteristic flavor develops.

carte au jour   (kart o zhur′) French   Bill of fare or menu for the day.

caviar   (cav ee ar′) French   Salted roe of sturgeon or other large fish. May be black or red.

chantilly   (shang te′ ye) French   Foods containing whipped cream.

charlotte   (shar′ lot) French   Dessert with gelatin, whipped cream, fruit, or other flavoring, in a mold, garnished with lady fingers.

chiffonade   (shee′ fahn ahd) French   With minced or shredded vegetables, as in salad dressing.

chill   To refrigerate until thoroughly cold.

chop   To cut food into fairly fine pieces with a knife or other chopping device.

choux paste   (shoo paste) French   Cream puff batter.

chowder   A thick soup of fish or vegetables and milk.

chutney   (chut′ ni)   A spicy relish made from several fruits and vegetables.

cilantro   The pungent leaf of the coriander plant, also known as *Chinese parsley*. Used to season Oriental and Mexican foods.

clarified butter   Melted butter from which the milk and water have been removed leaving pure butterfat. Clarification raises the smoke point of butter.

clarify   Make clear by skimming or adding egg white and straining.

cloche   (klosh) French   Bell, dish cover. *Sous cloche* (soo klosh), under cover.

coat   To cover entire surface with flour, fine crumbs, sauce, batter, or other food as required.

cocktail   An appetizer, either a beverage or a light, highly seasoned food, served before a meal.

coddle   To simmer gently in liquid for a short time.

compote   (kom′ poht) French   Mixed fruit, either raw or stewed in syrup; a stemmed serving dish.

condiment   An aromatic mixture, such as pickles, chutney and some sauces and relishes, that accompanies food.

convection   A method of heat transfer in which heat is transmitted through the circulation of air.

converted (parboiled) rice   A specially processed long grain rice that has been partially cooked under steam pressure, redried, then milled and polished.

consommé   (kon so may′) French   A clear broth that has been clarified, usually made from two or three kinds of meat.

court bouillon (cor boo yon′) French Seasoned broth in which fish, meat, or vegetables are cooked.

couscous Pellets of semolina usually cooked by steaming.

cream To mix fat and sugar until soft and creamy.

creole (kre′ ohl) French Foods containing meat or vegetables with tomatoes, peppers, onions, and other seasonings.

crepe (krayp) French Thin, delicate pancake, often rolled and stuffed, served as appetizer, entree or dessert. *Crepe suzette,* a small, very thin and crisp pancake served for tea or as dessert.

crisp To make foods firm and brittle, as in chilling vegetables or heating cereals or crackers in the oven to remove excessive moisture.

croissant (krwa sang′) French Crescent; applied to rolls and confectionary of crescent shape.

croquette (crow ket′) Mixture of chopped, cooked meat, poultry, fish, or vegetables bound with thick cream sauce, shaped, breaded, and fried.

croustade (krus tad′) A toasted case or shell of bread.

croutons (kroo tons′) Bread cubes, toasted, for use in garnishing soups and salads.

crudités (croo dee tays′) French Raw vegetables.

cube To cut into ½-inch squares.

curry (kur′ ee) Highly spiced condiment from India; a stew seasoned with curry.

cut in To cut a solid fat into flour with knives or mixer until fat particles are of desired size.

cutlet Thin slice of meat, usually breaded, for frying; also croquette mixture made in a flat shape.

deep fry To cook in fat deep enough for food to float.

deglaze To dilute and wash down pan juices by adding liquid.

de la maison (de lah may zon′) French Specialty of the house.

demitasse (deh mee tahss′) French Small cup of black coffee served after dinner.

dice To cut into ¼-inch cubes.

dot To scatter small bits of butter or margarine over surface of food.

dough A mixture of flour, liquid, and other ingredients, thick enough to roll or knead.

drawn butter Melted butter.

dredge To thoroughly coat a food with flour or other fine substance.

drippings Fat and liquid residue from frying or roasting meat or poultry.

du jour (doo zhoor′) French Of the day, such as soup of the day.

dust To sprinkle lightly with flour.

eau (oh) French Water.

eclair (ay klair′) French Finger-shaped cream puff pastry filled with whipped cream or custard.

egg and crumb To dip a food into diluted, slightly beaten egg and dredge with crumbs. This treatment is used to prevent soaking of the food with fat or to form a surface easily browned.

emulsion A mixture of two or more liquids, one of which is a fat or oil and the other is water-based, so that tiny globules of one are suspended in the other. Emulsions may be temporary, permanent, or semipermanent.

enchilada (en chee lah′ dah) Mexican Tortillas filled and rolled, served with sauce.

en cocotte (ahn ko cot′) French   In individual casserole.

entree (ahn′ tray) French   The main course of a meal or a single dish served before the main course of an elaborate meal.

EP   Edible portion. The weight of an item after trimming and preparation (as opposed to AP weight, or as purchased weight).

espagnole (ays pah nyol′) French   Brown sauce.

farci (far′ see) French   Stuffed.

fermentation   The breakdown of carbohydrates into carbon dioxide gas and alcohol, usually through the action of yeast on sugar.

filet or fillet (fee lay′) French   A boneless cut of meat, fish or poultry.

fines herbes (fen zerb′) French   A mixture of herbs, usually parsley, chervil, tarragon, and chives.

flake   To break into small pieces, usually with a fork.

flan   In France, a filled pastry; in Spain, a custard.

flambé (flam bay′) French   To flame, using alcohol as the burning agent.

florentine   A food containing or placed upon spinach.

fold in   To blend ingredient into a batter by cutting vertically through the mixture, and turning over and over by sliding the implement across the bottom of the mixing bowl with each turn.

frappé (fra pay′) French   Mixture of fruit juices frozen to a mush.

french fry   To cook in deep fat.

fricassee (frik a see′)   To cook by browning in a small amount of fat, then stewing or steaming; most often applied to fowl or veal cut into pieces.

frijoles (free hol′ ays) Mexican   Beans cooked with fat and seasonings.

fritter   A deep-fat fried batter containing meat, vegetables, or fruit.

frizzle   To pan fry in a small amount of fat until edges curl.

froid (frwä) French   Cold.

fry   To cook in hot fat. The food may be cooked in a small amount of fat (also called *sauté* or *pan fry*), or in a deep layer of fat (also called *deep-fat fry*).

garde-manger (garhd e mah zha′) French   Pantry chef/station. Responsible for cold food preparation.

garni (garnee′) French   Garnished. Garnish. An edible decoration or accompaniment to a food item.

gelatinization   A phase in the process of thickening a liquid with starch in which starch molecules swell to form a network that traps water molecules.

glacé (glah say′) French   Iced, frozen, or coated with sugar syrup.

glaze   To make a shiny surface. In meat preparation, a jellied broth applied to meat surface; in breads and pastries, a wash of egg or syrup; for doughnuts and cakes, a coating with a sugar preparation.

gluten   An elastic protein formed when hard wheat flour is moistened and agitated. Gluten gives yeast doughs their elasticity.

goulash (goo′ lash) Hungarian   Thick beef or veal stew with vegetables and seasoned with paprika.

grand sauce   One of several basic sauces that are used in the preparation of many other small sauces. The grand sauces are: demi-glace, veloute, béchamel, hollandaise, and tomato. Also called mother sauce.

grate   To rub food against grater to form small particles.

gratinée   (grah teen ay') French   To brown a food sprinkled with cheese or bread crumbs; or a food covered with a sauce that turns brown under a broiler flame or intense oven heat.

grease   To rub lightly with fat.

griddle   A heavy metal surface, which may be either built into a stove or heated by its own gas or electric elements. Cooking is done directly on the griddle.

grill   To cook by direct heat. May be open grid over a heat source or on a flat cooking surface such as a griddle.

grind   To change a food to small particles by putting through grinder or food chopper.

grits   Coarsely ground corn, served either boiled or boiled and then fried.

gumbo   A rich, thick Creole soup containing okra or filé.

herbs   Aromatic plants used for seasoning and garnishing of foods.

hollandaise   (hol' ahn days) French, of Dutch origin   Sauce of eggs, butter, lemon juice, and seasonings; served hot with fish or vegetables.

hors d'oeuvre   (oh durv') French   Small portions of food served as appetizers.

infusion   To steep an aromatic or other item in liquid to extract the flavor.

IQF   Terminology for Individually Quick Frozen.

Italienne   (e tal yen') French   Italian style.

jalapeño   A hot pepper used for seasoning Mexican food.

jardinière   (zhar de nyayr') French   Mixed vegetables in a savory sauce or soup.

jicama   Tuberous root used in salads.

julienne   (zhu lee en') French   Vegetables or other foods cut into fine strips or shreds.

jus   (zhoo) French   Juice or gravy.

kebobs   Marinated meat and vegetables cooked on skewers.

kippered   Lightly salted and smoked fish.

knead   To work dough with a pressing motion accompanied by folding and stretching.

kolach   (ko' lahch) Bohemian   Fruit-filled bun.

kosher   (ko' sher)   Food handled in accordance with the Jewish religious customs.

kuchen   (koo' ken) German   Cake, not necessarily sweet.

lait   (lay) French   Milk.

lard   To insert small strips of fat into or on top of uncooked lean meat or fish to give flavor or prevent dryness.

lebkuchen   (lab koo' ckhen) German   Famous German cake; sweet cake or honey cake.

leek   Seasoning vegetable resembling a large spring onion with wide leaves, always cooked.

legumes   The seeds of certain plants, including beans and peas, which are eaten for their earthy flavor and high nutritional value.

limpa   Swedish rye bread.

lox   Yiddish   Smoked salmon.

lyonnaise   (lee' oh nayz) French   Seasoned with onions and parsley, as lyonnaise potatoes.

macédoine   (mah say dwan') French   Mixture or medley of cut vegetables or fruits cut in uniform pieces.

maître d'hôtel   (mai tre doh tel′) French   Steward. *Maître d'hôtel butter,* a well-seasoned mixture of butter, minced parsley, and lemon juice.

marinade   (mah ree nahd′) French   Mixture of oil, acid, and seasonings used to flavor and tenderize meats and vegetables; French dressings often used as marinades.

marinate   To steep a food in a marinade long enough to modify its flavor.

marzipan   (mahr′ zi pan)   Powdered sugar and almond paste colored and formed into fruit and vegetable shapes.

mask   To coat a food with a thick sauce before it is served. Cold foods may be masked with a mayonnaise mixture or white sauce, which gels after chilling.

melt   To liquify by the application of heat.

meringue   (mah rang′)   Stiffly beaten egg white and sugar mixture used as a topping for pies or other desserts; or formed into small cakes or cases and browned in the oven.

meunière, à la   (meh nyair′) French   Floured, sautéed in butter and served with butter sauce and lemon and sprinkled with chopped parsley; usually refers to fish.

Milanaise   (me lan ayz′) French   Food cooked in a style developed in Milan, Italy. Implies the use of pasta and cheese with a suitable sauce, often béchamel.

mince   To chop food into very small pieces—not so fine and regular as grinding, yet finer than those produced by chopping.

minestrone   (mee ne stroh′ nay) Italian   Thick vegetable soup with beans and pasta.

mirepoix   (meer′ pwa) French   Mixture of chopped vegetables used in flavoring soup stock, usually 25% carrots, 50% onions, and 25% celery.

mise en place   (meez on plahss′) French   The preparation, organization and setup before production. Term means "everything in place."

mix   To combine two or more ingredients by stirring.

mocha   (moh′ ka)   Coffee flavor or combination of coffee and chocolate.

monosodium glutamate (MSG)   White crystalline material made from vegetable protein, used to enhance natural flavor of food.

Mornay   (mohr nay′) French   Sauce of thick cream, eggs, cheese, and seasonings.

mousse   (moose) French   Frozen dessert with fruit or other flavors, whipped cream and sugar; also a cold dish of pureed chicken or fish with egg whites, gelatin, and unsweetened whipped cream.

mulligatawny   (mul i ga taw′ ni)   A highly seasoned thick soup, of Indian origin, flavored with curry powder and other spices.

napoleons   Puff pastry kept together in layers with a custard filling, cut into portion-size rectangles, and iced.

Neopolitan   (also *harlequin* and *panachée*) Molded dessert of two to four kinds of ice cream or ices arranged in layers.

Nesselrode pudding   Frozen dessert with a custard foundation to which chestnut puree, fruit, and cream have been added.

Newburg, à la   Creamed dish with egg yolk added, flavored with sherry; most often applied to lobster, but may be used with other foods.

noisette   (nooa zet′) French   Nut-brown color; may imply nut-shaped. A small round piece of lean meat. *Potatoes noisette,* potatoes cut into the shape and size of hazelnuts and browned in fat.

oeuf   (oof) French   Egg.

oven spring   The rapid initial rise of yeast dough when placed in a hot oven. Heat accelerates the growth of the yeast, which produces more carbon dioxide gas and also causes this gas to expand.

paella (pä ay′ yah) Spanish   Dish with rice, seafood, chicken, and vegetables, usually served in a wide shallow pan in which it is cooked.

pan broil To cook, uncovered, on hot metal, such as a fry pan, pouring off the fat as it accumulates. Liquid is never added.

pan fry To cook in a skillet in a small amount of fat.

papillote (pah pe yote′) French   Meat, chicken, or fish cooked in a closed paper container.

parboil To boil until partially cooked, the cooking being completed by another method.

parch To cook in dry heat until slightly browned.

parchment Heat-resistant paper used in cooking for lining baking pans.

pare To cut off the outside covering, usually with a knife.

parfait (par fay′) French   A mixture containing whipped cream, egg, and syrup that is frozen without stirring. May be ice cream layered with fruit or syrup in parfait glasses.

parmigiana (par mee zhan′ ah) Italian   Parma style, particularly veal, chicken, or eggplant covered with tomato sauce, mozzarella cheese, and Parmesan cheese and browned under the broiler or in the oven.

pasta Italian   Any of a large family of flour paste products, such as macaroni, spaghetti, and noodles.

paste Soft, smooth mixture of a dry ingredient and a liquid.

pastrami (pahs tram′ ee) Yiddish   Boneless meat cured with spices and smoked.

pâté (pah tay′) French   Paste, dough; highly seasoned meat paste used as an appetizer.

pâté de foie gras (pah tay d′fwah grah′) French   Paste of fat goose livers.

patty shell Shell or case of pastry or puff paste used for individual portions of creamed mixtures.

peel To strip off the outside covering.

persillade (payr se yad′) French   Served with or containing parsley.

pesto Italian   A thick pureed mixture of an herb, usually basil, and oil used as a sauce for pasta. May also contain pine nuts, grated cheese, garlic and other seasonings.

petit pois (puh tee pooá) French   A fine grade of very small peas with a delicate flavor.

petits fours (pe teet foor′) French   Small fancy cakes frosted and decorated.

phyllo dough Greek   Extremely thin pastry dough that produces a flaky pastry.

picante A highly spiced tomato sauce used as a condiment with Mexican foods.

pilaf or **pilau** (pih lahf or pih low) Turkish   Dish of rice cooked with meat, fish, or poultry, and seasoned with spices. A technique for cooking grains, in which the grain is sautéed briefly in butter, then simmered in stock or water with various seasonings.

piquant (pee kahnt′) French   Sharp, highly seasoned.

pizza (peet′ zah) Italian   Flat yeast bread covered with tomato, cheese, and meat, or other toppings.

plank Hardwood board used for cooking and serving broiled meat or fish. *Planked steak,* a broiled steak served on a plank and garnished with a border of suitable vegetables.

poach To cook gently in a hot liquid, held just below the boiling point, the original shape of the food being retained.

polenta (poh lent' ah) Italian   Thick cornmeal mush; cheese is usually added before serving.

pollo (po' yo) Italian   Italian and Spanish/American term for chicken.

polonaise (po lo nays') French   Dishes prepared with bread crumbs, chopped eggs, browned butter, and chopped parsley.

pomme de terre (pom de tare') French   Potato; literally, apple of the earth.

pot-au-feu (poh toh fu') French   Meat and vegetables boiled together in broth.

pot roast   To cook large cuts of meat by braising.

potage (po tazh') French   Soup, usually of a thick type.

prawn   Large shrimp.

preheat   To heat oven or other cooking equipment to desired temperature before putting in the food.

proof   To allow yeast dough to rise.

prosciutto (pro shoot' toh) Italian   Ham, usually thinly sliced and served as an appetizer or as a component in veal dishes.

puff paste   Rich dough, made flaky by repeated folding and rolling.

pulse   The edible seeds of various leguminous crops (peas, beans, lentils).

puree (pu ray') French   Foods rubbed through a sieve; also a nutritious vegetable soup in which milk or cream is seldom used.

quiche (keesh)   Custard, cheese, and seasonings baked in a pie shell and served warm.

ragout (ra goo') French   A thick, well-seasoned stew containing meat.

ramekin (ram' e kin)   Small baking dish for individual portions.

rarebit   Mixture of white sauce, cheese, and seasonings.

ravioli (rav vee oh' lee) Italian   Bite-sized cases of pasta dough filled with finely ground meat, cheese, and spinach; served with a highly seasoned tomato sauce.

reconstitute   To restore concentrated foods to their normal state, usually by adding water, as in fruit juice and milk.

reduce   To boil down, evaporating liquid from a cooked dish.

refritos   Twice-cooked Mexican beans that are boiled once and fried once. Also called *refried beans*.

rehydrate   To cook or soak dehydrated foods or restore water lost during drying.

remoulade (ray moo lad') French   Pungent sauce made of hard-cooked eggs, mustard, oil, vinegar, and seasonings. Served with cold dishes.

risotto (ri sot' toh) Italian   Rice that has been sautéed with onion and other aromatics and then combined with stock. Adding stock slowly while stirring produces a creamy texture with the rice grains still al dente.

rissolé (ree sall') French   Savory meat mixture encased in rich pastry and fried in deep fat.

roast   To cook uncovered in oven by dry heat, usually meat or poultry.

roe   Eggs of fish.

rosette (roh zet') French   Thin, rich batter made into fancy shape with special iron and fried in deep fat.

roulade (roo lahd') French   Rolled thin piece of meat, usually stuffed and roasted or braised.

roux (roo) French   Browned flour and fat used for thickening sauces, stews, and soups.

sabayon (sa by on') French   Custard sauce with wine added.

salsa   A highly spiced tomato sauce used as a condiment with Mexican foods.

sauerbraten (sour brah' ten) German   Beef marinated in spiced vinegar, pot-roasted, and served with gingersnap gravy.

sauté (soh tay') French   To cook in a small amount of fat.

savory   Not sweet. Also a family of herbs.

scald   To heat a liquid to a point just below boiling; pour boiling water over or dip food briefly into boiling water.

scallion   An onion that has not developed a bulb.

scallop   To bake food, cut into pieces and cover with a liquid or sauce and crumbs. The food and sauce may be mixed together or arranged in alternate layers in a baking dish, with or without crumbs. *Escalloped* is a synonymous term.

scallopine (skol a pee' nee) Italian   Small flat pieces of meat, usually veal, sautéed and served in a sauce.

scone (scahn)   Scottish quick bread containing currants.

score   To make shallow lengthwise and crosswise slits on the surface of meat.

sear   To brown the surface of meat quickly at high temperatures.

semolina   Coarsely milled hard wheat endosperm used for gnocchi, some pasta, and couscous.

set   Allow to stand until congealed, as in gelatin and puddings.

shallot   Small onion having a stronger but more mellow flavor than the common variety.

shirr   To break eggs into dish, cover with cream and crumbs, and bake.

shortening   Fat suitable for baking or frying.

simmer   To cook in a liquid in which bubbles form slowly and break just below the surface.

skewer   Pin of metal or wood used for fastening meat or poultry while cooking; or long pins used for holding bits of food for broiling or roasting.

skim   To remove surface fat or foam from liquid mixture.

sliver   To cut into long, slender pieces, as in slivered almonds.

smorgasbord (smor gas bohrd') Swedish   Arrangement of appetizers and other foods on a table in attractive assortment.

sorbet (sor bay') French   Sherbet made of several kinds of fruits.

soubise (soo' bees) French   White sauce containing onion and sometimes parsley.

soufflé (soo flay') French   A light fluffy baked dish with beaten egg whites; may be sweet or savory.

soy sauce   Chinese sauce made from fermented soy beans.

spaetzle (spet' zel) Austrian   Fine noodles made by pressing batter through colander into boiling water or broth.

spoon bread   Southern corn bread baked in a casserole and served with a spoon.

springerle (spring' er le) German   A Christmas cookie. The dough is rolled into a sheet and pressed with a springerle mold before baking.

spumoni (spoo moh' nee) Italian   Rich ice cream made in different layers, usually containing fruit and nuts.

stabilizer   An ingredient added to an emulsion to prevent it from separating.

steam   To cook in steam with or without pressure. Steam may be applied directly to the food, as in a steamer, or to the vessel, as in a double boiler.

steam-jacketed kettle   A kettle with double-layered walls, between which steam circulates, providing even heat for cooking stocks, soups, and sauces.

steep   To cover with boiling water and let stand to extract flavors and colors.

stew   To simmer in a small amount of liquid.

stir   To mix food materials with a circular motion.

stir-fry   To cook quickly in oil over high heat, using light tossing and stirring motion to preserve shape of food.

stock   Liquid in which meat, fish, poultry or vegetables have been cooked.

stroganoff   (stro′ gan off) Russian   Sautéed beef in sauce of sour cream, with mushrooms and onions.

strudel   (stroo′ dl) German   Pastry of flaky, paper-thin dough filled with fruit.

table d'hôte   (tabl doht′) French   Meal at a fixed price.

tacos   (tah′ cos) Mexican   Rolled sandwiches of tortillas filled with meat, onions, lettuce, and hot sauce.

tamale   (ta mah′ lee) Mexican   Highly seasoned meat mixture rolled in cornmeal mush, wrapped in corn husks, and steamed.

tart   Small pie or pastry.

tartar sauce   Mayonnaise to which chopped pickles, onions, and other seasonings have been added; usually served with fish.

tender crisp   The point in cooking vegetables at which they are firm and slightly crisp.

terrine   (tay reen′) French   Tureen, an earthenware pot resembling a casserole. *Chicken en terrine,* chicken cooked and served in a tureen.

timbale   Thin fried case for holding creamed mixtures; or unsweetened baked custard with meat, poultry, or vegetables.

toast   To apply direct heat until the surface of the food is browned.

tofu   Bean curd.

torte   (tor′te) German   Rich cake made from crumbs, eggs, and nuts; or meringue in the form of a cake.

tortilla   (tohr tee′yah) Mexican   A round thin unleavened flour or cornmeal cake baked on a griddle.

toss   To mix ingredients lightly without crushing.

tournedos   (tur ne′ doe) Spanish   Small round filets of beef. French, a small cut from the tenderloin of beef.

trifle   English   Dessert made with sponge cake soaked in fruit juice and wine and layered with jam, custard, almonds, and whipped cream.

truffle   A dark mushroom-like fungus, found chiefly in France. Used mainly for garnishing and flavor.

truss   To tie or skewer poultry or meat so that it will hold its shape while cooking.

turnover   Food encased in pastry and baked.

tutti frutti   Mixed fruit.

velouté   (ve loo tay′) French   A rich white sauce, usually made of chicken or veal broth.

vinaigrette   (vee nay groit′) French   French dressing often with chopped eggs, capers, and herbs.

whip   To beat rapidly to increase volume by the incorporation of air.

Wiener schnitzel   (ve′ner schnit sel) German Breaded cutlets, frequently served with tomato sauce or lemon.

wonton   Stuffed dumplings cooked in chicken broth.

Yorkshire pudding   English Accompaniment for roast beef, a popover-like mixture baked in drippings of the roast.

zest   Peel of citrus fruits, such as orange or lemon, which contains aromatic oil.

zwieback   (tsvee′ bahk) German   Toasted bread, crisp and slightly sweet.

Index ▪

NOTE: **Boldface** page number indicates a recipe.

NOTE: **Boldface** page number indicates a recipe.

NOTE: **Boldface** page number indicates a recipe.

NOTE: **Boldface** page number indicates a recipe.

NOTE: **Boldface** page number indicates a recipe.

NOTE: **Boldface** page number indicates a recipe.

NOTE: **Boldface** page number indicates a recipe.

NOTE: **Boldface** page number indicates a recipe.

NOTE: **Boldface** page number indicates a recipe.

NOTE: **Boldface** page number indicates a recipe.

NOTE: **Boldface** page number indicates a recipe.

About the Authors .

GRACE SHUGART, M.S., professor emeritus of Hotel, Restaurant and Institution Management, and Dietetics at Kansas State University, graduated from Washington State University and earned a master's degree at Iowa State University. Her professional experience includes 24 years at Kansas State University, first as director of Residence Hall Foodservice and assistant professor of Institutional Management, then as professor and head of the Institutional Management Department from 1957 until her retirement. Mrs. Shugart has also served as food director of the cooperative dormitories and instructor in Institution Management at Iowa State University. She has held positions in hospital dietetics as well. Mrs. Shugart has been active in The American Dietetic Association, having served as delegate from Kansas, delegate-at-large, speaker of the House of Delegates, and president. She was also on the board of directors of The American Dietetic Association Foundation. She was a recipient of ADA's Medallion in 1978 and was named the Kansas Dietitian of the Year in 1977 by the Kansas Dietetic Association. In 1980, Mrs. Shugart was presented with the Marjorie Hulsizer Copher Award, ADA's highest award given each year to a member. Mrs. Shugart is a member of Women in Communications and holds membership in the honor societies of Phi Kappa Phi, Kappa Omicron Nu, and Phi Upsilon Omicron. Mrs. Shugart was presented with the Distinguished Home Economics Alumnus Award in 1978 and with the Alumni Achievement Award in 1982 by Washington State University. She is also a coauthor of the text *Foodservice in Institutions*.

MARY MOLT, M.S., R.D., L.D., is assistant director of Housing and Dining Services and instructor of Hotel, Restaurant and Institution Management, and Dietetics (HRIMD), Kansas State University. She holds a bachelor's degree from University of Nebraska–Kearney and a master's degree from Oklahoma State University. Ms. Molt has 20 years of professional experience at Kansas State University, with a joint appointment in academe and foodservice administration. Current responsibilities include overseeing supervised practice experiences for junior and senior students in the HRIMD department and directing management activities for three residence hall dining centers serving more than 8000 meals per day. Mary Molt is active in the American Dietetic Association, Kansas Dietetic Association, and the National Association of College and University Food Services (NACUFS). In 1981 and 1986 she was recognized with the NACUFS Richard Lichtenfelt Award for outstanding service to the association. Mary Molt holds membership in several honor societies including Delta Kappa Gamma, Kappa Omicron Nu, Phi Upsilon Omicron, and Phi Kappa Phi.

ISBN 0-02-410341-1

90000>